CHILD DEVELOPMENT

CHILD DEVELOPMENT

AN INTRODUCTION

SECOND EDITION

ROBERT F. BIEHLER

CALIFORNIA STATE UNIVERSITY, CHICO

HOUGHTON MIFFLIN COMPANY   BOSTON

DALLAS   GENEVA, ILLINOIS   HOPEWELL, NEW JERSEY   PALO ALTO   LONDON

The original impetus for this book and the basic orientation toward developmental psychology that influenced its form and content were supplied by professors at the Institute of Child Welfare (now the Institute of Child Development) at the University of Minnesota during the early 1950s. Dale B. Harris, who later served with distinction as professor of psychology and human development at the University of Pennsylvania, had a particularly positive and significant impact on my career in psychology. In grateful recognition of his inspiring influence as teacher and adviser, this book is dedicated to him.

Material from *The History of Childhood*, edited by Lloyd de Mause. New York: Psychohistory Press, 1974. Reprinted by permission of editor and publisher.

Material from *The Adolescent Experience* by Elizabeth Douvan and Joseph Adelson. New York: Wiley, 1966. Reprinted by permission of Elizabeth Douvan.

Material reprinted from *Childhood and Society*, 2nd ed., by Erik H. Erikson. By permission of W. W. Norton & Company, Inc., and the Hogarth Press, Ltd. Copyright 1950, © 1963 by W. W. Norton & Company, Inc.

Material reprinted from *Identity, Youth and Crisis*, by Erik H. Erikson. By permission of W. W. Norton & Company, Inc.

Material reprinted from *The Laws* by Plato, translated by A. E. Taylor. By permission of the publisher in the United States, E. P. Dutton & Co., Inc. and by the publisher in England, J. M. Dent & Sons, Ltd.

Cover and chapter opening photography by Jim Scherer.

Printed in the U.S.A.

Library of Congress Catalog Card Number: 80–82347

ISBN: 0–395–29833–4

CONTENTS

PREFACE

This second edition of *Child Development: An Introduction* generally follows the same pattern as the first edition. The original sixteen chapters, however, have been reduced to thirteen; the material within most chapters has been reorganized; the last chapters now cover youth as well as adolescence; and about two-thirds of the text is either new or substantially rewritten. The following outline presents a list of objectives that guided the preparation of this edition. Descriptions of features of the text designed to contribute to the achievement of these objectives follow each numbered point.

1.   Summarize and interpret scientific evidence on human development. Place primary emphasis on current research but do not neglect classic studies. Identify psychologists who were pioneers in establishing techniques of study or who first called attention to significant types of behavior.

Fifty-three percent of the articles or books referred to in the text were published since 1970, 26 percent were published since 1975.

In Chapter 2 a history of developmental psychology is outlined in the form of an imaginary diary. Eminent psychologists are introduced and their work is related to historical and cultural trends.

2.   Call attention to the impact of the *Zeitgeist* on research trends and interpretations. Make the reader aware that replacement of once-accepted ideas by new interpretations reflects a strength, rather than a weakness, of scientific study.

In the prologue changing ideas about development and child rearing are traced, in part, to the cumulative nature of science. Chapter 2 details ways certain studies attracted attention at particular times because of cultural and historical trends. Throughout the text speculations are offered about the possible influence of current events on researchers. In addition, a number of examples demonstrate how "revolutionary" findings reported in a groundbreaking study later came to be revised or rejected as additional research was reported.

3.   Do everything possible to encourage students to learn, remember, and apply scientific information about development. Encourage the reader to think of the book as a reference worth keeping.

In recognition of the value of structure in promoting learning and remembering, the organization of the text and of material within chapters is made as clear as possible. The overall organization of the text is explained in the prologue. The first three chapters provide background; Chapter 1 outlines conceptions of development and points out how these influence the ways information will be applied; Chapter 2 summarizes the history of scientific child study and describes methods developed by well-known psychologists; Chapter 3 outlines theories of human development.

Five clearly recognizable stages of development are discussed in the five Parts following the introductory chapters. Each of these Parts—from conception to the first month, the first two years, from two to five years, from six to twelve years, adolescence and youth—contains two chapters which summarize selected topics considered to be of special significance at that period in development.

At the beginning of each chapter instructional objectives (Key Points) are listed under major headings; these serve as advance organizers.

In recognition of the extremely high rate of forgetting that occurs when students feel obliged to learn hundreds of unrelated details in a book only well enough to be able to answer test questions, the Key Points are printed in color in the page margins to indicate significant sections of the text. (Many of the Key Points also function as a glossary.)

A Study Guide is offered to help assure learning and understanding. Designed to help students organize information about the Key Points and to learn these points quickly, easily, and thoroughly, the Study Guide can be used in preparing for exams or used in open book exams. To ease the mastery of difficult or hard-to-remember information, suggested study techniques and memorization aids are offered.

Frequent reviews, often presented in the form of tables, are used to tie together points, clarify age trends, and show the relationships between the conclusions of different theorists.

Suggestions that parents, teachers, and others who interact with children might follow in *applying* well-established findings are described in several chapters.

To motivate students to read the entire book carefully (and to recognize its potential value as a reference worth keeping and using), special efforts have been made to present the material as effectively as possible. Chapter, section, and page headings identify the age level and type of behavior being discussed. The illustrations have been carefully selected to clarify significant points. Annotated bibliographies of particularly valuable articles and books on important topics are provided at the end of each chapter. An index to these sources of additional information is supplied inside the front and back covers.

4. In addition to acquainting students with what psychologists have discovered about human development, encourage students to function as informed, objective, and critical observers.

At the end of the prologue readers are introduced to basic reference works and journals they might consult for detailed scientific information on development. They are also encouraged, in one of the Suggestions for Further Study at the end of the prologue, to make distinctions between scientific and unscientific articles.

The conclusion of Chapter 2 summarizes the methods of scientific child study and describes a number of ways these methods might be used by anyone who has contact with children.

The Suggestions for Further Study at the end of most chapters offer instructions for carrying out simple experimental and observational investigations. To make readers aware that these suggestions are not only for term projects, a section is included at the end of Chapter 2 outlining ways parents might systematically observe child behavior *after* they have completed course work.

5. Call attention to stages, patterns, interrelationships, and continuities in development. Emphasize the significance of individuality in development. Make clear how later behavior may—or may not—emerge from or be traceable to early behavior.

Following the first three chapters of background information, the book is organized by age levels. This organization is felt to be most effective in helping students grasp stages, patterns, continuities, rates, and individual differences in development—*and* call attention to specific types of behavior that are particularly significant during infancy, childhood, and adolescence.

Stage descriptions by Freud, Erikson, Piaget, and Sears are outlined in Chapter 3 and are used throughout as frames of reference in the discussion of types of behavior at the different age levels. To serve as advance organizers, the appropriate sections of the stage descriptions of each of these theorists are featured in the opening for each of the last five Parts of the text.

Speculations by various theorists regarding the question of continuity in individual development are summarized in at least one of the chapters in each Part.

Acknowledgments

I would like to acknowledge my indebtedness to Marjorie V. Roberts, who typed the various drafts of the manuscript for this book, and to the editors and artists of Houghton Mifflin Company, who supervised the transition of the final manuscript into a text. Dale B. Harris of Pennsylvania State University, Stewart Cohen of the University of Rhode Island, Phyllis Blumenfeld of the University of Michigan, Marion Perlmutter of the University of Minnesota, and Peggy Emerson of the University of Mississippi read the first draft of the manuscript and made suggestions for improving it. E. Duwayne Keller of the University of Connecticut, Jerry Willis of Texas Tech University, and Lynne M. Hudson of the University of Toledo read at least two drafts of the manuscript and made detailed suggestions which were particularly helpful. Duwayne Keller supplied so much information and so many references, in fact, that he deserves to be recognized as an "honorary coauthor."

Robert F. Biehler
California State University, Chico

PROLOGUE

What You Will Learn in This Book

Books on human development summarize scientific data regarding physical, mental, social, and emotional behavior. They also explain how these types of behavior change with age. Some texts on development are organized by subject areas, with age trends traced for each type of behavior. This book is organized by age levels, with significant types of behavior discussed for five age spans ranging from conception through adolescence and youth. The age-span frame of reference has been chosen to make clear continuities of development.

To help you understand how behavior changes with age, theories of development are outlined (in Chapter 3) as a prelude to the discussion of types of behavior at each of the five age levels. The stages outlined in this analysis of theories are then called to your attention in later chapters to enable you to place at least some trends into a framework.

One of the distinguishing characteristics of science is its cumulative nature. We currently enjoy marvels of space-age technology because present-day scientists, technologists, and inventors have taken advantage of discoveries made by earlier theorists. Similarly, we know more about human behavior today than at any previous time in history because contemporary researchers have benefited from the discoveries of their predecessors. A historical survey of developmental psychology (in Chapter 2) will permit you to examine the work of early developmental psychologists so that you will become aware of contributions that form the foundation for current understanding of development. In Chapter 2 you will meet notable psychologists and learn about their significant studies. When their work is mentioned in later chapters you will not only understand when, why, and how particular studies were carried out, you may also be inspired to carry out investigations of your own by using similar techniques.

Once you have learned about conceptions of development (Chapter 1), history, methods, and scientists (Chapter 2), and theories of development (Chapter 3), you will be prepared to trace development from conception through adolescence. Chapter 4 supplies information about heredity, prenatal development, and birth. Chapter 5 outlines characteristics of the neonate, or newborn infant. Chapters 6 and 7 are devoted to significant developmental changes during the first two years. Chapters 8 and 9 describe aspects of the development of children between the ages of two and five. Chapters 10 and 11 stress analyses of important types of behavior that appear between the years of six to twelve. Chapters 12 and 13 outline key features of development in adolescence and youth. The overall structure of this book is therefore easy to grasp. Three chapters of background information, two chapters each on the child from conception to the first month, from one month to two years of age, from two to five, from six to twelve, and from thirteen to the early twenties.

This book summarizes scientific information about human development. Whereas conclusions based on investigations carried out in a scientific manner are much more trustworthy than hunches based on subjective impressions, there are still problems faced by those who wish to apply the findings of scientists to behavior. You should, therefore, take into account certain complications and cautions.

Some Factors to Remember When Reading This Book

Recommendations Change as Knowledge Accumulates

As developmental psychologists observe behavior and read reports of studies by their colleagues they benefit from the cumulative nature of science. New ideas constantly replace old ones for a variety of reasons: results published by early theorists permit later researchers to begin at an advanced level of understanding; innovative methods of study are perfected and yield previously undiscovered data; scholars recognize interrelationships that earlier students overlooked; investigators carry out more complete and sophisticated experiments; theorists, through analyzing and synthesizing data, evolve more comprehensive or revolutionary sets of principles. An inevitable byproduct of the continual progression of scientific interpretations of development is that current books on child psychology and child rearing often contradict those published just a few years ago. A parent or teacher eager for definitive answers may sometimes find this unsettling and wonder about the wisdom of placing confidence in any book on child psychology. Nevertheless, the demand for expert opinion remains high.

Parents Seek Child-rearing Advice

To a greater extent than in most societies, American parents actively seek information—scientific or otherwise—about child rearing. America is essentially a meritocracy where a person's position in life may often be determined more by merit than family background. There is no denying that some Americans have greater opportunities to achieve success than others, but genuinely capable

In America there is a steady demand by parents for advice on child rearing. One explanation for this demand is that America is a meritocracy where individuals from all types of backgrounds can achieve success through their own efforts. Accordingly, many parents are eager to do everything they can to help their children develop in the most fulfilling way possible. Owen Franken/Stock, Boston.

individuals often work their way to the top through their own efforts regardless of their background. This characteristic of our society appeals especially to recent immigrants and to those from lower socioeconomic situations, but even in families that settled in America generations ago and have achieved wealth and status parents want to do the "right" thing to help their children make the most of their opportunities. If parents have enjoyed the fruits of their labors (or of the labor of their ancestors), they want to make it possible for their children to do the same.

A meritocratic society is based on open competition, however, and parents, in spite of themselves, may measure their success as child rearers by comparing their children's performance with that of others. If a neighbor's child does exceptionally well in some activity or seems to possess every virtue, parents may wonder if that child's parents know something about child rearing that they don't know. Obtaining information about children is not necessarily motivated only by the wish to help a child make the most of opportunities or to keep up with the Joneses, however. Parents may simply want to take advantage of available knowledge. If research specialists have engaged in painstaking study of development and subjected their conclusions to scrutiny by others, it makes sense to find out what they have discovered. Even though some parents may be skeptical about changing knowledge and even though motives may differ, most parents are interested in finding out what psychologists have to say about child rearing. This desire for information can be understood more completely by comparing parenthood in the 1880s (before developmental psychology existed as a discipline) with parenthood today.

Conventional Views of Child Rearing Have Changed

Parenthood in the 1880s   If you had been born one hundred years earlier, you would not have been confronted as a young adult with very many decisions regarding parenthood and child rearing. Unless you decided to join the ranks of the tiny minority of old maids and bachelors, it would never have occurred to you that there was any alternative to marriage. Once married, you and your spouse would have probably accepted as a matter of course that you would begin almost immediately to have a family. If you had had a child every year or so for several years you probably would have earned admiration and respect. If you had not had a child after two or three years of marriage, it is likely that relatives and friends would have suggested that you do something to remedy such an abnormal situation.

After the conception of a child, you would have made decisions about pregnancy and birth on the basis of what your parents had done or on the advice of other relatives, friends, or perhaps a family physician. Once your child was born, you would have adopted, without much thought or discussion, infant-care routines that had been practiced for generations. In the absence of books, magazine and newspaper articles, and television programs on techniques of child rearing, you would have simply done the "natural" thing or used techniques you remembered or observed. At the appropriate age, your sons and daughters would have learned and accepted traditional sex roles with little or no resistance— largely because of the unquestioning way you and your spouse had accepted your sex roles: the father was the breadwinner; the mother took care of the children and the house. You would have expected your children to be respectful and obedient to you and to other older people. Your children would have learned well-established patterns of adult behavior by observing and imitating your behavior and that of other elders.

All of this made life a lot simpler then. But life was also restrictive and precarious in many ways. Relatively few choices could be made, and the limited knowledge of medical practitioners as well as parents about many aspects of conception, prenatal development, birth, child care, and the nature of human development led to frequent miscarriages or stillbirths, high infant and maternal death rates, and much unnecessary unhappiness for both parents and children.

An American family in the 1880s. Culver Pictures

Parenthood in the 1980s   In the last one hundred years, and especially in the last thirty years, more knowledge has accumulated about human behavior and development than in all preceding periods of history. This knowledge has opened up unprecedented possibilities for making life free and full, but it has also made life much more complicated. For along with knowledge has come the need for making a large number of decisions. Consider just a few of the choices available to you that were not available to your great-grandparents.

Today, alternatives to formal marriage are being explored and accepted, and if you join in formal or informal matrimony with a member of the opposite sex, you may devote considerable thought to the question of having children. You may take into account such factors as the population explosion, ecological considerations, careers for both marriage partners, and the possibility that parenthood may take precedence over all other roles—particularly for the mother.

So many forms of birth control are available that you have the option of deciding when and how many children you will have. If you wish, you and your spouse (or prospective spouse) can have an analysis made to ascertain the possibility that incompatibilities in genetic structure might lead to abnormalities in your offspring. In addition to deciding on the number and timing of pregnancies, you may make an effort to determine the sex of each child. If an unwanted pregnancy occurs, or if some disease or condition known to cause abnormalities in fetal development occurs during pregnancy, you have the option

An American family in the 1980s. George Bellerose/Stock, Boston.

(under certain circumstances) of aborting the pregnancy. If a child is conceived and prenatal development is allowed to proceed, you will be able to choose from several theories and methods of prenatal care. By selecting a particular obstetrician, the *way* the delivery of the child occurs becomes a matter of choice.

After the child is born, if you become informed about current thinking on child rearing, you will discover that there is a great deal of information available. (Because you are several times more likely than your great-grandparents to finish high school and study at an institution of higher learning, you are much more likely to be aware of scientific information about development.) If you examine even a small amount of this information you are likely to find (for reasons just discussed) that interpretations conflict and that ideas about child rearing change in a very short period of time. If you have more than one child, and if you follow up-to-date recommendations, each of your offspring may be reared according to quite different guidelines. Simply being *exposed* to new and different ideas (through books, college courses, magazine and newspaper articles, or television programs) may cause you to frequently alter your opinions about child rearing.

As this brief comparison of parenthood in the 1880s and 1980s indicates, parents of one hundred years ago tended to follow a prescribed pattern, which limited choice but made child rearing straightforward and simple. There were few thoughts about whether what was being done was right or wrong, and most parents did not question that traditional techniques were the only ones to use. Today, few American parents slavishly follow traditional methods of child rearing. We have acquired an enormous amount of information about behavior and development and are in a position to make child rearing more effective than ever. But the extent, variety, and changeable nature of this information leads to speculations and doubts about whether some approaches are better than others. Unthinking but confident acceptance of tradition has been replaced by informed but sometimes insecure choice.

As a consequence of these various factors, you will need to exercise judgment and discretion when you attempt to apply scientific information to behavior. You will also need to take into account how assumptions regarding human nature influence the way knowledge may be applied.

Basic Assumptions May Influence Applications

Consider a question that has been debated for thousands of years: Is the newborn infant basically good, or evil, or simply blank, like an empty sheet of paper? If parents assume that children are born good, they will want to allow freedom for natural goodness to flourish. If parents assume that children are born evil, they will want to take pains to suppress inherent wickedness. If parents assume that the mind of a child is like a blank sheet of paper—ready to be written or drawn upon—they will want to think very carefully about the kind of child they hope to mold or shape.

Consider as well related questions that philosophers and scientists have pondered since they began to speculate about human behavior: To what extent is child behavior influenced by inherited predispositions? To what extent is behavior shaped by experiences? If parents assume a child inherits a unique combination of personality traits, they will want to make allowances for this individuality. They will rear each child in a different way, depending on the child's idiosyncrasies. If parents assume a child is primarily the product of experiences, on the other hand, they may think that all children will respond to the same experiences in the same way. They will expect a technique that worked with one child in a given situation to exert the same influence over all children in similar situations.

To illustrate the significance of these various assumptions and how they have influenced the use of knowledge about children, Chapter 1 surveys views proposed at different times in history.

Suggestions for Further Study

Journals Containing Reports of Research on Children

One of the goals of this book is to encourage you to become directly involved with scientific studies of development. It would be beneficial, therefore, if you were to become acquainted with journals in this field of study. Listed below are selected journals containing reports of research on children. Some are devoted exclusively to such research, others publish occasional articles describing studies relating to development. (Not all of these publications are journals in the strict sense. Some are annual collections made up of reviews of articles on a topic, or detailed reports of extensive research investigations.)

Adolescence
American Educational Research Journal
American Journal of Orthopsychiatry
Behavioral Science
Child Development
Developmental Psychology
Educational and Psychological Measurement
Exceptional Child
Genetic Psychology Monographs
Harvard Educational Review
Human Development
Journal of Abnormal Child Psychology
Journal of Applied Behavior Analysis
Journal of Clinical Psychology
Journal of Educational Psychology
Journal of Experimental Child Psychology
Journal of Experimental Education
Journal of Genetic Psychology
Journal of Home Economics

Journal of School Psychology
Journal of Social Psychology
Marriage and Family Living
Merrill-Palmer Quarterly of Behavior and Development
Mental Hygiene
Minnesota Symposia on Child Development
Monographs of the Society for Research in Child Development
Personality
Psychoanalytic Study of the Child
Psychological Monographs
Psychological Review
Psychological Reports
Psychology in the Schools
Psychology Today
Science
Scientific American
Vita Humana
Young Children

To become familiar with research in developmental psychology, you might examine recent issues of some of these journals. If you ever seek information on a topic by reading research reports, you might write abstracts of pertinent articles by following the outline below:

☐ Author of article
☐ Title of article
☐ Journal in which article appears (including date, volume number, and page numbers)
☐ Purpose (or description of problem)
☐ Subjects
☐ Procedure (or methods)

☐   Treatment of data

☐   Results

☐   Conclusions

☐   Are there any criticisms that you can make of the procedure or of the conclusions? (For example, were there enough subjects? were the subjects "selected" in any way? did the procedure seem to "favor" the predicted results? might you draw different conclusions than those noted in the article?)

Journals of Abstracts and Reviews

Browsing through professional journals is one way to deal directly with facts about development. In most cases, however, you are likely to want information relating to a specific question, and it would be too time-consuming to use a "browse" approach. The more efficient procedure is to find a recent article describing research on the point in question and refer to the bibliography of that article for other references. A variety of journals and reference works exists to assist you in doing this. The journals listed below consist of abstracts (brief summaries of results) of articles that appear in the type of journal listed in the preceding section.

Child Development Abstracts and Bibliography
Education Index
Exceptional Child Education Abstracts
Psychological Abstracts
PsycSCAN Developmental Psychology
Social Sciences Citation Index (Though it does not include abstracts, it can be used to find articles on a specific topic.)

The journal *Contemporary Psychology* provides reviews of new books in psychology, and the *Annual Review of Psychology* provides information reflected by the title—a specialist in each of several areas of psychology reviews significant studies that have appeared during a given year. The *Review of Educational Research* and the *Review of Child Development Research* feature articles that describe and analyze reports of studies on a particular theme.

To discover the nature of these indices and reference works, you might select a topic of interest, look in the index of one of the journals of abstracts (or scan the appropriate chapter in one of the *Reviews*) until you find a reference to a recent article. Look up that article and read it to discover if it provides relevant information. If it does, you can use the bibliography as a source of information about related articles.

The Developmental Psychologist's Bible

In 1933, a time of burgeoning interest in child development, Carl Murchison edited a *Handbook of Child Psychology* designed to provide advanced students and research workers with reviews of studies on various aspects of development. The original *Handbook* was eventually revised, and, in 1946, Leonard Carmichael edited a similar volume entitled *Manual of Child Psychology*. A second edition of the *Manual* was published under Carmichael's editorship in 1954, and a third edition, edited by Paul H. Mussen, appeared in 1970. The two editions of Murchison's *Handbook* and the first two editions of Carmichael's *Manual* reveal much of the history of child psychology. The third edition of Carmichael's *Manual,* edited by Mussen, is a comprehensive source of information about research carried out (for the most part) in the 1950s and 1960s. The fourth edition, published in 1980, and consisting of four volumes, summarizes research through the late 1970s. If you are interested in finding technical information about some aspect of development, in addition to examining journals of abstracts and annual reviews, you might also consult the editions of Carmichael's *Manual.*

ERIC

Thousands of articles are published each year on every conceivable aspect of psychology. To assist psychologists and educators in discovering what has been published on a specific topic in developmental or educational psychology, the Educational Resources Information Center (ERIC) has been established by the U.S. Office of Education. ERIC publishes three sources of information:

Current Index to Journals in Education—Annual Cumulation, which contains an index of articles in over three hundred education and education-oriented journals published in a given year. There are four sections in each volume: Subject Index (which lists titles of articles organized under hundreds of subject headings); Author Index; Journal Contents Index (which lists the tables of contents for each issue of journals published that year); and Main Entry Section (which provides the title, author, journal reference, and a brief abstract of articles published in journals covered by the *Index*).

Research in Education, which lists curriculum guides, catalogs, and the like; and papers, reports, and monographs not published in journals. The Document Résumé section presents descriptions of the documents arranged according to the ERIC classification scheme, together with information about where each can be obtained. There is also a Subject Index (titles of documents listed according to the ERIC classification), an Author Index, and an Institution Index.

ERIC Educational Documents Index, which lists titles of documents noted and abstracted in *Research in Education* and also in *Office of Education Research Reports.* Each document is classified under as many as five "Major Descriptors" (general categories) and perhaps also under "Minor Descriptors" (more specific categories).

As these descriptions indicate, for information on what is available in journals, you should refer to *Current Index to Journals in Education—Annual Cumulation.* For information about curriculum guides, pamphlets, and reports not published in journals, consult the *ERIC Educational Documents Index* for titles and *Research in Education* for descriptions and information about how to obtain such documents. You are urged to examine a recent issue of these publications to discover what is available in the ERIC network and how you might obtain information.

Popular versus Professional Reports

Because of the demand for information on child rearing, newspapers and magazines frequently publish articles on this subject. There are also many TV programs on aspects of development, and books on how to raise children often appear on the best-seller lists. There are often significant differences between such popularized discussions and the reports of experiments found in the journals described in the three preceding Suggestions.

Writers of newspaper or magazine articles, TV scripts, or popular books know they must catch and hold the interest of the reader or viewer. Consequently, many of them highlight the dramatic side of things, oversimplify, and exaggerate. They also are likely to assume that no one will take the trouble to check on what they say and may not be concerned about being completely accurate. In extreme cases, they may make a point by embellishing an incident or part of a report on children.

Psychologists who write reports of experiments in professional journals usually operate under a different set of guidelines. They are expected to describe exactly what they were interested in studying, the characteristics of the children they used as subjects, the procedures they followed, and how they obtained and evaluated their results. This makes it possible for the reader to decide whether their conclusions seem justified. If readers have doubts about the results, they can often replicate the experiment on the basis of the information provided. Scientific articles and books on development may be less dramatic than magazine, TV, and book coverage of this subject, but they are more likely to be accurate—simply because scientists usually tell how they got their evidence. (It sometimes happens that a scientist manipulates data or draws unsupported conclusions. Most of the time, however, such distortions are pointed out, sooner or later, by other scientists.)

To become aware of the often untrustworthy nature of magazine articles, TV programs, or popular books on aspects of development, select a report that arouses your interest, and evaluate it with reference to questions such as:

☐ Does the author (or narrator) indicate the number and background of the subjects who were studied?

☐ Is there detailed information regarding the procedures used?

☐ Are you told where you could read about the study and draw your own conclusions, or are you just told the name (and perhaps affiliation) of the investigator?

☐ Are statistical data supplied to back up the conclusions, or are you more or less asked to accept what is reported "on faith"?

☐ Are the conclusions interpreted in a tentative way, or does the author or narrator give the impression that they are clearly established or widely endorsed?

Changes in Child-rearing Practices

If you would like to read accounts of how approaches to child rearing have changed, look for one or more of these articles or books: "Sixty Years of Child Rearing Practices" by Celia Burns Stendler (*Journal of Pediatrics,* 1950, **36,** 122–134); "Trends in Infant Care Ideas" by C. E. Vincent (*Child Development,* 1951, **22,** 199–209); "Trends in Infant Care" by Martha Wolfenstein (*American Journal of Orthopsychiatry,* 1953, **33,** 120–130); or *Two Centuries of Child Rearing Manuals* (1968) by Samuel Z. Klausner.

The Demand for Child-rearing Advice

In "Popular Primers for Parents," an article which appears on pages 359–369 of the April 1978 *American Psychologist,* K. Alison Clarke-Stewart comments on the proliferation of primers for parents. It appears, she notes, that almost all parents read one such book, and many of them read more than five. She concludes, however, that most of the books show "little respect for parents' intellectual interest or competence" (p. 369), particularly because the authors rarely back up their suggestions with scientific evidence. Readers are not given the chance to draw their own conclusions; they are expected to take what is written on faith. In a brief comment on the Clarke-Stewart article, Robert J. Griffore (*American Psychologist,* February 1979, pp. 182–183) endorses her evaluation of parent primers and also points out ways some of the advice offered by certain authors might be expected, when interpreted with reference to findings of scientific studies, to lead to complications—if not undesirable forms of behavior.

PART ONE

BACKGROUND

This part consists of three chapters: Chapter 1, "Conceptions of Development"; Chapter 2, "History, Methods, Scientists"; and Chapter 3, "Theories of Development."

The background provided by these introductory chapters will make it easier for you to grasp descriptions of child development presented in the remaining five parts of the text.

For centuries, philosophers and scientists as well as teachers and thoughtful parents have speculated on human development.

Although some forms of child behavior seem to have stayed the same throughout recorded history (for example, anxiety, jealousy, play), other forms of behavior (for example, child-parent relationships) have changed as cultures and attitudes have changed.

KEY POINTS

Plato and Aristotle

Meritocracy: one's position in life determined by merit

Education should be arranged to fit different personalities

Fourteenth to Eighteenth centuries: from wickedness to innocence

Fourteenth century: inherent wickedness should be suppressed by punishment

Eighteenth century: inherent innocence should be protected and guided

John Locke: Children Learn from Experience

All knowledge from experience

The newborn's mind as a blank slate

Praise children for good behavior; ignore bad behavior

Jean Jacques Rousseau: Inherent Goodness

Fit education to child; offer instruction when child feels need for it

John B. Watson: Shaping Human Behavior

Behaviorism: scientists should base conclusions on overt behavior

Conditioning a child to fear a rat

B. F. Skinner: Shaping Behavior More Effectively

Conditioning a rat to press a bar in preselected ways

Pavlovian conditioning: involuntary action aroused by a previously neutral stimulus

Operant conditioning: voluntary behavior strengthened by reinforcement

Behavior determined by reinforced experiences, not by free choice

Behavior modification: reinforce desirable, ignore undesirable, behavior

Key to mental health: person's belief in ability to control own behavior

Abraham H. Maslow: Self Determination

Trust children; let them grow

Albert Bandura: Anticipatory Control

Anticipatory control: ability to preselect consequences

CHAPTER □ 1

CONCEPTIONS OF DEVELOPMENT

Some people possess a zest for living—they take advantage of their opportunities, get along with almost everyone they meet, and make positive contributions to society. Others are unhappy—they are unwilling or unable to use their abilities, incapable of forming friendships, and engage in activities that are destructive to themselves and others. From the time human beings first became intrigued by behavior, thoughtful individuals have asked: What are the causes of such differences in human behavior? Can't we use the knowledge we have accumulated to help more people enjoy life and take advantage of their abilities? Since experiences during childhood and adolescence apparently have a significant influence on later behavior, shouldn't it be possible to observe how children develop and how they are influenced by experiences, in order to find ways to help people live happy, fulfilling lives?

Many of the early thinkers who recorded their impressions of human behavior expressed dismay about widespread unhappiness, marital incompatibility, conflict between generations, selfishness, and aggression against others. Today, although we have found ways to conquer most diseases, ease physical suffering, make our lives remarkably comfortable, and even put a man on the moon, we have not substantially reduced the incidence of unfortunate and undesirable forms of human behavior. Part of the explanation, perhaps, is that we have not observed the development of children long enough, or carefully enough, or that we have failed to use the information we possess in the proper manner. This book summarizes past and present information on human development and various interpretations of how this information might be applied to the rearing of children. When you have finished it you should be able to draw your own conclusions about the extent and value of our knowledge of development. Then you will be able to decide how it might best be used by parents, teachers, nurses, social workers, and others who have contact with children.

Plato and Aristotle: Educating Ideal Citizens

Many discussions of the history of scientific study of human behavior begin with Plato and Aristotle. Their recorded observations on a variety of topics are studied today in dozens of separate university departments. Some of their speculations about human development, child rearing, and education are surprisingly modern; others are highly provocative.

Athens in 300 B.C. was similar in many respects to the United States of America in the 1980s. Corruption in politics had led to an erosion of confidence in government and to cynicism and distrust. Both Plato and Aristotle concluded that to save Athens it would be necessary to find an alternative to the democratic selection of leaders as well as ways of rearing and educating children so that they would not be tainted by the corruption of adult society.

Plato: Child Rearing by the State

Plato became convinced that the average citizen of Athens was incapable of making wise choices when given the opportunity to elect leaders. He also felt that many parents had succumbed to the moral decadence of Athenian society and were therefore unfit to raise children. But even parents who gave every appearance of being admirable and capable could not be trusted to rear future citizens of an ideal state, Plato concluded, because each husband and wife would use techniques that would differ in some respects from those used by every other couple. He pointed out that this would lead to confusing inconsistencies:

The privacy of home life screens from the general observation many little incidents, too readily occasioned by a child's pains, pleasures, and passions, which are not in keeping with a legislator's recommendations, and tend to bring a medley of incongruities into the characters of our citizens. (*Laws*, Book 7, Section 788)[1]

---

[1] Because there are so many different collections of the works of Plato and Aristotle, the references indicate section numbers (which should be the same in all editions) rather than page numbers (which apply only to a particular edition).

To make sure that most capable individuals would become leaders, to guarantee that children would not be exposed to parents who would set a poor example, and to avoid a "medley of incongruities" in the characters of the citizens of Athens, Plato decided that all children would have to be separated from their parents early in life. The state would then control child rearing and education. About every ten years all children would be subjected to exhaustive objective evaluations. Those judged least capable after the first stage would become workers. Those eliminated after the second stage would become managers and military leaders. The small number who survived the stringent screening process would first be given additional training and then be required to spend several years earning a livelihood and leaning about life from a citizen's point of view. When they reached the age of fifty, they would become the rulers of Athens.

Plato's ideal society was to be a *meritocracy,* and an individual's position in life would thus be decided by objectively determined merit. Every infant born in Athens would have an equal opportunity regardless of the social and economic position of the parents—or of the sex of the child. In stressing equality of opportunity, Plato anticipated a current trend in American society:

Meritocracy: one's position in life determined by merit

Education is, if possible, to be, as the phrase goes, compulsory for every mother's son. . . . And, mind you, my law will apply in all respects to girls as much as to boys; the girls must be trained exactly like the boys. . . . The present practice in our own part of the world is the merest folly; it is pure folly that men and women do not unite to follow the same pursuits with all their energies. In fact, almost every one of our cities in our present system is, and finds itself to be, only the half of what it might be at the same cost in expenditure and trouble. And yet, what an amazing oversight in a legislator! (*Laws,* Book 7, Section 804)

While girls and boys were to have the same basic education, Plato concluded that boys would need to be exposed to more carefully arranged and stringent instruction:

Now of all wild things a boy is the most difficult to handle. Just because he more than any other has a fount of intelligence in him which has not yet "run clear," he is the craftiest, most mischievous, and unruliest of brutes. So the creature must be held in check, as we may say, by more than one bridle—in the first place, when once he is out of the mother's and the nurse's hand, by attendants to care for his childish helplessness, and then, further, by all the masters who teach him anything. (*Laws,* Book 7, Section 808)

Plato gave this more complete explanation of what he meant by "holding the creature in check":

[Self-control] is the aim of our control of children, our not leaving them free before we have established, so to speak, a constitutional government within them and, by fostering the best element in them with the aid of the like in ourselves, have set up in its place a similar guardian and ruler in the child, and then, and then only, we leave it free. (*Republic,* Book 9, Section 591)

Many people believe that encouraging (or permitting) women to assume leadership roles is a product of modern thinking. In 300 B.C. however, Plato observed, "It is pure folly that men and women do not unite to follow the same pursuits with all of their energies." Plato would have been pleased that Margaret Thatcher (shown here campaigning) was elected Prime Minister of Great Britain. Philippe Achache/Gamma.

In reflecting upon how self-control might be established, Plato wrestled with a problem that still plagues parents and child psychologists: how can children be taught to control themselves without destroying their individuality and initiative in the process? In recent years proponents of strict and of permissive child rearing have debated this point. Here is Plato's opinion of the dangers of an extreme interpretation of either point of view:

While spoiling of children makes their tempers fretful, peevish, and easily upset by mere trifles, the contrary treatment, the severe and unqualified tyranny which makes its victims spiritless, servile, and sullen, renders them unfit for the intercourse of domestic and civic life. (*Laws,* Book 7, Section 791)

Aristotle: Allowing for Individual Differences

Aristotle, Plato's most outstanding pupil, shared his mentor's desire to create an ideal society. He agreed with Plato that Athens needed a state-controlled system of education because, as he put it, "the citizen should be molded to suit the form of government in which he lives" (*Politics,* Book 8, paragraph 1). He also agreed that a special kind of education should be given to the most capable individuals, who would become leaders. He differed from Plato, however, regarding state control of child rearing, which he felt was appropriate only for future leaders. He wanted most citizens to have opportunities for individual liberty and privacy and felt that the family provided personal and social stability. Plato was against having parents rear their own children because within the "privacy of home life" the different techniques used in each family would produce "incongruities." Aristotle felt that the "privacy of home life" should be *encouraged* and that the use of different techniques would be an advantage rather than a disadvantage because no single technique seemed likely to be effective with all children. Where Plato saw undesirable "incongruities," Aristotle saw desirable individuality:

Education should be arranged to fit different personalities

> There is an advantage . . . in private as against public methods of education. It is much the same as in medicine, where, though it is the general rule that a feverish patient should be kept quiet and take no food, there may be individual exceptions. Nor does a teacher of boxing teach all his pupils to box in the same style. It would seem then that a study of individual characters is the best way of making education perfect, for then each has a better chance of receiving the treatment that suits him. (*Nicomachean Ethics,* Book 10, Chapter 9, Section 1180)

Aristotle's desire to foster individuality and protect privacy and his conviction that the family was a more solid base for a stable society than the communal arrangement proposed by Plato led him to veto his mentor's suggestion that girls be educated exactly the same way as boys. In order for the family to function properly, Aristotle argued, females must devote themselves to child rearing and supervision of the home. The question "Is woman's place in the home?" was being debated just as energetically in 300 B.C. as in the 1980s.

From Infanticide to Socialization

Plato and Aristotle both described ideal societies. Their observations and suggestions regarding child rearing and education might lead you to expect that even though Greek children were to be exposed to firm control, most parents and teachers would usually be benign and supportive. Unfortunately, the treatment of children in Greece before the time of Christ (and in other societies during the same period) appears to have been anything but benign. In *The History of Childhood* (1974), edited by Lloyd de Mause, several historians report that until the eighteenth century the typical attitude of parents and teachers toward children centered on abuse rather than love. In summing up the general conclusions reached by the contributors to *The History of Childhood* de Mause notes, "The history of childhood is a nightmare from which we have only recently begun to awaken. The further back in history one goes, the lower the level of child care, and the more likely children are to be killed, abandoned, beaten, terrorized, and sexually abused" (p. 1). During the era when Plato and Aristotle recorded their ideas, for example, it was common for Greek parents of all classes (who were considered to be more enlightened and civilized than parents in any other part of the world at that time) to routinely kill children who were born with abnormalities, who were irritable, or who were simply considered to be superflous. (Healthy first-born sons were most likely to be spared, daughters—regardless of their family position or characteristics—were most likely to be eliminated. De Mause reports (p. 26) that one survey of Greek families in 220 B.C. listed 118 sons but only 28 daughters.) It was not until A.D. 400, de Mause concludes, that philosophers and church and political leaders began to speak out against infanticide. It took several centuries, however, for lethal and callous handling of children to be replaced by more humane treatment.

The contributors to *The History of Childhood* offered a number of explanations for the cruel treatment of children during the earlier periods of history. First, more babies were born than could be easily fed, housed, or eventually employed. In the absence of knowledge about techniques of birth control or abortion, infanticide was considered to be the most logical form of population control. (Even Aristotle recommended a law that no deformed child should be allowed to survive.) Population control is also the most logical explanation for the much greater tendency for parents to kill or fail to care for daughters.

Second, children were simply considered to be unimportant, perhaps because both parents had to devote so many hours to work, and perhaps because young children did not "earn their keep." Women of the lower classes had to work all day, every day, and a young child was seen as a nuisance. An early English proverb stated, "Who sees a child sees nothing."

Further, the contributors noted that the life expectancy of children born in most countries before the seventeenth century was about thirty years. During many periods of history as many as half of all infants were stillborn or died within a few months after birth. Parents may have developed a callous and fatalistic attitude toward young children because of the potential grief if the baby failed to survive.

Finally, infants are helpless, dependent on others, often difficult to care for, and in almost constant contact with at least one of the parents. Some historians speculated that parents of earlier times who lived under deplorable conditions and were forced to endure many hardships may have taken out their frustrations on young children as convenient scapegoats.

In the opening chapters of *The History of Childhood* de Mause traces the evolution of typical modes of child rearing during different periods of history. These trends are summarized in Table 1–1. The designations chosen by de Mause and the descriptions of typical ways parents reacted to children reveal a shift from indifference or out-and-out cruelty to recognition of children as precious individuals who should be protected and guided. When you examine Table 1–1 you might keep in mind that de Mause acknowledges that there were and continue to be substantial differences in the behavior of parents at any given time in history and that he is summarizing general trends. It seems reasonable to assume, for example, that quite a few parents before the time of Christ must have

Table 1–1
Evolution of Modes of Child Rearing

PERIOD OF HISTORY	DESIGNATION OF MODE OF CHILD REARING	CONCEPTION OF CHILD AND CHARACTERISTIC MODES OF CHILD REARING
Antiquity to fourth century A.D.	Infanticide	Children not perceived as humans with souls. Infants frequently killed or allowed to die. Little or no emotional involvement on part of parents.
Fourth to thirteenth centuries A.D.	Abandonment	Gradual acceptance of the idea that infants have souls, but little sense of parental responsibility. Children often placed in care of wet nurses or foster parents or indentured as servants.
Fourteenth to seventeenth centuries	Ambivalent	Children viewed as wicked as a result of literal interpretations of the doctrine of original sin. Parents suppress wickedness and mold proper behavior through strict instruction and punishment.
Eighteenth century	Intrusive	Children viewed as innocent as doctrine of original sin is interpreted more liberally. Marked improvement in the general level of child care.
Nineteenth to mid-twentieth centuries	Socialization	Children viewed with affection but are expected to learn to control selfish impulses and to acquire traits that will permit them to function satisfactorily in a particular culture. Child rearing becomes more preplanned. For the first time fathers active in child rearing.
Mid-twentieth century to the present	Helping	Children are viewed as being innately wise and are encouraged to develop their potentialities with the help of both parents who facilitate development more than they attempt to guide it.

Source: Adapted from descriptions by L. de Mause in *The History of Childhood,* (New York: Psychohistory Press, 1974), pp. 51–54.

responded positively to their children or else the human race would not have survived and sensitive and sympathetic individuals would not have argued against cruel treatment of children.

Conversely, as statistics on child abuse in America in the 1970s and 1980s reveal, some parents in our ultracivilized society still behave in the barbaric manner that most individuals "outgrew" hundreds of years ago. Even so, de Mause feels that he has summarized the most typical forms of child rearing at different periods of history. For reasons that will become clear as various conceptions and theories of development are discussed in these first three chapters, however, comparatively few contemporary psychologists agree with de Mause that the most characteristic form of child rearing in the 1980s stresses *helping* children rather than socializing them. The "helping" mode which de Mause regards as the form of child rearing used by enlightened parents during the last part of the twentieth century is based on the assumption that "the child knows better than the parents what it needs at each stage of life" and "there is no attempt at all to discipline or form 'habits'" (p. 52). While this extreme form of permissiveness is advocated by some psychologists and is popular with some parents, it is misleading to characterize it as the preferred approach to child rearing at the present time.

Before considering present-day interpretations of child rearing, however, it will be instructive to examine in greater detail the shift in attitudes toward children that took place between the fourteenth and eighteenth centuries.

From the Fourteenth to Eighteenth Centuries: From Wickedness to Innocence

The most noteworthy change in child-rearing attitudes between the fourteenth and eighteenth centuries was a shift from believing children to be inherently wicked to viewing them as innocent. Literal and extreme interpretations of the doctrine of original sin were widely accepted in Europe during the fourteenth to seventeenth centuries and are reflected by statements similar to these familiar verses from the King James version of the Bible:

I was shapen in iniquity; and in sin did my mother conceive me. (Psalms 51:5)

He that spareth his rod hateth his son: but he that loveth him chasteneth him betimes. (Proverbs 13:24)

Foolishness is bound in the heart of a child: but the rod of correction shall drive it far from him. (Proverbs 22:15)

The rod and reproof give wisdom: but a child left to himself bringeth his mother to shame. (Proverbs 29:15)

During this period of history, therefore, parents were told that the misbehavior of their children was due to innate wickedness. Their inherent sinfulness had not been sufficiently suppressed, and parents were encouraged to make frequent use of punishment.

Starting in the eighteenth century, however, a significant shift took place in thinking about the nature of infants and young children. Clergymen began to emphasize that baptism purified a child's immortal soul. They diverted attention from biblical descriptions of sin to statements similar to these verses from the King James version of the Bible:

> Except ye be converted, and become as little children, ye shall not enter the kingdom of heaven. (Matthew 18:3)

> Suffer the little children to come unto me, and forbid them not; for of such is the kingdom of God. (Mark 10:14)

> Train up a child in the way he should go: and when he is old he will not depart from it. (Proverbs 22:6)

Parents and teachers were told they should devote much care and thought to child rearing and education. The innocence of childhood was to be safeguarded and strengthened. Many philosophers expressed their ideas on the nature of behavior and development. Questions on such matters as the origin of ideas and the best methods of child rearing were debated by the leading intellectuals of Europe.

John Locke: Children Learn from Experience

Ideas Come from Experience

John Locke (1632–1704), the English philosopher, found it difficult to accept contemporary conclusions about ways human beings acquire knowledge. René Descartes and other philosophers of the 1600s argued that certain ideas, such as those of God, or of one's soul, or of axioms of geometry, were so inevitable and certain that they must be innate. Locke did not believe that ideas were simply "built-in" to the human organism and he spent almost twenty years building an alternative explanation, which he eventually published in his famous *Essay Concerning Human Understanding* (1690). Descartes, whose brilliance as a mathematician reflected his love of abstract thought, had engaged in pure reasoning to draw his conclusions about the mind. Locke, a practical man of medicine and politics as well as a philosopher, followed a much more down-to-earth procedure in seeking an answer to the question of the origin of ideas. He simply sat down next to the cribs of newborn infants and observed them. It is easy to understand why he concluded, "There is not the least

14th century: inherent wickedness should be suppressed by punishment

18th century: inherent innocence should be protected and guided

appearance of any settled ideas at all in them, especially of ideas answering the terms which make up those universal propositions that are esteemed innate principles" (Locke, 1690, Book 1, chapter 4, paragraph 2). Determining the kinds of innate ideas Descartes had in mind—thoughts of God, or one's soul, or a theorem of Pythagoras—by observing the behavior of a newborn infant might strike you as unfair and an impossibility, but Locke's *Essay* found a receptive audience, especially among thinkers who preferred empirical observation to abstract reasoning. They were particularly impressed by Locke's explanation of how ideas are acquired:

> Let us then suppose the mind to be, as we say, white paper, void of all characters, without any ideas; how comes it to be furnished? Whence comes it by that vast store which the busy and boundless fancy of man has painted on it with an almost endless variety? Whence has it all the materials of reason and knowledge? To this I answer in one word, from experience; in that all our knowledge is founded, and from that it ultimately derives itself. (1690, Book 2, chapter 1, paragraph 2)

All knowledge from experience

The newborn's mind as a blank slate

Locke's description of the mind of a child at birth as a "white paper" is similar to a concept proposed originally by Aristotle, who described the mind as a *tabula rasa* (blank slate). Locke accounted for the development of complex ideas, such as those Descartes considered to be innate, by reasoning that they were constructed when individuals *associated* simpler ideas. Locke's empirical approach, based on objective observation of behavior, and his concept of the association of ideas exerted a profound influence of philosophical, and later psychological, speculation in England and America.

Locke's Views on Child Rearing

Since Locke argued that experience and observation were the sources of all ideas, it was inevitable that he would be asked to describe the kinds of experiences he thought most likely to encourage proper development of a child's mind. A friend who had just become a father asked for such advice, and Locke supplied it in a long series of letters. The recipient showed the letters to several acquaintances, who pleaded with Locke to make it possible for others to profit from his wisdom. He agreed, and the letters were published under the title *Some Thoughts Concerning Education* (1693). In this book Locke pointed out that even though the mind was empty at birth, this did not mean a newborn baby lacked personality. He suggested that parents observe each child and try to adjust education to the child's unique personality.

Locke was impressed by the natural curiosity of children and urged parents to encourage it in them, "not only as a good sign, but as the great instrument nature has provided, to remove that ignorance they were born with, and which without this busy inquisitiveness will make them dull and useless creatures" (1964, p. 88). He recommended that parents be patient in answering questions and aware that

From the fourteenth to the seventeenth centuries parents were told to suppress the inherent wickedness of children by frequently punishing them. Starting around the eighteenth century, however, public figures such as John Locke began to argue that bad behavior might often be ignored rather than punished and that good behavior should be encouraged by praise. Culver Pictures.

children "hate to be idle . . . [and that] their busy humour should be constantly employed in something of use to them" (p. 95).

A particularly noteworthy point about Locke's advice to parents was his rejection of the "spare the rod and spoil the child" philosophy that had been unquestioningly accepted for hundreds of years as *the* basic principle of child rearing. Instead of punishment Locke recommended the use of praise and commendation, techniques that are the cornerstone of methods of child rearing advocated by several contemporary psychologists. The language in Locke's description of the use of reinforcement in child rearing and education is different from that used today, but the basic advice is the same:

Children (earlier perhaps than we think) are very sensible of praise and commendation. They find a pleasure in being esteemed and valued, especially by their parents, and those whom they depend on. If therefore the father caress and commend them, when they do well; show a cold and neglectful countenance to them upon doing ill; and this accompanied by a like carriage of the mother, and all others that are about them; it will in a little time make them sensible of the difference; and this, if constantly observed, I doubt not but will of itself work

Praise children for good behavior; ignore bad behavior

more than threats or blows, which lose their force, when once grown common. (1964, p. 37)

Locke's writings reflected an emerging view of humanity that was shared by many of his contemporaries. Instead of seeing children as depraved victims of original sin, many thinkers of Locke's time began to perceive them as rational and benevolent creatures. It seems likely that the shift from thinking of children as depraved to thinking of them as innocent which was underway in the 1700s would have continued regardless of the influence of any particular individual, but the change was accelerated by the appearance of one of the most controversial and persuasive philosophers in history, Jean Jacques Rousseau.

Jean Jacques Rousseau: Inherent Goodness

Rousseau's Background

Jean Jacques Rousseau was born in Geneva in 1712. His mother died giving birth to him, and his father abandoned him when he was ten. An uncle arranged for him to live with a clergyman while Rousseau served as an apprentice to an engraver, but he was cruelly treated and ran away, obtaining a series of jobs as a servant in households of the aristocracy. In 1742 he went to Paris, where, after initial failure, he succeeded in having a play and an opera performed. He first attracted widespread attention in 1750 when he published an essay in which he argued that civilization weakened men morally and physically and that only members of primitive societies—the "noble savages"—could escape corruption. This earned him considerable notoriety, which he maintained by writing additional essays, operas, and plays. His fame reached a peak when he published *Émile; or, On Education* (1762).

The Nature of Émile

Émile opens on this provocative note:

Everything is good as it comes from the hands of the Maker of the world but degenerates once it gets into the hands of man. . . . Not content to leave anything as nature has made it, [man] must needs shape man himself to his notions, as he does the trees in his garden. (Rousseau, 1762; reprinted in Boyd, 1962, p. 11)

It is easy to understand why people who had been reminded how evil and sinful they were almost every time they went to church responded favorably to a book that began with such a statement. But those who criticize the status quo and profess to have special knowledge about how to improve the world invite a "show-me" challenge. Rousseau was particularly vulnerable as a self-professed expert on teaching and child rearing because he had been a dismal failure as a teacher and because the five children he fathered (with his servant-girl mistress) were all placed in a foundling home. He nimbly outmaneuvered his critics by stating in the first chapter of *Émile:* "A man of high rank once suggested that I should be his son's tutor. But having had experience already I knew myself unfit and I refused. Instead of the difficult task of educating a child I now undertake the easier task of writing about it" (1962, p. 20). A significant point to remember about *Émile,* therefore, is that it describes the education of an imaginary child who is surrounded by individuals, conditions, and a society Rousseau was able to manipulate to suit his fancy. But even though many of the teaching techniques described in *Émile* are unrealistic and impractical, some of the points made are insightful and thought-provoking, and there have been educators in every era since the book appeared who have hailed it as the most important statement on education ever published.

Rousseau's Views on Child Rearing

In *Émile,* Rousseau explained how he thought education should be arranged to foster natural goodness. He recommended that the development of the individual should be the basic purpose of education, noting that "each mind has a form of its own in conformity with which it must be directed. If you are a wise man you will observe your pupil carefully before saying a word to him" (p. 42).

Though many of the techniques Rousseau described in *Émile* are contradictory and inconsistent, the general message is clear: parents and teachers should observe children closely and fit education to them, not attempt to induce children to learn what is beyond them; children should learn through their own experience and only when they feel a desire to learn; if children are screened from negative aspects of society, their natural goodness will assure that they will make wise choices about what they should learn.

Fit education to child; offer instruction when child feels need for it

It should be noted, however, that Rousseau recommended that children be *educated,* not left to develop *entirely* on their own. (This point is not always understood or stressed by some contemporary advocates of permissive child rearing.) After stating that "everything is good as it comes from the hands of the Maker of the world" and decrying the tendency for adults to try to shape children, Rousseau added:

> But under present conditions, human beings would be even worse than they are without this fashioning. A man left entirely to himself after birth would be the most misshapen of creatures. . . . He would fare like a shrub that has grown up by chance in the middle of the road, and got trampled underfoot by the passers-by. . . . All that we lack at birth and need when grown up is given us by education. (1962, p. 11)

By "present conditions" Rousseau meant the complexity of European civilization in 1760, a civilization that appears simple compared to the world in which we live.

In 1762 Jean Jacques Rousseau enthusiastically argued that children are inherently good and wise and that they should be allowed to develop with as little adult interference as possible. In 1960, A. S. Neill (shown here with his pupils) emphasized the same view in *Summerhill,* in which he described the school of that name he had established in England. Wide World Photos.

Rousseau's Natural View Not Popular in America

Rousseau's emphasis on human goodness and the virtues of nature appealed to the many Europeans of his day who were impatient with domination by religious dogma and bored with the artificiality of society. His argument for letting nature take its course did not have as much appeal in the United States, however. The citizens of the New World in the late 1700s and early 1800s did look upon the child as good rather than depraved. But they also fervently believed in the *perfectibility of human beings.* The abundant natural resources of the North American continent and the absence of the restrictive social structure of Europe made many Americans feel that the opportunities to better themselves—and their society—were unlimited. Believing they were masters of their own destiny, they were eager to provide their children with maximum opportunities for personal fulfillment. Alexis de Tocqueville, the perceptive French observer of the American scene, made this observation in his famous *Democracy in America* (1835):

They [the Americans] have all a lively faith in the perfectibility of man, they judge that the diffusion of knowledge must necessarily be advantageous, and the consequences of ignorance fatal; they all consider society as a body in a state of improvement, humanity as a changing scene, in which nothing is, or ought to be, permanent; and they admit that what appears to them today to be good, may be superseded by something better tomorrow. No natural boundary seems to be set to the efforts of man; and in his eyes what is not yet done is only what he has not yet attempted to do. (1835, part 1, chapter 18)

The achievements of American scientists, engineers, inventors, and manufacturers during the nineteenth century were both a product and an affirmation of this belief in the perfectibility of humans and their environment.

John B. Watson: Shaping Human Behavior

By the beginning of this century faith in the ability of science, technology, and "good old American know-how" to solve any problem had become so strong it influenced the thinking of those establishing departments of psychology in American universities. If human beings can conquer nature, fight disease, and make their lives more and more comfortable, they reasoned, why can't we improve human nature? Because American psychologists were interested in finding ways to change behavior, they endorsed John Locke's arguments that a child is born a blank slate and that all knowledge comes from experience. By assuming that a child was like a piece of clay, psychologists were free to seek ways to mold personality. When Ivan Pavlov described (in the early 1900s) how he had established what he called a conditioned reflex (or response) in dogs, John B. Watson, a particularly enthusiastic and enterprising American psychologist, was convinced that a technique was at hand for shaping human behavior in unlimited ways.

Pavlovian Conditioning

In his most famous experiment Pavlov induced a dog to salivate when a bell was rung by building up an *association* between the bell and food. If the bell was rung several times without food being presented, Pavlov reported that the response would disappear or *extinguish*. He also pointed out that once the dog was conditioned to salivate to the sound of the bell it would tend to salivate to other sounds such as a whistle; he referred to this as *stimulus generalization*. Such generalized responses could be overcome by supplying reinforcement after the bell was rung but never after a whistle was sounded. When this occurred Pavlov said that *discrimination* had taken place. Combining aspects of Locke's philosophy with Pavlov's principles of conditioning, Watson established a theory of human development and wrote a book explaining how parents should shape the behavior of their children.

Behaviorism

As a graduate student in 1903, Watson wrote a dissertation *Animal Education: The Psychical Development of the White Rat.* In American psychology at that time, when an experimenter had finished his observations of animal subjects he was expected to speculate about the state of the animal's consciousness. Watson objected to this, arguing that it was more sensible and scientific to concentrate on overt behavior, which could be observed and described objectively. He spent several years developing his arguments and eventually presented them in a paper entitled *Psychology as the Behaviorist Views It* (1913). He called himself a *behaviorist* to emphasize his belief that psychologists should base their conclusions exclusively on observations of overt behavior.

Behaviorism: scientists should base conclusions on overt behavior

While Watson was developing his views on behaviorism, he also studied infants. Since the scientific study of behavior was just beginning in the early 1900s, few controlled observations of children had been made. Watson was thus one of the first psychologists to concentrate on the study of newborn babies. Following the same empirical approach as Locke when the English philosopher examined Descartes's theory of innate ideas, Watson simply stimulated infants in various ways and described how they responded. He would expose each baby in a hospital nursery to the same series of experiences—holding their arms at their sides, for example, or making a sudden loud sound, or tickling their feet (Watson and Morgan, 1917)—and then describe their overt physical reactions. As he accumulated data, Watson began to speculate how one experience comes to be associated with another.

Albert and the White Rat

When he read about the experiments of Pavlov, Watson became convinced that the conditioned response was a more complete and satisfactory explanation of learning than the views of associationism that had been proposed up to that time. In a now classic experiment (Watson and Rayner, 1920) he demonstrated how human behavior could be conditioned. He encouraged an eleven-month-old boy named Albert to play with a white rat. When Albert began to enjoy this activity, Watson suddenly hit a steel bar with a hammer just as the child reached for the rat. In his observations of infants, Watson had discovered that a sudden, loud sound frightened most children. When Albert came to associate the previously attractive rat with the frightening stimulus, he not only responded with fear but generalized this fear to many other white and fuzzy objects.

Conditioning a child to fear a rat

"Give Me a Dozen Healthy Infants . . ."

The success of this experiment and similar experiments carried out by Pavlov and his colleagues in Russia led Watson to believe that by arranging sequences of conditioned responses he could control behavior in almost limitless ways. He was emboldened to make the following claim:

Give me a dozen healthy infants, well-formed, and my own specified world to bring them up in and I'll guarantee to take any one at random and train him to become any type of specialist I might select—doctor, lawyer, artist, merchant-chief and, yes, even beggarman and thief, regardless of his talents, penchants, tendencies, abilities, vocations, and race of his ancestors. (1925, p. 82; revised edition, 1930, p. 104)

Watson was confident that the application of science to child rearing would be as effective as the application of science to medicine and technology. Watson's skepticism about what happened to children when parents trusted to "intuition" was reflected in the dedication of his *Psychological Care of Infant and Child* (1928) to "the first mother who brings up a happy child."

Watson's impact on the study of child development was substantial but brief. Other psychologists discovered that the kind of learning he had demonstrated so dramatically with Albert applied only to essentially involuntary reflex actions (such as reacting in a fearful way). Furthermore, attempts to build sequences of conditioned responses were rarely successful. And many parents who purchased his book on child rearing were unwilling to play the role of objective scientist or engage in systematic shaping of behavior. (In an autobiographical sketch written toward the end of his career Watson noted that he was sorry he had written *Psychological Care of Infant and Child* because "I did not know enough to write the book I wanted to write" [1936, p. 286].)

Arnold Gesell: Maturation and Inner Determination

Starting in the 1920s, hundreds of studies of conditioned responses were carried out, and most of the learning theories developed in America were based on the principle of the association of ideas. In the 1930s, however, some developmental psychologists who had carefully observed infants were impressed by the uniformity of the sequence of types of behavior appearing at different age levels. They reasoned that the similarity in the behavior of children from widely different backgrounds could be accounted for only by assuming that development was controlled by innate tendencies. The man who was most energetic in promoting this view was Arnold Gesell. Gesell, together with his two chief associates Frances Ilg and Louise Ames (who became the directors of his research institute after his death), became convinced that Watson's failure to make good on his boast had demolished the belief that behavior could be systematically shaped. They argued for recognition of the inner determination of behavior and urged parents to acknowledge the inexorable nature of maturation. Children develop according to a built-in timetable, they maintained, and therefore "control" much of their own behavior. Ilg and Ames began their *Child Behavior* (1955) by observing, "Gone are the days when psychologists likened the child's body to a lump of clay which you the parent could mold in any direction you chose." When making this assertion they failed to consider the extent to which Americans believed in the perfectibility of human beings—or the energy and ingenuity of a psychologist named B. F. Skinner.

B. F. Skinner: Shaping Behavior More Effectively

In a survey of psychology departments conducted in 1967 (Myers, 1970, p. 1045) Skinner was chosen as the most influential American psychologist of this century. As the leading spokesman for the behaviorist-associationist-environmentalist position, Skinner argues that every personality is the product of environmental experiences. It is therefore appropriate to speculate about the experiences that shaped his own behavior. (The background of other theorists mentioned in this book is presented for the same reason: you are encouraged to theorize about causes of behavior, particularly the impact of childhood experiences, so it is reasonable to speculate about the backgrounds of those who have proposed theories of development. In addition, learning something about the personalities of theorists may encourage you to sample their writings.)

Skinner's Background

Skinner's father was a draftsman in a railroad shop in Susquehanna, Pennsylvania, when he met and eventually married the daughter of the foreman, a gentleman named Burrhus. He studied law as he worked and in time passed the bar examination. The Skinners settled in Susquehanna, and in 1904 the first of two boys born to the couple was named Burrhus Frederic (which explains the use of the initials B. F.). Young Fred, as he preferred to be called, was always building things; his projects included a merry-go-round, a water pistol, and a steam cannon capable of shooting plugs of potato and carrot over the roofs of houses. Fred attended a small school (his graduating class had eight students) and he came under the influence of a teacher who aroused his interest in literature, the subject he majored in when he entered Hamilton College. At the end of his freshman year, Skinner complained that the college was "pushing him around with unnecessary requirements," and by his senior year he reports he was "in open revolt" (1967, p. 392). One time he spread the (false) word that Charlie Chaplin was going to give a lecture at the college. Children thronged the railroad station, and—despite police roadblocks—four hundred carloads of people who

B. F. Skinner. New York Times Pictures.

mistook a football rally for the Chaplin lecture arrived on campus. On Senior Class Day he defiantly covered the walls of the auditorium with caricatures of the faculty. Despite all this, Skinner graduated.

At first he attempted a career as a writer, but became so dissatisfied with everything he wrote that he ended up spending most of his time playing the piano and building ship models. Since he found literature unrewarding, he decided to turn to science and chose to do graduate work in psychology at Harvard. His choice of psychology he attributes to a number of factors: an early interest in animals, a recollection of a troupe of performing pigeons he had seen at a county fair, curiosity about episodes of human behavior, and his discovery of books by Pavlov and Watson. The direction his theories ultimately took was determined by his early contact with graduate students who were enthusiastic about behaviorism and also involved in research on maze running in rats.

The Skinner Box

The inventiveness that had produced the steam cannon, his interest in trained animals, and the example set by Pavlov, Watson, and the graduate students he met at Harvard led Skinner to develop a device for investigating the way animals learn through associations. The *Skinner box*, as the apparatus came to be called, is a small enclosure that contains only a bar (or lever) and a tray. Outside the box is a hopper holding a supply of food pellets that are dropped into the tray when the

Conditioning a rat to press a bar in preselected ways

bar is pressed under preselected conditions (for example, when a tone is sounded). Each time the bar is pressed, a record is automatically made on a graph. An experimenter can set the controls of a dozen Skinner boxes, place a hungry rat in each, and engage in other activities while the rats and the machines carry out a series of experiments. Skinner later developed a slightly different apparatus for use with pigeons. In place of the bar, a disk (to be pecked) activates the food-supplying mechanism.

Operant Conditioning

Pavlovian conditioning: involuntary action aroused by a previously neutral stimulus

On the basis of principles derived from his experiments with rats and pigeons, Skinner developed a theory of *operant conditioning*.[2] He and other behaviorist-associationists had come to recognize that the kind of conditioning practiced by Pavlov and Watson was extremely limited, since an originally neutral stimulus (a bell or a white rat) simply came to arouse an essentially involuntary action (such as salivation or responding with fear). He argued that the kind of learning demonstrated by a rat or pigeon in a Skinner box was much more common and versatile. A voluntary action (pressing the bar or pecking the disk) could be strengthened by reinforcing the behavior under preselected conditions (when a tone was sounded, after a move in a given direction). Skinner proposed that behavior could be shaped in almost any way by supplying reinforcement in systematic fashion, and he supported his claim by teaching pigeons to —among other things—play table tennis and tap out tunes on a xylophone. These feats were accomplished by first reinforcing the behavior of a hungry pigeon when it voluntarily made a move in the desired direction (for example, pecking a bar on a xylophone) and then refining these movements by supplying food only when a specific sequence of actions occurred (pecking four bars on a xylophone in a particular order).

Operant conditioning: voluntary behavior strengthened by reinforcement

Science and Human Behavior

Once he had established the principles of operant conditioning, Skinner began to speculate, in the tradition of the American belief in perfectibility, on how these principles could be applied to human behavior. He observed, "The methods of science have been enormously successful wherever they have been tried. Let us then apply them to human affairs" (1953, p. 5). He proposed—in a less flam-

---

[2] Skinner chose the term *operant conditioning* to stress that an organism "operates" on the environment when it learns. This type of learning is also referred to as *instrumental conditioning* because what the organism does is instrumental in securing reinforcement. The type of learning first demonstrated by Pavlov is often referred to as *classical conditioning* because it was based on a "classic" experiment (an experiment that was an excellent demonstration of scientific methods and had a significant impact on later studies).

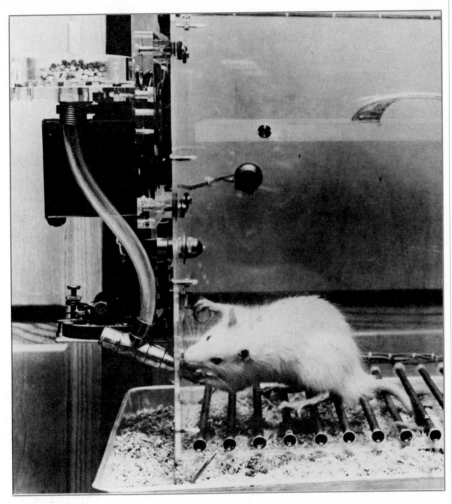

A rat in a Skinner box. The rat's behavior is reinforced with a food pellet when it presses the bar under conditions preselected by the experimenter. The rat does not respond in a reflexive manner, as is the case with Pavlovian conditioning, but engages in self-selected behavior. In the process of exploring the Skinner box, for instance, the rat is almost certain to touch the bar. When that occurs the experimenter supplies a food pellet, and bar-pressing behavior is reinforced. Eventually the rat may be reinforced only when a particular sequence of actions (for example, pressing the bar five times in succession) is performed. Courtesy of Pfizer, Inc.

boyant manner than Watson—that behavior could be shaped in a systematic way. In his novel *Walden Two* (1948) he describes a society based on principles of operant conditioning. The children in this society are placed in the hands of child-rearing specialists who systematically control the children's behavior in order to eliminate undesirable traits (such as jealousy) and encourage desirable ones (such as self-control and perseverance).

When Skinner had perfected the principles of operant conditioning, he was convinced that the basic weakness of Watson's approach had been overcome. Behavior shapers were no longer restricted to arousing reflex actions by substituting one stimulus for another; they were now capable of controlling any type of behavior. But for behavior control to be effective, Skinner argued, it would be essential to make a fundamental assumption about human nature that conflicted with the view of free will widely accepted since the Renaissance. Skinner concluded that the belief that human beings are capable of shaping their own destinies and that each person's behavior is a result of free choice was incompatible with a scientific analysis of behavior. In *Science and Human Behavior* (1953) he observed:

If we are to use the methods of science in the field of human affairs, we must assume that behavior is lawful and determined. We must expect to discover that what a man does is the result of specifiable conditions and that once these conditions have been discovered, we can anticipate and to some extent determine his actions. (1953, p. 6)

Skinner acknowledged that his proposal would be difficult for many people to accept because the view of humans as free agents was both well established and appealing. But he argued that the only way to make effective use of scientific knowledge was to endorse totally a view of environmental control. "A scientific conception of human behavior dictates one practice," he explained, "a philosophy of personal freedom another. Confusion in theory means confusion in practice. The present unhappy condition of the world may in large measure be traced to our vacillaton" (1953, p. 9).

Choice Between Planned or Accidental Reinforcement

As an organism emitted behavior, Skinner theorized, certain actions would be reinforced and strengthened; others would go unrewarded and be extinguished. Therefore, the behaving organism is controlled by reinforcing experiences, and those who supply reinforcements are in control of behavior. Children will act on their own, but the tendency to repeat certain acts will be determined by which acts are rewarded. If those in contact with a child did not reinforce behavior in a systematic way, Skinner mantained, development would be left to accidental reinforcements. Skinner did not ignore the possibility that inherited factors influence behavior, but he pointed out that these cannot be changed. He suggested that it is more sensible to concentrate exclusively on environmental experiences that *can* be arranged and altered. Skinner recommended that parents and teachers emulate the fictional child-rearing specialists of *Walden Two* by assuming that all behavior is determined by experiences and by doing everything possible to shape the behavior of children systematically.

Behavior determined by reinforced experiences, not by free choice

Behavior Modification

Shaping behavior according to the principles of operant conditioning is referred to as *behavior modification*. The parent or teacher who uses this technique first decides on specific types of behavior to be encouraged and discouraged. Then, instances of negative behavior are ignored, and all initial instances of positive behavior are reinforced by praise, candy, money, or tokens that can later be traded in for prizes.[3] The frequency of reinforcement is gradually decreased so that children eventually behave in the desired manner on their own. Suppose, for example, that parents want a three-year-old to stop throwing temper tantrums and to start putting toys away. As much as possible, temper tantrums are ignored, and the parents make sure that the child gains nothing from tantrums. Each time the toys are put away, by contrast, the child is given a hug or kiss, praised, or given a treat. If all goes well, the actions of the parents will modify the behavior of the child so that temper tantrums will disappear and toy-putting-away behavior will increase to the point where it can be maintained by only an occasional reward.

Behavior modification: reinforce desirable, ignore undesirable behavior

Controlled Behavior versus Free Choice

Many American psychologists agreed with Skinner's view in *Walden Two* and *Science and Human Behavior* that behavior is determined by reinforcement. They were not bothered by the assumption that humans are not free if this would lead to effective control of behavior. Some psychologists, however, urged those who endorsed Skinner's arguments to consider the implications of forcing a choice between controlled behavior and free choice. The psychotherapist Carl R. Rogers, for example, felt that Skinner's view of human behavior was a threat to efforts to improve mental health. In all of his therapeutic sessions Rogers tried to help his clients develop the conviction that they *could* control their own behavior. He pointed out that asking people to assume that they had little or no control over what happened to them was likely to shatter their self-confidence. Rogers engaged in a debate with Skinner (reported in *Science*, 1956, **124**, 1057–1066) and wrote *Learning to Be Free* (1963) in which he took issue with the argument that our behavior is controlled by reinforcement. While Rogers forcefully expressed his objections to Skinner's view, the psychologist who presented the most complete alternative to behaviorism was Abraham H. Maslow.

Key to mental health: person's belief in ability to control own behavior

---

[3] Note how the basic technique advocated by behavior modifiers of today is essentially the same as the advice offered by Locke in 1690: "If therefore the father caress and commend [children] when they do well; show a cold and neglectful countenance to them upon doing ill; and this accompanied by a like carriage of the mother, and all others that are about them; it will in a little time make them sensible of the difference" (1964, p. 37).

Abraham H. Maslow: Self-Determination

The fact that Skinner studied psychology at Harvard in the 1930s at a time when behaviorism and associationism were being explored influenced the development of operant conditioning. Maslow also started his career in psychology in a department with a behavioristic emphasis, but a series of events both personal and professional led him to develop a quite different conception of behavior.

Maslow's Background

Maslow's father, a Russian emigrant, settled in Brooklyn, New York, where he worked as a barrel maker. When he had accumulated some savings he wrote to a cousin in Russia and asked her to come to America and marry him. She accepted, and Abraham (born in 1908) was the first of seven children. He was shy, sensitive, and odd in appearance and later observed, "I was certainly neurotic, extremely neurotic during all my first twenty years—depressed, terribly unhappy, lonely, isolated, self-rejecting" (quoted in Wilson, 1972, p. 131). Things would have been much worse, he felt, if a kindly uncle had not provided sympathy and support. He also found satisfaction in school work and was an honor student at Brooklyn High School.

After graduation, his father urged him to prepare for a career in law, but Abraham was unable to generate any enthusiasm for the courses he took at City College of New York and later at Cornell University. Eventually his interest was aroused by a psychology course he took shortly after enrolling at the University of Wisconsin. There he earned a B.A. and a Ph.D. in psychology. He later taught at Brooklyn College for fourteen years.

Humanistic Psychology

Maslow insatiably sought new ideas in psychology. He met Max Wertheimer and Kurt Koffka, two of the founders of Gestalt psychology (based on the assumption that behavior should be studied by taking into account the interplay of forces acting on a person). He also met students of Freud, immersed himself in psychoanalysis in preparation for a career as a psychotherapist, and became fascinated by anthropology. These and other influences led him to champion *humanistic psychology*. The word *humanistic* emphasizes the great significance of such uniquely "human" qualities as thoughts, feelings, and attitudes. Such qualities are often difficult to study in a scientific manner because they are not always expressed in the form of observable behavior. Maslow and other humanistic psychologists believe, however, that feelings and attitudes are too important to ignore because of methodological complications.

Abraham H. Maslow (1908–1970) a few months before his death. Marcia Roltner.

Development as Free Choice

Maslow believed that American behaviorist psychologists had become so preoccupied with overt behavior and objectivity that they were disregarding some of the most important aspects of human existence. This conclusion was reinforced when his first child was born. Maslow observed later, "All the behavioristic psychology that I'd learnt simply didn't prepare me for having a child. A baby was so miraculous and so wonderful . . . all the work with rats . . . just didn't help at all" (quoted in Wilson, 1972, p. 146). Maslow found too that he was unable to accept Skinner's argument that a scientific view of human behavior required the assumption that humans are not free. He concluded that each individual possesses an essential inner nature: the behavior of a person is *not* dominated by external forces, individuals determine much of their own behavior. The acceptance of the behavioristic view leads to the conclusion that parents have the *responsibility* to shape the behavior of their children. Maslow's humanistic view, however, leads to this philosophy of child rearing:

In the normal development of the healthy child, it is now believed that, much of the time, if he is given a really free choice, he will choose what is good for his growth. . . . This implies that *he* "knows" better than anyone else what is good for him. A permissive regime means not that adults gratify his needs directly but make it possible for *him* to gratify his needs, and make his own choices, i.e., let him *be*. It is necessary in order for children to grow well that adults have enough trust in them and in the natural processes of growth, i.e., not interfere too much, not *make* them grow, or force them into predetermined designs, but rather *let* them grow and *help* them grow in a Taoistic rather than an authoritarian way. (1968, pp. 198–199)

This view of development repeats a point made earlier by Aristotle, Locke, and Rousseau: observe children carefully and allow for their individuality.

Bad Choosers and Good Choosers

Maslow felt children should be given freedom to grow and to make their own choices, but he emphasized that only when children feel comfortable, safe, loved, and accepted are they likely to choose wisely. He stressed this point by making a distinction between *bad choosers* and *good choosers*. When some children are allowed freedom to choose, they seem consistently to make wise choices; many children, however, frequently make choices that are self-destructive. Maslow explained this difference as the result of opposing sets of internal forces, one set impelling the child to seek safety, the other stimulating the child to seek growth. In Maslow's view parents should not try to shape behavior, but neither should they feel that children should be left entirely on their own. Maslow reasons that before children are likely to make wise choices their needs for physical comfort, safety, love, belonging, and esteem must be satisfied. Children cannot do this on their own. Others must minister to their physical demands, guard them from danger, show them that they are loved, make them feel that they are individuals worthy of esteem.

Limitations of Maslow's View

Books and articles by Rogers and Maslow called attention to some of the possible dangers of too literal an interpretation of Skinner's stress on external control. But Skinner answered his critics in numerous articles and eventually a book, *Beyond Freedom and Dignity* (1971), in which he reaffirmed the same basic points made earlier in *Science and Human Behavior*. He was more convinced than ever that the environment determines behavior: "As we learn more about the effects of the environment, we have less reason to attribute any part of human behavior to an autonomous controlling agent" (1971, p. 101). Skinner also disagreed with Maslow's plea that parents simply *let* and *help* their children grow. He noted: "The fundamental mistake made by all those who choose weak methods of control is to assume that the balance of control is left to the individual, when in fact it is left to other conditions" (1971, p. 99).

Skinner's point might be understood more completely by imagining parents who are eager to *help* their children grow (as Maslow recommends). While Maslow's observations about children determining their own behavior are superficially appealing, they are too vague to be of value to parents who are trying to decide when they should allow a child to make choices and when they should supply assistance or guidance. Suppose parents observe that their child has developed an extreme fear of dogs. They are quite sure the fear first became apparent just after the child was inadvertently knocked down by the neighbor's large, playful dog. In a situation such as this they can clearly benefit from Skinner's theory that behavior is controlled by external conditions. They might assume that the fear developed, not because of some inner tendency, but because the child associated dogs with painful and frightening experiences. Operating on this assumption, they might arrange for the child to engage in a series of positive, enjoyable experiences with dogs and thereby replace negative associations with positive ones. If the parents follow Maslow's advice too literally and do *not* interfere, the child *might* eventually overcome the fear if "accidental" positive experiences with dogs happened to occur. On the other hand, another unfortunate experience with dogs might make the fear so extreme that it will be generalized to other animals. Skinner argues that it is a mistake to leave such situations to chance, simply hoping that the child will eventually get over the fear. Parents who are impressed by Maslow's books may make every effort to satisfy the basic needs of their children. Even if they do succeed in satisfying love, belonging, and esteem needs, however, they may fail to help a child overcome something as specific as a fear. In many situations, therefore, it seems preferable to make a deliberate effort to replace unfortunate behavior with desirable behavior.

Albert Bandura: Anticipatory Control

Albert Bandura is every bit as enthusiastic as Skinner about the potential values of applying principles of operant conditioning to human behavior. (Among other things, he has demonstrated [Bandura, Grusec, and Menlove, 1967] how a child's fear of dogs can be overcome by arranging for the child to watch other children engaging in enjoyable interactions with dogs.) But Bandura, like Maslow and Rogers, was bothered by some of the same potential disadvantages of Skinner's extreme stress on external control. He felt that principles of operant conditioning might be rejected or ignored because the underlying assumptions stressed by Skinner were difficult for many people to accept.

Bandura concluded that behaviorists overemphasized manipulative control because they assumed that reinforcement influences behavior without the conscious involvement of the individual. (He notes: "Humans do not simply respond to stimuli, they interpret them" [1977, p. 59].) He was not convinced that human beings were as helpless as they were made to appear by those who interpreted the behaviorist view in an extreme way. Bandura suggests (1974) that human beings are capable of choosing how they will respond to many

*Anticipatory control:
ability to preselect
consequences*

situations because many types of human behavior are under *anticipatory control.* That is, children and adults are capable of observing the effects of their actions, and they are also able to anticipate what will happen under certain conditions. As a result, they are able to control their own behavior to a significant extent by imagining what might happen under given circumstances and then choosing between different situations and experiences.

To illustrate what Bandura means by anticipatory control, picture a tenth-grade boy who has developed quite a bit of skill as a musician and enjoys taking clarinet lessons from a much-admired teacher. The boy envies the attention earned by athletes, though, and decides to try out for the school football team. Unfortunately, he lacks ability, makes many mistakes, is ridiculed by teammates, and is ignominiously dropped from the squad after being publicly berated by the not-too-sensitive coach. As a result he develops a negative attitude toward sports. If an extreme behaviorist interpretation is made of these situations, it might be argued that the boy's attitudes toward music and sports are not due to deliberate choices on his part because they have been shaped by positive and negative experiences. If Bandura's concept of anticipatory control is taken into account, however, it might be reasoned that even though the boy's behavior *has* been shaped, he is in a position to control future experiences. If he is later given a choice between taking a physical education class taught by the football coach or performing in the school band, for example, he can control his own destiny by anticipating what is likely to happen in each situation and by selecting a course of action that is almost sure to be fulfilling rather than disagreeable.

Bandura's allowance for anticipatory control avoids the implication of Skinner's view that humans are almost always the "victims" of experiences. A limitation of Bandura's view is that it accounts for only certain types of behavior (choices between alternatives). All of the other conceptions discussed in this chapter, however, are similarly limited in that they can account for only some aspects of behavior. Accordingly, it will be of value to reexamine the various views that have just been discussed to gain a more complete and balanced picture of conceptions of human development.

Placing Conceptions of Development in Perspective

In Table 1–2 you will find a summary of the various conceptions of development discussed in this chapter. Factors that influenced each theorist are noted to call your attention to prevailing trends which had an impact on the thinking of each person. Criticisms are mentioned to emphasize that while each view clarifies certain aspects of behavior and development, each has certain limitations. Taken together the factors that influenced theorists and the criticisms of the points they emphasized reveal that each theorist reacted against certain prevailing ideas, often

Extreme behaviorist interpretations suggest that preferences (such as these students' choice for competitive sports or for playing in the band) are not due to deliberate choice but are shaped by positive and negative experiences. Albert Bandura, who favors a modified behaviorist position, suggests that individuals *can* often control their own behavior by anticipating what might happen under given circumstances and then choosing between different kinds of activities. Hugh Rogers/ Monkmeyer and David S. Strickler/Monkmeyer.

Table 1–2
Conceptions of Development—Summary

THEORIST	FACTORS THAT INFLUENCED THINKING	MAIN POINTS STRESSED	CRITICISMS AND LIMITATIONS
Plato	Bothered by decadence of Athens. Eager to produce a perfect society.	Establish a meritocracy by giving all children equal opportunities. Systematically place individuals in worker, manager, or leader categories. Establish self-control without squelching individuality.	Too regimented. Individual subordinated to the state. Family life eliminated.
Aristotle	Eager to produce a perfect society but bothered by disadvantages of a strict meritocracy.	Provide many kinds of education to allow for personality differences in children. Stress on family life.	Emphasis on family life relegated females to roles of homemaker and child rearer.
Locke	Unable to accept doctrine of innate ideas. Impatient with speculations that could not be checked. Concerned about negative impact of punishment.	Children learn from experience. Praise good behavior, ignore rather than punish bad behavior.	Tried to explain too much by stressing observation of behavior and the association of ideas.
Rousseau	Bothered by excessive rules of deportment in society and stress on proper behavior in every situation.	Assume children are naturally good. Fit education to the child. Let children decide what to learn and when to to learn it.	Description of the education of Émile too hypothetical and unrealistic. Children cannot anticipate what they will need to know in a complex society.
Watson	Irritated by prevailing view that psychologists should speculate about the thoughts of animals (and children).	Scientists should base conclusions on observations of overt behavior. Child behavior should be shaped through Pavlovian conditioning.	Failed to recognize limitations of Pavlovian conditioning. Too extreme (and optimistic) in advocating behavior shaping.

Table 1–2
Conceptions of Development—Summary

THEORIST	FACTORS THAT INFLUENCED THINKING	MAIN POINTS STRESSED	CRITICISMS AND LIMITATIONS
Skinner	Impatient with vague beliefs about how people make choices. Eager to apply science to human behavior, trace causes, shape desirable traits.	Assume that behavior is determined by identifiable causes. Shape behavior by taking into account causes and by making judicious use of precepts of operant conditioning.	Stress on external control is a threat to self-confidence (and perhaps mental health). Inherited predispositions largely ignored. Possibility that parents might squelch individuality.
Maslow	Birth of own child led to doubts about values of operant conditioning. Bothered by too much stress on objectivity.	Children determine much of their own behavior. Trust children, let them grow.	Those who wish to help children grow have no clear guidelines to follow. Too much is left to chance.
Bandura	Believed in principles of operant conditioning but was bothered by certain implications of the view that all behavior is under external control.	Ability of individuals to anticipate makes it possible to preselect consequences (and control own behavior). Children learn by imitating others.	Explains only one particular type of behavior (the way certain choices are made).

to the point of overreacting. Quite frequently, the overreaction of one theorist stimulated a different theorist to propose an alternate view. The conceptions of development summarized in this chapter were selected from the many recorded opinions to provide a balanced summary of significant observations.

Similar Ideas Have Been Stressed at Different Times

Table 1–2 demonstrates that similar ideas have been presented at different times. Quite often, however, these similar conceptions have been proposed for different reasons. Plato and Skinner, for example, both recommended systematic child rearing. Plato made this recommendation because he wanted to produce a perfect society. Skinner desired to apply science to human behavior and to shape desirable characteristics instead of simply *hoping* they would develop.

Locke, Watson, and Skinner all argued that those who wish to guide child development should make careful observations of overt behavior. Locke was in favor of this approach because he was unable to accept Descartes' doctrine of innate ideas. Watson reacted against the insistence of his mentors that he try to fathom the "psychical development" of rats. Skinner supported the behavioristic view because he reasoned that if "we are to use science in the field of human behavior, we must assume that behavior is lawful and determined." The only way to discover the determinants of behavior, he maintained, is through careful observation.

Aristotle, Rousseau, and Maslow all stressed that every child is unique and that personality differences should be recognized and encouraged. Aristotle supported the view because he was afraid Plato's ultrasystematic approach to education would limit individuality and destroy the family. Rousseau was reacting against the excessive formality of French society in the 1700s. Maslow felt that behaviorists were concentrating on experiences to the point of totally ignoring inborn tendencies.

Each Conception Is Relevant to Contemporary Society

Another point that emerges from an examination of Table 1–2 is that even conceptions propounded before the birth of Christ can be related to developments in the world of the 1980s.

Plato wanted all children, regardless of their sex or backgrounds, to have equal opportunities not only for self-fulfillment but for the good of society. In the 1960s Lyndon Johnson established or stimulated the later development of legislation intended to create a "Great Society" in America. Equal opportunity regulations of various kinds were established, affirmative action programs were instituted, laws were passed in an effort to reduce discrimination against females, Head Start and similar programs were funded.

Aristotle wanted to avoid what he felt were disadvantages of Plato's recommendations and sought a balance between individual freedom, the rights of others, and the good of society. He proposed that a variety of forms of education be made available so that teaching could be adapted to the unique personality of each child. He also stressed the values of child rearing in a family setting. Today, the leaders of the Soviet Union have established a meritocratic form of schooling that is quite similar to that recommended by Plato. Capable children are identified very early in life and placed in special institutions designed to accomplish two basic goals: (1) the development of special skills to a maximum; (2) the inculcation of loyalty to the state. This system of education has been highly successful in producing outstanding athletes, musicians, dancers, and scientists. But, as Aristotle predicted, it has severely limited individuality (which

Even though Plato and Aristotle recorded their ideas before the birth of Christ, some of their observations help explain events in the 1980s. Aristotle predicted, for example, that too much emphasis on standard education intended to inspire loyalty to the state or to shape officially endorsed forms of artistic expression would interfere with individuality and unique forms of personal expression. Many recent Russian defectors, such as Alexander Godunov, shown here dancing with Natalia Makarova and the American Ballet Theatre, have sought asylum in free societies for the very reasons emphasized by Aristotle. Wide World Photos.

is the main reason so many outstanding Russians have defected). At the present time in America there is great interest in alternatives to public school education, and private schools are proliferating. The voucher system, whereby parents would be able to use tax money to pay tuition at any school of their choice, is energetically endorsed by many citizens. A growing number of parents have decided to act as teachers and educate their children in the home because of dissatisfaction with public schooling.

Rousseau and Maslow argued in favor of permitting children as much freedom as possible to develop in their own way. In the 1970s parents who were disenchanted with what they considered to be excessive controls in our society banded together to form cooperative schools more or less patterned after A. S. Neill's Summerhill. This famous English school was based on the premise that "a child is innately wise and realistic. If left to himself without adult suggestion of any kind, he will develop as far as he is capable of developing" (Neill, 1960, p. 4). During the same decade many American schools and universities eliminated requirements and experimented with student selection of the curriculum. In the 1980s there is substantial evidence that many students who attended such schools did not acquire skills they need to handle common jobs in our society. Accordingly, there is currently considerable support for return to a prescribed curriculum in the schools.

Locke, Watson, Skinner, and Bandura all pointed out the futility of speculating about causes of behavior that could not be observed. They all recommended that parents and teachers try to be more systematic in encouraging desirable traits and minimizing the emergence of negative ones. In the last twenty years thousands of articles and books on behavior modification have been published. In many American schools, techniques of teaching derived from principles of behavior modification are used every day.

A "Meeting of Minds" (and Exchange of Ideas)

Points noted in these last two sections, as well as those recorded in Table 1–2 might be summarized and clarified by imagining a "meeting of minds." Steve Allen has presented a series of television programs of that title in which famous individuals from different periods of history engage in a roundtable discussion. If all of the individuals listed in Table 1–2 could be brought together on a television panel show, they might engage in an exchange of ideas something like this:

Moderator: Since you have seniority, Plato, perhaps you should have the privilege of kicking off this discussion.

Plato: Thank you. I believe it might be stimulating for me to mention an article I recently read in one of your news magazines in which the author argued that America is experiencing a loss of confidence and lacks leadership. Since conditions in present-day America seem to be quite similar to those in the Athens of my time, I would like to suggest that you follow the procedure I outlined in the volume of my writings titled *Laws* and establish a highly systematic meritocracy.

Aristotle: Even though you were my teacher, sir, and I admire you more than any man who ever lived, I feel obliged to point out that the plan you outline in *Laws* overlooks two very important things. First, the need to allow for personality differences in children. Second, the advantages of having children grow up in a family setting.

Skinner: I would like to suggest that both of my learned Greek colleagues read my novel *Walden Two.* In Chapters 12 through 17 you will find a description of a form of child rearing that is quite similar to that recommended in *Laws*. Children are not reared by their parents, most of whom do not have the time or training to do a proper job of it, but by trained specialists. One of the disadvantages of your emphasis on family life, if you will permit me to say so, Aristotle, is that you overlook Plato's argument that telling women their place is in the home is "folly." In my ideal society women bear children before they reach the age of twenty and then are encouraged to spend the rest of their lives making the most of their abilities.

Aristotle: I *have* read your book, Professor Skinner, and I am impressed by many of the policies you advocate. Even so, I find it difficult to accept your view that most parents would be willing to relinquish their ties with their children. I still believe that there are values that come from a close relationship between parents and children that cannot be achieved any other way.

Maslow: I'd like to go on record as being in agreement with Aristotle. When my first child was born I found that I was absolutely fascinated by watching different forms of behavior emerge. I didn't get the impression that "experts" of any kind had to *do* things to children. That's why I urge parents to *let* their children grow. It seems to me that parents can do a better job than anyone else of showing their children that they love and esteem them. Building up that sort of relationship can overcome many little "mistakes" in child rearing.

Skinner: All right, let's forget about the "experts" I described in *Walden Two* (who were fictional characters anyway). Let's concentrate on what might happen if parents, even loving ones, did just *let* their children grow. If that policy is followed, some lucky children will have fortunate experiences and will acquire desirable traits, less fortunate children will have negative experiences and be saddled with traits that will handicap them for the rest of their lives.

Bandura: I'd like to support that point. Those of us who have been interested in behavior modification have found that it is possible for parents to arrange experiences so that their children can overcome unfortunate traits, such as fears. Furthermore, parents can strengthen positive traits by supplying reinforcement and weaken negative traits by ignoring the behavior.

Watson: How I envy you psychologists of the post-1960 era. If I had only known what you know, I would have been able to convert more people to the idea of using psychological principles to do a better job of child rearing.

Locke: If you will permit me to say so, I was amused when I read some of the books published in the 1960s on your so-called behavior modification. They presented it as a revolutionary discovery. I hope you will not think it immodest of me to point out that I urged parents to use the same techniques in 1690.

Rousseau: I don't see why you should worry about being immodest, Dr. Locke! I was hugely amused when I read some of the books published in the 1960s urging parents to *let* their children grow. (I don't intend that as an insult, friend Maslow.) You scholars of the twentieth century might have saved yourself a lot of time and trouble if you had read my *Émile*. You know, just because a book is old does not mean that everything in it is worthless.

Skinner: Very true. Probably the greatest strength of scientific study is that the discoveries of one generation serve as the basis for more advanced discoveries by the next generation.

Watson: You can say that again.

Skinner: I would like to point out, though, that while behavior modification is similar to ideas first recorded in 1690 by Dr. Locke, it is based not on logical thinking but on principles that have been established experimentally.

Moderator: Well, gentlemen, I'm afraid our time is up. It seems fair to conclude, even after such a short exchange, that each of you has something important to say. To get a balanced picture, though, it would appear to be advantageous to examine the pros and cons of each of your views. Taken together, they help explain many things about human development.

This imaginary discussion sets the stage for topics to be discussed in the next two chapters. Chapter 2 consists of a history of the scientific study of development, a description of methods developed to study human behavior, and capsule descriptions of the types of studies carried out by many of the best-known developmental psychologists. Chapter 3 outlines the most completely thought-out theories of development.

Suggestions for Further Study

Historical Views of the Child and of Child Rearing

The History of Childhood (1974) edited by Lloyd de Mause consists of several historians' summaries of attitudes toward children and child rearing in different countries at different times in history. While many interesting observations are offered, particularly in the form of statements from early documents, you should be forewarned that most of the interpretations made by the authors stress a technical psychoanalytic point of view. Anyone who lacks sophisticated knowledge of Freudian theory is likely to experience problems comprehending some of the points made. Accordingly, if you refer to this book you may find it more instructive to focus on direct quotes from early sources rather than the interpretive comments supplied. The same suggestion applies to the *Journal of Psychohistory* which contains articles on the impact of child rearing on individuals and groups written from a psychoanalytic frame of reference.

A different historical analysis of child rearing is *Centuries of Childhood: A Social History of Family Life* (1962) by Philippe Ariès. While Ariès summarizes many interesting historical descriptions and offers some provocative hypotheses, his book has been criticized by other historians (including de Mause). A primary criticism is that he bases much of his theorizing about early child care on interpretations of art works. He argues, for example, that artists before the 1600s typically painted children as miniature adults and that this means they were not viewed as children. Critics have pointed out, however, that early artists other than those mentioned by Ariès *did* paint children as children.

Another book to consult if you would like to learn about changing views of childhood is *The Child* (1965) by William Kessen. This volume is made up of excerpts from the works of Locke, Rousseau, Darwin, Binet, Freud, Watson, Gesell, Piaget, and others. Kessen supplies commentary and points out how early views of the child were expounded by physicians and reformers, then philosophers and teachers, and most recently by specialists in developmental psychology.

Locke's Observations on Education

John Locke's reputation is based primarily on his *Essay Concerning Human Understanding*. If you would like to sample this famous treatise, read Chapters 1 and 2 of Book I, and Chapter 1 of Book II. (There should be at least one edition of this work in your library). These sections will give you a clear idea of his answer to Descartes's theory of innate ideas.

As a student of development you will probably find Locke's *Some Thoughts Concerning Education* of special interest. A particularly good selection of Locke's thoughts can be found in *John Locke on Education* (1964), edited by Peter Gay.

Rousseau's Views of Education

Jean Jacques Rousseau was an original thinker whose observations on development and education are still thought-provoking more than two hundred years after he wrote them. Although Rousseau was imaginative and innovative, he did not possess much intellectual discipline, and his original works tend to be disorganized, wordy, and repetitious. Therefore, you may respond more favorably to Rousseau if you read an edited version of *Émile* rather than a complete translation. Particularly recommended is *The Émile of Jean Jacques Rousseau* (1962), translated and edited by William Boyd.

Neill's Views on Child Rearing

Between 1940 and 1970 A. S. Neill functioned as a twentieth-century counterpart to Rousseau. Unlike Rousseau, however, Neill actually put his ideas into practice in a school he called Summerhill *before* he published his views on education and child rearing. In the first twenty-eight pages of Neill's first book, *Summerhill*, you will find a brief description of the school. On pages 95 to 116 and 155 to 171 you will find observations on Neill's philosophy of child rearing. Neill's *Freedom—Not License!* (1966) covers many of the same points on child rearing presented in *Summerhill*. For an account of how and why Neill developed his school, read his autobiography *Neill! Neill! Orange Peel!* (1972).

Watson's Views on Behaviorism and Child Rearing

John B. Watson seemed to have a knack for making provocative observations, and his articles and books sometimes outraged his readers. If you would like to sample his style and also learn about his views on behaviorism perhaps the best book to examine is *The Ways of Behaviorism* (1928), which is made up of articles originally written for *Harper's* magazine. In Chapter 1 he explains the nature of behaviorism. On pages 57–63 he describes how a child can be conditioned to fear a previously neutral stimulus and then reconditioned to overcome his fear. In the last chapter he explores the question, "Can the Adult Change His Personality?" For a more complete and technical discussion, examine *Behaviorism* (1925). The case for the famous claim that he could train any healthy child to become any type of specialist is made in Chapter 5 (p. 82). To discover the kind of child-rearing practices Watson urged parents to use, examine *Psychological Care of Infant and Child* (1928). In the introduction Watson acknowledges that behaviorists of that era did not know enough to do a completely satisfactory job of prescribing detailed techniques of child rearing, but he still voices the opinion that parents would do a better job if they tried to condition certain types of behavior. Chapter 1 asks parents to consider the question "Isn't it just possible that almost nothing is given in heredity and that practically the whole course of development of the child is due to the way I raise it?" (p. 15) and describes how Watson studied and conditioned infants. Chapter 2 is on "The Fears of Children and How to Control Them." Chapter 3 describes "The Dangers of Too Much Mother Love" and explains why parental behavior should "always be objective and kindly firm" and why handshaking should be substituted for kissing (p. 81). Chapter 4 is on "Rage and Temper Tantrums." Chapter 5 is on "Night and Daytime Care of the Child." Chapter 6 is on "What Shall I Tell My Child About Sex?" (Watson's answer to this question is "Not much," since he felt 75 percent of all parents of the 1920s were not competent to do the job themselves.) (If you are unable to find *Psychological Care of Infant and Child* in your library, exerpts from Chapters 2 and 3 are reprinted on pages 232–244 of *The Child* [1965] by William Kessen.)

Behavior Modification

Watson's efforts to shape behavior were not very successful primarily because he used Pavlovian conditioning as a model. When Skinner demonstrated principles of operant conditioning and it became possible to shape any kind of behavior emitted by an organism, techniques of behavior modification were introduced. If you would like to learn more about how parents and teachers might use these techniques, look for one of these books: *For Love of Children* (1970) by Roger W. McIntire, *Living with Children: New Methods for Parents and Teachers* (1976) by Gerald R. Patterson, *Applying Behavior Analysis Procedures with Children* (1977) by B. Sulzer-Azaroff and G. R. Mayer.

Skinner on Behaviorism

B. F. Skinner has developed a more sophisticated version of behaviorism than the original conception developed by Watson. The publication of Skinner's *Beyond Freedom and Dignity* (1971) led to almost as much controversy as the appearance of some of Watson's books. *Beyond Freedom and Dignity* appeared in condensed form in the August 1971 issue of *Psychology Today.* The book was widely advertised and offered as a selection by several book clubs. Critical reviews aroused considerable interest, which was intensified by Skinner's numerous television appearances. If you would like to discover for yourself what caused the furor, you are urged to read either the *Psychology Today* condensation or the book itself.

Another way to sample Skinner is to read excerpts (particularly the first and last chapters) from *Science and Human Behavior* (1953), his earlier book on behaviorism. The same basic arguments are presented in both books, but some students have reported that the earlier analysis is easier to understand than *Beyond Freedom and Dignity.* Still another way to learn about Skinner's views is to read *About Behaviorism* (1974), which is essentially a reply to critics of *Beyond Freedom and Dignity,* or *The Skinner Primer* (1974) by Finley Carpenter, which interprets Skinner's view as well as those of his critics. For information about Skinner's own account of factors that shaped his personality and early career, see the first volumes of his autobiography *Particulars of My Life* (1976) and *The Shaping of a Behaviorist* (1979).

A Debate Between Skinner and Rogers

When B. F. Skinner's views on the application of science to human behavior attracted support from many American psychologists in the 1950s, Carl R. Rogers felt impelled to call attention to what he considered to be dangers and limitations. A debate between Skinner and Rogers was arranged at the 1956 convention of the American Psychological Association, and the remarks of the two participants were published in *Science,* 1956, **124,** 1057–1066. An augmented version of Skinner's arguments, titled "Some Issues Concerning the Control of Human Behavior," appears in his *Cumulative Record* (1961), pp. 23–36; a more complete presentation of the counterarguments of Rogers is presented in an essay titled "Learning to Be Free," which originally appeared in *Conflict and Creativity* (1963), edited by S. M. Farber and R. H. L. Wilson, and is also reprinted in *Person to Person* (1967), edited by Rogers and Barry Stevens.

Maslow's Views on Humanistic Psychology

Abraham H. Maslow is generally acknowledged as the leading spokesman for humanistic psychology. He explains his reasons for preferring this view of psychology in *Toward a Psychology of Being* (2nd ed., 1968), *Motivation and*

Personality (2nd ed., 1970), and in *The Farther Reaches of Human Nature* (1972). If you would like to gain a reasonably complete grasp of his observations, read Chapters 1, 2, 3, 4, and 14 of *Toward a Psychology of Being* or the preface, Chapter 1, Chapter 2, and the appendixes of *Motivation and Personality*. (If you would prefer to read an interpretation of these works by a leading Maslow scholar, look for *The Third Force* [1970] by Frank Goble.)

A Biographical Sketch (and Interpretation) of Maslow

If you would like to learn more about the influences that led Abraham Maslow to form his view of development, read Part II (pp. 129–202) of *New Pathways in Psychology: Maslow and the Post-Freudian Revolution* (1972) by Colin Wilson. The first chapter in this section of Wilson's book is a biographical sketch of Maslow's early life highlighted by personal recollections Maslow tape-recorded just before his death in 1970. The second chapter is an account of Maslow's professional career and how he was stimulated to develop his theories of development and growth motivation. Wilson reviews articles and books by Maslow, adds comments about the work of other psychologists, and proposes his own extension of Maslow's theory. The biographical sketch is the strongest section of this book, but in the first chapter Wilson gives a brief overview of Maslow's theory. In Part I, he traces the philosophical background of varying conceptions of behavior and development, including views of Locke and Freud. A briefer, but more penetrating, analysis of Maslow is presented in *A. H. Maslow: An Intellectual Portrait* (1973) by Richard J. Lowry.

Evaluating a Scientific Utopia

In *Walden Two* (1948), B. F. Skinner describes a fictional utopia based on his approach to a science of human behavior. It is a fascinating story, and you might read it to see whether you would like to live in the sort of world he imagines. (Descriptions of how children are reared are in Chapters 12 to 17.) If you read *Walden Two,* consider these questions: What aspects of *Walden Two* strike you as most appealing? What aspects would you find difficult to accept? Do you think real people would react to the utopia as the characters in the novel do? Can you come up with an improved utopia of your own? (To compare your hypotheses regarding *Walden Two* to actual experiences with such a community, read *A Walden Two Experiment: The First Five Years of Twin Oaks Community* [1973] by Kathleen Kinkade or excerpts in *Psychology Today,* January and February 1973.)

KEY POINTS

Baby biography: detailed record of infant behavior

Baby biographies often insightful but unsystematic, irregular, subjective

Coefficient of correlation: index of relationship

Test: responses to standard questions compared to a key

Questionnaires: children reveal knowledge or opinions by writing answers

Questionnaires provide much data but are subjective, difficult to evaluate

Time sampling: behavior recorded after observing children for a short period of time

Matched-group experiment: similar groups exposed to different conditions

Rating scales: observers judge behavioral traits

Longitudinal approach: same children are studied over a period of time

Longitudinal approach reveals age trends, but selection of subjects is crucial

Sociometric technique: children indicate which playmates they like

Clinical interview: child's initial responses determine later questions asked

Clinical interview flexible but subjective

Projective techniques: ambiguous stimuli used to study personality

Standardized interview: responses to standard questions

Interviews provide much information, but it may be inaccurate, distorted, difficult to interpret

Base-line experiment: behavior observed before and after conditions imposed

Cross-sectional approach: characteristics of children of different ages measured

Some age-groups used in cross-sectional studies may be atypical

Scientific methods: sampling, control, objectivity, publication, replication

CHAPTER □2

HISTORY, METHODS, SCIENTISTS

To help you understand developmental psychology, this chapter examines those who proposed different hypotheses about development, when and why those hypotheses were proposed, and how they were tested. You will learn about the history of research on development; the methods used by those who originated or made especially effective applications of various research techniques; and the names, personalities, and interests of many of the outstanding scientists who have studied development. Without this background this book (or any other book on development) might strike you as a hodgepodge of studies and names. With it, you should be able to appreciate the sequence and continuity of research, fit reports of studies into a framework, and be capable of recognizing and evaluating methods of investigation. Furthermore, as suggested in the Prologue, you should feel as though are meeting old acquaintances when you later encounter the names of many of the scientists. All of the studies, theories, and scientists mentioned in this chapter either have already been mentioned or will be discussed more completely later. Information is duplicated in this and other chapters to strengthen your grasp of the structure of developmental psychology. This chapter traces the sequence of discoveries and the methods devised to analyze development. Discussions in other chapters emphasize different aspects of the points mentioned here.

An Imaginary Diary

To experience history as if it were actually happening, imagine that it is 1880, that you are the youngest offspring of a wealthy American family, and that you have just graduated from college. Your older brothers and sisters have assumed the responsibilities expected of them by taking positions in the family business and by rearing children who will perpetuate the proud family name. You have always been an independent soul, however, and you are not the least bit enthusiastic about becoming a vice president or committing yourself to a life of domesticity. You have been granted a *substantial* annual living allowance by an eccentric aunt who always admired your spirit, and so you are independently wealthy and free to do as you like. At college, you drifted rather aimlessly until an inspiring teacher aroused your interest in human development. He did this so effectively you have decided to spend the rest of your life functioning as a free-lance scholar of development. Since you want to keep some sort of permanent record of what you discover, you are going to keep a journal, just as Charles Darwin kept a record of what he observed and thought on his five-year voyage aboard H.M.S. *Beagle*. Your first entry, appropriately enough, records an interview with Darwin.

The Theory of Evolution Arouses Interest in Development
Downe, Kent, England—July 1, 1881[1]

I visited Charles Darwin at his home today. He is seventy-two years old and very frail and weak, but I was still impressed by the forcefulness of his personality.

He showed me the famous journal he kept aboard the *Beagle*, and that is one of the main reasons I am recording these words. I haven't the slightest conviction that anything I write on these pages will ever have the impact on people's lives that Darwin's works have had, but I find it enjoyable to think about things, and that is reason enough to record my ideas.

When I ponder how Mr. Darwin's books have changed the way we look at the world, I marvel at how relaxed I was this afternoon, a tribute to his kind and considerate manner. I wish all my relatives who were so shocked to hear that I was going to meet that "blasphemous heretic" could have eavesdropped on our conversation. As I see it, the theory of evolution doesn't force people to choose between the Bible and Darwin; it's simply a matter of two alternative explanations for the same thing. My relatives love to read the opening chapters of Genesis with its marvelous description of how God created the world and Adam and Eve, and I enjoy reading it, too. But at the same time, I am fascinated by the

---

[1] A few slight liberties have been taken with the sequence of actual events, and dates and locations have sometimes been deduced from incomplete information. Such minor inaccuracies should not alter the significance of the information provided, however.

Left, Darwin on the veranda of his home, Down House, shortly before his death.
Right, Darwin with his eldest son, William ("Doddy"). Courtesy of Down House, Downe, Kent.

theory that over a period of millions of years mutations occurred and organisms produced progeny that differed in various ways and that some of these differences contributed to survival more than others did. It doesn't bother me to speculate that my ancestors might have been related in some ways to apes rather than being descendants of Adam and Eve. After all, if that *is* the case, we can take pride in thinking that only the most intelligent and capable offspring born to generation after generation of our remote ancestors survived.

One thing that excites me about Darwin's view is the idea of looking for relationships between animal and human behavior. I am also fascinated by the possibility that if I observe primitive tribes I may get an inkling of how I might have lived and behaved thousands of years ago. What intrigues me most of all, though, is to study the development of the child. Perhaps we can find ways to help or accelerate the evolution of humans into more perfect beings. There's no doubt about it; my decision to spend the rest of my life studying development was irrevocably affirmed when I talked with Charles Darwin today.

*Baby biography:
detailed record of
infant behavior*

Just before I left, Mr. Darwin showed me what he called a *baby biography*, a detailed record of the early behavior and development of his first-born child, William Erasmus (nicknamed "Doddy"). He made the original notes thirty years ago but recently revised them for publication in the journal *Mind* after he read a similar description made a hundred years ago by a German, Dietrich Tiedemann, and more recent descriptions of the same type by another German, named Wilhelm Preyer, and by a Frenchman, Hippolyte Taine. I found the biography very interesting, but it seems to me it may be more useful as a source of ideas to study than as an acceptable scientific record. For one thing, Doddy Darwin is certainly not an average child (nor were the children of the other baby biographers, I imagine). And even though his father is an extremely observant man, it was not possible for him to keep a continuous record of all of Doddy's behavior. Consequently, Mr. Darwin probably picked out certain types of behavior in his son and ignored others. The same must be true of the other baby biographers, and, too, each observer probably was influenced by his expectations and also by the fact that the baby was, after all, his child. But a highly detailed diary of the behavior of one child does provide certain kinds of information (such as subtleties and sequences in behavior) that more objective analyses of large numbers of children cannot.

*Baby biographies
often insightful but
unsystematic,
irregular, subjective*

As we parted, Mr. Darwin gave me a letter of introduction to his cousin Sir Francis Galton. He pointed out that Sir Francis is independently wealthy and devotes all of his time and energy to studying whatever interests him, and that he and I therefore have a lot in common.

The Emergence of Measurement and Statistics
London, England—July 10, 1885

I met Sir Francis Galton today at his Anthropometric Laboratory in the South Kensington Museum. (He gave his laboratory that name because he is making an effort to measure as many characteristics of humans as he can.)

Sir Francis is such a brilliant and energetic man I was a bit intimidated by him at first (for some reason, his bushy eyebrows made me feel insignificant), but he talked so rapidly and enthusiastically about his various studies I soon got over my awestruck shyness. I had read his *Hereditary Genius* before we met, and while there is no doubt he proves that eminent men have eminent children, I'm not sure he proves that heredity is the only cause. The home environment of a child and the example set by the parents are just as plausible explanations for a line of famous people in the same family as heredity is, but I didn't say anything about that to Sir Francis. Many people think he is one of the most intelligent men in the history of the world, and I had no intention of engaging in a debate with him. In any event, he was eager to tell me about science and statistics, and so the subject never came up.

He admonished me to be a true scholar and to make accurate measurements and use scientific methods. As an example, he showed me some data on the heights of fathers and sons. First he spread out several pages of figures of heights and pointed out that it is almost impossible to make much sense of them. He demonstrated that calculating the *mean* by adding up all the measures and dividing by the number of them provided information about averages, but to discover more revealing trends he has developed what he calls a *scatter diagram*. He drew this sample of it, which makes it possible to record the heights of fathers and sons in such a way that the relationship between them becomes immediately apparent:

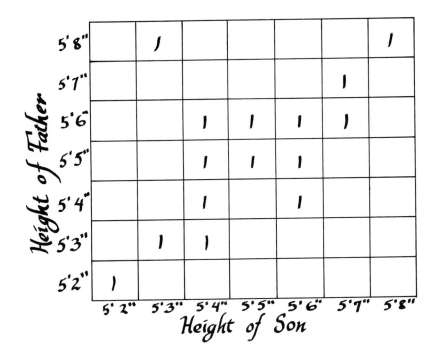

To make one of these scatter diagrams all one has to do is put a tally in the box indicating the height of father and son. If the tallies are arranged in a diagonal line from the bottom left corner to the top right corner, the relationship is a strong one. But if the tallies scatter so that no discernible pattern is apparent, there is little or no relationship. Sir Francis has developed what he calls the *coefficient of correlation* (or correlation coefficient), a numerical value between +1.0 and −1.0 reflecting how strong the relationship is and whether it is positive or negative. A negative value doesn't mean there is a *lack* of relationship (which is indicated by 0), it indicates a *reversed* relationship. That is, a large amount of a characteristic in one individual will be related to a small amount in the other member of the pair

Coefficient of correlation: index of relationship

being compared. He showed me a formula for calculating the index that he is working out in conjunction with a mathematician named Karl Pearson. (The formula for it is a bit complex, so I won't record it here.)

Sir Francis also showed me figures and diagrams that demonstrate what he calls *regression toward mediocrity*. He has found that tall fathers tend to have sons slightly shorter than themselves, and that short fathers have slightly taller sons. (Since the regression does not always make a person "mediocre" in a literal sense, other scientists have suggested it would be better to call this *regression toward the average or mean*.) Because regression is found when correlation coefficients are calculated, Sir Francis refers to correlations by the abbreviation *r* (for regression).

I was still trying to assimilate all this information when Sir Francis got started on the subject of measurement. He wants to measure, in the most objective and accurate manner possible, the capacities and abilities of large numbers of people. Since a typical subject will cooperate in providing such measurements for a short period of time only, he has devised various kinds of *tests*. Tests consist of a series of brief questions or situations which the person is asked to answer or perform. Sir Francis pointed out that each individual is exposed to the same situations or asked the same questions in exactly the same way and that responses are measured by various devices or recorded in writing. Answers to written questions can be analyzed by comparing them to a key of correct answers. The number of correct answers can then be totaled, and the result is a numerical index of a particular ability. At the present time Sir Francis is working on a mental test, and he mentioned that he had heard rumors that some psychologists in France are doing the same. As we parted, he suggested that I travel to Paris in the near future and check up on the rumor. I left Sir Francis with one thought dominating all others: there is a tremendous amount of variability in human beings, and I would like to try to find some of the factors that make people develop in such different ways.

Test: responses to standard questions compared to a key

Development of an Effective Test of Intelligence
Paris, France—April 5, 1905

I spent a fascinating day with Alfred Binet and his colleague Théodore Simon. The rumor Sir Francis Galton had heard turned out to be true. Monsieur Binet has been attempting to measure mental ability for several years and recently perfected a very satisfactory test of intelligence. He told me that the previous year he had been approached by the Minister of Public Instruction of Paris and asked if it would be possible to devise a means for determining if some school-children lacked the intelligence to benefit from instruction in regular classrooms. Monsieur Binet explained that his goal was to devise a measuring scale that could be administered in a short period of time and would yield a numerical index of intelligence. The goal was achieved by making up a series of tests of increasing difficulty and arranging them by age levels.

Monsieur Binet arranged a demonstration of his test for me. He invited a ten-year-old girl to accompany him to a quiet room, shook hands with her, and asked her to explain the meaning of certain words "to awaken her curiosity and pride," as he put it. Then, he began the test by asking her to answer simple questions. One I remember involved pieces of paper with lines of different lengths drawn in ink. The girl was asked to tell which line was longer. A more difficult question involved supplying a missing word in a sentence. Still another test consisted of definitions of progressively more difficult words. Monsieur Binet continued to ask questions until the girl was unable to answer several of them in succession. At that point he thanked her and told her that she should not feel disappointed about missing some questions because they were intended for much older children. After the young lady left, Monsieur Binet scored the answers she had given, and her *mental age*—calculated by assigning so many months credit for correct answers—was computed.

Widespread Use of the Questionnaire
Worcester, Massachusetts—January 4, 1906

I have spent many years in Europe, partly because so much has been happening there, partly because I have not wished to listen to my family ask me when I am going to settle down. Now that I have finally returned to these shores it is apparent that my fellow Americans have been showing their characteristic energy and ingenuity in pursuing the study of children. The center of activity at the moment seems to be Clark University, and that is why I am here in Worcester. I had dinner tonight at the home of G. Stanley Hall, the president of the university. What an indefatigable researcher, organizer, and administrator he is. He has established one of the first psychological laboratories in this country, founded the American Psychological Association and several journals in psychology, and carried out hundreds of studies—in addition to running the university. Many of his studies make use of *questionnaires,* which also have been used by Sir Francis Galton and some German researchers.

President Hall explained to me that he first used the questionnaire when he became curious about whether children think of things in the same way as adults. He asked hundreds of elementary schoolchildren to answer a list of questions (one I remember was "What happens when the sun sets?") and discovered that children do not really understand many things adults have assumed they understood. (This discovery has led to quite an upheaval in education.) He gave me a copy of his report "The Contents of Children's Minds" and of his two-volume work *Adolescence,* which is fascinating.

A particularly intriguing hypothesis derived from Darwin's theories is that "ontogeny recapitulates phylogeny." This elegant phrase means the development of each individual organism (ontogeny) passes through the same stages (from

Questionnaires: children reveal knowledge or opinions by writing answers

creeping to walking, for example, and from control by the lower brain to control by the cortex) as humanity has in its development (phylogeny). President Hall obtained much of his data on adolescence through questionnaires; this is obviously a quick and easy way to obtain information, but I can't help thinking that it may not always be appropriate. How can you be sure that all children will interpret the questions the same way or that what they write really reflects what they think? I also wonder if it is possible to evaluate and analyze their responses with a high degree of accuracy. Perhaps the Binet-Simon test or its equivalent may be a better way to get some types of information because the questions bring out specific answers that can be evaluated by referring to detailed standards.

Questionnaires provide much data but are subjective, difficult to evaluate

At dinner tonight I sat next to Lewis Terman, one of President Hall's graduate students. When I mentioned my views on questionnaires and tests to him, he warmly shook my hand and said he had already come to the same conclusion. He told me the title of his thesis was "Genius and Stupidity" and that he was at work on an intelligence test. Needless to say, he was excited and fascinated when I reported what Binet and Simon were doing. Across the table at dinner was another graduate student, Arnold Gesell. He was writing his thesis on jealousy in animals and children, but he told me he was eager to begin a detailed study of growth in infants.

As we enjoyed afterdinner coffee in front of the fire, President Hall announced plans to invite some of Europe's most famous psychoanalysts, notably Sigmund Freud, to a conference to be held three years from now, in 1909. Freud's fame had just begun to spread when I left Europe, and although I had read his book on dreams, I had never heard him speak or met him, and so I eagerly accepted an invitation to attend the conference.

Sigmund Freud Tells Americans About Psychoanalysis
Worcester, Massachusetts—September 10, 1909

I am here for the conference at Clark University. Thanks to great good fortune I journeyed here on the same train with Sigmund Freud, and we met in the dining car. He told me he was extremely pleased to receive the invitation to the conference because he does not feel his work has been accepted by most European scientists. (While he is gratified by America's recognition, he confessed that he did not like our country very much and was eager to get back to Vienna.) I had to cut short our conversation because the smoke from his cigar began to nauseate me. I was tempted to ask him if he smoked so much because of unfortunate infantile experiences. I held my tongue, which was fortunate, because when I congratulated him after his address tonight, he invited me to visit him in Vienna.

In his address, Freud described how he encourages his patients to talk about their childhood experiences and the extent to which these seem to involve sexual impulses. I must say I admire Freud's courage in suggesting that sex plays an important role in our behavior.

Front row, left to right, Sigmund Freud, Stanley Hall, and Carl Jung; *back row, left to right,* A. A. Brill, S. Ferenzi, E. Jones; at Clark University, Worcester, Massachusetts, in September 1909. Culver Pictures.

Before John Locke wrote his *Essay Concerning Human Understanding,* the child was pictured as saturated with original sin. Locke made him empty. Then Rousseau wrote *Émile* and made the child innocent and pure. Now Freud has added a generous dash of sex. Suddenly, children appear more interesting (and real) than they have seemed before. Freud has made us admit to ourselves (if we are honest) that as children we *did* think about differences between the sexes and about where babies come from and that it is logical to expect that almost all children do the same. I'm not convinced sex *dominates* the lives of all children to the extent that it may have dominated the lives of some of Freud's neurotic patients, but sexual impulses are important, and it is time we accepted that fact.

Many people seem to think of Freud as merely a "sex fiend," but I believe posterity will recognize not only the significance of sexual impulses but also the importance of his conception of the unconscious and his views of early childhood. I know I understand some of my own thoughts, feelings, and actions better now that I accept the possibility they are influenced in part by memories I can't consciously recall. And my ideas of development have certainly been jumbled by Freud's description of psychosexual stages. After meeting Darwin I became so excited about his theory of evolution I agreed with G. Stanley Hall that we should study childhood to discover if it is a recapitulation of the origin of our species. Now I realize that we were heading toward a dead end. Freud has stimulated us to move in a new direction—we should study childhood to understand the behavior of an individual as a child and as an adult.

I do think it's unfortunate, though, that Freud has based his theory entirely on recollections of his adult patients because I know from personal experience that some of my memories of childhood are not very accurate when I compare them to what my parents report actually happened. I seem to have filled in and rounded off my recollections, and I'm sure Freud's patients have done the same. But that makes the study of children and how they are influenced by their early experiences all the more important.

Behaviorism, Objectivity, and Behavior Shaping
Baltimore, Maryland—October 5, 1917

I've had a very unsettling day. Just as I thought I was getting some insight into the conscious and unconscious processes of myself and others, I have been told that such speculations are worthless because they are not scientific. I met John B. Watson in his office at Johns Hopkins University this morning, and he did his best to make me see the error of my ways and to convert me to what he calls behaviorism. I agree with Watson that psychologists should be as systematic and objective as possible—that's the same message Sir Francis Galton impressed upon me thirty-five years ago—but I feel uncomfortable about studying *only* overt behavior. In any event, Watson has made me appreciate once again the significance of infancy. Darwin first aroused my interest in infant behavior when he showed me his baby biography. Now Watson has convinced me that I should make some systematic observations of infants. Those of us in developmental psychology have been so busy developing and administering tests and questionnaires we've ignored subjects who aren't old enough to speak or write. It's time we made up for that oversight, and Watson's methods are certainly an improvement over some aspects of the baby-biography approach (although an observer who makes an effort to be ultraobjective and concentrates only on overt behavior will probably miss some of the subtleties described by the baby biographers).

I accept Watson's argument that a behavioristic approach is a valuable method to use in studying children, but I'm not sure I share his faith in our ability to shape behavior. There is no denying he produced a fear reaction in little Albert, but does that mean he could really produce a lawyer, doctor, or thief? And even if he could, does he have the right to try? As I said, it's been a very unsettling day. If psychologists do succeed in finding ways to shape all kinds of behavior, how and when should they use that knowledge? I'll have to do a lot of thinking before I come up with a satisfactory answer to that question.

Maturation, Ages, and Stages
New Haven, Connecticut—March 7, 1926

I renewed my acquaintanceship with Arnold Gesell today at his Clinic of Child Development at Yale University. He has carried out his plan to study stages of

Gesell's photographic dome. Gesell is shown here with a mother and infant inside the dome. Cameras, riding on metal tracks that bisected the quadrants of the dome, were moved as needed to photograph the child's activities. Observers could also watch from outside unseen by the child, since the dome was encased in a one-way-vision screen. Gesell Institute of Human Development, New Haven, Conn.

development, which he mentioned to me when he was a student at Clark University. He is making motion pictures of the behavior of infants as they respond to standard conditions. Frame-by-frame analyses have provided an extremely detailed description of sequences of behavior in infants. The sequence seems to be amazingly uniform in all children, and Gesell is convinced that development is almost entirely the result of maturation (that is, growth processes that seem to occur independently of experience). This certainly contrasts with Watson's stress on shaping or training that has dominated thinking about children for the last ten years. Gesell told me of an experiment he and a colleague, Helen Thompson, are carrying out with a pair of identical twins. One was given training in skills starting at six months; the other was not given training until about eighteen months, yet both seem to be performing equally well at two years. Gesell maintains that development is mediated by a genetic timetable and that all the shaping in the world won't change the rate of growth to any significant extent.

Studies of the Impact of the Environment
Iowa City, Iowa—September 29, 1930

I spent an interesting day talking with the staff of the Iowa Child Welfare Research Station at the State University. The research station was established in 1917 through the efforts of Mrs. Cora Bussey Hillis, who spearheaded a drive to persuade the Iowa legislature to finance a research institute for the purpose of making scientific studies of development. (Laura Spelman Rockefeller made a substantial financial contribution, too.) It appears that Mrs. Hillis, a practical midwesterner, wanted to take advantage of the scientific study of development. She argued that in addition to doing something about child labor and other forms of child abuse, Americans should try to discover the most effective approaches to child rearing.

At the research station, Beth Wellman, H. M. Skeels, and M. Skodak are trying to determine if nursery school instruction has an impact on intelligence-test scores (they have found evidence that it does). They are also studying children in institutions. In one case they discovered that infants who were given a great deal of attention by mentally retarded older girls developed faster than those left in their cribs. (It looks as if there are exceptions to Gesell's argument that experience has no effect on the rate of maturation.)

Observational Studies of Development
Minneapolis, Minnesota—October 10, 1930

Today I took the short train ride from Iowa City to Minneapolis to visit the Institute of Child Welfare here at the University of Minnesota. The institute was established shortly after the Iowa Research Station and is directed by John E. Anderson. He is an empiricist to the core and has attracted students interested in carrying out very thorough observational studies. Mary Shirley, for instance, is using a baby-biography approach not with one infant, but with twenty-five of them. She started out observing and testing her subjects every day, and now she observes them once a week. She intends to continue the study until they are two years old. This approach has an advantage over the baby biography because twenty-five times as many subjects are being studied. But, even when she observed the babies every day, Shirley was unable to match the detailed descriptions of Darwin and the other baby biographers.

Another researcher, Mildred Parten, is studying the social behavior of pre-school children. She first observed them in free play and wrote descriptions of the types of behavior they engaged in. She believes that six categories account for almost all types of nursery school social behavior: unoccupied behavior, solitary play, onlooker behavior, parallel play (where the child plays *alongside* another child but not really with him), associative play (where the child plays with other children, but there is no division of labor and no organization of activity), and cooperative or organized play (where the child plays in a group organized for some purpose, as in a game). Parten uses a variation of what is called the *time-sampling technique* (a method first used by W. C. Olson in studying nervous habits). She selects a child and observes him for one minute. At the end of that time, she classifies his play into one of the six categories. Then she observes another child for a minute, classifies her behavior, and so on. Over a period of days, she accumulates twenty such samples for each child.

Time sampling: behavior recorded after observing children for a short period of time

The Interplay of Maturation and Learning
Detroit, Michigan—October 20, 1930

After the uneventful train ride from Minneapolis to Detroit, I looked forward to interviewing specialists in the study of nursery school education at the Merrill-Palmer Institute. Josephine Hilgard has performed an interesting study of the interrelationships between maturation and learning in young children. Hilgard selected two groups of fifteen nursery school children each and matched them according to chronological age, mental age, sex, and their initial ability at three tasks: buttoning, climbing, and cutting with scissors. Then, one group received twelve weeks of intensive training in these three skills, while the other group received no training. At the end of twelve weeks, when both groups were tested to determine their skill in the three tasks, the experimental (practice) group was superior in all three skills. (Because of the nature of the tasks, precise measurements could be made. For example, a stopwatch was used to determine the exact time a child took to climb up and down a short ladder.) At that point, the control group, which previously had been given no training, was exposed to just four days of supervised practice. On the last day of that week, when both groups were tested once again, the two groups had become equal in ability. Up to a point Hilgard agrees with Gesell's emphasis on maturation, but she also notes that general practice in a variety of skills probably contributed to the development of the abilities she measured.

Matched-group experiment: similar groups exposed to different conditions

Extended Research of Parent-Child Relationships
Yellow Springs, Ohio—November 1, 1930

Before leaving the midwest I decided to pay a visit to the Fels Research Institute here in Yellow Springs. Lester W. Sontag, the director, explained the ambitious undertaking he has instituted. Close to one hundred children have been selected, and their behavior—as well as that of their parents—will be studied. Furthermore, the behavior of their children, and their children's children, will be recorded and analyzed.

Sontag and his associates have developed *rating scales* to record behavior. Observers are given detailed descriptions of different types of behavior. Then, after watching the behavior of parents and children in different situations, the

Rating scales: observers judge behavioral traits

observers mark their ratings on lines representing gradations between opposite types of behavior. As the children mature, an effort will be made to relate the characteristics of children to the child-rearing practices used by their parents. Dr. Sontag feels that this approach will yield insight into the continuity of development and long-term cause-and-effect relationships. He is philosophical about the fact that the most important conclusions of the study may not be drawn until after his death. He gave me a copy of a list of all the scales they intend to use in rating parent behavior and also a detailed set of instructions observers will use in rating one type of behavior.

Extended Research of All Aspects of Growth
Berkeley, California—January 21, 1932

To complete my tour of institutes established to study development, I have come to the West Coast. Here at the University of California three impressive studies are under way. Each started out as a short-term investigation, but each has now been converted to a continuing research program similar to the study at the Fels Institute.

Jean Walker Macfarlane is directing an investigation referred to as The Guidance Study because its original aim was to determine the impact of guidance supplied to parents. The initial sample consisted of every third child born in Berkeley during an eighteen-month period in 1928 and 1929. Sixty percent of these children were selected for study and divided into experimental and control groups. When the children in the experimental group reached the age of twenty-one months, their parents were supplied with extensive information on child-rearing procedures. The parents of the children in the control group received no instruction. The behavior of children in both groups was measured in a variety of ways and their parents were interviewed. Instead of terminating the study as originally planned, Macfarlane has decided to transform it into a long-term investigation of personality development. She intends to obtain cumulative measures of physical and mental growth and personality development up until the time her subjects are eighteen years old, and then conduct follow-up studies when they are thirty to forty years of age.

Five years ago Nancy Bayley initiated an intensive investigation of development in the first fifteen months after birth (an approach very similar to that being used by Shirley at Minnesota). At the end of that age span she decided to continue her research indefinitely. The investigation, which is called the Berkeley Growth Study, began with a sample of seventy-four white, full-term, healthy, hospital-born babies of English-speaking mothers. The major emphasis of this study is physical and mental growth, but personality and social factors will be measured as well.

Harold E. Jones and Herbert R. Stolz have just begun an intensive study of the

Fels Parent Behavior Rating Scale No. 7.2

Serial sheet no.

1	2	3	4	5	6	7	8	9	10	Number
6/9/40	6/15/40	6/21/40	6/7/40	6/20/40	6/10/40	6/14/40	6/17/40	6/10/40	6/13/40	Period of observation
M	M	M	M	M	M	M	M	M	M	Ratee
122	86	122	25	50	14	32	52	110	86	Age in months at end of period
Jane Calhoun	Dave Able	Ivene Lott	Anita Bauer	Tommy Westy	Susan Darley	Paul Stanley	Betsy Larson	Marilyn Foote	Susan Bone	Child

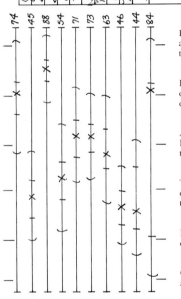

Acceptance of child
(devotion-rejection)

Rate the parent's acceptance of the child into his own inner circle of loyalty and devotion. Does the parent act in such a way as to indicate that the child is considered an intimate and inseparable partner? Or does the parent act as though he resents the child's intrusion and rejects the child's bid for a place in his primary area of devotion?

Consider all evidence which in any way may impinge upon the child as acceptance–rejection, however subtle, vague, or indirect. It is not the parent's true feeling, but his *attitude*, as a functioning unit in the child's environment, which we are rating.

Parent's behavior toward child connotes utter devotion and acceptance into his innermost self, without stint or suggestion of holding back in any phase of his life.

Parent clearly accepts child. Includes child in family councils, trips, affection, even when it is difficult or represents considerable sacrifice.

A "charter member" of the family but "kept in his place." Parent accepts child in general, but excludes him from certain phases of parent's life.

Tacit acceptance. Excludes child so frequently that to the child the rejection attitude may seem to predominate even though parent takes acceptance for granted.

Parent's predominant tendency is to avoid, repulse, and exclude the child, but without open rejection.

Child openly resented and rejected by parent. Never admitted to inner circle. Made to feel unwanted, ostracized.

										Score
										Tolerance
										Range
1	2	3	4	5	6	7	8	9	10	Number

Rater: M J H   Date of rating: 6/26/40

Scored by: A   Date: 9-17-40
Checked by: A   Date: 10-17-40
Tabulated by: A   Date: 11-18-40

Rater's remarks: (continue on back of sheet)

One of the Fels Parent Behavior Rating Scales. (Instructions for rater.) From "The Appraisal of Parent Behavior," Alfred L. Baldwin, Joan Kalhorn, and Fay Huffman Breese, *Psychological Monographs*, No. 299, 1949, **63**, No. 4.

adolescent development of approximately two hundred fifth- and sixth-graders in Oakland. Physiological changes at adolescence are a major emphasis of this investigation, but social relations and teachers' appraisals of classroom behavior also will be analyzed. Even though the original plan was to terminate the study when the students graduate from high school, this investigation also will be extended.

Longitudinal approach: same children are studied over a period of time

The Fels Institute research and the three studies underway here at Berkeley make use of the *longitudinal approach*. The Fels and Berkeley researchers are enthusiastic about this technique because the same subjects will be studied from infancy through childhood, adolescence, and adulthood. This approach avoids the weaknesses of retrospective analyses (such as Freud's descriptions of what his patients recalled about childhood experiences), provides maximum information about the overall process of growth, and permits evaluation of the accuracy of predictions of later behavior. On the basis of early observations, the Berkeley researchers plan to record their impressions of what individual children will be like as adults and then check up on their predictions.

Longitudinal approach reveals age trends, but selection of subjects is crucial

While they extol all the advantages of the technique, they point out that there are also certain disadvantages. A considerable amount of patience, energy, money, and cooperation is needed to embark on a longitudinal study. Staff turnover, lack of cooperation from subjects (particularly those who may move out of the vicinity), and a delayed payoff for their efforts may make it difficult for them to persevere. They also realize that all of their results will be based on the behavior of a small group of subjects, and if that group is atypical in significant ways, the results may not apply to other groups or individuals.

Intelligence Testing
Palo Alto, California—February 3, 1932

It was only a short trip from Berkeley to Stanford University, where I once again talked with Lewis Terman, my dinner companion at G. Stanley Hall's house nearly thirty years ago. He has been busy following up on the topic of his doctoral dissertation "Genius and Stupidity." His major accomplishment is the Stanford-Binet Intelligence Scale, an exceptionally effective test patterned after the Binet-Simon scale. (I like to think my telling Terman of my visit with Binet and Simon had something to do with this.) A major improvement he has made over the original Binet test is to report scores by dividing mental age by chronological age and multiplying by 100. (This score, called the *intelligence quotient*, or IQ, is based on a concept first proposed by the German psychologist W. Stern.)

Terman has also instituted a longitudinal study of gifted children. He asked teachers from all over California to help him pick out close to two thousand intellectually gifted children, and with the assistance of Melita Oden he plans to study them for at least thirty years.

Sociometric Techniques Are Introduced
New York, New York—November 10, 1934

This afternoon I spent an hour with Jacob Moreno, an Austrian psychiatrist who recently moved here. He has developed what he calls the *sociometric technique* which involves asking members of a group to indicate which individuals they like best. Moreno showed me some sociometric diagrams he drew after asking elementary school students to list the classmates they like best. The diagrams call attention to stars (the most popular children) and isolates (those who are not chosen at all).

Sociometric technique: children indicate which playmates they like

Awareness of the Importance of Early Experience
Vienna, Austria—February 10, 1937

Reading newspaper accounts of the rise to power of Adolf Hitler has made me realize that this might well be my last chance to accept Sigmund Freud's invitation of over twenty years ago. So, here I am in Vienna. Hitler seems on the verge of taking over Austria, and Freud's life is in danger. Despite that fact and also the fact that he is painfully ill from cancer, he greeted me warmly. He told me that since 1909 when I first heard him speak, he had altered and expanded his psychoanalytic view of development and that he was more convinced than ever that early experiences influence later behavior. As I left his study, I met his daughter Anna and two of her most promising students, Erik H. Erikson and Peter Blos, who have just completed their psychoanalytic training and are thinking about emigrating to America. I gave each of them my card and asked them to contact me if they carry out their plan to move to the United States.

Use of the Clinical Method to Study Children's Thinking
Geneva, Switzerland— March 1, 1937

To get away from some of the war tension in Europe I have journeyed to Switzerland. My main purpose, though, is to make the acquaintance of Jean Piaget. He has been engaged in the study of the thinking processes of children and has developed what he calls the *clinical method*. The original idea for this technique grew out of baby biographies he wrote of his own children. At first, Piaget simply described the behavior of his children, just as Charles Darwin kept a diary of the development of his son Doddy. In time, however, he began to record not only spontaneous behavior but also the reactions of his children to simple "experiments." (One of the first experiments he tried involved a game where he hid a matchbox under a pillow and observed and recorded the reactions of his son.) Eventually, Piaget concluded that he might present more complex problems to different children. He wanted to allow maximum scope for individual interpretations, so he let each child's answers determine the nature and direction of the interview. This approach made it possible for Piaget to probe for the reasoning used by the child. Probing for reasons behind actions and answers is the distinguishing feature of the *clinical interview,* and I imagine Piaget selected this term for his technique because it is something like interviews in psychological clinics where patients are asked to explain and discuss their behavior.

After conducting hundreds of clinical interviews, Piaget has come to the conclusion that intellectual development in children follows a definite pattern, and he is in the process of describing stages and substages.

While I am excited about Piaget's work, I can't help wondering if some of the patterns of cognitive development he is reporting can be attributed more to his orderly mind than to children's thinking. The clinical interview certainly permits Piaget to follow up on points that emerge as he questions his subjects. At the same time, the very flexibility of the technique opens up the possibility that Piaget might interpret answers and ask questions that "lead" to responses that fit his expectations.

Clinical interview: child's initial responses determine later questions asked

Clinical interview flexible but subjective

The Potency of Group Identity
London, England—November 10, 1945

Now that World War II is finally over, I am once again able to visit Europe. I renewed my acquaintance with Anna Freud today. She and her father escaped from Austria in 1938 just before Hitler took over. Her father died a year later in London, but she has continued his work and is specializing in the psychoanalytic study and treatment of children. She is doing some interesting research on how war orphans may develop such a strong sense of group identity that they are able to compensate for lack of maternal care. She suggested that I contact a fellow psychoanalyst, René Spitz, who is carrying out a study of the impact of lack of maternal care on infant behavior.

The Importance of Mothering
London, England—November 15, 1945

René Spitz told me today of his study of babies reared in institutions. Spitz first became interested in this area of research when he noticed the behavior of infants who had been separated from their mothers by the war. If mothers were killed in air raids or worked in war industries, their infants were often placed in hospital nurseries. Despite the fact that the children were given excellent physical care under hygienic conditions, many of them failed to develop normally, and some showed signs of deep depression.

In an effort to analyze the causes of such behavior, Spitz is comparing the development of babies being reared in the nursery of a penal institution for delinquent girls and in a foundling home. The babies in the penal-institution nursery are being cared for by their mothers and are free to move around and explore. The foundling-home babies, on the other hand, are given only minimal care by nurses and are confined to cribs covered with sheets. During the first months of life, no major differences in the babies were apparent, but by the end of the first year, the foundling-home infants were noticeably retarded in development. They were also much more susceptible to disease, and some infants became so depressed it was difficult to keep them alive. Spitz attributes his findings to lack of mothering, a point that has also been made by Margaret Ribble, an American, in her recently published book *The Rights of Infants*. It seems possible, though, that the retardation could also be due to lack of stimulation.

Sigmund Freud is dead, but interest in the impact of early experience on child development has never been greater than it is right now. Some psychologists are suggesting that the first months and years of life may be of tremendous significance in development and that if young children fail to receive proper care or stimulation, they may never be able to make up for it later.

Imprinting and Species Survival
Altenburg, Austria—December 10, 1945

While in London I heard about some studies of bird behavior being carried out by an Austrian naturalist named Konrad Lorenz. I made inquiries and have been invited to his delightful retreat in the country. Lorenz specializes in observing birds, fish, and animals in their natural habitats, a type of study called *ethology*. In the course of his observations of birds Lorenz discovered that a newly hatched gosling will adopt as its mother any moving object it sees a few hours after it is hatched. This is called *imprinting,* and it occurs during a brief *critical period*. There are undeniably substantial differences between birds and humans, but perhaps imprinting is related to the sort of behavior described by Spitz. If a human infant is not given proper care during the first critical months of life, perhaps the chances for survival may be lessened.

Lorenz and his fellow ethologists point out that certain types of "instinctive" behavior (such as imprinting in birds) help assure that a species will be perpetuated. If newly hatched goslings do not follow the mother, they might not be fed or cared for. Lorenz hypothesizes that during the course of evolution goslings that inherited a tendency to follow the mother were more likely to survive and that this trait has been passed on from generation to generation. This is certainly an intriguing theory, and it leads to all kinds of fascinating speculations about human behavior.

Psychoanalytic Study of Adolescence
Boston, Massachusetts—January 20, 1946

Meeting Anna Freud and René Spitz made me wonder if any Americans are carrying out research based on psychoanalytic principles. By happy coincidence, last week I received a note from Peter Blos inviting me to visit him in Boston.

Konrad Lorenz being followed by goslings who adopted him as their "mother" since he was the first moving object they saw during a critical period shortly after they were hatched. Thomas McAvoy, Time-Life Picture Agency.

Both he and Erik H. Erikson carried through on their plan (mentioned when I met them at Freud's home) to settle in America.

Blos is specializing in the treatment of adolescents and plans one day to write a psychoanalytic interpretation of adolescence based on direct experience with them, not on what adults remember about that period of their lives (which was the approach Freud used). He told me that Erikson is doing research at the University of California, so I will make another cross-country trip to find out what Erikson is up to.

Projective Techniques
Berkeley, California—February 3, 1946

Today Erik Erikson showed me how he is studying play constructions made by subjects of the Berkeley Growth Study. (All of the longitudinal studies I learned

Projective techniques, such as the Rorschach inkblot test and the Thematic Apperception Test (where subjects are asked to make up stories while looking at provocative pictures) are used to induce children to reveal personality tendencies without being aware of it. Sybil Shelton/Monkmeyer.

about on my previous visit are still going strong.) The Berkeley researchers wanted some data on unconscious as well as conscious aspects of adolescent behavior, and they have made use of several *projective techniques*. These methods are designed to confront subjects with ambiguous stimulus situations so that they cannot deliberately distort their responses. On a test or questionnaire, particularly one that taps personality variables, subjects may read some significance into a

Projective techniques: ambiguous stimuli used to study personality

question and then answer accordingly. Projective techniques make it very difficult for subjects to do this, and so they "project" their thoughts and feelings in an undistorted way when they respond.

The Berkeley Growth Study researchers have already used the Rorschach inkblot test (where subjects are asked to describe what they see in a series of inkblots) and the Thematic Apperception Test (where subjects are shown pictures of ordinary and provocative situations and asked to make up a story about them.) Erikson is using a doll-play technique to gain further insight into the unconscious thoughts and feelings of adolescent children. He asks each subject to take an assortment of dolls, houses, cars, animals, furniture, blocks, and the like and "make a scene out of an exciting movie." He has found that boys arrange action scenes but that girls are more likely to create domestic tableaus.

Before coming to Berkeley, Erikson did anthropological research with two American Indian tribes and he told me that he has come to the conclusion that Freud's tendency to stay in Vienna prevented him from becoming aware of the importance of cultural differences when he proposed his description of stages of psychosexual development. Erikson is at work on a modification of Freud's description of stages that will emphasize psycho*social* behavior and trace how it is influenced by the culture in which a child lives.

Maternal Care Appears to Be Essential
London, England—February 12, 1951

I am back in London to talk with John Bowlby of the Tavistock Clinic and Institute of Human Relations. Bowlby is just completing a report for the World Health Organization on infants reared in institutions. He has concluded that the overall development of a child deprived of maternal care between six months and three years of age will be retarded and that the effects of early deprivation will be permanent. Even if the child is given extra stimulation and attention later in life, Bowlby feels there is no way to make up for care not supplied earlier. It looks as if there *are* critical periods in human behavior similar to those Lorenz found in goslings.

Compensating for Lack of Maternal Care
London, England—February 15, 1951

Since I was in London, I called on Anna Freud. She has been busy carrying out and accumulating reports of psychoanalytic studies of children. I asked her what she thought of Bowlby's conclusion about maternal care. I was a bit surprised to learn that she is not convinced that lack of mothering will inevitably lead to problems or irreversible deficits. She has completed her study of war orphans and has concluded that the children were able to compensate for lack of contact with adults by developing a strong sense of group identity. Perhaps Bowlby has made the picture seem bleaker than it is in his eagerness to bring about reform of institutional care. Certainly we need to do everything possible to provide warm and consistent care for children in institutions, but it may be misleading and defeatist to argue that there are *no* ways to compensate for lack of maternal care.

As I was speculating about Bowlby's hypothesis just now I suddenly remembered reading about some studies being carried out at the University of Wisconsin. I believe they are attempting to trace factors that lead to the development of love between infant monkeys and their mothers. As soon as I return to America I must make a trip to Madison.

Studies of Love in Infant Rhesus Monkeys
Madison, Wisconsin—April 10, 1956

I am visiting the primate laboratory here at the University of Wisconsin. Harry F. Harlow, the director, showed me around and described some of his research. His initial experiments were intended to determine if love between mother and child is based on associations built up when the baby is fed. To analyze this problem he constructed some substitute mothers made out of wire and cloth. Newborn baby monkeys were taken away from their real mothers and reared in cages containing the substitutes. Observation of the behavior of the monkeys suggests that love may be more a function of *comfort* than of feeding. When his monkey subjects grew up, Harlow discovered that they showed little affection for each other. It was difficult to induce females to conceive, and the few that did have babies showed no interest in them. Harlow suggests that this may have been due to lack of mothering during a critical period early in the lives of the monkeys. John Bowlby surveyed studies of the impact of institutionalization on human infants; Harlow has performed experiments with monkeys; both have concluded that lack of maternal care early in life may have a permanent impact.

Inducing Infants to Learn
Providence, Rhode Island—January 6, 1963

I am at Brown University to observe the work of Lewis Lipsitt and his associates. They have developed an ingenious device for determining if it is possible to establish an operant conditioned response in infants. A checkerboard pattern is projected on a screen over the subject's head, and a nipple, wired to an electronic apparatus that controls the image, is inserted in the baby's mouth. (It functions much the same way as a remote-control tuning gadget for a television set.) The experimenter projects a dim picture, and the infant can brighten it by sucking on the nipple. The four-month-old I observed today was quite adept at fine tuning, but I couldn't help thinking that technology deserved most of the credit. I also found myself wondering if this study may be partly an expression of the current interest in accelerating development. Before long American babies may be expected to start to learn the moment the umbilical cord is cut.

Harry F. Harlow in the Primate Laboratory at the University of Wisconsin. Courtesy of the Primate Laboratory, University of Wisconsin.

Analyzing Child-rearing Practices
Stanford, California—March 10, 1963

I am back at Stanford University to learn about the work of Robert R. Sears and his colleagues. He has specialized in research on parent-child relationships. Sears began his career at the Iowa Child Welfare Research Station. The fact that the research station was established by the Iowa legislature for the purpose of applying science to improving the welfare of children undoubtedly influenced Sears, because his research has been aimed at supplying information that might be used by parents as well as scientists.

Sears endorses the view that child behavior is primarily the product of experiences. If this assumption is accepted, then it follows that much child behavior is the product of the parents' child-rearing techniques. Therefore, if relationships can be established between techniques used by parents and different types of child behavior, Sears reasons that informed parents could encourage the development of selected traits in their children.

At Iowa, Sears supervised a study by Barbara Merrill Bishop, who developed a technique for rating child and parent behavior. Bishop elaborated on Parten's basic procedure in her study of preschool social behavior in Minnesota. Bishop first observed mothers and their children interacting in a variety of situations and wrote descriptions of the types of behavior each engaged in. Once these categories were established, she sat behind a one-way vision screen and observed a mother and child interacting during thirty-minute play sessions. Every five seconds a light flashed in the observation booth, and at each flash Bishop classified mother and child behavior by marking a record blank that listed all of the categories. Analysis of the records revealed considerable variation in the way mothers and their children interact.

From Iowa, Sears moved to the Harvard University Laboratory of Human Development, where he supervised a study of patterns of child rearing. He and his colleagues Eleanor E. Maccoby and Harry Levin trained ten women to conduct intensive *standardized interviews* of almost four hundred mothers of five-year-old children. The mothers were asked to respond to a lengthy series of questions about their own behavior as well as that of their children. The interview records were analyzed by two independent raters with reference to 188 scales which provided information about child-rearing practices used by different women and the impact these had on children. Through the use of interviews a substantial amount of data from a large number of mothers was obtained, but this method has limitations. For one thing, there is no way of being certain that the mothers gave true descriptions or even that they were able to remember accurately incidents that occurred years or months earlier. And when the responses were classified, further distortions might have occurred. Even so, this study supplies an abundance of information about child-rearing practices and their impact.

Standardized interview: responses to standard questions

Interviews provide much information, but it may be inaccurate, distorted, difficult to interpret

From Harvard, Sears came here to Stanford. In collaboration with Lucy Rau and Richard Alpert he has combined the observational techniques Bishop used at Iowa with the interview method he used at Harvard to analyze the impact of different child-rearing practices. The behavior of preschool children was observed and classified into categories, and the children also were interviewed. Both mothers and fathers were interviewed, and they were also observed interacting with their children. All data were analyzed, and close to two hundred variables for children and an equal number for parents were coded and compared. Unfortunately, relatively few clear-cut relationships have been established to date, but the methods developed by Sears and his colleagues are sure to pave the way for valuable research of the same type.

Observational Learning and the Importance of Imitation
Stanford, California—March 15, 1963

Before leaving Stanford I observed an experiment directed by Albert Bandura. Bandura agrees with the basic assumption of John B. Watson and B. F. Skinner—that much of behavior is determined by experiences—but he is foremost in pointing out that the kind of operant conditioning achieved in Skinner's rat

1. First of all we'd like to get a picture of the family. How many children do you have?
   1a. How old are they?
   [If more than one child] In this interview we want to talk mostly about X, since he's in the kindergarten group we are working with.

2. Has X been with you all his life, or have you been separated from him at any time?
   2a. [If separated] For how long? How old was he then?

3. And how about his father—has X been separated from his father at any time?
   3a. [If separated] For how long? How old was X then?

4. Now would you think back to when X was a baby. Who took care of him mostly then?
   4a. How much did your husband do in connection with taking care of X when he was a baby?
   4b. Did he ever change the baby's diapers? feed him? give him his bath?

5. All babies cry, of course. Some mothers feel that if you pick up a baby every time it cries, you will spoil it. Others think you should never let a baby cry for very long. How do you feel about this?
   5a. What did you do about this with X?
   5b. How about in the middle of the night?

6. Did you have time to spend with the baby besides the time that was necessary for feeding him, changing him, and just regular care like that?
   6a. [If yes] Tell me about what you did in this time. How much did you cuddle him and sing to him and that sort of thing?

7. Do you think that babies are fun to take care of when they're very little, or do you think they're more interesting when they're older?

8. Now would you tell me something about how the feeding went when he was a baby?
   8a. Was he breast-fed?
   8b. [If not] How did you happen to decide to use a bottle instead of breast feeding?
   8c. [If yes] For how long?
   8d. [If yes] Did you go directly to the cup or did you use a bottle?
   8e. And how about weaning him (from the bottle) (from the breast) to a cup? When did you start this?
   8f. How did you decide it was time to begin this?
   8g. How did you go about this?
   8h. How did he react to being taken off the bottle (breast)?
   8i. Had you been giving him liquid from a cup before?
   8j. How long did it take to get him to give up the bottle (breast) completely?

9. There has been a lot of talk about whether it is better to have a regular feeding schedule for a baby, or to feed him whenever he is hungry. How do you feel about this?
   9a. How did you handle this with X?
   9b. [If schedule] How closely did you stick to that schedule?

10. Have you had any problems about X eating enough, or eating the kinds of food he needs?
    10a. What do you do about it?

Portion of interview schedule devised by Sears, Maccoby, and Levin. *Source:* Robert R. Sears, Eleanor Maccoby, and Harry Levin, *Patterns of Child Rearing* (Evanston, Ill.: Row, Peterson, 1957).

In experiments supervised by Albert Bandura children were first shown a film depicting an adult assaulting a Bobo doll in a variety of ways (top row of photographs). Then, the children were frustrated (by being interrupted while playing with some highly desirable toys) and taken to a play room containing a Bobo doll. Most of the children responded by imitating the aggressive actions they had seen in the film (middle and bottom rows of photographs). Courtesy of Albert Bandura.

and pigeon experiments accounts for only selected aspects of child behavior. Certainly some kinds of behavior are acquired when a child's activity is reinforced either deliberately or accidentally, but Bandura emphasizes that many other types of behavior are acquired when children imitate a model. In some cases children may see the model rewarded for some action; in other cases they will simply imitate the behavior because it seems appealing.

Bandura has devised several experiments to demonstrate how imitation of models leads to the development of different kinds of behavior. The one I observed this morning was quite dramatic. A four-year-old girl was shown a film depicting an adult assaulting an inflated doll. Then she was allowed to play with some very attractive toys and, just when she was thoroughly enjoying herself, was abruptly interrupted and taken to a room that contained the inflated doll (as well as many other playthings) she had seen in the film. According to a widely endorsed theory in American psychology, frustration is supposed to lead to aggression, and Bandura predicted that the frustrated child would not only be primed to vent her aggression, she would do so by imitating the models she had viewed in the film. Sure enough, the little girl I observed used every assault technique she had seen in the movie.

Bandura believes the results of his experiment can be generalized to television. He argues that a child who is frustrated in a real-life situation may express aggression by imitating types of behavior seen on television programs. There may be some truth to this hypothesis, but I see quite a difference between hitting an inflated doll made expressly for the purpose of being hit and, say, attacking or killing another human being. Even if there are significant differences between behavior in experimental and real-life situations, Bandura has called attention to the influence of models and the potential impact of television. He wants to alert parents to the possibility that their children may learn aggressive forms of behavior from watching too many television programs that feature violence.

Base-line experiment: behavior observed before and after conditions imposed

Some of the experiments that have been carried out by Bandura and other psychologists who are interested in the impact of different kinds of experiences on child behavior make use of the base-line experimental technique. Children are first observed to establish their "natural" (or base-line) level of behavior of a particular type. Then, they are exposed to conditions arranged by the experimenter, and their behavior is observed again. When studying aggressive reactions, for example, it is important to first find out the level of aggressiveness a child exhibits in ordinary play before measuring the number of aggressive responses exhibited after the subject has been exposed to a frustrating experience.

Cross-sectional Study of Moral Development
Chicago, Illinois—April 6, 1963

I have come to the University of Chicago to talk to Lawrence Kohlberg who has just completed a fascinating pilot study of moral development. When Kohlberg was a graduate student he read about Jean Piaget's observations on the moral thinking of children. He became so intrigued by the subject he decided to make it the topic of his doctoral dissertation. In a book published in 1932 and in several subsequent articles Piaget theorized that the moral reasoning of young children is different from that of older children. Kohlberg decided to carry out a systematic analysis of Piaget's hypothesis by asking ten-, thirteen-, and sixteen-year-old boys to respond to what he calls *moral dilemmas.* (In the moral dilemma Kohlberg showed me this afternoon I was asked to identify with a man who must decide whether or not to break the law in order to save the life of his wife.) Each boy was asked to describe his reactions to ten moral dilemmas and his tape-recorded responses were later scored for thirty aspects of morality. In addition, the level of moral reasoning was evaluated.

Cross-sectional approach: characteristics of children of different ages measured

This kind of study is called *cross-sectional* (or *normative*) because age differences are established by studying a sample of children at different ages. An advantage of the cross-sectional approach over the longitudinal approach is that information about age differences can be obtained in a short period of time. Furthermore, a specific aspect of behavior can be studied in detail, and if an important variable is overlooked in an initial study, a supplementary investigation is a simple matter. The biggest problem is selecting subjects at different age levels who share the same basic characteristics.

In his study, Kohlberg made an effort to select boys who had approximately the same IQ, but he did not attempt to control other potentially significant factors (such as parental attitudes toward morality). Accordingly, there is the possibility that some of the age differences reported by Kohlberg may not be solely due to differences in age but to differences in the background of each group. Kohlberg is aware of this weakness and he told me that he plans to carry out a longitudinal follow-up study by asking the same boys to respond to moral dilemmas every few years.

Some age-groups used in cross-sectional studies may be atypical

Piaget Recommends Self-Directed Learning
Worcester, Massachusetts—February 10, 1967

I am back at Clark University just short of sixty years since I heard Sigmund Freud give a lecture here. This time the lecture is to be delivered by the most famous child psychologist of this era, my old friend Jean Piaget. Piaget invited me to join him in his hotel room just after he arrived, and I asked him what he thought about attempts by American psychologists to show children how to progress through his stages at an accelerated pace. He replied that he thought these attempts were unfortunate, and he doubts that development can be speeded up to any appreciable extent or that any gains made will be permanent. He feels that children must develop their own conceptions of things and that trying to teach them ideas "ahead of schedule" will produce only artificial and superficial understanding. He is more in sympathy with the approach to education that is becoming popular in England just now.

Some elementary school teachers in that country are using his theory as the basis for what they call *open education*. The main feature of the approach is to encourage children to learn through their own exploration and from each other. The open approach is almost the opposite of some of the programs established in this country to speed up learning. Here the teacher supplies complete direction. Having talked with Piaget, the world's leading exponent of "self-education," perhaps I should make an appointment to visit at some future date with B. F. Skinner, the man who has inspired more attempts at systematic instruction than any other individual in history.

Renewed Interest in Behavior Shaping
Cambridge, Massachusetts—October 21, 1971

I visited B. F. Skinner at Harvard University today. It was very kind of America's most eminent psychologist to take time to talk to an ancient eccentric, but apparently I am something of an institution now, and he was probably curious to meet me. In the last ten years more attempts to shape child behavior have been made than at any other time—many more than when Watson tried to convert us all—and Skinner has supplied the basic technique. I asked him why he had not been content to remain a laboratory scientist but instead had risked describing how people might shape behavior in his novel *Walden Two* and in his just-published *Beyond Freedom and Dignity*. He replied that he was upset about an attitude toward science that was common after the end of World War II. Many people of that era blamed scientists for the atomic bomb and the threat of nuclear war between Russia and the United States, he said, and he wanted to emphasize that just because a few discoveries have been misused is no reason to condemn all scientific advances. He believes that if we use scientific knowledge in a consistent manner we will be able to solve most of the problems that beset us.

After we talked in his office Skinner drove me to his home to show me how much his granddaughter enjoys the Air Crib he designed. At first glance it looks a bit like a king-sized Skinner box, but it is really a very sensible alternative to the crib and playpen. It has glass sides so the child can look out; the temperature is kept constant; and the baby is free to move around without restraint. Professor Skinner is obviously a man who believes in applying what he has learned.

The Infant Takes the Center of the Stage
Loch Lomond, Scotland—September 11, 1975

I am on the shores of this beautiful Scottish lake to observe the proceedings of a conference being held at a country house owned by the University of Strathclyde. The theme of the conference is "Mother–Infant Interaction," and psychologists who have specialized in the study of this topic have journeyed here from all over Great Britain as well as from Germany and the United States. As I examine books and articles currently being published on child development I am struck by the extent to which this appears to be the era of the infant. I get the impression that many more experiments and observations are being carried out on infant subjects today than at any previous time in the history of developmental psychology.

In the United States it seems that the main interest is in *The Competent Infant*, at least that is the title of a virtual encyclopedia of studies on infancy edited by Joseph Stone, Henrietta Smith, and Lois Murphy. Interestingly enough, psychologists in Great Britain are fascinated by the "human" qualities of infants. Most of the papers being presented at this conference, sponsored by a Scottish university, are concerned with subtle interactions between infants and mothers—with the infant being the star performer and the mother acting more as a responsive audience.

I suppose the interest of Americans in seeking sources of competence may be yet another manifestation of our basic urge to try to improve things. Educational techniques with older children haven't seemed to produce impressive gains in abilities, so perhaps American psychologists have concluded that we haven't started early enough. In any event, I occasionally get the impression that some

B. F. Skinner's granddaughter Lisa in the Air Crib originally used by her mother (shown here caring for her). Richard Phillips.

researchers who study infants are motivated by a desire to take credit for what their subjects do. If they can report detecting a form of behavior in infants at an earlier age than in any previously observed babies, they may attract a bit of notoriety.

I suppose the main reason for current interest in infants, though, is not too different from the source of the controversy generated by Charles Darwin way back when I first started to study child development. Darwin made us think about factors that influence different forms of human behavior. How much are they due to inherited predispositions that emerged as humans evolved? How much are they due to experiences and learning? The newborn child is perhaps the best possible subject to study if someone is interested in trying to track down sources of human behavior. Initial environmental experiences are just then exerting their influence on brand-new human beings.

World-wide Interest in Welfare of Children Expressed
Washington, D.C.—January 14, 1979

I am in Washington to attend a meeting of the United States National Commission for the International Year of the Child. Growing awareness of the impact of early experiences on later behavior and of the deplorable conditions under which children in many parts of the world mature has prompted leaders from hundreds of countries to join in proclaiming 1979 The International Year of the Child. I was shocked to be told this morning that 95 percent of the children in the world are not immunized against common contagious diseases. And in developing nations, more than half of the children in the five- to fifteen-year age range do not attend any kind of school. The United States commission has pointed out, however, that even in our highly developed society some children are at an extreme disadvantage compared to others. (For one thing, over two million American five- to fifteen-year-olds do not attend any kind of school.) The group I met with this morning discussed the eight areas that the commission feels need particular attention: child nurturing; education; health care; juvenile justice; development through recreation, play, and cultural activities; fostering equal opportunity and cultural diversity; impact of the media; and children around the world.

I find it interesting to recall that the current desire to use scientific knowledge to foster optimum development in children was the driving force that led to the formation of many American university departments of child development in the 1920s and 1930s. The biggest difference between 1930 and 1980, though, is that today there is much greater awareness of the impact on child development of environmental and cultural differences. The psychologists of the 1930s studied mostly middle-class white American children, usually because such children were readily available as subjects. In the fifty-year period since those first departments of child development were established we have accumulated an enormous amount of information about all kinds of children. The basic question they faced in the thirties is still the same today, though: How can we use scientific information to help children make the most of their capabilities?

If, as you have been asked to imagine, you had been twenty-one in 1881, you would have been one hundred and twenty in 1980. It is unlikely that a person over a hundred would still be active as a scholar, but it is not impossible. If you had been an eighteen-year-old college freshman in 1909, however, at the time of Freud's visit to America and in a decade when child psychology was being established as an organized field of study, you would have been eighty-nine in 1980. Therefore, disregarding the accounts of meetings with Darwin and Galton—who were not really developmental psychologists—one individual *could* have personally interacted with all of the leading scientists who have specialized in the study of development. Jean Piaget was fourteen in 1909 and already taking an active interest in science; since he died in 1980, it is fair to say that the scientific study of development has been taking place for only one lifetime.

Summary: Trends and Methods in Developmental Psychology

To help you grasp the points that have been recorded in this imaginary diary, four summaries are provided in this section: a decade-by-decade outline of research trends, characteristics and values of science, a review of methods for studying different types of child behavior, and methods you might use to study behavior.

A Decade-by-Decade Outline of Research Trends

The first summary consists of a decade-by-decade analysis of significant trends in developmental psychology. Since thousands of studies of children have been carried out each year, it is clearly impossible to summarize all research interests that appeared during any particular period of time. The points listed are not intended to reflect a complete outline of all significant developments, therefore, but of trends selected to supply an overview of the kinds of topics developmental psychologists have studied at different times.

☐ 1880   Darwin's various books on the theory of evolution arouse great interest in the scientific study of human development.

☐ 1890   Galton reports accurate measurements of many human characteristics and introduces the development of statistical techniques for analyzing them.

☐ 1900   Influential pioneers publish works that have a profound influence on later psychologists: Binet develops an effective intelligence test; Freud writes and lectures on psychoanalytic theory; Hall establishes several journals of psychology in America and makes extensive use of questionnaires to study child and adolescent behavior.

☐ 1910   Watson publishes his articles and books on behaviorism, reflecting and influencing stress on learning by association and on objective observation that are hallmarks of American psychology.

☐ 1920   Gesell studies infant behavior and concludes that early behavior is so universal and predictable it must be controlled by an inner timetable of growth.

☐ 1930   Institutes for the study of children's development become well established and highly productive at Iowa, Minnesota, Berkeley, Stanford, and elsewhere. Such departments are often funded because it is reasoned that scientific information should be used to improve the well-being of children.
Piaget's observations on children's thinking stimulate considerable research and speculation.

☐ 1940 The critical period concept, based on observations by Lorenz and other ethologists, arouses the interest of developmental psychologists in the significance of early experiences on later behavior.

☐ 1950 Bowlby reports on world-wide studies of infancy and stresses the need for early stimulation and effective mothering.

☐ 1960 Studies of operant conditioning lead to discussions of when and how parents and teachers should use behavior modification techniques with children.

☐ 1970 Many developmental psychologists publish articles revealing the competence of human infants. Others call attention to ways mothers influence infants and vice versa.

The desire to use psychological knowledge to help children is stressed, just as it was in the 1930s. In the 1970s, however, there is much greater interest in tracing how different kinds of environmental conditions influence child behavior and development.

Characteristics and Values of Science

Many of the characteristic strengths and values of science can be emphasized by taking into account some of the limitations of casual observation (and of unsystematic applications of such observations to behavior and development) and by noting how the scientists described in the imaginary diary attempted to correct for these weaknesses.

Limitations of Unsystematic Observation   Those who make unsystematic observations of human behavior and development may be easily led into drawing false conclusions. The first plausible explanation that comes to mind may be treated as if it is the only possible explanation. A single episode may lead to a generalization that will be mistakenly applied to superficially similar situations. The reactions of a child in a given situation may be due primarily to unrecognized idiosyncratic factors which may never occur again. The behavior of one child under certain circumstances may not be compared to that of other children in the same circumstances. Unsystematic observers are especially prone to note only evidence that fits their expectations and ignore evidence that does not. The conclusions of parents observing their own children may be distorted by wishful thinking and other subjective factors. If what others have learned is ignored, each set of parents will have to learn everything through experience. In the process, they may make many of the mistakes others made before them and fail to find out about techniques others found successful.

Strengths of Scientific Observation   Those who study development scientifically are more likely to acquire trustworthy information than a casual observer is and to apply what they learn more effectively because they follow these procedures:

☐ In most cases, a representative *sample* of children is studied so that individual idiosyncrasies are cancelled out.

☐ An effort is made to note *all* plausible hypotheses to explain a given type of behavior, and each of these is tested under controlled conditions. If all factors but one can be held constant in an experiment, the researcher may be able to trace the impact of a given condition by comparing the behavior of those who have and those who have not been exposed to it.

☐ Observers make special efforts to be objective and to guard against being misled by predetermined ideas, wishful thinking, or selected evidence.

☐ Observations are made in a carefully prescribed systematic manner, which makes it possible for observers to compare reactions.

☐ Complete reports of experiments—including descriptions of subjects, methods, results, and conclusions—are published in professional journals. This makes it possible for other experimenters to replicate a study to discover if they obtain the same results.

☐ The existence of reports of thousands of experiments makes it possible to discover what others have done, which can then serve as a starting point for one's own speculations.

☐ Techniques that have proven to encourage desirable aspects of development can be described. Situations likely to lead to difficulties in development can be identified, checked, double-checked, and called to the attention of others.

Scientific methods: sampling

control

objectivity

publication

replication

Methods for Studying Different Types of Child Behavior

The summary of strengths of scientific observation that you have just examined calls attention to a point you may have noted as you read about the psychologists' methods mentioned in the imaginary diary: there are different approaches to studying children in scientific ways. Sometimes spontaneous child behavior is studied in natural settings, sometimes the responses of children to questions or stimuli are recorded, sometimes children are observed behaving under conditions controlled by an experimenter. The following reviews the methods described in this chapter and reflects these different approaches of study.

Methods for studying spontaneous behavior in natural settings

☐ Baby Biography—Detailed descriptions of infant behavior are recorded.

☐ Time Sampling—Specific types of behavior are categorized after observing a child for a short period of time.

    ☐ Rating Scales—Judgments about different types of behavior are made after a child has been observed over an extended period of time.

Methods for recording children's reactions to questions or stimuli

    ☐ Sociometric Techniques—Children are asked to indicate their feelings about acquaintances.

    ☐ Questionnaires—Children are asked to reveal their opinions or knowledge by writing answers to a series of specific questions.

    ☐ Clinical Interview—Children are asked to explain certain phenomena. Initial answers determine later questions asked by the examiner.

    ☐ Standardized Interview—Children are asked to express opinions or supply information by responding to a standard series of questions presented and recorded by an examiner.

    ☐ Tests—Answers supplied by children to a standard series of questions are evaluated with reference to precise scoring standards.

    ☐ Projective Techniques—Children are asked to respond to ambiguous pictures, stories, or assortments of play objects. Inferences about personality tendencies are drawn from their responses.

Methods for studying children behaving under controlled conditions

    ☐ Experiments—Groups of children with similar characteristics are exposed to different conditions arranged by the experimenter. Ways a change in one variable affects another variable or variables are recorded as precisely as possible.

Methods for obtaining information regarding age trends

    ☐ Cross-sectional Approach—Characteristics of children of different ages are measured or recorded.

    ☐ Longitudinal Approach—Characteristics of a single group of children are measured or recorded at different stages of their development.

Methods You Might Use to Study Development

This final summary highlights methods of study described in the diary. Instead of reviewing the studies already noted, the methods are described as if you are using them to gain more systematic and objective information about the behavior of your own child. This approach is used not only to give you a different perspective but also to make you aware that after you complete this course you can become a do-it-yourself researcher.

    Whenever you want the most accurate answers available to questions about human development you should consult the information sources described in the Suggestions for Further Study at the end of chapters. Quite often, however, you may be curious about the behavior of particular children in a particular environment at a given point in time. In such situations you might follow procedures such as those described in the following paragraphs.

When your first child is born (which we will assume is a girl), you find yourself so fascinated by her behavior you decide to write a *baby biography*. Whenever you have the time, you sit down next to her crib or playpen and write down detailed descriptions of what she does, adding interpretive comments about what might have caused the behavior.

When your daughter is a preschooler you are often entertained by her comments about the people and things she encounters. You find yourself wondering just how much she understands so you make up a *questionnaire* and ask her to describe her impressions and interpretations of things in her immediate environment.

Some of your daughter's answers strike you as remarkably perceptive, and you find yourself wondering how sharp she is compared to the other boys and girls in the neighborhood. To find out, you make up a simple *test* consisting of questions about your neighborhood (for example, the names of people who live in different houses, which family has the biggest dog, where the nearest fire hydrant is) and ask your daughter and several of her friends to respond. Then, you ask an acquaintance who does not know any of the children to evaluate the responses of each child by referring to scoring standards you supply. Finally, you add up the number of points earned by each child and compute a "Neighborhood Knowledge" score.

When you examine these scores you assume that older children should know more about the neighborhood than younger ones since they have been around longer. To acquire information relating to this point you prepare a *scatter diagram* showing the relationship between the scores of all children who took your test and their ages in months. (If you are mathematically inclined you might also calculate a *correlation coefficient.*)

The test scores earned by the younger and older children who come to play in your backyard do not seem to be too noticeably influenced by age, since the tallies scatter all over your diagram. You hypothesize that this may be the case because the difference between the youngest and oldest children you tested is only thirty-six months. Accordingly, you ask neighborhood children up to the age of fifteen years to take your test. When you compare the scores of children of all ages, you *do* find that there is a definite relationship between neighborhood knowledge and age. You realize, however, that the rough age norms which you have established by using a *cross-sectional* approach may not be very accurate because some of your subjects do not seem to be typical of their age-group. (You got the impression that the ten-year-old you tested was preoccupied and you know that the fifteen-year-old is in a gifted child program in school.) So you decide to do a *longitudinal* investigation and ask each child below the age of five to take your test every two years.

You have a large backyard and many neighborhood children congregate there for play. As you watch them one afternoon you get the impression that some children are leaders, others followers, still others independent souls. You decide it would be interesting to find out which children assume each of these roles. You realize that it would be impossible to write down everything that every child says or does, so you decide to carry out a *time-sampling* study. You list the names of all the children who are frequent visitors to your backyard on a sheet of paper and draw three columns opposite the names. You head the columns: "Tells others what to do," "Does what others say," "Plays without paying much attention to others." You watch the first child on your list for a minute and put a check mark in the appropriate column if one of the three kinds of behavior is observed. Then you record the behavior of the next child, and so on. You do this for thirty minutes on three different afternoons and total up the tallies in each column. You discover that you now have a quite clear picture of leaders, followers, and independent types.

Your time-sampling study causes you to wonder about the different personality characteristics of your daughter's playmates. So, you develop a home-made *rating scale* by listing pairs of traits (such as confident-anxious, daring-cautious, active-sedentary) on either side of a piece of paper and connect them with lines containing equally spaced divisions. Then, you ask your spouse and a friend to watch the neighborhood children for several afternoons before putting a mark on the lines indicating how much or little of a characteristic they think each child displays. Finally, you compare your ratings with the other ratings to see if you and your two fellow observers have reached similar conclusions.

While you are observing children in the backyard preparatory to making your ratings you speculate about who the most popular children are. To find out you carry out a *sociometric* study by asking each child to tell you the name of the playmate he or she likes the best.

One day as you watch a television show with your daughter you wonder if what she sees on TV influences her behavior to the extent that she would go out and immediately imitate some of the actions she has seen. (You recall that after watching Western movies as a child you frequently got out your cap pistol and went in search of playmates to organize a gunfight game.) You happen to notice that a Western titled "Duel of the Gunfighters" is scheduled to be shown on a local TV channel the next day. This prompts you to set up a simple *experiment* featuring experimental and control groups. You make a few telephone calls and find out that three children in the neighborhood always plant themselves in front of a TV in one of their homes and watch that channel at that time. You invite them to come to your backyard for ice cream and play just after they watch the movie. The next day, at the time these three children are watching the Western, you persuade your daughter and two of her friends to watch a rented movie about baby animals. You invite them to join the other children in the backyard for ice cream as soon as the movie is over. On a table next to the counter from which ice cream is served you place several cap pistols as well as some stuffed animals. After making sure everyone has a generous helping of ice cream, you move to a remote part of the yard to record the kinds of games the children engage in immediately after they finish their treat.

When your daughter reaches the sixth grade you become aware that she suddenly seems to be very concerned about right and wrong behavior. You ask her how she feels about different rules and laws and why they should be obeyed. You let her initial answers determine the questions you ask as your interview proceeds since you have decided to use the *clinical inteview* to probe her thinking.

When your daughter is in the ninth grade you realize that she now keeps to herself thoughts that she expressed openly when she was younger. She also seems very concerned about making a good impression. Both of these tendencies make you wonder if it would be possible to get her to reveal her inner feelings without being aware of it. Your realize that your own knowledge of specialized tests is too limited but wonder what sorts of tendencies might come to the surface if your daughter was asked to respond to a *projective test* given by a trained psychometrist.

When your daughter nears the end of the high school years she sometimes engages in discussions with you regarding social, moral, and political issues, causing you to wonder if there is a "generation gap" in your family and in other families you know. To find out, you list questions about contemporary topics (such as legalizing marijuana), jot down your own responses, and then *interview* your daughter, several of her friends, and their parents. You summarize and analyze the different responses to see if any trends emerge.

If you do become intrigued by child development to the point of making systematic observations such as those just described, sooner or later you will probably find yourself trying to relate one conclusion to other conclusions. In other words, you may make an effort to develop a *theory* about certain forms of human behavior so that you can tie together separate conclusions. A theory based on the sorts of observations just described would not be too elegant, but it would represent an attempt on your part to *explain* how children develop. In that sense, you would share the goal of psychologists whose work is summarized in the next chapter, which consists of a description of the best-known theories of human development.

Suggestions for Further Study

History of Developmental Psychology

If you are interested in history, you may enjoy reading *A History of Experimental Psychology* (2nd ed., 1950) by Edwin G. Boring. In addition to summarizing discoveries and movements, Boring describes the personalities of those who influenced the development of psychology and how they were in turn influenced by the culture in which they worked. (His book served as inspiration and model for this chapter.) The impact of Darwin and Galton is outlined on pages 468–488. In Chapter 9, Boring traces the philosophical bases of modern psychology and explains the influence of, among others, Locke. In Chapter 21 he describes how American psychology developed. (The sections most relevant to developmental psychology appear on pages 505–523.) The emergence of behaviorism under John B. Watson is noted on pages 641–645; the development of psychoanalysis is outlined on pages 706–712.

For a brief history of developmental psychology, look for "Historical Beginnings of Child Psychology" by Wayne Dennis (*Psychological Bulletin*, 1940, **46**, 224–225). For an explanation of how Watson's behaviorism came to be favored and how it then gave way to the experimental analysis of behavior, see "The Learning Theory Tradition and Child Psychology" by Sheldon H. White, Chapter 8 in Volume 1 of *Carmichael's Manual of Child Psychology* (3rd ed., 1970), edited by Paul H. Mussen. An especially interesting account of the history of child study is presented in *The Child* (1965) by William Kessen, who intertwines his own observations with excerpts from works by physicians, philosophers, and psychologists. The earliest account he quotes (by John Locke) was published in 1693. The most recent (by Jean Piaget) appeared in 1947. Wayne Dennis has edited a collection of articles published between 1728 and 1948, titled *Historical Readings in Developmental Psychology* (1972), which includes reports of many of the studies mentioned in this chapter. Robert R. Sears discusses "Your Ancients Revisited: A History of Child Development" on pages 1–74 of *Review of Child Development Research*, 1975, **5**, edited by E. M. Hetherington. Milton J. E. Senn provides "Insights on the Child Development Movement in the United States" in a *Monograph of the Society for Research in Child Development,* 1975, **40**, (3–4, Serial No. 161).

Methods of Child Psychology

This chapter (and the suggestions that follow) supplies information about specific techniques of studying children. If you would like to read a brief general description of such methods, consult "Methods of Child Psychology" by John E. Anderson, Chapter 1 in *Manual of Child Psychology* (2nd ed., 1954), edited by Leonard Carmichael (pp. 1–59). For a more comprehensive analysis, examine *Handbook of Research Methods in Child Development* (1960), edited by Paul H. Mussen. The first two chapters, by Alfred Baldwin and William Kessen, are devoted to general considerations and problems. The remaining twenty chapters describe specific techniques.

Baby Biographies

Charles Darwin's baby biography of his son Doddy appeared in the British journal *Mind* in 1877. This journal is not likely to be available in your library, but the article was reprinted in *Readings in Child Psychology* (1951), edited by Wayne Dennis, pp. 54–64. (At the end of the article [pp. 64–67] Dennis supplies references for sixty-four other baby biographies.) The article is also reprinted in *The Child* (1965) by William Kessen (pp. 118–129). In addition, Kessen provides excerpts from baby biographies written by Wilhelm Preyer (pp. 134–147) and Hippolyte Taine (pp. 181–182). Baby-biography material that is directly related to several later sections of this text can be found in *The Origins of Intelligence in Children* (1952) by Jean Piaget, in which he supplies observations of his children to illustrate the principles and stages of his theory of development. If you read the descriptions of Darwin or Piaget (or of some other baby biographer), you might note the kind of behavior described. Or, if you would prefer to function as a baby biographer yourself, keep a record of the actions and reactions of an infant over a period of time, summarize your conclusions, and assess the vaue of your research.

Binet's Observations on Intelligence Testing

To learn how Alfred Binet developed his test of intelligence and why he devised the techniques he used, read "The Measurement of Intelligence" by Binet and Simon reprinted in *The Child* (1965) by William Kessen (pp. 188–208). Because this account was written at a time when psychologists were just beginning to refine tests, it is an especially revealing analysis of the problems faced by those who attempt to measure intelligence.

Questionnaires

Ever since G. Stanley Hall inquired into the contents of children's minds, psychologists have asked children to respond to questionnaires. It is a quick, easy way to get information, and the results are often interesting and sometimes unsettling. A commonly used research technique is to administer a questionnaire developed several years ago and compare the responses of children at that time with those given by children of the same age today. If this strikes you as interesting, you might ask a group of five- to six-year-old children to respond to the questions below, originally asked by C. A. Probst in the early 1930s. (For complete details, see the article "A General Information Test for Kindergarten Children," *Child Development*, 1931, **2**, 81–95. The figure in parentheses after each question is the percentage of kindergarten children who answered each query correctly in 1931.)

1 How many pennies in a dime? (22)
2 What time of year do flowers grow outdoors? (99)
3 How many eggs in a half dozen? (12)
4 What time or what o'clock is it at noon? (30)
5 What do bees make that we eat? (59)
6 A baby dog is called a pupppy; what is a baby cow called? (26)
7 What do we eat that grows on vines? (29)
8 Who makes money by cutting hair? (96)

9   Where does coal come from? (32)
10   What is a thermometer for? (50)

Comment on the differences between the number of correct answers from the kindergarten children of the 1980s and the number from the 1931 group.

The questions noted above ask children to supply factual information. Questionnaires are also used to tap opinions. The Gallup and Harris polls of public opinion on current affairs illustrate this approach. If you are interested in how adolescents feel about current issues, you might make up a list of questions followed by "Agree" and "Disagree," and ask them to respond. The same questions might be submitted to some of your college classmates and to older adults, particularly parents of teenagers.

Gesell's Maturational View of Behavior

An early presentation of Arnold Gesell's maturational view of development appeared in his *Infancy and Human Growth* (1928). A later, more concise analysis can be found in "The Ontogenesis of Infant Behavior," Chapter 6 of *Manual of Child Psychology* (2nd ed., 1954), edited by Leonard Carmichael (pp. 335–373). After observing the development of children over a period of years Gesell and his associates became convinced that they had succeeded in plotting a series of stages that describe the typical behavior of children at different age levels from birth to sixteen years. These are reported in several books, the most concise of which is a paperback, *The Gesell Institute's Child Behavior* (1955) by Frances L. Ilg and Louise Bates Ames (two of Gesell's colleagues who assumed leadership of his research institute when he died). The main theme of the book is summed up in this statement, "Our observations of child behavior have led us to believe that almost any kind of behavior you can think of . . . develops by means of remarkably patterned and largely predictable stages" (p. 13). To get an idea of the Gesell Institute's view of development, including the stages typical of different age levels, read the first two chapters of *Child Behavior.*

Shirley's The First Two Years

Mary Shirley's study of twenty-five infants during their first two years was carried out in the early 1930s, but it remains a classic because of her skill and thoroughness as an observer. She reported her observations and conclusions in three University of Minnesota *Institute of Child Welfare Monographs.* Volume I (1931) describes posture and locomotor development. Volume II (1933) describes intellectual development, and Volume III (1933) analyzes personality manifestations. If you would like to find out more about the nature of development during the first two years, examine one or more of these.

Time Sampling

Observing social behavior can be quite fascinating. If you would like to make a systematic record of some aspect of interactions between children, the time-sampling technique is easy and enjoyable. One way to proceed would be to use Parten's classifications of the social behavior of nursery school children. (For details of her descriptions and techniques, see her article "Social Participation Among Preschool Children," *Journal of Abnormal and Social Psychology*, 1932, **27**, 243–269.) Or select some form of behavior that is of interest (for example, elementary school playground interaction, high school between-class behavior). To develop your own list of observational categories, simply observe children of the age you have selected as they engage in a particular type of behavior and write down what they do. Eventually, you should be able to describe five or so categories that cover most aspects of their behavior. At that point, pick out a child to observe for ten seconds. At the end of that time put a check mark in the appropriate column opposite the child's name. Then select another child, observe him or her for ten seconds, record the behavior, and so on. If you sample behavior on several different occasions, you will have a record of the types of behavior engaged in by different children. Parten's technique is just one of many types of time sampling. A summary of several variations of the basic technique is presented on pages 92–104 of "Observational Child Study" by Herbert F. Wright, Chapter 3 in *Handbook of Research Methods in Child Development* (1960), edited by Paul H. Mussen.

Sociometric Techniques

Time sampling is a method for obtaining information about overt social interaction. For example, you might check on friendships by tallying the number of times children play together during twenty-second observations of their behavior. If you would like to obtain some information about *subjective* factors in social behavior, you might make use of *sociometric techniques*. (For Jacob Moreno's account of how he developed and used this technique, see pages 92–174 of his *Who Shall Survive?* [1934, 1953].) The simplest way to do this is to ask elementary school children to write down the name of the person they like the best in their class. (If you act as a teacher aide, you could add that question to a math or spelling quiz. Or, if you ask permission to observe in an elementary grade classroom, you might ask the teacher to add the question to a written exercise.) However you obtain the names of the most-liked children, the most graphic way to record the choices is to use what is called a *target diagram*, described by M. L. Northway in *Sociometry*, 1940, **3**, 144–150. First, count up the number of times the most popular child's name is mentioned. Then, take a compass and draw that number of concentric circles, as illustrated below. (In this example, it is assumed the most popular child was named four times.)

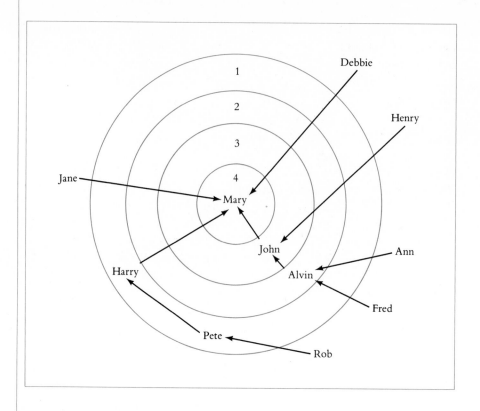

Put the name of the four-choice child in the center, or 4, circle; the names of any three-choice children in the 3 circle, and so on. Place the names of children not chosen at all outside the largest circle. Finally, draw a line with an arrow showing each child's choice (as illustrated above). If you follow this procedure, you will be able to pick out quickly the *stars* (those in the center) and the *isolates* (those on the outside) and also be able to see whom each child chose. If you would like more information about sociometric techniques, look for *Sociometry in the Classroom* (1959) by Norman Gronlund or examine issues of the journal *Sociometry*.

Longitudinal Studies

If the longitudinal approach strikes you as interesting, you might want to examine one of the classic studies of this type. *The Course of Human Development* (1971), edited by Mary Cover Jones, Nancy Bayley, Jean W. Macfarlane, and Marjorie P. Honzik, provides comprehensive coverage of the three longitudinal investigations carried out at the University of California. *Birth to Maturity* (1962) by Jerome Kagan and Howard A. Moss is a description of an analysis of Fels Research Institute data. *The Gifted Group at Midlife: Thirty-five Years' Follow-up of the Superior Child* (1959) by Lewis M. Terman and Melita Oden summarizes the findings of the Stanford "Genetic Studies of Genius." Jerome Kagan provides an overview of longitudinal research carried out in this country in an article that begins on page 1 of Volume 35 of *Child Development* (1964). L. W. Sontag (1971) describes "The History of Longitudinal Research: Implications for the Future" in *Child Development*, 1971, **42**, 987–1002.

Techniques for Studying Interpersonal Behavior

Many interesting studies have been done of interactions between children playing together and between children and their parents. For a concise account of such methods, see "Interpersonal Behavior" by William W. Lambert, Chapter 20 in *Handbook of Research Methods in Child Development* (1960), edited by Paul H. Mussen (pp. 854–917). Lambert describes techniques used to study mother-child interaction (pp. 904–906), and also gives an account of methods of studying child-child interactions involving aggression, dominance, submission, dependence, and sympathy (pp. 893–903). If you are interested in how interpersonal interactions are studied, you might either outline the methods described by Lambert or use some of the techniques mentioned to carry out a simple study of your own. For a comprehensive analysis of research of parent-child relationships see "Observational Studies of Parent-Child Interaction: A Methodological Review" by H. Lytton which starts on page 651 of *Child Development*, 1971, **42**.

Interviews

If you are interested in feelings and attitudes, you might want to interview some students or parents. (Generally speaking, you are more likely to get responses of greater depth and variety if you interview older children or adults.) To carry out an interview study of adolescents, make up a short list of questions and ask some high school students to respond. (For examples of the kinds of questions you might ask, see pages 429–449 of *The Adolescent Experience* [1966] by Elizabeth Douvan and Joseph Adelson. One advantage of using some of the questions developed by Douvan and Adelson is that you can compare the responses of your subjects to the summaries in *The Adolescent Experience*.) Another approach would be to ask children of different ages to respond and compare their answers. If you would like to interview parents, see pages 491–501 of *Patterns of Child Rearing* (1957) by Robert R. Sears, Eleanor Maccoby, and Harry Levin for sample questions.

Items from Interview Schedule for Girls Devised by Douvan and Adelson

1   What are the things you'll have to decide or make up your mind about in the next few years?

2   We find that some girls have a kind of plan or picture of what they'll do

when they get out of school. What ideas do you have about the way you want things to work out for you?

3 Do you want to get married some day?

4 Could you tell me a little about the kind of person you'd like to marry?

5 What kind of work would you like your husband to do?

6 Are there any girls you wouldn't go around with?

7 What do you think makes a girl popular with boys?

8 What do you think about dating?

9 What do you think about the idea of going steady?

10 Now, I'm going to show you some pictures about a girl, her parents, and her friends. In each picture someone has just said something and another person is going to answer. What do you think the answer would be?

Picture 1. What would the parents say?
Picture 2. What would the girl say?
Picture 3. What would the girl say now?

11 Most parents have some ideas about how they want their children to behave. What are the most important things your parents expect of you?

12 Very often girls your age disagree with their parents about something. What disagreements do you have with your parents?

13 Jane sometimes wishes that her parents were different—more like the parents of her friends. What does she have in mind?

14 A girl is told by someone that a close friend of hers has said unkind things about her. What does she do about it?

15 Gladys feels terrible because she did something she thought she would never do. What do you think it would be?

16 What would she do about it?

17 Would she talk it over with anyone?

18 Would you tell me whether or not you agree with the following statements?

The husband ought to have the final say in family matters.

It is only natural and right that men should have more freedom than women.

A man should help his wife with some of the work around the house.[2]

Projective Techniques

If you are intrigued by methods that attempt to tap the unconscious or at least make it difficult for a subject to distort responses, you might want to discover

[2] Elizabeth Douvan and Joseph Adelson, *The Adolescent Experience* (1966), pp. 441–444. Schedule developed by the University of Michigan Survey Research Center.

more about projective techniques. One way is to actually take a Rorschach or TAT test. (Check with a professor who teaches a course in projective techniques and ask if any students need practice subjects.) Another way to gain information is to read "Projective Techniques" by William E. Henry, Chapter 15 of *Handbook of Research Methods in Child Development* (1960), edited by Paul H. Mussen (pp. 603–644). More comprehensive treatment of such techniques can be found in *Handbook of Projective Techniques* (1965), edited by Bernard I. Murstein, or *Projective Techniques in Personality Assessment* (1968), edited by A. I. Rabin.

If you would like to find out how children respond to play constructions, buy or borrow an assortment of small figures, animals, buildings, and the like and follow the procedure used by Erik Erikson (described on pages 98–108 of *Childhood and Society*) by asking children to construct an exciting scene out of an imaginary film or TV show. Describe the nature of the scenes and what the children say about them, and perhaps contrast the scenes made by younger and by older children, or by boys and by girls, or compare your subjects' scenes with the constructions made by Erikson's subjects.

Laboratory-experimental Study of Child Behavior

A concise account of the application of experimental techniques to the study of development is provided by Sidney W. Bijou and Donald M. Baer in Chapter 4 of *Handbook of Research Methods in Child Development* (1960), edited by Paul H. Mussen (pp. 140–200). They note that "The essential concept involved in the definition of experimental technique is that of control" (p. 140) and that measurement of changes in variables should ideally be done by mechanical means (to eliminate human error). They point out that it is necessary in setting up conditions of control to take into account the child's present environment, history of interaction with past environments, and genetic endowment; and they comment on some of the problems involved when an experimenter sets out to do this. Topics covered by Bijou and Baer include how to obtain subjects of different ages, sampling considerations, and a variety of investigative procedures. If you would like to acquire knowledge of the laboratory-experimental method, an excellent way to do it would be to outline the Bijou and Baer chapter in the *Handbook of Research Methods in Child Development*.

Skinner's Air Crib

B. F. Skinner describes "My Experiences with the Baby Tender" in *Psychology Today* (1979), **12** (10), 28–40, an excerpt from *The Shaping of a Behaviorist* (1979), the second volume of his autobiography.

KEY POINTS

Freud: *Stages of Psychosexual Development*

Libido: basic instinctual energy with strong sexual component

Oral, anal, phallic, latency, and genital stages

Anaclitic identification: boys and girls strive to be like mother

Defensive identification: boys try to be like father so as to acquire admired qualities

Conscious: what a person is aware of at a given moment

Preconscious: memories stored in the mind that can be recalled

Unconscious: memories stored in the mind that cannot be recalled at will

Id: source of the libido

Ego: screens and controls expression of libidinal energy

Superego: one's conscience

Defense mechanisms: control primitive impulses and protect ego

Erikson: *Stages of Psychosocial Development*

Trust vs. mistrust

Autonomy vs. doubt

Initiative vs. guilt

Industry vs. inferiority

Identity vs. role confusion

Piaget: *Stages of Cognitive Development*

Organization: combine and systematize impressions

Adaptation: adjust to the environment

Equilibration: seek coherence and stability

Assimilation: incorporate conceptions into store of ideas

Accommodation: modify ideas

Scheme: organized pattern of behavior or thought

Conservation: ability to recognize that properties stay the same despite change in appearance

Decentration: ability to consider more than one quality at a time

Operation: mental action that can be reversed

Sensorimotor stage: acquire first schemes through sense impressions and motor activities

Preoperational stage: form many schemes but not able to mentally reverse actions

Concrete operational stage: capable of mentally reversing actions but generalize only from concrete experiences

Formal operational stage: able to deal with abstractions, form hypotheses, engage in mental manipulation

Learning Theory

Features of learning theory: behaviorism, experimentation

Imitation and observation in social learning

Reciprocal relationship between child and parents

CHAPTER □3

THEORIES OF DEVELOPMENT

The outline of conceptions of development presented in Chapter 1 will help you comprehend how different assumptions influence the application of knowledge about children. The survey of history and methods offered in the preceding chapter will help you understand how and why different points of view developed at particular times. In this chapter theories of development will be outlined to help you place specific facts into a pattern, and descriptions of stages will be summarized to contribute to your understanding of the sequence of development.

On the following pages you will find descriptions of stage theories proposed by Sigmund Freud, Erik H. Erikson, and Jean Piaget, and an analysis of learning theory (which many American psychologists feel is the most satisfactory way to explain development). To provide background, factors that influenced the development of those who proposed each theory are included in each section.

Freud: Stages of Psychosexual Development

Childhood and Education

Sigmund Freud was born in 1856 in Freiberg, Austria (now Příbor, Czechoslovakia). His father was a wool merchant who married twice. Sigmund was the first child born to the second wife, who was twenty-one at that time. Sigmund's father was then forty, twice the age of Sigmund's mother. The father was known as a gentle man who combined a sense of humor with skepticism and was once described by Freud in a letter to his future wife as "always hopefully expecting something to turn up." Sigmund's mother (who lived to be ninety-five) was pretty, had a lively personality, and was alert and intelligent. Shortly after she gave birth to Sigmund she met an old peasant woman in a pastry shop who informed her that she had brought a great man into the world. The young mother firmly believed this prediction and treated Sigmund as the indisputable favorite of all her children.

Among the events in Sigmund's childhood that might have contributed to his later theorizing were these:[1] at the age of two he still wet his bed, which did not bother his mother but led his father to scold him; he experienced considerable jealousy when his brothers and sisters were born since he then had to share his mother's love with others; at about the same time he suspected that his father was on more intimate terms with his mother than he and was therefore a rival for her affections.

When Sigmund was four, the family moved to Vienna. His parents provided his first lessons, but he eventually was enrolled in a private school where he did so well he was admitted to high school a year early. He was the outstanding student in the school and graduated with high distinction. The careers open to a Viennese Jew at that time were business, law, or medicine, and Sigmund chose the last without great enthusiasm. He entered the University of Vienna at the early age of seventeen, specializing in physiology out of admiration for the professor who taught that subject. After he earned his M.D. degree he became an intern at the General Hospital of Vienna, where he served for several months in the psychiatric clinic. He eventually was chosen lecturer in neural pathology and in time won a grant to study in Paris with the most famous neurologist of that era, Jean Martin Charcot.

Charcot was experimenting with the use of hypnosis to treat a type of hysteria in which the patient developed a paralysis of some sort. Freud became intrigued by this technique, and when he returned to Vienna he entered practice with Josef Breuer, who also made use of hypnosis in treating patients suffering from hysteria. One of these was a young woman who had developed paralyses of three limbs, disturbances of sight and speech, and a severe nervous cough (among other things) as a consequence of nursing her critically ill father. One day, Anna O. (as the famous young lady is referred to in histories of psychoanalysis) spontaneously described to Breuer how a particular symptom had developed. As she did so, the symptom disappeared. The next day, Breuer hypnotized Anna and urged her to tell him about the development of other symptoms, and they also disappeared. In her waking state, Anna was unable to trace the development of most of her

---

[1] For a comprehensive analysis of factors that influenced Freud, see *Freud and His Followers* (1974) by Paul Roazen.

Left, Sigmund Freud, aged 8, with his father, Jakob Freud. *Right,* Sigmund at 16 with his mother, Amalie. Sigmund Freud Copyrights Ltd.

paralyses, but once hypnotized, she was able to grasp and explain the connection between experiences and symptoms.

The Development of Psychoanalysis

In the process of treating Anna, who was very attractive and intelligent, Breuer developed a strong attachment to his patient which she began to reciprocate. When he became aware of this Breuer broke off the treatment. Anna's reaction was to become convinced, to the point of showing all the appropriate symptoms, that she was giving birth to a child fathered by her therapist. This incident caused Breuer abruptly to take his wife to Venice on a second honeymoon. When he returned to Vienna, he chose to practice other types of medicine.

Freud, however, continued to treat cases of hysteria. In time, he became dissatisfied with hypnosis because not all patients could be hypnotized and because cures induced by hypnosis were only temporary. He decided to make more systematic application of the technique that Anna used spontaneously by asking his patients simply to talk about whatever thoughts popped into their minds. As his patients engaged in such *free association,* Freud observed that dreams and recollections of childhood experiences were frequently of special importance and that unhappy or embarrassing experiences were sometimes so difficult to recall that he had to help the patient overcome *resistance* to talking about them.

Because it was assumed at that point in the development of understanding of disturbed behavior that only females experienced hysteria (medical practitioners of that time believed the condition was linked to the uterus), Freud saw only female patients. As he listened to them describe recollections of early childhood experiences, Freud became aware that almost all of his patients reported sexual fantasies, and several of them imagined that they had been seduced by their fathers. This led him to conclude that sexual factors were a normal, not an abnormal, feature of development.

At this stage of his career, Freud experienced considerable anguish and depression because of lack of professional recognition and difficulties in developing his conception of behavior. He therefore decided to psychoanalyze himself. As he examined his own early experiences, he was impressed by recollections of sexual wishes. Eventually, insights from his own analysis and his treatment of others led him to form a comprehensive theory of psychosexual development.

The Nature of Libidinal Energy

Libido: basic instinctual energy with strong sexual component

To explain behavior Freud proposed that human beings are born with a basic instinctual energy, the *libido*. He was convinced that this basic energy was characterized by a strong sexual component, but he defined "sexual" to include many types of pleasurable sensations, not just those centering on the genital organs. The libido constantly moves and flows, and the behavior of an individual is determined by the way it is distributed. Sometimes libidinal energy may become concentrated on a part of a person's own body; sometimes it is attached to another person or a particular object; sometimes it may become blocked and accumulate.

The key to understanding behavior, Freud suggested, is to determine how libidinal energy is being expended. Some of Freud's patients, for example, seemed unable to keep from gorging themselves on food and drink; others were excessively concerned about neatness and cleanliness. Freud concluded that such behavior might be accounted for by assuming that libidinal energy had become attached to a particular part of the person's own body. When he observed the behavior of children (primarily his own, since he had no child patients), remembered his own childhood, and listened to his patients free-associate, Freud became convinced that libidinal energy was likely to become concentrated on different parts of the body at different age levels. He eventually developed a detailed description of stages of libidinal, or psychosexual, development.

Stages of Psychosexual Development

Oral stage

The period from birth to two years Freud called the *oral stage* because the infant is particularly concerned about feeding, uses the mouth to examine objects, and gains satisfaction from such activities as sucking a thumb or pacifier. During the *anal stage* two- to three-year-olds are preoccupied with toilet training and may experience pleasure as they experience the processes of elimination. Four-year-olds are at the *phallic stage* because they become curious about anatomical differences between the sexes, the origin of babies, and the sexual activities of parents. Children may also discover that manipulating the genital organs provides a pleasurable sensation. Freud concluded that the libido is not concentrated on any particular part of the body between the age of six or so and the time of puberty, and so he called this the *latency period*. Psychosexual development terminates at adolescence in the *genital stage* when libidinal satisfaction centers on the genital organs.

Anal stage

Phallic stage

Latency period

Genital stage

Fixation and Attachment of Libidinal Energy

Freud hypothesized that if a child had a traumatic experience, or a series of disagreeable or abnormal experiences, during one of the stages of development, libidinal energy might become *fixated*. If fixation occurs, the person is predisposed to reduce tension later in life by resorting to the forms of behavior that were of greatest significance during earlier stages of development. A child who is weaned too early, for example, may experience urges to eat and drink to excess as an adult; a child who is exposed to severe toilet training may manifest a compulsive concern about cleanliness in adulthood.

These stages and the concept of fixation account for ways libidinal energy might become centered on the person's own body. Other aspects of development Freud explained by suggesting that libidinal energy would become cathected (attached) to particular individuals who would literally become *love objects*. He assumed that libidinal energy in an infant would be attached to the mother. Freud noted, however, that many of his female patients revealed in their free associations that they had experienced a strong attraction toward their fathers early in their lives. Furthermore, when Freud analyzed himself, he recalled that he had first gone through a stage when he adored his mother and feared and hated his father but that eventually he came to want to be like his father. To explain these trends in child behavior Freud proposed the *Oedipus complex*,[2] which refers to the tendency for a child (around the age of four) to attach libidinal energy to the

---

[2] If you are not familiar with the Greek myth of Oedipus or the play Sophocles based on it, you may wonder why Freud chose the term. Oedipus was separated from his parents at birth. At adulthood, without realizing it, he engaged in battle with his father and killed him. He then married, also without realizing it, his mother. When he discovered what he had done, he blinded himself. Strictly speaking, *Oedipus complex* refers to the love of the boy for his mother and his hostility and fear of his father. The love of a girl for her father (and her feeling of rivalry with the mother) is sometimes called the *Electra complex*, after a woman in another Greek myth who avenged the murder of her father by persuading her brother to kill their mother. In many discussions, however, *Oedipus complex* is used to refer to behavior of both male and female children.

parent of the opposite sex and to experience feelings of hostility and rivalry toward the parent of the same sex. If development proceeds normally, the Oedipus complex is resolved when the child of five or so comes to *identify* with the parent of the same sex.

Anaclitic and Defensive Identification

Anaclitic identification: boys and girls try to be like mother

To account for changes in the attachment of libidinal energy Freud introduced the concept of *identification*. He distinguished between two types, anaclitic (literally translated: "leaning-up-against-type") and defensive (also called aggressive). *Anaclitic identification* occurs when children pattern their behavior after the primary caretaker, in almost all cases the mother. The mother provides care when the infant is completely dependent (and must therefore "lean" on her for care and sustenance). Freud thus hypothesized that the child, when capable of a certain amount of independent behavior (around the age of two), gains a measure of security by engaging in some of the activities of the person who had previously provided care. In a sense, the child's own behavior becomes a substitute for some of the satisfactions originally supplied by the parent.

Defensive identification: boys try to be like father so as to acquire admired qualities

Defensive identification enters the picture when the child is old enough to recognize sex differences (usually around the age of four years or so). Even when she becomes attracted to the father, the girl continues to identify with the mother, and she encounters few difficulties at this stage. But the boy must *transfer* his tendencies toward identification from the mother to the father. Freud proposed that this switch involves *defensive* behavior on the part of the boy because the Oedipus complex causes him to fear and resent his father, who is perceived as a rival. To overcome these feelings, the boy makes efforts to be like his father so that he might vicariously acquire some of the qualities he envies. (In slang terms, defensive identification means "If you can't lick 'em, join 'em.")

One of the most significant and far-reaching aspects of Freud's theories was his revolutionary suggestion that the attachment or fixation of libidinal energy takes place without conscious awareness on the part of the individual. To explain how this occurs, Freud made a distinction between three levels of consciousness.

Levels of Consciousness

Conscious: awareness

Preconscious: memories

Unconscious: unrecallable memories

The three levels of consciousness proposed by Freud are the conscious, the preconscious, and the unconscious. The *conscious* level consists of all mental processes that a person is aware of at a given moment. The *preconscious* (sometimes also called the *foreconscious*) consists of memories stored in the mind that can be readily recalled, particularly by the association of ideas. The third level, which comprises the largest part of the mind, is the *unconscious*. This is made up of memories that may influence thinking and behavior but cannot be recalled (except under such special circumstances as dreams, hypnotic states, or free associations).

Freud proposed that up to the age of four or so both boys and girls would strive to be like the mother because such *anaclitic* (leaning-up-against) identification would produce a sense of secur-ity. After they reached the age of four, Freud felt, boys would begin to engage in *defensive* (if you can't lick 'em, join 'em) identification and try to be like their fathers in order to acquire qualities they admired and envied. ©Erika Stone 1980. Leonard Freed/Magnum.

Freud felt that many types of behavior could be explained in terms of conflicts between levels of consciousness. To clarify the nature of these conflicts he proposed that personality is made up of three sets of forces or structures: the id, ego, and superego. The *id* is the source of the libido and is entirely unconscious. It is guided by the *pleasure principle* (the seeking of gratification and the avoidance of pain) and is primitive and illogical. The *ego* is partly conscious and partly unconscious. Its primary function is to screen and control the unconscious impulses emanating from the id and to determine how and when libidinal energy will be expressed. The ego is governed by the *reality principle,* which means that it involves rational analysis of the situations an individual must cope with. The *superego* is essentially one's conscience. It consists of the moral values of a society acquired primarily through identification with parents and other adults. The superego influences how individuals act in situations involving moral judgments and how they feel about moral decisions that have been made. Freud hypothesized that when children identified with their parents, they would think of actions as right or wrong by imagining how their fathers and mothers would evaluate those actions and respond to them.

Id: libido

Ego: controls libido

Superego: conscience

Defense Mechanisms

To further explain how conflicts are handled, Freud suggested several *defense mechanisms* that are called into play, usually in an unconscious way, when primitive impulses need to be controlled, when accumulating libidinal energy must be released, or when the ego needs to be protected. *Repression* is one of the most common of these mechanisms. Individuals who have had painful experiences will resist remembering them and tend to suppress the memories in the unconscious level of the mind. In some cases, threatening desires may be controlled by *reaction formation,* where individuals assume forms of behavior opposite to those they are struggling to master. (Individuals who are apprehensive about their own strong sexual desires, for example, may lead a crusade against pornography). Or some individuals may resort to *projection* and attribute to others types of behavior they are reluctant to recognize in themselves. Or individuals may engage in *sublimation* by diverting libidinal energy from sex objects to interests and activities that have no direct connection with sex—art or sports, for instance. In situations that individuals feel may be threatening to the ego if they analyze their behavior objectively, they may resort to *rationalizations* by giving "good" reasons for behavior that is weak or unacceptable. If individuals become frustrated and angry because of their inadequacies, they may resort to *displacement* and divert their hostility from themselves to others. Another reaction to frustration takes the form of *regression,* where individuals resort to forms of behavior that provided satisfaction at earlier stages of development.

Defense mechanisms: control primitive impulses or protect ego

Most contemporary psychologists acknowledge the value of Freud's description of mechanisms, even though they may not be willing to accept the idea that

One of the most significant defense mechanisms proposed by Freud is *repression*. Even though a person may not be able to recall a disagreeable childhood experience (because the experience is "pushed" into the unconscious), the memory may be stored in the mind and later influence behavior in ways unrecognized by the individual. Irene B. Bayer/Monkmeyer.

libidinal energy is involved or that a primitive id is engaged in a battle with a superego.

Freud's Theory in Perspective

The Impact of Freudian Theory Freud's impact on the study of human development was diverse. His emphasis on the impact of sex drives on behavior opened up an entirely new area of research. His stage descriptions, particularly of the oral and anal periods of libidinal development, stimulated many observational studies of feeding and toilet training. His theories on the impact of infantile experiences on later behavior led psychologists to study infants and young children intensively and to plan longitudinal investigations in an effort to trace cause and effect relationships. His suggestion that behavior was often controlled by unconscious memories and his description of defense mechanisms contributed to understanding types of child behavior that had previously been difficult to interpret. The technique of psychoanalysis was used by many psychotherapists and led to the development of alternative forms of therapy.

In many respects, however, Freud's impact on American psychology was "indirect" in the sense that investigations were often stimulated by skepticism regarding his theory. Psychologists in this country were bothered by the fact that most of Freud's speculations were based on recollections of child behavior by an extremely small, atypical group of adult subjects. They were also reluctant to accept statements based on abstract theorizing rather than objective observation. Even when psychologists published data that led to doubts about aspects of Freudian theory, however, they contributed to the understanding of human development.

In evaluating Freud's theory you should remember that he was attempting to explain aspects of behavior that had not been previously understood. In his eagerness to make his explanations as clear as possible he sometimes resorted to rather extreme and fanciful concepts. The term Oedipus complex, for example, arouses visions of overwhelming passion that are appropriate in Greek tragedy but a bit difficult to imagine in the behavior of a four-year-old boy. The postulation of an id, ego, and superego suggests that our minds are the site of violent battles between elemental forces. And at first glance, his description of stages of development may seem too far-fetched to take seriously. But in light of Freud's own childhood—and aspects of the development of a typical child—his description of stages makes considerable sense.

The Impact of Freud's Own Experiences   First, consider Freud's childhood. He experienced difficulties in toilet training. He adored his admiring mother, who was twenty years younger than her husband, which contributed to the feeling that his father was a rival for his mother's affection. Next, consider the development of a typical child. The most important and pleasurable feature of an infant's life is feeding. Most two-year-olds are concerned about toilet training; most four- and five-year-olds are curious about anatomical differences between the sexes and the origin of babies. At adolescence, particularly in boys, the sex drive is more highly developed than at any other stage of development. Those who have repressed or forgotten an unhappy childhood incident may not be aware that their behavior is being influenced by it until they remember it (spontaneously or with the assistance of a therapist), talk about it, and understand and accept it. Freud discovered and demonstrated this as he practiced psychoanalysis. When his patients were helped to recall and discuss childhood experiences or the onset of hysterical symptoms, their abnormal behavior diminished.

Freud ventured into completely new territory and, as is the case with any explorer, he was forced to fill in gaps where his initial impressions were incomplete. Because he suggested, at a time when there was great prudery about sex, that sexual memories and fantasies influence behavior, his theories were reviled, derided, and misinterpreted. Critics cast aspersions on Freud's own sex life and implied that the analyst needed more help than his patients. Some theorists (for example, Margaret Ribble, 1943) were so impressed by his emphasis on the possibility of fixation that they advocated ultrapermissive child rearing and admonished parents *never* to interfere with an infant's behavior for fear it would cause a traumatic experience which would lead to neurosis later in life. (Chapter 6 of Ribble's *The Rights of Infants* is "Babies Must Not Be Thwarted.") Freud should not be blamed for extreme interpretations of psychoanalytic theory made by others.

Using Freudian Principles to Understand Behavior   Today, after sixty years of examination of Freud's proposals, relatively few psychologists completely endorse all aspects of his theory. But obviously the points regarding the typical child can assist those seeking to understand development. The way a child is fed and toilet trained, the way parents react to curiosity about sex, the adolescent's experiences with sexual exploration—all may have a significant impact on development. Early experiences retained in the memory but not recalled may influence later behavior in such a way that individuals will not be aware of the reasons they act as they do.

If a literal interpretation is avoided, postulating three levels of consciousness, or a basic sexual energy, or the existence of an id, ego, and superego can clarify understanding of many types of behavior. There are undoubtedly times in the life of a child (or an adult) when it *does* seem that a battle is taking place between primitive impulses and rational control. (A child who is tempted to steal a candy bar from a store, for example, may experience conflicting impulses aroused by the primitive desire to devour something delicious and the awareness that it is improper to take things without paying for them.) The idea that libidinal energy becomes attached to love objects is not so far-fetched, either. Falling head-over-heels in love could well be described as a flowing of a massive amount of libidinal energy from one person to another. And taking into account defense mechanisms, with or without reference to the libido, id, or superego, can explain many types of behavior.

Therefore, even though Freudian theory in its pure form may have limitations, interpretations based on it serve to illuminate many aspects of development and behavior. Furthermore, several theorists have based *their* interpretations of development on Freudian principles, and an understanding of their views will be facilitated by an awareness of the original theory. For all of these reasons, Freud's observations will be referred to frequently in the chapters that follow. To help you grasp the overall structure of Freud's theory, the various stages, structures, and mechanisms are summarized in Table 3–1.

Whereas Freud's theory illuminates some types of development, it does not touch on other aspects of behavior. At this point, therefore, it is appropriate to examine the views of Erik H. Erikson, a psychoanalyst who has used Freud's observations as a starting point for evolving a theory of psycho*social* development.

Table 3–1
Summary of Freudian Theory

Libidinal development

Basic sexual energy (libido) is concentrated on parts of the body, objects, or individuals. Libidinal development proceeds according to this sequence:

Birth to two years	Oral stage	Mouth is center of satisfaction.
Two to three years	Anal stage	Concern about toilet training.
Three to four years	Phallic stage	Curiosity about sex differences.
Around four to five years	Oedipus complex	Libidinal energy concentrated on parent of opposite sex leads to fear of parent of same sex, who is seen as rival (also explained by switch from anaclitic to defensive identification).
Six to eleven years	Latency period	Resolution of Oedipus complex when child identifies with parent of same sex; libidinal energy not concentrated on any particular part of body, object, or person.
Puberty	Genital stage	Sensual satisfaction through genital organs; libidinal energy concentrated (typically) on member of opposite sex.

Negative experiences (traumatic or repeated) may *fixate* libidinal energy at a particular stage and lead to permanent personality traits.

Levels of consciousness

Conscious	Everything a person is aware of at a given moment.
Preconscious	Memories a person is not thinking of at the moment but that can be recalled.
Unconscious	Memories that cannot be recalled but that may influence behavior.

Table 3–1	
Summary of Freudian Theory	

Structure of personality

Id	Unconscious and primitive source of libido, guided by pleasure principle.
Ego	Screens and controls libidinal energy, guided by reality principle.
Superego	Conscience.

Defense mechanisms

To control primitive impulses of the id and protect the ego, it may be necessary for the person to resort to *defense mechanisms:*

Repression	Resisting recollection of painful memories.
Reaction formation	Assuming forms of behavior opposite to those that are of concern.
Projection	Attributing to others types of behavior that are difficult to acknowledge in oneself.
Sublimation	Diverting libidinal energy from sex objects to activities not related to sex.
Rationalization	Giving "good" reasons for behavior that is weak or unacceptable.
Identification	Adopting the characteristics of others as if they are one's own.
Displacement	Diverting feelings of hostility from self to others.
Regression	Resorting to immature forms of behavior when frustrated.

Erikson: Stages of Psychosocial Development

Childhood and Early Career

Erik H. Erikson was born in 1902 near Frankfurt, Germany. His parents were Danish, but shortly before Erik was born they separated and his mother left

Erik H. Erikson. Photograph © 1975 by Jill Krementz.

Copenhagen to stay with friends in Germany. She remained in Germany after her son was born, settling in Karlsruhe, where she later married the boy's pediatrician. The second marriage was a happy one, and Erik's mother frequently invited artists of different kinds to her home so that the boy not only had the opportunity to hear his stepfather discuss medicine but was also introduced to the aesthetic aspects of life.

In contrast to Freud, Erikson was not an outstanding student in high school, primarily because he preferred self-directed study to a formal curriculum. When he left high school his stepfather urged him to go into medicine, but finding it difficult to decide on a career, he instead spent a year wandering around Europe. When he returned to Karlsruhe he entered a local art school and after a year enrolled in an art school in Munich. After two years in Munich he moved to Florence, Italy, where he met a friend from high school days, Peter Blos, who was then a writer but was destined to become an eminent psychoanalyst.

At the age of twenty-five, Erikson returned to Karlsruhe, intending to become an art teacher. His meeting with Blos, however, was the first in a series of incidents that channeled his career in a much different direction. Blos had left Florence to study in Vienna, where he met Dorothy Burlingham, a wealthy American who had taken up residence there so that she could study with Freud and be analyzed. Her four young children had accompanied her, and she asked Blos to tutor them. After two years Blos was given the freedom, responsibility, and financial backing to establish a school for the Burlingham children, as well as other American and English children living in Vienna. Blos realized he could no longer handle all the teaching himself and invited Erikson to join him. Erikson accepted the invitation, and the two young men established a school that stressed individual learning and considerable freedom of choice and self-direction for the students.

Because Mrs. Burlingham was a close friend of the Freud family, Erikson soon became acquainted with the famous psychoanalyst. He made a favorable impression and was invited to enter psychoanalytic training. Shortly after Erikson completed his psychoanalytic internship, Hitler came to power, and Freud and his followers were obliged to leave Vienna. Erikson first considered moving to Denmark, but an encounter with an analyst who had returned to Vienna for a visit after establishing practice in Boston led him to choose America instead.

Despite the fact that he held no formal degree (because he dropped out of high school before graduating and because psychoanalytic training was not provided in an institutional setting), Erikson was offered a position at the Harvard Medical School. He also was appointed to the staff of a guidance clinic for children and he engaged in private practice. His association with Harvard led to contacts with several outstanding anthropologists, and when he later moved to Yale he continued to have opportunities to explore the subject. One of the Yale anthropologists told him of an opportunity to study Sioux Indians living in South Dakota. Erikson immediately took advantage of this chance to study child rearing in a self-contained society. His research on the Sioux was so rewarding that Erikson subsequently studied the Yurok Indians of the Northern California coast.

At this stage of his career World War II broke out. Erikson settled in San Francisco, taught at the University of California at Berkeley, and also served as a clinician in a hospital for war veterans. In addition, he continued to work with children as part of a research project at the university and he also engaged in private clinical practice. As he sorted out his observations of Indians, war veterans, and normal and abnormal children, Erikson began to conclude that Freud's description of development was incomplete. Unlike Carl Jung and Alfred Adler, two of Freud's early disciples who had made such substantial departures from psychoanalytic doctrine that their relationship with the master became bitter and hostile, Erikson remained faithful to the theory and the man. His main reservation about Freudian theory was that not enough allowance was made for cultural influences.

The Evolution of Erikson's Theory

As he pondered the behavior of the Sioux and Yurok, Erikson was struck by the extent to which many of their adjustment problems seemed to result from a lack of continuity between their tribal history and their existence in twentieth-century America. He hypothesized that the Indians found it difficult to develop a consistent identity. He was unable to explain this conflict in terms of Freud's concept of libidinal energy and began to formulate an augmented psychoanalytic theory that centered on the ego of the individual and the culture in which he lived.

This conception of development was supported by therapeutic interviews with war veterans. He concluded that many of them were experiencing difficulties reconciling their activities and attitudes as soldiers with the activities and attitudes of their prewar civilian life. He used the term *identity confusion* to describe this condition, a problem that the veterans shared with the Indians—lack of a consistent conception of ego or self.

The hypotheses formulated to explain the behavior of Indians and servicemen were corroborated by his research and by clinical interviews with children. Eventually Erikson worked out a complete, consistent conception of development which he describes in Chapter 7 of *Childhood and Society* (1963) and Chapter 3 of *Identity: Youth and Crisis* (1968). He proposes that in addition to the psycho*sexual* stages described by Freud there are psycho*social* stages of ego development in which children establish a series of orientations to themselves and their social world.

The Epigenetic Principle

Erikson bases his description of personality development on the *epigenetic principle*. In fetal development certain organs of the body appear at certain specified times and eventually "combine" to form a child. The personality, says Erikson, develops in a similar way: "Anything that grows has a ground plan, and . . . out of the ground plan the parts arise, each part having its time of special ascendancy, until all parts have arisen to form a functioning whole" (1968, p. 92). Erikson hypothesized that just as the parts of the body develop in interrelated ways when the human organism is *in utero,* the personality of an individual forms as the ego progresses through a series of interrelated stages. All of these ego stages exist in the beginning in some form, but each has a critical period of development. In Erikson's view, personality development is seen as a series of turning points, which he describes in terms of dichotomies of desirable qualities and dangers. He does not mean to imply by this scheme that only positive qualities should emerge and that any manifestation of potentially dangerous traits is undesirable; he emphasizes that a *ratio* in favor of the positive is to be sought. Only when the positive quality is outweighed by the negative do difficulties in development arise.

Stages of Psychosocial Development

The following designations, age ranges, and essential characteristics of the stages of personality development are proposed by Erikson.

Trust vs. mistrust | Birth to one year | Trust vs. mistrust | Consistency, continuity, and sameness of experience lead to trust. Inadequate, inconsistent, or negative care may arouse mistrust.

Two to three years	Autonomy vs. doubt	Opportunities to try out skills at own pace and in own way lead to autonomy. Overprotection or lack of support may lead to doubt about ability to control self or environment.	*Autonomy vs. doubt*
Four to five years	Initiative vs. guilt	Freedom to engage in activities and to use language to express new understandings leads to initiative. Restrictions of activities and parents' failure to respond to comments and questions lead to guilt.	*Initiative vs. guilt*
Six to eleven years	Industry vs. inferiority	Being permitted to make and do things and being praised for accomplishments lead to industry. Limitation on activities and criticism of what is done lead to inferiority.	*Industry vs. inferiority*
Twelve to eighteen years	Identity vs. role confusion	Recognition of continuity and sameness in one's personality, even when in different situations and when reacted to by different individuals, leads to identity. Inability to establish stability (particularly regarding sex roles and occupational choice) leads to role confusion.	*Identity vs. role confusion*
Young adulthood	Intimacy vs. isolation	Fusing of identity with another leads to intimacy. Competitive and combative relations with others may lead to isolation.	
Middle age	Generativity vs. self-absorption	Establishing and guiding next generation produces sense of generativity. Concern primarily with self leads to self-absorption.	
Old age	Integrity vs. despair	Acceptance of one's life leads to a sense of integrity. Feeling that it is too late to make up for missed opportunities leads to despair.	

Erikson's Theory in Perspective

Erikson's description of early stages of psychosocial development calls attention to important relationships between children and their parents. His analyses of behavior during the school years and at adolescence highlight significant facets of the emergence of an individual's self-concept and the establishment of relationships with peers. But the types of behavior Erikson stresses at each level are certainly not the *only* important factors to consider in attempting to comprehend psychosocial development. The capsule summaries just presented indicate only the essence of stages that are described much more completely in *Childhood and Society*. Even so, the types of behavior emphasized at each stage were apparently chosen because they seemed important to Erikson himself or helped him understand the behavior of individuals he observed.

Although he occasionally carried out research investigations, most of Erikson's conclusions are based on highly personal and subjective interpretations that have never been substantiated by controlled investigations. As a result, there have been no checks on the tendency to generalize from personal experiences. To cite just one example, Erikson lacked clear occupational goals and drifted aimlessly through adolescence and young adulthood. It is not surprising, therefore, that he later emphasized the significance of occupational choice and the need to establish a sense of identity during the high-school years. Just because Erikson had strong identity problems centering on confusion about vocational choice during his high-school years, though, does not mean that all adolescents will be equally concerned. It seems likely that some young people will be more preoccupied with problems involving relationships with parents or peers than with identity as defined by Erikson. In interpreting Erikson's descriptions of psychosocial stages, therefore, it will be prudent to keep in mind that he is emphasizing types of behavior that are *likely* to be important. The qualities highlighted by Erikson may not be crucial in the development of all children, and types of behavior he does not mention may be of much greater significance in some cases.

Another factor to consider in Erikson's theory is eagerness to select types of behavior that were congruent with the epigenetic principle. He deliberately chose types of behavior that were interrelated in order to convey that personality emerges as a functioning whole. One consequence of this emphasis on relatedness is that several of the stages—particularly those at two to three years, four to five years, and six to eleven years—seem to stress the same basic qualities. *Autonomy, initiative,* and *industry* all emphasize the desirability of permitting and encouraging children to do things on their own. *Doubt, guilt,* and *inferiority* all focus on the need for parents and teachers to provide sympathetic support.

If you keep these reservations in mind, however, you are likely to discover that Erikson's observations will clarify important aspects of development. His stages will be discussed more completely in several of the chapters that follow.

Freud stressed psychosexual development. Erikson concentrates on psychosocial development. Another important facet of human development centers on

Erikson suggests that preschool-age children will first develop autonomy and later acquire a sense of initiative if they are given opportunities to try out skills and engage in independent activities. Terry Evans/Magnum.

intelligence and thinking. At his death in 1980, the Swiss psychologist Jean Piaget had spent fifty years studying cognitive forms of development.

Piaget: Stages of Cognitive Development

Childhood and Early Career

Piaget was born in the small university town of Neuchâtel, Switzerland, in 1896. His father was a professor of history who specialized in medieval literature, and young Jean was brought up in a scholarly atmosphere. His main boyhood interest was observation of animals in their natural habitat, an interest he pursued with considerable energy and sophistication—he published his first "professional" paper at the age of eleven. (He had seen an albino sparrow in a park and reported this in a nature magazine.)

When he entered school, Piaget concentrated on the biological sciences. A series of articles on shellfish so impressed the director of the natural history museum in Geneva that the fifteen-year-old Jean was offered the post of curator of the mollusk collection. Since he had not finished high school he felt obliged to decline this offer. A vacation with his godfather, a scholar specializing in philo-

Jean Piaget (1970). Yves De Braine/Black Star.

sophy who urged Jean to broaden his horizons and study philosophy and logic, resulted in Piaget's fascination with *epistemology*, the branch of philosophy concerned with the study of knowledge.

After graduating from high school, Piaget entered the University of Neuchâtel and earned undergraduate and graduate degrees in natural science, the Ph.D. being awarded when he was twenty-one. At that point he became intrigued with psychology and studied that subject in Zurich, where he was introduced to Freudian theory and wrote a paper relating psychoanalysis to child psychology. From Zurich he went to Paris to study abnormal psychology. Shortly after he arrived, he obtained a position at the Binet Laboratory and was assigned the task of developing a standardized French version of some reasoning tests developed in England. As he recorded the responses of his subjects Piaget found that he was much more intrigued with wrong answers than correct ones. He became convinced that thought processes of younger children are basically different from those of older children and adults. His lifelong fascination with biology and his interest in studying the nature of knowledge led him to speculate about the development of thinking in children.

Shortly thereafter, an appointment as director of research at the Jean Jacques Rousseau Institute in Geneva permitted Piaget to concentrate full time on the study of cognitive development. He did not feel that he could gain the kind of information he wanted by placing subjects in rigidly controlled experimental situations. So, as he had done earlier in studying animals, he first observed the spontaneous behavior of his own children (and wrote baby biographies), then observed children in natural play situations. Eventually, he developed a series of questions and tasks to be presented to children in interview fashion, a technique of study he called the *clinical interview*. As he recorded his impressions, Piaget gradually evolved descriptions of the development of all aspects of thought.

Basic Principles of Piaget's Theory

The conception of intellectual development Piaget arrived at after a lifetime of study reflects his basic interests in biology and epistemology. He postulates that human beings inherit two basic tendencies: *organization* (the tendency to systematize and combine processes into coherent systems) and *adaptation* (the tendency to adjust to the environment). Piaget believes that just as the biological process of digestion transforms food into a form which the body can use, intellectual processes transform experiences into a form the child can use in dealing with new situations. And just as the biological processes must be kept in a state of balance (homeostasis), Piaget believes intellectual processes seek a balance through the process of *equilibration*. Equilibration is a form of self-regulation that children use to bring coherence and stability to their conception of the world and to comprehend inconsistencies in experience.

Organization: combine and systematize impressions

Adapation: adjust to the environment

Equilibration: seek coherence and stability

To grasp these principles of Piaget's theory, imagine an infant who has just reached the crawling stage and is in the process of meeting one entirely new experience after another when put down on the living room floor for the first time. As the infant moves around the floor, dozens of new objects (tables, chairs, lamps) and experiences (a startled yell from father when about to pull a lamp over) are encountered. Piaget mantains that because of the basic tendencies of organization, adaptation, and equilibration, an infant will be inclined to system-atize, combine, and adjust to objects and experiences encountered. Such attempts to establish coherence and stability take place through the operation of two processes: assimilation and accommodation. *Assimilation* refers to the process by which elements in the environment are incorporated in the child's store of ideas about things. The infant exploring the living-room floor for the first time will gradually build up physical and mental conceptions of table, chair, lamp, and so forth by combining tactile and visual impressions of these objects. Initial impres-sions, however, are bound to be oversimplified. Sooner or later the infant will discover that chairs in the dining room, for example, are not the same chairs in the living room. Accordingly, it is frequently necessary for children to modify conceptions and alter their responses to things, which is the process Piaget refers to as *accommodation*. As children assimilate (incorporate) and accommodate (mod-ify) their conceptions of objects and experiences they establish organized patterns of behavior and thought which Piaget refers to as *schemes*. Schemes can be behavioral (for example, how to grasp objects) or intellectual (for example, realizing that there are different kinds of chairs).

Assimilation: incorporate conceptions into store of ideas

Accommodation: modify ideas

Scheme: organized pattern of behavior or thought

These various tendencies and principles can be illustrated by the example of an infant's experiences with balls of different kinds. From interaction with objects previously encountered, the child of ten months or so will have *organized* the separate skills of looking and grasping into the capability of visually directed reaching. Therefore, when a ball is encountered for the first time, the child benefits from past experience when reaching for it and trying to pick it up. If no previous attempts have been made to pick up an object that rolls, the first efforts may be unsuccessful, so the child will need to *accommodate* to the new object—altering grasping techniques already mastered. As success in doing this is achieved, this new feature will be *assimilated* into a scheme for picking up objects. If the first ball is small and hard, the child will think this typical of all balls until other balls of different sizes and qualities are encountered. When this happens, the need to maintain equilibration will lead the child to reduce inconsistencies between the original and later experiences with balls by assimilating (incorporating) and accommodating (modifying) the earlier scheme for "ball." In time, a cognitive conception of "ball" will be developed that will permit the handling of all types of balls and an understanding of their common qualities.

The Nature of Operational Thought

Organization, adaptation, assimilation, accommodation, and equilibration are basic principles of Piagetian theory. Other principles are based on differences between the thinking of younger and older children, differences that became apparent as Piaget used the clinical interview. In the clinical interview children are asked to explain the reasoning behind their answers. The use of the method can be illustrated by what is probably the best known of all experiments devised by Piaget.

A child is taken to a quiet place by the experimenter, and then water (or juice, or beans, or whatever) is poured into two identical glasses until the child agrees each contains an equal amount. Then, water is poured from one of these glasses into a tall, thin glass. At that point the child is asked "Is there more water in this glass (the experimenter points to the tall, thin glass) or this one?" Immediately after the child answers, the experimenter asks "Why do you think so?" If the child's response is evasive or vague, the experimenter continues to probe until the underlying thought processes become clear.

In carrying out this experiment (and many others similar to it) with children of different ages, Piaget discovered that children below the age of six or so maintain that there is more water in the tall, thin glass than in the short, squat glass. Even though they agree at the beginning of the experiment that the water in the two identical glasses is equal before the pouring takes place, young children stoutly insist that after the water has been poured, the taller glass contains more. When asked "Why do you think so?" many preschool children immediately and confidently reply "Because it's taller." Children over the age of six or so, by

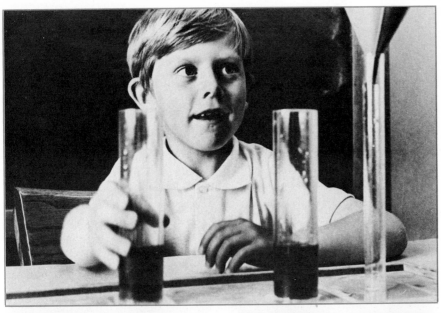

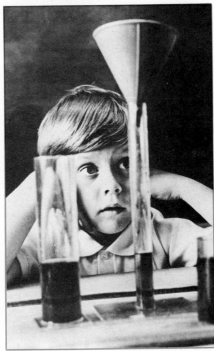

A child reacting to one of the procedures Piaget developed to reveal the nature of preoperational thought. Children below the age of six or so tend to concentrate on one quality at a time and are unable to mentally reverse actions. As a consequence, they are likely to maintain that if liquid is poured from one container into another of a different shape, the quantity of the liquid will be changed. New York Times Pictures.

contrast, are more likely to reply, "Well, it *looks* as if there's more water in this one because it's taller, but they're really the same."

Piaget proposes three principles—conservation, decentration, and operation—to account for this striking difference between the thinking of younger and older children. *Conservation* refers to the idea that certain properties of objects (such as volume or mass) remain invariant despite transformations in their appearance. (The amount of water stays the same even though it looks higher—or bigger—in the tall, thin glass than in a short, squat glass.) *Decentration* refers to the ability of a child to consider more than one characteristic of an object at the same time. (The younger child concentrates only on height and equates it with bigness. The older child can take into account height *and* volume.) The concept of *operation* explains the way conservation is mastered. Piaget describes an operation as "an interiorized action which modifies the object of knowledge" (1964, p. 8). The most distinctive aspect of an operation is its *reversibility*—awareness that conditions can be mentally reversed. That is, the child can imagine what conditions were like before they were altered. An operation can be defined, therefore, as a mental action that can be reversed. (An older child might "solve" the water experiment by mentally pouring water back from the tall, thin glass into the original container.)

Conservation: some properties remain unchanged

Decentration: consider more than one characteristic at same time

Operation: mental reversal

Stages of Cognitive Development

After carrying out clinical interviews with many children, Piaget concluded that there are recognizable stages of cognitive development. These stages follow a continuous but often zig-zag pattern. That is to say, children do not suddenly "jump" from one stage to the next. Their cognitive development follows a definite sequence, but they may occasionally use a more advanced kind of thinking or revert to a more primitive form. The *rate* at which a particular child proceeds through these stages varies, but Piaget believes the *sequence* is the same in all children. There are four basic stages which will be outlined here. Detailed analyses of substages will be presented in later chapters.

Sensorimotor Stage   Infants and young children up to the age of two years acquire understanding primarily through sensory impressions and motor activities, and so Piaget calls this the sensorimotor stage. During the first months of postnatal existence, infants develop schemes primarily by exploring their own bodies and senses because they are unable to move around much on their own. After they learn to walk and manipulate things, however, toddlers get into everything and build up a sizeable repertoire of schemes involving external objects and situations. Before the age of two years, most children are able to use schemes they have mastered to engage in mental, as well as physical, trial and error behavior.

Sensorimotor Stage: acquire first schemes through sense impressions and motor activities

Preoperational Stage The thinking of preschool children centers on mastery of symbols (such as words), which permits them to benefit much more from past experiences. Piaget believes that many symbols are derived from mental imitation and involve both visual images and bodily sensations. Even though their thinking is much more sophisticated than that of one- and two-year-olds, preschool children tend to center attention on only one quality at a time and are incapable of mentally reversing actions. Because they have not yet reached the point of engaging in operational thought, Piaget uses the term *preoperational* to refer to the thinking of two- to seven-year-olds.

Preoperational stage: form many schemes but not able to mentally reverse actions

Concrete Operational Stage Children over the age of seven are usually capable of mentally reversing actions, but their operational thinking is limited to objects that are actually present or that they have experienced concretely and directly. For this reason, Piaget describes the stage from seven to eleven years as that of *concrete operations*. The nature of the concrete operational stage can be illustrated by the child's mastery of different kinds of conservation.

By the age of seven most children are able to correctly explain that water poured from a short, squat glass into a tall, thin glass is still the same amount of water. Being able to solve the water-pouring problem, however, does not guarantee that a seven-year-old will be able to solve a similar problem involving two balls of clay that are transformed in shape. A child who has just explained why a tall glass of water contains the same amount as a short one may inconsistently maintain a few moments later that rolling one of two equal-sized balls of clay into an elongated shape causes it to become bigger. Primary grade children tend to react to each situation in terms of concrete experiences. The tendency to solve problems by generalizing from one situation to a similar but not identical situation does not occur with any degree of consistency until the end of the elementary school years. Furthermore, if asked to deal with a hypothetical problem, the concrete operational child is likely to be stymied. Seven-year-olds are not likely to be able to solve abstract problems by engaging in mental explorations. The usually need to physically manipulate concrete objects, or recollect specific past experiences, to explain things to themselves and others.

Concrete operational stage: capable of mentally reversing actions, but generalize only from concrete experiences

Formal Operational Stage When children *do* reach the point of being able to generalize and to engage in mental trial and error by thinking up hypotheses and testing them "in their heads," Piaget says they have reached the stage of *formal operations*. (The term *formal* reflects the development of *form* or structure of thinking. It might also be thought of as emphasizing the ability of the adolescent to *form* hypotheses.) Even though they can deal with mental abstractions representing concrete objects, twelve-year-olds are likely to engage in haphazard trial and error behavior when asked to solve a problem. It is not until the end of the high-school years that adolescents are likely to attack a problem by forming

Formal operational stage: able to deal with abstractions, form hypotheses, engage in mental manipulation

hypotheses, mentally sorting out possible solutions, and systematically testing the most promising leads.

To help you grasp the sequence of these four stages, here is a brief outline indicating the age range and distinguishing characteristics of each:

Birth to two years	Sensorimotor	Development of schemes primarily through sense and motor activities.
Two to seven years	Preoperational	Gradual acquisition of ability to conserve and decenter, but not capable of operations and unable to mentally reverse actions.
Seven to eleven years	Concrete operational	Capable of operations, but solve problems by generalizing from concrete experiences. Not able to mentally manipulate conditions unless they have been experienced.
Eleven years	Formal operational	Able to deal with abstractions, form hypotheses, solve problems systematically, engage in mental manipulations.

Piaget's Theory in Perspective

The Scope and Impact of Piagetian Theory   Norman S. Endler, J. Philippe Rushton, and Henry L. Roediger III (1978) tallied the number of times different psychologists were mentioned in the *Social Sciences Citation Index*. (This index supplies data regarding individuals mentioned in articles appearing in over 180 psychology journals.) Sigmund Freud topped the list (p. 1074) with 1,426 mentions, Jean Piaget was second with 1,071. (These were the only two individuals mentioned over one thousand times. Most of the psychologists on the list of one hundred most frequently noted behavioral scientists had two or three hundred citations.) The fact that Piaget was mentioned in recent psychology journals many more times than any other living psychologist indicates the impact his work has had on theorists in all parts of the world.

There are several reasons Piaget was mentioned so frequently in psychology journals. His observations on cognitive development are very comprehensive and he had published articles for over fifty years which have stimulated thousands of studies by others. His views on cognitive development also serve as the inspiration for many variations of what is called *open education*, a type of schooling that was at a peak of popularity in the mid-1970s. Furthermore, many psychologists, particularly in America, are highly critical of certain aspects of the methods he used and of his theories. As noted at the end of Chapter 2, Piaget had studied cognitive development for as long as psychology has been a recognized branch of scientific endeavor. Except for Freud, no other psychologist has so dominated an area of specialization within psychology. Any book on human development, therefore, should contain an analysis of the work of Piaget.

Piaget's Impact on Education   Starting in the 1960s, elementary grade teachers in various parts of the world (particularly Great Britain) adopted certain educational procedures that were based on aspects of Piaget's theory. (The general approach to teaching they used was often called open education, but the same term was, and continues to be, applied to a variety of styles of teaching that are not based on the theory of Piaget.) Teachers who were impressed by the pedagogical possibilities of Piagetian principles often used the following techniques:

☐   Manipulation of materials—in recognition of the concrete thinking of children below the stage of formal operations.

☐   Pupil interaction—in order to permit children at the same level of cognitive development to explain things to each other in terms that are mutually understandable.

☐   Teacher interaction with individual children—to allow for the fact that different children in a class are certain to be at different levels of cognitive development.

☐   Opportunities for children to explain their reasoning—to encourage children to gain greater understanding of what they are learning and to make it possible for teachers to arrange instruction to harmonize with the thinking of individual pupils.

☐   Learning centers arranged for self-instruction—to make it possible for children to discover things on their own (due to the impact of the tendency toward equilibration).

Although initial enthusiasm for open education has faded a bit as unforeseen problems have become apparent, at least some techniques used by many contemporary teachers might be traced directly or indirectly to Piaget.

Criticisms of Piaget's Theory   Many American psychologists, particularly those who think of themselves as behaviorists, have criticized Piaget for his reliance on the clinical interview. Piaget preferred to obtain information from children by letting their answers determine the course of interviews. He felt that flexible interviews reveal subtleties and idiosyncracies not likely to be discovered through the use of more structured procedures. Unfortunately, there is no way to determine the extent to which give and take between interviewer and child, or later interpretations of what is said by the child, will be influenced by the preconceptions of the examiner. John H. Flavell, author of a highly regarded book on Piaget, observes "Piaget's writings seem to have a penchant for symmetry and neatness of classification" (1963, p. 38). It seems possible that some principles and stages described by Piaget are as much a product of his tendency to order ideas systematically as of actual child behavior.

Piaget has provided himself with a built-in safeguard against those who suggest that cognitive development is not organized just as he says it is—he simply maintains that they have not used the clinical method as sensitively as he has. This kind of reasoning led Flavell to observe "the reader of Piaget's writings has to take more on faith—faith in Piaget's experimental skill, theoretical ingenuity, and intellectual honesty—than would be the case for the bulk of child psychology publications" (p. 31). In the years since that statement was made, however, hundreds of psychologists have carried out impeccably scientific studies to test many of Piaget's hypotheses and have supplied impressive evidence to lend support to many of his basic arguments. Even so, it is possible that Piaget filled in gaps and smoothed out rough spots to produce a consistent picture of this unfolding of children's thinking. If you make allowance for the subjective and interpretive aspects of Piaget's theory, however, you are likely to find that you gain insight into many types of children's thought processes. Statements children make that would baffle a person ignorant of Piagetian theory may make sense to you.

As you read these accounts of the stage theories of Freud, Erikson, and Piaget, you may have been struck by the fact that all three are Europeans. (Erikson has been an American citizen for over forty years, and his theorizing has certainly been influenced by his experiences in this country. His early and most significant professional training, however, took place in Europe.) Even though there have been and continue to be more developmental psychologists in this country than in any other, no individual American has proposed a theory that approximates the scope of the descriptions provided by Freud (and Erikson) or Piaget. Several Americans have offered analyses of aspects of development, but their conclusions do not take the form of a comprehensive theory. Arnold Gesell (1928, 1954) for example, analyzed early neuromuscular development, and Jerome Bruner (1966, 1973) has speculated about cognitive development. Their observations, though, are not nearly as comprehensive as those of Freud or Piaget. There *is* a theory that is widely endorsed by American developmental psychologists, but it consists of a set of related principles proposed by several different researchers.

Learning Theory

The view of development widely endorsed by American psychologists is not derived from the theorizing of Freud, Piaget, or any other individual. It is based instead on a set of principles proposed by several psychologists. Most of the experiments from which the principles were derived focused on the ways organisms learn as associations between stimuli and responses are built up. That is why interpretations of behavior and development based on these principles are referred to as *stimulus-response theories* or as the *learning-theory* view of development.

Learning theory differs from Freudian and Piagetian theory in several ways. The first has already been mentioned—it is made up of principles proposed by several different psychologists. Second, Freud and Piaget attempted to develop comprehensive theories made up of interrelated concepts. Learning theory, by contrast, consists of principles derived from experiments carried out by researchers who endorsed a common set of assumptions. These principles, however, have not been combined to form a single, organized theory. Third, Freud and Piaget specifically concentrated on proposing a theory of *development* made up of *stages* of development. While it is possible to use learning-theory principles to analyze specific aspects of development, it is difficult to use them to clarify interrelationships or to highlight continuities of growth. It is possible and profitable to interpret human development in terms of learning-theory principles, but this is done by concentrating almost exclusively on ways children learn. Characteristics of learning theory will become more apparent when basic features and assumptions are examined.

Features of Learning Theory

In *Theories of Child Development* (1967) Alfred L. Baldwin notes two distinctive features of learning theory: (1) the behaviorist view that all conclusions drawn by psychologists should be based on observations of overt behavior and (2) the establishment of principles through controlled experimentation, preferably involving simple and uncomplicated forms of behavior. Many American psychologists of the 1920s and 1930s felt uncomfortable when they learned about psychoanalytic theory. They felt Freud was too unrestrained in theorizing and they resolved to be more rigorous and scientific. When John B. Watson published his papers and books outlining the behaviorist view, many American psychologists enthusiastically supported his arguments. Freud could propose new concepts as rapidly as his fertile imagination could supply them. American theorists, who wanted to make sure they could support and defend their conclusions by referring to impressive empirical data, proceeded at a much more deliberate pace. This may be a major reason learning theory is made up of principles proposed by different researchers—no single individual had time to establish more than a few essential conclusions.

The clinical interview used by Piaget involves the accumulation of data under semicontrolled conditions, but the Swiss psychologist is not as constrained as most American researchers when it comes to interpreting what is observed. Piaget is

Features of learning theories: behaviorism, experimentation

eager to build a comprehensive theory and does not hesitate to propose hypotheses that cannot be conclusively substantiated by observations alone. He is willing to postulate, for example, that assimilation and accommodation are inherited tendencies. American psychologists are not satisifed with such an explanation. They prefer to assume that behavior is learned and they hope to discover how this occurs.

The nature of differences between the theorizing of Europeans and Americans is analyzed in (and illustrated by) Baldwin's *Theories of Child Development.* He devotes at least one chapter (often two or three) to theories proposed by Sigmund Freud, Jean Piaget, Kurt Lewin, Fritz Heider, and Heinz Werner. All of these men were educated in Europe and all proposed theories of development arrived at primarily through deductive reasoning (although Piaget and Lewin used observational methods in gathering data to use as the basis for many of their speculations). Baldwin summarizes the contributions of American psychologists in three chapters outlining different aspects of learning theory. In addition to evaluating theoretical speculations, which is the general approach he takes in the other chapters, Baldwin devotes considerable attention in his analysis of learning theory to descriptions of specific *experiments.* The chapters outlining the theories proposed by Europeans feature a portrait of the particular individual who developed each view. The chapters on learning theory feature portraits of *eight* American psychologists—John B. Watson, Clark L. Hull, B. F. Skinner, Neal E. Miller, John Dollard, Albert Bandura, Richard H. Walters, and Robert R. Sears. (These men are featured in Baldwin's discussion of learning theory, but several dozen other psychologists are also mentioned.)

Because there is no universally agreed upon set of learning-theory principles, every discussion of them will vary, depending on the points selected. An exhaustive analysis would need to include mention of hundreds of researchers and examination of subtle variations of principles and subprinciples. The discussion that follows is based on brief mention of one or more significant contributions made by the eight psychologists pictured in Baldwin's account. The particular points emphasized were chosen because they have relevance to topics mentioned in this book. If you read other, more detailed analyses of learning theory (see the Suggestions for Further Study at the end of this chapter for articles and books to consult), you should expect to encounter principles proposed by psychologists other than those mentioned below. (Other aspects of the work of those men will also be stressed.)

Learning-Theory Principles Proposed by Watson, Hull, and Skinner

John B. Watson was instrumental in establishing the learning-theory tradition in American psychology. In his articles and books he stressed the need for objectivity, the value of observing only overt behavior, the advantages of the experimental method, and the significance of associations between stimuli and responses. Learning is often defined as a change in behavior as a result of experience, and Watson urged his colleagues to analyze changes in behavior as objectively as possible. Even though he left academic life in midcareer and is sometimes ridiculed because he made exaggerated claims for Pavlovian conditioning, Watson still deserves credit for introducing concepts that have dominated American psychological theorizing.

Clark L. Hull (1943) became one of the leaders of the learning-theory movement when Watson left academic life. In the 1930s and 1940s Hull carried out dozens of experiments and proposed a series of postulates that significantly expanded the learning theory view. One of these that has special relevance to developmental psychology is the concept of *secondary reinforcement*. Hull suggested that any stimulus present with a *primary reinforcer* (something that leads to the satisfaction of a physiological drive such as hunger) might come to function as a *secondary reinforcer* (arouse the same response as the primary reinforcer). A baby offered milk by his mother, for example, will associate the mother's facial expression and the tone of her voice with the satisfaction of hunger. Subsequently, her smiles and murmured expressions of endearment may arouse a response in the child similar to that originally produced by food.

The work of B. F. Skinner was described in detail in Chapter 1. To review, he expanded understanding of the significance of reinforcement (particularly the impact of different schedules of reinforcement), extinction, generalization, and discrimination; called attention to basic differences between Pavlovian and operant conditioning, and demonstrated the extent to which behavior is shaped by reinforcement. He also speculated about how principles of operant conditioning could be applied to child rearing in his novel *Walden Two* (setting the stage for the emergence of behavior modification) and introduced programmed instruction into the schools.

Aspects of learning theory proposed by Watson, Hull, and Skinner made it possible to explain many types of behavior, but critics pointed out that some forms of behavior cannot be traced to either primary or secondary reinforcement. Accordingly, Neal Miller, John Dollard, Richard H. Walters, Albert Bandura, and Robert R. Sears proposed what has come to be called *social-learning theory*.

Social-Learning Theory

Social-learning theorists stress imitation and reinforcement. In many respects identification and imitation are similar, since both refer to the tendency for children to acquire more mature forms of behavior by acting as their parents (or older children and other adults) act. In speculating about how reinforcement influences behavior, social-learning theorists sought ways to overcome the limitations pointed out by critics of the early work of Hull and Skinner. Their solution was to suggest that *imitative* behavior may be acquired in a variety of ways.

Imitation and observation in social learning

The Significance of Imitation and Observation   In *Social Learning and Imitation* (1941), for example, Neal E. Miller and John Dollard point out that it is not essential for children to have their own spontaneous actions reinforced in order to acquire a new pattern of behavior. Miller and Dollard suggest that children can learn when they are reinforced at a time their behavior *matches* that of another person. A boy might be praised by his mother, for example, when imitating some form of desirable behavior displayed by an older brother. Albert Bandura and Richard H. Walters agree with Miller and Dollard regarding the significance of imitation, but in *Social Learning and Personality Development* (1963) they argue that merely *observing* another person might be sufficient to lead to a learned response. They point out that reinforcement is not always necessary.

Anticipatory Control Makes Choices Possible   In addition to carrying out experiments to determine how children learn through imitation, Bandura took the lead in proposing that learning theorists be more flexible in making allowance for conscious control of one's own behavior. He was disturbed by the tendency of critics (such as Aldous Huxley in *Brave New World* and George Orwell in *1984*) to imply that *all* psychologists supporting the learning-theory view were suggesting that individuals have little control over their behavior. John B. Watson made his famous "Give me a dozen healthy infants" statement (1925, p. 82), and B. F. Skinner argued "The environment determines the individual" (1953, p. 118), and these rather extreme interpretations of the learning-theory view alarmed those impressed by the warnings of Huxley and Orwell. Many people came to the conclusion that psychologists intended to treat human beings much the same way Pavlov treated his dogs.

As noted in Chapter 1, Bandura concluded that overemphasis on manipulative control was due to the behaviorist assumption that reinforcement influences behavior without the conscious involvement of the individual. He suggests (1974) that human beings are capable of choosing how they will respond to many situations because many types of human behavior are under *anticipatory control*. Because children and adults are capable of observing the effects of their actions and are also able to anticipate what will happen under certain circumstances, they are able to control their own behavior to a significant extent.

Studies of Dependency and Identification   Robert R. Sears first studied dependency (Sears, Maccoby, and Levin, 1957) and later identification (Sears, Rau, and Alpert, 1965). Sears began with the assumption that child behavior is learned. He then reasoned that parents have control over many factors that influence childhood learning and that they have the primary responsibility for helping children move from dependency to independence. Sears studied dependency because he hoped to discover how associations established when a child was dependent on the parents might influence later behavior. He analyzed identification because he felt this was perhaps the most significant way children acquire more mature forms of behavior. Sears hypothesized that children would first behave like their parents because they wanted to be like their parents and that eventually they would recognize that the behavior was desirable in itself.

More than any of the other learning theorists mentioned in this section Sears stresses child-parent interaction. In addition, Sears has made more of an effort than his fellow learning theorists to seek out continuities of human development. Although Sears himself has not referred to specific stages of growth, Henry W. Maier (1978) analyzed his writings and concluded that it is possible to delineate three social learning *phases of development* described by Sears.

Phase I lasts for approximately the first sixteen months of infancy. Innate needs, such as hunger, produce tensions the infant seeks to reduce, initially through trial and error. A hungry baby may fuss and cry, for example, and learn that such behavior causes a parent to supply food along with signs of affection. The child is reinforced by the parent's reactions and learns that certain types of behavior bring about certain types of responses. (This example emphasizes the reciprocal relationship between child and parent behavior, a significant aspect of Sears' theorizing.)

Reciprocal relationship between child and parents

Phase II extends from the end of the second year of life to the time the child enters school. During these years the child moves from dependence to a considerable degree of independence. Furthermore, the child learns many forms of social behavior by identifying with and imitating parents.

Phase III begins when the child goes off to school and is influenced by the reactions of teachers and of peers.

In his articles and books Sears makes clear, more than other learning theorists, why the term *social-learning theory* was chosen to refer to that particular set of ideas regarding human development. He stresses that child behavior is the result of learning but that much of this learning is social in that it occurs when children interact with parents, teachers, and peers. What the child learns is also social in the sense that acquired forms of behavior make it possible for one individual to interact in satisfying ways with other individuals.

Learning Theory in Perspective

Principles of Learning Theory   Freud, Erikson, and Piaget provide us with comprehensive, integrated, stage-by-stage analyses of development. American psychologists have supplied an assortment of loosely related principles, many of which were proposed to highlight aspects of learning. Perhaps the best way to summarize the essence of learning theory as it applies to development, therefore, is simply to list selected points (and their practical implications) emphasized by the psychologists Baldwin features in his analysis.

☐ *Watson*—Child behavior is shaped by experiences. Since parents are in a position to arrange experiences for their children, they are in a position to shape child behavior.

☐ *Hull*—A stimulus present when a primary reinforcer (such as food) is supplied may come to function as a secondary reinforcer. Parents should therefore be aware that associations may have wide-ranging impact on behavior.

☐ *Skinner*—Behavior that is reinforced will be strengthened; behavior that is not reinforced will tend to disappear. Behavior is shaped by reinforcement. Instead of permiting reinforcements to occur in an accidental or haphazard manner, parents should be systematic in supplying them, first by selecting desired behavior and then by taking steps to strengthen it. If parents hope to extinguish behavior by ignoring it, they should be as consistent as possible in withholding reinforcement.

☐ *Miller, Dollard, Bandura, Walters*—Children learn many forms of behavior by observing models. Parents should therefore set a good example, expose their children to models with desirable characteristics, and minimize their exposure to models that behave in undesirable ways (such as characters in violent television programs).

☐ *Bandura*—Children are capable of observing the effects of their actions and they are able to anticipate what will happen under certain circumstances. As a result, they are able to control their own behavior to a significant extent.

☐ *Sears*—The development of a child is significantly influenced by the child-rearing methods used by parents. It is therefore desirable to attempt to discover the techniques of parents of children with positive qualities and to remain aware of the ways children move from dependency to independence. Since children acquire many forms of behavior by identifying with their parents, mothers and fathers should behave in ways they would like their children to emulate.

This list of contributions to understanding of behavior by leading learning theorists makes it clear that many aspects of child behavior and development can be clarified by taking into account principles of this theory. But American psychologists (perhaps for reasons first noted by de Tocqueville in his observations on perfectibility) have been interested not only in understanding, they have sought ways to *apply* what they have discovered.

Applications of Learning-Theory Principles

Principles of learning theory have been and continue to be applied to child rearing, education, and psychotherapy in a variety of ways. Behavior modification techniques based on these principles can be used by parents to teach toilet training in a day (Azrin and Foxx, 1976), to make child rearing more systematic and effective (McIntire, 1970; Patterson, 1976; M. Hall et al., 1977), and to enhance intellectual development in preschoolers (Engelmann and Engelmann,

1968). Programmed instruction, where learning is shaped by presenting stimuli (questions) designed to elicit correct responses (answers) that are immediately reinforced, is widely used in American schools. Sometimes programs are presented by teaching machines or computers; sometimes they are presented in workbook form. Teachers can use behavior-modification methods to help disadvantaged children prepare for school (Engelmann, 1969), to become more aware of ways they influence the behavior of their students (R. V. Hall, 1974; Sherman and Bushell, 1975), and to establish constructive classroom control without resorting to punishment (Andersen, 1974). Therapists can use behavior-modification techniques to help children overcome abnormal or self-destructive forms of behavior (Lovaas, 1974; Krumboltz and Thoreson, 1976). Personnel in correctional institutions can use principles of learning theory to help delinquents learn acceptable forms of behavior (Cohen and Filipczak, 1971). Adolescents can use behavior-modification methods on themselves to control weight (Abramson, 1977) or overcome a "broken heart" (Wanderer and Cabot, 1978). (These last techniques represent a recent trend in applications of learning theory principles: having individuals learn to control their own behavior.)

Limitations of Learning Theory

Even though principles of learning theory are used in all of the ways just described (and in other ways as well), there are significant limitations of this theory. First of all, as noted earlier, the principles described in this section do not really represent a *theory* as they are not interrelated in a comprehensive way. Furthermore, with the exception of Sears (among the eight psychologists mentioned by Baldwin in his analysis of learning theory), most learning theorists have been more interested in particular types of behavior than in the overall process of human development. In addition, children learn to use certain aspects of language and to engage in novel thinking (both highly significant forms of behavior) in ways that cannot be traced either to the formation of conditioned responses or to imitation of others. A final criticism (recognized by some leading exponents of this view, such as Bandura) centers on the extent to which the child is sometimes pictured as a more or less passive organism manipulated almost entirely by experiences or the responses of others.

Taking Advantage of All Theories

No single theory described in this chapter offers a complete framework for interpreting child behavior. Taken together, however, they can be of considerable value in helping you to gain insight into development as you consider different stages and types of behavior.

Freud's description of psychosexual stages, for example, may help you understand how feeding, toilet training, awareness of knowledge of sex differences, and the impact of puberty may influence development. His analysis of levels of consciousness may help you comprehend possible causes of many different types of normal and abnormal behavior.

Erikson's description of psychosocial stages may call your attention to significant aspects of parent-child relationships and to personality characteristics likely to contribute to smooth and favorable development at different age levels.

Piaget's description of stages should assist you to make quite sophisticated analyses of cognitive development and help you understand differences between the thought processes of younger and older children.

Learning theory explains how parents might encourage desirable behavior and avoid inadvertently strengthening behavior they would prefer to discourage. Learning theory also explains how children may generalize responses from one situation to another and how they may be influenced by models. Social-learning theory may clarify your understanding of the ways children move from dependence to independence, how they learn by identifying with others, and how different approaches to child rearing may influence personality.

As you read the account of development from conception through adolescence provided in the remainder of this book, you are urged to try to relate specific studies and isolated facts to one or more of the theories just described. The more you do this, the more likely you are to understand and remember what you learn about development. To help you relate what you read to the theories just described, two summaries are presented in Tables 3–2 and 3–3. Table 3–2 outlines the contributions and the limitations of each of these theories. Table 3–3 lists features of development that Freud, Erikson, Piaget, and Sears suggest are likely to be significant at each of the age levels discussed in later parts of this book. (Sears has been chosen to represent learning theorists because it is possible to identify phases of development in his writings.)

Starting with the next chapter, relevant sections of Table 3–3 will be recalled at the beginning of each of the remaining parts of this book to remind you of the types of behavior that theorists have suggested are of particular significance for the span of years covered by those chapters.

Suggestions for Further Study

Sigmund Freud and His Theories

If you would like to find out more about Sigmund Freud and the development of his theories, the best source to consult is *The Life and Work of Sigmund Freud* (1953) by Ernest Jones. Jones was a member of Freud's inner circle of close associates, and his three-volume work is considered to be the definitive biography

Table 3–2
Contributions and Limitations of Theories of Development

THEORIST	CONTRIBUTIONS TO UNDERSTANDING OF CHILDREN	LIMITATIONS
Freud	Early experiences may influence later behavior, even if they are not remembered. Potential importance of infant feeding and toilet training. Impact of identification with parents. Significance of sexual impulses. Understanding of abnormal behavior and of defense mechanisms. Techniques of psychotherapy.	Based on recollections of a small number of extremely abnormal adults. Speculations not based on objective observations.
Erikson	Relationships with parents and peers are of great importance. Certain types of feelings about self are of critical importance at different stages of development.	Types of relationships stressed at different age levels are those that seemed particularly significant to Erikson. They may not be significant to all children.
Piaget	The thinking of younger children differs in significant ways from the thinking of older children. Parents and teachers should take into account a child's level of cognitive development. Certain educational techniques can be based on Piagetian theory.	The clinical method may be too subjective to supply accurate data. Piaget may have made cognitive development seem more orderly than it actually is.
Sears (and other learning theorists)	Much child behavior is learned, and parents have control over many factors that influence childhood learning. The way parents guide children from dependence to independence is of significance. Children learn many types of behavior by identifying with and imitating parents, other adults, and peers.	Learning theory principles are difficult to interrelate and do not shed light on continuities of development. It is not possible to explain significant types of behavior (such as some aspects of language acquisition) in terms of learning theory principles.

of Freud. Volume I, *The Formative Years and the Great Discoveries,* is likely to be of greatest interest to a student of developmental psychology. (An abridged version of the Jones biography was edited by L. Trilling and S. Marcus, [1961].) A briefer account of Freud and his theory is offered by Paul Roazen in *Freud and His Followers* (1974).

Table 3–3
Summary of Age Trends Stressed by Theorists

	FREUD	ERIKSON
First two years	Oral stage. Mouth is center of satisfaction. The way an infant is fed may influence later behavior. Libidinal energy attached to mother due to anaclitic identification.	Trust vs. mistrust. Parents should encourage a sense of trust by providing consistent, supportive care.
Two to five years	Anal and phallic stages. Children are first concerned about toilet training, then they are curious about sex differences. Libidinal energy attached to parent of opposite sex around age of four.	Autonomy vs. doubt. Initiative vs. guilt. Children should be allowed to try out skills, set own pace, encouraged to engage in self-selected activities.
Six to twelve years	Latency period. Children tend to identify with parent of same sex. Libidinal energy not attached to any part of body or person.	Industry vs. inferiority. Children should be encouraged to do things and be praised for their accomplishments.
Adolescence	Genital stage. Concern about sexual relations. Libidinal energy typically concentrated on member of opposite sex.	Identity vs. role confusion. Adolescents need to establish a sense of identity, particularly with regard to sex roles and occupational choice.

Several books by Freud himself are available in inexpensive paperback form. Two short volumes which together provide quite complete coverage of his life and theories are *An Autobiographical Study* (1935; paperback ed., 1963) and *An Outline of Psycho-Analysis* (1949). A comprehensive one-volume collection of several of Freud's works is available in *The Basic Writings of Sigmund Freud* (1938), edited and translated by A. A. Brill.

Psychoanalytic Views of Childhood

Sigmund Freud had only limited contact with children and based his theory of development on recollections of his own childhood and on statements made by his adult patients. A number of followers later specialized in treating children,

Table 3–3
Summary of Age Trends Stressed by Theorists

PIAGET	SEARS	
Sensorimotor stage. Development of schemes primarily through sense and motor activities.	Phase I. Infant seeks to reduce biological drives and learns that certain types of behavior bring about certain responses. Infant-care techniques used by parents shape initial responses of child.	First two years
Preoperational stage. Rapid accumulation of schemes, acquisition of abilities to conserve and decenter, but unable to mentally reverse actions.	Phase II. Preschool child interacts with parents and is influenced by their reactions. Child identifies with and imitates parents. Child-rearing techniques used by parents, particularly in dealing with dependency, are of significance.	Two to five years
Concrete operational stage. Children become capable of mentally reversing actions but can solve problems only by generalizing from concrete experiences.	Phase III. When a child enters school, behavior is shaped by the responses of teachers and classmates. The child identifies with and imitates selected adults and peers.	Six to twelve years
Formal operational stage. Many adolescents become able to deal with abstractions, form hypotheses, solve problems systematically, engage in mental manipulations.	In adolescence behavior may be shaped as much by reactions of peers as by reactions of adults. Identification with and imitation of admired peers is of significance.	Adolescence

however, and a substantial body of psychoanalytic literature on childhood and adolescence has accumulated. Among psychoanalysts who have concentrated on children are Anna Freud (daughter of Sigmund), René Spitz, Margaret Ribble, Melanie Klein, Sibylle Escalona, Sylvia Brody, and Selma Fraiberg. To sample the writings of these and other psychoanalysts who have concentrated on development, browse through one or more of the annual volumes of *The Psychoanalytic Study of the Child* or look for these books: *Normality and Pathology in Children: The Writings of Anna Freud* (1965); *The First Year of Life* (1965) by René Spitz; *The Rights of Infants* (1943) by Margaret Ribble; *Contributions to Psychoanalysis, 1921–1945* (1948) by Melanie Klein; *Prediction and Outcome* (1959) by Sibylle Escalona and G. M. Heider; *Anxiety and Ego Formation in Infancy* (1970) by Sylvia Brody and Sidney Axelrad; and *The Magic Years* (1959) by Selma Fraiberg.

If you sample any psychoanalytic interpretations of aspects of development, you might keep in mind that many of Freud's most loyal followers thought of Freudian doctrine as sacred and were unwilling to question any of his basic pronouncements—even though Freud himself frequently altered his views as he had new insights. Because some psychoanalytic writers are essentially "true believers" in what they think of as almost a religion, they may rigidly adhere to Freudian principles and resort to some rather elaborate and fanciful interpretations to explain certain types of behavior. They also are less than completely open minded about criticism, and you may encounter some rather sharp and ill-tempered remarks about those who offer alternative explanations. As you read articles or books by psychoanalysts, therefore, take into account the background and nature of Freudian doctrine in an effort to place in perspective what may occasionally strike you as extreme or one-sided interpretations.

Erikson's Description of Development

Erik Erikson's books are of considerable significance in speculating about development and education. In the first six chapters of *Childhood and Society* (2nd ed., 1963) he describes how studying American Indians and observing patients in treatment led to the development of his Eight Ages of Man (described in Chapter 7). In the final chapters of this book, Erikson analyzes the lives of Hitler and Maxim Gorky with reference to his conception of development. Erikson comments on many aspects of his work in an interview with Richard I. Evans, published under the title *Dialogue with Erik Erikson* (1967). For a concise biography of Erikson and a capsule description of his stages of development, read "Erik Erikson's Eight Ages of Man" by David Elkind, which appeared in the 5 April 1970, issue of the *New York Times Magazine*. For a comprehensive analysis of Erikson, his theory, and its significance, examine *Erik H. Erikson: The Growth of His Work* (1970) by Robert Coles.

Piaget's Theory of Cognitive Development

Since Jean Piaget has probably exerted more influence on theoretical discussions of development and on educational practices than any living psychologist, you may wish to find out more about him. Of his own books, you might consult *The Language and Thought of the Child* (1952), *The Origins of Intelligence in Children* (1952), and *The Psychology of the Child* (1969), which was written in collaboration with Bärbel Inhelder. H. E. Gruber and J. J. Vonèche have edited *The Essential Piaget: An Interpretive Reference and Guide* (1979), which Piaget describes in the foreword as "the best and most complete of all anthologies of my work." An inexpensive paperback that provides a biography of Piaget and an analysis of his work is *Piaget's Theory of Intellectual Development: An Introduction* (2nd ed., 1979) by Herbert Ginsburg and Sylvia Opper. Other books about Piaget are

Piaget for Teachers (1970) by Hans Furth; *Piaget for the Classroom Teacher* (1978) by Barry J. Wadsworth; and *Understanding Piaget* (1971) by Mary Pulaski. A brief, highly readable account of Piaget and his theories is David Elkind's "Giant in the Nursery: Jean Piaget," which originally appeared in the 26 May 1968, *New York Times Magazine* and is reprinted in Elkind's *Children and Adolescence: Interpretive Essays on Jean Piaget* (1970).

Learning Theory

A particularly insightful analysis of learning (or stimulus-response) theory can be found in Chapters 14, 15, and 16 of Alfred Baldwin's *Theories of Child Development* (1967). Another analysis is offered by Sheldon H. White in "The Learning Theory Tradition and Child Psychology," Chapter 8 of *Carmichael's Manual of Child Psychology* (3rd ed., 1970), edited by Paul H. Mussen (Vol. I, pp. 657–702). A more complete account of learning theory, with emphasis on how its principles might be applied in education, is presented in *The Psychology of Learning Applied to Teaching* (2nd ed., 1971) by B. R. Bugelski. For a general account of learning theory, see *Learning: A Survey of Psychological Interpretations* (3rd ed., 1977) by Winfred F. Hill.

Social-Learning Theory

Alfred Baldwin offers a concise analysis of social-learning theory in Chapter 15 of *Theories of Child Development* (1967). Albert Bandura and Richard H. Walters explain their interpretation of this version of learning theory in *Social Learning and Personality Development* (1963). Robert R. Sears gives the rationale for his analyses of child-rearing practices in the first chapter of *Patterns of Child Rearing* (1957), written in collaboration with Eleanor E. Maccoby and Harry Levin. He explains why he studied identification in the first chapter of *Identification and Child Rearing* (1965), written in collaboration with Lucy Rau and Richard Alpert. Albert Bandura summarized his reasons for proposing an alternative to a strict behaviorist interpretation of learning theory in his presidential address for the 1974 convention of the American Psychological Association. The address, "Behavior Theory and the Models of Man," was reprinted in the December 1974 issue of *American Psychologist*. Bandura provides a detailed analysis of how a particular type of behavior is learned in *Aggression: A Social Learning Analysis* (1971). In *Social Learning Theory* (1977) he offers an outline of the nature of this view of behavior and development.

PART TWO

FROM CONCEPTION TO THE FIRST MONTH

This part consists of two chapters: Chapter 4, "Heredity, Prenatal Development, Birth"; and Chapter 5, "The Neonate."

During the first month of postnatal existence an infant is referred to as a *neonate*. Theorists whose work is summarized in Chapter 3 consider the following types of behavior and relationships with others to be of significance during the first month of life (and throughout the first two years):

□ Freud: Oral stage. Mouth is center of satisfaction. The way an infant is fed may influence later behavior. Libidinal energy attached to mother due to anaclitic identification.

□ Erikson: Trust versus mistrust. Parents should encourage a sense of trust by providing consistent, supportive care.

□ Piaget: Sensorimotor stage. Development of schemes primarily through sense and motor activities.

□ Sears: Phase I. Infant seeks to reduce biological drives and learns that certain types of behavior bring about certain responses. Infant care techniques used by parents shape initial responses of child.

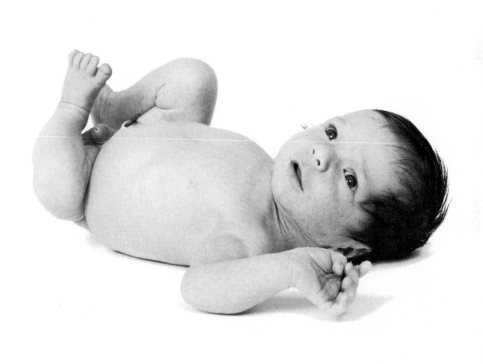

KEY POINTS

Heredity

Chromosomes: threadlike particles containing genes

Genes: units of hereditary transmission

DNA (double helix model of DNA molecule)

Germ cells (egg and sperm)

Meiosis: cell division reducing number of chromosomes in germ cells

Dominant and recessive genes

Genotype: genetic makeup

Phenotype: physical appearance

X or Y chromosome determines sex

Sex-linked recessive traits

Phenylketonuria (PKU): inherited metabolic disorder causing mental retardation

Down's syndrome (Mongolism): mental retardation caused by chromosomal abnormalities

XYY males tall, violent, low intelligence

Prenatal Development

Mitosis: cell division leading to multiplication of cells

Amnion: fluid-filled sac in which embryo and fetus develop

Placenta: membranous organ that partially envelops amnion (and fetus)

Embryo: prenatal organism from time nourishment by placenta begins

Ribonucleic acid (RNA) carries instructions, assembles chemicals

Fetus: prenatal organism from third month after conception to birth

Poor maternal nutrition influences physical and intellectual development of child

Infectious diseases contracted by mother may cause fetal abnormalities

Smoking during pregnancy has significant adverse effect on fetus and newborn baby

Excessive drinking during pregnancy may cause physical and mental defects in child

Interaction of Rh-positive and Rh-negative blood causes abnormalities

Extreme extended anxiety during pregnancy may cause complications

Birth

Average labor for first-borns 14 hours

Natural childbirth intended to reduce tension in mother

Natural childbirth may reduce, but not eliminate, pain

Low-birth-weight infants from disadvantaged backgrounds most likely to experience problems

CHAPTER ▫4

HEREDITY, PRENATAL DEVELOPMENT, BIRTH

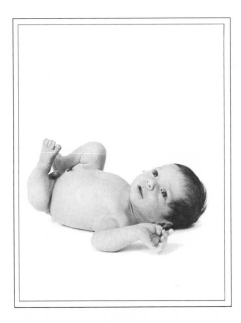

At the moment your life began, you were a single cell about the size of a pinpoint. If that cell could have been compared microscopically to all the other cells of future human beings conceived that day in all parts of the world, it would have been indistinguishable from the rest. At the present time, your body contains approximately sixty trillion cells—all of them produced by that original tiny organism. Depending on the function, they resemble similar cells in other human beings. But (unless you are an identical twin) the basic structure of your cells and the way they are arranged is absolutely unique. You are now easily distingishable from all the other people in the world conceived the same day you were. Yet your facial features, the color of your hair and eyes—many of the characteristics that make you unique—were determined the moment that original cell was formed. When you think about the great complexity of that original cell, it is almost impossible to comprehend. How did that unique cell become formed in the first place, and how did it become transformed from a single cell into sixty trillion cells—each of which has the same basic structure but each of which also has a special function? Some at least partial answers to these questions are offered in this chapter.

Heredity

Basic Units and Processes of Hereditary Transmission

Chromosomes and Genes   The single cell that is the beginning of a human being is created when a sperm fertilizes an egg (or ovum).[1] These two cells are different from all others in the body. In human beings, all cells, with the exception of sperm and egg cells, contain forty-six chromosomes. *Chromosomes* are threadlike particles contained in the cell nucleus, each of which contains approximately—depending on the estimate you accept—between one thousand and twenty thousand *genes.* (Geneticists have not yet developed techniques for actually counting genes.) Genes are the units of hereditary transmission that determine the traits that make each individual unique.

Chromosomes: particles containing genes

Genes: units of hereditary transmission

DNA   The search for the structure of genes led to an intense and exciting competition culminating in the Nobel Prize. M. H. F. Wilkins and F. H. C. Crick of England and James D. Watson, a young American, won the prize when they developed a model of the molecular structure of the chemical *deoxyribonucleic acid* (called DNA for short). They proposed that a gene is a segment of DNA and that the DNA molecule is in the form of a double helix (coil). Each strand of the helix (see Figure 4–1) consists of four repeating chemical subunits, which may be arranged in a different order. The double helix made it possible to explain how the fertilized egg subdivides and reproduces itself while simultaneously producing different types of cells. The Watson-Crick model suggests that as the fertilized egg divides and subdivides, the two strands in the DNA molecule uncoil, each strand taking with it the exact pattern it needs to reproduce itself.

DNA (double helix model of DNA molecule)

Germ Cells   Sperm and egg cells develop by a process different from that of all other cells because of their potential for combining. Each of these *germ* cells (given that name because they are the basis for growth—like a germinating flower seed) must contain twenty-three chromosomes, half the usual number. The germ cells develop in the reproductive organs—the testes in males, the ovaries in females. It is estimated that several hundred million sperm are produced by the testes every four or five days. The ovaries contain (from the time of birth) an estimated 400,000 eggs. One of these (usually) is released about every twenty-eight days. (Approximately 300 to 400 eggs are released during a woman's fertile years.) Before the germ cells can produce a new human being they must go through a process of maturation.

Germ cells (egg and sperm)

[1] For the sake of clarity, the terms *germ cell, egg, ovum,* and *sperm* are used in this book. If you have previously studied genetics and reproduction, or if you read other books on this subject, you may find it helpful to keep in mind that germ cells are also called *sex cells, reproductive cells,* or *gametes;* that sperm cells are also called *spermatozoa* (the singular form of which is *spermatozoon*); and that the fertilized egg is also called the *zygote.*

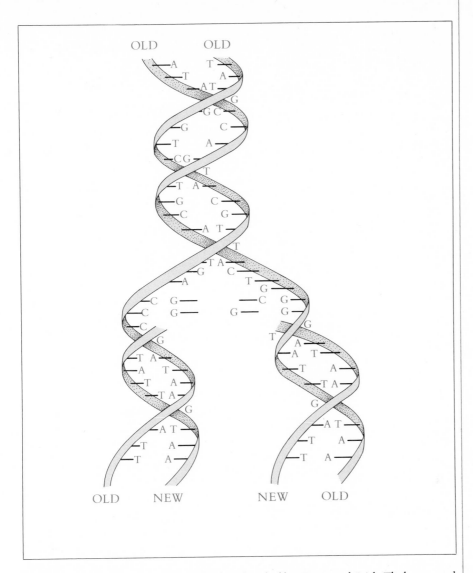

Figure 4–1   A segment of the DNA molecule as described by Watson and Crick. The letters stand for the pairs of chemicals that make up each rung in the double helix model. *A* stands for adenine, *T* stands for thymine, *C* for cytocine, *G* for guanine. As the DNA molecule unwinds, the rungs separate, attract duplicate chemical partners, and thus form duplicate genes. From J. D. Watson, *The Double Helix* (New York, Atheneum, 1968), p. 211. © 1968 by J. D. Watson.

Meiosis (Reduction Division)   At the beginning of the maturational process, there are twenty-three pairs of chromosomes in each sperm and egg. As the germ cells develop, a special kind of cell division called *meiosis* (or *reduction division,* since the number of chromosomes is reduced) takes place. During meiosis, the

Meiosis: cell division reducing number of chromosomes in germ cells

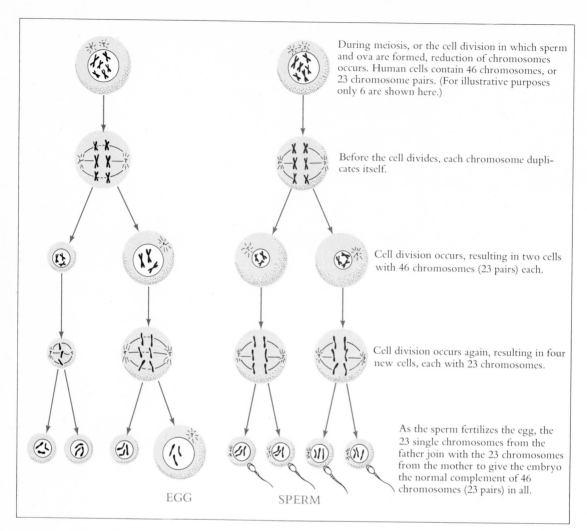

During meiosis, or the cell division in which sperm and ova are formed, reduction of chromosomes occurs. Human cells contain 46 chromosomes, or 23 chromosome pairs. (For illustrative purposes only 6 are shown here.)

Before the cell divides, each chromosome duplicates itself.

Cell division occurs, resulting in two cells with 46 chromosomes (23 pairs) each.

Cell division occurs again, resulting in four new cells, each with 23 chromosomes.

As the sperm fertilizes the egg, the 23 single chromosomes from the father join with the 23 chromosomes from the mother to give the embryo the normal complement of 46 chromosomes (23 pairs) in all.

EGG   SPERM

Figure 4–2   The development of germ cells.

chromosomes of each germ cell first arrange themselves into pairs, with each pair containing one chromosome from the mother and one from the father. These pairs separate, and then separate again, but the second time they divide lengthwise so that one-half of the original forty-six chromosomes are retained in each new cell. (See Figure 4–2.)

Aspects of Hereditary Transmission

Mendelian Principles of Hereditary Transmission   Our understanding of genetics is based on the laws of hereditary transmission proposed around 1860 by the Austrian monk, Gregor Mendel. Mendel experimented with two strains of peas in the monastery garden. Some of these had red flowers; others had white flowers. He discovered that if he mated purebred red and white plants, all the plants produced would be red. When these red plants were mated with each other, however, they produced (on the average) one white plant for every three red ones. After experimenting with several strains of peas for a period of eight years, Mendel proposed the following principles of hereditary transmission.

1   The individual units of heredity (genes) remain essentially constant even when passed from one generation to the next.

2   Genes are found in pairs, one from the mother and one from the father. In some cases both are alike, but sometimes they are different and one will be *dominant* over the other. (Genes for red flowers in pea plants, for example, are dominant over those for white, so the gene for white flowers is called *recessive.*) The red gene is called dominant because whenever the pair of genes that determine flower color in pea plants consists of one red and one white, the flowers will always be red.

Dominant and recessive genes

3   When germ cells are formed through meiosis, the pairs of genes separate from each other, which explains why the dominant gene may not appear in all sperm or egg cells produced. This separation occurs in a random manner, so it is not possible to predict the kind of gene any particular germ cell will contain.

A considerable amount of much more sophisticated research on genetics has been carried out in the hundred and some years since Mendel published his findings. Although his basic principles still stand, scientists have learned that the interaction of dominant and recessive genes may take place in a variety of ways.

Impossible to Predict Chromosome Combinations   Chance seems to determine which members of the chromosome pairs will be given to any egg or sperm, which explains why a child may or may not resemble the father, the mother, or neither. (A. Scheinfeld [1972] has estimated that there are sixty-four trillion possible arrangements of chromosome combinations and [1956] that the probability that a particular sperm will unite with a particular egg is one in three hundred trillion.) One egg, for example, may contain eighteen chromosomes from the woman's mother and five from her father; another egg, the opposite; still another, eleven from the mother and twelve from the father, and so forth. Making accurate prediction more unlikely, some genes may "skip" one or more generations—they remain in the genetic structure but do not always influence development. Finally, it has been found that many characteristics depend not just on pairs of genes but also on complex combinations of genes. It is now known that at the beginning of meiosis, when the chromosomes become arranged in pairs, genes may *cross over* to opposite chromosomes. As a result, a new combination of genes may be formed in any chromosome. Consequently, it is impossible to predict how close parents will come to producing a child with a clear-cut combination of their characteristics. It may happen, but it probably will not. From time to time (in Hitler's Germany, for example), efforts have been made to mate ideal males and females to produce superbabies. The difficulty of succeeding in attempts to breed children with the best traits of each parent is characterized by a statement attributed to George Bernard Shaw. It is reported that a famous actress wrote to him and proposed that they mate and produce a child. She argued, "With your brains and my beauty, it should be a marvel." Shaw declined the offer, pointing out, "Suppose it has your brains and my beauty?"

Genotype and Phenotype The concepts of genotype and phenotype help clarify the nature of hereditary transmission. *Genotype* refers to the genetic makeup of the individual, which, because of recessive traits, may differ from the person's physical appearance—the *phenotype*. (*Pheno* is derived from a Greek word which means *to show*, so the phenotype is *what shows*.) Two brown-eyed parents, for example, who each have recessive blue-eye genes may have a child with blue eyes if the pair of genes that determines eye color is made up of a recessive gene from each parent. If only their phenotype is considered, their production of a blue-eyed child would seem impossible, but if account is taken of their genotype, it is readily understood.

Genotype: genetic makeup

Phenotype: physical appearance

Aspects of Sex Determination

How the Sex of the Child Is Determined Because the germ cells divide twice, four cells are produced from each original cell when meiosis takes place. Within each germ cell there is a pair of chromosomes that will determine the sex of the child if conception takes place. When the original germ cell divides to produce two cells of twenty-three pairs of chromosomes each, and then these daughter cells divide again, this pair of chromosomes (as do all other pairs) splits. In women, all four of these cells contain an X (or female) chromosome. Only one of these—which contains the yolk of the original cell—is a genuine egg cell, capable of being fertilized; the other three (called polar bodies) are absorbed and secreted. In men, however, the pairs of chromosomes that determine sex contain one X and one Y (male). When the first cell division takes place, each new cell contains an X and a Y, but when the second split occurs, the sperm cells which are produced contain *either* an X or a Y chromosome. If a sperm with an X chromosome fertilizes the egg, the child will be a girl. If a sperm with a Y chromosome fertilizes the egg, the child will be a boy. Thus the sperm determines the sex of the child, which indicates how unfair it is when a king blames his queen for not producing a male heir.

X or Y chromosome determines sex

Males Have Greater Mortality Rate Because of the way meiosis takes place (through splitting of chromosomes), there are an equal number of X and Y

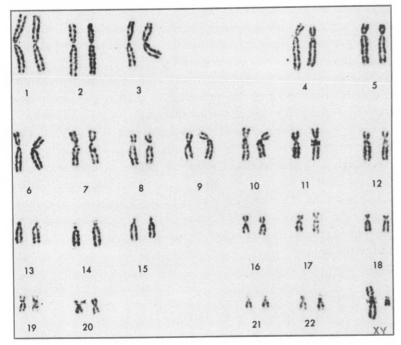

Sex-chromosome pairing. This photograph of chromosomes in male and female cells has been cut up so that they could be arranged in pairs. Note that the pair of sex chromosomes for the male consists of an X and a Y and that the Y chromosome is noticeably smaller. The fact that the Y chromosome contains fewer genes accounts for the greater tendency of males to be born with sex-linked recessive traits, such as color blindness, diabetes, and hemophilia. Courtesy of Dr. Melvin M. Grumbach, University of California, San Francisco.

sperm. However, for some yet to be explained reason, more eggs are fertilized by Y (male) sperm. It has been suggested that since the Y sperm is slightly lighter, it is faster, and therefore it is more likely to reach the egg first. While this leads to an intriguing picture of X and Y sperm engaged in a mad race up the Fallopian tube toward the egg, it does not explain *why* the Y sperm is lighter, or why the heavier X (female) sperm wins the race as often as it does. Whatever the reasons, an estimated 130 to 170 males are conceived for every 100 females (Scheinfeld, 1958). The ratio of male to female *births,* however, is aproximately 106 to 100. According to U.S. Census figures for 1970, by the age of twenty-five, females outnumber males 100 to 95; by the age of sixty-five, there are approximately 100 females to every 72 males. These changes in the ratio of males and females are due, obviously, to the greater mortality rate of males. It is estimated that during the prenatal period, 50 percent more male fetuses die; during the first month after birth, 30 percent more male babies die; and the proportion of male deaths over female increases from 44 percent between the ages of five to nine, to 70 percent between the ages of ten to fourteen, to 145 percent between the ages of fifteen and nineteen (Scheinfeld, 1958).

Hypothesis: Stronger Females Survived   Your first reaction to these figures might be to attribute the higher mortality rate in males to greater participation in potentially lethal activities starting early in life and to greater stress because of wage-earning responsibilities later in life. While these hypotheses might account for more deaths after birth, they do not account for the higher *prenatal* death rate. (A male fetus cannot engage in dangerous activities while in the mother's uterus, nor be inclined to worry about getting promoted to the vice presidency of a business concern.) Perhaps the most plausible explanation for the greater durability of females is "evolutionary." It has been suggested that the female must be strong enough to nourish and carry the fetus through the prenatal period in order to insure the survival of the species. During the course of evolution, it is hypothesized, stronger females survived, while males, whose role in procreation does not require that kind of strength and endurance, were not selected for these qualities. Perhaps the "natural" need for a greater supply of expendable males to insure the survival of the species is the reason the male sperm is lighter and more likely to fertilize the egg.

Genetic Abnormalities

Sex-linked Recessive Traits   The Y chromosome has fewer genes than the X, which opens up the possibility that some X genes may remain unmatched when the egg and sperm unite. This may lead to undesirable consequences if the X chromosome of the fertilized egg contains a gene for some physical defect. If a fertilized egg destined to become a female human being receives an X chromo-

If a defective gene is in the X chromosome (as in color blindness) —

FEMALE

CARRIER   SONS   DAUGHTERS

 XX   XY   XY   XX   XX

With two X's, a female   One in two   One in two   One in two   One in two
carrier usually has a   gets mother's   gets mother's   gets mother's   gets the normal
normal X gene to block   bad X gene   normal X   bad X and is   X and cannot
the bad one and is   and has the   and is not   a carrier like   pass on defect.
herself normal.   defect.   defective.   mother.

AFFLICTED   SONS   DAUGHTERS

 XX   XY   XX

Only when a female gets an   Every one of her sons will   Every daughter will be a
X with a bad gene from   have the same defect.   carrier of the gene.
both parents will she
develop the defect.

MALE

AFFLICTED   SONS   DAUGHTERS

 XY   XY   XX

With only one X, male has   Every son gets father's Y,   Every daughter gets the
no normal gene to block   so every son is free of the   father's bad X and is a
the bad one and develops   defect and cannot pass on   carrier (like woman at top
the defect.   the bad gene.   left of page).

Figure 4–3   Sex-linked inheritance. Adapted from Amram Scheinfeld, *Heredity in Humans* (Philadelphia, Lippincott, 1972).

some with a recessive gene that might lead to some physical anomaly, the other X chromosome will be likely to have a corresponding gene that will block its effect. But the Y chromosome does not carry genes that match all those in the X, and so undesirable genes in the X chromosome of an egg destined to be a male will not

Sex-linked recessive traits

be blocked. Examples of such *sex-linked recessive traits* are red-green color blindness and hemophilia (a condition in which the blood does not clot). These conditions rarely occur in females because they appear only when *both* X chromosomes of the female contain the appropriate gene. With males, however, the gene need only exist in the single X chromosome, and the trait will appear because there is no corresponding gene in the Y chromosome to block it.

In addition to conditions caused by unmatched genes in X and Y chromosomes, other defects may be caused by specific defective genes or chromosomal abnormalities.

Phenylketonuria (PKU)   An abnormality thought to be caused by two recessive genes is phenylketonuria or PKU. This condition was first discovered in 1934 by a Norwegian physician, Asbjørn Følling, whose attention was called by a female patient to a musty odor emanating from her two mentally retarded children. She asked if the odor might have something to do with the retardation. When Følling tested the urine of the children, he found a peculiar substance he eventually identified as phenylalanine, a compound found in protein. Subsequent research led to the conclusion that in children with PKU the enzyme that normally metabolizes phenylalanine does not function properly. As a result, the compound increases in the body tissues and leads to chemical changes that cause injury to brain cells. After years of experimentation a special diet was perfected that contains a minimum amount of phenylalanine. It soon became apparent, however, that a child with PKU had to be put on the diet immediately after birth, or brain damage would result. The presence of PKU can be detected by using a simple test, which means that it is possible to begin the diet in time—provided the test *is* made. The condition is found only once in every ten to twenty thousand births (Kopp and Parmelee, 1979), and some physicians feel that checking for PKU is not worth the trouble. Accordingly, laws have been passed in many states to make the PKU-test a mandatory part of every hospital delivery. If no such law exists in a given area, parents of newborn children are well advised to insist that a PKU-test be made.

Phenylketonuria (PKU): inherited metabolic disorder causing mental retardation

Down's Syndrome (Mongolism)   One of the most common chromosomal abnormalities is *Down's syndrome* (a condition also called Mongolism). It is characterized by several distinctive physical traits and mental retardation and occurs approximately once in 500 to 600 births (Reed, 1975, p. 70). This condition is caused by an extra chromosome in pair number twenty-one of the fertilized egg (Jacobs et al., 1959). In most cases of Mongolism the extra chromosome results from the failure of the two chromosomes in pair number twenty-one to separate when the egg is formed. Such a condition is much more likely to occur in older women and may be due to endocrine changes that take place with age (German, 1970). Other explanations are that ova produced by an older woman (which have been present in her body since birth) are slower to fertilize, and that older women have had a longer period of exposure to toxic

Down's syndrome (Mongolism): mental retardation caused by chromosomal abnormalities

agents such as viruses and radiation. A much less common type of Down's syndrome is the result of a *translocation* chromosome abnormality. Here one parent has a genotype where part of chromosome number twenty-one has become transferred or relocated to chromosome number fifteen (sometimes number twenty-two) (Carter et al., 1960). In contrast to the more common type of Mongolism, the translocation type is caused by an abnormality in the genotype of the mother or father.

Missing or Extra Sex Chromosomes   Other chromosomal abnormalities involve missing or extra sex chromosomes. In some cases, a normal egg is fertilized by a sperm not containing a sex chromosome, or an egg without an X chromosome is fertilized by an X-bearing sperm. The result is a female with an XO chromosome combination. Lack of a second X chromosome causes stunted growth and blocks breast development and menstruation. This condition is called Turner's syndrome and occurs approximately once in every 2,500 female births (Reed, 1975, p. 81).

In other cases, an egg having an extra X chromosome is fertilized by a Y sperm producing a male with an XXY chromosome combination. This leads to a condition called Klinefelter's syndrome, which is characterized by nonfunctioning testes, deficiencies in male hormone production, enlarged breasts, and perhaps, mental retardation. This syndrome occurs approximately once in every five hundred male births (Reed, 1975, p. 82).

A chromosomal abnormality called to public attention in the mid-1960s occurs in males with an XYY genetic structure. It was discovered (Jacobs et al., 1965) that an extra Y chromosome was found in the cells of male criminals who were unusually tall, subject to periods of excessive violence, and of low intelligence. The discovery soon became publicized when lawyers argued that their XYY clients could not be held reponsible for criminal acts (including murder) because they had no control over their actions as a result of the chromosomal imbalance. In some early cases, this argument was successful, but as more research was carried out, it was discovered that the XYY pattern did not always lead to criminal tendencies. (A model citizen and family man in Australia was found to be an XYY type when he volunteered to give blood.) Lissy R. Jarvik, Victor Klodin, and Steven S. Matsuyama (1973) analyzed all available data on the XYY pattern and reported that it appeared about once in every thousand births, that a few XYY men were unaffected by the condition, but that fifteen times as many XYY men as genetically normal men became criminals.

XYY males tall, violent, low intelligence

Techniques for Analyzing Genetic Structure

New techniques for making genetic analyses are constantly being developed, and in the near future obtaining information about the infant's genotype may become a routine feature of hospital deliveries. If parents learn that their newborn son has an XYY pattern, they might take special pains during the course of his development to help him control his aggressive tendencies. There is also the possibility they could find out about the presence of an XYY pattern (or any other atypical chromosomal pattern) *before* the baby is born.

Genetic Analysis   Within the last few years, techniques of genetic analysis have developed to the point where it is now possible to estimate the likelihood that any man and woman might produce a child with a genetic problem of some sort. According to the National Genetics Foundation, you might benefit by a visit to a genetic counselor if you fall into either of these categories: you are parents of a child with a genetic disease or a birth defect and you are thinking about having another child; your family has any history of genetic disease, and you are thinking of having children.

Several hundred genetic counseling centers have been established in the United States, and about fifty of these are members of the National Genetics Foundation's network of genetic counseling and treatment centers. (If you would like information, write to the National Genetics Foundation, 9 West 57th St., New York, New York 10019.) When couples visit one of these centers, first, a family history is drawn. Second, chromosomal analyses of tissue culture cells are made. Such analyses might reveal missing or extra sex chromosomes, indicating the possibility, for example, that a boy with an XYY genetic structure might be born. If genetic counselors detect such abnormalities, they might be able to predict that there is a probability (perhaps one in four) that a child will be born with a particular type of defect. Instead of simply "gambling" in such a situation, it would be possible for the woman to conceive and then request that an analysis be made of the genetic structure of the fetus, preferably sixteen weeks after conception. The technique for doing this is caled *amniocentesis.*

Amniocentesis   A physician performs amniocentesis (Friedmann, 1971) by inserting a long, hollow needle in the expectant mother's abdomen to draw off some of the amniotic fluid, which contains cells shed by the fetus. These cells can be analyzed to determine the genotype of the developing organism. If the fetus does have a chromosomal pattern known to cause a particular form of abnormality, the parents can consider aborting the pregnancy.

The National Institute of Child Health is conducting a study through the Amniocentesis Registry to determine the risks entailed when the procedure is used. Comparison of children born to 1,040 women who underwent amniocentesis with children of 992 women who did not (Brody, 1977) led to the preliminary conclusion that there were no significant differences between babies in both groups up to the age of one year. In an earlier, less extensive survey (Etzioni, 1973), it was reported that women undergoing amniocentesis might suffer mild bleeding or easily treatable infection and perhaps be inclined to miscarry. On the basis of evidence reported so far, therefore, it appears that amniocentesis is a safe procedure, although it does require considerable skill on the part of the physician. Prospective parents who weigh the pros and cons of having amniocentesis performed might take into account that it has proved 99 percent accurate in predicting the existence of some types of fetal abnormalities. (They should also take note that it may take several days to get an amniocentesis report back and that in some states the time allowable for an abortion is the twentieth week after conception.)

Attempting to Preselect the Sex of a Child

A number of techniques for attempting to preselect the sex of a child have recently been proposed (Rorvik and Shettles, 1970). One of these involves having the woman use a vinegar and water douche (to increase vaginal acidity, favoring conception of a girl) or a baking soda and water douche (to increase vaginal alkalinity, favoring conception of a boy) just before intercourse. (Some physicians recommend against the use of such douches.) Another is based on the hypothesis that if the mother conceives just after ovulation a boy is more likely to be born. Controlled studies (Glass and Kase, 1973) have not provided proof that sex-determination is possible. Even so, some couples are convinced that they preselected the sex of their child. This is not absolutely certain, of course, since they might have had boys or girls of a "chosen" ratio no matter what they did.

Still another way the sex of a child might be controlled is through *parthenogenesis* (virgin birth). This technique, which has been used successfully with rabbits, involves activation of a female's egg so that it fertilizes itself. Since the egg carries only X chromosomes, every child produced by this technique will be a girl.

Before prospective parents consider using any technique of sex determination, they might ask themselves some questions. Will such an attempt be sensible family planning or primarily an attempt to try to control what has previously been uncontrollable? Is it wise to alter "nature's balance"? What criteria should be used in deciding whether to have a male or female? Would the choice of one or the other imply that one sex is better than another and lead to friction over sexual equality? If a couple makes every effort to conceive a male (for example), and a female is born, will they resent the child because it is living proof they have been unsuccessful? As these questions suggest, there are arguments for letting the father's sperm fight it out for themselves as they race up the Fallopian tube.

Prenatal Development

Period of the Ovum (Fertilization to about Two Weeks)

Meiosis and Mitosis Approximately once every twenty-eight days (usually about midway in the menstrual cycle) an ovum is released in one of a woman's two ovaries. The egg produced in the ovary moves down the Fallopian tube (also called the oviduct) toward the uterus. If sperm are ejaculated into the uterus

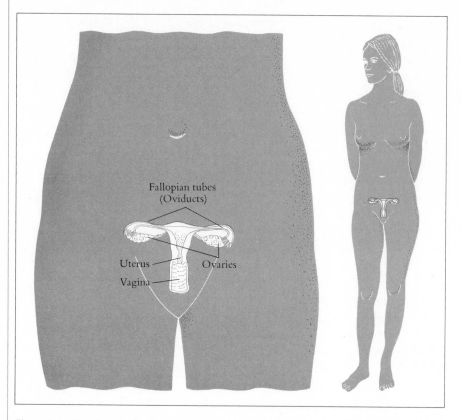

Figure 4–4   Female reproductive system.

during the three to seven days the ovum is in the Fallopian tube, they are attracted to the egg by a hormonal force which draws them into the tube. If one of the sperm enters the egg, the surface is changed so that no other sperm can enter. At the moment of penetration the nuclei of the two cells merge, and a new cell is produced which contains twenty-three pairs of chromosomes, one half from the mother, the other half from the father. At that moment, the sex and heredity of the new organism are determined. The germ cells are produced by *meiosis,* the process of reduction division leading to egg and sperm cells each containing twenty-three chromosomes. When these two cells unite to form a fertilized egg of forty-six chromosomes, *mitosis,* a different process of cell division, begins. First the original cell divides to produce two cells identical in genetic structure; each of these divides to produce two cells, and so on until the sixty trillion cells that make up a human being have been produced. Mitosis accounts for the multiplication of cells; the double helix model of DNA accounts for the development of different types of cells. Various types of cells form as the strands of DNA unravel (each strand consists of different combinations of the four basic chemical subunits) and then recombine.

Mitosis: cell division leading to multiplication of cells

IDENTICAL TWINS

—result from the same
single egg and single
sperm.

After the egg begins to
grow it divides into equal
halves with duplicated
chromosomes.

The halves go on to
become two babies
with exactly the same
hereditary factors.

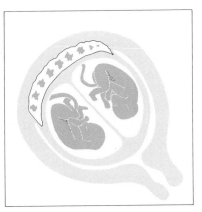

Identical twins are always
the same sex (either two
boys or two girls). They
usually look much alike.
They have exactly the same
eye color, hair color, hair
form, blood types, and all
other hereditary traits.

FRATERNAL TWINS

—result from two different
eggs, fertilized by two
different sperms.

The two different
fertilized eggs develop
separately into two
different embryos.

The two embryos grow into
two babies with different
hereditary factors.

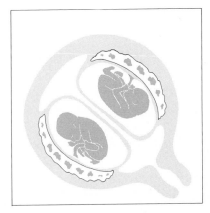

Fraternal twins may be
either of the same sex
(two boys or two girls) or
different in sex (a boy
and a girl). They may be
different in looks, coloring,
hair form, blood types, and
other hereditary traits.

Figure 4–5   How twins are produced. Adapted from Amram Scheinfeld, *Heredity in Humans.*

Types of Twins   Occasionally *two* eggs are released in the ovaries. If both of
these are fertilized and then mature, twins will be born. Less frequently, when the
first cell division of the fertilized egg occurs, the chromosome will separate and

form two separate cells—each with exactly the same genetic structure. Still less frequently, three or more eggs may be produced (particularly if the mother has taken drugs to increase the likelihood of conception), and each will be fertilized. Or two or more eggs may be produced and fertilized, and one or more of these may split to produce two identical cells. If all of these mature, three or more children may be born. Children who develop from separate eggs and are born at the same time are called *fraternal;* those who develop from a single fertilized egg are called *identical.*

The Amnion   By the time the fertilized egg reaches the uterus, it has divided several times and formed a spherical cluster of several dozen cells. This cluster floats in the uterus while it continues to divide. After seven to ten days it burrows into the lining of the womb and attaches itself. As cell division continues, fingerlike extensions called *villi* develop. The *amnion,* a fluid-filled sac in which the developing organism will float, also begins to form at this time. The amnion serves to protect and cushion the organism throughout prenatal development.

Amnion: fluid-filled sac

Period of the Embryo (from Three to Eight Weeks After Conception)

The Placenta and Umbilical Cord   During the third week after conception, the villi multiply and interlock with the tissues of the uterus to form the *placenta* and the umbilical cord. The placenta is a membranous organ that lines the uterine wall and partially envelops the embryo. The umbilical cord emanates from the placenta and connects with the embryo at the navel. It contains two arteries and one vein that nourish the developing organism and remove its wastes. Up until this time, the fertilized egg has been sustained by its own yolk. Now it is nourished by the mother, and when this occurs, the organism is referred to as the *embryo.* The mother's blood flows into the placenta and the umbilical cord from arteries in the wall of the uterus and provides food and oxygen to the developing organism. Consequently, alterations in the mother's blood stream may affect the development of the embryo. If the mother contracts a virus or takes a drug, for example, her blood chemistry may be altered in such a way that the process of cell division is distorted. The incredible sensitivity and complexity of the chemical balance involved in DNA molecules, which are to produce trillions of cells, explain why an estimated one-third of all pregnancies may miscarry. If there are abnormal genes in the fertilized egg, or if something triggers an incorrect sequence of chemical reactions, the embryo or the villi or amnion may not develop properly, and growth will cease. J. M. Tanner (1970, p. 89) estimates that 30 percent of all embryos are aborted, usually without the mother's knowledge, because of such abnormalities of development. He reports that chromosomal abnormalities are found in between 3 and 4 percent of fertilized ova but in

Placenta envelops embryo

Embryo: prenatal organism from time nourishment by placenta begins

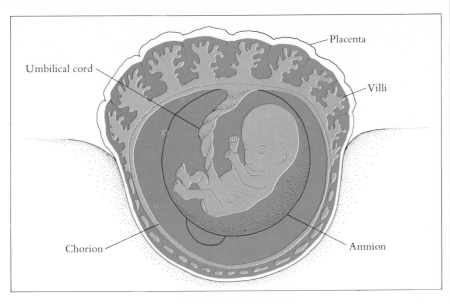

Figure 4–6   A three-month-old fetus in the uterus, showing the amnion, villi, placenta, and umbilical cord.

only .25 percent of newborn infants. These figures indicate that 90 percent of all fertilized eggs containing chromosomal abnormalities are aborted spontaneously.

The Roles of DNA and RNA in Cell Division   If development proceeds normally, once the embryo is implanted in the uterine wall cell division occurs at a rapid pace. It is during this period that development seems most remarkable since cells of specific types become recognizable as cell division continues. This occurs because the DNA in the genes leads to the formation of amino acids, which in turn form proteins that cause the development of different types of cells.

As the cells of the embryo divide, the two strands of the DNA molecule unwind, taking along half of each rung in the ladderlike structure. Each strand then reacts to chemical processes to form a new double helix. The information coded in the nucleus of the new cell must be communicated to the rest of the cell, however, if specialized cells are to form. This function is performed by another substance in the genes, *ribonucleic acid* (RNA). There are two basic types of RNA, *messenger,* which carries from the nucleus instructions regarding the type of cell to be formed, and *transfer,* which collects the necessary chemicals and assembles them. The two types of RNA work together to determine which amino acids will produce proteins necessary for the development of different types of specialized cells.

Ribonucleic acid (RNA) carries instructions, assembles chemicals

Critical Nature of Embryonic Development   As the process of cell division takes place, the embryo begins to differentiate into three distinct layers:

☐ The *endoderm* (inner layer), from which will develop the lungs, liver and intestines

☐ The *mesoderm* (middle layer), from which will develop the muscles, bones, circulatory, and excretory systems

☐ The *ectoderm* (outer layer), from which will develop the skin, hair, teeth, and the nervous system

Three weeks after conception, the heart of the embryo begins to beat. It is not until about eight weeks after conception, however, that the embryo (which is now about an inch long) begins to assume a more or less human form. Most of the organs of the body appear during this period, and the development of the nervous system is especially rapid, which is why this period is the most crucial. During this stage of embryonic development, chemical changes in the mother's blood stream caused by viruses or drugs are most likely to lead to abnormalities of development, affecting the particular organ in the process of being formed.

Period of the Fetus (Third Month After Conception to Birth)

Fetus: prenatal organism from third month after conception to birth

From the start of the third month after conception until birth, the developing organism is called the *fetus*. During this period the fetus increases in size and the organs and nervous system mature to the point where the fetus becomes capable first of activity and eventually of independent existence. The mother may sense fetal movements at the end of about sixteen weeks of development, even though the fetus is only five inches long at this time.

An organism that reaches the fetal stage without suffering any aberrations in development is not likely to suffer any damage during the remaining months it grows in the uterus. The amnion provides a very effective cushion against virtually any kind of external onslaught. In 1963, for example, a woman in Wales who was three months pregnant was struck by lightning. She gave birth to a normal baby six months later (reported in Tanner and Taylor, 1969, p. 31).

Perhaps the most important point in the fetal period is around twenty-eight weeks after conception when the child may be *viable* (capable of life) if born. Even though viable, the baby born prematurely must be cared for in an incubator, which serves as a substitute uterus. The degree of care needed usually depends on the degree of prematurity. A child born twenty-eight weeks after conception will need considerable care to survive, and a slower rate of development during the first five years will be likely. A child born just a few weeks before full term may not need special care or show any retardation in later development. Birth weight seems to a key factor in the adaptability of premature infants—the lighter the child at birth, the greater the likelihood of susceptibility to infection and a slower rate of development.

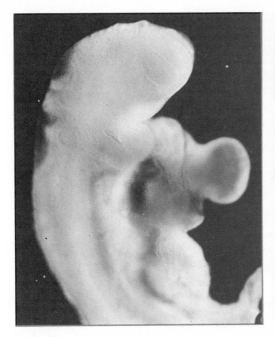

30 days, ⅕ inch

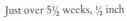
Just over 5½ weeks, ½ inch

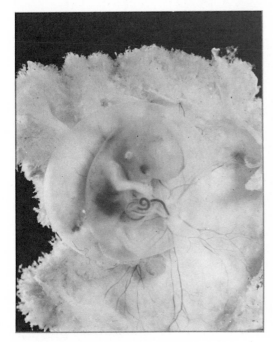

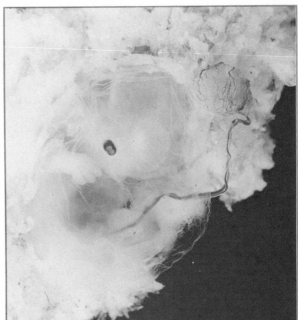

11 weeks, 2 inches

14 weeks, about 4 inches

The developing embryo and fetus. Photographs by Lennart Nilsson, *A Child Is Born* (New York, Seymour Lawrence [an imprint of Dell Publishing Co.], 1967.). Used by permission of Delacorte Press/Seymour Lawrence.

Length of fetus

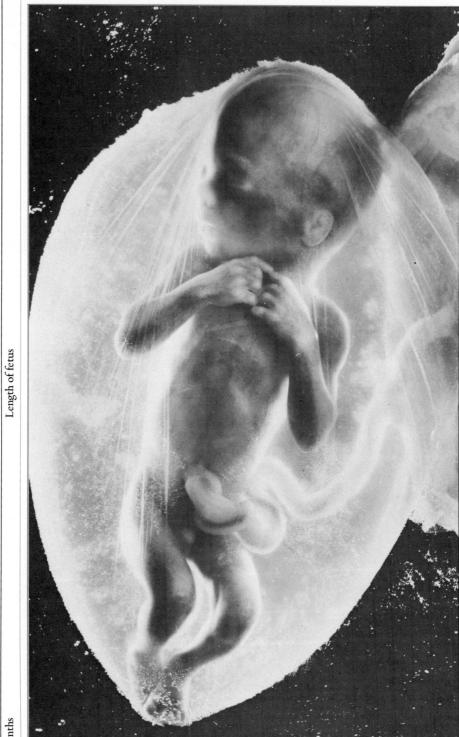

30 days

5½ weeks

11 weeks

14 weeks

4 months

Over 4 months, 8 inches

Factors That Influence Prenatal Development

According to the latest available data (see Table 4–1), the infant mortality rate in the United States is higher than that in many other technological societies (some of which are considered to have poorer medical care and facilities). Additional data noted in Table 4–2 reveal, however, that the infant mortality rate for whites in this country is significantly lower than the rate for other races. Some explanations for these figures become apparent when factors that influence prenatal development and birth are examined. Among conditions that may cause

Table 4–1

Infant Deaths (per 1,000 Live Births) in Various Technological Societies

Sweden	8.0
Denmark	8.9
Japan	9.3
Netherlands	9.5
Norway	10.5
Switzerland	10.7
France	11.4
Finland	12.0
Eastern Germany	13.1
United Kingdom	14.0
Ireland	14.1
Australia	14.3
United States	15.2

Source: Demographic Yearbook, 1978. Department of Economic and Social Affairs, United Nations. (Rates are those reported in 1976 or 1977)

Table 4–2

Infant, Fetal, and Maternal Death Rates (per 1,000 Live Births) for Whites and Other Races in the United States in 1976

Infant deaths	15.2
Whites	13.3
Other races	23.5
Maternal deaths	12.3
Whites	9.0
Other races	26.5
Fetal Deaths	10.5
Whites	9.3
Other races	15.2

Source: Statistical Abstract of the United States, 1978.

abnormalities in the development of the ovum, embryo, and fetus are poor diet, infectious diseases, drugs, Rh blood factors, age of mother, and emotional factors. There may also be birth complications. Each of these will be discussed separately. Before they are described, however, you are reminded of two points mentioned in the discussion of prenatal development up to this juncture: the incredibly complex nature of the chemical processes involved in the unraveling and re-formation of DNA molecules, and the importance of the first three months of development. Since the nervous system and organs of the embryo are formed during the first three months after conception (Moore, 1977), this is the most crucial period of the entire life cycle. Yet the expectant mother usually does not know she is pregnant until several weeks after fetal development begins. (It is now possible, however, to purchase an early pregnancy test in drug stores.)

Nutrition   After the placenta and umbilical cord form, the development of the embryo is sustained by the mother's blood stream. Therefore, factors affecting the mother's health also affect the health—or more importantly the development—of the embryo and fetus. One of the most significant factors in health is nutrition, and what the mother eats is of considerable importance. The significance of the expectant mother's diet first attracted widespread attention during World War II when pregnant women in Europe were forced to live under conditions of near starvation. Analyses of reports from various countries (Keys et al., 1950) led to the conclusion that poor maternal diet slowed the growth of the fetus, particularly during the last four months of pregnancy. Evidence was also reported (Ebbs et al., 1942) that expectant mothers with poor diets were more likely than those with adequate nutrition to miscarry, have premature infants, or experience prolonged labor. Subsequent investigations carried out in the 1950s did not always corroborate the findings of the wartime studies. In an analysis of all research carried out through the 1960s, the Committee on Maternal Nutrition, National Research Council (1970) concluded that it was difficult to separate diet from other factors, particlarly when studying women from lower socioeconomic levels. Researchers (Cravioto, DeLicardie, and Birch, 1966) in Mexico, however, *were* able to control nonnutritional factors quite effectively. They found evidence leading to the conclusion that when both mother and child had poor diets, children were likely to be below average in height and weight and also earn lower scores on an intelligence test. Furthermore, an analysis of children who developed under prenatal and postnatal conditions of extreme malnourishment led Myron Winick (1976, pp. 16–17) to conclude that brain-cell division might be substantially slowed to the point that the later intellectual capability of the child would be affected.

Poor maternal nutrition influences physical and intellectual development of child

Despite the difficulties in interpreting inconsistent data, the Committee on Maternal Nutrition of the National Research Council concluded that there is sufficient evidence regarding the impact of nutrition to support the following recommendations (1970, pp. 132–133):

Women who expect to bear children should strive to maintain an adequate diet *throughout* the child-bearing years, not just during pregnancy.

As soon as a woman knows she is pregnant, she should seek advice from a physician or public health agency regarding proper diet while she is carrying the fetus.

An average weight gain of twenty to twenty-five pounds is considered reasonable and desirable during the course of pregnancy. Attempts to limit weight gain to less than twenty pounds may lead to malnutrition that could adversely affect both the mother and the fetus.

Routine use of vitamins during pregnancy is of doubtful value, and excessive use of a few vitamins (for example, vitamin D) might lead to fetal abnormalities. Some supplements (especially iron and folic acid), as well as vitamins recommended by a physician for special nutritional deficiencies, may be beneficial.

A point not stressed by the Committee on Maternal Nutrition but which might be added because of a report that has been published since the committee made its recommendations, is that expectant mothers should not drink more than a cup or so of coffee a day. Paul S. Weathersbee (1975) found some evidence that women who drank more than six cups of coffee a day when pregnant had a much higher-than-average tendency to miscarry.

Infectious Diseases It is now clearly established that if an expectant mother contracts certain infectious diseases during the first months of pregnancy, abnormalities in fetal development may occur. The best-known of these diseases is Rubella (German measles). In some states, laws have been passed to assure that all girls will be immunized against this disease. In other states a woman will not be issued a marriage license until she provides proof of immunization. Other infectious diseases known to lead to aberrations in fetal development are syphilis, gonorrhea, and polio. Influenza and mumps may also lead to abnormalities but apparently not to the same extent as the other diseases noted.

Infectious diseases contracted by mother may cause fetal abnormalities

Tranquilizers and Aspirin The potential negative impact of drugs on fetal development is now widely recognized because of the thalidomide tragedy. You have probably read newspaper reports of legal judgments in several countries requiring the manufacturer of this drug to pay parents large sums of money to provide their children with special prosthetic devices, treatment, care, and education. If you are not sure what led to these payments, a brief history will fill in the details.

In 1960, a West German drug firm placed on the market a nonprescription sleeping pill and nausea preventive called thalidomide. It was used by many pregnant women to alleviate morning sickness. A tremendous increase in the number of children born with deformities of the limbs, heart, and digestive tract, led to an investigation, which revealed that the abnormalities appeared in babies born to women who had used thalidomide between the fourth and sixth weeks after conception. (Frances Kelsey, an alert member of the Food and Drug Administration, prevented the drug from being sold in this country. Some obstetricians, however, gave their patients free samples distributed by a company applying for the rights to sell thalidomide in the United States, and some Americans purchased it abroad.)

The thalidomide tragedy stimulated substantial interest in the possibility that other drugs taken by expectant mothers might cause aberrations in fetal development. The Food and Drug Administration, for example, has been carrying out an extensive study of the impact of aspirin. It does not appear that aspirin causes stillbirth, low birth weight, birth defects, or infant death. There is some evidence, however, that women who take aspirin the last three months of pregnancy may experience prolonged labor and have longer-than-average clotting and bleeding times. The Food and Drug Administration has also issued a warning (Zimmerman, 1976) that some widely sold tranquilizers may cause cleft palate and other defects in a child if the mother takes them during the first months of pregnancy. The manufacturers of the tranquilizers have disputed the warning, claiming that the drugs were carefully tested before they were placed on the market.

LSD and Heroin   Studies (for example, McGlothlin et al., 1970) of the impact of LSD and heroin on fetal development have proven inconclusive, largely because so many of the mothers who used these drugs also were heavy smokers, had extremely poor diets, and/or suffered from infectious diseases of various kinds. The absence of clear-cut evidence linking use of LSD and heroin to birth defects should not be interpreted as indicating that these drugs are harmless, however. One aspect of drug use which has become apparent, even when evidence is inconclusive or contradictory, is that some expectant mothers (or the unborn children they carry) are much more (or less) resistant to drugs than others. Not all women who took thalidomide during the first weeks of pregnancy had deformed babies, yet some women who have taken milder drugs have had children born with abnormalities. The same has proven true of LSD, heroin and other drugs. Accordingly, many obstetricians recommend that as soon as a woman has reason to believe she is pregnant, she should avoid as much as possible the use of any and all drugs.

Tobacco   *Smoking and Health: A Report of the Surgeon General* (1979) reviews over two hundred studies of relationships between smoking, pregnancy, birth and the behavior of infants and children. The general conclusions are summarized in the introduction to the entire *Report:*

Smoking during pregnancy has significant adverse effect on fetus and newborn baby

The weight of the evidence demonstrates that smoking during pregnancy has a significant adverse effect upon the well-being of the fetus and the health of the newborn baby.

There is abundant evidence that maternal smoking directly retards the rate of fetal growth and increases the risk of spontaneous abortion, of fetal death, and of neonatal death in otherwise normal infants. More important, there is growing evidence that children of smoking mothers may have measurable deficiencies in physical growth, intellectual development, and emotional development that are independent of other known risk factors. Children of mothers who smoke during pregnancy do not catch up with children of nonsmoking mothers in various stages of development. (P. ix)

As is the case with drugs, it is difficult to separate cause from effect in analyzing these findings. It has been suggested (Frazier et al., 1961) that three possible explanations for the relationships between maternal smoking and low-birth-weight infants are:

1 The expectant mother's appetite may be diminished when she smokes, leading to poor nutrition (which is known to cause fetal abnormalities).

2 Smoking may constrict the placental blood vessels, decreasing the oxygen supply to the fetus.

3 Women who smoke may do so because they are anxious and tense, and anxiety and tension may directly or indirectly cause low-birth-weight infants (perhaps due to premature birth).

Marijuana Research on the possible adverse effects of marijuana use on fetal development is difficult to assess. For every study that seems to supply evidence that marijuana causes birth defects or chromosomal anomalies that might cause abnormalities in children not yet conceived, there is likely to be a study that leads to the opposite conclusion. (For a review of such contradictory studies, see Brecher, 1973, pp. 451–463.) A major difficulty in evaluating such research is that many individuals who use marijuana also use other drugs. Among possible negative effects of marijuana (Tinklenberg, 1975) that might influence heredity or prenatal development are damage to chromosomes, delayed genetic damage, fetal brain damage, and abnormalities in sex differentiation in male fetuses. Marijuana might also adversely affect the capability of the parents to care for newborn infants if account is taken of the antimotivational syndrome produced in some marijuana users (who must make an effort to carry out even routine tasks), and the possibility that marijuana may intensify neurotic or psychotic tendencies. Even if there is no clear-cut proof that such abnormalities are caused by marijuana, it would seem that a woman who expects to bear a child should avoid use of this drug (as well as LSD and heroin) before, during, and just after pregnancy.

Alcohol It has been found (Hanson, Jones, and Smith, 1976; Rosett and Sander, 1979) that women who are chronic alcoholics have a much greater tendency than average to bear children with a variety of physical and mental defects. (This is often referred to as the Fetal Alcohol Syndrome, abbreviated FAS.) Furthermore, even when children of alcoholic mothers are placed in excellent foster homes, they do not seem to show noticeable improvement, suggesting that prenatal damage caused by alcohol is permanent. The possibility of fetal damage traceable to alcohol is not restricted to chronic drinkers. James W. Hanson (1977) reported that 12 percent of the babies born to women who consumed a average of two ounces of 100-proof alcohol a day before and during pregnancy were born with defects. Only 2 percent of a control group of women who drank lightly or not at all had similar defects. Two qualifications similar to those noted in evaluating research on smoking may also apply to drinking:

1   Alcohol consumption decreases appetite, which may lead to a poor maternal diet before and during pregnancy.
2   Women who drink heavily may do so because they are tense, if not neurotic, and tension may directly or indirectly cause prenatal complications.

Radiation   The dropping of the atom bomb on Hiroshima revealed the potentially harmful nature of radiation. Fifteen pregnant Japanese women who had been within a mile and a half of the explosion gave birth to babies with damaged brains and skulls. Alerted by this discovery, as well as by other evidence that was accumulating, medical scientists found that pregnant women who had received heavy doses of X rays, either for treatment of some kind or to determine the placement of the fetus in the uterus, gave birth to babies with malformed eyes and brains. Expectant mothers are now urged to avoid exposure to X rays. If an obstetrician desires information about fetal position, a recently developed device that sends sound waves through the expectant mother's body can be used to produce a picture that is equivalent to an X-ray plate.

Rh Blood Factors   Each individual's blood has a genetically determined characteristic referred to as the Rh factor (because it is found in all rhesus monkeys). If the father's genetic pattern contains Rh-positive (which is a dominant gene), and the mother's Rh-negative, complications may develop because the fetus will have Rh-positive blood, but it will need to be nourished by the mother's Rh-negative blood. Any interaction between fetal and maternal bloodstreams—such as bleeding during the process of birth—leads to the development of antibodies which attack the red corpuscles in the blood of the fetus. The production of antibodies is instituted only when some of the baby's blood interacts with the blood of the mother. This rarely occurs during a first pregnancy, which means Rh-factor incompatibility is usually a problem only with second or later pregnancies. A physician usually is able to make an estimate of the extent of antibody activity. If the activity seems potentially dangerous

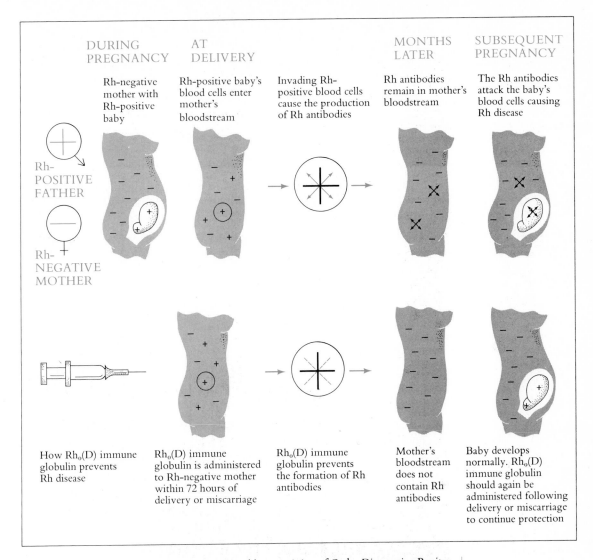

DURING PREGNANCY	AT DELIVERY		MONTHS LATER	SUBSEQUENT PREGNANCY
Rh-negative mother with Rh-positive baby	Rh-positive baby's blood cells enter mother's bloodstream	Invading Rh-positive blood cells cause the production of Rh antibodies	Rh antibodies remain in mother's bloodstream	The Rh antibodies attack the baby's blood cells causing Rh disease

Rh-POSITIVE FATHER

Rh-NEGATIVE MOTHER

| How Rh$_0$(D) immune globulin prevents Rh disease | Rh$_0$(D) immune globulin is administered to Rh-negative mother within 72 hours of delivery or miscarriage | Rh$_0$(D) immune globulin prevents the formation of Rh antibodies | Mother's bloodstream does not contain Rh antibodies | Baby develops normally. Rh$_0$(D) immune globulin should again be administered following delivery or miscarriage to continue protection |

Figure 4–7   How Rh disease develops. Reprinted by permission of Ortho Diagnostics, Raritan, New Jersey (1975).

early in pregnancy, an intrauterine blood transfusion may be provided. If the risk does not seem too great, the transfusion may be given immediately after birth. There is also the possibility that antibody production can be blocked by treating the mother with gamma globulin (Freda et al., 1966).

Age of Mother   In his fictional utopia *Walden Two*, B. F. Skinner suggested that early marriage would be encouraged so that childbearing would be completed before the age of twenty. (Children in his utopia were also to be reared by specialists, not by their parents, to make it possible for a married woman to pursue a career free of the responsibilities of motherhood.) While this scheme sounds reasonable and desirable, it may not be practical because it appears that the best age (from a physiological point of view) for a woman to bear a child is between twenty and twenty-nine (Daly et al., 1955). At the age Skinner proposed women should have babies the reproductive apparatus may not be fully developed, and some of the hormones needed for reproduction have not reached optimum levels. (In addition to physiological maturity, account should also be taken of psychological maturity and readiness to deal with the responsibilities of child rearing.) The woman who wants to pursue a career first and have children later also faces something of a dilemma. Developmental abnormalities, miscarriages, and still-births increase with age and are particularly likely in women over thirty-five. The likelihood that a woman under twenty-five will have a Mongoloid child, for example, is 1 in 1,500. Between the ages of twenty-five to thirty-four it is 1 in 1,000; between the ages of thirty-five to forty-five it is 1 in 150; and over forty-five it is 1 in 38. (Hamerton et al., 1961; Knoblock and Pasamanick, 1962). (These figures reveal that an older woman is more likely to have a Mongoloid child, but they also indicate that the great majority of older mothers have normal babies.)

Also related to age of the mother is the likelihood of having twins (which may be looked upon either as an advantage or a disadvantage). A woman of thirty-five to thirty-nine who has already borne a number of children has a 1 in 50 chance of giving birth to fraternal twins. For a woman of fifteen to nineteen who has not previously had a child, the chances are 1 in 200. One explanation for the greater tendency for an older woman to have twins is that hormonal changes in women over thirty-five cause ovulation to become irregular. The ovaries of a woman beyond this age may release no egg one month, two the next.

Emotional Factors   If a woman experiences extreme or continued anxiety or unhappiness during pregnancy, there is a possibility that glandular changes associated with emotion may alter her blood chemistry (Sontag, 1941). If this occurs, the development of the fetus may be affected, particularly if emotional reactions are extreme within the first few weeks after conception (Stott, 1971). L. T. Strean and A. Peer (1956), for example, found evidence that a child may be born with a cleft palate if the expectant mother experienced emotional stress between seven and ten weeks after conception. (This condition might also be due to heredity or to the influence of a drug or virus at the critical stage of fetal development.)

R. C. McDonald (1968) concluded that emotional factors were most likely to be associated with abnormalities in fetal development when these characteristics were found in the expectant mother: extreme anxiety, high levels of dependency, sexual immaturity, ambivalent feelings about pregnancy. McDonald noted, however, that many anxious women *do* have normal pregnancies and deliveries. He hypothesized that endocrine changes likely to cause complications in preg-

Extreme, extended anxiety during pregnancy may cause complications

nancy and birth may occur only when a woman experiences a very high degree of anxiety over a extended period of time. Generalizing from animal studies, R. L. Webster (1967) has suggested that anxious mothers may eat less and that some complications of prenatal development may therefore be due to poor nutrition.

A factor to consider in evaluating the impact of prenatal stress is that a woman who is emotionally upset during pregnancy may be quite likely to feel the same way after her baby is born. Therefore, some abnormalities in infant behavior might be attributed to postnatal care, not to prenatal stress. This point is underscored by studies of colic in infants (Stewart et al., 1954; Lakin, 1957), in which it was found that insecure women who were unaccepting of their role as mothers were much more likely to have babies characterized by excessive crying and digestive upset. Maternal tenseness and anxiety during pregnancy is one explanation for the colicky behavior of the infants. Another possible explanation is that the colic was caused by the tense and anxious way the mother cared for the infant after birth.

Birth

In addition to factors that might lead to abnormalities in the development of the ovum, embryo, and fetus, problems may occur during the process of birth. A description of the birth process will reveal some of the ways delivery of the fetus may lead to complications.

The Birth Process

Position of the Fetus   Approximately nine months after conception, the fetus has increased in size and complexity from a single barely visible cell to a recognizably human creature weighing about seven and one-half pounds. In order to accommodate to the uterus this sizeable organism assumes a position of maximum compactness with the legs tucked up and crossed. Sometime before birth, most fetuses assume a head-down position, with the chin close to the chest, which favors passage through the pelvis and vagina. Some fetuses, however, assume a head-up position (called breech presentation) or even an oblique position (transverse lie). When the head (or rump) of the fetus settles into the pelvis, it is referred to as the *lightening* because the change in position reduces pressure on the upper abdomen of the mother and she experiences it as a lightening effect. This may take place gradually over a period of days or shift quite abruptly and noticeably. In a woman carrying her first child it usually occurs two to four weeks before delivery. In a woman who has previously given birth, it may not occur until labor begins.

Labor and Delivery The exact causes of the onset of labor are unknown, but it is apparently triggered by hormonal changes as well as reactions of the uterus when it has been stretched to a maximum point (Reynolds and Danforth, 1966, pp. 458–465). The mother becomes aware of these changes when contractions of the uterus produce labor pains. At first spaced about ten to fifteen minutes apart and of mild intensity, these contractions become more frequent and intense as labor continues. The beginning of labor is also indicated by the appearance of a clot of mucus that had formed a plug in the cervix and was released as the cervix dilated; frequently, the amniotic sac bursts at the beginning of labor. The duration of labor may vary from three to twenty-four hours and still be considered normal (Bryant and Danforth, 1966, p. 519), but the average time for first-born babies is fourteen hours.

Average labor for first-borns: 14 hours

The placement of the body and head of the fetus is an important factor in determining ease of delivery. The opening in the mother's pelvis is usually an inch smaller than the circumference of the head of the fetus, but the skull bones of the fetus overlap in such a way that the head can be molded without damage to the brain. The size of the head is smallest when the fetus is in the head-down, chin-to-chest position, and the compression of the skull takes place most expeditiously in this type of delivery. Once the head slips through the pelvis, it must pass through the vagina. The tissues of the vagina have become softened during pregnancy and can be stretched to a considerable extent, but if the attending physician thinks they may be torn as the fetus emerges, a small incision (which can be easily stitched after delivery) may be made to enlarge the opening. (The medical term for this procedure is *episiotomy*.)

Natural and Surgical Adjustments to Facilitate Birth The uterus seems to come equipped with a slowing-down mechanism that controls the size of the fetus and adjusts it to the size of the mother. If a small mother is carrying a child genetically programmed to become a 6-foot 6-inch, 280-pound adult, for example, the rate of fetal growth is slowed during the last months of pregnancy. This built-in feature of prenatal growth was demonstrated by the mating of a male-female pair and a female-male pair each consisting of a large horse and a small pony. The pair in which the mother was a horse had a large newborn foal; the pair in which the mother was a pony a small foal. In a few months, however, both foals were the same size, and at maturity both were about halfway between their parents in size (Tanner, 1970, p. 91).

Many obstetricians use a specially designed instrument called the *forceps* to grip the unborn baby's head and help pull the child through the pelvis. Some doctors use the forceps only if the fetus appears to be in distress due to oxygen deprivation or pressure on the head or if there is prolonged labor. Other physicians make routine use of forceps during the final stages of delivery, particularly in first births. Proponents of routine use of forceps (for example, Guttmacher, 1973, pp. 217–218) argue that use of the instrument spares the fetal head from prolonged pressure and relieves the mother of much of the strain of the last stage of labor.

Stages of birth. During the first stage of labor the cervix dilates to permit passage of the baby's head from the uterus. *Top left,* the baby's head is beginning to pass through the pelvic opening and is being slightly molded by the pressure. During the second stage of labor the baby begins passage through the vagina. Note how the head is beginning to turn toward the mother's back. *Top right,* the amniotic sac has not yet ruptured and bulges in front of the baby's head. The mother can speed the second stage of labor by tightening her abdominal muscles in concert with the contractions of the uterus. *Middle left,* the amniotic sac has ruptured and the crown of the baby's head appears at the outlet of the vagina. *Middle right,* toward the end of the second stage, the baby's head emerges. Notice how the baby's body has turned. *Bottom,* as the baby's head emerges the contractions continue, the rest of the body slides out, and the baby is born. The third stage of labor, the delivery of the afterbirth (the placenta, the amniotic and chorionic membrances, and the rest of the umbilical cord) takes about 20 minutes. Reproduced with permission from the *Birth Atlas,* published by Maternity Center Association, New York.

If the mother's pelvis is small or oddly shaped, or if the head of the fetus is large, or if uterine contractions are weak or absent, or if the fetus does not assume a head-down and chin-to-chest position (to mention only some of the reasons), delivery may be prolonged or complicated. The obstetrician may then resort to Caesarean section (used in from 5 to 12 percent of all deliveries [DeCosta, 1966, p. 668]). This operation consists of incising the lower abdomen of the mother, cutting into the uterus, and removing the fetus.

Use of Anesthesia

Depending on the mother's anatomy and attitude, the position of the fetus, and other factors, labor may involve considerable pain. Up until 1853, when Queen Victoria inhaled chloroform during the birth of her son Leopold (her seventh child), there was widespread opposition to any kind of pain relief during delivery. This opposition was due to the belief (promulgated by male theologians) that pain suffered by a woman during birth was punishment for original sin. (No doubt many women of earlier times wondered if God had been completely fair and had provided males with a sufficiently demanding way to atone for *their* original sin. Eve ate the apple first, but Adam also disobeyed, and his punishment consisted of working for his bread and putting up with a few thistles and thorns.)

In 1690 John Locke persuaded many of his countrymen to empty the human organism of sin in his *Essay on Human Understanding,* but a hundred years earlier a female resident of Edinburgh who had obtained a medicine to relieve pain during childbirth was burned at the stake by order of King James VI (Speert, 1966, p. 19) because she had violated the biblical injunction "In sorrow thou shalt bring forth children" (Genesis 3:16). If King James had given birth to nine children, as Victoria did, he might have felt differently about the matter. (He might have also listened to biblical scholars who pointed out that the word that had been translated "sorrow" might also have been translated "labor," leading to the implication that a woman was expected to *work* at giving birth but not necessarily to suffer pain.)

The first use of anesthesia for childbirth took place in Britain in 1847. James Young Simpson, the physician who used it, was widely and bitterly attacked but proved to be as adept at finding divine sanction for his view as his critics were in discovering biblical passages to uphold theirs. He pointed out that verses 21 and 22 of the second chapter of Genesis describe how the Lord prepared Adam for the ordeal of the creation of Eve from one of his ribs by causing him to slumber. Thus the only time in history a man gave birth, he was completely anesthetized. Queen Victoria's use of chloroform effectively silenced much of the opposition in Britain and America (particularly since she knighted Simpson, who served as her anesthetist). As a variety of different anesthetics were perfected, some form of pain relief came to be used in most hospital deliveries, often to excess.

Natural Childbirth

Early Development of the Natural Childbirth Movement In 1914 Grantly Dick-Read, a London physician, was called to assist a poor woman who was having a baby. He prepared to give her an anesthetic, but she declined it. After the baby had been born he asked her why she had not taken advantage of the anesthetic, and she replied, "It didn't hurt, it wasn't meant to, was it, doctor?" (1959, p. 7). The woman's innocent question stimulated Read to observe how different women responded to delivering a child. Some were obviously in need of an anesthetic, but others seemed to be remarkably calm and apparently without pain. He became convinced that for many women the pain of labor was due primarily to tension and fear aroused by stories of agonizing childbirth told by relatives and friends.

Read gradually evolved an approach he called *natural childbirth*. Designed to reduce tension in the expectant mother, detailed information about anatomy and physiology was provided so that she would be completely aware of the entire process of prenatal development and birth and of the emotional and physical rewards of relaxed and conscious childbirth. Training in relaxation, breathing, and general physical fitness was also designed to reduce tension and ease delivery. Read encouraged the expectant mother to think about managing the birth of her child on her own. He also recommended that the father play an active role in both prenatal preparation and delivery.

Natural childbirth intended to reduce tension in mother

There was considerable initial resistance to Read's suggestion that pain during childbirth was not inevitable, but by the time the first edition of his *Childbirth Without Fear* was published in the United States in 1944, his previous books had attracted many followers. Women who had used the technique and successfully achieved natural childbirth were particularly enthusiastic and were eager to spread the word. It should be noted, though, that apparently only half of Read's patients achieved completely natural birth. Richard D. Bryant and David N. Danforth note (1966, p. 527) that Read is reported to have given an anesthetic to 242 of 481 of his patients.

Emergence of the Psychoprophylactic Method At about the same time natural childbirth was becoming popular in America, a different way to reduce pain at birth was being developed in Russia. The Soviet doctors who developed the method began with the same assumption as Read—that pain was not an inevitable part of labor—but they used Pavlovian principles to explain how many women had been conditioned to be tense during labor. They hypothesized that stories of agonizing childbirth led women to build up an association between pain and labor. The Russian doctors reasoned that if pain *was* a conditioned response, replacing it with a different, positive response should be possible. In time, they developed what has come to be called the *psychoprophylactic method* (abbreviated PPM) to accomplish this purpose. One technique encourages the expectant

Expectant parents learning techniques of natural childbirth in a Lamaze class. Elizabeth Hamlin/ Stock, Boston.

mother to substitute a new response (breathing) for fear or pain when a uterine contraction occurs. By concentrating on breathing, the woman also inhibits awareness of pain, just as a skier competing in a slalom race might not be aware she has injured herself because of her intense concentration on completing the course as rapidly as possible. The PPM aproach was adopted by the Russian government as the official method of childbirth in 1951, and it was introduced in France shortly after by Fernand Lemaze (1958), who learned of it on a visit to Russia. It was publicized in this country by Marjorie Karmel (1959), a young American woman who was introduced to PPM by Dr. Lamaze when she sought an obstetrician because her baby was due while she was in Paris.

Natural Childbirth Methods Do Not Always Eliminate Pain   In the years since the Read and PPM methods were introduced in this country it has become apparent that some women *are* able to have painless childbirth. But, as the statistics regarding Read's own practice of the method reveal, this is not true of all women, no matter how faithfully they follow instructions or how fervently they believe in the method. Consequently, some proponents of the technique (for example, Chabon, 1966) now stress that a woman *may* experience no pain but that in choosing natural childbirth she should concentrate primarily on taking an active part in the birth of her child and do her best to minimize the use of drugs and surgical intervention. Many obstetricians stress that a woman in labor should feel free to request or authorize assistance if she feels she needs it. Her own anatomical and physiological characteristics, and those of the fetus she is carrying, may make it necessary to have the attending physician provide an anesthetic and play an active role in the delivery.

Natural childbirth may reduce, but not eliminate, pain

Preparing for Natural Childbirth   The term *natural childbirth* no longer refers only to the Read method but refers to any approach that stresses the preparation of the mother and father for childbirth and their participation in the process. For this reason many advocates of the method prefer the term *prepared* birth to natural birth. In practice, such approaches often combine techniques recommended by Read with aspects of PPM. Couples who elect to try natural childbirth attend classes for eight to twelve weeks before the delivery date. They learn how the mother can control specific groups of muscles she will use during labor and how she can use different breathing patterns at different stages of the birth process. They visit the hospital and become familiar with the delivery room and the procedure that will be followed. The husband assists and coaches during the training period and also at the time of delivery. (The husband may assist in the delivery by helping his wife pace breathing patterns, spotting tense muscle groups, and timing labor contractions.)

Drugs Taken During Labor May Have Long-Term Effects

One of the major arguments offered by enthusiasts for natural childbirth is that drugs taken by the mother during labor will have an undesirable influence on the newborn baby (Tanzer and Block, 1972, pp. 42–58). In a review of research on this question, Watson A. Bowes and several associates (1970) found that medication given to the mother during labor had a significant retardant effect on sensorimotor functioning of the infant for as long as four weeks after birth. The researchers concluded, however, that this was "transient narcosis" and that there were "probably few long-term untoward effects" (1970, p. 23). The baby may take up to four weeks to overcome the effects of drugs given to the mother because a dosage sufficient to anesthetize an adult has a much greater impact on a seven-pound infant, whose bloodstream must be detoxified by the immature liver and kidneys (Brazelton, 1970, p. 2).

In a later review of studies on the impact of drug use, Yvonne Brackbill concludes that "the effects of obstetrical medication are *not* transient" (1979, p. 109, italics added). Brackbill later notes, however, that the most reliable studies she cites did not extend beyond the first twelve months. Her statement that the effects of drugs are "not transient," therefore, might be qualified by the phrase "up until the end of the first year." It appears, then, that her conclusion is not really in conflict with that of Bowes and his associates who considered long-term effects. Since there is the possibility that drugs taken at the time of delivery may have at least a temporary impact on child behavior, Brackbill feels that the mother, rather than the obstetrician, should make the decision about use of medication during labor. (She notes [pp. 115–116] that there is evidence that particular doctors and hospitals follow a "standing order" policy where evey woman who enters a delivery room is given a standard series of drugs at prescribed intervals.)

Final Stages of the Birth Process

Once the baby's head emerges, the physician checks to make sure the umbilical cord has not wound itself around the neck and, if this problem does not need to be dealt with, supports the head and assists the passage of the shoulders through the vagina. After the shoulders are through, the rest of the body emerges rapidly, and the moment the entire body is outside the mother's body is the official time of birth. Some physicians cut the cord immediately because they feel it is easier to care for the newborn baby in a crib. Others, who believe that it is desirable to make sure the baby receives all the blood in the cord, wait until the cord stops pulsating. (If the mother has received large amounts of drugs during labor, the cord may be cut as soon as possible to minimize the amount of blood interchange between mother and baby.) Once the baby is born, the placenta is expelled, often with the physician's assistance, and the birth process is complete.

The final stages of labor and delivery may cause a shortage of oxygen (anoxia) in the fetus that may lead to damage of the cells in the brain stem (Teuber and Rudel, 1962), and some form of cerebral palsy may result. Brain damage may also be caused by asphyxia, and if the infant does not begin to breathe spontaneously, a slap on the buttocks may be given or various types of resuscitation apparatus may be used. The functioning of the infant is usually evaluated with reference to the Apgar Scoring Method (Apgar et al., 1958), which involves rating heartbeat, respiratory effort, muscle tone, reflex irritability, and color. A healthy baby has a heart rate over one hundred, a strong cry, is active, cries when the sole of the foot is slapped, and appears completely pink. If the infant fails to meet one or more of these criteria, the physician may supply various treatments depending on the diagnosis of the problem.

Pre-Term Birth

Between 7 and 8 percent of all births in the United States occur before full term. The term *premature baby* is commonly used to refer to such infants, but many scientists and medical practitioners prefer the term *low-birth-weight infant* or *short-gestation-period infant*. Furthermore, it has been suggested (Kopp and Parmelee, 1979) that it may be helpful to distinguish between *small-for-dates infants* who have low birth weights regardless of the time of delivery and *pre-term infants* who are born before the expected date but whose weights *are* appropriate for their gestational age. The reason for this distinction is that low birth weight appears to be more predictive of difficulties in development than early birth per se.

Among the possible causes of pre-term birth are maternal health and nutritional status prior to and during pregnancy; maternal age, height, and weight; weight gain; smoking; use of drugs during pregnancy; uterine problems; and lack of prenatal care (Bergner and Susser, 1970). Many of these factors are related directly or indirectly to poor economic and social conditions, and the percentage of pre-term births is higher for disadvantaged mothers than for those from more

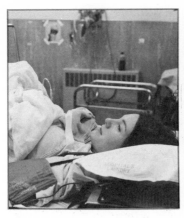 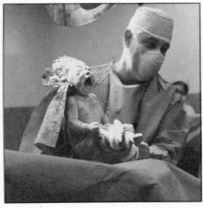 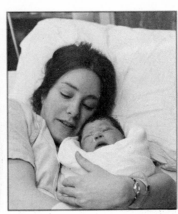

In the early stages of labor this mother practices breathing and relaxation techniques she learned in prenatal classes. This helps her reduce the amount of drugs needed to reduce pain and allow her to be conscious and aware when the baby is born. Susan and Terry Moor.

favored backgrounds. (For reasons to be discussed more completely in later chapters, it appears that low-birth-weight infants who are reared in good environments often overcome early signs of retardation in development [Sameroff and Chandler, 1975], but this may not be the case for infants who are reared in poor environments. Thus, it is important to consider home background in assessing the long-term as well as the immediate effects of pre-term birth.)

Up until the 1970s investigation of the early and later development of pre-term infants led to the conclusions (Crowell, 1967) that many of them were likely to be retarded in physical and mental growth, suffer speech difficulties, and have poor visual acuity. Starting in the late 1960s, however, detailed investigations of pre-term infants revealed that such conclusions needed to be analyzed and qualified. It was discovered, for instance, that routine hospital procedures used with pre-term infants often caused preventable problems. In the 1940s and 1950s, for example, many pre-term infants were kept in incubators with high oxygen levels and low temperatures, fed on diluted formulas (because of imperfect methods of tube feeding) and handled as little as possible (to reduce the possibility of infection). In time it was discovered that excessive amounts of oxygen caused a type of blindness, that nutrients from the diluted formulas were diverted from growth to maintenance of body temperature (leading to near starvation), and lack of handling retarded physical, cognitive, and emotional growth. In the 1970s, excellent hospital care of pre-term infants has eliminated these conditions. Temperature and oxygen levels in specially designed incubators are carefully monitored, care is taken to supply an adequate diet, and the infant is physically handled (without having to be removed from the specially designed incubator) and stimulated at frequent intervals. As a result of such practices, the number of pre-term infants who develop physical, cognitive, speech, or visual anomalies has been substantially reduced.

Low-birth-weight infants from disadvantaged backgrounds most likely to experience problems

In summarizing research on pre-term infants Claire B. Kopp and Arthur H. Parmelee (1979, pp. 47–59) report that infants who are below average in weight for their gestational age and whose mothers come from disadvantaged back-grounds are most likely to exhibit developmental anomalies of various kinds. They also report that when satisfactory care is provided, pre-term infants later appear to earn average scores on intelligence tests, but that boys, in particular, may experience problems in school. Finally, they note that there is often unevenness in some of the ways pre-term infants mature.

It is not possible on the basis of available data to pinpoint the source of these various characteristics. In some cases behavioral anomalies may be due to the prenatal conditions or birth complications noted earlier in the summary of possible causes. In other cases, the way parents treat pre-term infants may perpetuate, retard, or shape particular traits. Mary Shirley (1939), for instance, speculated that some of the characteristics of children who had been born pre-term might have been intensified by the tendency for parents to be overpro-tective and anxious when handling such infants. And in some cases it appeared that the same parents later seemed to feel obliged to urge the child to make up for a slow start. (If such types of parental behavior do occur, they might account for some of the unevenness of development noted by Kopp and Parmelee.)

If account is taken of all the factors influencing prenatal development that have just been discussed, the statistics reflecting the high infant mortality rate in the United States (Tables 4–1 and 4–2) become understandable. Many women have poor nutrition (partly because they have been encouraged by advertisers to make frequent use of highly processed convenience foods or food substitutes). Expec-tant mothers may not be aware of the potentially harmful impact of infectious diseases, drugs, Rh factor incompatibility, or maternal age. Poorly educated women are less likely to know about such factors, and the high cost of medical care may mean the mother of limited financial means will receive no medical attention or advice until the time of birth—if then. But if parents are well informed and take advantage of their knowledge of genetics, prenatal develop-ment, and birth, they can do much to assure that their offspring will begin life as healthy, full-term infants. The behavior and characteristics of such infants will be described in the next chapter.

Suggestions for Further Study

Genetics

If you would like to find out more about heredity and genetics, two books by Amram Scheinfeld are highly regarded: *Your Heredity and Environment* (1965) and *Heredity in Humans* (1972). You might also look for *The Genetic Code* (1962) by Isaac Asimov. Gerald E. McClearn provides a concise analysis of "Genetic Influences on Behavior and Development" in Chapter 2 of *Carmichael's Manual of Child Psychology* (3rd ed., 1970), edited by Paul H. Mussen.

DNA

If you saw the film (or read the novel by Irving Wallace) *The Prize,* you may know of the potential for high drama in discoveries that lead to a Nobel Prize. This was certainly true of the discovery of DNA. In the 1950s, biochemical research led to the conclusion that the nucleic-acid molecule carried the genetic code, but the details of how the code was passed from one generation to the next were yet to be found. Hundreds of scientists worked at finding the answer, and James D. Watson and F. H. C. Crick, using a technique of X-ray diffraction developed by the English physicist M. H. F. Wilkins, were the first ones to propose a satisfactory explanation. For their efforts, they were awarded the Nobel Prize for medicine and physiology in 1962. For a brief account of their work, see Chapters 7 and 8 of *The Genetic Code* (1962) by Isaac Asimov. For a more extensive, highly personal account, peruse *The Double Helix* (1968) by Watson.

Conception and Contraception

If you have questions about the nature of conception and how it might be controlled, an extremely detailed analysis is presented in *Human Reproduction: Conception and Contraception* (1973), edited by E. S. E. Hafez and T. N. Evans. Among the chapter titles in this book are (chapter number is given in parentheses): Fertilization (6), Ovulation Detection (11), Oral Contraceptives (15), Effects of Oral Contraceptives (23), Sociological and Psychological Aspects of Family Planning (32), Biomedical, Social, and Legal Implications of Fertility Control (33). Less technical accounts of many of the same topics are provided in *Birth Control and Love* (1969) by Alan F. Guttmacher; *Birth Control* (1970) by Garrett J. Hardin; and *Woman's Choice: A Guide to Contraception, Fertility, Abortion, and Menopause* (1970) by Robert H. Glass and Nathan G. Kase.

Birth

If you would like more information about the process of birth, consult *Textbook of Obstetrics and Gynecology* (1966), edited by David N. Danforth. Normal pregnancy is described in Chapters 8, 9, and 10; abnormal pregnancy in chapters 11–15; normal labor in Chapters 16, 17, and 18; abnormal labor in Chapters 20–27. A number of books have been written expressly for expectant parents. One of the best of these is *A Child Is Born* (1966) with a series of remarkable photographs by Lennart Nilsson and an informative text by Axel Ingelman-Sundberg and Claes Wirsén. Another excellent book of the same type is *A Baby Is*

Born (1964), a simplified and popularized version of the *Birth Atlas* (5th ed., 1960), published by the Maternity Center Association. A list of exercises and a general set of guidelines for the expectant mother can also be obtained from the Association (Maternity Center Association, 48 E. 92nd Street, New York, New York, 10028). A book providing descriptions of several methods of childbirth, a list of childbirth education associations (by states, pp. 195–201), and an extensive bibliography is *Methods of Childbirth* (1972) by Constance A. Bean. A comprehensive book written by one of America's most respected obstetricians is *Pregnancy, Birth, and Family Planning: A Guide for Expectant Parents in the 1970s* (1973) by Alan F. Guttmacher. A popular, inexpensive paperback is *Pregnancy and Chilbirth* (1979) by Tracy Hotchner.

Prenatal Development and Care

Not so many years ago a common belief was that an expectant mother could influence the later development of her unborn child if she exposed herself to certain experiences and environments. (If a mother hoped her child would become a musician, for example, she would attend concerts and recitals during her pregnancy.) There is no proof that such a prenatal regime ever had the intended effect, but recent scientific discoveries have called attention to a number of factors and conditions that *do* seem to influence the development of a fetus. The most important of these have been outlined in this chapter, but for more complete information you can examine *The Child Before Birth* (1978) by Linda Ferrill Annis.

For practical suggestions regarding such matters as diet, exercise, and the like, see *Guide for Expectant Parents* (1969) by the Maternity Center Association; *Preparing for Childbirth: A Manual for Expectant Parents* (1969) by Frederick W. Goodrich, Jr.; or contact your local county health department for pamphlets published by such agencies as the Children's Bureau, Office of Child Development, U.S. Department of Health, Education and Welfare (Washington, D.C. 20201); the Public Affairs Committee (381 Park Avenue South, New York, N.Y. 10016); or The National Foundation—March of Dimes (600 Third Avenue, New York, N.Y. 10016). (Addresses are provided in case you are unable to obtain publications of these organizations from a local source.)

Natural Childbirth

If you would like more information about natural childbirth, these books are recommended: *Childbirth Without Fear: The Principles and Practice of Natural Childbirth* (2nd ed., 1959) by Grantly Dick-Read; *Painless Childbirth: Prophylactic Method* (1958) by Fernand Lamaze; *Thank You, Dr. Lamaze: A Mother's Experiences in Painless Childbirth* (1959) by Marjorie Karmel; *Natural Childbirth and the Christian Family* (1963) by Helen Wessel; *Six Practical Lessons for an Easier*

Childbirth (1967) by Elizabeth Bing; *Awake and Aware: Participating in Childbirth Through Prophylaxis* (1969) by Irwin Chabon; and *Why Natural Childbirth?* (1972) by Deborah Tanzer and Jean Libman Block.

Information and educational materials are available from these organizations:

☐ American Society for Psychoprophylaxis in Obstetrics (APO)
7 West 96th Street
New York, N.Y. 10025

☐ International Childbirth Education Association (ICEA)
P.O. Box 5852
Milwaukee, Wisconsin 53220

☐ Maternity Center Association
48 East 92nd Street
New York, N.Y. 10028

You might keep in mind while reading books by some of the more enthusiastic proponents of natural childbirth that their commitment to the technique may lead them to select reports emphasizing the advantages of natural childbirth (when it is successful) and call attention to the undesirable aspects of delivery involving drugs and assistance by the attending physician. On the other hand, some obstetricians who are highly critical of natural childbirth give the impression that they may distrust the technique partly because the physician takes a subordinate role to the mother. Objective reviews of all available evidence on topics such as use of anesthesia during labor (for example, Bowes et al., 1970) provide a more balanced view than articles or books written by adherents to a given point of view.

In addition to reading about natural childbirth, you might talk to a mother who tried the method or arrange to sit in on a group meeting for expectant parents.

KEY POINTS

Views of the Neonate

Birth trauma (Rank and Leboyer)

First relationship gives personality its original slant (Ribble)

Rooting, grasp, and Moro reflexes

Subcortical reflexes controlled by lower brain

Waning of subcortical reflexes may account for crib death

Man-in-miniature view of neonate

System-of-reflexes view of neonate

Developing-organism view of neonate

Neonatal Learning

Pavlovian conditioning of neonates

Operant conditioning of neonates

Perceptual Development in the Neonate

Neonates prefer to look at contrasty curved patterns

Habituation: soothing effect of continuous stimulation

The Social Nature of Neonates

Types of cries: rhythmical, mad, pain

Interactional synchrony: neonates synchronize movements to spoken words

Neonates respond to their mothers (and their voices)

View of the neonate as capable but immature

Individual Differences in Neonatal Behavior

Infants respond to soothing in consistent ways

Behavior of baby may influence mother's reactions

Realizing some infant behavior is innate could lessen guilt

Reproductive risk high in disadvantaged homes, when parents are anxious

Initial Parent-Child Relationships

Encouraging a sense of trust (Erikson)

Accommodation and the revision of sucking schemes

Only repeatedly reinforced behavior likely to be retained

Evolutionary explanation for attachment (Bowlby)

CHAPTER □5

THE NEONATE

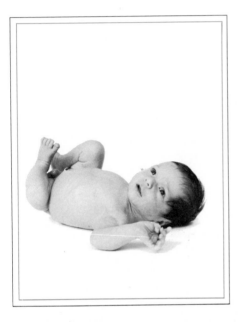

If a sperm fertilizes an egg and the process of cell division takes place without being interrupted or distorted, approximately nine months later a child will be born. After the newborn baby emerges from its mother's body and the umbilical cord is cut, the baby begins to function as an independent human being. The official time of birth is the moment the baby is completely clear of the mother's body. Independent existence might be said to begin when the baby takes its first breath, sometimes on its own, sometimes in response to a slap by the attending physician. Once breathing begins, the onset of the process causes the valves in the heart to alter the pattern of the circulation of the blood. In the uterus the blood was circulated to the placenta for aeration. When the baby is separated from the placenta, the blood is pumped to the lungs to be aerated.

From birth to the age of one month the baby is called a *neonate* (from the Latin *neo*, "new," and *natus*, "born").[1] The average newborn baby weighs a few ounces over seven pounds and is twenty inches long (boys, on the average, are slightly larger than girls), but because the legs are drawn up, the baby looks smaller. By adult standards the body looks out of proportion, since the head accounts for a quarter of total length (compared to a tenth in a mature individual). Once the birth process is over, the baby sleeps much of the time—as much as twenty hours a day. When awake and active, behavior appears aimless, diffuse, and uncoordinated. Yet this seven-pound, out-of-proportion, sleepy, and apparently disor-

---

[1] In an early definitive analysis of the neonate, Karl C. Pratt (1954) notes that authorities differ as to the duration of the neonatal period. Some hold that it extends only to the end of the first week; others maintain it lasts until the end of the third month. He concludes that most developmental psychologists use the term to refer to the infant during the first month of life.

ganized organism possesses all of the equipment needed to survive.

To a casual observer any particular newborn infant may not be readily distinguishable from others delivered the same day in a large hospital (which is one reason an identifying wristband is attached and a footprint is taken). But within a few hours or days the infant begins to manifest distinctive characteristics. Some of these take the form of physical traits; others are behavioral expressions of various types. One baby in a hospital nursery may be quiet, another active, still another irritable. The fact that personality differences are apparent from the moment of birth leads us back to questions that were discussed in Chapter 1. Is the infant born a blank slate, or does the newborn child possess inherited predispositions that exert a significant influence on behavior from the moment of birth? Another question to consider centers on the degree of sensitivity of the neonate. Some theorists believe the newborn infant is significantly and permanently influenced by initial experiences. Others argue that the neonate has an incompletely developed nervous system and is unlikely to respond to subtle variations in handling as an older child or adult would.

Views of the Neonate

Neonatal Sensitivity

Rank and Leboyer: Birth Trauma The view that the neonate is especially sensitive was first emphasized by psychoanalysts. Otto Rank (pronounced *Rahnk*), one of Freud's early pupils, was so impressed by his mentor's theories on early experience that he proposed the concept of *birth trauma*. Rank (1929) argued that separation from the mother was such a traumatic experience to the infant that it caused an anxiety that became the basis for all subsequent anxiety, including neurotic behavior as an adult. Freud did not endorse this view, but it was accepted by some of Rank's colleagues.

Birth trauma (Rank and Leboyer)

Rank proposed his birth-trauma theory in 1929. In the mid-1970s Frederick Leboyer, a French obstetrician, attracted a great deal of publicity with basically the same argument. In *Birth Without Violence* (1975) Leboyer maintains that the bright lights and rough treatment that are features of many hospital births cause a birth trauma. (He backs up his argument by noting personal recollections of how he reacted to his own birth.) When Leboyer delivers a baby he insists on dim lights and a quiet atmosphere. The emerging infant is handled with great tenderness and placed on the mother's bare stomach as soon as birth is complete. The newborn infant is then stroked and massaged until the umbilical cord stops pulsating and breathing is established, after which a leisurely warm bath is given. Many obstetricians have pointed to some possible disadvantages of the Leboyer approach, such as the difficulty of examining a baby placed on the mother's abdomen in a dimly lighted room. They note that potential complications might go undetected under such circumstances. Furthermore, researchers have presented evidence (to be summarized later in this chapter) that newborn infants do not appear to be neurologically mature enough to experience an emotional reaction such as the extreme trauma described by Rank and Leboyer.

Even if the *baby* may not be neurologically mature enough to be bothered by bright lights and less-than-gentle treatment at the time of birth, it is possible that a more serene delivery room atmosphere might be beneficial to the mother (and perhaps the father, if he is assisting). Many women who gave birth in the 1950s and early 1960s (before natural childbirth techniques became popular) resented the sterile, impersonal, "baby-factory" atmosphere of some hospital delivery rooms. If they had looked forward to the birth of a child as a moment to be treasured they were understandably bitter when doctors and nurses treated the arrival of their child as a routine matter to be handled in much the same fashion as the assembly of a stereo amplifier. It seems possible, therefore, that some (perhaps much) of the enthusiasm for Leboyer's book might be attributed to expectant parents' desires to make the birth of their child something memorable. Instead of assuming that a newborn baby is mature and sophisticated enough to be aware of subtleties in the way it is handled, however, it may be preferable to concentrate on the feelings of the parents regarding the atmosphere of the delivery room. That many parents of the 1980s *are* interested in the way their child is delivered is indicated by the number of books on the subject as well as by new interest in home delivery, midwifery, and birthing rooms in maternity hospitals. Furthermore, psychologists (for example, Klaus and Kennell, 1976) are speculating on the impact of post-birth experiences on the parents (as contrasted with the psychoanalytic interpretations of Rank and Leboyer which stress the reactions of the infant). There is some evidence (to be summarized and evaluated in Chapter 7) that the attachment parents feel for a baby may be strengthened if they have skin-to-skin contact with their child a few hours after it is born.

Ribble: The Rights of Infants The psychoanalytic interpretation of the sensitivity of the neonate and infant that has gained the greatest amount of acceptance and publicity over the years is offered by Margaret Ribble in *The Rights of Infants* (1943). Ribble, an M.D., began her career as a member of the staff of the Boston Children's Hospital. In the course of diagnosing and treating children suffering from behavior disorders not traceable to known organic causes, she noticed a condition called *marasmus* (Greek for "wasting away"). Some of the babies she observed were so unresponsive and listless that they sometimes refused to take food and appeared to be actually wasting away. Ribble concluded that a common factor in the backgrounds of these babies was lack of mothering. After making these observations she spent two years studying in Europe with eminent psychoanalysts, including Anna Freud. When she returned to this country, Ribble observed over six hundred infants in three maternity hospitals in New York City.

On the basis of her observations of disturbed and normal infants and her interpretation of psychoanalytic theory, Ribble concluded that the way a child is mothered the first days and weeks of its life is of crucial importance, and she presented this view in *The Rights of Infants*. While the book makes a strong case for early mothering, Ribble fails to provide any acceptable evidence to substantiate her claims. She simply notes that she observed certain types of behavior and backs up most of her points by describing extreme case histories. It is possible to "prove" any point by selecting extreme cases. Therefore, her observations should be interpreted as speculative hypotheses.

On the opening page of *The Rights of Infants,* Ribble states the basic theme of the book, "the experiences of infancy determine in no small way the evolution of individual personality" (1943, p. 3). She amplifies this point by saying "It is the first relationship of life which activates the feelings of the baby and primes his dormant nervous system into full functional activity, giving to each individual personality its original slant" (p. 13). In Ribble's view, the newborn infant is an extremely delicate organism that must be given careful mothering. In commenting on the importance of mothering, Ribble observes "Until the higher levels of the brain mature, the mother must act as the child's brain; that is, by judicious use of her loving attention she must stimulate within the infant the activities which he cannot start in motion for himself" (p. 53). She later observes (in a chapter titled "Babies Must Not Be Thwarted") "The human infant in the first year of life should not have to meet frustration or privation, for these factors immediately cause exaggerated tension and stimulate latent defense activities" (p. 72).

First relationship gives personality its original slant (Ribble)

The Rights of Infants was a best seller when it was first published, and Ribble's argument that the infant is extremely sensitive and that initial experiences are of great significance was endorsed by many theorists and parents. Other psychologists, however, found evidence that led them to conclude that the neonate is essentially a reflex organism too immature to be significantly or permanently influenced by experiences such as parent-child relationships during the first month.

The Neonate as a Reflex Organism

Survival Reflexes   Ribble maintains that the newborn infant must be assisted to breathe, suck, and sleep properly. Another view is based on the fact that neonates come equipped with reflex actions that permit them to do much to maintain their own survival and comfort. Breathing—with or without assistance—ordinarily begins just after birth, and most babies will obtain nourishment the first time they are exposed to a breast or bottle. This occurs because of two reflexes. If the cheek of a newborn baby is touched, the baby's head will turn to that side. This reaction is called the *rooting reflex,* and its importance can be easily understood—in order to eat, the child must find the source of food. Once the rooting reflex causes the mouth to come into contact with the nipple of the breast

Rooting reflex

or bottle, the *sucking reflex* is activated. Some babies start to suck immediately; others may need to be "primed" by having the nipple moved around in the mouth.

The neonate also possesses some reflexes that might serve a protective function. The newborn infant may exhibit a *withdrawal* reflex involving sudden jerking away of the legs when the sole of the foot is stimulated. Neonates blink their eyes shut if an object is moved close to the face and also "defend" themselves against an approaching object by pulling the head back and moving their hands in front of their bodies (Bower, Broughton, and Moore, 1970).

Subcortical Reflexes   Still other reflexes illustrate the nature of the development of the brain and nervous system. If a pencil or similar object is placed in the palm of the neonate's hand, the *grasp* reflex will cause the fingers to tighten around it. If the sole of the foot is stroked, the toes may fan upward and outward in the *Babinski* (or plantar) response (named after J. Babinski, the French doctor who first described it in 1896). (Karl C. Pratt [1954, p. 260] points out that there is considerable variability in the Babinski response and that lack of a "classic" pattern does not necessarily indicate any abnormality in development.) If there is a sudden sound or movement (someone knocking over a can of powder, for example, or bumping the table when changing a diaper), a baby lying on his or her back will respond with the *Moro reflex* (named after E. Moro, the German doctor who first described it in 1918) by first stretching out the arms and legs and then bringing them together.

Grasp reflex

Moro reflex

To account for the fact that the grasp and Moro reflexes were present in the behavior of neonates but had pretty much disappeared by the age of five or six months, Myrtle McGraw (1943) suggested that the original reflexes were activated by lower and older parts of the brain. Since the older parts of the brain are below the cortex, reflexes controlled by the lower brain are called *subcortical*. McGraw hypothesized that when the cortex developed and began to function more actively the subcortical control of the nervous system was inhibited. This explanation is now widely accepted, and if the grasp and Moro reflexes do not diminish or disappear by the time an infant is six months old, it may be taken as an indication that the brain and nervous system are not developing normally.

Subcortical reflexes controlled by lower brain

Crib Death May Be Due to Waning of Subcortical Reflexes   Even though this chapter is devoted to development during the first month of life, this is an appropriate place to discuss crib death, also referred to as the *sudden infant death syndrome* (SIDS). Crib death is the unexplained death of an infant that typically takes place between the second and fourth months after birth. An ostensibly healthy baby simply stops breathing, usually in the night, without apparent cause and without giving any signs of having struggled or suffered. Approximately two out of every thousand children born in America are victims of crib death. Even though the condition has been analyzed extensively, no

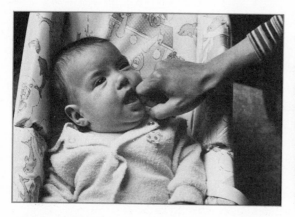

The rooting reflex

The sucking reflex

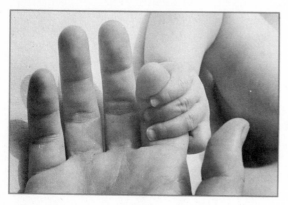

The grasp reflex

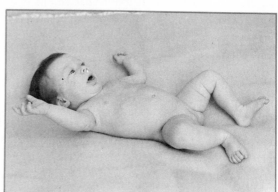

The Moro reflex

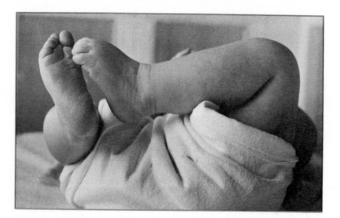

The withdrawal reflex

Some of the significant reflexes of the new born infant. Photographs, top to bottom, by David Nudell; David Nudell; Roy Pinney/Monkmeyer; Lew Merrim/Monkmeyer; Nolan Petterson/ Black Star.

widely accepted or proven explanation has yet been proposed, which means that no satisfactory prescription for prevention has been offered.

After studying fifteen crib-death cases matched with control infants, Lipsitt, Sturner, and Burke (1979) reported that the crib-death infants had low Apgar scores, low birth weights, and were kept in the hospital longer than average after being born. Furthermore, their mothers were often reported to be anemic. Careful analysis of records also led to the conclusion that the crib-death infants had respiratory anomalies of various kinds. After completing a different analysis of SIDS infants, Naeye, Messmer, Specht, and Merritt (1976) concluded that crib-death victims tend to be temperamentally lethargic. It appears, then, that crib-death infants are below normal in general physical tone and alertness which may make them more vulnerable when respiratory problems develop. As for the timing of crib death, Lewis P. Lipsitt (1979) speculates that the tendency for crib death to occur between two and four months of age suggests that this is a period *Waning of subcortical* when subcortical reflexes are beginning to be supplanted by voluntary or learned *reflexes may account* reactions. Thus, the infant is at an in-between stage of development. If respira- *for crib death* tory problems occur (for example, mucus blocking the nasal passages), an infant may not struggle to gasp for breath because built-in defensive reactions are disappearing and learned protective reactions are not yet well established.

On the basis of current knowledge it would appear that mothers might minimize the likelihood of crib death by following the suggestions offered in the preceding chapter regarding diet and health practices during pregnancy. Parents might also stimulate the neonate in a variety of ways and frequently respond to the infant's behavior (by using techniques to be described in Chapter 7), since the lethargy typical of some crib-death infants may have been due to the tendency for their parents to ignore them or react negatively to their behavior (Lipsitt, 1979).

The Neonate as a Developing Organism

In Chapter 4 of the second edition of the *Manual of Child Psychology* (1954), Karl C. Pratt reviewed research on the neonate up to the early 1950s. In his summary *Views of neonate* he noted different basic interpretations. He referred to the psychoanalytic view of Rank and Ribble as a "man-in-miniature" interpretation because adult re- *Man-in-miniature* sponses were attributed to the infant. Another conception he called the "system-of-reflexes" view because some psychologists were so impressed by the nature of *System-of-reflexes* subcortical reflexes that they assumed that the behavior of the neonate was dominated by the lower parts of the brain and that voluntary actions controlled by the cortex would not develop until later. Pratt himself favored a view of the neonate as a "developing organism." He was reluctant to attribute adult responses *Developing-organism* to newborn infants but at the same time he was convinced that the neonate was more than a system of reflexes. He suggested that the diffuse and uncoordinated appearance of the neonate's behavior was due to a tendency toward generalized responses. Pratt hypothesized that a stimulus might arouse a variety of responses the newborn infant was unable to control in a specific way. As development proceeded, Pratt suggested, maturation of nerves and muscles and practice in controlling the body would make it possible for the infant to make more specific or differentiated reactions.

After reviewing research completed before 1954 Pratt concluded that the newborn infant is sensitive to visual, auditory, olfactory, gustatory, thermal, pressure, and pain stimuli but that sensory development is incomplete. He pointed out, however, that there was insufficient evidence to draw firm or detailed conclusions about the sensitivities and capabilities of the neonate. He finished his review with this statement:

The important need in the study of neonatal behavior and development is to obtain increasingly accurate and detailed descriptions of the infant's responses and the stimulating conditions under which they are obtained. This should include further exploration of the possibilities of learning. (Pratt, 1954, p. 280)

In the twenty-five years since Pratt made that appeal, hundreds of psychologists have carried out the kinds of studies he recommended, and their conclusions have led to new conceptions of neonatal behavior. Present-day psychologists are interested in studying the infant because they believe they have detected previously undiscovered indications of sensitivity and capability. Descriptions of a sampling of informative studies will illustrate the nature of techniques and the conclusions of recent research on infancy.

Neonatal Learning

Pavlovian Conditioning

A number of investigators have succeeded in establishing Pavlovian conditioned responses in neonates. In Pavlovian conditioning (illustrated by John B. Watson's famous experiment with Albert and the white rat described in Chapter 1), an essentially involuntary reflex action comes to be actuated by a previously neutral stimulus. In order to establish Pavlovian conditioned responses in neonates, the experimenter must use stimuli that a newborn baby can respond to and also must arouse reflex actions that are part of the infant's repertoire. In a review of studies of Pavlovian conditioning, H. E. Fitzgerald and Yvonne Brackbill (1976) note that neonates have been conditioned to respond to a variety of sounds, mild electric shock, and lights. Types of reflex actions that have been successfully aroused by such stimuli are heart-rate changes, blinking, sucking, and foot withdrawal.[2] The apparatus pictured here illustrates how a Pavlovian condi-

Pavlovian conditioning of neonates

---

[2]It should be noted that not all psychologists are convinced that genuine conditioned responses have been clearly established in neonates. Arnold Sameroff and Patrick Cavanagh (1979), for example, argue that what some researchers call *learned* responses might more properly be classified as types of behavior that occur when an infant is in a *state of preparedness to react*.

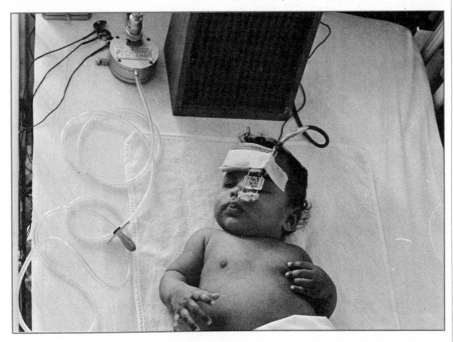

Pavlovian conditioning of an infant. A gentle puff of air (which causes the eye to blink) is produced by the mechanism attached to the baby's forehead. A tone is paired with the air puff. After a number of such presentations, the tone itself elicits the eye blink. Photograph by Jason Lauré. Courtesy of Lewis P. Lipsitt.

tioned response can be established in neonates. As soon as they are born, infants respond to puffs of air directed at the eyes by reflexively blinking the lids closed. After a puff of air directed at the eyes is associated several times with a tone sounded through a loudspeaker close to the baby's head, the neonate will blink when the tone is sounded, even though the puff of air is omitted.

Pavlovian conditioning involves an essentially involuntary response. The organism responds but without exerting any deliberate control over the actions. A much more significant kind of learning occurs when an organism makes precise movements in response to a specific stimulus and does this when it wants to.

Operant Conditioning

Learning that involves strengthening actions *initiated* by an organism occurs when operant conditioned responses are established. In his experiments with rats and pigeons, B. F. Skinner reinforced responses that were emitted spontaneously. When the rat pressed the bar or the pigeon pecked the disk, it was not engaging in an involuntary reflex action (as was the case with salivation in Pavlov's dog subjects), its behavior was under its own control. In order to establish operant conditioned responses, therefore, it is necessary to reinforce types of behavior that

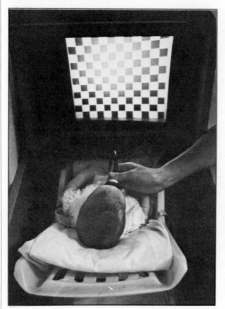 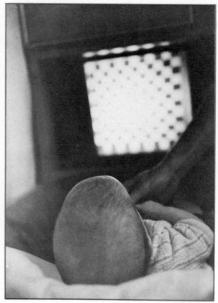

Operant conditioning of infants. Experiments like this one indicate that the behavior of very young infants can be shaped by reinforcement. The nipple on which this four-month-old is sucking controls the brightness of the pattern projected on the screen. When the infant sucks at a rapid rate, the picture becomes brighter and reinforces the higher frequency of sucking behavior. E. R. Siqueland and C. A. DeLucia, "Visual Reinforcement of Nonnutritive Sucking in Human Infants," *Science* 1969, **145**, 1144–1146. Photos taken in laboratory of Einar R. Siqueland at Brown University by Jason Lauré.

can be initiated and controlled by the organism. The newborn human infant is not capable of making very many responses of this type, but nonnutritive sucking and head turning fit this description.

Operant conditioning of neonates

In one of the earliest studies of operant conditioning, Hanus Papoušek (1967) conditioned head-rotation movements in neonates. A bit later Reuben E. Kron (1966) used an apparatus for controlling and recording sucking behavior in newborn infants. Kron found that as early as the first day of life infants would alter their sucking pattern when the flow of milk was turned on or off. He concluded that the day-old infant is capable of developing an operant conditioned response. Lewis P. Lipsitt has supervised or stimulated a series of infant-conditioning studies. Einar R. Siqueland and C. A. DeLucia (1969), for example, were able to establish nonnutritive-sucking responses in babies as young as one month of age by using an apparatus (pictured here) that allowed the infants to alter visual patterns when they sucked on a nipple wired to a slide projector. These studies and many others of the same type (reviewed by Sameroff and Cavanagh, 1979, pp. 355–362) indicate that neonates are capable of acquiring learned responses as soon as they can control their own behavior.

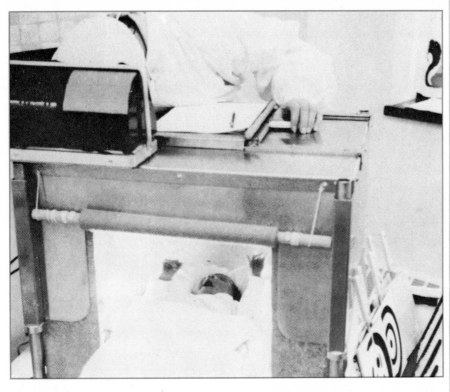

The infant "looking chamber" used in Fantz's study of perception in young infants. The experimenter peers through a small hole in the screen and observes the reflected image on the infant's eyeball. This technique makes it possible to record the amount of time infants look at different patterns. Photograph by Dr. Robert Fantz.

Perceptual Development in the Neonate

Responses to Visual Patterns

Robert L. Fantz developed an ingenious technique for studying how infants respond to visual patterns. (His methods triggered dozens of studies and led to new appreciation of the responsiveness of infants.) Fantz constructed a comfortable crib with a depression designed to hold an infant's head in a steady position. This crib was placed within an enclosure topped by a screen upon which cards could be placed. Fantz would settle an infant in the crib and attach to the screen cards on which different patterns had been drawn. Immediately after attaching the patterns, Fantz peered through a small hole in the screen and observed the reflected image on the surface of the infant's eyeball. This made it possible to determine the amount of time the infant concentrated on each pattern.

In an early study Fantz (1958) observed preferences between two patterns. In a subsequent study (1961) he measured duration of gaze for patterns presented in succession. His findings led him to conclude that during the early months of life infants can concentrate on one-eighth-inch stripes at a ten-inch distance, that they prefer patterns to plain colors, that they can differentiate among patterns of similar complexity, and that they show interest in a pattern similar to a human face. In a later study Fantz (1963) found that neonates from ten-hours- to five-days-old attended more to a schematic face and a concentric circle pattern than to unpatterned colored squares. (Some theorists [for example, Bowlby, 1958] have hypothesized that neonates have an innate preference for human faces. Fantz joins with Cohen, De Loache, and Strauss [1979, p. 416], who reviewed many studies, in concluding that this hypothesis is not supported by available evidence. These researchers believe that a face just happens to be one type of stimulus that infants respond to.)

Neonates prefer to look at contrasty curved patterns

In yet another investigation (Fantz and Miranda, 1975) Fantz reported that neonates prefer curved patterns with a high degree of contrast and that they appear to concentrate on the outer contours of patterns. The studies of Fantz and others (reviewed by Cohen, De Loache, and Strauss, 1979) who have used the same technique make it clear that immediately after birth infants are capable of making differential responses to visual patterns.

Neonatal Responses to Sounds

A number of investigations (reviewed in Spears and Hohle, 1967, pp. 88–99; and Kessen, Haith, and Salapatek, 1970, pp. 319–325) have revealed that the neonate is quite sensitive to sounds. Some of the most interesting studies of the newborn infant's response to auditory stimuli have centered on analysis of what is called *habituation*.

Habituation The first time a tone (or similar stimulus) is sounded, neonates are likely to respond by blinking their eyes, turning their heads, or either stopping or starting crying. But if the tone continues to be sounded at regular intervals it is likely to produce a soothing (habituating) rather than an arousing effect. This occurs, presumably, because the baby responds primarily to novel stimuli and ignores or filters out stimuli that have become "habitual" and because steady stimulation appears to induce relaxation. (One significant lesson from this tendency is that students of neonatal behavior should not present too many similar stimuli at one time. The cause of an infant's decreased responsiveness toward the end of a session may be more habituation than the characteristics of the stimuli.) Extensive research (reviewed by Kessen, Haith, and Salapatek, 1970, pp. 339–346; and Spears and Hohle, 1967, pp. 92–94 and 98–99; and Berg and Berg, 1979, pp. 325–330) has been carried out on aspects of habituation. Some of the most intriguing studies center on the soothing effect of continuous sounds.

Habituation: soothing effect of continuous stimulation

The Soothing Effect of Continuous Sounds What present-day psychologists refer to as habituation was recognized by mothers before the time of Christ. In his *Laws* (380 B.C.) Plato observed "You know, when mothers want to put

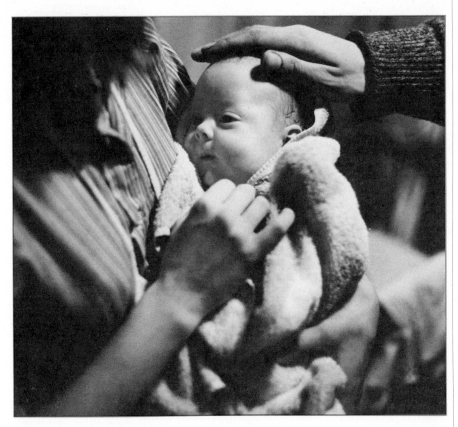

Some parents assume that a neonate should not be encumbered with clothing. Studies of habituation suggest, however, that infants who are continuously stimulated, as by clothing or covering, may be soothed by the soft material. David A. Krathwohl.

fractious babies to sleep, the remedy they exhibit is not stillness, but its very opposite, movement—they regularly rock the infants in their arms—and not silence, but a tune of some kind" (Book VII, Section 790). The effect of soothing techniques mothers had used for thousands of years was recorded in systematic fashion by scientists as soon as psychology became established as a field of study.

Before the beginning of this century Francis Warner mentioned how sounds soothe in *The Children: How to Study Them* (1887–1888). Thereafter, aspects of the phenomenon were periodically analyzed. L. A. Weiss (1934), for example, reported evidence that any sound had a greater calming effect on a neonate than no sound. New interest in this aspect of habituation was aroused when Lee Salk (1960, 1962) published reports that, compared to neonates cared for in a quiet room, neonates exposed to a recorded heartbeat gained weight, cried less, and were more content. This finding was consistent with previous results and might not have attracted attention except for the fact that Salk reported the heartbeat had the soothing effect but a metronome and a recorded lullaby did not. Since this finding conflicted with the results of the Weiss study (and other investigations as well), Yvonne Brackbill and several associates (1966) replicated the Salk study under carefully controlled conditions. Their results did not support Salk's hypothesis about the special soothing quality of a heartbeat but were consistent with Weiss's conclusion that any sound is more soothing than no sound.

The Social Nature of Neonates

When neonates are observed intensively and sensitively, certain types of behavior that can be interpreted as "social" become apparent.

Studies of Smiling and Crying

Peter H. Wolff has systematically used the baby-biography approach introduced by early students of child behavior. Instead of making observations of his own children, however, Wolff selected neonates in hospital nurseries and observed them comprehensively and objectively for up to eighteen hours a day.

Types of Smiles   In an early report Wolff (1963) described the development of smiling behavior. He noted that within two to twelve hours after delivery all of the eight neonates he observed manifested what resembled a smile. He also found that smiles appeared during sleep and suggested they might function as spontaneous nervous system discharges. By making sounds of various kinds Wolff also managed to elicit smiles when infants were drowsing. An interesting aspect of this discovery was that elicited smiles appeared, almost invariably, seven seconds after the stimulus.

Social smiles aroused by the sight of a person's face did not appear until the third week. Such smiles were noticeably different from reflex smiles and were also aroused by the sound of a human voice (and to a lesser extent a bell and a bird whistle). An important change taking place in the fourth week was the initiation of what Wolff considered to be genuine eye-to-eye contact that was not only an especially effective smile-inducer but also a potent attention-arresting stimulus.

Types of Cries   In still another report Wolff (1969) described crying behavior. He concluded that what is sometimes referred to as the "hungry cry" might better be termed a *rhythmical cry*, since it follows a regulated pattern and is not always associated with hunger. This type of crying can usually be distinguished from a *mad cry*, which is also rhythmical but noticeably more energetic. Even more easy to distinguish is the *pain cry*. This begins with an extended shriek followed by several seconds of complete silence and total inactivity as the baby recovers breath and is then followed by energetic crying and considerable activity. Wolff made tape recordings of the various cries of the infants he was studying, visited the

Types of cries: rhythmical, mad, pain

homes of the babies, and asked mothers to busy themselves about the house while he "observed" the neonates in their own rooms. Instead of observing the baby, however, Wolff played the tape recordings. He found that when he reproduced the pain cry mothers would drop whatever they were doing and rush into the room. They responded either not at all or in a leisurely manner when the rhythmical or mad cries were played.

By the second week Wolff found that interruption of feeding and being naked were likely to lead to crying. (Simply draping a blanket or diaper over an unclothed baby seemed to diminish crying caused by nakedness, a bit of information parents might find useful at bath and changing time). Wolff also found that he could induce a two-week-old neonate to cease soft crying by attracting interest with a moving object or a human voice. He also observed that fussy neonates may *begin* to cry when presented with a stimulus (for example, a face or voice) that would make them smile if they were contented. Apparently, attempting to soothe a fussing infant by resorting to tried-and-true smile producers may lead to crying rather than relaxation. (Perhaps the infant uses cries to communicate the message: "I'm not in the mood for play.") During the third week of life babies develop a *fake* cry characterized by moaning sounds probably intended to attract attention. Some babies seem to engage in such crying when they are content, apparently just for the sake of experimenting with making sounds.

Smiles and Cries as Forms of Communication   It seems fair to say that the smiling and crying of neonates function as their earliest forms of communication. Wolff's discovery that social smiles are more likely to be aroused by a human voice than a bell or bird whistle suggests that even a three-week-old infant expresses a response to fellow humans. The various types of cries also might be interpreted as attempts on the part of the neonate to tell others about personal feelings. The fact that mothers "tricked" by Wolff responded to the recorded pain cries indicates how effectively a neonate can inform others of distress. The fake cry is perhaps the most "social" of all, since it might be interpreted (in some cases, at any rate) as an attempt on the part of the babies to induce others to interact with them.

The "Human" Nature of Neonates

T. G. R. Bower argues (1977b, p. 20) that newborn babies realize they are human beings and possess specific responses elicited only by other human beings. He bases this contention (in part) on observations that week-old babies will imitate others. Bower reports that if a mother (or other adult) holding a week-old baby sticks out her tongue, flutters her eyelashes, and opens and closes her mouth, the infant will mimic each of these actions in turn. Furthermore, in Bower's estimation, the baby shows signs of enjoying such "games."

Neonatal Responses to Speech   Other evidence to back up the hypothesis that neonates are social beings is in their responses to voices. When two humans talk to each other, they tend to make bodily movements as they speak and listen. Because the listener frequently synchronizes his or her movements with those of the speaker (for example, by nodding the head, altering facial expression), this phenomenon is called *interactional synchrony*. W. S. Condon and L. Sander (1974) found that newborn babies only twelve hours old synchronized head and body movements to "live" voices as well as tape recordings of spoken English and spoken Chinese. Such synchronized movements did *not* seem to be aroused by tape recordings of isolated vowel sounds or tapping noises. It appears, then, that newborn babies have a built-in tendency to respond to the human voice. Furthermore, Peter D. Eimas and associates (1971) and P. A. Morse (1972) found that by the age of one month, infants are not only responsive to speech but are able to perceive quite fine distinctions in vocal production. The neonate's ability to recognize rather subtle differences in speech patterns probably accounts for the fact that G. Carpenter (1975) reported that two-week-old babies recognized their mothers—and their mothers' voices.

Interactional synchrony: neonates synchronize movements to spoken words

Neonates Recognize Their Mothers (and Their Voices)   Carpenter first had the mother of each infant subject peer through a porthole over a crib. Then, an adult not known to the baby stood behind the porthole. In some experimental situations, the mother's voice was broadcast through a loudspeaker as she peered through the porthole and talked to her child. In other situations, a recording of a different adult's voice was played as the mother made lip movements. The neonates in this experiment spent significantly more time gazing at their mothers than at strangers. In addition, they showed signs (turning the head away from the porthole) of being bothered when the stranger's voice was associated with the mother's face. And some of the subjects in this study indicated that they were disturbed if their mothers simply stared at them through the porthole in a speechless way. Apparently, by the age of two weeks human infants expect their mothers to talk to them.

Neonates respond to their mothers (and their voices)

How Capable Is the Neonate?

Relatively recent discoveries that neonates can learn, perceive differences in visual patterns, and respond selectively to human voices (among other things) reveal that newborn babies are substantially more capable than earlier psychologists believed. T. G. R. Bower, who has specialized in the study of infant behavior, recounts (1977b, pp. 27–28) how he had to overcome his own skepticism regarding the capabilities of neonates. Bower confesses that when mothers told him that their two- and three-week-old children reached out toward things, he politely refused to believe them because such behavior had not been reported in scientific journals. It was only after he happened to observe his three-week-old nephew reach out toward an object in his crib that Bower became less dominated by his preconceptions. He discovered that when he put objects in the cribs of neonates, many of them did indeed make reaching movements. This unsettling experience led Bower to conclude that up to the late 1960s, psychologists (including himself) who had studied neonates, apparently had put their subjects in empty cribs. The primary reason infants observed scientifically up to the late 1960s did not exhibit reaching behavior, therefore, seemed to be that they had nothing to reach for.

Bower: Newborn Infants Realize They Are Human

Bower was profoundly influenced by the discovery that neonates could do a lot more than he originally thought they could. Perhaps more than any other scientific student of infant development he has stressed that newborn babies interpret their perceptions in knowledgeable ways. He qualifies his assertion that neonates "know" by suggesting that it is not self-conscious thinking identical to adult thinking. He still maintains, however, that when babies "defend" themselves against an approaching object, for example, they must "know" that the object is potentially harmful (1977b, p. 29). It is tempting to share Bower's enthusiasm for neonatal precocity, but the defensive response of newborn babies *could* be yet another subcortical reflex. That is, the tendency for neonates to pull back their heads and move their arms in front of their bodies might serve a protective function. Instead of being a voluntary act carried out because the infant "knows" that trouble is looming, therefore, defensive arm movements might be reflexes initiated by lower parts of the brain.

Reevaluating Conceptions of the Neonate

Information published during the last twenty-five years about the capabilities of neonates makes it possible to reevaluate the bundle-of-reflexes and man-in-miniature views of the neonate described by Karl C. Pratt in 1954. It is obvious that the newborn baby is much more than a mere collection of reflexes. But it also seems unlikely that a human infant experiences anxiety, as Rank maintained, at the time of birth. Being able to recognize the mother's face, or stare at one pattern in preference to another, or suck on a nipple to focus a picture are impressive feats for a two-week-old baby to perform. But the abilities to carry out such actions hardly serve as proof that neonates have a brain sufficiently developed to store memories that will influence behavior dozens of years later. Neither does Ribble's assertion that neonates are so delicate and sensitive they must be assisted to breathe, eat, and sleep seem defensible. On the contrary, newborn babies appear to be more than capable of handling such routine matters with ease—to the point that they actively seek to interact with other humans and objects around them.

View of the neonate as capable but immature

Disadvantages of Assuming Neonates Are Molded

It would seem that Bower's view of infants as functioning human beings in their own right is closer to the truth than Ribble's conception of newborn babies as passive organisms whose behavior is entirely molded—for good or ill—by the way the mother cares for it. Bower's conception of the neonate is not only more in harmony with recent scientific reports, it is also much more reassuring to parents. Ribble's view of the mother-child relationship is based on the assumption that the infant's behavior is almost entirely the product of mothering. Parents who endorse this view may feel pleased with themselves if their newborn child is easy to care for and displays the kinds of behavior they had anticipated (such as responding positively to being cuddled). But if the infant acts in ways that do *not* fit preconceived notions about how babies should behave (such as being irritable or responding negatively to cuddling) the parents may become preoccupied with the thought: What are we doing wrong? Instead of assuming that they are responsible for all of a baby's behavior, parents might prefer the view that neonates are not only quite capable organisms, they also have personalities of their own. Parents might also consider the possibility that *their* behavior is shaped by the kinds of behavior that their baby exhibits.

As noted in Chapter 3, one limitation of psychoanalytic theory is that human beings are pictured as the victims of circumstances. Humanistic psychologists such as Carl Rogers and Abraham Maslow and certain learning theorists such as Albert Bandura argue that children are able to control much of their own behavior. The social-learning theorist Robert Sears also stresses the *reciprocal* nature of human relationships. Concentrating on ways parents shape child behavior tends to obscure the likelihood that the child—even during the first month of life—shapes parent behavior. A number of investigations provide evidence you might use in evaluating these points.

Individual Differences in Neonatal Behavior

Differences in Irritability and Soothability

The hypothesis that certain types of neonatal behavior are not entirely shaped by the parents is supported by hundreds of studies which are reviewed in *The Effect of the Infant on Its Caregiver* (1974), edited by Michael Lewis and Leonard Rosenblum; and *Child Effects on Adults* (1977) by Richard Q. Bell and Lawrence V. Harper. To illustrate the nature of this research, two frequently cited investigations by Beverly Birns will be described.

Some Babies Are Consistently Soothable   In her first investigation Birns (1965) exposed 30 two- to five-day-old babies to a soft tone, a loud tone, a cold disk, and a sweetened pacifier. She found consistent differences in response intensity to these stimuli and also observed that reactions to different stimuli tended to lead to essentially the same state of arousal. That is, one infant would respond in an intense way regardless of whether it was exposed to a tone, cold disk, or sweetened pacifier; another would respond in a consistently mild way. The results of the study led Birns to carry out a follow-up investigation with Marian Blank and Wagner H. Bridger (1966). In this study 30 two- and three-day-old babies were taken out of the nursery an hour before feeding time on the assumption that they would be in an irritable mood. Their irritability was further aroused by flicking the soles of their feet. At that point efforts were made to soothe them by offering a sweetened pacifier, sounding loud and soft continuous tones, gently rocking their bassinets, and immersing their feet in warm water.

The behavior of the babies was also observed when no attempts at soothing were made. Some infants were easily aroused to a high level of irritability and did not respond markedly to any of the attempts at soothing; others became only moderately irritated and were easily soothed. Furthermore, one soothing stimulus turned out to be as effective as any other.

Infants respond to soothing in consistent ways

The differences in sensitivity to stimulation and in soothability described by Birns appeared so soon after birth that the way the babies were handled is not likely to have caused these differences. Moreover, if infants were as sensitive to techniques of handling as Ribble suggests they would presumably alter their behavior in response to different stimuli. One would certainly expect that a pacifier (providing direct oral satisfaction) would arouse more of a reaction than placing an infant's foot in warm water. Yet the babies observed by Birns responded to a variety of stimuli in a consistent way. The results of these studies therefore lend support to the conclusion that some babies have an innate tendency to accept or resist mothering.

Impact of Baby's Behavior on the Mother   In summing up the conclusions of her second study, Birns states:

One need only observe a few infants to become aware of the different feelings evoked by a "baby who cries no matter how hard you try to calm him" and one who quiets within moments of soothing. The baby's behavior thus may affect the mother's feelings toward him. In addition, the mother-child relationship may be influenced by how effectively the mother responds to her child's individual predispositions. (1966, p. 321)

Behavior of baby may influence mother's reactions

Rudolph Schaffer and Peggy Emerson (1964) carried out another frequently mentioned study supporting the view that inborn differences in infants may influence maternal behavior as much as mothering techniques may influence the child. They studied two groups of one- to two-year-old children. One group responded favorably to being cuddled by their mothers; the other group reacted negatively. The researchers were unable to detect any consistent differences in the way the cuddlers and noncuddlers had been handled by their mothers. They did discover, however, a distinctive cluster of traits for each type. Cuddlers were quiet and inactive, slept more, and liked soft playthings. Noncuddlers were restless and wakeful, stood and walked earlier, and disliked being confined in any way. The extent to which each type had these traits, together with lack of evidence that they had been produced by any identifiable child-rearing practices, suggests that the tendency to respond positively or negatively to cuddling may be due to innate factors.

The Significance of Individuality

In the 1930s individuality in infant behavior was reported by Mary Shirley (1933) and Arnold Gesell (1937) after they had made intensive observations of several infants. Both of these theorists concluded that such differences were due to inherited predispositions. Nevertheless, interpretations of Freudian theory (such as Ribble's *The Rights of Infants*) and the emergence of learning theory led many psychologists in the following decades to emphasize the impact of parental behavior on child behavior and to minimize the significance of the impact of the child's behavior on the parents. Recently, some of the problems the parent-as-shaper view may cause have been called to the attention of scientists and parents.

Are Consistent Personality Differences Apparent in Neonates?   In *Behavioral Individuality in Early Childhood* (1963), Alexander Thomas and several colleagues point out that the American emphasis on experience and the psychoanalytic view of development both stress an environmental view of the determination of personality. Concluding that this view is one-sided because it fails to take into account the child's own characteristics, Thomas and his associates decided to carry out a longitudinal study to discover the extent to which personality differences appear at birth and how stable such differences are during the span of development. They reasoned that if clear-cut differences were apparent at birth and if these personality tendencies seemed constant over a period of years, a reasonable conclusion would be that such tendencies were influenced to a considerable extent by inherited predispositions.

   To test this hypothesis, Thomas and his colleagues selected 130 infants and asked their parents to describe how the babies behaved in specific situations. These descriptions were then analyzed with regard to such qualities as rhythmicity, adaptability, intensity, persistence, and distractability. *Behavioral Individuality in Early Childhood* describes the results of the investigation up to the time the children were two years old. At that stage of their research they concluded "Each child has an individual pattern of primary reactivity, identifiable in early infancy and persistent throughout later periods of life" (p. 84). The authors point out that this implies all infants will not respond in the same way to particular child-rearing practices.

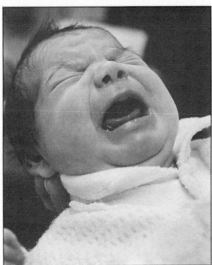
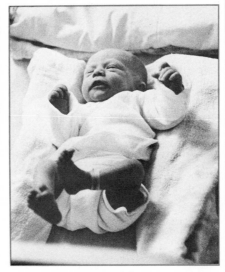

Newborn infants display wide differences in behavior. It is possible that distinctive patterns of neonatal behavior are produced by experiences during the prenatal period and at the time of birth. Another explanation is that each infant's behavior pattern arises primarily from inherited predispositions. Chuck Isaacs; Hanna Schreiber/Rapho Photo Researchers; © Michael Philip Manheim 1969.

Does Neonatal Behavior Influence Parental Behavior?   Thomas and his associates point out that most children appear to be quite adaptable, which is one explanation for the ability of different generations of infants to survive some of the diametrically opposed infant-care techniques advocated in the last fifty years. They hasten to add, however, that there have always been infants who have not responded positively to whatever regime has been popular, and parents of such children should adapt their approaches to the child rather than attempt to force the "atypical" baby to conform. They also stress the same point made by Birns: their observations convince them that a baby's primary reaction pattern is likely to influence the attitudes and reactions of his parents, especially when the baby asserts individuality right from the moment of birth. Thomas and his associates concluded their report with this statement, which many parents may find reassuring:

> The knowledge that certain characteristics of their child's development are not primarily due to parental malfunctioning has proven helpful to many parents. Mothers of problem children often develop guilt feelings because they assume that they are solely responsible for their children's emotional difficulties. This feeling of guilt may be accompanied by anxiety, defensiveness, increased pressures on the children, and even hostility toward them for "exposing" the mother's inadequacy by their disturbed behavior. When parents learn that their role in the shaping of their child is not an omnipotent one, guilt feelings may lessen, hostility and pressures may tend to disappear, and positive restructuring of the parent-child interaction can become possible. (p. 94)

Realizing some infant behavior is innate could lessen guilt

Birns and Thomas and his colleagues emphasize that an infant may influence the parents as much as they influence the infant. If attempts at soothing an irritable neonate are not successful, or if a child reacts negatively to cuddling, originally confident parents may begin to feel anxious and apprehensive about their skill at handling the baby. If they resort to a variety of methods recommended by different authorities, none of which brings about an improvement, they may despair and panic. Thomas and his colleagues suggest that parents consider the possibility that the behavior of the child is due to inborn temperament and adjust their infant-care techniques to the personality of the child. (A policy that was advocated by Aristotle before the birth of Christ and by Rousseau in 1760.)

Adapting Child-rearing Techniques to Temperament

In 1970, fourteen years after the start of the study reported in *Behavioral Individuality in Early Childhood*, Thomas, Chess, and Birch provided a follow-up report. In the years between the earlier book and the 1970 report, the researchers continued to acquire information about their subjects and how they reacted to child-rearing techniques used by parents. After analyzing the accumulated data, Thomas, Chess, and Birch concluded: "Our long-term study has now established that the original characteristics of temperament tend to persist in most children over the years" (1970, p. 104). They qualify this statement by noting: "Of course a child's temperament is not immutable. In the course of his development the

Table 5–1
Types of Child Temperament and Effective Child-Rearing Techniques

TYPE OF TEMPERAMENT	CHARACTERISTICS OF CHILDREN	EFFECTIVE CHILD-REARING TECHNIQUES
Easy (found in 40 percent of sample)	Positive mood, regularity in bodily functions, moderate reaction tendencies, adaptable, positive approach to new situations	Many different approaches will bring about a favorable response. Main danger is to avoid having children become used to only one approach. Prepare children for variety of reactions from others (for example, teachers).
Difficult (found in 10 percent of sample)	Negative mood, irregularity in bodily functions, intense reaction tendencies, slow to adapt, withdrawal from new situations.	Treat children objectively, patiently, nonpunitively, consistently. Essential requirement for parents is to recognize need for unusually painstaking handling.
Slow to warm up (found in 15 percent of sample)	Somewhat negative in mood, low intensity of reaction, slow to adapt, likely to withdraw from new situations.	Allow children to adapt to environment at own pace, but when children show interest in new activity, encourage them to try it.

Source: Based on research carried out by Alexander Thomas, Stella Chess, and Herbert G. Birch reported in "The Origin of Personality," *Scientific American,* 1970, **223:** 102–109.

environmental circumstances may heighten, diminish or otherwise modify his reactions and behavior" (p. 104). They also point out that "not all children in our study have shown a basic constancy of temperament" (p. 105) and suggest that *inconsistency* of temperament may be a basic characteristic of some children. (Essentially the same conclusions are reaffirmed by Thomas and Chess in a still later follow-up report, *Temperament and Development* [1977].)

While some of their subjects were unpredictable and some did not fit patterns shared with others, Thomas, Chess, and Birch concluded that most children they observed manifested one of three clusters of traits. Each of these types seemed to respond favorably to certain child-rearing techniques. A summary of the types of temperament and general child-rearing techniques appropriate to each is presented in Table 5–1.

The Concept of Reproductive Risk

Thomas and his colleagues divided their subjects into three general categories. Other psychologists and pediatricians have devised neonatal assessment scales to make it possible to make detailed evaluations of infant behavior. One of the most highly regarded of these is the Brazelton Neonatal Behavioral Assessment Scale (BNBAS) developed by T. Berry Brazelton (1973). A trained observer rates a neonate on factors such as neurological intactness, interactive capacities, social attractiveness, and need for stimulation. The Brazelton Scale has proven to be effective in identifying children who are rated high in terms of what is often referred to as a *continuum of reproductive casualty* or *reproductive risk.* These terms call attention to the tendency for certain types of complications occurring during the prenatal period and at birth to cause problems later in development. The Brazelton Scale was devised to identify children who seem likely to experience difficulties because of abnormalities that take place during the reproductive process.

In an analysis of reproductive risk Arnold Sameroff and Michael Chandler (1975) conclude that four factors are frequently mentioned as likely to lead to later disorders in development: anoxia (oxygen deficiency), prematurity, newborn status, and socioeconomic influences. They reviewed studies of the later behavior and adjustment of children who were judged to be high in reproductive risk due to the influence of the first three factors and concluded that the effects of anoxia, prematurity, and low ratings on neonatal assessment scales often were overcome—provided the children were reared in middle- or upper-income homes by parents who did not manifest high levels of anxiety. Children who were reared in disadvantaged environments, or by parents of any economic level who were rated high in anxiety, were much less likely to overcome early handicaps. (Sameroff and Chandler note that there is evidence that many children of high-anxiety parents contributed to the insecurity of the parents because they were difficult to care for.)

Reproductive risk high in disadvantaged homes, when parents are anxious

Sameroff and Chandler support the hypothesis originally proposed by Waddington (1966) that humans come equipped with self-righting tendencies. They conclude, however, that these self-righting tendencies are most likely to produce a positive effect when the child is reared in a favorable physical and psychological environment. If the environment is poor and/or if the parents are unable to provide confident care, the child may be unable to overcome early handicaps. If a child has characteristics of the difficult children described by Thomas and his associates, though, even upper-class parents with good intentions may lose confidence in their abilities to provide satisfactory care.

The studies of Birns and of Thomas, Chess, and Birch, as well as analyses of reproductive risk, call attention to the significance of early child-parent relationships. In Chapter 3, speculations by leading theorists were described, and a summary of points they considered to be of importance at different age levels was provided (Table 3–3). The sections of this summary that relate to neonates were repeated on the opening page of this Part of the text. Points stressed by each theorist reveal different facets of the first relationship between parents and their newborn child.

Initial Child-Parent Relationship

Freud: The Importance of Feeding

The neonate is at the oral stage of psychosexual development. It is difficult to argue with Freud's observation that a newborn baby gains many kinds of satisfaction from sucking. The biological need for food must be satisfied and infants must suck to obtain food. Since sucking leads to the reduction of hunger, it is an activity which the infant is eager to repeat. Furthermore, sucking is the first coordinated activity that comes under the infant's control. At first, sucking is a reflex activity, but before the end of the first month infants are able to control sucking movements (as indicated by the operant conditioning experiments described earlier in this chapter). Thus, babies satisfy physiological needs and learn how to control their own behavior by using mouth and lip movements. Freud is certainly correct, then, in maintaining that humans begin life with an oral orientation.

The impact of early sucking experiences on personality development is more difficult to evaluate, however, particularly when Freud's concept of libidinal energy is taken into account. Freud suggested that libidinal energy might become fixated, and Ribble argued that a baby's initial experiences with feeding give personality its original slant. Before you draw any conclusions about Ribble's hypothesis, examine the analyses of first experiences to be presented in the remainder of this section, particularly in the review of observations by Piaget and Sears. (In addition, you should read about research relating to the impact of breast and bottle feeding that will be summarized in Chapter 7.)

Erikson: The Significance of Trust

The first stage in Erikson's description of psychosocial development is *trust versus mistrust.* Erikson suggests that the basic psychological attitude to be learned by infants is that they can trust their world. He notes (1963) "The . . . sense of trust . . . implies not only that one has learned to rely on sameness and continuity of the outer providers, but also that one may trust one's self and the capacity of one's own organs to cope with urges" (p. 248). Erikson then comments on the nature of the parent-child relationship: "The amount of trust derived from earliest infantile experience does not seem to depend on absolute quantities of food or demonstrations of love, but rather on the quality of the maternal relationship" (p. 249). (The exact nature of this quality is difficult to describe but sensitivity and confidence appear to be basic components.)

Encouraging a sense of trust (Erikson)

Erikson suggests that if the parents establish a relationship of trust and tenderness, the infant will respond positively. If the parents are anxious, insecure, or hostile, mistrust and negative feelings may be produced. If you are impressed by the observations of Erikson, you may be wondering how parents should behave in accordance with them. Consider the case, once again, of a child who is difficult to soothe from the moment of birth. If parents attribute behavior primarily to experiences, they may become anxious—and communicate their anxiety to the child. If parents consider the possibility of inherited predispositions, on the other hand, they may not be so inclined to blame themselves for certain types of infant behavior. They may have to work harder at being confident and tender with an active and independent neonate than with a baby born placid and responsive, but acceptance of the existence of a unique personality in the newborn child may help them maintain their trust in themselves, which will be communicated to the child.

Piaget: Formation of First Schemes

The first cognitive concept formed by many infants is probably a scheme for sucking. Even as a newborn baby engages in reflexive sucking for the first time, sensory and motor impressions are combined. In time, the baby establishes a scheme for sucking. The initial scheme is modified, however, as the baby engages in different kinds of sucking activities. If the baby's thumb comes into contact with the mouth, for example, the tendency to accommodate will cause the infant to revise the original scheme which was established when a nipple was sucked. The Piagetian principle of accommodation might be used in evaluating Ribble's argument that initial experiences are of critical importance. Ribble maintains, in effect, that an infant's original set of ideas about feeding will remain unaltered and will influence later behavior. If the tendency for humans to accommodate is taken into account, however, it might be expected that the baby will continually revise schemes that center on sucking and feeding.

Accommodation and the revision of sucking schemes

Suppose, for example, that a new mother suffers from the physical and emotional letdown many women experience just after giving birth (often referred to as the *postpartum blues,* described in Yalom, 1968). She wants to breastfeed her baby, but does not feel very enthusiastic about it or satisfied with the way she handles the feeding. She also has the impression that the baby is tense and incompletely satisfied during initial feeding sessions. An extreme psychoanalytic interpretation might lead to the expectation that such less than satisfying initial feeding experiences will have a permanent negative impact on the child's behavior later in life. A Piagetian interpretation might lead to the expectation that subsequent positive experiences (when the mother is less depressed and more skillful) are likely to cause the baby to modify original impressions of feeding.

Sears: Infant Care Techniques Shape Initial Responses

Learning theorists such as Sears have concentrated on ways infants learn to associate certain types of parental behavior with satisfaction of biological needs. When neonates obtain food, for example, they will build up associations between

Social-learning theorists such as Robert R. Sears trace attachment behavior to associations built up during the first months of life. John Bowlby hypothesizes that in the course of evolution particular members of our species survived because mother and infant both had tendencies to be close to each other. Patricia Hollander Gross/Stock, Boston.

the satisfaction of hunger and the way they are handled by the parents. Some learning theorists (for example, Gewirtz, 1961, 1972; Bijou and Baer, 1965) feel that even idiosyncratic differences in ways infants respond to their mothers can be explained in terms of learning-theory principles. They reason that a mother who cuddles her baby when she feeds will shape cuddling behavior; a mother who smiles as she feeds her baby but does not establish close physical contact will cause her child to become responsive to indirect rather than physical signs of affection.

It seems clear that the way a baby is handled will influence behavior. The extent to which initial learned associations will be retained is less clear. One of the basic principles of learning theory is reinforcement, which means that most types of behavior are learned only after they have repeatedly led to satisfaction of some kind. It might be reasoned, therefore, that the types of reactions that a young child learns will be those that are built up through associations that are repeated over a period of time. If that is the case, it would be logical to expect that experiences throughout infancy, not just those during the first months of life, will shape responses.

Only repeatedly reinforced behavior likely to be retained

Early learning theorists tended to concentrate exclusively on ways parents shape infant behavior. As evidence has accumulated supporting the view that newborn infants are not merely passive recipients of stimuli but active organisms capable of self-initiated behavior, many theorists (whose work is summarized in

Lewis and Rosenblum, 1974; Bell and Harper, 1977) have joined Birns and Thomas in calling attention to ways infants shape their parents. A theorist who has been particularly interested in the reciprocal nature of early parent-child relationships is the British psychologist John Bowlby. He offers an explanation for individual differences in infant and parent behavior that is not based on either libidinal energy or learning through association of stimuli and responses.

Bowlby: Evolutionary Explanation of Attachment

Bowlby (1969) suggests that the word *dependency* (which was used by early psychoanalysts and learning theorists) has a negative connotation and that it refers primarily to the extent to which one individual relies on another for satisfaction of needs. While this is certainly one aspect of early infant-parent relationships, Bowlby feels that *attachment*—where the infant actively seeks to be close to the parents—is more important since attachment involves reciprocal interaction. Bowlby explains his view of the development of attachment in *Attachment* (Volume 1 of *Attachment and Loss* [1969]). In the preface, he explains how he was stimulated to do research which eventually led to the book when he was asked by the World Health Organization to summarize research on the impact of institutionalization on children. He concluded that an essential aspect of human development is that "the infant and young child should experience a warm, intimate, and continuous relationship with his mother (or permanent mother substitute) in which both find satisfaction and enjoyment" (1969, pp. xi–xii). This is the same basic point emphasized by Ribble and Erikson; and Bowlby acknowledges that many of his conclusions are in harmony with Freudian theory. He differs from Freud, however, in his explanation of how attachment behavior develops. Freud proposed that an infant becomes attached to the mother when she becomes the first external object to which libidinal energy is directed.

Evolutionary explanation for attachment (Bowlby)

Bowlby bases his explanation of attachment behavior on Darwin's theory of evolution. He proposes that in the course of evolution particular members of our species survived because mother and infant both possessed innate tendencies to be close to each other. These tendencies included such infant behavior as crying, smiling, and clinging, which elicited caretaking responses in the mother. Bowlby hypothesizes that during the long period of history when human beings lived in small nomadic groups infants born with tendencies that aroused a caretaker response were most likely to survive. Babies who did not evoke caretaker responses were more likely to die because of lack of adequate care or protection from predators.

Bowlby acknowledges the findings of Birns, Schaffer and Emerson, and Thomas and his associates regarding differences in the degree to which infants engage in types of behavior likely to arouse a maternal response. He also suggests that the infant's attachment behavior will become progressively weaker if the caretaker does not adequately respond. One explanation for the wide differences in infant attachment behavior is that some babies inherit weaker tendencies to smile, vocalize, and seek attention and cuddling than others. During the nomadic period of human history some infants who inherited few attachment tendencies survived apparently because their mothers happened to possess compensatingly strong maternal tendencies. Another explanation for differences in the degree of attachment (to be discussed in Chapter 7) is that conditions and experiences immediately after the birth of a child may strengthen or weaken the mother's attitudes toward the infant. Finally, Bowlby's explanation for attachment helps explain why at least some parents have always reacted positively to infants, even during periods of history when infanticide and abandonment were common. In Chapter 1 the often callous attitudes toward children that were typical up to the eighteenth century were outlined. The point was also made that some parents during these periods of history must have reacted positively to their children or the human race would not have survived nor would more humane attitudes toward child rearing have emerged. Bowlby's evolutionary explanation of attachment can be used to account for atypical sensitivity even during periods when the prevailing attitude toward children varied from cruelty to indifference.

While attachment behavior is initially manifested during the first month of interaction between infant and parents, reciprocal relationships become clearer over more extended periods of time. Before drawing any conclusions about the various theories of attachment behavior or the significance of early parent-child interactions, therefore, it is desirable to consider the nature of development during the first two years and to examine evidence regarding the impact of child care during this period. These topics will be discussed in the next two chapters.

Suggestions for Further Study

Characteristics and Behavior of the Neonate

For more complete information on the neonate, an excellent source regarding studies done before 1950 is "The Neonate," by Karl C. Pratt, Chapter 4 in *The Manual of Child Psychology* (2nd ed., 1954), edited by Leonard Carmichael. For more recent research examine Chapter 3 of *The Competent Infant* (1973), edited by L. Joseph Stone, Henrietta T. Smith, and Lois B. Murphy. Chapter 3 of *The Competent Infant* consists of excerpts from thirty-five recent studies of the neonate. Other sources to consult for similar information are *Behavior in Infancy and Early Childhood* (1967), edited by Yvonne Brackbill and George G. Thompson; and *Infancy and Early Childhood: A Handbook and Guide to Early Development* (1967), edited by Yvonne Brackbill. The first book is a collection of sixty-three articles by different psychologists; the second consists of eight chapters in which research in a specific area is reviewed by one or more authorities. Many of the articles and sections of the reviews summarize information on the neonate. Still another excellent reference is *Carmichael's Manual of Child Psychology* (3rd ed., 1970), edited by Paul H. Mussen. No specific chapter is devoted to the neonate (as was the case with the second edition, in which Pratt's account appears), but you can find information on behavior during the first month of life by examining appropriate sections of chapters devoted to specific types of behavior. For reviews of research up to the late 1970s consult *Handbook of Infant Development* (1979) edited by Joy D. Osofsky.

Ribble's The Rights of Infants

Margaret Ribble's *The Rights of Infants* was purchased by an impressive number of mothers when it was first published in 1943 and it still attracts readers. If you would like to read her psychoanalytic interpretation of infant development, sample sections of Chapter 1 ("The Right to Mother"), in which she argues that "the experiences of infancy determine in no small way the evolution of individual personality" (p. 3), Chapter 3 ("Sucking"), in which she emphasizes the vital importance of breast feeding (pp. 31–34), Chapter 4 ("Learning to Feel"), where the importance of rhythmic movement is stressed (pp. 38–39), or Chapter 9 ("Babies Must Not Be Thwarted").

Infant Perception

Infant Perception: From Sensation to Cognition (1975), edited by Leslie B. Cohen and Philip Salapatek, reviews thousands of studies of all aspects of perception in infants. Volume I covers basic visual processes, Volume II describes studies in the perception of space, speech, and sound. A briefer analysis of early perceptual development is provided by T. G. R. Bower in *The Perceptual World of the Child* (1977).

The Social Nature of the Neonate

T. G. R. Bower summarizes evidence to back up his contentions that neonates realize they are human and that they are social creatures in *A Primer of Infant Development* (1977). He also discusses other aspects of early development in this readable and interesting book.

"Average," "Quiet," and "Active" Infants

In *Infants and Mothers: Differences in Development* (1969), T. Berry Brazelton, a pediatrician and professor at the Harvard Medical School, makes the point that all babies are different by describing the month-by-month development during the first year of "average," "quiet," and "active" infants. He describes not only the behavior of the babies but also the reactions of their parents. In the process, he explains many aspects of development and child care that are of concern to parents. The three types of babies are described as actual infants (even though they are hypothetical composites), and their behavior and the actions and thoughts of their parents are presented. This makes it possible for the reader to identify with the parents and share their fears and triumphs as they cope with and enjoy the development of their children. Comments by Brazelton are inserted as if the parents had turned to an ever present physician whenever a problem or question developed. As you read, you therefore learn about general trends in development, the wide range of differences in the behavior of normal babies, the degree to which an infant's personality influences the parents, and also pick up bits of wisdom and advice from a pediatrician with twenty-five years of experience helping parents and babies to understand each other.

Behavioral Individuality in Early Childhood

In *Infants and Mothers,* Brazelton describes how differences in infant behavior bring about varying reactions from parents by presenting composite case histories based on impressions gained during twenty-five years of medical practice. The same point—that every infant is unique—is made with reference to controlled research in *Behavioral Individuality in Early Childhood* (1963) by Alexander Thomas et al. This book is an account of a study where 130 infants were intensively observed for the first few years of their lives to determine the extent to which initial biological characteristics determined their individuality. The results provide evidence that newborn infants display characteristics that not only vary to a considerable extent but are also quite stable during the first two years of life. The authors suggest that this means efforts to find a single set of ideal child-rearing guidelines may be ill advised. The research is described in Chapters 1 through 6, theoretical and practical implications are presented in Chapters 7 and 8. The follow-up study by Thomas, Chess, and Birch, which includes recommendations for dealing with three types of children, can be found on pages 102–109 of *Scientific American,* 1970, **223**, no. 2. A summary and analysis of their own and related research on child-parent interactions is presented by Thomas and Chess in *Temperament and Development* (1977).

Attachment and Dependency

For more information about theories accounting for the development of attachment and dependency, you can consult the concise summary of major research and theories on this question in "Attachment and Dependency" by Eleanor E. Maccoby and John C. Masters, Chapter 21 in Volume 2 of *Carmichael's Manual of Child Psychology* (3rd ed., 1970), edited by Paul H. Mussen. *Attachment and Dependency* (1972), edited by Jacob L. Gewirtz, is made up of papers by American psychologists who have made significant contributions to the study of these two phenomena: Robert R. Sears, Robert B. Cairns, Leon J. Yarrow, Mary D. S. Ainsworth, and Gewirtz. The most completely developed single theory of the development of attachment is that of the English psychologist John Bowlby. He explains how he came to develop his evolutionary view and presents evidence to support it in *Attachment,* Volume I of *Attachment and Loss* (1969). To gain familiarity with Bowlby's theory, read the preface and Chapter 1, in which he explains his basic point of view, and sample sections of Chapters 11 through 17 for details of his conception of how attachment behavior develops.

Ethology and Developmental Psychology

Ethology is defined in dictionaries as the study of animal behavior. As a result of studies by naturalists such as Konrad Lorenz and psychologists such as John Bowlby, however, the term is now frequently used to refer to analyses of adaptive behavior (such as imprinting and the development of attachment behavior). For a more complete understanding of the ethological view of development read "Ethology and Developmental Psychology" by Eckhard H. Hess, Chapter 1 of *Carmichael's Manual of Child Psychology* (3rd ed., 1970), edited by Paul H. Mussen. Hess outlines basic concepts of ethology which has as its major premise "the notion that the study of behavior begins through the compilation of as complete an inventory as possible of all the behaviors of the organism in, and in relation to, its natural environment, throughout its entire life cycle" (1970, p. 2). He explains how the ethological approach first developed from the work of zoologists who studied the natural behavior of animals and later came to be used by psychologists who were dissatisfied with learning-theory interpretations that minimized the possibility of innate behavior. The bulk of the chapter is devoted to a review of significant studies by ethologists.

Observing the Behavior of a Neonate

If you have the opportunity to observe a neonate (perhaps your own, perhaps the newborn child of a relative or friend), you might find it of interest to make observations and records of the following types of behavior:

☐ Smiles—Make a sound (perhaps by humming or whistling softly) when the baby is in a drowsy state. Then, count "One thousand and one, one thousand and two," and so on for up to ten seconds to see if a smile appears. (Wolff found that many neonates he observed smiled seven seconds after hearing such a stimulus.) Watch for *social* smiles (in response to a familiar face) around the third week. Look for eye-to-eye contact in conjunction with smiles around the fourth week.

☐ Cries—See if you can identify the following types of cries during the first month. (If you have the opportunity, you might keep a record of the number of each type of cry you observe and how long each lasts every time it is noted.)

Rhythmical—regular pattern (often associated with hunger).

Mad—rhythmical but energetic.

Pain—a shriek, followed by a few seconds of silence as the breath is recovered, followed by extremely energetic crying.

Fake—sobs that do not seem to be stimulated by any particular condition (except perhaps the desire to arouse a response from others)

☐ Responses to faces and voices—Place your face close to the baby's face and stick out your tongue, open and close your mouth, and flutter your eyelashes. Observe the neonate closely to see if any effort is made to imitate your actions.

☐ Interactional Synchrony—Talk to the baby in a rhythmical way (perhaps by reciting a nursery rhyme with emphasis on the rhythm). Watch the baby closely to see if interactional synchrony is exhibited by making head and body movements in time with your utterances.

☐ Reactions to the Mother's Voice and Face—Have the mother talk to the baby from a position where she cannot be seen, than have a stranger do the same. Observe the infant to see if the mother's voice arouses more of a response than the stranger's. (If possible, carry out several trials with the mother and stranger taking turns talking first.) Have the mother and a stranger individually stand within the baby's line of vision. Keep a record of the amount of time the baby watches each face.

☐ Reciprocal shaping—Closely observe all interactions between the baby and either of the parents. Record interactions where one individual's behavior seems to shape the behavior of the other member of the pair. (If the baby emits a fake cry, for example, and stops when the mother or father picks up and cuddles the infant, you might conclude that the infant is shaping parental behavior.)

PART THREE

THE FIRST TWO YEARS

This part consists of two chapters: Chapter 6, "The First Two Years: Physical and Cognitive Development"; and Chapter 7, "The First Two Years: Child-Parent Relationships."

Theorists whose work is summarized in Chapter 3 consider the following types of behavior and relationships with others to be of significance during the first two years:

□ Freud: Oral stage. Mouth is center of satisfaction. The way an infant is fed may influence later behavior. Libidinal energy attached to mother due to anaclitic identification. Beginning of anal stage. Concern about toilet training.

□ Erikson: Trust versus mistrust. Autonomy versus doubt. Parents should encourage a sense of trust by providing consistent, supportive, care. Children should be allowed to try skills.

□ Piaget: Sensorimotor stage. Development of schemes primarily through sense and motor activities.

□ Sears: Phase I. Infant seeks to reduce biological drives and learns that certain types of behavior bring about certain responses. Infant care techniques used by parents shape initial responses of child.

KEY POINTS

Growth and Motor Development

Target-seeking tendency: child deprived of food later catches up

Cephalocaudal growth: from head to tail

Proximodistal growth: from inside to outside

Sequence of motor development: head, arms, hands, legs

Perceptual Development

Dishabituation: attention to new stimulus

Dishabituation reveals maturation of cortex

Procedure of visual cliff experiment

Infants decline to venture over visual cliff

Maturation and Learning

Early development controlled by maturation (Gesell)

Maturation makes learning possible (Dennis)

One-year-olds can learn many skills (if maturation has taken place)

More mature children learn more rapidly

Current emphasis: respond to behavior initiated by child

Early Language Development

More attention, less crying in infants

Functions of language

Vocal contagion: child vocalizes with parent

Mutual imitation: parent and child repeat sounds initially made by child

First word: child emits sound, is reinforced, builds association

Holophrastic speech: one-word communications

Telegraphic speech: nonessential words omitted

Pivot words: all-purpose words

Deep structure and surface structure: actual and apparent meaning

Piaget: Stages of the Sensorimotor Period

Formation of primitive schemes

Primary circular reaction: satisfying bodily activity repeated

Functional assimilation: tendency to use a capability

Object concept: object exists even when not perceived

Secondary circular reaction: intentional duplication of activity involving an object

Interrupted actions continued; part sensed as whole

Coordinated schemes: separate skills combined to achieve goal

Tertiary circular reactions: exploration; interest in novelty

Final stage: thought replaces activity; delayed imitation

CHAPTER ▫6

THE FIRST TWO YEARS:

PHYSICAL AND COGNITIVE DEVELOPMENT

During the first four weeks of their lives infants are capable of responding to their world and their caretakers in a variety of ways. While the capabilities of one- to four-week-old babies are much greater than earlier psychologists supposed, neonates are unable to produce more than a few simple responses on their own and must be cared for by others. Before their second birthdays, however, normal children will have learned how to walk and talk, two skills that lead to an extremely important shift in the nature of their existence. Children who can move about on their own, engage in verbal interchanges with others, and use words as a basis for formulating conceptions of objects and experiences are now independent individuals. Because there is reason to believe that a child's earliest experiences with others will substantially influence the kind of independent personality he or she will become, there has been a great deal of speculation about the significance of early child care. In the two chapters that make up this part, the key aspects of development just noted will be discussed. In this chapter, early motor, perceptual, language, and cognitive development will be analyzed. In the next chapter, varying views on the nature, significance, and impact of caretaker-child interactions during the first two years will be summarized.

Growth and Motor Development

Factors That Influence Growth

The anatomical and neurological changes during the first two years in the life of a child are considerable and varied. The average infant, who weighed a bit more than seven pounds and was twenty inches long at birth, weighs about twenty pounds and is approximately thirty inches tall at the age of one year. After the first year, average weights and heights do not supply very helpful information about growth because of several factors. At most age levels, boys, on the average, are heavier and taller than girls; but girls, on the average, mature at a more rapid rate. (It has been estimated [Garai and Scheinfeld, 1968] that in terms of maturity, the newborn girl is equivalent to a four- to six-week-old boy.) Because of genetic and prenatal influences, some children will be taller and heavier than others, some will be shorter and lighter, some will be slow or rapid maturers. Genetic factors also have much to do with body build, but extremely good or poor nutrition may have an impact on weight and sometimes height (Greulich, 1957). Improved nutrition, along with better health practices and living conditions, probably accounts for the progressive increase in size of American and some European children during the last one hundred years (Malina, 1979). This is known as the *secular trend*,[1] and although it is still continuing in many countries, it appears to be leveling off in developed societies, such as the United States, England, and Japan (Roche, 1979).

The Impact of Emotional Factors on Growth   There is also a possibility that emotional factors may influence growth. Elsie M. Widdowson (1951) discovered this when she decided to study what would happen if orphanage children who were on a diet that provided only 80 percent of needed calories were given extra amounts of bread, jam, and sugar. Children in one orphanage were given the supplemented diet for six months; those in another were not When she compared records at the end of the experiment, Widdowson was startled to find that the children on the extra-calorie diet had gained *less* weight than those in the control group. When she searched for an explanation, she discovered that a supervisor who was an extremely strict disciplinarian had taken over the enriched-diet orphanage the same day the experiment began. The children were severely and publicly rebuked for even minor offenses at mealtime. Widdowson concluded that even though more nutritious food was available, the

---

[1] Here *secular* refers to a trend that lasts from century to century or extends over a period of time.

Continuing tensions at the dinner table may affect a child's growth in height or weight. © Michael Philip Manheim.

children did not eat much of it because they were tense and upset almost every time it was served.

A different type of situation where emotional upset may lead to slowing of growth occurs in children living in homes where family relationships are tense and hostile. Such a home environment may produce a condition called *deprivation dwarfism* (Powell, Brasel, and Blizzard, 1967; Gardner, 1972). Children in homes characterized by friction may eat and drink compulsively and become fat, but they may fail to gain in height, apparently because psychological stress leads to a "switching off" of the growth hormones (Tanner, 1970, p. 142). It is possible, then, that if parents habitually berate children at mealtime, or use the supper table as a battleground for airing grievances, or continually snipe at each other and their offspring, children may not achieve their genetic potential in height.

Nationality Differences in Rate of Maturation   The rate of maturation varies from one country and geographic area to another. M. Geber and R. F. A. Dean (1957) and F. Falkner and several associates (1958) found that African black infants are advanced in skeletal maturation, and a number of investigations (reviewed by Corwell, 1967, p. 166) have yielded data indicating that black children in Africa and the United States are also advanced in motor development for about the first two years. While the *average* European child lags behind African infants, some nationality groups are more precocious than others. C. B. Hindley and four other European researchers (1966) compared the age of walking of children from five cities. Children from Brussels and Stockholm started to walk a month earlier, on the average, than those from Paris, London, and Zurich. Such differences in rate of motor development might be attributed to differences in opportunities for exercise or amount of encouragement, to nutrition, or to genetic factors.

Gentically Controlled Individual Growth Patterns   There are wide variations in growth rates between children, therefore, but a quite consistent pattern of growth characterizes each individual child. The child who is a fast maturer of a particular body build, for example, will be consistent in rate and structure. In a study carried out in Britain, A. Merminod (1962) found that the height of two-year-olds (who are almost exactly half their adult height on the average) correlates approximately 70 percent with ultimate height. The extent of genetic control over growth is emphasized by what J. M. Tanner refers to as a *target-seeking tendency*:

Target-seeking tendency: child deprived of food later catches up

Children, no less than rockets, have their trajectories, governed by the control systems of their genetical constitution and powered by energy absorbed from the natural environment. Deflect the child from its growth trajectory by acute malnutrition or illness, and a restoring force develops so that as soon as the missing food is supplied or the illness terminated the child catches up toward its original curve. When it gets there, it slows down again to adjust its path onto the old trajectory once more. (Tanner, 1970, p. 125)

The tendency to return to an original growth curve after a short period of deflection has been referred to as *canalization* by C. H. Waddington (1957). The mechanism is not completely understood, but it appears that females are "better canalized" than males (Tanner, 1962, p. 127). That is, a girl who is subjected to poor nutrition or emotional stress is less likely to show a slowing of growth than a boy in the same situation. It is also clear that it is difficult for a child to make up for *extended* deprivation, particularly when it occurs early in life.

The pattern of growth for the body as a whole tends to be consistent, then, but it is also cyclical. For some reason yet to be understood, the rate of gain in height between March and August during a child's growth years is as much as two and one-half times as great as in the fall and winter months. On the other hand, two-thirds of the annual gain in weight takes place between September and February (Tanner and Taylor, 1969, p. 137). Not all parts of the body follow the same rate of growth, however. The brain completes 95 percent of its growth by the age of ten, for example, while the heart may not reach its ultimate size until after the age of twenty. At birth the head accounts for one-quarter of total length, the legs for one-fifth, but by the age of two the head accounts for less than a fifth, the legs for one-third of total height.

Principles of Developmental Direction

Even allowing for all of these variations, the overall growth of the body and nervous system follows a lawful pattern. Development proceeds from the head

Prehension. The ability to pick up small objects with the thumb and fingers occurs only after fine muscle control has developed. Ellen Lieberson.

region to the extremities, which is referred to as *cephalocaudal growth* (from the Latin *cephalus* meaning "head" and *cauda* meaning "tail"). It also proceeds, simultaneously, from the interior of the body to the exterior, which is referred to as *proximodistal growth* (from the Latin *proximus* meaning "nearest" and *distantia* meaning "remote").

Cephalocaudal growth: head to tail

Proximodistal growth: inside to outside

One of the clearest examples of these principles of growth is the development of *prehension,* which refers to the ability to pick up a small object (such as a small block) by using the thumb and fingers. H. M. Halverson (1931) made motion pictures of how young children sitting in a high chair responded when a block was placed in front of them. He found that if he placed the block in the palm of a two-month-old infant, the grasp reflex would be activated. Such reflexive grasping disappeared by the age of four months, as the cortex gained ascendancy over the lower brain. For the next two months or so the child was unable to do much more than brush the block back and forth in an uncoordinated way. Not until the age of seven months could the child actually grab the block in the palm with any degree of consistency or precision, and the ability to use fingers and thumb to pick up the block was not achieved until the ninth month. This sequence occurs because—in keeping with cephalocaudal and proximodistal development—the nerves and muscles nearest the head and spinal cord mature before those of the extremities of the body. Another way of expressing this principle is to say that large-muscle control precedes fine-muscle control. In picking up a block, a child learns to control the muscles involved in palming an object before achieving finger control.

Figure 6–1   Sequence of Mastery of Locomotor Behavior. *Source:* Mary M. Shirley, *The First Two Years*, Institute of Child Welfare Monograph No. 7, Minneapolis, University of Minnesota Press, Copyright 1933, renewed 1961 by the University of Minnesota.

The Development of Motor Skills

The most obvious and dramatic illustration of the nature of physical development is provided by the mastery of locomotor behavior. On the basis of an intensive study of children during their first two years, Mary Shirley (1933) described the sequence illustrated in Figure 6–1. As you can see, in keeping with the principles of developmental direction, the child first acquires the ability to hold up the head, then refines the use of arms and hands, and finally gains control of legs and feet.

Sequence of motor development: head, arms, hands, legs

When you examine the ages at which Shirley observed the locomotor activities depicted in Figure 6–1, you should take account of the fact that she was an objective observer watching each of her subjects for only a short period of time. Parents, who have almost constant contact with their young children and are

Table 6–1

Age Placement in Months for Items from the Bayley Infant Scale of Motor Development (with Comparison to Ages Reported by Shirley)

SKILL	AGE IN MONTHS	AGE REPORTED BY SHIRLEY
Lifts head at shoulder	0.1	0.1
Dorsal suspension—lifts head	1.7	2.0
Sits with support	2.7	4.0
Sits alone momentarily	5.4	6.0
Walks with help	9.9	11.0
Stands alone	11.3	14.0
Walks alone	11.8	15.0
Walks upstairs with help	18.7	
Walks upstairs alone, marks time	22.7	
Walks downstairs alone, marks time	22.9	
Ascending short steps, alternate feet, unsupported	31.0	
Descending short steps, alternate feet, unsupported	49.0	

Sources: Ages reported by Nancy Bayley: "Comparisons of Mental and Motor Test Scores for Ages 1–15 Months by Sex, Birth Order, Race, Geographical Location and Education of Parents," *Child Development,* 1965, **36:** 379–411. Ages reported by Mary M. Shirley: *The First Two Years,* Institute of Child Welfare Monograph No. 7, Minneapolis, University of Minnesota Press, © Copyright 1933, renewed 1961 by the University of Minnesota.

"rooting" for them to stand and walk as early as possible, are likely to encourage and arouse more effort than a dispassionate visitor. They also are likely to give credit for a good try and to be lenient in determining exactly when a particular skill is mastered. Consequently, if parents compare the motor performance of their child to the age levels described by Shirley, they may conclude that they have a remarkably precocious baby. It is preferable to concentrate on the *sequence* of skills depicted in Figure 6–1, rather than use the noted age levels for estimating rate of development. For that purpose, a test of infant development would be more appropriate.

On the basis of her initial observations of the sixty-one subjects of the Berkeley Growth Study, Nancy Bayley (1936) reported age placements for over one hundred motor skills on what was originally called the California Infant Scale of Motor Development. She later used this information to standardize the Bayley Infant Scale of Motor Development (1965, 1969) by testing nearly fifteen hundred infants. Table 6–1 depicts some items and age levels from this scale. (To facilitate comparison, the age levels for skills reported by Shirley are also supplied.) As you can see, the age levels described by Bayley are consistently earlier than those noted by Shirley, perhaps because Shirley recorded behavior only when it occurred during one of her observations, whereas Bayley arranged for the babies she studied to attempt all the skills on her scale.

The sequence of motor development described by Shirley and Bayley can be explained by taking into account the principles of cephalocaudal and proximo-distal growth. These principles also help explain aspects of perceptual develop-ment. The nerves and muscles that control the sense organs mature rapidly during the first few months of postnatal existence, equipping the infant with sensitive sight, hearing, and touch. Furthermore, the increasing ability of babies to handle objects makes it possible for them to add significant cues to their perceptions of people and things around them.

Perceptual Development

Responses to Visual Patterns

Changes in Visual Perception During the First Two Years In the twenty years since Robert Fantz developed the basic technique for recording visual responses of infants, hundreds of studies have been carried out to determine the kinds of patterns that young children prefer to look at as they mature. After reviewing his own research, as well as dozens of other studies carried out by others, Fantz, Fagan, and Miranda (1975) concluded that the difficulty neonates experience in concentrating on details of patterns (noted in the preceding chapter) is due to immaturities of the eye and nervous system. By the time they are two months of age, though, maturation of the eyes and brain, as well as practice using the eyes, equip babies to differentiate between distinctive features of a pattern. The acquisition of the ability to distinguish between details seems to predispose two- to five-month-old infants to respond to patterns that are made up of many elements, angles, and contours. At about the age of five months, a third phase in the development of visual perception takes place when infants show a preference for three-dimensional objects over two-dimensional pictures or photographs. Fantz hypothesizes that this preference is due to experiences with reaching, grasping, and manipulation of objects. It appears that once babies have handled something, they prefer to look at the real thing instead of a picture of it.

The kinds of differences Fantz found between the visual perception of one- and two-month-old infants were highlighted by research carried out and analyzed by Philip Salapatek (1975). Salapatek found that one- to four-week-old babies concentrate on a single feature of a pattern, usually at the edges of the design. Salapatek concluded that the visual scanning of neonates might be thought of as reflexive sensory discharge activated by peripheral parts of the stimulus pattern that stand out. By the end of the second month, however, and increas-

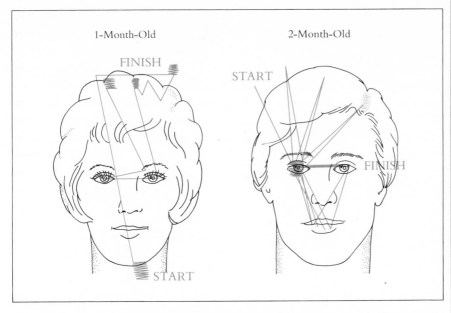

Figure 6–2   Schematic plots of visual scanning of a real head by 1- and 2-month old infants. The lines drawn over these representations of a human face record the eye movements made by 1- and 2-month old infants as they watched an adult who leaned over them. As you can see, the 1-month-old baby concentrated on the top and bottom edges of the head; the 2-month-old focused on internal features, particularly the eyes. *Source:* Philip Salapatek, "Pattern Perception in Early Infancy." In L. B. Cohen and Philip Salapatek, eds., *Infant Perception: From Sensation to Cognition,* Vol. 1, *Basic Visual Processes* (New York: Academic Press, 1975), p. 201.

ingly thereafter, infants reveal that they become intrigued by internal features of a pattern. These differences between the scanning behavior of one- and two-month-old babies will become clear if you examine Figure 6–2.

Changes in visual perception from four months to two years are illustrated by a study carried out by R. B. McCall and Jerome Kagan (1967). They exposed infants to a photograph of the face of a smiling man, a jumbled version of the same photograph (the mouth upside-down on the forehead, an eye in the chin, etc.); stylized, simplified line drawings of a face and a jumbled face; and also clay masks with all, few, and jumbled features. McCall and Kagan found that the duration of attention to these stimuli decreased from four to thirteen months but increased toward the end of the second year. They hypothesized that the child of twelve months or so had been exposed to many more stimuli than a three-month-old, and so the faces were not as intriguing to the one-year-old. They concluded that two-year-olds showed interest in the faces, particularly the distorted versions, because they had acquired language, which helped them analyze what they were looking at. Some two-year-olds, for example, asked about what had happened to the man whose mouth was placed upside-down in the forehead—had someone hit him or thrown a pie at him?

These studies indicate, then, that during the first two years children not only become capable of focusing their eyes more precisely, they also begin to interpret what they see.

Dishabituation: Familiarity Leads to Boredom   Studies of infants' responses to patterns also reveal an interesting aspect of habituation. When the subjects in the experiments just described became bored with looking at a particular pattern, they were showing that they had become habituated to it. When a different pattern was presented, their interest perked up. This transfer of interest from an old to a new stimulus is called *dishabituation*. It indicates that the infant has learned to differentiate clearly between patterns. Visual habituation seems to appear around the age of ten weeks, suggesting that the cerebral cortex takes that long to mature to the point where the infant can clearly remember visual patterns. (Up to that time, infants do not seem to get bored watching the same stimulus.) This assumption is based on the reasoning that in order for babies to get bored by an old stimulus and become excited about a new one, they have to have recorded a representation of the first pattern in their brains. Support for this hypothesis is supplied by a report of an infant born without a cortex (Brackbill, 1971) who failed to show dishabituation and by a study (Super, 1972) where one group of ten- to sixteen-week-old infants was shown a moving ball and another group was not. The next day, when both groups were shown the ball, those who had seen it the previous day became bored faster.

Dishabituation: attention to new stimulus

Dishabituation reveals maturation of cortex

Aspects of Depth Perception

The studies by Fantz and others indicate that as early as two months after birth an infant is able to perceive depth. An intriguing aspect of this capability was provided by the research of E. J. Gibson and R. R. Walk (1960), who devised what is called the "visual cliff" experiment.

The Visual Cliff Experiment   Gibson and Walk constructed a platform about four feet above the floor. On top of this platform they placed a sheet of heavy plate glass which extended on either side. On one side it covered a second platform which was the same height as the first; on the other, it extended over the floor. Six-month-old infants were placed on the center platform, and their mothers tried to persuade them to crawl toward them. When the mothers cajoled their children to crawl onto the platform of the same height, they happily complied. When the mothers attempted to entice their children to crawl over the glass several feet above the floor, however, the infants refused. Younger babies did crawl over the visual cliff, possibly because they were not mature enough to be able to focus their eyes on the floor. In a subsequent study, Walk (1966) found that babies were less likely to crawl over the glass when a highly visible checkerboard pattern was placed on the floor. When a grey pattern was substi-

Procedure of visual cliff experiment

Infants decline to venture over visual cliff

The visual cliff experiment. *Developmental Psychology Today,* First edition. Copyright © 1971 by Ziff-Davis Publishing Co. Reprinted by permission of CRM Books, a division of Random House, Inc.

tuted, which made perception of depth more difficult, many infants crawled across the glass. Babies were also more likely to go over the cliff when the pattern was raised to a few inches under the glass.

Is Depth Perception Innate?   The results of these studies led to speculation about the interplay of heredity and environment. Does depth perception develop as the result of experience, or is it an inborn tendency that emerges as the nervous system matures? Walk discovered, in his follow-up investigation, that children with more rapid locomotor development, and, therefore, with greater experience with falling, were less likely to crawl over the visual cliff. This might be interpreted as support for the hypothesis that the behavior is learned. On the other hand, since human infants are not able to crawl or focus their eyes too efficiently until they are several months old, finding out how they might respond to the visual cliff at birth—before they had acquired a backlog of experiences—is impossible. Chickens and goats, though, *are* capable of locomotor activity a and have well-developed visual acuity. When Gibson and Walk used animals as subjects, they declined to venture out over the cliff at a period ir lives (a few hours after birth) when they could not have had any experience with falling. This might be interpreted as support for the hypothesis that not only depth perception but also awareness of the danger of heights are built-in features of many organisms, including human infants. The innate fear hypothesis is supported by John Bowlby (1973) who suggests that avoidance of heights is an inborn tendency that favored survival during early stages of the evolution of human beings. Joseph J. Campos and several associates (1978) question Bowlby's explanation, however. Campos and his colleagues analyzed several visual cliff studies and concluded that, while human infants do perceive depth before they can locomote, they do not manifest a fear of height until some time after they can move around on their own.

The question of built-in versus acquired behavior has been debated for years. During some decades the hypothesis that certain forms of behavior are innate has attracted wide support. At other times the majority of psychologists have endorsed the blank-slate view and argued that almost all behavior is learned. A review of some of the classic studies of maturation and learning will reveal not only the nature of evidence and arguments on both sides of the question but also how support for opposing views has shifted.

Maturation and Learning

Psychologists of the 1930s who made the first carefully controlled observational studies of samples of children were impressed by the degree to which the behavior of the young child seemed to be dominated by built-in factors.

Gesell: Maturation Determines Early Behavior

Early development controlled by maturation (Gesell)

Arnold Gesell was the chief proponent of the maturational view in American psychology. His studies of infant and child behavior during the 1930s led him to conclude that early development was due almost entirely to maturation. Many other psychologists joined him in reacting against the extreme behaviorist-associationist-environmentalist position of John B. Watson. The focusing on maturation during this era might be accounted for by the fact that the investigators were studying infancy, a stage of development when physical and neurological growth is most rapid and dramatic, and by the discovery that Watson's boast about shaping behavior was based on an incompletely developed theory of learning. There is no denying he proved that he could condition a child to fear an animal, but Pavlovian principles could not explain many other forms of behavior.

Watson's extreme views on shaping behavior may have contributed to a counterreaction.

In any event, for a decade or so after Gesell published his most important book and Shirley reported her observations of development during the first two years, there was a great deal of emphasis on permitting development to *unfold*. A number of classic studies were carried out to discover if arranging experiences or providing training made any difference in the rate of development. Watson had argued that a child would develop properly only if the parents arranged experiences to produce behavior. A number of psychologists of the 1930s supported the hypothesis that a child would develop just as rapidly and satisfactorily during the first few years if parents simply allowed and encouraged maturation to take place.

Dennis: Maturation Makes Learning Possible

Wayne and Marsena Dennis thought of a way to test Gesell's hypothesis regarding the impact of maturation on early development. They heard of two Pueblo Indian tribes: one still used the traditional cradleboard; the other did not. They visited these tribes and concluded that in terms of diet, basic child-rearing practices, and similar factors, they were essentially identical. The only difference was that for the first nine months of their lives the children of one tribe spent almost all day on the cradleboard, which prevented them from exercising their limbs. Children in the other tribe were allowed complete freedom of movement. The Dennises simply noted the age that babies in each tribe started to walk. When they computed averages, they discovered that the cradleboard babies walked a day earlier than the noncradleboard babies (Dennis and Dennis, 1940).

The Dennises also carried out a study (1941) in which two girls whose mother was unable to care for them were reared under controlled conditions where stimulation was minimized. Up to the age of nine months the behavior of the girls was similar to that of infants growing up under normal conditions. The similarities were not only in motor activities but in smiling and laughter as well—despite the fact that the Dennises had neither smiled nor laughed in the presence of the girls. The first sign of retardation in development appeared when the girls were placed in sitting and standing positions. They were unable to match the performance of infants who were being given a substantial amount of handling and assistance by their parents. On the basis of their observations of the two girls (and their comparison of the Pueblo Indian tribes) the Dennises concluded that practically all the responses of the first year of life were self-generating, but the retardation in sitting and standing led them to suggest that learning also played an important part in locomotor development. They summed up both points in this statement: "While maturation is a major factor in infant development, its importance lies chiefly in making learning possible" (1951, p. 130).

Maturation makes learning possible (Dennis)

The Impact of Early and Later Training

McGraw's Study of Johnny and Jimmy   About the same time the Dennises were observing their twin girl subjects, Myrtle McGraw (1935) decided to analyze relationships between maturation and learning. She had read reports by Gesell in which he argued that maturation was so important during the first years of life that training and practice would make little difference. When Gesell published an article (Gesell and Thompson, 1929) in which he described how one of a pair of identical twins failed to learn locomotor skills any faster than his brother even when exposed to early training, McGraw accepted it as a challenge. She received permission from the parents of twin boys to use them as subjects in an elaborate experiment. The experiment began when the boys were less than a year old. At that time, doctors believed they were identical twins. A few months after the experiment was under way, however, it became apparent that they were *not* identical. Consequently, the results of the study were not as simple to interpret as they would have been if the boys had possessed identical genetic makeups.

The basic approach McGraw followed was to give one twin (Johnny) intensive practice in a number of skills early in life. When the other twin (Jimmy) was several months older, he was given similar training but he was more mature by then. The skills of the two boys were then compared immediately after training was completed and again after an interval of three or four years.

Starting at the age of two months, Johnny and Jimmy spent the hours from nine until five, five days a week, at a medical center. Johnny was given training by McGraw, Jimmy stayed in a crib or a playroom. It is apparent that McGraw wanted to test Gesell's hypotheses with a vengeance, because she taught Johnny how to roller skate and swim before he was a year old. As a matter of fact, by the age of sixteen months, Johnny was so expert on wheels he would skate through a tunnel from the building of the medical center where McGraw's experimental room was set up to another building which housed the swimming pool. Johnny was also given training in riding a tricycle, climbing, and jumping off pedestals (among other things).

While it took only a few weeks for McGraw to train Johnny to skate, swim, climb, and jump, it took almost ten months of training before he became proficient on a tricycle. At this point, he was twenty-two months old, which was the age Jimmy started training sessions. Jimmy learned how to manipulate a tricycle as well as Johnny after just a few weeks but did not become as proficient in skating, swimming, climbing, or jumping, even after months of training. In analyzing the causes of these differences, McGraw (1939) had to take into account that since the boys were not identical twins, there was a possibility genetic factors played a part. She also discovered that the parents of the boys seemed to feel obligated to make a bigger fuss over Jimmy to compensate for all the attention Johnny was receiving from McGraw. This seemed to lead to differences in the attitude of the boys toward the experiment and some of the activities.

Despite these complications, it seems clear that McGraw demonstrated that very young children could be taught skills no one had previously thought possible. Johnny's exploits did not necessarily disprove Gesell's hypothesis (or conflict with the conclusions of Dennis), however, since it could still be argued that learning took place only after maturation had set the stage. Johnny's accomplishments might seem less startling if it is assumed that no one had ever thought of teaching an eleven-month-old child to roller skate and swim before McGraw came along. It might be argued that roller skating is basically the same as walking and that swimming occurred because movements originally due to subcortical reflex were maintained through exercise and repetition. When Johnny was put on a tricycle and asked to develop a skill which involved a pattern of movements not related to locomotor or reflex activities, he experienced difficulties—until the maturation of his nerves and muscles made learning possible. (The skill Gesell and Thompson taught their twins was ladder-climbing, which also involves a pattern of movements and which also could not be learned until maturation set the stage.) Finally, some of Johnny's superiority in skating and swimming seemed to have been a function of such factors as being used to falling (since he had just learned to walk), a lower center of gravity (since he was shorter than Jimmy at the time training began), and a lack of awareness of potential danger (Jimmy was older and wiser when he began training).

One-year-olds can learn many skills (if maturation has taken place)

Hilgard: Older Children Learn More Rapidly   The same basic experimental design utilized by McGraw was followed by Josephine Hilgard who carried out an experimental study (1932) of interrelationships between maturation and learning. Hilgard arranged for one group of two- and three-year-old children to be given training for twelve weeks in buttoning, ladder climbing, and the use of scissors. A matched control group was given no specific training. At the end of the twelve-week period, the trained group did better at the skills. The control group, then three months older than the experimental group had been at the onset of its training, was given just one week of instruction. At the end of this week the control group was as proficient as the experimental group, which had received three months of training at an earlier age level. Hilgard concluded that general physiological maturation, plus experiences other than the specific training, had contributed to the faster development of the skills by the control group.

More mature children learn more rapidly

From Readiness to Acceleration to Responsiveness

During the 1930s, books by Gesell stressing the significance of maturation, Shirley's descriptions of the unvarying sequence of stages in locomotor development, articles by the Dennises, and the Hilgard study all contributed to the concept of *readiness*. Many psychologists and educators became convinced that children would learn only after physical and neurological development, plus the normal experiences of childhood, had prepared them to learn. Tests were devised to determine if children were ready to enter first grade, and when children were rated as immature, their parents were advised to have them spend another year in kindergarten. In the 1950s and 1960s this view came to be widely rejected, and faith in the importance of learning was renewed. Some psychologists urged parents to do everything possible to accelerate physical as well as intellectual development. Books and articles outlined techniques parents might use to teach one- and two-year-olds to walk, talk, and even read (Doman, 1964) much earlier than they would on their own. (Explanations and evaluations of this trend will be presented in Chapter 9.)

Within the last few years studies revealing previously unrecognized capabilities of infants and young children seem to have led to a compromise in which parents are urged to provide encouragement and guidance but not instruction intended to try to speed up development. In the 1930s and 1940s Gesell more or less told parents that child behavior would unfold in a particular way at a particular point in development no matter what they did. In effect, parents were told to play the role of interested spectators. In the 1960s some psychologists told parents they should shape behavior as systematically and as rapidly as possible. It was argued (Engelmann and Engelmann, 1968) that if children were stimulated to master sequences of physical and mental skills early in life, they would be more capable and competent later in life. In this period the parent was seen as the molder and accelerator of development. In the 1970s many of the psychologists whose work is being summarized in these chapters on development during the first two years have put the child back in the central position. But, unlike Gesell, they have been intrigued about subtle ways parental reactions are likely to foster maturing forms of behavior initiated by the child. And unlike proponents of preschool instruction, they have suggested that young children should not be stimulated too much because they need time to develop skills and sort out experiences on their own. (Their reasons for stressing this point will be explained in the next chapter.)

Current emphasis: respond to behavior initiated by child

Differences of opinion between theorists who urge parents to attempt to accelerate learning and those who are so impressed by newly discovered capabilities of young children they urge parents to permit children to take the lead are illustrated by recent studies of language development.

Early Language Development

Responses to Sounds

The preceding chapter described both the tendency for neonates to respond to a human voice by synchronizing their movements with the speech sounds and their ability to recognize their mothers' voices. Peter D. Eimas discovered that infants are also capable of making very fine distinctions between quite similar sounds. In collaboration with several associates (Eimas et al., 1971) he exposed one- and four-month-old babies to recorded speech sounds. The infant subjects were able to keep the recordings turned on by sucking on a nipple which contained a switch. At the beginning of an experimental session a baby could hear a *pa-pa* sound coming from a loudspeaker. Most subjects responded with interest and sucked vigorously on the nipple to keep the recording playing. They became bored with the sound (and/or tired of sucking) very quickly, however, and at that point the recording was switched from *pa-pa* to *ga-ga*. As soon as the infants heard the new sound they perked up and their rate of sucking increased significantly.

Eimas reasoned that in order for this change of interest to occur, the babies had to be able to distinguish between *pa* and *ga*. These results led Eimas (1975, p. 224) to suggest that *linguistic feature detectors* are part of the innate structure of human organisms. Eimas also observed that the built-in ability of an infant to perceive quite fine distinctions in human speech more or less paves the way for the acquisition of the ability to speak. If infants had to learn how to distinguish between sounds before they could utter similar sounds, the entire process of language development would take much longer than it does.

We use sounds to communicate with others, and children (and animals as well) seem to have an inherent urge to do this very early in life. Once an infant initiates vocal behavior, the way language develops will be shaped by reinforcements (such as the utterance of a similar sound accompanied by a smile from a parent), and certain types of verbal behavior will be strengthened.

Crying

The most noticeable sound uttered by the newborn infant is the cry. Throughout the first two years, and less frequently later in life, children use this form of vocal communication—as Wolff noted in his descriptions of rhythmical, mad, pain, and fake cries—to express their desires (for food or attention) or displeasure.

Theory: Crying Will Diminish if Reinforcement Is Withheld In terms of the principles of operant conditioning, a child who is attended to by the parents presumably would have crying behavior reinforced, whereas one whose crying behavior was ignored would have that type of activity extinguished. B. C. Etzel and J. L. Gewirtz (1967) offered supporting evidence when they selected as subjects for a simple experiment a six-week-old and a twenty-week-old infant staying at a children's hospital. Both babies had been picked up regularly by attentive nurses when they cried. The experimenters asked the nurses to ignore all crying for a period of days and reported that there was a significant decrease in the amount of crying at the end of the experimental period.

Practice: Babies Cry Less When "Reinforced" Before you assume this means that it is a simple matter to control the crying behavior of children by withholding reinforcement, the results of some other studies should be considered. C. A. Aldrich and several associates (1945a, 1945b) observed crying behavior in hospital nurseries and concluded that the main cause was hunger. They also discovered that prolonged crying spells were almost three times as frequent in the hospital as at home. (Home babies had about four prolonged crying spells a day, and their total crying time per day was rarely more than an hour.) These findings led Aldrich to hypothesize that the home babies cried less because they received more attention. With the cooperation of several associates (1946), he increased the amount of time nursery babies were cared for from 0.7 hours a day to 1.9. The mean amount of crying dropped from 113 to 55 minutes per day. Mary D. Ainsworth (1972) corroborated these findings. She studied infant-mother interactions in twenty-six families and concluded that babies whose mothers responded promptly to crying from the outset tended to cry little and had developed a variety of other modes of communication by the end of the first year. Not responding to cries in the hope of not spoiling the child tended to have exactly the opposite effect.

More attention, less crying in infants

Moral: It Is Difficult to Precisely Shape Infant Behavior Taken together, these studies might be interpreted as indicating that parents wishing to experiment with shaping crying behavior on a short-term basis might make limited use of behavior-modification techniques and ignore all crying for a period of time; they may enjoy temporary success. However, it might be expected that responding to an infant's cries most of the time will reduce the amount of crying and perhaps lead to greater peace of mind and body for infant *and* parents. If parents resolutely refuse to respond to crying for an *extended* period of time in an effort to extinguish such behavior, the baby might go hungry (and express displeasure ever more vocally as the hunger pangs increase in intensity), or perhaps lack of reinforcement will cause the infant to develop a sense of mistrust (which Erikson believes should be avoided as much as possible). This illustrates a problem sometimes encountered when operant-conditioning principles are applied to child behavior. An experimenter who shapes the behavior of a rat or pigeon in a Skinner box can usually control the situation so that only one variable is reinforced or not. The human infant is much more complex than a rat or pigeon, however, and withholding reinforcement with the intention of extinguishing one response may inadvertently shape other types of behavior or extinguish desired activities in unintentional or unexpected ways.

Cooing and Babbling

Fortunately for everyone concerned, most babies spend much more time cooing and babbling than crying. Cooing may start as early as the third week after birth; babbling usually begins between three to six months of age. One of the most fascinating aspects of infant babbling is that during the first months of their lives, infants seem to be capable of producing all of the sounds of all of the languages in the world (Lenneberg, 1967). The average six-month-old baby, in fact, is capable of producing sounds in foreign languages more accurately than an adult. (Infants can do this spontaneously as they experiment with making sounds but cannot reproduce foreign language words on cue.) The explanation for the difference in vocal flexibility between six-month-old babies and adults is that as we use speech we tend to restrict ourselves to producing sounds found only in our native tongue. This tendency to focus on particular sounds does not appear only after a child has acquired the ability to form words, it is apparent in the babbling of infants as early as seven or eight months after they are born. Before the end of the first year young children tend to produce only sounds that they hear because twelve-month-old babies apparently are not as versatile at vocalizing as they were six months before. The fact that early vocal production is shaped even before a baby is aware of what is happening underscores the degree to which listening to others and having them respond to sounds we make influence language development.

The Functions of Language (Private or Public)

After listening carefully to the vocal production of children during the first years of their lives, M. A. K. Halliday concluded that they use language in seven different ways. He designates each as a *function* of language and labels and describes them as follows (1975, pp. 19–21):

□ Instrumental (or "I want") function—used by the child to gain satisfaction of needs, for example, a twelve-month-old girl says "Milk" to indicate she wants some.

Functions of language

□ Regulatory (or "Do as I tell you") function—used by the child to control the behavior of others, for example, a fourteen-month-old boy says "Up" to get his father to pick him up.

□ Interpersonal (or "Me and you") function—used by the child to interact with others, for example, an eleven-month-old girl who has just learned to say "Hi" greets everyone and anyone with that salutation several times in succession.

□ Personal (or "Here I come") function—used by the child to express awareness of personal feelings, of participation, or of pleasure, for example, a three-year-old boy says "I like ice cream" when eating his favorite dessert.

□ Heuristic[2] (or "Tell me why") function—used by a child to acquire information, for example, a two-year-old girl says "What's that?" when she first sees a zebra in a zoo.

---

[2] If you have never encountered the word *heuristic* before, it means helping to discover or learn.

☐ Imaginative (or "Let's pretend") function—used by the child to create an environment of her or his own, for example, a three-year-old boy says "I'm Superman."

☐ Informative (or "I've got something to tell you") function—used by the child to tell others about a recent observation or discovery, for example, a three-year-old girl tells her father "I saw a doggy."

After recording the language repertoire of a ten-month-old boy, Halliday concluded that even though the child did not use a single word listed in an English dictionary, he used "words" of his own in instrumental, regulatory, interactional, and personal ways. To request someone to hand him a toy bird, for example, the child said "Bih." This sound was used consistently to refer to the toy bird, and his parents readily understood what the child was trying to convey, particularly when he underlined his meaning with gestures and facial expressions. By the age of eighteen months Halliday's subject was noticeably more proficient and came to use the imaginative function as well.

It appears that normal babies develop prespeech languages of their own provided they have opportunities to interact with at least one interested adult who is willing to try to interpret their utterances. The uniqueness of each child's private language was emphasized when T. G. R. Bower (1977b, p. 143) observed that even identical twins use different noises to secure the same purpose.

The ability of a young child to communicate effectively by using his or her own private language may, paradoxically, retard the use of the first word and of subsequent vocabulary acquisition. A child with easily educated parents may be able to express most of the functions of language described by Halliday by making exclusive use of her or his own language. Only when the parents make an effort to substitute real words for the child's private words is it likely that the child will begin to use utterances that are recognizable to nonfamily members. The momentous occasion when a child first uses a bona fide English word *as* a word usually takes place around the first birthday.

The First Word

A very plausible explanation for the way children reach this important plateau in language development has been proposed by Jean Piaget (1952a) on the basis of observations of his own children. Like all normal babies, Piaget's daughter Lucienne spontaneously began to emit sounds early in life. When she was slightly less than two months old Lucienne would sometimes increase her vocal activity in response to sounds made by her father. She was unable to reproduce the exact sounds he made, but the fact that she was stimulated to "talk" led Piaget to refer to her reaction as *vocal contagion*. She did not really talk *back* but talked along *with* her father, as if his vocalizing activity was contagious. By the time she was three months old, Lucienne was able to imitate sounds made by her father, provided

Vocal contagion: child vocalizes with parent

she had just made them herself. Piaget called this *mutual imitation,* emphasizing that it could only take place if Lucienne had instituted the interchange and if both father and daughter made mutual (or similar) sounds. Eventually Lucienne used a recognizable sound in the presence of her father to refer to a specific object.

This sequence may become clearer if you imagine that a mother and baby have engaged in mutual imitation involving the sound *ma-ma.* That is, the mother hears the baby spontaneously emitting the *ma-ma* sound as the child plays at babbling. The mother picks up the cue and says "ma-ma" just after the baby does. That prompts the baby to repeat "ma-ma" several times, which arouses an equal number of *ma-ma* responses from the mother. After this "duet" has been refined over a period of time the mother points to herself and says "ma-ma." The child responds with the same sound, and if the mother responds to this behavior with smiles or expressions of delight, the child may associate the sound with her. When the child consistently associates the sound *ma-ma* with the mother, a word has been learned.

The learning theorist explains the acquisition of the first word in much the same way as Piaget, differing only in the terms used. Instead of referring to *vocal contagion* and *mutual imitation,* a learning theorist would point out that the sequence just described is an excellent illustration of *operant conditioning.* First, the child emits sounds of its own volition. Then, particular sounds (for example, *ma-ma*) are reinforced when the parent makes similar sounds, smiles, plays with the child, and so forth. Reinforcement strengthens the tendency of the child to use the *ma-ma* sound, and when this response is well-established, the parents build up an association between the sound and an appropriate object (the mother) by enthusiastically reinforcing the child when the sound is used to refer to the object. In *Verbal Behavior* (1957) B. F. Skinner offers an analysis of the development of language based on sequences of emitted sounds and reinforcements.

While the acquisition of the first word can be explained quite adequately in terms of imitation and reinforcement, such is not the case with many aspects of early language development. Even two-year-olds, for example, speak and understand sentences they have never heard their parents say. They also put together words in ways that have never been reinforced.

Mutual imitation: parent and child repeat sounds initially made by child

First word: child emits sound, is reinforced, builds association

Aspects of Early Language Acquisition

Language Acquisition Device (LAD)   To account for the ability of children to use language in "unlearned" ways, Noam Chomsky (1968) has proposed that language development is based on innate tendencies which make up what he calls the *language acquisition device* (LAD). This term is intended to convey that certain tendencies inherited by all children cause them to begin to use words in essentially the same manner. (Some psychologists prefer to say the child is *wired* or *programmed* to behave in certain ways.) Chomsky felt obliged to postulate the

LAD when he analyzed the speech of young children from various parts of the world. He concluded that they all seemed to develop the same type of grammar and that this grammar differed from that of adults to the extent that short sentences uttered by parents would be modified by children to be consistent with their own way of talking.

Research on early language development carried out since Chomsky first proposed the LAD has not clearly substantiated his claim that there is a universal form of grammar used by all children everywhere. Even so, there are recognizable differences between the sentence structure used by children just beginning to talk and sentences uttered by older children who have learned the rules of language usage.

Holophrastic Speech   Once a child learns to use one or more words, a single word may be used to communicate a variety of messages. Such use of language is called *holophrastic* speech. (*Holo* is Greek for *whole,* so holophrastic speech refers to the use of a single word as a whole "phrase.") A matter-of-fact "Milk," uttered by a fourteen-month-old just after a glass of milk is placed on the table, may be translated by a perceptive parent as "That's a glass of milk." An urgent "Milk," uttered as a child entreatingly pats the refrigerator door, will be taken as "I want a glass of milk." A tentative "Milk," uttered just after an accidental push of a glass of milk off of a table, might be interpreted as "Oops. The glass of milk fell on the floor. Now how do you suppose that happened?" (Such an interpretation might be justified if the child first gazes sadly at the mess on the floor and then slowly transfers that sorrowful gaze to the parent.)

Holophrastic speech: one-word communications

These various possible interpretations of a child's use of holophrastic speech reveal the extent to which initial attempts to convey meaning through speech depend on the listener's awareness of the situation. If a parent is not able to see the situation or gestures accompanying the word, the meaning may not be clear. In order to use speech to communicate without resorting to other cues, it is almost always necessary to combine words into at least rudimentary sentences, for example, "That's milk," "Sally want milk," "Milk fall."

Telegraphic Speech and the Use of Pivots   Many of the two-word utterances used by children are called *telegraphic* because they resemble telegrams in which nonessential words have been left out. "Milk fall," for example, gets the point across even though the child leaves out words that would be included by an adult using correct grammar. After analyzing the speech of young children, Martin D. S. Braine (1963) concluded that many telegraphic utterances may be formed from a quite limited pool of words. This occurs because an all-purpose word (called a *pivot* by Braine) may be used in essentially the same way with a variety of other words (called *open-class* words). One child studied by Braine, for example, said "Allgone vitamins," "Allgone eggs," "Allgone watch," "Allgone

Telegraphic speech: nonessential words omitted

Pivot words: all-purpose words

sticky" (after washing his hands), and "Allgone outside" (after the front door was closed). In this case *allgone* is the pivot word, and *vitamins, eggs,* and so on are open-class words.

Consistently Used Rules or Groping Patterns?   In addition to proposing the LAD, Chomsky (1965) has hypothesized that as children acquire language, they use what he refers to as *transformational grammar*—a grammar made up of rules for putting words together. Almost all psycholinguists of the 1960s and early 1970s seem to have been influenced by the idea that children follow rules when they begin to speak, because most of the psycholinguists searched for consistencies in the speech of two-year-olds. Telegraphic speech and pivot words, for example, were originally thought to be formed according to discernible patterns. More recent studies of the speech of young children cast doubt on the validity of Chomsky's hypothesis regarding use of rules. Martin D. S. Braine, who thought he had detected consistently applied rules in children's use of pivot and open class words in 1963, came to a different conclusion in 1976. He reviewed all the studies he could find of records of the spontaneous speech of young children from several countries and decided that there is little evidence that two-year-olds follow rules as consistently as he and other students of language had first thought. Braine suggests that children exhibit certain patterns when they begin to put words together but that they do not seem to consistently use the rules described by Chomsky or other psycholinguists (for example, Bloom, 1970; Schlesinger, 1975). Braine coined the term *groping patterns* to call attention to the tentative way children experiment with word combinations to express ideas.

In a commentary appended to Braine's 1976 article, Melissa Bowerman (yet another psycholinguist who has described [1973] apparent rules of grammar used by young children) points out that he may not have made sufficient allowance for a distinction Chomsky has made between deep structure and surface structure.

Deep Structure and Surface Structure   Telegraphic utterances often make it possible for a person who is not aware of what a child is doing to grasp what he or she means, but that may not always be the case. A boy who says "Allgone outside" in one situation, for example, may mean that the front door is closed. In a different situation the same telegraphic utterance may be intended to convey that *all* of his brothers and sisters have *gone* outside. This distinction between what children seem to say and what they actually mean was stressed by Chomsky. He urged students of language to remain aware of differences between *deep* structure (what is actually meant) and *surface* structure (what is apparently said).

Bowerman suggests that in his analysis, Braine assumed a very direct relationship between what children said and what they meant. She notes that other psycholinguists believe that "deep structure is richer than surface structure" (1976a, p. 101). It may be the case, therefore, that two-year-olds understand

Deep structure and surface structure: actual and apparent meaning

rules of grammar, and want to use them, but that they have not yet acquired the vocabulary to say what they mean in a way that is clearly understandable to someone else.

In many respects, the most significant feature of early language development is the way children gradually learn to use accepted forms of grammar to unmistakably convey deep structure. Since such mastery of language takes place after the age of two (but quite amazingly before the age of five), observations on how it occurs will be presented in Chapter 10 in discussing development during the two- to five-year age span.

The ability of children to use words, even single words, to convey ideas reveals that they are beginning to form concepts. The most complete explanation of how this occurs has been proposed by Jean Piaget. Accordingly, it is time to take a detailed look at his description of the first stage of cognitive development.

Piaget: Stages of Sensorimotor Period

To help you grasp the overall structure of Piaget's description of stages in early cognitive development, here is a brief review of the basic concepts of his theory that were described in Chapter 3.

Piaget believes human beings inherit two basic tendencies: organization (the tendency to combine processes into coherent systems) and adaptation (the tendency to adjust to the environment). Adaptation occurs through two complementary processes: assimilation (the tendency to incorporate experiences into one's view of the world) and accommodation (the tendency to modify one's conceptions in response to new or inconsistent experiences). These various tendencies lead to the development of schemes (organized patterns of behavior). Piaget refers to the first two years as the *sensorimotor* period because the child develops schemes primarily through sensorimotor activities. There are six stages in this period.

Stage 1: Birth to One Month

The sucking behavior of the neonate illustrates how the infant begins to develop schemes. Piaget began to observe his children immediately after they were born by sitting next to the cradle and making detailed descriptions of their behavior. He recorded how the rooting and sucking reflexes were aroused the first time the babies had an opportunity to feed; he then noticed that as early as the second day variations of these basic responses began to appear. The first variation was that the babies made sucking movements between feedings; the next was that they would suck almost anything that touched their lips (for example, their thumbs or a blanket). Before the end of the first month they engaged in sucking for the sake of

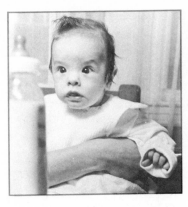

The development of schemes. The infant in these photos has associated the sucking scheme with the nursing bottle. Excerpted from *Infants and Mothers: Differences in Development*, T. Berry Brazelton, M.D. Copyright © 1969 by T. Berry Brazelton, M.D. Reprinted by permission of Delacourt Press/Seymour Lawrence.

exercise (thumb sucking) in addition to sucking for the sake of food. From these changes in behavior Piaget concluded that as early as the first days of life the baby assimilates and accommodates to form schemes regarding sucking activities.

Formation of primitive schemes

Stage 2: Primary Circular Reactions

Primary Circular Reaction   After the first month, the complexity of the behavior of the child develops at an accelerated pace, basically through what Piaget refers to as the *primary circular reaction,* which takes place when the infant engages in an activity (by chance or the intervention of his parents) that leads to a satisfying state of affairs. The infant seeks to repeat such satisfying activities and when it succeeds in doing so, the act becomes part of its repertoire of behavior.

Primary circular reaction: satisfying bodily activity repeated

The primary circular reaction is illustrated by the way Piaget's children came to engage in thumb sucking. The hand of the young child is frequently held close to the mouth, probably because the arms and hands are usually tucked up close to the face in the fetal position, which young infants continue to assume after birth. Piaget noticed that when the thumb or fingers of one of his children first came into contact with the lips, the sucking reflex was activated. Once this occurred, the infant tried to move his hand to his mouth, and by the end of the first month, he was mature enough to be able to do this. (On one occasion, when his son Laurent was one month old, Piaget moved the infant's hand from his mouth to his side thirteen times in succession. Each time, Laurent moved it back to his mouth.) At first, Piaget's children sucked any part of the hand, but they quickly developed a preference for the thumb, perhaps because it is the most nipplelike appendage available. Another aspect of his children's sucking behavior that

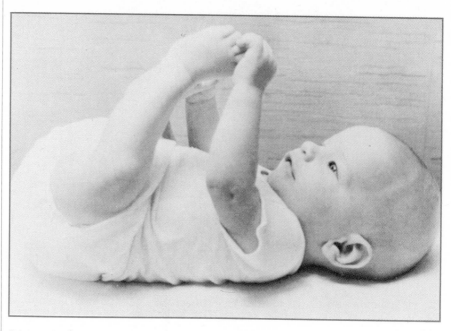

Primary circular reactions involve repeated movements or manipulations of the child's own body. Excerpted from *Infants and Mothers: Individual Differences in Development*, T. Berry Brazelton, M.D. Reprinted by permission of Delacourt Press/Seymour Lawrence.

attracted Piaget's attention was their tendency to anticipate sucking before feeding actually started. At first, almost any contact with the mother aroused this response. In time, it began only when the child was held in the customary feeding position.

Functional Assimilation   Piaget believes the self-starting aspect of human behavior is due to curiosity and the inborn tendency of the child to seek stimulation. When children become capable of an activity, an inherited tendency makes them do it. This is what Piaget terms *functional assimilation*. Observing how his children looked at objects, Piaget noticed that at the age of one month Laurent would spend as long as an hour looking at fringe on his cradle. When he was two weeks older, Laurent engaged in systematic visual exploration of his bassinet. By the third month he was more likely to look at things, such as a toy hanging from the top of the bassinet, that were moderately novel. This progression from fixed attention, to visual exploration, to interest in novel objects led Piaget to conclude that children come equipped with a tendency to use their eyes, that they seek stimulation, and that they quite early in life develop schemes based on visual perception. This last conclusion is based on the reasoning that Laurent must have developed a quite consistent conception of what his bassinet was like to be capable of recognizing the addition of something new when the toy was

Functional assimilation: tendency to use a capability

attached. (Piaget's account of the development of schemes provides an explanation for the types of perceptual behavior observed by Fantz and those who recorded the reactions of infants to patterns and faces. After children develop a scheme for a pattern they are likely to be attracted to variations that call their attention to new details.)

What Piaget refers to as functional assimilation has been observed and described in different terms by many other psychologists. Robert W. White (1959), for instance, analyzed various views of motivation that had been proposed in American psychology up to the mid-1950s and concluded that too many of them led to the assumption that children had to be stimulated to learn or even respond. White rejected this conception and proposed instead that human beings are born with built-in curiosity and manifest a desire to interact with their environment. (The same point had been made by Locke in 1690 and Rousseau in 1762.) He referred to this tendency as a drive toward *competence* or *effectance*. Observations of normal human infants (or of puppies or kittens) tend to support White's argument that young organisms have an urge to explore and try out their abilities. The same tendency has also been demonstrated many times under controlled conditions. Anneliese F. Korner and Evelyn B. Thoman (1970), for example, observed what happened when infants who were crying in their cribs were picked up and placed on the shoulders of their mothers. In most cases the babies stopped crying quite abruptly when they were provided with the opportunity to just look around. The chance to satisfy the drive of curiosity by engaging in visual exploration was strong enough to take their minds off whatever had been bothering them in their cribs. Taking into account the likelihood that the only thing the infants were able to see when in their cribs was either the ceiling or the side of the crib, it is possible that many of them were crying out of sheer boredom.

Harriet Rheingold, who has made a career of studying infants and young children in many different kinds of situations, endorses the hypothesis that boredom bothers babies. She notes (1973, p. 183) that placing a child in a nonstimulating environment (such as an empty crib) often leads to fussing and crying. When she observed infants in institutions, Rheingold reports that she was impressed by the apparently irrepressible (at first) urge of infants to occupy themselves, even when they had practically no playthings to handle or objects or people to look at. Children who have access to many interesting objects seem to possess an innate urge to explore with zest and enthusiasm whenever the opportunity arises. In an experiment with twelve- and eighteen-month-old children Rheingold (1973) arranged for the mothers to carry their children into a room, put them down on the floor, and then simply sit and watch as the infants amused themselves in two adjacent playrooms containing toys. All of the children left their mothers within seconds and explored the rooms with considerable energy. Rheingold believes that the children deserved to be called *enterprising* because they took the initiative to discover and interact with the playthings on their own. Furthermore, they obviously got a great deal of pleasure out of it.

Stage 3: Secondary Circular Reactions

Object concept: object exists even when not perceived

The Object Concept   From the fourth to the tenth month, the major change in the intellectual development of the child consists of adding to reactions centering on the body (initial or *primary* reactions) and to those involving the external environment (later or *secondary* reactions). Awareness of the external environment is illustrated most clearly by what Piaget calls the *object concept:* understanding that an object continues to exist even when it is no longer perceived. (Such understanding is also referred to as *object constancy* or *object permanence.*) Piaget formulated this concept when he observed Laurent's reactions as his mother came to the bassinet and then left it. At first, Laurent would stare at her when she was present but almost immediately look away when she left. It seemed apparent that his reaction was "Out of sight, out of mind." After he was four months old, however, Laurent would continue to stare at the spot she had vacated, and when he was a bit older, he would look in the direction of his mother's voice (when he was not able to see her). By his behavior he revealed that he had developed a scheme of "mother" which involved both visual and auditory stimuli. Not until Laurent actively searched for his absent mother, however, by looking around and listening intently, did Piaget feel that a true object concept had developed. By these actions, Laurent was revealing that his scheme of "mother" had sufficiently developed that he understood that she continued to exist even when he could not see or hear her.

Secondary circular reaction: intentional duplication of activity involving an object

Interrupted actions continued; part sensed as whole

Intentional Duplication of Initially "Accidental" Activities   The key aspect of secondary circular reactions is the ability of the child to reproduce activities involving objects (not just bodily movements) initially discovered by chance. This takes place by a sequence of events similar to that leading from vocal contagion to mutual imitation in the development of vocalization. When Laurent accidentally discovered that he could make a sound by hitting a rattle, for example, he repeated the act. Another feature of this stage is the ability of the child to interrupt an act and then return to it. Lucienne, for example, was playing with a small box one day when Piaget came up to her crib. She turned her attention to him for a few minutes, but then confidently reached for the box and resumed play with it. Still another feature that appears toward the end of this stage is the ability to recognize an object that is partially hidden. When nine-month-old Laurent's rattle was completely hidden by a cloth, he acted as if it no longer existed. But when one end of it protruded from the cloth, he reached for it.

During the stage of secondary circular reactions, then, the child shifts from concentrating on her or his own body to interest in the external environment; object concepts develop which lead the child to understand that something continues to exist even though it is not being perceived; chance actions leading to satisfaction are repeated; an activity that is interrupted will not be forgotten; and

Development of object concept. In the first two photos the concealed toy no longer exists for the infant. The child in the last four photos, however, has formed an object concept. The toy continues to exist even though he cannot perceive it, which enables him to search for and find it. George Zimbel/Monkmeyer.

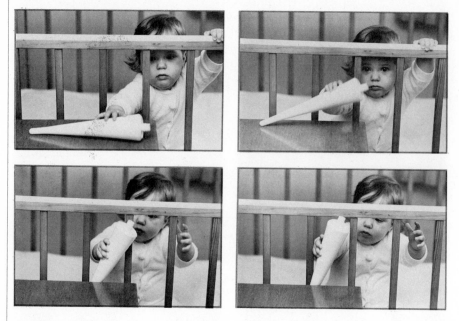

Coordination of secondary schemes occurs when a child combines separate skills to achieve a particular goal. This child coordinates skills of picking up and rotating objects to solve the problem of getting a long object through the bars of the crib. George Zimbel/Monkmeyer.

sensing only part of an object may be sufficient to permit the child to react to it as a whole.

Stage 4: Coordination of Secondary Schemes

As noted in discussing cephalocaudal and proximodistal development at the beginning of this chapter, the average child develops the ability to pick up an object between thumb and fingers (prehension) at around nine months. By the time children have matured to the point where they can manipulate objects with considerable precision and control, they have also reached the point where their interactions with the environment have produced a sizable repertoire of schemes, paving the way for new combinations of schemes.

Piaget became convinced that schemes became coordinated as he watched his children cope with problems such as searching for a matchbox hidden in a hand or under a pillow. In dealing with such novel situations, Laurent and Lucienne would try techniques they had previously developed through spontaneous activities. In the course of manipulating objects, for example, they would pick up pillows. When the box was placed under the pillow, they would apply the previously learned skill (picking up an object just for its own sake) to the new situation (picking up a pillow to search for an object). This switch from playful to purposeful manipulation is the major feature of Stage Four, and it explains why the stage is referred to as *coordination of secondary schemes:* separate skills learned in interacting with the environment are put together or coordinated to achieve a specific goal. Other changes during this stage are the development of the ability to imitate actions (provided the child has already mastered them through spontaneous activity) and more sophisticated understanding of the object concept.

Coordinated schemes: separate skills combined to achieve goal

Stage 5: Tertiary Circular Reaction

Shortly after their first birthdays, children begin to perfect their locomotor abilities, and when they are able to walk, their investigation of the environment takes on greater self-direction. They no longer must limit themselves to objects made available by others (or within crawling distance); they can roam around and explore things on their own. The degree to which children at this age actively seek new and interesting things is the key feature of the *tertiary circular reaction stage.* The first type of circular reaction centers on the infant's own body; the second on external objects or events; the third is characterized by exploration and interest in novelty.

Tertiary circular reactions: exploration; interest in novelty

Piaget explains the fifteen-month-old's fascination with novelty for its own sake by suggesting that the large number of schemes built up during the first year make the child familiar with many things. Schemes become so clearly established that children are capable of recognizing objects and events that do not fit into their growing conception of the world. The tendencies to seek equilibration, and to assimilate and accommodate, stimulate the child to examine new objects carefully and either incorporate them into an existing scheme or form a new one. The child's acquisition of the ability to move around and seek out new objects and situations coincides with the development of tertiary circular reactions.

This potential for both physical and mental exploration leads children to engage in constant manipulation of their world and explains why children of this age explore with unrelenting vigor wastebaskets, objects on coffee tables, knobs on television sets, pots and pans in lower cupboards, and the like. As they investigate things, children expand their understanding of relationships between themselves and the objects they handle, thereby learning to institute and imitate all kinds of actions, not just those which happen to be similar to actions done on their own immediately preceding the acts they imitate.

Stage 6: Beginning of Thought

Children in Stage Five have built up a repertoire of schemes that make it possible for them to deal with new situations by trying out a variety of techniques mastered in the course of exploring their environment. Before they are two years of age children usually will show the first signs of substituting thinking for action. A fifteen-month-old child confronted with a problem is likely to run through a

Tertiary circular reaction. The active seeking out and manipulating of new objects is characteristic of this stage. James R. Holland/Stock, Boston.

Final stage: thought replaces activity; delayed imitation

series of physical actions in an effort to find a solution. Two-year-olds, on the other hand, may hesitate and by eye movements indicate that they are engaging in mental trial and error. Another kind of behavior providing evidence that a cognitive image has been formed is imitation of an action hours or days after the model was observed. Lucienne, for example, observed a little boy engage in a temper tantrum. She was quite fascinated since she had never before seen such behavior. When she wanted to get out of her playpen the next day, she did an

The beginning of thought. The two-year-old can solve some problems by mental rather than physical activity. © 1980 Erika Stone.

excellent imitation of the screaming and foot stamping she had observed. The final characteristic of this stage is that object concepts now function as mental images. If an object is removed from sight, children will clearly show they comprehend that it still exists.

Summary of Sensorimotor Stages

The basic changes which take place as a child progresses through these stages can be summarized as follows:

- *Birth to one month*—development of variations of reflex activity (of sucking, for example) indicates formation of primitive schemes.
- *One to four months*—visual exploration progresses from staring, to scanning, to looking at moderately novel objects. Such activities indicate formation of primary circular reactions: schemes based on exploration by children of their own bodies and senses.

☐ *Four to ten months*—object concept (permanence) begins to develop as children come to realize that things continue to exist even though they are not present to sense. The switch in emphasis from exploration of their own bodies and senses to exploration of physical environment leads children to secondary circular reactions: spontaneous reactions involving external objects or events are deliberately repeated.

☐ *Ten to twelve months*—development of many schemes through secondary circular reactions paves the way for combining them. Children have developed enough awareness of their bodies and environment to engage in purposeful manipulation.

☐ *Twelve to eighteen months*—development of ability to walk, increased skill at manipulating things, understanding of many schemes, and recognition of novelty all lead to active exploration of the environment (tertiary circular reaction).

☐ *Eighteen to twenty-four months*—experience with exploration and manipulation equip the child with enough clearly established schemes to be able to engage in mental manipulation; that is, actions can be thought out.

When this description of stages is related to the basic principles of Piaget's theory, the overall picture becomes clearer. The inherited tendencies for children to organize experiences and adapt to their environment account for the self-starting aspects of their behavior. As they use their senses, infants assimilate similar experiences into schemes. When a new experience is encountered, children accommodate to the novelty and revise their view of that general type of experience. At first the schemes center on sense activity; later they are based on experiences with people and objects. In time, children comprehend that objects do not exist just in their senses but have a separate reality. After children have formed a repertoire of experiences, they coordinate previously separate schemes. As they encounter new experiences, they continue to assimilate and accommodate, and they eventually reach the point where their understanding of the world permits them to think out, not act out, solutions to simple problems.

In contrast to the extreme learning-theory view, which sometimes leads to the assumption that parents must induce and supervise learning, Piaget's view is that children are capable of learning many things on their own. He acknowledges that parents supply essential assistance, feedback, and encouragement, but his principle of functional assimilation emphasizes that children come equipped with a built-in urge to use their abilities. The tendency for a child to use a newly acquired ability is confirmed and illustrated by the vocal behavior of young children. In one study (Bell, 1903) it was discovered that a three-year-old uttered 15,230 words in a single day. Evidence that this was not a rare occurrence was provided by a later study (Brandenburg and Brandenburg, 1919) where the single-day word count for a four-and-a-half year-old was 14,930. Children functioning at this level of verbal output will utter over a million words in less than seventy days and by the time they enter school will be well over the 10 million mark. Instead of feeling that they must stimulate verbal (and other types of) behavior, therefore, many parents may wonder how they can diminish it.

Two-year-olds can get around on their own, form concepts, think, solve problems, and communicate with others. All of these capabilities make them truly independent, and their independence makes it clearer than ever that each child is a distinct personality. Certain personality traits of two-year-olds, in fact, are so well established that they may still be recognizably distinctive at young adulthood. This point was established when personality sketches of nineteen children written when they were two years old were compared with an independently prepared set of sketches written when they were seventeen. The first personality sketches were prepared by Mary Shirley after she had studied the nineteen babies intensively for the first two years of their lives. The later sketches were written by Patricia Neilon (1948) after she studied personality test data, analyzed rating scales, and interviewed the subjects as well as their mothers. Neilon asked several graduate students and professors to try to match the sketches of the two- and seventeen-year-olds. They succeeded remarkably well, although the sketches of some subjects were easier to match than others.

Awareness that a child's personality has already taken a distinctive form by the age of two years leads us back to speculations about the interplay of heredity and environment. To what extent are personality traits traceable to inherited predispositions? How much do a child's earliest experiences shape personality? Partial answers to these questions can be sought by analyzing the significance of early child–parent relationships, the topic to be covered in the next chapter.

Suggestions for Further Study

Physical Growth During the First Two Years

If you would like more complete information about growth and physiological development, consult *Carmichael's Manual of Child Psychology* (3rd ed., 1970), edited by Paul H. Mussen. Chapter 3, "Physical Growth," by J. M. Tanner, describes growth curves of various kinds, summarizes data on prenatal and adolescent growth, notes differences between early and late maturers, explains the endocrinology of growth, and reviews studies of the impact of heredity and environment on growth. Chapter 4, "Physiological Development," by Dorothy H. Eichorn, is a quite technical discussion of physiological aspects of development, describing in detail how the various bodily processes begin to function as the fetus develops. Circulation, respiration, metabolism, temperature, and neurophysiology are analyzed.

Motor Development During the First Two Years

"Infant Motor Development" by David H. Crowell, Chapter 3 in *Infancy and Early Childhood* (1967), edited by Yvonne Brackbill, supplies background information about interpretations of motor development derived from behaviorism, the maturation hypothesis, and Piagetian theory. The development of motor skills is outlined, and motor responses of various kinds are described. An extensive bibliography is provided to give you access to more information.

Sensory and Perceptual Processes During the First Two Years

For more complete information about the development of sensation and perception, consult "Sensory and Perceptual Processes in Infants" by William C. Spears and Raymond H. Hohle, Chapter 2 in *Infancy and Early Childhood* (1967), edited by Yvonne Brackbill; "Sensory and Perceptual Development" by Herbert L. Pick, Jr., and Anne D. Pick, Chapter 11 in *Carmichael's Manual of Child Psychology* (3rd ed., 1970), edited by Paul H. Mussen; or *Infant Perception: From Sensation to Cognition*, Volumes I and II (1975), edited by Leslie B. Cohen and Philip Salapatek.

Infancy: General Surveys of Information

One excellent source of information on infancy is "Human Infancy: A Bibliography and Guide" by William Kessen, Marshall M. Haith, and Philip H. Salapatek, Chapter 5 in *Carmichael's Manual of Child Psychology* (3rd ed., 1970). The authors present a history of research on infants, describe methods for studying infants, provide sample items from four infant tests (pp. 304–305), summarize views of the infant (an assembly of reflexes, a sensory surface, a learner), and review research on sucking, habituation, and early vision. The bibliography at the end of the chapter covers *eighty-five* pages. Another excellent compilation of information on early development is *Infancy and Early Childhood* (1967), edited by Yvonne Brackbill. Each of the eight chapters in this book consists of reviews of important studies by specialists in different aspects of early development. For comprehensive reviews of recent research, consult the *Handbook of Infant Development* (1979), edited by Joy D. Osofsky.

Early Language Development

Early research on language development concentrated on the establishment of norms. A substantial number of observational studies carried out in the 1930s and 1940s are reviewed in "Language Development in Children" by Dorothea McCarthy, Chapter 9 in *Manual of Child Psychology* (2nd ed., 1954), edited by Leonard Carmichael. More recent research has explored the significance of the acquisition of language. An excellent review of these studies is provided in

"Language Development: The First Four Years" by Freda G. Rebelsky, Raymond H. Starr, Jr., and Zella Luria, Chapter 5 in *Infancy and Early Childhood* (1967), edited by Yvonne Brackbill. Another excellent analysis is provided by Paula Menyuk in *The Acquisition and Development of Language* (1971). Still another excellent analysis is presented in "Structure and Variation in Child Language" by Lois Bloom, Patsy Lightbown, and Lois Hood, a *Monograph of the Society for Research in Child Development* [1975, **40**, (2, Serial No. 160)].

The Sensorimotor Period

If you would like more complete information about Piaget's description of the sensorimotor period of intellectual development, read pages 26–71 of *Piaget's Theory of Intellectual Development: An Introduction* (2nd ed., 1979) by Herbert Ginsburg and Sylvia Opper. Other books you might consult are *Understanding Piaget* (1971) by Mary Pulaski; and *Piaget's Theory of Cognitive Development: An Introduction for Students of Psychology and Education* (1971) by B. J. Wadsworth. If you would like to read Piaget's own account of cognitive development, including excerpts from his baby biographies of his own children, see *The Origins of Intelligence in Children* (1952).

KEY POINTS

How Critical Are the First Two Years?

Imprinting: attachment to mother during critical period

Method devised by Harlow to study attachment

Contact comfort more important than feeding

Hypothesis: early isolation may block development of love

Institutionalized babies retarded in development

Retardation of institutionalized children due to restricted opportunities

Longer the deprivation, greater the retardation

Psychoanalytic Interpretations of Child Rearing

How infant fed is important factor, not whether breast- or bottle-fed

No clear-cut evidence toilet training has predictable or identifiable influence

Erikson's Stress on Trust and Autonomy

Important to foster trust and autonomy, minimize mistrust, shame, and doubt

Learning-Theory Views of Child Rearing

Children need to learn they can get others to respond

Behavior-modification approach to toilet training has advantages

Aspects of Mother-Infant Relationships

Many types of infant behavior arouse positive responses

Early skin-to-skin contact may promote attachment

Maternal critical-period hypothesis tentative, not clearly established

Fathers may be influenced as much as mothers by early contact

Sex-typed and androgynous parents likely to respond to infants in different ways

Child abusers express aggressive impulses freely, were abused themselves

Child abusers must cope with frustrations, often live in social isolation

Abused children often premature, sick, given to crying

Effective mothers have a good sense of timing

Infants and mothers need to take turns

Infants need to learn they can produce consequences

Effective mothers handle babies well, take delight

May be unwise to overstimulate infants

Stranger and separation anxiety typically appear before end of first year

Securely attached infants perceive mother as accessible, responsive

Securely attached infants likely to explore, respond positively to others

Separation anxiety may be caused by understanding of person permanence

Stranger anxiety may be caused by inability to assimilate or accommodate new schemes (people)

Multiple caretakers should provide consistent care

Mothers of competent children, talk, respond, enrich, enourage, explain

CHAPTER ⬚7

THE FIRST TWO YEARS:

CHILD-PARENT RELATIONSHIPS

In Chapter 5 various hypotheses regarding the significance of experiences at birth and during the first four weeks of postnatal existence were summarized. Research strongly suggests, however, that because the neonate is such an immature organism, it seems unlikely that those early experiences will have a permanent impact on later behavior. But during the first two years of their lives, normal children have acquired an extensive repertoire of skills that permit them to function independently. In fact, some theorists maintain that what occurs during that time makes changes during any subsequent period of development seem insignificant by comparison. Michael Lewis, for example, observes "The infant, although limited in its response repertoire, is a highly complex and sophisticated organism. And while growth characterizes all living things, the rapid rate of growth most characterizes these early years. At no time in its history will the human being again experience more dramatic, intense and dynamic change" (1967, p. 17). And T. G. R. Bower begins a book on infancy with "Few would dissent from the proposition that infancy is the most critical period of development, the period in which the basic frameworks of later development are established" (1977b, p. vii).

How Critical Are the First Two Years?

Bower's use of the word *critical* calls attention to the most controversial question about development during the first two years: Is this a critical period in human existence? When psychologists speak of *critical periods* they use the term in a quite specialized way, a point which will become clear as research underlying the concept is reviewed.

Studies of Imprinting in Birds

Konrad Lorenz, the most famous ethologist of our time, has observed a variety of animals in their native habitats for over forty years. (In recognition of his research, he was awarded a Nobel Prize in 1973.) The type of animal behavior described by Lorenz that has particularly aroused the interest of developmental psychologists is *imprinting*. Lorenz noticed that newborn goslings will adopt as their mother any moving object they encounter in the first few hours after they are hatched. This tendency to *imprint* (or form) an attachment to another object occurs during a very short period of time, which is, therefore, a *critical period* in development.

Imprinting: attachment to mother during critical period

In the years since Lorenz first described imprinting in goslings, hundreds of similar observational studies have been carried out. Some studies do support the critical period hypothesis. Eckhard Hess (1964), for example, made detailed experimental analyses of the nature of imprinting in birds and concluded that the critical period occurs within the first hours after birth and that the strength of the imprinting depends on the amount of effort the newly hatched gosling must make to get to the mother object. Quite often, however, observations of birds other than goslings have led to the conclusion that critical periods are not as universal as they first seemed (Lorenz, 1970, pp. 124–132). Furthermore, factors that seem to favor imprinting (for example, the ways young birds develop increasing familiarity with the mother) suggest that the effort factor Hess considered to be of such significance is only part of the story. After reviewing many studies of imprinting, Robert Hinde (1973, pp. 150–157) concluded that it might be preferable to substitute the term *sensitive period* for critical period. Hinde joins other students of animal behavior in stressing the point that experiences occurring early in life involve *probabilities* that certain forms of learning may take place. There is a *tendency* for some species of birds to imprint an attachment to another bird, person, or moving object they follow around a few hours after they hatch, but such learning does not always occur.

While imprinting has frequently (though not invariably) been demonstrated in birds, it is unwise to generalize from bird to human behavior. A key factor in the imprinting of goslings is the ability of the newly hatched bird to follow the mother (or mother object) around. Obviously, a human infant cannot engage in such behavior. But monkeys—which resemble humans much more than birds do —*are* able to move about on their own shortly after birth. Because of the close resemblance of monkeys to humans, Harry F. Harlow embarked on a series of studies of monkey behavior that has aroused a great deal of interest. One of the most dramatic conclusions reached by Harlow after studying monkey behavior related to critical periods. To understand the sequence and nature of his research, it will be helpful to trace the motives that originally stimulated him to study infant monkeys.

Harlow's Studies of Monkeys

In keeping with the blank slate view and stress on experiences, many American psychologists (for example, Gewirtz, 1961; Bijou and Baer, 1965) explain the development of behavior involving attachment in terms of principles of operant conditioning. They hypothesize that attachment between infant and mother is due to associations built up early in life between feeding and the types of behavior associated with it. If the mother cuddles the infant, smiles at it, and murmurs endearing words as she feeds it, presumably these stimuli will later arouse positive feelings in the child because they will be associated with the satisfaction of hunger.

Contact Comfort a Key Factor   Harlow (1958) decided to test this hypothesis. He constructed several cages, each containing two imitation monkey mothers made out of wire mesh. One of these was covered with a towel and had a different head than the other; both types were designed so that a nursing bottle could be inserted in the "chest." Several baby monkeys were taken from their mothers just after they were born. Half of them were put in cages where a bottle of milk had been inserted in the wire mother, the other half in cages with the bottle inserted in the cloth-covered mother. Since baby monkeys are quite mature, shortly after birth they were able to crawl to the bottle protruding from the substitute mothers and feed themselves. Harlow hypothesized that if the theory of association between feeding and later behavior was correct, the baby monkeys should have shown a marked preference for the kind of mother that nursed them. He discovered, however, that all of the babies, even those nursed by a wire mother, spent almost all of their nonfeeding time on the cloth mother. In addition, when they were exposed to frightening stimuli, either in their cages or in an experimental room, they invariably ran to the cloth mother. Harlow argued that this disproved the theory that feeding is of crucial importance in the development of later behavior and suggested instead that the basic factor was *contact comfort.* The baby monkeys seemed to respond more to the physical sensation of contact with a motherlike towel than to food.

Method devised by Harlow to study attachment

Contact comfort more important than feeding

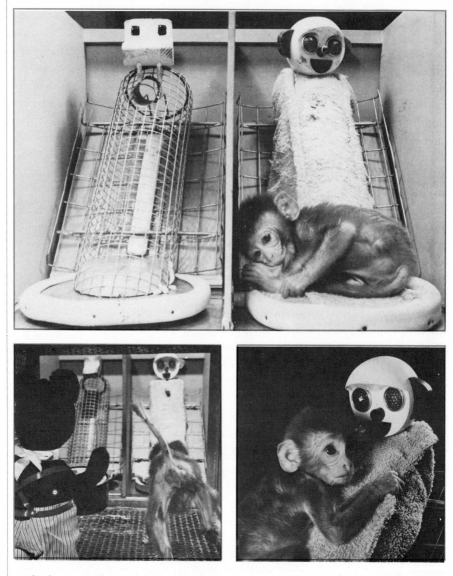

Harlow's experiments to test the hypothesis that attachment is based on associations built up when an infant is fed. Harlow discovered that baby monkeys spent more time with the cloth-covered mother and ran to it when frightened even when they had been fed from the wire mother. He concluded that contact comfort was more important than feeding as a source of affection between mother and child. Primate Laboratory, University of Wisconsin.

Critical Period in Development of Love In subsequent studies, Harlow (1964) found that monkeys who had been reared on the substitute mother sometimes developed extreme forms of abnormal behavior early in life; and when they were mature, females showed no interest in copulating and had difficulty conceiving. Furthermore, if these females did have babies, they did not behave toward them in a maternal way. In setting up his experiments, Harlow separated the monkeys from their mothers, and this factor seemed to take on increasing significance. Lack of contact with the mother (or other monkeys) apparently prevented the development of normal social and maternal behavior. Harlow found, for example, that if monkeys were isolated for as long as six-to-twelve months after birth, they did not respond in any way to other animals. This discovery led Harlow to propose a critical period in the development of affection: if a baby monkey had no contact with other monkeys during the first months of its life, it would never respond to others. By comparing the maturation rates of monkeys and humans, he extrapolated his results and proposed (in a documentary film, "Mother Love," shown on television in 1960) that if human infants do not learn to love during the first two years, they may never learn to love.

Hypothesis: early isolation may block development of love

Harlow's conclusion that contact comfort is of greater importance than feeding can be substantiated by his evidence. It may not be prudent, however, to accept his hypothesis that human infants who do not learn to love during the first two years may be incapable of ever responding to others with love. In fact, Harlow himself later modified his views about the critical nature of early experiences when he and his colleagues (Ruppenthal et al., 1976) discovered that motherless monkeys later overcame the effects of early deprivation if they were given opportunities to interact with other monkeys.

It would be illegal and unethical for a psychologist to test Harlow's hypothesis by deliberately rearing human infants without any contact with human care-takers. There are, however, certain unfortunate situations in which babies are reared under extremely deprived conditions. In some orphanages the care provided has not been very different from the sort of treatment endured by Harlow's monkeys.

Human Infants in Deprived Environments

In most countries today the need to provide proper care and stimulation for children in institutions is well recognized, but this is a quite recent development. For example, the records of the Dublin Foundling Home indicate that between 1775 and 1800, of the 10,272 children admitted, 45 survived (Kessen, 1965). And even during this century, one of the major orphanages in Germany reported a mortality rate of over 70 percent for children during the first year of life (Spitz, 1945). Thus, the negative impact of a deprived environment on human development has been recognized for years. Not until controlled studies were carried out, however, did the causes of retardation become apparent.

Spitz: Pioneering Investigation of Institutionalization   Movements toward social reform and humane treatment of less fortunate individuals in the last century led to improved conditions in orphanages such as the Dublin Foundling Home. Providing better food, living conditions, and medical care did much to reduce the mortality rate. Eventually, however, it became apparent that some children failed to develop normally even when reared under close to ideal physical and medical conditions. Margaret Ribble was instrumental in calling attention to this fact, but an Austrian physician named René Spitz was primarily responsible for publicizing the negative impact of marasmus. Spitz, like Ribble, had noticed the wasting-away of motherless babies kept in hospital nurseries, and he decided to obtain some systematic data on the condition. He found two groups of babies being reared in institution nurseries: infants in a prison nursery who were cared for by their inmate mothers, or by full-time mother substitutes, and provided with an abundant supply of toys; and infants in a foundling home who were isolated in cribs covered with sheets and were handled only at feeding time. It should come as no surprise that the foundling-home babies scored considerably lower on a scale of infant development.

Institutionalized babies retarded in development

Spitz had taken motion pictures of the foundling-home infants in their cribs, and when these were shown, public outcry led to substantially improved conditions. Even after a year of better care, however, most of the children were still retarded. This led Spitz to conclude that early deprivation had had an irreversible negative impact on development.

Surveys and Analyses of Institutionalization   In the years since Spitz published his report, dozens of other studies of the impact of institutionalization have been carried out in all parts of the world. (John Bowlby [1952] was asked by the World Health Organization to survey such studies.) Sally Provence and Rose C. Lipton (1962), for example, made detailed observation of seventy-five babies during and after time spent in an institution, and Wayne Dennis (1960, 1973) supervised a series of studies of orphans in Lebanon. Most investigators reported substantial retardation of development, and many were convinced that early losses were irreversible. Other psychologists, however (for example, Pinneau, 1955; Casler, 1961) criticized the methods and conclusions of some studies; still others offered evidence that institutionalization does not always lead to retardation (Bowlby, Salter, Boston, and Rosenbluth, 1956; Rheingold and Baley, 1959; Rheingold, 1961; Tizard and Hodges, 1978). Finally, Anna Freud and Sophie Dann (1951) found that children reared in a concentration camp were later able to overcome early extreme negative experiences.

Negative Conditions That May Affect Institutionalized Children   In evaluating the studies of the impact of institutionalization, you might take into account some observations by William R. Thompson and Joan E. Grusec (1970, p. 606) who reviewed a large number of investigations of this type. Thompson and Grusec point out that the institutionalized children who were the subjects of many of the studies carried out in the 1950s and 1960s may have been atypical (compared to home-reared children) in a variety of ways. They speculate that it is likely that many of the mothers of such children were unwed or were deserted by their husbands. For these, as well as other reasons, it seems reasonable to assume that many women who gave up their newborn children were dismayed about becoming pregnant and perhaps were anxious, tense, or depressed during pregnancy. In addition, it is likely that such expectant mothers made little effort to maintain an adequate diet, limit smoking and use of drugs, or guard against infectious diseases—particularly if they had made the decision to place the child in an institution as soon as they learned they were pregnant. Finally, it is likely that the mothers of many institutionalized children received little or no medical advice and care during pregnancy and at the time of birth.

All of these factors may have had a negative impact on institutionalized children during the prenatal period and at birth. But the kind of treatment they received *after* they had been placed in orphanages is probably of even greater significance (for reasons that will become clear when disadvantaged children are discussed in Chapter 9). While most theorists agree on the negative impact of the inadequate care typical of many orphanages before the World Health Organization and similar agencies brought about improvements, they differ about *why* such care retarded development.

Institutionalized Children Have Restricted Learning Opportunities
Some theoriosts (for example, Spitz, Ribble) attribute retardation in institutionalized children to lack of adequate mothering during the first few months of life, while others (for example, Rheingold) attribute it to lack of stimulation or restricted learning opportunities. After reviewing all available data on the subject up to 1970, Thompson and Grusec came to this conclusion:

> The fact that a number of investigators have not discovered negative effects in *all* children raised in institutions, *in spite of the fact that they had all suffered maternal deprivation,* means that other explanations for these effects, where they occur, must be sought. A likely explanation lies in the suggestion that children in institutions suffer from perceptual deprivation and restriction of learning opportunities. (1970, p. 607)

Retardation of institutionalized children due to restricted opportunities

Impact of Institutionalization: Conclusions
Mary Ainsworth (1962) has pointed out that in practice it may be impossible to make a distinction between maternal and perceptual deprivation and lack of learning opportunities since a caretaker supplies most of the stimulation for the infant. Ainsworth has specialized in the study of early parent-child relationships, and on the basis of a thorough review of the literature on deprivation and separation, she came to these conclusions (1962, pp. 153–154):

1 Infants seem capable of recovering from a single, brief depriving separation experience, but may become vulnerable to future threats of separation.

2 Even after a fairly prolonged deprivation experience in early infancy, provi-

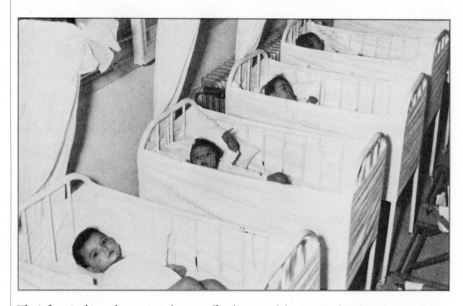

The infants in this orphanage in Lebanon suffered maternal deprivation, but they also were hampered by perceptual deprivation and restriction of learning opportunities. (They spent much of their time in cribs with sheets attached to the sides.) Psychologists differ in their opinions regarding which of these factors accounts for the fact that children reared in institutions are retarded in development. Wayne Dennis, *Children of the Crèche* © 1973. By permission of Margaret W. Dennis, Doswell, Virginia.

sion of stimulation before a child is twelve months old is likely to lead to rapid and dramatic improvement, although language development may lag behind intellectual and personality functioning.

Longer the deprivation, greater the retardation

3   Prolonged and severe deprivation that begins early in the first year and continues for as long as three years is likely to lead to severe retardation in intellectual, personality, and language functioning. As a general rule, the longer the deprivation experience, the greater the retardation and the poorer the prognosis for recovery.

4   Impairments in language and in the capacity for strong and lasting interpersonal relationships appear to be particularly resistant to attempts at reversing the effects of deprivation, although intensive therapeutic efforts early in life may be successful.

In a later review that included studies carried out in the 1960s and 1970s, Michael Rutter (1979) reaffirmed many of Ainsworth's conclusions. However, he expressed greater optimism about the ability of some children to later overcome the impact of early deprivation. He also agreed with Thompson and Grusec that perceptual deprivation and restricted learning opportunities (especially in the area of linguistic interaction) are probably more significant than maternal deprivation as explanations for retarded development in institutionalized children. Rutter was impressed by the range of differences in reactions to institutionalization. Some children who are placed in excellent homes, who develop close relationships with foster parents, who have positive personality traits, and who have favorable experiences in school, seem capable of overcoming an extremely poor start. Other children, however, may have quite positive experiences while institutionalized, only to encounter many problems later in life because of conflicts with foster parents and/or exposure to negative conditions (such as living in a disadvantaged environment) after leaving the orphanage.

Rutter's observations on the significance of parent-child relationships lead to the question: Which techniques of infant care appear to be most effective? To answer that question it will be helpful to take a closer look at interpretations of the impact of early experience by Freud, Erikson, and learning theorists.

Psychoanalytic Interpretations of Child Rearing

Freudian Views on the Significance of Feeding

Significance of the Oral Stage To review points noted earlier in discussing the neonate in Chapter 5, Freud proposed that during the first months of their lives humans were at the oral stage of psychosexual development. He believed that unfortunate experiences with feeding might cause an individual to become preoccupied later with food or fingernail biting or a desire to acquire possessions (to note only a few types of oral behvaor). O. Fenichel (1945) and Lois B. Murphy (1973) have provided detailed accounts of the phases of the oral stage and the types of adult behavior psychoanalysts believe are likely to be produced by certain types of feeding situations. It is extremely difficult to prove or disprove Freudian theories regarding the oral stage because all organisms must continue to eat throughout their lives in order to survive. How can anyone be sure that only feeding experiences during the first two years produced a particular type of behavior?

Breast-Feeding versus Bottle-Feeding It is possible to at least partially evaluate Freudian interpretations of the significance of oral behavior by comparing the later behavior of breast-fed and bottle-fed infants. M. I. Heinstein (1963) carried out a carefully planned longitudinal study of feeding practices and reported that there were no significant differences in the later behavior of bottle-fed or breast-fed children. It was discovered, however, that boys who had been breast-fed by mothers classified as "cold" had above-average adjustment problems. This finding supports a conclusion reached by others (for example, N. R. Newton, 1951): the important point seems to be *how* the baby is fed, not whether fed at the bottle or breast. The mother's attitude toward the child as reflected in the total feeding situation appears to be the crucial factor.

How infant fed is important factor, not whether breast- or bottle-fed

This hypothesis may explain why B. C. F. and C. H. Rogerson (1931) found that breast-fed babies tend to be less neurotic and to make better progress in school than bottle-fed babies while Heinstein did not, and why A. R. Holway (1949) found a relationship between duration of breast-feeding and later adjustment, but W. H. Sewell and P. H. Mussen (1952) and C. H. Peterson and F. Spano (1961) did not. An evaluation of the impact of methods of feeding should include examining the factors that might have contributed to the mother's choice of method. For example, mothers who decide to breast-feed their children may do so out of a desire to be especially conscientious about child rearing. This concern and solicitude may be shown not only in the feeding situation early in life but also in many later aspects of child rearing. Therefore, later child personality traits cannot be attributed only to feeding experiences during the first few months.

Pros and Cons of Breast- and Bottle-Feeding   In the absence of unequivocal evidence, the choice between bottle- and breast-feeding must be made in terms of preference. Those who favor breast-feeding argue that it is "nature's way" and that it provides an especially satisfying experience for both mother and child; that mother's milk is superior to any other kind, not only because of nutritional value but because of the presence of antibodies that improve the child's resistance to infection; and that it is simpler than mixing formulas and sterilizing bottles. Those who favor bottle-feeding argue that with the bottle held at the breast, communication between mother and child is essentially the same as it is in breast-feeding; that because of the use of insecticides, additives, and preservatives in food production and processing, the mother's milk may be contaminated in various ways; that mother's milk will vary from time to time, but the formula can be consistently controlled to provide maximum nutritional value for a particular child; and that breast-feeding may be inconvenient for the mother and other family members.

The conclusions that can be safely drawn from the debate over breast-feeding can be applied to Freud's observations on the oral stage. Feeding and sucking are of considerable importance to the child, and the way parents handle such behavior may influence the development of personality, even if this influence is not completely predictable or traceable.

Freudian Views of the Significance of Toilet Training

The same reasoning applies to Freud's analysis of the significance of toilet training. (As children approach their second birthdays, they enter the anal stage of psychosexual development.) For several months after birth, elimination takes place involuntarily. Toward the end of the second year the muscles and nerves have developed to the point where the average child can control the processes of elimination. When that time comes, the child is confronted with one of the most

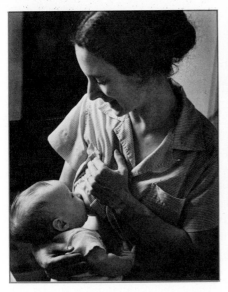

A number of arguments can be offered in support of either breast- or bottle-feeding. Advocates of breast-feeding, for example, stress empathy between mother and infant. Bottle-feeding, on the other hand, can be handled by any member of the family. Ellis Herwig/Stock, Boston; Nicholas Sapieha/Stock, Boston.

difficult tasks yet encountered—exerting control over a natural function for personal comfort and the convenience of others. There is no doubt that many children around the age of two years *are* more concerned about toilet training than any other aspect of their lives. Also, children probably experience elements of sensual satisfaction as they relieve themselves or handle their genital organs. But how can anyone be sure that toilet training has a permanent impact on personality?

As was the case with the oral phase, there is no clear-cut evidence to support the psychoanalytic view (described in detail in Fenichel, 1945) that a particular approach to toilet training leads to identifiable adult personality traits. E. J. Anthony (1957) and L. Despert (1944) found some evidence that children subjected to coercive toilet training before the first birthday were inclined to be rigid and compulsive; Robert R. Sears and several associates (1953, 1957) and the Berkeley Growth Researchers (Macfarlane, Allen, and Honzik, 1954) found that harsh toilet training was related to negativism and aggression later in life; but H. Beloff (1962) concluded that child personality traits showed more association with the personality of the mother than with her method of toilet training.

Freud's observations on the importance of the oral and anal phases of development seem to have some validity, therefore, but there is no proof that specific feeding and toilet-training practices will produce the personality traits attributed to them in psychoanalytic theory.

No clear-cut evidence toilet training has predictable or identifiable influence

Erikson's Stress on Trust and Autonomy

Important to foster trust and autonomy, minimize mistrust, shame, and doubt

In discussing the neonate in Chapter 5, the first stage of Erikson's description of development, trust versus mistrust, was used to provide insight into initial parent-child relationships. For the remainder of the first year and the beginning of the second, the development of trust continues to be important. Toward the end of the second year, however, when a major concern of the child is toilet training, the basic consideration of the parents is to help the child to develop a sense of *autonomy* and avoid a sense of *shame* or *doubt*.

In contrast to Freud, Erikson points out that children at the age of two years are mastering their entire musculature, not just the muscles which control elimination. But he agrees with Freud that toilet control is likely to be of special significance. If parents are impatient with children and try to shame them into mastering the processes of elimination, children may feel not only inadequate but evil as well. The development of at least a degree of shame, however, is desirable. You are reminded that in describing his stages as dichotomies, Erikson does not mean to imply an all-or-nothing choice. He believes that both qualities at each stage are necessary but that the positive factor should be more highly developed than the negative. One-year-olds (at the trust-versus-mistrust stage) should not develop an uncritical trust in everything; they should learn that some aspects of their world are untrustworthy. Two-year-olds should develop a sense of autonomy and independence. However, they should also begin to learn that in some situations they should be ashamed of their actions and experience a sense of embarrassment. Thus children need to have "the autonomy of free choice" at a time when they are literally standing on their own feet and mastering their bodies, but they must also be given full assistance in learning discretion and control.

While Erikson's observations on trust and autonomy seem eminently sensible and supply excellent general guidelines for some aspects of child rearing, it is not possible to substantiate these qualities as the most crucial features of early parent-child relationships. Furthermore trust and autonomy are extremely elusive and complex qualities. It does seem logical to assume, however, that a child who first develops a sense of trust and then acquires a sense of autonomy will be off to a good start in adapting to experiences that will be encountered later.

Learning-Theory Views of Child Rearing

John B. Watson's initial enthusiasm regarding the application of learning-theory principles to child rearing led him to believe he could shape behavior any way he chose. It soon became apparent, however, that his boast about converting any "well-formed infant" into a doctor, lawyer, or whatever was an empty claim because of the limitations of classical conditioning.

Skinner on the Potential Values of Scientific Child Rearing

After B. F. Skinner used operant-conditioning techniques to induce rats and pigeons to learn complex sequences of behavior he concluded that the limitations of classical conditioning had been overcome. In his novel *Walden Two* Skinner described how child-rearing specialists would arrange experiences and use rein-forcement (or lack of it) to shape desirable forms of behavior and extinguish undesirable traits. For instance, Skinner offers a description of how the child-rearing specialists at his fictional utopia would cause their charges to acquire a tolerance for annoying experiences. At the age of three, children are given a lollipop that has been dipped in powdered sugar (so that a single touch of the tongue can be detected). The children are told that they may eat the lollipop later in the day—provided it has not already been licked. At first, the children are encouraged to recognize that putting the lollipop out of sight will make it much easier to resist temptation. Eventually, however, the children are required to wear the lollipops around their necks for several hours at a stretch. When they are a bit older the children are taken for a long walk at a time when they are hungry and then required to stand in front of tantalizingly aromatic bowls of soup for five minutes. Skinner suggests that such techniques could be used to systematically build frustration tolerance in all children, not just those lucky enough to have had a favorable sequence of experiences. He also claims that such undesirable emo-tions as envy and jealousy could be virtually eliminated by arranging appropriate experiences and withholding reinforcement.

Limitations and Complications of Scientific Child Rearing

Skinner wrote *Walden Two* in 1948, shortly after he had established the basic principles of operant conditioning. He speculated about what *might* happen under ideal and carefully controlled conditions. In the thirty-some years since Skinner recorded his speculations, hundreds of psychologists and parents have actually used behavior modification techniques, but on a much more modest scale than the fictional child rearers of *Walden Two*. As noted in Chapter 3, behavior-mod-ification techniques are often effective when efforts are made to change quite specific types of behavior (such as a fear of dogs). It is a simple matter to arrange for a fearful child to observe other children having positive experiences with dogs. It is essentially impossible, however, to control circumstances to the point that a child will meet frustrations, for instance, only in prearranged situations. Accord-ingly, it would appear that operant-conditioning techniques are most likely to be effective when used selectively and systematically to shape or alter specific types of behavior.

Parents might be well-advised to limit their use of behavior modification techniques to occasional shaping of selected types of child behavior not only because of the likelihood of failure if they endeavor to shape general personality traits, but for more significant reasons as well. One potential danger of child-rearing techniques that involve an element of manipulation by parents was noted in the preceding chapter in reviewing the report by Etzel and Gewirtz (1967) that they had reduced infant crying by asking nurses to withhold reinforcement. If parents try to shape a seemingly simple type of infant behavior such as crying by withholding reinforcement, they may inadvertently shape more complex and significant types of behavior in unfortunate ways. That is, parents who make a resolution not to respond to an infant's cries may (or may not) temporarily reduce crying, but they may also retard infant development and cause unfortunate parent-child relationships. There are compelling reasons (as Erikson and others have stressed) to encourage infants and young children to develop the feeling quite early in life that *they* can shape the behavior of others. It is highly desirable for a baby to feel that it can sometimes "control" the parents—or at least get them to respond in predictable ways. If parents attempt too much behavior shaping, a child may fail to develop trust, autonomy, or initiative.

Children need to learn they can get others to respond

Making Judicious Use of Behavior Modification

Even so, it may be desirable for parents to make occasional use of principles of operant conditioning. Parents may find that they can use these techniques, for example, to help their children move quickly and smoothly through an important phase of the anal stage of psychosexual development. At the time Freud proposed his stages, toilet training was often a lengthy and anxiety-filled process for child and parents alike. (His own father was upset, for instance, because Sigmund wet his bed at an age when it was assumed he should have achieved control.)

Nathan H. Azrin and Richard M. Foxx describe ways parents can use behavior-modification techniques to teach *Toilet Training in Less Than a Day* (1976). In Chapter 4 of their book they describe how parents can begin training by first using a doll that wets to demonstrate this basic sequence: drinking lots of beverages, lowering loose-fitting training pants, sitting on a potty chair, urinating, being praised, being given a treat, emptying the pot in the toilet, flushing the toilet, putting the pot back in place. Next, the child is instructed to inspect the doll's pants to determine if they are dry and to carry out the sequence of actions with the doll that the parent has just demonstrated. (This part of the procedure takes advantage of the impact of imitation.) When actual training begins the child is encouraged to drink at least a cup of beverages an hour. Several favorite beverages are kept handy and the child is offered a drink every few minutes, often with the announcement that the drink is a reward for staying dry. (The purpose of plying the child with drinks is to increase the frequency of urination, learning

Helping the doll to the potty.

Figure 7–1   From *Toilet Training in Less Than a Day*. Copyright © 1974 by Nathan H. Azrin and Richard M. Foxx. Reprinted by permission of Simon & Schuster, a Division of Gulf & Western Corporation.

trials, and rewards. Learning is more likely to take place when several trials and reinforcements occur in quick succession.) The child is encouraged to follow the procedures that had been demonstrated with the doll by lowering the training pants and sitting on the potty chair. The moment that the child urinates, he or she is enthusiastically praised, given a treat, offered a drink, and given nonverbal praise in the form of smiling, clapping, hugging, and kissing. The child is also reminded how pleased "friends-who-care" (for example, grandma) will be.

Azrin and Foxx report that many parents who have followed these procedures have helped children achieve toilet training in a very short period of time (provided they first checked on the child's readiness and then followed instructions diligently). Because the behavior-modification approach to toilet training takes such a short period of time, and because it stresses the support and approval of the parents, it seems to be reasonable to assume that children who respond are not likely to suffer a fixation of the libido because of problems in learning to

Behavior modification approach to toilet training has advantages

control urination. Instead, Azrin and Foxx maintain, children are delighted with their new skill, and the sense of independence they experience often promotes initiative and confidence in other areas of behavior.

Sears: Stress on Reciprocal Interactions

Robert R. Sears believes that during the first phase of development infants seek to reduce biological drives. In the process, they learn that certain types of behavior bring about certain responses from others. Sears also emphasizes ways infant-care techniques used by parents influence the responses of the child. Thus, he calls attention to the reciprocal nature of early child-parent interactions.

If the child-rearing methods used by parents influence child behavior, it makes sense to try to discover the techniques used by parents of children who display desirable forms of behavior. In one of the comprehensive research projects he supervised early in his career (Sears, Maccoby, and Levin, 1957), Sears used interviews to obtain information about ways parents cared for their children during the first months of their lives. As noted in Chapter 2, information supplied in interviews, particularly data based on recollections, is not very trustworthy. In the years since Sears carried out his pioneering investigation, however, many psychologists have made detailed analyses of child-caretaker interactions during the first months of life in an attempt to discover how mothers who seem to have an excellent relationship with their offspring establish and maintain that relationship. Recent studies of this type point to the conclusion that the key to excellent early child-caretaker relationships is the mother's ability to coordinate and adapt her behavior to that of the infant. Descriptions and speculations relating to the nature of this parent-child coordination will now be presented.

Aspects of Mother-Infant Relationships[1]

Innate Qualities That Favor Mother-Infant Relationships

Characteristics of Infants That May Stimulate Caregiving   Some students of infant behavior (for example, Bowlby, 1969; Ainsworth, 1972) have been struck by the extent to which many forms of behavior that emerge during

---

[1] The term *mother* is used in preference to *caretaker*, *caregiver*, or *parents* in most of this discussion because even in the 1980s the mother still takes the primary responsibility for infant care in almost all homes. Furthermore, most studies of early interactions have involved mothers and their own infants. It would therefore be inaccurate to use *parents* in discussing such research and unnecessarily vague to use *caretaker*. The frequent use of *mother*, though, is not meant to exclude fathers from caregiving, nor is it meant to place all the responsibility for caregiving on mothers. As you will learn a bit later in this chapter, there appear to be strong reasons to believe that fathers can be as nurturant as mothers.

the first months of life seem to "equip" a baby to arouse positive responses from others. Several such types of behavior were mentioned in the preceding two chapters:

☐ Under certain circumstances, the rooting, sucking, and grasp reflexes may give a mother the feeling that her baby is eager to interact with her.

☐ Newborn infants come equipped with a rudimentary smile. And genuine social smiles, unmistakably stimulated by and directed to others, appear within the first months of postnatal existence.

☐ Very early in their lives infants seem to enjoy interacting with others, a form of activity that often appears to be a game involving two participants.

☐ Infants pay special attention to visual patterns that are circular and have high contrast. Such patterns are very similar to a human face which means that early in their lives, infants are likely to regard their parent's faces more frequently than other stimuli.

☐ As early as a few days after they are born infants respond to human voices by synchronizing their movements with the speech sound they hear.

☐ The infant's babbling begins spontaneously, and before the end of the first year most babies use sounds to communicate with others.

Many types of infant behavior arouse positive responses

Such forms of behavior might be interpreted as built-in qualities that predispose mothers to want to care for their children. Konrad Lorenz (1943) was one of the first theorists to point out that the behavior and appearance of babies of any species makes them extremely appealing. (How do you react, for example, when you see one or more puppies or kittens?) Lorenz speculated that physical and behavioral characteristics of many newborn organisms may have emerged and been retained due to evolutionary survival-of-the-fittest tendencies. John Bowlby (1969) has expanded on Lorenz's point regarding the extent to which human babies seem to be "designed" to encourage positive responses from mothers.

Characteristics of Humans That May Predispose Them to Provide Care   There is some evidence that humans develop a tendency at the time of puberty to respond to infants. W. Fullard and A. M. Rieling (1976) asked males and females who ranged in age from seven years through adulthood to indicate their preference for photographic slides of infant and adult faces. Beginning at the age of twelve and continuing through adulthood, females reported that they preferred the picture of the baby. At around the age of fourteen, boys began to indicate a preference for the picture of the infant. This tendency, however, was not found to the same extent in adult males. Fullard and Rieling acknowledge the possibile impact of social factors on the behavior they studied. It is suggestive, though, that the tendency for older humans to become attracted to infants' faces appears at puberty when they become capable of conceiving children.

Daniel Stern (1977, pp. 27–28) reports that anecdotal evidence, as well as more systematic data he is in the process of collecting, leads to the conclusion that starting in childhood humans seem primed to respond to infants. Stern also reports that such caretaker tendencies are stronger and more extensive in females than males. Because virtually all children have observed mothers caring for infants, it is impossible to determine the extent to which this sex difference is due to inherited predispositions, how much it is influenced by observation and imitation.

Individual Differences in Caregiving

Even though there may be a tendency for many females (as well as some males) to be positively attracted to infants, there are substantial individual differences in the strength of this tendency. Some women, for example, eagerly seek motherhood and report that they feel disappointed and unfulfilled when they no longer have young children to care for. Other women make up their minds quite early in life that they do not wish to bear children or care for them. Among women who do bear children, there are substantial differences in caretaking behavior that appear as they take on the responsibilities of motherhood.

Differences in the responses of mothers to their children suggest that no universal "instinct" of mothering is present (or becomes activated) in all women who give birth. A number of explanations can be proposed to account for the fact that some mothers love their children and are sensitive to their needs, while others are indifferent. (Some of these explanations were noted in Chapter 5 in the analysis of the research of Birns and Thomas.)

The Impact of Contact with the Newborn Infant The attitude of a woman toward her child may be influenced by experiences the first few hours after birth. John H. Kennell, Diana K. Voos, and Marshall H. Klaus (1979) reviewed studies comparing the later behavior of mothers who had considerable skin-to-skin contact with their newborn infants with that of mothers who were prevented by hospital routine from having more than occasional contact (for example, at feeding time). They found that during subsequent infant physical exams, early-contact mothers stood near their infants and also soothed crying to a significantly greater extent than limited-contact mothers. During feeding session the early-contact mothers displayed more eye-to-eye contact and fondling. In addition, the early-contact mothers displayed a significantly greater tendency to breast-feed their babies longer than limited-contact mothers. Kennel, Voos, and Klaus suggest (p. 794) that skin-to-skin contact of mother and infant should begin during the first twelve hours after birth (indicating that the researchers feel this is a critical period in the formation of attachment). It is possible, therefore, that the degree of attachment between infant and parents may be traceable to the opportunity for contact with each other immediately after birth. One of the

Early skin-to-skin contact may promote attachment

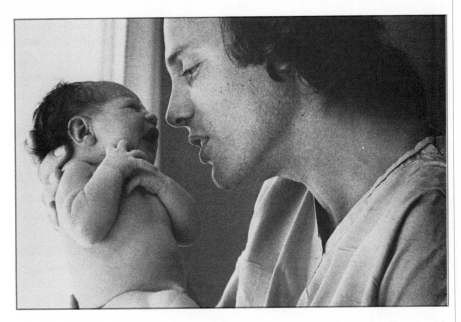

Some psychologists suggest that mothers and fathers are more likely to form an attachment with their child if they have contact with the infant the first few hours after birth. © Hella Hammid/ Photo Researchers.

features of the delivery procedure favored by Frederick Leboyer (mentioned in Chapter 5), specifically the practice of placing the newborn baby on the mother's abdomen, may have more of an immediate impact on the mother than the infant. (Also, if the mother develops a strong feeling of attachment, her responsive child care during the first months may lead to the kinds of infant behavior Leboyer attributes to the baby's response to being born.)

Evaluation of the Maternal Critical-Period Hypothesis Before expectant parents assume that they can more or less guarantee that they will develop a strong attachment to a child by arranging for skin-to-skin contact immediately after birth, however, a number of points should be considered. First of all, the studies on which Kennell, Voos, and Klaus base their conclusions have involved small numbers of mother–infant pairs (sometimes as few as five), and not all potentially significant factors have been controlled (for example, the attitudes of the mother regarding pregnancy, birth, and child care; whether the infant was judged easy or difficult to care for). Second, it is possible that when more comprehensive and carefully controlled studies are carried out, a modification of the maternal critical-period hypothesis as now stated will emerge. As noted in discussing the research of Lorenz and Harlow, initial reports of imprinting in birds and of critical periods in monkeys and humans were revised as research data accumulated. When original studies were repeated, it was concluded that sensitive, rather than critical, periods occur and only under certain circumstances.

A similar revision of the maternal critical-period hypothesis might be anticipated as follow-up investigations of early interaction are carried out. Some researchers (for example, Leiderman and Seashore, 1975; Clarke and Clarke, 1976; Whiten, 1977), in fact, have already reported evidence that leads to the conclusion that contact the first few hours after birth is not necessarily as significant as Klaus and Kennell suggest it is. Furthermore, Michael Rutter (1970) points out that many foster parents develop a close relationship with adopted children even though they may not have had any contact with them until they were several months, or even years, old. After reviewing research on the impact of initial parent-child contacts on later behavior Rutter concluded, "It seems unlikely that . . . events in the neonatal period have an inevitable lasting impact on mother-child relationships" (1979, p. 294). Finally, there is no proof that the kinds of child-handling tendencies found in early-contact mothers (for example, more extensive breast-feeding) have a significant impact on later behavior. Evaluations of Freud's hypothesis about the significance of the oral stage of psychosexual development, for instance, led to the conclusion that breast-feeding per se does not seem to have a predictable impact on a child's later behavior and personality.

Maternal critical-period hypothesis tentative, not clearly established.

Even though there currently may not be unequivocal proof of a maternal critical period, parents who are eager to develop a close relationship with a new baby might try to arrange for both mother *and* father to handle their child shortly after it is born. The reason both parents might wish to be present at the birth of their child is that there is evidence (Parke, 1979) that fathers who participate in the delivery (as in the Lamaze method) and who handle newborn infants are often at least as nurturant as mothers. Parke reports, for example, that fathers who had early contact with a baby were just as responsive as mothers to the infant's signals and were equally adept at bottle-feeding. (It appears, though, that fathers seem to identify more with sons than daughters, particularly first-born sons. Parke summarizes research evidence indicating that during the first three months of infant-parent interactions fathers vocalize more with boy babies and stimulate them more than girl babies.)

Fathers may be influenced as much as mothers by early contact

Prospective parents might make arrangements to try to have immediate contact with their newborn child by following natural childbirth procedures and by selecting an obstetrician who will cooperate. If circumstances and complications prevent immediate contact, however, parents who had hoped to handle their newborn baby might keep in mind this point: in most American hospitals in the 1950s and 1960s very few mothers had contact with their newborn children because the mothers were under sedation and/or prevented by hospital routine from handling their infants except at prescribed feeding times. Yet many of these mothers must have formed a strong attachment to their children because there is no evidence that there was a marked decrease in maternal responsiveness on a large scale during those decades. It would appear, then, that early contact may

Males classified as sex-typed feel comfortable when taking part in masculine activities such as football but may feel self-conscious when engaging in traditionally feminine activities such as child care. Males rated high in psychological androgyny, by contrast, are able to move between such roles without experiencing doubts or difficulties. Ellis Herwig/Stock, Boston; Christa Armstrong/ Rapho Photo Researchers.

encourage the formation of attachment between parent and child, but it is not essential.

The Impact of Sex-typed or Androgynous Tendencies

Because many mothers who failed to experience immediate contact with their newborn infants still formed a strong attachment, there seem to be several factors other than early contact that may influence infant-parent relationships. Due to interactions between inherited predispositions (such as hormonal balances), cultural sex stereotypes, and experiences, some women (and men) may be more attracted to and comfortable with infant-care responsibilities than others. Sandra Bem (1975, 1976) has studied the extent to which individuals can be classified as *sex-typed* (the tendency to exhibit forms of stereotyped masculine or feminine behavior) or high in *psychological androgyny*[2] (the integration of both masculine and feminine traits in the same individual). Sex-typed females, for example, respond favorably when asked to care for an infant but may refuse to try to nail two boards together (because it is a "masculine" rather than "feminine" form of behavior). Sex-typed males may be extremely reluctant to handle a baby or even wind a package of yarn into a ball (apparently because they will be made to

Sex-typed and androgynous parents likely to respond to infants in different ways

[2] Androgynous, spelled with a *y*, means possessing both male and female characteristics. Androgenous spelled with an *e*, refers to the impact of the male sex hormone, androgen.

appear "effeminate"). Adults of both sexes who are rated high in psychological androgyny appear able to move between masculine and feminine roles without difficulty or self-consciousness.

Furthermore, some individuals appear to be *undifferentiated* (that is, low in both masculinity and femininity), others Bem classifies as feminine males (low in independence), masculine males (low in nurturance), feminine women (low in independence), or masculine women (low in nurturance). It would seem logical to assume that the response of any father or mother to skin-to-skin contact with a newborn baby (as well as later interactions) would depend on the tendencies that have been described by Bem. A sex-typed female would presumably be more likely to form an attachment than an undifferentiated woman or one classified as a masculine woman. A sex-typed male might not be influenced by early contacts or might even refuse to handle the child. A male classified high in psychological androgyny, by contrast, might respond positively to early contact and enjoy sharing infant-care responsibilities with the mother.

The Impact of Experiences During Pregnancy   Other factors that might influence a woman's reaction to early contact with a newborn baby include her attitude toward pregnancy, the amount of discomfort she suffered during pregnancy, and the ease or difficulty of labor and birth. Furthermore, a new mother might discover after the first few days that she resents, rather than enjoys, the responsibilities of infant care. (This might be particularly true if she has been employed.)

Characteristics of the child may also shape the mother's attitudes toward child care. If the baby is attractive, easy to care for, and responsive, a woman classified by Bem as masculine might be won over. If the baby is unattractive, difficult to care for, and given to uncontrollable crying and unpredictable demands, a sex-typed woman who had looked forward to motherhood might become disenchanted.

Factors such as early contact, sex-typed tendencies, or the characteristics of the child account for some of the differences in the degree of attachment between infant and parents. Further insight into differences in parental responsiveness can be supplied by comparisons of extreme parent types: those who abuse their children and those who are rated as particularly sensitive and effective.

Characteristics of Parents Who Abuse Their Children

In the last few years dozens of articles and books (for example, Helfer and Kempe, 1974) on the *battered child syndrome* have revealed that a substantial number of parents physically mistreat their children. In a review of books and articles on child abuse R. D. Parke and C. W. Collmer (1975) note that hypotheses regarding causes can be summarized under three headings: psychiatric, sociological, and social-situational.

Parke and Collmer report that the authors of the first articles on child abuse (published in the 1950s and 1960s) often suggested that basic causes were traceable to characteristics of child abusers that became apparent when psychiatric analyses were made. Among traits frequently found in parents who abused their children were low self-esteem, self-centeredness, rigidity, impulsiveness, immaturity, and hypersensitivity. Parke and Collmer note that while child abusers often display one or more of these traits, no consistent pattern that characterizes such parents as a group has emerged. The most common factor appears to be a tendency to express aggressive impulses too freely (Spinetta and Rigler, 1972). There *is* consistent evidence, however, that child abusers were themselves abused as children and that their parents were often demanding and aggressive individuals who disregarded their children's needs.

Child abusers express aggressive impulses freely, were abused themselves

One of the sociological explanations for child abuse focuses on the American attitude toward violence. Murders occur ten times more frequently in this country than in England (Geis and Monahan, 1975). The assault and battery rate in America is about five times the rate in Canada (Steinmetz, 1974). In a survey of middle-class American families, 93 percent of the parents reported that they used physical punishment (Stark and McEvoy, 1970). Violence is featured on American television to a much greater extent than it is in any other country. In one survey (Gerbner, 1972), for example, over 75 percent of all drama programs shown on network television contained violence. It is not possible to determine precisely how the various trends indicated by these statistics are related to child abuse, but some theorists (for example, R. J. Gelles, 1973) hypothesize that the extent to which violence permeates our society might predispose parents to resort to physical aggression when angered by the behavior of a child.

A widely accepted theory in psychology is that frustration leads to aggression (Dollard, Doob, Miller, Mowrer, and Sears, 1939). Those who provide sociological explanations of child abuse suggest that individuals who are likely to experience frequent feelings of frustration because of such factors as unemployment, poverty, and crowded living conditions may be particularly inclined to react with violence when the behavior of a child adds yet another frustration or irritation. In addition, it appears that child abusers often live in self-imposed social isolation, that is, with little or no contact with neighbors or relatives. As a result, the child is more likely to be in lengthy contact with parents, which increases the possibility of annoyance. Furthermore, the absence of other people may cause parents to feel less inclined to control their anger since they will assume that they will be unobserved if they beat a child.

Child abusers must cope with frustrations, often live in social isolation

Social-situational interpretations of child abuse emphasize that the experiences of parents who were abused by their parents predispose them to be punitive themselves. If physical punishment used by such parents causes the child to stop annoying behavior, the tendency toward punitiveness is reinforced. Furthermore, if the child builds up an immunity to habitual forms of punishment, the parents may feel obliged to resort to more extreme physical abuse. Other social-situa-

Abused children often premature, sick, given to crying

tional explanations of child abuse focus on characteristics of the victims. Infants born prematurely (who are difficult to care for and may have a variety of abnormalities), children who are sick, and babies who cry excessively are frequent victims of parental violence. One of the reasons premature babies are frequent victims of parental abuse may be that such infants are often placed in an incubator during the first weeks of postnatal existence (A. Leifer et al., 1972). The mother is thus prevented from having contact with her child during what may be a maternal sensitive period. This may account, in part at least, for her failure to later develop strong feelings of attachment.

A variety of techniques for attempting to prevent and control child abuse have been developed. These include parent group discussions, home support programs, hotline services (where a frustrated parent can talk to a sympathetic and supportive listener), crisis nurseries and drop-off centers (where a child can be left until a frustrated parent on the brink of resorting to physical abuse is able to gain control), and educational programs designed to provide information about techniques that might be used to control violent tendencies and replace them with non-punitive reactions.

The parent who abuses a child is at one end of a continuum of negative and positive caretaker characteristics. At the other end is the parent who appears to have strong positive feelings about the child and who is especially effective in promoting child development. Several investigators have sought to identify techniques used by sensitive, successful mothers in caring for their babies.

Techniques Used by Sensitive, Successful Mothers

Stern: Repetition, Timing, Optimal Stimulation   Daniel Stern (1977) has spent years poring over videotapes of the facial and bodily activities involved in early mother-child interactions. Such analyses have led him to conclude that an *episode of engagement* (pp. 79–80) between mother and infant typically involves the intention on the mother's part to maintain the baby's attention or enter into some sort of game (for example, peek-a-boo) to arouse pleasure. Usually the mother will repeat a brief routine of speech and physical movements (for example, saying "You're a sweetie-pie" while nuzzling the baby's face) several times in succession. In order to interact successfully with a baby, Stern concluded that mothers must have an excellent sense of timing, engaging in a particular type of activity at the precise moment the baby seems ready for it. Even the most sensitive mother, however, is sure to encounter periods of time when the baby is either not in the mood for play or the mother misinterprets the infant's signals. An important point about a successful episode of engagement appears to be gauging the amount of stimulation the baby can handle at a given point in time. Sometimes a mother may confront the infant with too many verbal and physical stimuli. In other cases, she may not stimulate the baby appropriately to arouse a

Effective mothers have good sense of timing

Sensitive, successful mothers are able to maintain a baby's attention in playful activity and arouse a sense of pleasure. Ken Heyman.

positive response. Just as the mood of the baby governs the success or failure of a particular interaction, so the mood of the mother plays a part. If the mother is tired or tense, she may be less sensitive than usual. Or if she fails to get a response from her baby after several minutes of effort and experimentation, she may experience the feeling that she is being rejected by her child and lose her enthusiasm for play.

Schaffer: The Need to Take Turns   H. Rudolph Schaffer (1977a) is another psychologist who has made detailed analyses of mothering. He agrees with Stern that successful mothers are exceptionally adept at picking up subtle cues to gauge the mood of a baby and that they have an excellent sense of timing. In addition, Schaffer stresses the need for mother and infant to take turns—after the baby started an interchange. Most successful mother-baby interactions apparently begin with the mother's response to some spontaneous activity of the infant. (This is the same sequence Piaget observed in language development. Parents must imitate sounds that are first uttered by the child.) If the mother's response stimulates the child to build up to a smile and perhaps reach out or engage in some other form of activity, it seems important for the mother not to interrupt the baby's behavior as it builds toward a crescendo. Instead, she should act as an interested, receptive audience until the baby has "performed" and at that point respond enthusiastically.

Infants and mothers need to take turns

Finally, Schaffer emphasizes that it is extremely important for babies, quite early in life, to acquire the feeling that they can produce consequences. This is the same point noted earlier in discussing the view of Skinner, Sears, and Erikson regarding the extent to which parents can (and should) control child behavior. Schaffer argues (1977a, p. 56) that withholding all reinforcement when babies cry, for instance, would be likely to cause children to develop a sense of helplessness. The infant uses cries and other forms of behavior to communicate needs and desires. If no one responds, the baby is likely to take on characteristics of children reared in deprived environments. In Schaffer's opinion, therefore, it is perhaps more important for children to learn before the end of the first year that *they* can successfully use behavior-modification techniques on their parents than for the opposite to occur.

Infants need to learn they can produce consequences

Ainsworth: Control, Contact, and Delight   Mary Ainsworth is another psychologist who has concentrated on the study of mother-infant interaction. She analyzed her own work and that of others (Ainsworth and Wittig, 1972) and concluded that the following factors seemed to favor development:

1   The provision of an environment that helps the child develop the feeling of having some control over what happens. (This is the same point stressed by Schaffer.)
2   Seeing things from the infant's point of view and responding promptly and appropriately to the baby's signals.
3   Frequent and sustained physical contact, especially during the first year of life, including the ability to soothe the baby's discomfort through physical handling.
4   The establishment of feelings of mutual delight between mother and child.

Effective mothers handle babies well, take delight

Bower: The Disadvantages of Overstimulation   T. G. R. Bower is still another specialist in the study of the responses of infants to others. Bower believes, as do Sears and Schaffer, that it is a mistake to bombard infants with stimuli. Overstimulation might take the form of too much interaction, trying to induce babies to respond to something they are not ready to respond to, and prolonging or overemphasizing a particular interaction. Bower believes that babies overburdened with people, things, and experiences, may be faced with interpretive problems beyond their capabilities. The concept that an infant needs time to sort out experiences helps explain why mothers who are willing to take turns seem to have successful interactions with their children.

May be unwise to overstimulate infants

Support for Bower's hypothesis is supplied by Burton L. White's research studies of the impact of stimulation on infant development. In an early investigation (White and Castle, 1964), week-old institutionalized infants were given twenty minutes of extra handling a day. At the end of thirty days developmen-

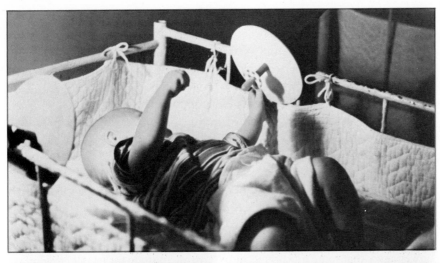

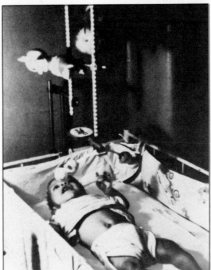
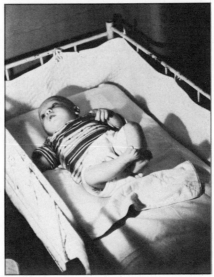

White and Held's study of the impact of different crib environments on reaching behavior. Infants in two-disk cribs developed reaching behavior faster than those in the multiple-toy or plain cribs, apparently because they concentrated their attention on the single within-reach object. By permission from B. L. White.

tal-test ratings of the handled infants were compared to ratings of nonstimulated babies. The only difference was a greater amount of visual attention shown by the stimulated infants. This prompted White (1967) to provide another group of institutionalized infants with extra stimulation by enabling them to look out of their cribs, or at intriguing objects suspended over their cribs, or at patterned crib bumpers. Compared to control infants, who were placed in plain cribs with high sides, the rich-environment babies showed greater visual attentiveness as well as accelerated reaching behavior.

In an effort to determine the effectiveness of different kinds of enrichment, White and Held (1966) placed one group of infants in the rich-environment cribs, another group in cribs that were equipped on each side with large disks from which pacifiers projected, still another group in plain cribs with high sides. The infants in the two-disk cribs developed reaching behavior faster than those who had been placed in the rich-environment cribs, who, in turn, were ahead of the control-group babies. Apparently the rich-environment infants had so many things to look at that they neglected to reach for objects. The babies in the two-disk cribs, on the other hand, concentrated all of their attention on the single, within-reach object attached to either side of their cribs.

Variations of Mother-Infant Interactions   Stern, Schaffer, Ainsworth, and Bower agree that some mothers seem to have an aptitude for interpreting infant behavior, timing their responses, and allowing for instantaneous changes in interest and mood. But it may also be that some mothers are simply luckier than others. In discussing the neonate in Chapter 5 mention was made of the conclusion of Alexander Thomas and his associates that babies could be classified into three general types: easy, difficult, and slow to warm up. Mothers who are fortunate enough to have an easy baby will probably be more successful at satisfying interactions than mothers of difficult infants. It is entirely possible, of course, that some mothers might at least partly "produce" difficult babies in just a few days of mistimed, ineffective handling and that some babies are slow to warm up because the mother doesn't know how to establish successful episodes of engagement.

It would be a mistake to assume, however, that babies and mothers are entirely consistent in their interactions. Not only do mother and child have good and bad days and minute-by-minute changes in mood; there are likely to be changes in relationships over time. Schaffer (1977a, p. 53) points out that the way mothers treat and handle their children changes as the infant matures. Furthermore, there is evidence (Moss, 1967 and Lewis, 1972) that mothers tend to treat girls differently from boys, particularly as the children grow older. Before the age of three months mothers cuddle boys and girls about the same extent. After three months, girls are cuddled to a significantly greater extent. (Moss hypothesizes that mothers may be positively reinforced by the responsiveness of female infants and negatively influenced by the irritability of many male infants.)

A mother may respond to her baby, therefore, not only in terms of the infant's personality traits but also because of its sex and changes in behavior that occur as development takes place. The impact of rapid physical and cognitive develop-ment also causes *children* to alter their patterns of response to their mothers (and other adults) during the first two years. During the first two years, for example, most children exhibit sometimes disconcerting responses to strangers and to being separated from their mothers.

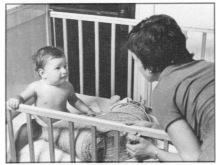

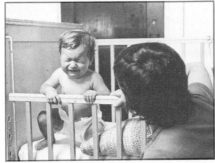
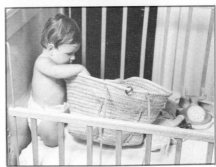

Stranger anxiety often appears at around eight months. This child is frightened by the appearance of a strange person and does not begin to relax until the stranger—who represents a drastic departure from the scheme for mother—withdraws. Philip Jon Bailey.

Stranger and Separation Anxiety

For the first half year of their lives most babies may not object if they are picked up by someone other than the mother. But starting around the age of six months or so, infants may stare or "freeze" when approached by someone they have never seen before. René Spitz (1965) was one of the first psychologists to comment on this phenomenon. He noticed that by eight months of age infants showed such a marked fear of strangers that he concluded it was a feature of normal development (referred to as *eight-month anxiety*) during the first year. At about the same time Mary Ainsworth carried out an intensive study of infants in Uganda and reported (1967) that they not only showed a fear of strangers, they also displayed anxiety (before their first birthdays) when separated from their mothers. Since the mid-1960s when stranger and separation anxiety were first described by Spitz, Ainsworth, and others, hundreds of reports on these two types of infant behavior have been published. Four of the most carefully planned of these investigations were carried out by Ainsworth, Blehar, Waters, and Wall (*Patterns of Attachment,* 1978). Over one hundred infants approximately one year old were observed in laboratory as well as home situations. (A summary of the sequence of situations the infants were exposed to in the controlled environment

Stranger and separation anxiety typically appear before end of first year

Table 7–1
Description of Procedures Used by Ainsworth
in Studying Stranger and Separation Anxiety

NUMBER OF EPISODE	PERSONS PRESENT	DURATION	BRIEF DESCRIPTION OF ACTION
1	Mother, baby, & observer	30 secs.	Observer introduces mother and baby to experimental room, then leaves. [Room contains many appealing toys scattered about]
2	Mother & baby	3 min.	Mother is nonparticipant while baby explores; if necessary, play is stimulated after 2 minutes.
3	Stranger, mother, & baby	3 min.	Stranger enters. First minute: Stranger silent. Second minute: Stranger converses with mother. Third minute: Stranger approaches baby. After 3 minutes mother leaves unobtrusively.
4	Stranger & baby	3 min. or less[a]	First separation episode. Stranger's behavior is geared to that of baby.
5	Mother & baby	3 min. or more[b]	First reunion episode. Mother greets and/or comforts baby, then tries to settle him again in play. Mother then leaves, saying "bye-bye."
6	Baby alone	3 min. or less[a]	Second separation episode.
7	Stranger & baby	3 min. or less[a]	Continuation of second separation. Stranger enters and gears her behavior to that of baby.
8	Mother & baby	3 min.	Second reunion episode. Mother enters, greets baby, then picks him up. Meanwhile stranger leaves unobtrusively.

[a]Episode is curtailed if the baby is unduly distressed.
[b]Episode is prolonged if more time is required for the baby to become re-involved in play.

Source: Ainsworth et al., *Patterns of Attachment* (Hillsdale, N.J.: Lawrence Erlbaum Associates, 1978), p. 37.

of the laboratory is presented in Table 7–1.) Observers tape-recorded a play-by-play account of what each baby and mother did, and in some cases, still or motion pictures were made of the baby's activities. The various records of infant and mother behavior were then coded, tabulated, and analyzed.

Individual Differences in Stranger and Separation Anxiety   Ainsworth and her associates designed their investigation to shed light on several incompletely answered questions about stranger and separation anxiety. As soon as these two types of behavior were first described, some psychologists (for example, Schaffer and Emerson, 1964) reasoned that they indicated that an infant had formed an attachment to the mother. This hypothesis seemed valid since both types of behavior reveal that an eight-month-old infant is noticeably upset when the mother disappears or is replaced by a stranger. It soon became apparent, however, that not all infants reacted in the same way or to the same degree. The response of the child seems to depend on the situation. M. Lewis and J. Brooks (1975), for example, exposed seven- to nineteen-month-old children to strange adults and children at close range and at a distance. They found that strange adults who came close to the children were quite likely to arouse a fear response, but if adult strangers remained at a distance, no signs of fear appeared. They also discovered that strange *children* of about the same age, whether near or far, aroused a *positive* reaction.

Ainsworth and her associates arranged the sequence of situations listed in Table 7–1 to seek causes of individual differences in both stranger and separation anxiety. After analyzing the tabulated results they concluded that consistent patterns of infant-mother interaction were found in both laboratory and home situations and that these influenced how the child reacted in the experimental situations.

In their first investigations Ainsworth and her associates identified three patterns of infant-mother interaction which they designated as Groups A, B, and C. In later studies, when the types of child and maternal behavior became more clearly established, terms that described the behavior of the infants in each group were added to supplement the original alphabetical designations. In Table 7–2 you will find a summary of infant behavior, maternal characteristics, and the infant's hypothesized perception of the mother for each of the three groups.

As you can see, Group B (securely attached) infants responded to the sequence of stituations described in Table 7–1 by initially exploring freely when the mother was present (Episode 2). They tended to be cooperative and outgoing when a stranger joined the mother (Episode 3) but were visibly upset when separated from the mother (Episodes 4 and 6). When the mother returned (Episodes 5 and 8) Group B babies responded with obvious relief and made strenuous efforts to establish physical contact with her. The mothers of these securely attached babies were judged to enjoy bodily contact with their infants, to be responsive to the baby's signals, and to have a good sense of timing (for

Table 7–2

Differences in Mother-Infant Interaction Reported by Ainsworth

TYPE OF INFANT BEHAVIOR	INFANT BEHAVIOR BEFORE, DURING, AND AFTER SEPARATION FROM MOTHER	BEHAVIOR AND CHARACTERISTICS OF MOTHER	INFANT'S HYPOTHESIZED PERCEPTION OF MOTHER
Group B securely attached (about 70% of sample)	Active exploration when alone with mother. Visibly upset by separation. Respond strongly to mother's return, eagerly seek physical contact, quickly soothed. Cooperative and outgoing with strangers (when mother present)	Enjoy bodily contact with baby. Responsive to baby's signals. Good sense of timing.	Mother perceived as accessible and responsive. Mother serves as secure base from which to explore.
Group C anxiously attached and resistant (about 10 percent of sample)	Anxious even when alone with mother, disinclined to explore. Upset by separation. Make strong efforts to gain contact with mother but simultaneously display anger or resentment. Likely to be distressed when strangers approach (even when mother is present)	Seem to enjoy bodily contact with baby but not skilled in interacting with baby. Not sensitive to baby's signals. Poor sense of timing.	Infant lacks confidence in mother as an accessible and responsive person. Infant expects to be frustrated rather than comforted when upset. Mother does not function as a secure base from which to explore, which leads to anxiety and limits exploration.
Group A anxious and avoidant (about 20 percent of sample)	Disinterested and perfunctory exploration when alone with mother. Show little distress when separated. Avoid contact with mother when reunited. Not excessively wary of strangers, but avert gaze from mother (as if ignoring her) when strangers approach.	Do not enjoy bodily contact with infant. Rigid and compulsive. Little emotional expression. Impatient, resentful, or angry when baby interferes with own plans and activities.	Infant expects that efforts to gain comfort will be rebuffed. When subjected to stress, infant defends self by avoiding contact. Mother not recognized or acknowledged as a supportive person.

Source: Ainsworth, Blehar, Waters, and Wall, 1978; Ainsworth, 1979a, Ainsworth, 1979b.

example, they knew when to pick the baby up and when to put the baby down). On the basis of the responses of Group B babies in the experimental episodes, Ainsworth and her associates concluded that they appeared to perceive the mother as an accessible and responsive person and as a secure base from which to explore. They seemed to be confident that the mother would be available to provide support if needed and that she would do this effectively.

Securely attached infants perceive mother as accessible, responsive

The mothers of anxiously attached and resistant (Group C) babies seemed to have good intentions and to be eager to provide physical contact, but they lacked the sensitivity and timing of Group B mothers. Ainsworth and her associates hypothesized that Group C babies have learned that their mothers are inept, which causes such children to be both anxious and resistant. They do not feel that they can count on the mother for satisfactory support and are angry and resentful about it.

The mothers of Group A babies were noticeably different from the other mothers. They seemed to have an aversion to physical contact and sometimes revealed that they had negative feelings about their children. They were rigid, reserved, impatient, and self-centered. Ainsworth and her colleagues concluded that the basic response of infants to such mothers was to try to avoid contact. Group A babies did not exhibit anger or resentment about the mother's ineffectiveness but acted disinterested, uninvolved, and withdrawn.

The Dynamics of Stranger and Separation Anxiety   The studies of Ainsworth and her colleagues reveal that the response of a child to separation or strangers depends on relationships with the primary caretaker. These studies also reveal how the behavior of infants depends on the situation and on the pushes and pulls of conflicting tendencies. The interplay of forces acting on a child can be understood more completely if the speculations of psychologist Kurt Lewin are mentioned before the results of the Ainsworth investigations are discussed further.

Kurt Lewin was a Gestalt psychologist. *Gestalt* is a German word that can be translated as *pattern* or *configuration*. It emphasizes that psychologists should study the whole situation instead of concentrating on specific aspects of behavior. Gestalt psychology is also called *field theory* because psychologists who favor this position believe that it is desirable to trace how psychological *fields of forces* influence behavior. (Analyses of fields of forces were originally made by physicists who studied magnetic and other types of fields of physical forces.) Lewin (1954) developed a system for diagramming how human behavior is influenced by positive and negative forces and by the direction of these forces. He also proposed the concept of the *life space*. As Lewin defined it, the life space of an individual consists of everything one needs to know about a person in order to understand her or his behavior in a specific psychological environment at a particular time.

Field theory principles and diagrams can be used to illustrate the behavior of Group A, B, and C babies as described by Ainsworth and her colleagues. In her own evaluation of these differences Ainsworth (1979b) concentrates on two dimensions of child behavior: security versus anxiety; and absence of conflict versus presence of conflict regarding close bodily contact. When infants are exposed to the episodes listed in Table 7–1 they experience conflicting tendencies. They seek the security of the mother when they first enter the strange experimental room but they are also tempted to explore and play with the attractive toys. They are intrigued by the stranger but may feel apprehensive. They are eager for bodily contact after being separated from the mother but they may not (in the case of Group A and C babies) expect that the contact will be comforting. These two types of conflicts are depicted in Lewin-style diagrams in Figures 7–2 and 7–3. The pluses and minuses in these diagrams indicate the presence and strength of positive and negative (or approach and avoidant) forces. The arrows indicate the direction of the push and pull forces. The line encircling the drawings represents the boundary of the life space of the child at the particular moment.

Securely attached infants likely to explore, respond positively to others

The diagrams in Figure 7–2 illustrate why a securely attached (Group B) child is eager to explore a new environment and also likely to respond positively to a stranger when the mother is present. There is little conflict between security and anxiety because the child is confident that the mother will supply support if needed. The child feels free to approach the toys or stranger because the mother is perceived as responsive and accessible. The diagrams of the behavior of anxiously attached and resistant babies (Group C) and anxious and avoidant babies (Group A), by contrast, reveal how much conflict they experience. They are tempted to explore and intrigued by the stranger but have conflicting feelings because they do not perceive the mother as a secure or trustworthy person. The anxiously attached and resistant child (Group C) responds to the conflict by expressing anger and resentment toward the mother. The anxious and avoidant child (Group A) responds to the conflict by avoiding contact and engaging in uninvolved interaction with the toys and mild interest in the stranger.

The diagrams in Figure 7–3 call attention to conflict (or lack of conflict) regarding physical contact with the mother. Group B children do not experience conflicting push-pull forces when reunited with their mothers. They perceive the mother as a supportive person and eagerly seek contact with her. Group C and Group A babies, by contrast, are subjected to conflicting feelings. They feel a strong need for comfort but anticipate (on the basis of previous experiences) that the comfort will not be provided. The anxiously attached and resistant child reacts to this conflict with anger and resentment; the anxious and avoidant child tries to reduce anxiety by avoiding contact and by attempting to minimize involvement.

The results of the investigations of stranger and separation anxiety by Ainsworth and her associates provide supplementary insights regarding negative and positive types of caretaker behavior discussed a bit earlier. Mothers who enjoy bodily contact with their infants, who are responsive to the baby's signals, and who have a good sense of timing promote security in their children. The child

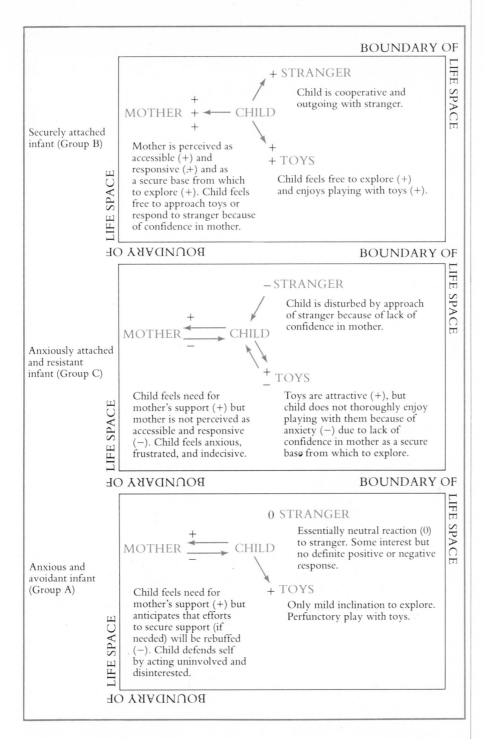

Figure 7–2 Diagrams of the life space of infants shortly after entering a room containing their mothers, toys, and a stranger. (Illustrating security vs. anxiety as described by Ainsworth.)

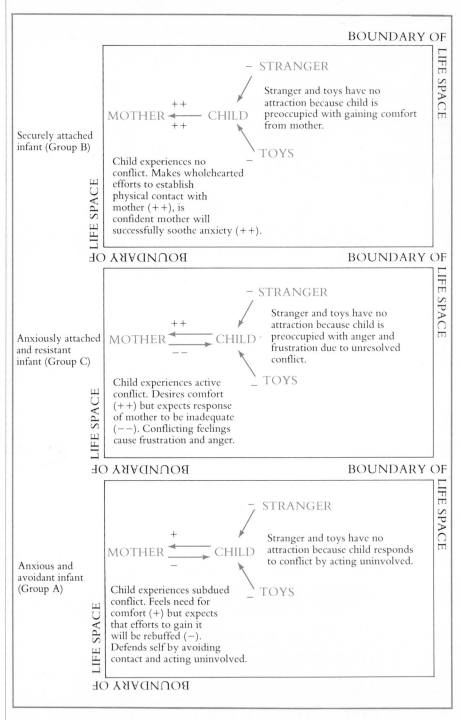

Figure 7–3 **Diagrams of the life space of infants just after they were reunited with their mothers. (Illustrating absence vs. presence of conflict as described by Ainsworth.)**

who perceives the mother as an accessible and responsive person thinks of her as a secure base from which to explore. As a consequence, such babies are likely to feel eager and confident about trying new experiences and to react positively to strange individuals (when the mother is present). (In Eriksonian terms such babies have acquired a sense of trust. In Piagetian terms their tendencies to assimilate, accommodate, and form schemes are unfettered.) Well-meaning mothers who are not able to interpret a baby's behavior properly or who respond inappropriately or ineffectively are likely to arouse anger and resentment in their children. Because the children of such mothers experience conflicting feelings, they may be disinclined to explore and be wary of strangers. These tendencies may hamper their cognitive and social development. Mothers who have an aversion to bodily contact, who are rigid and compulsive, and who are resentful when child-care responsibilities interfere with their own plans and activities, may cause their children to withdraw and to avoid contacts of all kinds. (In Eriksonian terms Group C and A babies mistrust their mothers. In Piagetian terms their preoccupation with anxiety or their avoidance and withdrawal behavior may limit their tendencies to assimilate and accommodate because the range of experiences to which they expose themselves is limited.)

Explaining Stranger and Separation Anxiety in Piagetian Terms

Ainsworth and her associates note (p. 21) that their explanation of individual differences in stranger and separation anxiety presupposes that an infant has developed to the point of understanding object (or person) permanence as described by Piaget. That is, one-year-olds may become fearful when a stranger "displaces" the mother because they assume the mother no longer exists. Similarly, a child who experiences separation anxiety may conclude that when the mother is no longer in sight, she has disappeared forever.

Separation anxiety may be caused by understanding of person permanence

It should be noted that some researchers (for example, Brossard, 1974) have failed to find a relationship between fear of strangers and measures of object or person permanance. Even if psychologists have not yet established a statistically significant relationship between fear of strangers and object permanence, however, Piaget's observations still clarify both stranger and separation anxiety. It might be reasoned, for instance, that eight-month-old children display a fear of strangers because they have developed schemes to account for the limited environment in which they exist. That is, they have developed conceptions of their mothers, their cribs, their playpens, the floor of the kitchen and living room, and so on. If they are unable to assimilate and accommodate people, objects, or surroundings which do not fit into these schemes, they may become frightened. (Lewis and Brooks account for the positive reaction of children to other children by hypothesizing that the child has developed a *self-scheme* and therefore is not upset when exposed to someone of similar size and shape.) In a few months, experiences with more people, objects, and places lead to more varied schemes, and the child becomes sophisticated enough to take strangeness in stride.

Stranger anxiety may be caused by inability to assimilate or accommodate new schemes (people)

Most observational and experimental studies of separation anxiety have involved the disappearance of the mother for quite short periods of time. In some cases, however, the separation of child from mother may be more extensive or even permanent (as when a mother is hospitalized or is killed in an accident). When John Bowlby, who has specialized in the study of attachment (1969), observed the extreme reactions of one- and two-year-olds to such severe or complete separations, he became convinced that a child needs to develop a close relationship with the mother if normal development is to take place (1973). The hypothesis proposed by Bowlby leads to the questions: Can someone other than the mother function as the primary caretaker? Can two or more people share the responsibility of child rearing without harming the child?

Can More than One Person Function as "Mother"?

As noted earlier in this chapter, psychoanalysts such as Spitz and Ribble have argued that institutionalized babies are retarded in development and may suffer permanent personality and intellectual damage because they have been deprived of contact with their mothers. In their review of studies of institutionalization, however, Thompson and Grusec point out that not all institutionalized babies displayed retardation. This suggests that maternal deprivation is not necessarily harmful. M. Rutter (1972, 1979) compared the behavior of children reared by their mothers with that of children who never had the opportunity to develop a long-term relationship with a single caretaker. The conclusion he drew is similar to that of Thompson and Grusec: lack of contact with the mother (or single caretaker) does not necessarily cause problems in development.

Nor does it seem to be necessarily harmful for a young child to grow up without forming a strong bond with a single caretaker. Rudolph Schaffer and Peggy Emerson (1964) found that most infants seemed capable of forming a number of attachments at the same time. Furthermore, satisfying attachments were formed with adults of varying ages and of both sexes. Michael E. Lamb (1979) reports that seven- to thirteen-month-old infants show no preference between their mothers and fathers, although the mother may be sought more frequently when the child is frightened. The fact that the mother appears to be preferred in stress situations has led some theorists (for example, Bowlby, 1969; Ainsworth, 1979a) to suggest that there is a *hierarchy* of attachment figures. Under normal circumstances infants may respond equally well to several familiar caretakers. If infants are distressed or ill, however, they seem to seek the person they have identified as the primary caretaker (usually the mother).

It appears, then, that a child can develop quite satisfactorily even though a strong attachment to the biological mother is never formed. If the natural mother lacks skill in establishing satisfactory interactions or dislikes or rejects the motherhood role for any reason, it seems reasonable to conclude that it might be better for the child if some other person or persons took over as caretakers. A key factor in the success of multiple caretaker relationships, however, seems to be the *consistency* of care. As long as the child is able to build up expectations that certain types of care will be provided by certain individuals, it does not seem to make a crucial difference how many people supply that care.

Support for the view that multiple caretakers can do an effective job if they are consistent is provided by a study conducted by Herbert and Gloria Leiderman (1974). They found a natural experimental situation in an East African village where children in one group of homes were reared by two or more caretakers. In another group, children in essentially similar homes were reared by their mothers. The Leidermans concluded that the children who were reared by multiple caretakers did not display any abnormalities in development. In fact, the greater stimulation provided by multiple caretakers seemed to favor cognitive development in some ways.

Multiple caretakers should provide consistent care

Evaluations of Day Care

One of the most significant developments in American society in the 1970s and 1980s has been the increasing number of women employed outside the home. New conceptions of sex roles, the availability of a variety of methods of birth control, concern about overpopulation, the desire to augment family income during a period of inflation, and other factors have contributed to the tendency for women to seek some form of employment. At the present time, approximately one-third of all American mothers who live with their husbands and have children under the age of three have some sort of job (L. W. Hoffman, 1979, p. 859). (The proportion of employed mothers is higher in single-parent homes, and single-parent families are on the increase.) It is clear, then, that many young children are placed in some sort of day care arrangement for at least part of most working days. Even though this chapter is about one- and two-year-olds, it seems appropriate to discuss day care at this juncture. It should be kept in mind, though, that the following analysis is based on studies of the impact of day care on children up to the age of five years.

Elva Poznanski, Annette Maxey, and Gerald Marsden (1970), Helen Bee (1978), and Jay Belsky and Laurence D. Steinberg (1978) reviewed research and concluded that if day care is provided by trained personnel responsible for small numbers of children, no negative effects on child behavior become apparent. There may be a tendency in children of working mothers to be more dependent in middle childhood, and boys in particular may experience some problems of sex-role identification. On the other hand, children who are cared for by parent-substitutes are somewhat more likely than home-reared children to do well in school and to develop nonstereotyped conceptions of male and female roles.

The general conclusion that day care *can* be as favorable as home care should be interpreted with caution, however. For example, a study often cited in support of

Day care in Hungary, *top*, and Israel, *bottom*. Current research indicates that if consistent care is provided by trained personnel to small numbers of children no negative effects on child behavior become apparent. Ken Heyman.

this conclusion (Caldwell, Wright, Honig, and Tannenbaum, 1970) was carried out by supervisors who noted that they were "acutely aware" of the possible risks involved (such as retardation in development similar to that found in institutionalized children), and they took special pains to try to provide faultless care. This study could be misleading if the assumption is made that all substitute parents will be equally devoted to providing ideal care. (In their review, Belsky and Steinberg conclude [1978, p. 929] that evidence accumulated up to 1978 is grossly inadequate to assess the impact of day care.)

In making a decision about day care or about the choice of a parent-substitute, therefore, parents would be well advised to obtain detailed information about the individuals who will care for their child. Another impotant factor for parents to consider is the mother's attitude toward her role. Women who liked their jobs were rated in one study (Yarrow, Scott, de Leeuw, and Heinig, 1962) as more adequate mothers than nonworking housewives who would have preferred a career. If a woman feels she might *resent* serving as a full-time mother, therefore, it might be preferable for her to work at least part-time and arrange for others to care for her children a few hours a day.

Regardless of who interacts with a young child, there seem to be certain infant care techniques that are likely to encourage optimum development.

Effective Infant-Care Techniques (The First Ten Months)

Here is a review of techniques that have been used by caretakers who seem to do an especially effective job promoting positive development during the first ten months of an infant's life.

Daniel Stern's analysis of mothering suggests these qualities as likely to arouse positive responses in infants:

- ☐ Using repitition.
- ☐ Timing responses to arouse and maintain an infant's attention.
- ☐ Correctly estimating the amount of stimulation to supply at a given moment.
- ☐ Taking into account rapid mood changes.

Rudolph Schaffer found that effective caretakers were skilled at using the following techniques with infants:

- ☐ Interpreting the state of the infant at any given moment.
- ☐ Letting the child initiate activities and then responding in ways that extend and expand on those activities.
- ☐ Taking turns, in the sense that the infant has ample opportunities to express himself or herself.
- ☐ Arranging conditions and providing responses so that the baby develops the feeling she or he can produce consequences.

Mary Ainsworth found that sensitive mothers exhibited these qualities:

- ☐ Seeing things from the baby's point of view and responding promptly and appropriately to the baby's signals.

☐ Providing sustained physical contact and using contact to soothe the baby's discomfort.

☐ Establishing feelings of mutual delight.

Effective Infant-Care Techniques (Ten to Twenty-four Months)

All of the techniques just summarized are appropriate for use with infants who have not yet learned to walk and talk. As they approach their first birthdays and develop locomotor and language skills, children function as quite different organisms than they did when they were babes in arms.

Because of his interest and experience in studying infant reactions to stimulation, Burton L. White was asked to direct a project (the Harvard Preschool Project; funded by the Head Start Division of the Office of Economic Opportunity) to discover if certain experiences during the first six years of life could be structured so that children would be better prepared for schooling. White and his associates began their task by first describing the characteristics of six-year-olds who possessed overall *competence* and those who did not. After specific abilities leading to competence were defined, the Harvard researchers attempted to discover the kinds of experiences that led to these abilities by making detailed observations of thirty-four families: half selected because they seemed likely to produce competent children; the other half selected because they seemed likely to have children below average in competence. The way parents handled their children in the home was observed at length, and the abilities of the children were measured in a variety of ways. Mothers of children who were rated as highly competent used the following types of child-care techniques (White and Watts, 1973, pp. 242–243):

Mothers of competent children talk, respond, enrich, encourage, explain

1 Talked to the child often and in understandable terms.

2 Made the child feel that what she or he was doing was interesting.

3 Provided many objects for the child to play with and arranged for the child to have access to a variety of situations.

4 Led the child to expect that help and encouragement would be supplied most, but not all, of the time.

5 Demonstrated and explained to the child primarily when the child asked for instruction and assistance.

The Infant as Instigator, the Caretaker as Responder

An analysis of these various techniques leads to the conclusion that during the first two years of child-adult interactions, effective caretakers are very adept at responding to activities intitated by the child. This responsiveness appears to be especially important during the first year of life, as revealed by the list of effective

Parents who interact with their children in a variety of ways, show interest in what they do, show that achievements are admired and appreciated, and communicate love in a warm and sincere way are likely to encourage competence in their offspring. Anna Kaufman Moon/Stock, Boston.

techniques reported by Stern, Schaffer, and Ainsworth, but it also appears to be significant later as well. Examination of the techniques used by the successful mothers described by White and his associates leads to the conclusion that throughout the first three years effective caretakers encourage the child to explore and interact. Explanations seem to be more effective when the child asks for them.

The concept of the child as the instigator and the caretaker as responder is in direct contrast to the blank-slate view in which it is assumed that children develop because of what caretakers *do* to them. If Bower's contention that it is undesirable to overburden infants with stimuli is accepted, it appears that it may even be counterproductive to do too much to young children. It may be preferable to make stimuli and experiences available to the child and then react with interest and support when the baby responds in some way. The qualities that make a caretaker an effective responder revolve around sensitivity to how the child feels at a given moment. Taken together, the effective infant-care techniques just summarized also promote the feeling on the child's part that he or she has some influence over events and other people. (This is the point that Schaffer considers to be of paramount importance.)

Does Caretaker Effectiveness Change as Children Mature?

While it may be desirable to encourage an infant to develop a feeling of control over others and its environment, there will inevitably come a time—usually before the age of two years—when the child will have to begin to learn that he or she must also defer to the wishes of others. The necessity for learning that sometimes it is necessary to take into account the desires of others leads to an interesting question about effective child care: Will parents who are sensitive to a baby's needs and capable of responding effectively to the baby's behavior be equally adept at handling a three-year-old who balks at restrictions, or a ten-year-old who has difficulty getting along with others, or a fifteen-year-old who resents authority?

It seems likely that an ability to see things from the child's point of view will serve a caretaker well in all of these situations, but there are certainly significant differences between the types of behavior just noted and the behavioral repertoire of a six-month-old infant. Parents who find that they just don't seem to see things the way an infant sees them, accordingly, might console themselves with the thought that they may be more successful dealing with an older child. Some educators choose to teach preschool children, others prefer to teach the primary, elementary, or high school grades. It seems likely that most teachers choose a particular grade level because they feel an affinity for children of that age. Perhaps many parents also have an affinity for a particular age level. Unlike teachers who are presented with a new batch of students the same age each September, however, parents have no choice in the matter and must interact with children throughout the span of development. The need to deal with a child at all ages may cause problems. Perhaps only rarely will a caretaker be equally effective in dealing with children of all ages.

If it is true that some parents have aptitudes for interacting with infants while others have a knack for handling older children, the question arises: Can those who are not "natural" caretakers with children of a particular age level learn how to become more skillful? It seems likely that at least some of the qualities necessary for successfully interacting with infants (to take the age level being analyzed in this chapter) can be acquired by referring to the conclusions of Stern, Schaffer, and Ainsworth. Any parent who is willing to try can let the child instigate activities, respond promptly, and use repetition when responding. It may be, however, that not all parents will be able to properly interpret a baby's signals or correctly assess rapid changes in mood. (Group C mothers in the Ainsworth studies, for instance, had good intentions but were ineffective.) If this is the case, caretakers may simply have to do the best they can when they are a bit baffled by the behavior of an infant and console themselves with the hope that they may have greater empathy with the child when she or he is older.

Supportive and Early Intervention Programs

It may be possible, though, for parents who sense that they are not skilled in handling an infant, particularly one that Thomas and Chess would classify as difficult, to improve their child-rearing skills. A number of *supportive programs* for infants and parents have been developed in the last few years. Dorothy S. Huntington notes (1979, p. 849) that such programs are often designed to accomplish the following goals: release guilt about a child's behavior, enhance the self-esteem and self-image of parents, encourage the development of inner controls in place of physical reactions (particularly with parents who have physically abused their children), supply understanding and awareness of individual differences between children and the nature of their needs, provide new ways of interacting with a child.

Several psychologists have developed *early intervention programs*, primarily for use with lower-class, educationally deprived mothers. (Several such programs are described by Beller, 1979.) One of the best known of these is the Florida Parent Education Program developed by Ira J. Gordon (1969). The basic goals of the Florida program are to enhance the cognitive and personality development of the child and to promote the mother's self-esteem and her conviction that she can affect what happens to her and her child. Women from the community were trained by Gordon and his associates to visit socially and economically disadvantaged mothers in their homes and teach them games and exercises that were developed by taking into account Piaget's observations on cognitive development. Games played with young children involve letting the child pick up objects while the mother comments on what is being done (to make the child more aware of the sensorimotor activities involved). Later games are designed to promote understanding of concepts such as object permanence (for example, the mother pulls a doll attached to a string from under a blanket).

When the later cognitive and social behavior of children who had been through the Florida program was compared with that of control children who had not, it was reported (Gordon and Guinach, 1974) that the early training had produced lasting gains in intellectual functioning but not in personality traits. It was also reported that mothers were most likely to report enhanced feelings of self-esteem and control if they had been trained to teach other mothers the techniques.

Evaluating the Critical-Period Hypothesis

The First Two Years as a Critical Period in the Formation of Love

At the beginning of this chapter reasons for assuming that the first two years are critical were outlined. Mention was made of the observations of imprinting by Lorenz, of Harlow's studies of monkeys, and of the various investigations of the impact of institutionalization of human infants. Many of the psychologists who carried out pioneering studies in this area of behavior hypothesized that the first two years of life might be a critical period in the formation of love or attachment between child and parents. Subsequent investigations led to the conclusion that animal and human infants deprived of love may overcome this early handicap with proper care and favorable experiences. Relationships established during the first two years, however, are still considered to be of great significance in the formation of love. In the 1970s, some psychologists proposed that the first two years may also be a critical period in the establishment of competence.

The First Two Years as a Critical Period in the Formation of Competence

In the course of making observations of mother-child interactions, Burton White and his colleagues concluded that the age span from ten to eighteen months is a critical period in the development of a sense of competence. White became so convinced of the critical nature of early experience that he wrote *The First Three Years of Life* (1975) to explain to parents how they might foster competence in their children. (The book is composed of descriptions of typical behavior, recommended child-rearing practices, and appropriate "educational" materials for age levels up to three years.) In the concluding chapter of the book White observes that people frequently ask him questions such as: "Is it really all over by three? Isn't there anything else I can do? Can't I compensate for mistakes?" He then notes, "Answering these questions is rather difficult for me because to *some extent* I really believe it *is* too late after age three" (1975, p. 257). He qualifies this statement by adding that the flexibility of human beings declines with age.

White's observations on the significance of the first years of a child's life in the establishment of competence bring us back to the question raised at the beginning of this chapter: How critical *are* the first two years? Now that you are familiar with the abilities acquired by children during the first two years and with observations regarding parent-child relationships, you may wish to formulate your own answer to that question. Here are some arguments for and against the critical period issue that you might consider as you draw your conclusions.

Reasons for Viewing the First Two Years as Critical

Certain psychoanalysts and some learning theorists emphasize the importance of the first two years because they believe that the child is born a blank slate. If this assumption is accepted, it seems reasonable that the very first experiences in life will have a greater impact on shaping behavior and personality than experiences that come later.

Descriptions of imprinting by Lorenz and other ethologists have led to speculation that the tendency for birds to acquire strong attachments to a mother-object a few hours after being hatched may also be found in humans.

Harlow's early experiments with monkeys reared in isolation led him to believe that if organisms do not establish attachments early in life, they may never be able to establish attachments.

White and his associates suggest that the ten- to eighteen-month age span is a critical period because it is during this stage that children develop the capacity for receptive language, learn to walk and get into things, and develop a clear sense of identity. White and his associates argue that the way caretakers handle the behavior of the child on the verge of independence will determine the nature of many subsequent parent-child relationships.

Reasons for Questioning That the First Two Years Are Critical

There is abundant evidence (noted in earlier chapters and mentioned again in this chapter) to substantiate the view that children are not born blank slates. Even before birth, children express themselves in individual ways, and immediately after birth definite personality characteristics can be recognized. There is reason to doubt, therefore, that infants have no control over the way their behavior is shaped. It seems more sensible to assume that even neonates will respond (or not respond) selectively to experiences in terms of inherited predispositions. If it were really true that experiences during the first months determine personality, it would be logical to expect that infant behavior would constantly change. Any new or different experience would push the personality in the process of being formed in a new direction. It is quite clear that this is not the case.

Some studies of institutionalization (for example, Rheingold, 1956; Tizard and Hodges, 1978) reveal that children who are placed in good environments after having spent the first years of their lives under deplorable conditions are able to make up for a bad start.

There is reason to assume that at least some techniques of child rearing used by parents during the first months of a child's life will be basically similar to those they use as the child matures. Parents who use strict toilet-training practices, for example, might be expected to insist on cleanliness throughout childhood. It is therefore impossible to prove that only certain experiences occurring at a particular stage of development are *the* causes of personality tendencies that become apparent later in life.

Some psychoanalytic and extreme learning theory interpretations of early childhood lead to the assumption that if a child behaves well and develops satisfactorily during the first two years, it is entirely due to child-rearing techniques used by the parents. (If the child develops symptoms of childhood neurosis or psychosis, on the other hand, the fault lies squarely with the parents.) The evidence presented by Thomas and his associates that starting at birth infants can be classified into easy, difficult, and slow to warm up suggests that the cause and effect relationship may often be reversed. That is, easy infants may make their parents look good, difficult infants may shape the behavior of potentially capable parents in unfortunate ways. Perhaps some of the competent (or incompetent) behavior observed in the children studied by White and his colleagues was due not so much to the mother's actions as the child's own inherited predispositions.

With few exceptions, most types of learning, even in mature adults, require repeated reinforcement. If a response is not reinforced from time to time, it will extinguish. Accordingly, it might be assumed that early experiences that are not repeated will tend to be forgotten. And if only repeated experiences are likely to have a permanent impact, they will need to occur and be reinforced over a substantial period of time, not just during the first two years.

Some Final Observations on the Critical-Period Hypothesis

The points just noted are not intended to belittle the quite amazing accomplishments of human beings during the first two years of their lives. It seems reasonable to assume, as Erikson (in particular) has stressed, that children who get off to a good start will be well prepared to cope with problems they encounter later. And even though early experiences may not *dominate* later development, they certainly influence the child. The child's initial reactions to people and experiences, in turn, influence the attitudes and behavior of those who care for it. Perhaps the most prudent conclusion to draw about the significance of the first two years is that while this is undeniably an important and eventful stage of development, stages that follow are also important and eventful. During the years from two to five, for example, children learn to interact with other children, characteristic responses to different types of interpersonal relationships become clearly established, most adult forms of language are acquired, and cognitive development proceeds at a remarkable rate. These significant types of behavior will be discussed in the next two chapters.

Before turning to the discussion of two- to five-year-olds, however, a summary of types of behavior that appear during the first two years will be presented.

Summary: Development During the First Two Years

At the end of the preceding chapter the six stages of the sensorimotor period of cognitive development as described by Piaget were outlined. Because the formation of a child's first schemes is such a significant aspect of development, many other types of behavior can be interpreted with reference to intellectual development. It is possible to propose an explanation of stranger anxiety, for example, by taking into account the inability of a child to assimilate or accommodate new schemes. And separation anxiety becomes more understandable if the concept of object (or person) permanence is referred to. Thus, important forms of early emotional behavior can be related to the child's growing awareness of others. Furthermore, early forms of *social* behavior can also be understood by taking into account stages of cognitive development. A young child's interactions with others are based primarily on impressions (schemes) of familiar and unfamiliar individuals. In addition, language development is often as much social as intellectual since it represents a desire to communicate with others.

Many of the most significant types of behavior that appear during the first two years can be summarized, therefore, by noting when different types of cognitive, emotional, and social behavior appear. In Table 7–3 you will find such a summary. The age levels selected are those that reflect the timing of the six stages of the sensorimotor period of cognitive development. Most of the types of behavior noted in Table 7–3 have been discussed in this and the preceding chapter, but descriptions of some types of emotional and social behavior noted in Table 7–3 are based on studies that have not been previously mentioned. The ages at which different types of anger appear, for instance, and of self-affection and self-assertion are derived from comprehensive discussions of such types of behavior by L. Alan Sroufe (1979). These types of behavior are included in the summary because they have either been noted in discussing significant developmental trends (for example, infants react with fear or anger to strangers or separation) or because they are related to types of behavior that have been analyzed in detail.

If you will contrast the types of behavior noted in Table 7–3 that appear during the *first* twelve months and the *second* twelve months of life, the growing independence of the young child becomes apparent. Up to the age of one year the child depends on others, particularly the mother. Even when one-year-olds strike out to explore on their own, they need to use the mother as a secure base. But during the second year of life the rapidly maturing child becomes more independent in many ways. Mastery of locomotor abilities and the acquisition of language skills both contribute to dramatically widened horizons. Perhaps more important, children become increasingly aware that they are independent beings. They exhibit self-affection, recognize that they exist as autonomous organisms, and begin to assert themselves. All of these significant tendencies become more

Table 7–3
Comparison of Stages of Cognitive, Emotional, and
Social Development During the First Two Years

MONTHS OF AGE	COGNITIVE DEVELOPMENT (PIAGET STAGES)	EMOTIONAL DEVELOPMENT	SOCIAL DEVELOPMENT (INCLUDING LANGUAGE)
0–1	*Stage 1* Variations of reflex activity. First primitive schemes.	Reflexive smiles. Generalized expressions of distress.	Initial impressions of others. Beginning of preferential responses to caretakers.
1–4	*Stage 2* Primary circular reactions. Exploration of own body and senses.	Social smile. Expressions of pleasure and rage.	Establishment of reciprocal interactions with caretakers. Vocal contagion (vocalizing *with* parents) and mutual imitation.
4–10	*Stage 3* Secondary circular reactions. Object concept (permanence). Intentional repetition of originally spontaneous activities.	Delight, joy, laughter. Social responsiveness. Wariness of strangers, initial signs of separation anxiety. Initial signs of anger.	Infant initiates social exchanges, engages in social games, makes an effort to elicit social responses. Exploration from secure base (i.e., close proximity to mother).
10–12	*Stage 4* Coordination of secondary schemes. Switch from exploration of own body to exploration of objects leads to combining of schemes, purposeful manipulation.	Clear expressions of anger. Well-established fear of strangers. Definite anxiety (particularly when separated from mother).	First word uttered. Continued and more extensive exploration from secure base.

apparent during the two- to five-year span, which will be discussed in the next two chapters.

Suggestions for Further Study

Books by Konrad Lorenz

In 1973, Konrad Lorenz was awarded a Nobel Prize for his studies of animal behavior. In *King Solomon's Ring* (1952) Lorenz describes many of his early observations and experiments with animals, including his first observations of

Table 7–3

**Comparison of Stages of Cognitive, Emotional, and
Social Development During the First Two Years**

MONTHS OF AGE	COGNITIVE DEVELOPMENT (PIAGET STAGES)	EMOTIONAL DEVELOPMENT	SOCIAL DEVELOPMENT (INCLUDING LANGUAGE)
12–18	*Stage 5* Tertiary circular reactions. Rapidly developing abilities to walk and talk lead to greatly increased exploration and formations of schemes.	Elation in mastery. Angry moods, petulance. Immediate fear reactions.	Telegraphic speech and groping patterns (in putting together words). Beginning of self-assertion as infant overcomes fear of strangers and of separation anxiety.
18–24	*Stage 6* Beginning of thought. Repertoire of schemes expands to point that child can sometimes engage in mental, rather than physical, manipulation.	Self-affection. Shame. Defiance. Purposeful anger.	In use of language, increasing ability to convey deep structure (express what is meant). Increasing awareness of self. Emergence of a sense of separateness. Increasing self-assertion.

Source: Stages of cognitive development derived from Piaget, 1952a, 1952b. Stages of emotional and social development derive from Sroufe, 1979, pp. 473, 476–477. Arrangement of Table patterned after Sroufe, 1979, pp. 467–477.

imprinting. (You will find them at the beginning of Chapter 5, "Laughing at Animals.") Almost any part of this book is enjoyable and instructive, but Chapter 8 ("The Language of Animals") and Chapter 11 ("Morals and Weapons") are especially interesting. The latter chapter examines a theme developed more completely in *On Aggression* (1966) — the nature of aggression in animal and man. Sample Chapter 3 ("What Aggression Is Good For"), Chapter 13 ("Ecce Homo!"), or Chapter 14 ("Avowal of Optimism"). Other books by Lorenz are *Studies in Animal and Human Behavior* (Vol. I, 1970; Vol. II, 1971) and *Civilized Man's Eight Deadly Sins* (1974). On pages 124 to 132 of the first volume of *Studies in Animal and Human Behavior* you will find a summary of observations on imprinting.

Harlow on Love

Harry F. Harlow summarizes his research on the responses of monkeys to various kinds of substitute mothers in *Learning to Love* (1971) and in *The Human Model: Primate Perspectives* (1979) written with Clara Mears. A more concise analysis of most of the same studies is presented in an article by Harlow in *Determinants of Infant Behavior*, Vol. 4 (1969), edited by B. M. Foss. An entertaining interview with Harlow appeared in the April 1973 issue of *Psychology Today,* beginning on page 65.

Studies of Early Experience

An extensive review of studies of early experience is provided by William R. Thompson and Joan E. Grusec in Chapter 7 of *Carmichael's Manual of Child Psychology* (3rd ed., 1970), edited by Paul H. Mussen. M. Rutter analyzes research on maternal deprivation carried out between 1972 and 1978 in an article that begins on page 283 of *Child Development,* 1979, **50.**

The Impact of Institutionalization

If you are interested in the impact of institutionalization on development, there are several specific studies you might examine in addition to the review by Thompson and Grusec. The article by René Spitz that did much to arouse interest in the potentially lethal effect of institutional care starts on page 53 of Volume I of *Psychoanalytic Study of the Child* (1943), edited by Anna Freud. In *Maternal Care and Mental Health* (1952) John Bowlby presents a comprehensive review of early studies of institutional living from all parts of the world. For reports of intensive, carefully controlled investigations, see *Infants in Institutions* (1962) by Sally Provence and Rose C. Lipton, or *Children of the Crèche* (1973) by Wayne Dennis.

Skinner on Ideal Child Rearing

B. F. Skinner presents his fictional view of the way babies living in a scientific utopia might be shaped by child-rearing experts in Chapters 12 through 17 of *Walden Two* (1948).

Freud and Erikson on the First Two Years

One of the most complete explanations of Freud's interpretation of the significance of the oral and anal stages of development is provided in *Psychoanalytic Theory of Neurosis* (1945) by O. Fenichel. Erikson's account of the significance of the early stages of psychosocial development can be found in Chapter 7 of his *Childhood and Society* (2nd ed., 1963) or Chapter 3 of his *Identity: Youth and Crisis* (1968).

Infant-Mother Interaction

Two brief, readable books on the nature of successful interactions between infants and their mothers are *Mothering* (1977) by Rudolph Schaffer and *The First*

Relationship (1977) by Daniel Stern. T. G. R. Bower offers his views on early relationships in Chapters 1, 4, and 9 (in particular) of *A Primer of Infant Development* (1977b). Mary Ainsworth summarizes her conclusions on the subject in "The Development of Infant-Mother Attachment" in *Review of Child Development Research*, Vol. 3, edited by B. M. Caldwell and H. N. Ricciutti (1974). A collection of short papers by many of the individuals just noted, plus other students of early relationships, can be found in *Studies in Mother-Infant Interaction* (1977b), edited by Rudolph Schaffer.

Attachment

John Bowlby's analysis of the development of attachment behavior is presented in his *Attachment*, Volume I of *Attachment and Loss* (1969). Discussions of attachment by Robert R. Sears, Robert B. Cairns, Mary D. Ainsworth, and Jacob L. Gewirtz are to be found in *Attachment and Dependency* (1972), edited by Gewirtz. A concise summary of research and theories is presented in "Attachment and Dependency" by Eleanor E. Maccoby and John C. Masters, Chapter 21 in Volume II of *Carmichael's Manual of Child Psychology* (3rd ed., 1970), edited by Paul H. Mussen.

Stranger Anxiety

The subtleties and ramifications of stranger anxiety are explored by L. Alan Sroufe in an article that begins on page 731 of *Child Development*, 1977, **48**; and in *Patterns of Attachment: A Psychological Study of the Strange Situation* (1978) by Mary D. Ainsworth, Mary C. Blehar, Everett Waters, and Sally Wall.

Separation Anxiety

John Bowlby presents an exhaustive analysis of separation in *Separation: Anxiety and Anger*, Volume II of *Attachment and Loss* (1973). Reviews of studies of separation are provided by William R. Thompson and Joan E. Grusec on page 623 of Chapter 7 in Volume I of *Carmichael's Manual of Child Psychology* (3rd ed., 1970), edited by Paul H. Mussen, and by Eleanor E. Maccoby and John C. Masters on pages 104–105 of Chapter 21 in Volume II of the same work.

Day Care

A collection of articles on the effects of different types of alternative care provided when mothers are employed (plus other articles on the role of fathers in child development and related topics) is presented in *Social Issues in Developmental Psychology*, 2nd edition (1978), edited by Helen Bee. A critical review of studies of day care is presented by Jay Belsky and Laurence D. Steinberg in an article that begins on page 929 of *Child Development*, 1978, **49**.

The Harvard Preschool Project

For more information about the Harvard Preschool Project look for *Experience and Environment: Major Influences on the Development of the Young Child,* Vol. I (1973) by Burton L. White and Jean Carew Watts. The background of the project is outlined in Chapter 1; the basic strategy is described in Chapter 2; the design and methods of the project are explained in Chapters 3, 4, 5, and 8; case studies are presented in Chapters 7 and 10; conclusions and implications are offered in Chapters 11 and 12. (The critical nature of the ten- to eighteen-month period is described on pages 237–240; an outline of "most effective child-rearing practices" is presented on pages 242–244.) Appendixes provide complete details and instructions for the various measurement techniques used and individual subject data.

A later summary is provided in *The Origins of Human Competence: The Final Report of the Harvard Preschool Project* (1979) by White, B. T. Kaban, and J. S. Attanucci. No new conclusions are offered except for some incompletely supported speculations about the significance of birth order on the emergence of competence.

White presents his ideas on early child rearing in a book addressed to parents in *The First Three Years of Life* (1975). He gives his opinions on the values of various types of play equipment and comments on typical forms of behavior that appear during the first three years.

Father-Infant Interaction

Recent trends in our society have led to greater tendencies for fathers to interact with infants and young children. Ross D. Parke offers a comprehensive review of research on this subject in Chapter 15 (pp. 549–590) of the *Handbook of Infant Development* (1979), edited by Joy D. Osofsky. Among other things, he notes that fathers may be as influenced as mothers by contact with a newborn baby (p. 561), that fathers treat male babies differently from female babies (p. 566), and that father-infant attachment can be just as strong as mother-infant attachment (p. 570).

Other comprehensive sources of information about father-child interaction are *The Father: His Role in Child Development* (1974) by D. Lynn, and *The Role of the Father in Child Development* (1976), edited by Michael E. Lamb.

The Effects of Infants on Their Parents

White (and many other psychologists) have concentrated on ways parents influence child behavior. In the 1970s, some students of development concluded that it was time to examine the other side of the coin. Two collections of articles tracing ways that infants shape their parents are *The Effect of the Infant on Its*

Caregiver (1974), edited by Michael Lewis and Leonard A. Rosenblum, and *Child Effects on Adults* (1977) by Richard Q. Bell and Lawrence V. Harper.

Supportive and Early Intervention Programs

For descriptions and analyses of programs designed to help parents of young children to become more confident and effective, see "Supportive Programs for Infants and Parents" by Dorothy S. Huntington, Chapter 26 (pp. 837–851) of the *Handbook of Infant Development* (1979), edited by Joy D. Osofsky. For descriptions and analyses of programs designed to supply help and instruction to parents of disadvantaged children, see "Early Intervention Programs" by E. Kuno Beller, Chapter 27 (pp. 852–894) of the same volume.

PART FOUR

TWO TO FIVE

This part consists of two chapters: Chapter 8, "Two to Five: Personality Development"; Chapter 9, "Two to Five: Cognitive Development."

Theorists whose work is summarized in Chapter 3 consider the following types of behavior and relationships with others to be of significance during the years from two to five:

□ Freud: Anal and phallic stages. Children are first concerned about toilet training, then they are curious about sex differences. Libidinal energy attached to parent of opposite sex around the age of four.

□ Erikson: Autonomy vs. doubt. Initiative vs. guilt. Children should be allowed to try out skills, set own pace, encouraged to engage in self-selected activities.

□ Piaget: Preoperational stage. Rapid acquisition of schemes, mastery of abilities to conserve and decenter, but unable to mentally reverse actions.

□ Sears: Phase II. Preschool child interacts with parents and is influenced by their reactions. Child identifies with and imitates parents. Child-rearing techniques used by parents, particularly in dealing with dependency, are of significance.

KEY POINTS

Genetic Influences on Personality Development

Schizophrenia much more likely in pairs of
identical than fraternal twins

Hypothesis: autism due to unsatisfactory
child-parent relationships

Hypothesis: autism due to inherited
predispositions

The Influence of Parents on Personality Development

Authoritative parents: self-reliant, competent
children

Authoritarian parents: insecure, hostile children

Permissive parents: dependent, immature
children

Authoritative techniques: encouragement, limits
(with explanations), appreciation, affection

Authoritative parents serve as models, help
children set standards

The Influence of Peers on Personality Development

Peers serve as models, reinforcing agents

From 2 to 5, children move from parallel to
associative and cooperative play

The Acquisition of Sex Roles

Sex-typed behavior in preschoolers influenced
more by attitude of parents than by models

Children imitate types of behavior exhibited by
many models

Cognitive awareness contributes to learning of
sex roles

Androgenized girls develop masculine traits
despite being treated as girls

Aggressive Behavior

Frustrated children tend to imitate aggressive
acts

Hypothesis: viewing TV leads to aggressive
behavior

Surgeon General's report: not all studies support
hypothesis that viewing TV leads to violence

Aggressive behavior strengthened by
reinforcement, observation

Prosocial Behavior

Relationship between sympathetic and aggressive
behavior

Children who express distress more likely to help
others in distress

Sympathetic models likely to be imitated are
warm, express pleasure

Prosocial behavior encouraged by discussion,
models, pleasure

Emotional Factors in Personality Development

Between 2 and 5, "physical" fears decrease;
"imaginary" fears increase

Fears may be overcome by explanations,
example, positive reconditioning, confidence

Preventing fears by allowing freedom to explore

Anxiety may be minimized by providing
support, satisfying needs, encouraging
independence

CHAPTER □8

TWO TO FIVE:
PERSONALITY
DEVELOPMENT

Human infants begin life as dependent beings. They engage in many types of behavior that help them respond in ways that contribute to their survival, but if others do not care for them, they will die. (They influence the behavior of their caretakers in many ways, but they are still dependent on them.) Infants also begin life as egocentric creatures. They are concerned primarily about satisfaction of their own needs, and the quickness and devotion with which these needs are satisfied (in most cases) during the first months of life reinforce this self-centeredness. In the short time between birth and the second birthday, children move from dependency on others to the capability of an impressive amount of self-directed behavior. Two-year-olds have excellent vision and highly developed senses; they can walk, manipulate things, feed themselves, control their processes of elimination (most of the time), and use words to express wants and desires. They have overcome most of the anxiety experienced as one-year-olds when separated from their mothers and are eager to explore new experiences on their own. They begin to seek and enjoy the companionship of their age-mates and start to interact with individuals outside their immediate family. All of these skills, abilities, and tendencies infuse two-year-olds with a sense of power and independence.

325

This sense of autonomy is a mixed blessing, however. Parents who have been delighted by almost all their offspring's accomplishments during the first year begin to realize that some of the tendencies and abilities appearing after that time may lead to complications and even trouble. Most parents are proud and excited when a one-year-old daughter or son begins to walk or says a first word. When a two-year-old refuses to follow a request to cease some activity, however, parental delight may turn to anger or dismay. An eleven-month-old who grabs a floorlamp and brings it down with a crash after having taken a few wildly uncoordinated but incontestably independent steps is not likely to be looked upon as a troublemaker. In fact, the parents may brag about the incident. But a two-year-old who deliberately knocks over a lamp in retaliation for being forcibly restrained from banging on the piano (after having spat out "No" to a request to stop) is almost sure to arouse a much different response.

When children become capable of moving around, getting into things, and expressing themselves verbally, they are confronted for the first time with the realization that they must sometimes subordinate their wishes to the wishes of others. They discover that their parents no longer cater to all their desires. And as they begin to play with siblings or peers, they realize that a certain amount of give-and-take is expected and that they cannot always have their own way.

Socialization and Personality

Starting around the age of two, then, children learn that they are expected to move from self-centered dependence to independent coexistence. They also learn that only certain types of behavior are considered appropriate in certain situations. The way these types of behavior develop and are influenced by parents is called the process of *socialization*.

Psychologists have sought information about the various ways a child acquires social forms of behavior. They have studied how children identify with and imitate parents and peers and how they learn to adapt to group interaction. Some of the ways socialization takes place will be discussed on the next few pages, but the organizational theme of this chapter is the emergence of *personality*. Most definitions of personality stress that it is made up of a unique combination of characteristics that determine how individuals respond to experiences, how they get along with others (and cause others to react to them), and how they get along with themselves. Developmental psychologists are particularly interested in trying to trace the causes of personality development to determine whether some types of early experiences are likely to enhance the appearance of desirable forms of behavior, whether other experiences may predispose the child to later encounter difficulties in adjustment.

A particularly helpful description of factors that determine personality has been proposed by Henry A. Murray and Clyde Kluckhohn (1948). They describe

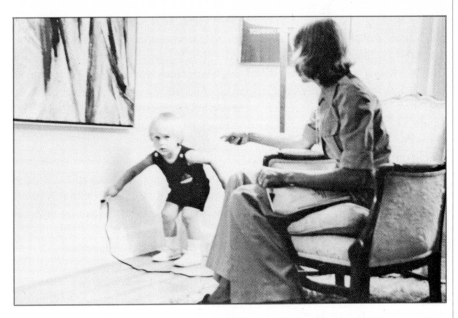

Two-year-olds are eager to engage in a great deal of independent behavior but must learn that they cannot always have their own way. Philip Jon Bailey.

four types of personality determinants: constitutional, group membership, role, and situational. *Constitutional* determinants are inherited characteristics and predispositions (sex, height, facial features, body chemistry, and so on). *Group membership* determinants include the general culture (for example, American, French, Japanese) in which a child is reared and all the cultural subgroups that influence personality development (such as class, family, peer group, friends). *Role* determinants include not only the general, more or less permanent self-concept of a person but also the specific and variable roles assumed in different situations (reflected, for instance, in the behavior of a boy who feels self-conscious when he writes a poem in English class as contrasted with his behavior as captain of the football team). *Situational* determinants are all the experiences of the individual that contribute to the development of personality—not only frequently repeated experiences that have a cumulative impact but also traumatic or especially significant single experiences that alter the entire course of a person's life. Some of the ways these various factors interact to determine personality will be explored in the sections that follow.

Genetic Influences on Personality Development

Murray and Kluckhohn describe the constitutional factors that determine personality. The research of Beverly Birns (1965) and Alexander Thomas and his associates (1963, 1970) (noted in Chapter 6) support the view that differences in the behavior of newborn infants are due to innate tendencies. Researchers who assume that differences in children are due almost entirely to the way they are treated by their parents suggest that a given set of techniques used by parents will usually lead to particular characteristics in children. This line of reasoning does not allow for the possibility that inherited predispositions may cause children exposed to exactly the same child-rearing techniques to respond in quite different ways.

The question of how much personality is influenced by inherited tendencies has been debated since the time of Plato and Aristotle. Prevailing opinions have changed as new research has been reported. As well, any particular theorist is influenced by determinants of her or his own personality, including cultural trends, the influence of teachers and colleagues, and experiences that had a significant impact on professional development. Research on personality development is also complicated by the fact that there is no way to analyze the complete genetic endowment of any individual. The presence of gross chromosomal abnormalities (such as an extra chromosome) can be determined, but there is no way to examine genes. The similar traits of individuals with an extra chromosome lend support to the conclusion that behavior is influenced by genetic factors, but it is impossible to trace precise cause-and-effect relationships.

The search for relationships between behavior, heredity, and experiences is further complicated by the difficulty of evaluating types of behavior manifested at different age levels and by different individuals. Observers may be able to agree that a newborn baby is active or quiet or that a preschooler is aggressive or timid. But they may find it much more difficult to evaluate the behavior of an adolescent or adult who has learned to disguise feelings and to express them in subtle and sometimes misleading ways. Despite such complications, there is reason to believe that many aspects of personal and social development may be influenced by inherited predispositions. Recent evidence, for example, supports the hypothesis that hyperactivity (Ross and Ross, 1976) and stuttering (Kidd, Kidd, and Records, 1978) are influenced by genetic factors. Furthermore, it appears that many less extreme traits of personality such as sociability, activity, and impulsivity are similarly influenced by inherited predispositions (Buss and Plomin, 1975). Some of the most convincing evidence of the impact of genetic factors on personality is supplied by studies of schizophrenia and speculations about autism.

Studies of Schizophrenia

Schizophrenia is the most common childhood psychosis. It is characterized by a number of traits including seclusiveness, irritability when disturbed, daydreaming, bizarre behavior, few personal interests, sensitivity to comments and criticism, and physical inactivity. There are usually three stages when such behavioral characteristics are likely to appear: the first two years of life, from three to four-and-one-half years, and from ten to eleven-and-one-half years (Bender, 1960).

F. J. Kallman (1946) carried out a classic study in which he attempted to trace the degree to which schizophrenia is caused by inherited predispositions. Comparing the incidence of schizophrenia in identical twins and fraternal twins—a method followed by many researchers who have been interested in the nature-nurture question—Kallman concentrated on families with an institutionalized member who was one of a pair of twins. He discovered that both members of pairs of identical twins were classified as schizophrenic 69 percent of the time, both members of pairs of fraternal twins 11 percent of the time. Gottesman and Shields (1966) carried out a similar study in Great Britain and also summarized the results of eight investigations of the same type (including the Kallman study). They concluded that when one twin is schizophrenic, the chances of the other member of the pair also being schizophrenic are five times greater for identical than for fraternal twins. (Gottesman and Shields reaffirm their conclusions in *Schizophrenia and Genetics* [1972].)

Schizophrenia more likely in pairs of identical than fraternal twins

Those who favor the hereditarian position argue that these figures provide conclusive proof that schizophrenia is due to a considerable extent to inherited predispositions. Environmentalists point out, in rebuttal, that the likelihood of both twins being institutionalized in fraternal pairs of the same sex is greater than in opposite-sexed fraternal pairs, which suggests that experiences play a part. D. Rosenthal (1959) has suggested that those who study the causes of schizophrenia should keep in mind that there are different types of this psychosis; one may be due primarily to genetic factors; others to environmental causes. Furthermore, it appears that there are a variety of genetic causes of schizophrenia (Kaplan, 1972).

Differing Explanations of Autism

A form of psychosis very similar to schizophrenia, *infantile autism* was first described by the eminent psychiatrist Leo Kanner (1942). He encountered a number of cases where infants were unresponsive to adults, language development was severely if not completely impaired, and behavior was dominated by an obsessive insistence on the maintenance of sameness. Children with this condition exhibit the characteristic pattern of symptoms very early in life. Some theorists argue that autism is caused by profoundly unsatisfactory child-parent relationships. Bruno Bettelheim (1967, 1974), for example, suggests that autistic behavior is the result of the development of strong feelings of what Erikson would refer to as mistrust on the part of the young child. Another theorist who traces autism to the inability of parents to establish a sense of trust in the child is Niko Tinbergen, an ethologist whose studies of seagulls earned him the Nobel Prize. Tinbergen proposes an explanation similar to Margaret Ribble's hypothesis that the neonate is substantially influenced by initial parent-child relationships.

Hypothesis: autism due to unsatisfactory child-parent relationships

Some theorists argue that autism, characterized by lack of responsiveness, is due to unsatisfactory child-parent relationships. Other theorists believe that autism is due to inherited predispositions. Ted Polumbaum.

Tinbergen observes "parents of autistic children are odd in some way—either strained or apprehensive or overserious" (1974, p. 75) and he suggests that autism is caused by the way these parents handle their children in infancy.

Hypothesis: autism due to inherited predispositions

Other psychologists, however, believe that autism can be traced to inherited predispositions. If allowance is made for a genetic factor in autism, a different explanation for the "odd" behavior of the parents becomes apparent. (An explanation related to speculations about causes of schizophrenia, noted above.) The parents of an autistic child may recognize that their newborn infant manifests strange behavior from the moment of birth, and this causes them to *become* strained, apprehensive, and overserious. This interpretation is favored by O. Ivar Lovaas, who has had notable success using behavior-modification techniques to treat autistic children. Lovaas reports (1974) that his impression of the parents of autistic children who are brought to him for treatment is positive. He believes that the odd behavior of their children causes them to lose faith in their abilities as child rearers and to blame themselves for the child's condition.

The opinion of Lovaas is similar to that stressed by Birns and by Thomas and his associates: some children seem to be born with tendencies that make them difficult to care for. If parents become convinced that infant and child behavior is entirely due to the way they handle their children, it is almost inevitable that they will experience feelings of guilt and a loss of confidence when undesirable forms of child behavior appear.

This brief outline of a few typical studies of the impact of constitutional factors on personality illustrates the difficulty of separating nature from nurture. Both inherited predispositions and environmental experiences obviously have an impact on personality. It is not possible, however, to determine precisely how much each factor contributes to a particular tendency.

The second set of personality determinants described by Murray and Kluck-hohn is made up of relationships with members of various groups. The most significant group for almost all children is the family, and emerging relationships with parents are obviously the most important. Because parents feel kinship with their children, their reactions to questionable forms of behavior may often be tempered by eagerness to foster positive development. Individuals who are not related to a child, however, have no reason to allow for inadequacies in interpersonal relationships. Accordingly, a child's first interactions with peers, either in the neighborhood or in preschool settings, may lead to difficulties in learning to get along with others. Each of these types of relationship—those with parents and with peers—will be discussed separately.

The Influence of Parents on Personality Development

Because the child from two to five years old is capable of independent behavior and mature enough to attend nursery school, the preschool years provide an exceptional opportunity for studying parent-child relationships. Researchers can observe children interacting during free-play periods in a nursery school (an ideal situation for obtaining evidence regarding personality differences) or in home situations and then compare descriptions of child behavior with information obtained from parents about their child-rearing practices. Furthermore, actual interactions between parents and their children in home and experimental situations can be recorded. Dozens of studies of this type have been carried out. Many early investigations were reviewed and analyzed by E. S. Schaefer (1959); studies carried out during the subsequent decade were reviewed by Wesley C. Becker (1964). Investigations by Diana Baumrind not only substantiate findings of many early studies, they also stand out because of the clarity of the implications that can be drawn from her conclusions. Baumrind's research, therefore, will be stressed in this analysis of parent-child relationships during the preschool years.

Three Types of Child Rearing

In one study Baumrind (1967) asked teachers and independent observers to rate the behavior of three- and four-year-olds who had been selected because of particular types of behavior patterns. Their parents were interviewed, and observers visited homes and recorded all parent-child interactions where one person tried to influence another during the period from dinner to bedtime. All of these impressions were analyzed and compared, leading eventually to descriptions of techniques used by mothers classified into three basic types. The techniques of control used by each type of mother and the types of child behavior associated with each included the following patterns:

Authoritative parents: self-reliant, competent children

☐ *Authoritative* mothers established firm control but gave reasons for restrictions. They respected the child's wishes but also expected the child to take into account the needs of others. They were warm, supportive, and loving. Their children were likely to be socialized and independent, self-reliant, explorative, assertive, and competent.

Authoritarian parents: insecure, hostile children

☐ *Authoritarian* mothers set absolute standards and used punitive techniques to enforce them. They did not permit their children to challenge restrictions but presented them as inviolable rules. They were not very affectionate. Their children were likely to be somewhat discontented, insecure, and hostile under stress.

Permissive parents: dependent, immature children

☐ *Permissive* mothers were nonpunitive, acceptant, and made few attempts to shape behavior. They tended to be disorganized and ineffective in running the household. A maximum amount of self-regulation was encouraged. Their children were likely to be dependent, immature, and to lack self-reliance or self-control.

Authoritative Techniques of Child Rearing   From her original sample Baumrind (1971) selected children who clearly exhibited the three patterns of behavior she had noted in her earlier studies and made detailed analyses of the control techniques used by parents of each type. Children who were rated as competent, mature, independent, self-reliant, self-controlled, explorative, affiliative, and self-assertive were found to come from homes where parents used an authoritative approach made up of techniques that can be converted into the following guidelines:

Authoritative techniques: encouragement, limits (with explanations), appreciation, affection

1   Permit and encourage the child to do many things independently.
2   Urge the child to try to achieve mature and skilled types of behavior.
3   Establish firm and consistent limits regarding unacceptable forms of behavior; explain the reasons for these as soon as the child is able to understand; listen to complaints if the child feels the restrictions are too confining; give additional reasons if the limits are still to be maintained as originally stated.

Permissive parents may feel that a policy of noninterference will encourage optimum development in their child. Diana Baumrind found, however, that too much self-regulation seemed to cause children to become dependent, immature, and lacking in self-reliance and self-control. Philip Jon Bailey.

4   Show that the child's achievements are admired and appreciated.

5   Communicate love in a warm and sincere (but not excessive) way.

Explanations for the Advantages of Authoritative Approaches   Some of the reasons authoritative child-rearing techniques seem to lead to competence in children are revealed by Baumrind's analysis of the three approaches she discovered and described. Parents of competent children were *authoritative* because they had confidence in their abilities as parents. They therefore provided a model of competence for their children to imitate. When they established limits and explained reasons for restrictions they encouraged their children to set standards for themselves and to think about *why* certain procedures should be followed. And because the parents were warm and affectionate, their positive responses were valued by their children as rewards for mature behavior. *Authoritarian* parents, by contrast, made demands and wielded power, but their failure to take into account the child's point of view, coupled with their lack of warmth, led to resentment and insecurity on the part of the child. Children of authoritarian parents did as they were told, but they were likely to do so out of compliance or fear, not out of a desire to earn love or approval. Permissive parents were likely to appear disorganized, inconsistent, and unsure of themselves, and their children

Authoritative parents serve as models, help children set standards

were likely to imitate such behavior. Furthermore, such parents did not demand much of their children, nor did they discourage immature behavior.

Autonomy, Initiative, and Child-Rearing Techniques

Baumrind's conclusions regarding the impact of authoritative, authoritarian, and permissive child-rearing approaches can be related to the stages of psychosocial development proposed by Erikson. The child of two and three years of age is at the autonomy vs. doubt stage, the four- and five-year-old is at the initiative vs. guilt stage. Erikson suggests that autonomy is most likely to develop if children are encouraged to do what they are capable of doing at their own pace and in their own way—but with judicious supervision by parents. He suggests that initiative is most likely to develop if children are given freedom to explore and experiment and if parents take time to answer questions. Erikson's suggestions for parental behavior are very similar to techniques used by the authoritative parents observed by Baumrind. Such parents encouraged their children to set standards for themselves, were warm and affectionate, and responded positively to the child's accomplishments.

It would seem likely that two- and three-year-olds might experience doubts about their capabilities if their parents were either authoritarian (causing the child to feel insecure) or permissive (serving as disorganized models). In addition, it seems likely that authoritarian parents might cause their children to experience shame if they made excessive demands (regarding toilet training, for instance). Four- and five-year-olds might be expected to experience guilt if authoritarian parents made too many demands and failed to take into account the child's point of view. Permissive parents might inadvertently foster guilt because of inconsistencies in child-rearing practices and because their behavior seems to encourage dependency and immaturity in children.

This discussion of ways that child-rearing techniques influence personality development calls attention to the fact that the family is usually the most important group to which a two- to five-year-old belongs. But as soon as a child begins to interact with age-mates, particularly in school, the peer group takes on increasing significance. Relationships with peers, therefore, often have an important impact on personality development.

The Influence of Peers on Personality Development

Friendships and Popularity

Two- to five-year-olds who attend nursery school are convenient subjects for study, and dozens of analyses of social interaction have been made. Some researchers make use of observational methods of different kinds (particularly time sampling); others prefer sociometric techniques (in which members of a group indicate which individuals they like best); some combine the two. Studies of the consistency of playmate choices (reviewed by Witryol and Thompson, 1953) indicate that friendships become more stable with age. Two- and three-year-olds tend to flit from one playmate to another and select a different classmate on successive sociometric interviews, but five-year-olds may be faithful to one or two companions for an extended period of time. The personality traits of preschool children chosen frequently by their peers include friendliness, sociability, social visibility, and outgoingness (Hartup, 1970, p. 388). Children who seek assistance from peers and are eager for their approval tend to be more popular than those who seem interested primarily in attracting attention. Preschoolers seem to like having a playmate seek their help or approval but are bothered by someone who pesters them. Several studies (reviewed by Hartup, 1970, p. 393) have provided evidence that brighter children are more popular than those below average in intelligence. As early as three years of age, children tend to prefer playmates of the same sex (Moore and Updegraff, 1964), but there are many bisexual friendships.

Peers as Reinforcers and Shapers

This discussion of factors that may contribute to popularity emphasizes that when children begin to interact with peers they are influenced for the first time by the reactions of individuals other than parents and siblings. In his description of motivation Abraham H. Maslow stresses that needs (such as love, belonging, and esteem) that set the stage for self-actualization can be satisfied only by others. Therefore, when children enter a social group, their behavior comes under the influence of members of that group. They are eager to win signs of approval and affection, and their behavior will be shaped by reinforcement from their peers. Consequently, many of the hypotheses accounting for the way parents influence socialization also apply to the way children influence each other; they may imitate models who are rewarded or who reward them or recognize that peers are engaging in forms of behavior that seem worth emulating.

V. J. Crandall and several associates (1958) studied the ways nursery school children complied with or conformed to the demands of their peers and of adults. They discovered that peer-compliant children were readily influenced by the opinions of others and were likely to seek praise and attention from others. But they were also rated as energetic, spontaneous, friendly, and relaxed. Children who were more adult-compliant were rated as nonaggressive and withdrawn. The child who seeks approval from peers appears to engage in easygoing, relatively nonaggressive give-and-take, while the child who seeks adult approval appears to be anxious and submissive. Part of the reason some children from this study sought adult approval might have been that they were unable to secure peer approval. Perhaps the need for belongingness was satisfied in the peer-compliant group but not in the children who sought adult approval. If so, peer approval was reinforcing, and so it was desired.

There seems to be a tendency for nursery school children who are eager to gain peer approval to imitate the behavior of classmates. W. W. Hartup and B. Coates (1967), for example, arranged for preschoolers to observe a child (a confederate of the experimenters) who was very generous in sharing things. The sharing behavior of many of the children increased, particularly in those the model had previously responded to in a favorable way. The results of this study reveal that peers serve both as models and as important reinforcing agents.

Peers serve as models, reinforcing agents

Age Trends in Social Interactions with Peers

Two- to five-year-olds seem to gradually build skills necessary for interacting with others. At first they prefer to keep to themselves, observing playmates from a distance. Next, they play more or less independently *beside* others. Eventually they engage in cooperative types of play in which specific roles are assigned. This sequence was first described by Mildred Parten (1932), who observed the free play of children in a nursery school and noted the types of social behavior they engaged in. Eventually, she was able to write quite precise descriptions of these six types of behavior.

- ☐ *Unoccupied behavior*—Children do not really play at all. They either stand around and glance for a time at others or engage in aimless activities.
- ☐ *Solitary play*—Children play alone with toys that are different from those used by children within speaking distance. They make no attempt to interact with others.
- ☐ *Onlooker behavior*—Children spend most of their time watching others. They may make comments on the play of others but do not attempt to join in.
- ☐ *Parallel play*—Children play *beside,* but not really with, other children. They use the same toys in close proximity to others, yet in an independent way.
- ☐ *Associative play*—Children engage in rather disorganized play with other children. But, there is no assignment of activities or roles; individual children play in their own ways.
- ☐ *Cooperative play*—Children engage in an organized form of play where leadership and other roles are assigned. The members of the group may cooperate in creating some project, dramatize some situation, or engage in some sort of coordinated enterprise.

Having developed these descriptions, Parten then used the *time-sampling* technique. She observed a one-minute sample of the behavior of the child selected. At the end of that time, she classified the child's play into one of the six categories. She then repeated this procedure with another child, and so on. Over a

Parallel play. Children play *beside* but not really with others. Guy Gillette/Photo Researchers.

Associative play. Children engage in dis-organized play with others. No roles are assigned because the play remains unstructured. David S. Strickler/Monkmeyer.

Cooperative play. Roles are assigned as children engage in structured play activities. Lyn Gardiner/Stock, Boston.

period of days she accumulated a record of the types of play engaged in, consisting of twenty such samples for each child. An analysis of these records showed that two-year-olds were most likely to engage in *parallel* play (they played *beside*, but not really with, others). Older children were more likely to enjoy *associative* or *cooperative* play (they interacted with others first in somewhat disorganized ways, eventually by engaging in coordinated activities and by assigning specific roles).

K. E. Barnes (1971) carried out a replication of Parten's study and compared the social behavior of preschool children of this generation with the descriptions of the behavior of children observed forty years earlier. The time samplings obtained by Barnes indicated that young children of the 1970s were much less

From 2 to 5, children move from parallel to associative and cooperative play

socially oriented than those of the 1930s. Barnes hypothesized that the time contemporary children spend watching television, plus the decrease in family size, might account for the change toward more self-centered behavior.

The fact that children begin to assume roles when they engage in cooperative play calls attention to the third group of personality determinants noted by Murray and Kluckhohn. All of the roles assumed by a child may influence personality development, but a particularly significant role depends on each child's perception of behavior appropriate for males and females in our society. Because of questions raised by feminists, there is considerable interest in ways that sex roles are acquired. A number of theorists have proposed explanations for what psychologists commonly refer to as *sex-typed behavior*—activities or interests that reflect stereotyped conceptions of masculinity and femininity.

The Acquisition of Sex Roles

Explanations Accounting for Sex-typed Behavior

Freud: Importance of Identification   In his theory of development, Freud emphasized the importance of identification. He distinguished between two types, *anaclitic* (leaning-up-against-type) and *defensive* (or aggressive). Freud proposed that anaclitic identification occurs when the child of two or so, who has been completely dependent on his or her mother the first few months of life, imitates some of her activities. He reasoned that two-year-olds may become apprehensive about certain aspects of their newfound independence and seek security by engaging in some of the activities performed by the person who has previously cared for them. This explanation may account for the identification behavior of two-year-olds, but at the age of three or four, when children typically become aware of sex differences, boys begin to identify with their fathers. Defensive identification was proposed to explain this switch. As noted in Chapter 3, Freud hypothesized that the four-year-old boy (who is experiencing the Oedipus complex) fears and resents his father as a rival. The boy realizes the father is more powerful and so he identifies with the "aggressor" and tries to become more like him. By doing this, the boy defends himself against anxiety.

Sears: Identification and Child Rearing   Robert R. Sears, Lucy Rau, and Richard Alpert carried out an ambitious study (reported in *Identification and Child Rearing*, 1965) in an effort to evaluate Freud's theory of identification. They considered this an important area for research because they felt it might yield a unitary process that would account for several types of behavior that become established early in a child's life—particularly sex typing and formation of adult roles. Sears was one of the originators of social-learning theory, and he was interested in analyzing the development of identification in terms of stimulus-response principles. He hypothesized that since the young child must be cared for by others, the development of sex-appropriate and adultlike behavior would be strongly influenced by early *dependency* in the child. He also theorized that if there were a unitary process that accounted for sex typing, the formation of adult roles, and other types of behavior, there would be considerable consistency in child behavior, traceable to child-rearing practices.

To test these hypotheses Sears and his colleagues obtained information on 40 four-year-olds attending a summer nursery school. The children were observed in free play and in experimental and doll-play situations and were then interviewed, as were both fathers and mothers. The mothers were observed interacting with their children in standard situations. In one phase of the study, for example, the mother was asked to fill out a questionnaire in a room where her child had nothing to do—which caused most children to pester their mothers. In another phase the child was asked to solve a jigsaw puzzle with or without the mother's help. (Both of these situations made it possible to evaluate the degree of dependency shown by a child.)

When all the data were processed and analyzed, Sears and his colleagues found more consistency in the behavior of girls than boys. They concluded that this could be interpreted as support for Freud's concept of anaclitic identification. The children being studied were four years old, which meant the boys theoretically were experiencing the Oedipus complex and in a process of shifting from anaclitic to defensive identification. The researchers failed, however, to find evidence that dependency was a unitary process. They observed "By age four, *overt dependency behavior* does not reflect a unitary drive or habit structure that can be interpreted as the unique source of reinforcement for all the other behaviors we have studied" (1965, p. 249).

Regarding the development of sex-typed behavior, a comparison of child behavior and parental practices led Sears and his colleagues to conclude: "Children of both sexes initially adopt feminine-maternal ways of behaving" (p. 261) due to a monitoring process based on the mother's responsiveness and also to direct instruction (not always intentional or verbalizable). "The boy develops a cognitive map of the male role at some point in his first three or four years and begins to shape his own behavior toward that role" (p. 261). The boy is able to do this more effectively if male models (particularly the father) are available. In contrast to the influence of the mother on the development of feminine behavior, the *responsiveness* of the male model is not an important factor. "Masculinity and femininity both appear to be more influenced by parental attitudes toward the control of sex and aggression than by any aspect of the availability of the behavior of models" (p. 261). If the parents encouraged freedom of expression and were nonpunitive, both boys *and* girls were likely to develop masculine traits.

Sex-typed behavior in preschoolers influenced more by attitude of parents than by models

Even though Sears concluded that dependency did not appear to be a unitary trait, his results might be interpreted as support for the Freudian concepts of anaclitic and defensive identification. At first, both boys and girls adopt forms of behavior exhibited by the mother, particularly if she responds positively to them. It seems quite reasonable to explain this as identification that involves dependency on (or anaclitic identification with) the primary caretaker. Around the age of three or four, the boy begins to imitate the father's actions, but masculine behavior will be practiced even though the male model does not respond to the child. It seems plausible to explain this by suggesting that the boy identifies with the father not because he feels dependent, but because he hopes to acquire some of the father's envied power. The same explanation might account, in part at least, for the tendency of a girl who is not "protected" by the mother to imitate masculine types of behavior.

Bandura: Impact of Imitation   At the same time Sears was evaluating the impact of identification on social learning, Albert Bandura began a series of investigations of the influence of observational learning. Bandura has observed (Bandura and Walters, 1963) that what personality theorists (such as Freud and Sears) called *identification* is labeled *imitation* by experimental psychologists. Bandura believes that both terms might be referred to as *observational learning*. Bandura suggests thinking of the three terms as synonyms, instead of drawing fine distinctions between them. Bandura also believes that attempts to explain all types of behavior in terms of traditional stimulus-response principles, with emphasis on reinforcement of specific acts, are not completely satisfactory. He feels that more allowance should be made for changes in behavior due to observation and imitation, with or without reinforcement.

Bandura and his colleagues carried out experiments (Bandura, Ross, and Ross, 1963a, 1963c) to discover the kinds of models most likely to be imitated. They concluded that individuals who supplied rewards or who were perceived as possessing power were often—but not always—imitated. They also discovered that some types of behavior may be imitated in the absence of any apparent reinforcement. Regarding the learning of sex-typed behavior Bandura and his colleagues observed:

Theories of identificatory learning have generally assumed that within the family setting the child's initial identification is confined to his mother, and that during early childhood boys must turn from the mother as the primary model to the father as the main source of imitative behavior. However, throughout the course of development children are provided with ample opportunities to observe the behavior of both parents. When children are exposed to multiple models they may select one or more of them as the primary source of behavior, but rarely reproduce all the elements of a single model's repertoire or confine their imitation to that model. (1963a, p. 534)

Children imitate types of behavior exhibited by many models

Preschool children begin to acquire sex-typed behavior by imitating older members of the same sex. Frank Siteman/Stock, Boston; Erika Stone.

Other studies of the same type (reviewed by Walter Mischel, 1970, pp. 29–39) have supported Bandura's conclusion that sex-typed behavior is often learned through imitation of a variety of models and in the absence of any form of tangible reward.

Kohlberg: Cognitive Awareness of Sex Differences   Lawrence Kohlberg (1966) points out that by the age of five, children have definite awareness of sex differences. (Freud based his explanation for the Oedipus complex on the same observation.) Kohlberg suggests that children of that age also have come to acquire knowledge of stereotypes about masculinity and femininity. (This hypothesis is similar to the conclusion of Sears that "The boy develops a cognitive map of the male role at some point in his first three or four years and begins to shape his own behavior toward that role" (1965, p. 261). Many aspects of the development of sex-role behavior, therefore, might be attributed simply to observation and the desire of a boy or girl to behave the way a man or woman does. A boy, aware that he is a male, who sees an older brother shave, watches college and professional athletes on television, or observes his father mow the lawn will think of these as masculine activities and tend to imitate them. A girl, aware that she is a female, who sees an older sister put on lipstick, observes the behavior of females depicted on television programs, and observes her mother cook dinner will think of these as feminine activities and tend to imitate them. As Bandura's conclusion suggests, children are exposed to so many models that the emerging self-concept of any particular child is likely to be a synthesis of many impressions. Sears, Bandura, and Kohlberg offer explanations for the way sex-role behavior may be learned. There is some evidence, however, that certain aspects of the behavior of males and females in our society may be due to innate biological differences between the sexes.

Cognitive awareness contributes to learning of sex roles

Biological Influences on Sex-typed Behavior

The basic problem in speculating about the causes of what have come to be called male and female traits is that under ordinary circumstances it is impossible to separate completely biological from environmental causes. The infant *must* be cared for, and the child cannot be reared in a vacuum. It is thus inevitable that he or she will have occasion to see how other males or females behave. The development and use of pregnancy hormones in the 1950s, however, inadvertently led to a situation where biological and environmental factors relating to sex differences could be examined separately. Before use of these hormones was discontinued, it was discovered that some women treated with them (to prevent unwanted abortion) gave birth to masculinized daughters, that is, females in whom the influence of the androgens (hormones that develop and maintain masculine traits) caused the development of male sex organs. In several cases, this condition was diagnosed at birth, and the masculine sexual organs were surgically modified. While the surgery corrected the external physical aspects of masculinization, it did not cancel out the continued impact of the androgens. Masculinization could be controlled with injections of cortisone so that the girls grew up with a female physique, and most were eventually capable of bearing children. These girls, therefore, as they matured, saw themselves and were seen as girls, yet they continued to be influenced by the androgens. This situation provided an excellent opportunity for studying the origin of sex differences.

John Money and Anke Ehrhardt (1972) found twenty-five androgenized girls (ranging in age from four to sixteen years) and matched each of these with a normal girl of the same age, socioeconomic background, IQ, and race. All fifty girls and their mothers were asked a standard series of questions and were given tests of sex-role preferences. The purpose of the study was to see if "prenatal androgens may have left a presumptive effect on the brain, and hence subsequent behavior" (1972, p. 98). It was discovered that the fetally androgenized girls manifested *tomboyism* to a much greater extent than the control group. The androgenized girls were much more likely to engage in activities involving energy expenditure and competitiveness; they preferred clothes that were utilitarian and functional (and avoided fashionable dresses); they were indifferent to dolls and later to human infants; but they were attracted to toy cars, trucks, and guns. Many of the control girls, by contrast, loved to play with dolls and took every opportunity to get close to human infants.

Androgenized girls develop masculine traits despite being treated as girls

Furthermore, all twenty-five of the controls said (in reply to a question) that they wanted to have babies of their own when they grew up. One-third of the androgenized girls, on the other hand, said they would prefer not to have children, and although the remainder did not reject the idea, they were not enthusiastic about it either. When asked whether they would prefer a career to marriage (and being a housewife) when they grew up, the majority of the androgenized girls chose a career first. The majority of the control girls answered that they felt marriage was the most important goal of the future, and the older girls in the sample showed a high interest in romance and boy friends. The androgenized girls, by contrast, took little interest in dating.

Money and Ehrhardt concluded, "The most likely hypothesis to explain the various features of tomboyism in fetally masculinized genetic females is that their tomboyism is a sequel to a masculinizing effect on the fetal brain" (p. 103). They theorized that this effect strengthened pathways in the brain that led to competitive energy expenditure (not necessarily aggression) and weakened those that led to maternal behavior. Money and Ehrhardt also analyzed several other types of cases where bisexual abnormalities had occurred. In summing up the significance of their research on hermaphroditism, they stressed the degree to which behavior seems to be controlled by genetic factors—if the fetal brain is androgenized, masculine traits will appear regardless of what the parents and others do.

Environmental Influences on Sex-typed Behavior

Money and Ehrhardt stress biological influences on sex-typed behavior, but environmental factors obviously influence the emergence of such forms of behavior. You may recall, for example, from the preceding chapter Howard Moss's conclusion (1963) that starting as early as three months after their children are born, mothers tend to cuddle girls more often than they cuddle boys. As soon as they come home from the hospital male and female babies are not only treated differently, the environments in which they spend much of their time are arranged differently. Harriet Rheingold and Kaye Cook (1975) examined the furnishings and playthings in the rooms of boys and girls under the age of six.

Boys' rooms contained many more "educational" toys (for example, construction sets) and "instructional" decorations (for example, informative posters). Girls' rooms contained large numbers of dolls, and decorations featured flowers and ruffles. Boys in books do different sorts of things than girls. Many female characters on TV shows engage in decidedly different kinds of activities than males. Many of the women depicted in TV commercials appear to be primarily concerned about such monumental problems as clean laundry and dirty ovens. The tendency Bandura demonstrated for children to imitate models, and the growing awareness of male-female differences stressed by Kohlberg serve to strengthen the impact of "traditional" sex roles. Even though there may be a tendency for the fetal brain of a child to be "masculinized" or "feminized" by hormones, therefore, the impact of experiences shaping masculine or feminine behavior might cancel out such tendencies. (A more complete description of the nature and causes of sex-typed behavior will be presented in discussing sex differences in the behavior of six- to twelve-year-olds in Chapter 10.)

This brief review of different interpretations of the causes of sex-typed behavior reveals that such forms of behavior are influenced by biological *and* environmental factors. Even though it may not be possible to delineate specific causal factors, there is evidence of clear-cut differences in the social interactions of males and females as soon as they engage in group activities.

Aggressive Behavior

Seymour Feshbach (1970, p. 190) summarized the results of fourteen observational studies of the social behavior of two- to five-year-olds. Boys were judged more aggressive in nine of these studies. In the remaining five studies, no significant sex differences were reported, but some of these investigations concentrated on forms of behavior such as verbal quarreling, verbal disapproval, and tattling. These last findings lend support to the conclusion (based also on other studies reviewed by Feshbach) that when girls engage in aggressive behavior, they do so in indirect ways. In their analysis of Fels Research Institute data, Jerome Kagan and Howard A. Moss (1962) found that aggressiveness was significantly more stable in males than females from birth to fourteen years. There is quite consistent evidence, therefore, that boys tend to be more aggressive than girls. The extent to which these differences are due to innate biological tendencies, experiences, imitation, or social expectation is impossible to determine on the basis of data currently available.

Differences Between Hostile and Instrumental Aggression

Sex differences in aggressive behavior have been revealed in analyses of types of reactions to anger-producing situations. As he studied aggressive behavior and

Dozens of studies support the conclusion that boys engage in more aggressive behavior than girls.
Elizabeth Hamlin/Stock, Boston.

reviewed research on the subject, Feshbach (1970) found it helpful to distinguish between two basic types of aggression. *Hostile* (or person-oriented) *aggression* is directed at other children and is provoked by behavior that threatens self-esteem (for example, a boy tells another boy "You're stupid") or is interpreted as intentional (for example, a girl is convinced that another girl deliberately hit her). *Instrumental aggression* is aimed at attaining or retrieving some object or privilege and is usually provoked when some goal-directed activity is blocked (for example, a boy pushes a playmate away from a pile of blocks he needs to complete a miniature castle). Willard Hartup (1974) observed aggressive inter-actions between preschool children and first graders. He found that the younger children engaged in aggressive interactions more frequently but that most of these were of the instrumental type. Hartup speculates that younger children may not respond to comments that would provoke a response from an older child because they have not yet developed a clear self-concept and are not aware of the intention of malice. As they grow older, children engage in fewer aggressive acts, but they are more likely to be provoked by threats to their self-esteem. They not only have formed a concept of themselves, they are also better able to interpret what is on the other person's mind. When preschool children are on the receiving end of derogatory remarks they use physical means of responding as frequently as they use verbal reactions (for example, counter-threats or derogatory remarks). Primary grade school children, on the other hand, use physical retaliation only about 20 percent of the time. Hartup also found that boys engaged in more aggressive acts than girls but that this difference was due almost entirely to differences in the amount of hostile aggression: boys were more likely to attack persons when angered.

Television and Aggressive Behavior

Bandura's Studies of the Impact of Imitation   In one of their series of experiments designed to test the impact of imitation of models on child behavior, Albert Bandura, D. Ross, and S. A. Ross (1963b) arranged for five-year-old children to observe models engage in aggressive acts. The children first saw a live female adult attack an inflated plastic figure (often called a Bobo doll) with her fist, her foot, a hammer, and a cap pistol; throw it up in the air; and sit on it while pummeling its face. The same sequence of acts was then depicted in a film of an adult and in a cartoon, both of which simulated television programs. Each child who had observed the model and seen the films, as well as each child in a control group who had not, was then frustrated (by being interrupted just when enjoying play with some very attractive toys) and taken to a room that contained an identical inflated figure and many other toys.

Frustrated children tend to imitate aggressive acts

When social-learning theory was being formulated several psychologists (Dollard, Doob, Miller, Mowrer, and Sears, 1939) proposed that frustration leads to aggression. Bandura and his colleagues took this hypothesis into account and reasoned that the children who had been interrupted were likely to react with aggression. On the basis of their previous research on the impact of imitation, they predicted that the aggressive reactions to frustration would be patterned on those of the models the children had observed. The reactions of the children in the experimental and control groups supported the frustration-aggression hypothesis as well as the prediction that aggressive acts would be imitated. Children in both groups engaged in aggressive acts. However, those who had observed the model attacked the inflated figure not only more frequently but often in exactly the same way and in the same sequence as the model. The experimenters suggested that these results might also apply to television viewing and argued that a child who is frustrated and reacts in an aggressive way will tend to engage in violent acts similar to those seen on television programs. A five-year-old who watches a cartoon where one character hits another over the head with a board, for example, may carry out the same action if frustrated by a playmate shortly after seeing the cartoon. A teenager frustrated to the breaking point may grab a gun and start shooting, imitating the behavior seen thousands of times in Western, war, and crime television programs.

Hypothesis: viewing TV leads to aggressive behavior

The Bandura study (and several others like it, reviewed by Feshbach [1970, pp. 211–214]) is accepted by some theorists as proof of a link between television and violence. Critics point out, however, that the inflated figure used in many of these studies is expressly designed to be hit and kicked and that children are well aware of this. Simply because children imitate the way a model hits a toy designed for the purpose of being hit does not prove that they will hit other children. Children who hit the inflated figure in the same way as the models might have been simply trying out some new assault techniques for use with Bobo dolls, techniques they had not tried before that looked like fun.

In a follow-up study, Bandura, Ross, and Ross (1963c) demonstrated that children are more likely to imitate a model they see rewarded and less likely to imitate one they see punished. Young children who realize that aggressive acts often lead to retaliation are likely to learn quite early in life to inhibit aggressive acts—even when they see these acts performed by models who escape unscathed (which may occur on television programs).

Children may also seek and enjoy opportunities to vent their frustration on an object, such as an inflated toy, that cannot fight back. Freud called this *displacement*, and it is a common feature of human behavior. If you are severely berated by a policeman who stops you for speeding, you may curb your aggressive feelings while in his presence (to avoid getting a ticket) but smash the flowerpot you trip over when getting out of your car in the garage. Those skeptical of the significance of the Bandura studies as proof of a link between television and violence argue that there is reason to doubt that the behavior of children in an experimental situation makes it possible to predict how they will react in spontaneous, everyday situations.

The Surgeon General's Report on Television and Violence When Robert Kennedy was assassinated, however, even congressional leaders who had been skeptics became convinced of the need for a careful review of all research on causes of violence in our society. They appointed The Surgeon General's Advisory Committee on Television and Social Behavior and asked its members to review all available information on the link between television and violence. Their conclusions are reported in a five-volume set of documents issued under the general heading *Television and Social Behavior* (1972). A summary report is titled *Television and Growing Up: The Impact of Televised Violence* (1972). The general conclusion of the committee is that some studies support the hypothesis that television viewing leads to violence and others do not. Some critics of the report have argued, however, that the members of the committee were not selected in a way that guaranteed a balanced combination of views and backgrounds. Others (for example, Liebert and Neale, 1972) have questioned the interpretation of some studies and the general conclusion of the committee.

Surgeon General's report: not all studies support hypothesis that viewing TV leads to violence

Even if the link between television and aggressiveness has not been clearly established to the satisfaction of all who have analyzed research on this question, Bandura's studies offer a basis for speculation about why some children are more likely to engage in aggressive behavior than others and why different forms of aggressive behavior are chosen. A possible explanation for abnormal aggressive tendencies might be that the particular child is experiencing many more frustrations than others of the same age. A possible explanation for choice of a particular type of aggressive reaction may be traced to recent exposure to models who reacted in a way that impressed the child. Bandura's results also might account for some aspects of sex differences in aggressiveness. Most violence depicted in films and television is exhibited by male characters, and boys are more likely than girls to identify with male characters (Maccoby and Wilson, 1957).

The Reinforcement of Aggressive Behavior

Another explanation for the tendency of some children to be more aggressive than others has been proposed by G. R. Patterson, R. A. Littman, and W. Bricker (1967). These researchers emphasize the extent to which aggressive behavior on the part of preschool children is reinforced by the reactions of peers. Visualize a boy who is spending his first day in a nursery school. He sees a beautiful tricycle on the playground and runs toward it, arriving simultaneously with a little girl. The girl tentatively grabs the handle bars, the boy gives her a hearty shove, causing her to stumble backwards and fall. The girl, frightened and upset, huddles on the ground and starts to whimper. The boy triumphantly mounts the tricycle and rides away. A few minutes later, another boy who had been an interested spectator of the scuffle—and who had never previously thought of using physical force against playmates—shoves the same little girl away from an easel when he wants to paint a picture. He is both surprised and pleased when he easily gets the easel all to himself. Patterson and his colleagues suggest that such interactions cause tendencies toward aggressiveness to be strengthened either through direct reinforcement or observation.

Aggressive behavior strengthened by reinforcement, observation

Patterson also found (1976a) that aggressive behavior is frequently reinforced in the home. He compared children referred to clinics because of excessive aggressive tendencies with children of the same age, sex, and background who had low levels of aggression. Both sets of children were observed in home and school situations interacting with parents, siblings, and peers. Patterson discovered that excessively aggressive children grow up in home situations that involve a great deal of aggression on the part of all family members. Parents and siblings of the aggressive children frequently expressed disapproval, either verbally or physically. They were also likely to tease the child or make demands. Furthermore, when the child responded with anger, the reactions of other family members often tended to reinforce the behavior. They might laugh, give the aggressive child their undivided attention, comply with the child's demands, or react aggressively themselves. When children in the aggressive group aroused an angry response from other family members, a reciprocal reinforcement pattern often developed leading to several quick "rounds" of aggressive and counter-aggressive acts.

Patterson stresses reinforcement in his analysis of highly aggressive children and their families, but other explanations might also be considered. It is possible that all family members in aggressive homes share similar inherited predisposi-

If parents frequently express disapproval of their children, they may not only arouse hostility but also provide a hostile model for the child to imitate. Vivienne Lapham/DPI.

tions that cause them to react with abnormal degrees of anger when they are frustrated. In addition, the possibility that either or both parents serve as aggressive models who are imitated by their children should be taken into account.

Aggressive behavior stands out because of its very nature. But young children also spontaneously engage in helpful, cooperative, and generous forms of behavior. Such types of behavior are called *prosocial* by psychologists. (When someone is *pro* something, they are in support of it; most forms of prosocial behavior are supportive.) Because prosocial behavior leads to positive relationships between individuals, psychologists have been interested in how it develops and how it might be encouraged.

Prosocial Behavior

Factors That Arouse Helping Behavior

A pioneering investigation of the prosocial behavior of preschool children was carried out by Lois Barclay Murphy (1937). She arranged for teachers in several nursery schools to keep records of sympathetic, cooperative, imitative, and aggressive forms of behavior exhibited by three-year-olds. She discovered that certain children, particularly popular children who cried loudly and dramatically, seemed to attract sympathetic responses more than others. An interesting finding was that children who displayed considerable sympathetic behavior also displayed high levels of aggressive behavior. It appeared that the same sort of tendencies that prompted a child to make an overt sympathetic response (for example, trying to comfort a sufferer with a hug) also prompted physical assertiveness in different situations. Murphy also observed the reactions of three-year-olds to a situation where a two-year-old was placed in a playpen with no toys. She found that some children remained aloof to the predicament of the two-year-old while others made a variety of attempts to help, and if these failed, made remarks intended to console the child. A final technique devised by Murphy involved asking children to respond to pictures showing children crying or in uncomfortable, dangerous, or painful situations. Most of the children revealed that they identified with the plight of the subjects of the pictures, but their interpretations were made primarily in terms of actual experiences they had had in similar situations.

In the forty-odd years since Murphy wrote her report, dozens of similar studies of prosocial behavior have been carried out. Many of these were reviewed by James H. Bryan (1975), who found that the relationship between helping behavior and aggressiveness first noted by Murphy has been corroborated repeatedly. Bryan also reported that children who expressed distress in everyday activities were more likely to help someone else in distress, suggesting that children who have strong feelings about their own plight have feelings almost as strong about the plight of others. Another factor that contributed to the inclination to help others was the amount of pleasure experienced in helping situations. Apparently, if the victim who is helped responds with gratitude, and/or if the child enjoys playing the role of "savior," helping behavior is reinforced. Bryan found that in some studies girls were reported to be more generous than boys. He speculated that this might be due to a tendency for girls to have had more experience being helped by parents and teachers. Bryan also reported that older children are more likely to help peers.

Another psychologist who specializes in the study of prosocial behavior is Martin L. Hoffman. Hoffman (1978) has described stages in the development of the ability of preschoolers to identify with the distress of others. This helps explain why older children are more likely than younger ones to help peers. At the first stage (up to about the end of the first year), children are unable to differentiate self from others. If ten-month-old children observe someone else in distress, they may respond as if they had suffered the painful experience themselves. If another child is observed to fall and cry, for example, an eleven-month-old observer may also cry and seek comfort from a parent. At the second stage (around the end of the first year), after children have achieved person permanence and are aware of others as separate entities, they assume that a sufferer's feelings are identical to their own. Hoffman describes an incident (p. 241), for instance, where a thirteen-month-old child observed an adult looking sad and offered the person his favorite doll.

At around the age of three or so children are able to engage in rudimentary role taking, that is, they are sometimes able to put themselves in another person's place. Before the end of the preschool years most children are able to clearly recognize signs of happiness and sadness. They realize as well that the feelings of others may differ from their own. Children also become capable of experiencing guilt. Two-year-olds may feel guilty when they become aware that something they have done has caused another to suffer. After the age of three or so children may also feel guilty when they realize that they did not act in a sympathetic way when they should have. Sometimes, however, the preschooler may feel sympathetic toward someone else but not know exactly *how* to help. Hoffman suggests that the basic reason preschoolers are unable to completely comprehend the feelings of others is due to preoperational and egocentric thinking, both of which will be discussed in the next chapter. (A more complete summary of Hoffman's description of age changes in empathy and how the stages he has described are related to the stages of cognitive development noted by Piaget will be presented in Chapter 11 when theories of moral development are summarized.)

Television and Prosocial Behavior

Even though there is disagreement about the extent to which television viewing causes violence, there is no question that children imitate aggressive actions they see on television shows. Several investigators have been intrigued by the question: Do children learn *positive* forms of behavior when they watch television shows?

In his review, Bryan summarizes a number of studies in which the impact of models on prosocial behavior has been measured. He reports that models engaging in helping behavior who are most likely to be imitated are perceived as warm individuals who express happiness about their altruistic behavior (for example, "I really felt good when I helped that little old lady pick up her groceries"). Furthermore, models (such as parents) are more likely to encourage helping behavior if they are consistent about practicing what they preach, and if they are in a position to dispense rewards.

Sympathetic models likely to be imitated: warm, express pleasure

Aletha H. Stein and Lynette K. Friedrich (1975) were interested in the extent to which actual television shows influence child behavior. They arranged for three- to five-year-olds to watch violent programs ("Batman" and "Superman"), neutral programs (nature and circus features), and several episodes of "Mr. Rogers' Neighborhood" (which uses a low-key approach calling attention to a variety of positive types of behavior). Simply viewing the "Mr. Rogers" episodes led to increases (in some children) in cooperative behavior, task persistence, rule acceptance, tolerance of delay, and verbalization of feelings. The children were less attentive to the "Mr. Rogers" programs than to the violent or neutral programs, which helps explain why Stein and Friedrich found that asking them to comment on what they were viewing or to act out similar situations seemed to increase the impact of the prosocial messages.

Implications of Research on Prosocial Behavior

If the various studies of prosocial behavior are examined for the purpose of developing guidelines for parents and teachers eager to encourage helpfulness and related traits in preschool children, the following suggestions emerge:

Prosocial behavior encouraged by discussion, models, pleasure

1   Invite children to talk about situations in which they have suffered in some way (to make them aware of their feelings and to encourage them to recognize similar feelings in others).

2   Express pleasure when helping someone else and encourage children to become aware of and to express the pleasure they feel when they help others.

3   Do not berate a young child for not showing sympathy in situations where you think it is justified. Unless the child has had personal experiences of a similar type, he or she may not possess the cognitive maturity to be able to comprehend how the sufferer feels.

4   Try to serve as a positive model to be imitated by exuding warmth and pleasure when helping others, being consistent, and rewarding acts of kindness.

5   Watch TV programs such as "Mr. Rogers' Neighborhood" *with* children, and encourage them to talk about the desirable actions that are depicted and perhaps also act out similar situations.

So far in this chapter, personality determining factors that can be classified as constitutional, group membership, and role determinants have been discussed. The only group of determinants proposed by Murray and Kluckhohn that has not been mentioned is the situational category. Situational determinants include not only frequently repeated experiences that have a cumulative impact but also traumatic or especially significant experiences that may alter the course of a person's life. It is not possible to identify or analyze all types of experiences that shape the personality of two- to five-year-olds, but experiences centering on fear and anxiety are often of special significance. Fear experiences frequently occur when children are on their own (or feel that way). Consequently they reveal personality traits in quite direct ways. Most children are apprehensive about new situations and anxious to please their parents and their peers as they become aware of themselves and the kinds of reactions they arouse from others. Accordingly, an analysis of anxiety will shed light on very significant aspects of early development.

Emotional Factors in Personality Development

Fear

Age Trends in Fears   Arthur Jersild and F. B. Holmes (1935a) carried out a series of classic studies of fear in young children. Subsequent investigations have not been as comprehensive nor have they produced any contradictory data. Even though these studies were carried out forty years ago, therefore, they are still valuable as sources of information about the fears of young children. Jersild and Holmes collected some data by exposing subjects to fear-provoking stimuli under experimental conditions. The investigators found that from the ages of two to five, children showed a decrease in fear of noise, strange objects and persons, pain, falling, sudden loss of support, and sudden movement. During the same age span, there was an increase in fear of imaginary creatures; the dark; animals; ridicule; and threat of harm (for example, from traffic, deep water, fire, or other potentially dangerous situations). These latter fears develop as children gain greater awareness of things and become capable of anticipating potential danger.

Between 2 and 5, "physical" fears decrease; "imaginary" fears increase

Overcoming Fears   In addition to studying age trends in fear, Jersild and Holmes (1935b) examined the effectiveness of different ways of dealing with fear. They concluded that ignoring the child, ridiculing or punishing, or forcing the child into the feared situation did more harm than good. Methods that were effective in helping the child overcome fear included the following:

1   *Explaining the situation.* The child who is afraid of thunder, for example, might be less frightened if told that it is caused by hot and cold clouds bumping together.

2   *Setting an example.* This is most likely to be effective if the child sees other children the same age who are not afraid in a particular situation. If older children or adults show no fear, the two- to five-year-old may not be inclined to imitate their behavior. Three-year-olds who are afraid of large dogs, for example, may be unimpressed if their father fearlessly pats a Great Dane because they are likely to think, "If I were that big, I wouldn't be afraid either." But if a child the same age pats the dog, a three-year-old might be emboldened to try it. Albert Bandura and F. L. Menlove (1968) showed films to preschoolers who were afraid of dogs. One of the films depicted a five-year-old playing happily with a dog; another showed models of various ages interacting with dogs. Both films were effective in reducing fear reactions, although the multiple-model version appeared to have a greater impact, which may have been due more to seeing the fearless behavior repeated than to the different ages of the models. Perhaps most effective of all would be a film or a "live" situation in which several children

Fears may be overcome by explanations, example, positive reconditioning, confidence

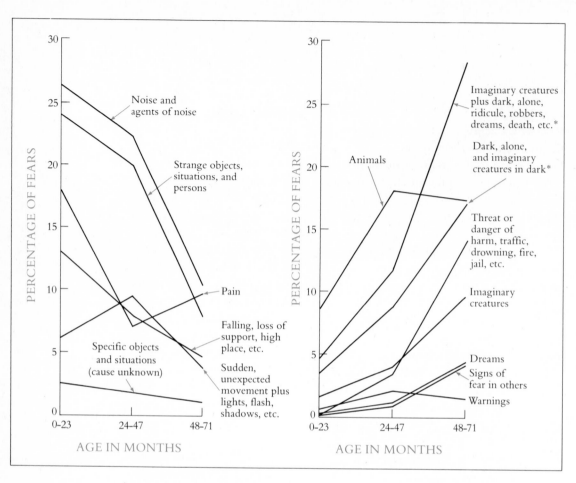

Figure 8–1   Age trends in fears based on 146 observations of children for periods of 21 days and occasional records of 117 additional children. Starred items represent a cumulative tally of two or more categories that also are depicted separately. Reprinted by permission of the publisher from Arthur T. Jersild and Frances G. Holmes, *Children's Fears* (New York: Teachers College Press, 1935).

the same age as the fearful child show fearless behavior with dogs.

3   *Positive reconditioning.* This is a technique Mary Cover Jones (1924) used to help a child overcome a fear similar to that Watson produced in Albert. Albert developed the fear in the first place because he associated the rat with a frightening stimulus (a loud, unexpected sound). To help a child overcome a fear this process can be reversed so that positive associations are substituted for negative ones. For a fear such as Albert's, for example, a feared animal might be put in a cage some distance from the child at a time ice cream and candy are served. There is the potential danger in this

technique, however, that the association might develop in a way opposite to that intended. Instead of overcoming fear of the animal, the child might generalize the fear of animals to ice cream, food in general, or eating. Accordingly, it may be preferable simply to let the child adapt to the feared object. For example, a caged animal might be put in a far corner of the room where a child is playing. Over a period of time the child might be allowed to approach the cage and examine the animal.

Helping the child gain confidence in dealing with the feared object or situation. Perhaps the most effective way to help a child overcome a fear is to teach him or her to become competent in dealing with it. A child who is afraid of the dark, for example, might be supplied with a night light wired to a bedside switch. When the switch is pushed, the child, in effect, controls the dark. Or a child who is fearful of dogs might be given a puppy and helped to train it.

Preventing Fears   As part of their studies of fear, Jersild and Holmes also analyzed how fears might be prevented from developing in the first place. They found that a common factor in many of the fears of young children was the sudden or unexpected nature of a stimulus. Suppose, for example, a mother or father decides to clean the living room floor in the presence of a young child who has not been exposed to a vacuum cleaner. If, without warning, the vacuum is turned on a few feet away from the child, the unexpected loud noise might easily lead to a fear reaction. A more prudent course of action would be to turn on the vacuum in another room and gradually move it closer to the child. Or suppose a relative gives a two-year-old a jack-in-the-box for Christmas. If the child is permitted to unlatch the top the first time, the doll figure that suddenly pops up may cause fear of the toy. A better course of action would be to hold the toy for the child and release the top slowly at first. Once the child understands how it works, the doll can be popped up more quickly. Under these circumstances, the child is more likely to delight in playing with the toy.

The most difficult variation of giving a warning occurs when an element of pain may be involved. A common example is a visit to the doctor or dentist. If the parents say "It won't hurt a bit" and it does hurt, children may lose faith in the parents and the doctor and generalize their fear to all situations involving medical treatment. On the other hand, if the parents go too far in describing how much it is going to hurt, children may become so tense the pain will be magnified.

If a child must undergo surgery, it is now standard practice in many hospitals to take children on a dry run of the entire procedure the day before, explaining what will be done, where they will go, how they will feel when it's over, and what can be done to control pain. This policy was established when it was discovered thirty or so years ago that some children who went into surgery unprepared and had to spend several days in a hospital (at a time when visiting hours were severely restricted) were haunted by the experience the rest of their lives.

An effective technique for preventing or minimizing some types of fears is to give advance information about situations and experiences likely to make a child feel apprehensive or afraid. Dani Carpenter/The Picture Cube.

Another aspect of fear prevention was neatly illustrated by an experiment carried out by D. G. J. Schramm (1935). Young children were placed in a chair so that their movements were restricted. Then, one at a time, a frog, a rabbit, a rat, and a parakeet were placed on a tray that was moved toward the children. Almost all of the children acted afraid, and some were terrified. A different group of children the same age were then allowed to roam around a room where the same animals were placed in the middle of a table. The children could approach or ignore them as they wished. None of these children showed any fear. These results suggest that if parents allow children to approach a potentially frightening situation in their own way and at their own pace, problems might be minimized.

But if children feel they are trapped and have no way of avoiding the situation thrust upon them, even a relatively innocuous object or experience may induce a panic reaction. A well-meaning father, for example, was pushing his three-year-old daughter (who was apprehensive about dogs) in the miniature fire engine she had inherited from an older brother. A large, amiable neighborhood dog ambled onto the scene, and the father decided this was a golden opportunity to help his daughter learn to like dogs. He energetically pushed the fire engine toward the dog. The little girl started to scream and tried to climb out, but her father shoved her back, telling her all the while about the "nice doggie." By the time they were close to the dog the little girl was screaming uncontrollably, and the puzzled father had to carry her into the house, where it took the mother twenty minutes to calm her down. If he had been aware of the Schramm study, he might have realized that his daughter felt helpless, while she saw the dog as powerful. If the father had held the dog on a leash and permitted the daughter to approach the controlled animal on her own, she might have felt *she*, not the dog, was in control of the situation.

Anxiety

The Nature of Anxiety   Jersild and Holmes concluded that perhaps the best fear preventative was the development of a sense of security. One way to define security is as an absence of anxiety. Jersild (1968, pp. 348–365) has pointed out some key differences between fear and anxiety. He notes that fear is usually a reasonably rational (legitimate) response to a tangible threat or danger. Anxiety, on the other hand, involves inner conflict that may appear irrational to others. Furthermore, fears are likely to disappear if children learn how to handle them. But anxiety may persist even after children gain knowledge and experience; they must gain insight into the "inner" danger and develop confidence in their ability to handle it.

In his analysis of anxiety Jersild calls attention to philosophical and theoretical accounts. The Danish philosopher Sören Kierkegaard presented a view of anxiety that anticipated certain contemporary interpretations. In *Either/Or* (English translation by W. Lowrie, 1949) and *Sickness Unto Death* (English translation by W. Lowrie, 1951), he described the significance of inner conflict aroused by decisions each individual must make in determining her or his own personality. Kierkegaard's ideas of inner conflict may have influenced Freudian theory. Kierkegaard's emphasis on the significance of decisions that will influence a person's development is similar to Abraham Maslow's conception of development as a series of choices between safety and growth—the child is torn between a desire to risk something new and the security of playing it safe. Kierkegaard's argument for being oneself is related in some ways to Erikson's stage of identity versus role confusion; in this stage young adults hoping to escape the negative impact of role confusion must make choices that will help them establish a sense of identity.

Explanations of Anxiety In Freud's view, the early dependency of the child on the mother accounted much for anxiety. He attributed stranger and separation anxiety to the child's fear of losing the love and protection of the mother. Freud also proposed that anxiety may be produced by conflicts between the id, ego, and superego. A child may experience anxiety when confronted by a conflict between a need for gratification and conditions in the environment that limit its satisfaction. A child in a store, for example, whose parents have said they will not buy a much desired toy may suffer anxiety in the struggle between the desire to steal the toy and awareness that it is wrong to take things without paying for them.

Another explanation for the development of anxiety is provided by Maslow's description of needs. Almost all of the infant's needs are anticipated and quickly satisfied. But when children begin to be independent and become aware of previously undiscovered complexities, there may be a sharp increase in situations where their deficiency needs remain unsatisfied. Three-year-olds may become concerned about physical or psychological safety, for example, or occasionally doubt that their parents love them. When they begin to interact with peers, they may yearn for their playmates' approval. When they are bested in a quarrel, or discover that they are less capable in some activities than playmates, their need for esteem may be frustrated. Any time children have doubts about safety, about being loved or accepted by peers, or about their abilities compared to others, they may experience feelings of anxiety.

Still another explanation for causes of anxiety is provided by Erikson's description of the stages of autonomy versus doubt and initiative versus guilt. Two-year-olds are in the process of establishing themselves as autonomous individuals. They need to develop feelings of independence as they assume responsibility for their own behavior. But there are bound to be experiences that cause these budding individualists to doubt their ability to handle everything on their own. Despite occasional setbacks and moments of doubt, however, most three-year-olds remain undaunted and are eager to initiate activities and explore new experiences. If preschoolers are allowed to try out their powers and if their parents are patient in answering questions, Erikson suggests, the children will develop a sense of initiative and self-confidence. If children are made to feel their questions and activities are a nuisance, they may feel guilty about trying to do things on their own and experience anxiety.

Minimizing Anxiety If the observations of Freud, Maslow, and Erikson are taken into account, the following factors can be listed as possible causes of anxiety in two- to five-year-olds: fear of losing love and protection of the mother;

conflict between desires and social codes and restrictions; concern about physical and psychological safety; lack of acceptance by others; threats to self-esteem; experiencing too much shame or doubt; being made to feel guilty about trying to do things on one's own. The following guidelines might be offered as ways to minimize the development of anxiety in children:

- ☐ Avoid withholding love as a means of punishment for misbehavior.
- ☐ Continue to provide support and protection even as the child makes efforts to assert independence.
- ☐ Help children cope with conflicts between desires and restrictions. (If a child takes something from a store without paying for it, for example, explain gently but firmly why the object must be returned or paid for, instead of berating or punishing the child.)
- ☐ Do everything possible to make the child feel secure, not only by arranging for physical safety but also by establishing the feeling that parents are always available to provide love and support. Give extra support and reassurance when a child has unfortunate or belittling experiences with peers.
- ☐ Guard against making a child feel excessively ashamed of misdeeds.
- ☐ Be patient when a child is eager to try doing things alone and do not provide assistance unless it is asked for or absolutely essential.
- ☐ Respond positively to expressions of initiative even if these cause extra effort and bother for older members of a household.
- ☐ Set realistic goals for a child and avoid being hypercritical of incomplete achievement.

Anxiety may be minimized by providing support, satisfying needs, encouraging independence

Now that you have become acquainted with some of the factors that influence personality development during the years from two to five, you might reconsider the argument that the first two years are *the* most critical period of development. During the preschool years, parents must find workable ways to socialize children. Child-rearing techniques for two- to five-year-olds are substantially different from those used during the first two years, particularly because the types of behavior that must be learned and controlled are so much more complex. Also during the preschool years, children discover how they are perceived by peers. Many roles of different kinds are established, and characteristic patterns of aggressive and prosocial behavior emerge. But in addition to the forms of behavior just noted, there are significant changes in cognitive development during the two- to five-year span. The two-year-old has just learned to solve problems by thinking things out and can communicate only in rather limited ways. By the age of five, however, children have expanded their intellectual horizons substantially. They have also acquired most forms of adult language. These accomplishments will be described in the next chapter.

Suggestions for Further Study

Genetic Influences on Behavior

A concise review of research on behavior genetics is provided in "Genetic Influences on Behavior and Development" by Gerald E. McClearn, Chapter 2 in *Carmichael's Manual of Child Psychology* (3rd ed., 1970), edited by Paul H. Mussen. More complete coverage of this complex field is provided in *Behavioral Genetics: Method and Research* (1969), edited by M. Manosevitz, G. Lindzey, and D. D. Thiessen; and *Genetic Theory and Abnormal Behavior* (1970) by D. Rosenthal. Evidence supporting the hypotheses that activity level, emotionality, and sociability have a genetic component is offered by Arnold H. Buss and Robert Plomin in *A Temperament Theory of Personality Development* (1975).

Interpretations of Autism

If you would like to examine the interpretations of autism offered by Niko Tinbergen and O. Ivar Lovaas, you will find Tinbergen's explanation of an environmental view in an interview with Elizabeth Hall that begins on page 65 of the March 1974 issue of *Psychology Today*. The genetic view of Lovaas (as well as a description of his behavior-modification approach to improving the behavior of autistic children) appears in an interview with Paul Chance that begins on page 76 of the January 1974 issue of *Psychology Today*. A comprehensive analysis of the nature and causes of autism is presented in *Autism: A Reappraisal of Causes and Treatment* (1978), edited by Michael Rutter and E. Schopler.

Child Rearing

Because of the complexity and subtlety of the processes involved, studies of the impact of child-rearing practices are difficult to summarize. The brief comments in this chapter reflect general conclusions, and you may wish to examine one or more of the actual studies mentioned for further information. The details of the methods and conclusions of such investigations can be found in *Patterns of Child Rearing* (1957) by Robert R. Sears, Eleanor E. Maccoby, and Harry Levin; *Identification and Child Rearing* (1965) by Robert R. Sears, Lucy Rau, and Richard Alpert; *Birth to Maturity: A Study in Psychological Development* (1962) by Jerome Kagan and Howard A. Moss; or "Child Care Practices Anteceding Three Patterns of Preschool Behavior" by Diana Baumrind, *Genetic Psychology Monographs*, 1967, **75**, 43–88; or "Current Patterns of Parental Authority," *Developmental Psychology Monographs*, 1971, (1), 1–103, also by Baumrind. In *Child Rearing* (1968), Marian Radke Yarrow, John D. Campbell, and Roger V. Burton describe a replication of the Sears study (described in *Patterns of Child Rearing*) and also present a summary and critique of other research on child rearing. More recent research is reviewed in "Parent-Child Relations" by

Barclay Martin in *Review of Child Development Research*, 1975, **4**, edited by Frances D. Horowitz.

Social Class and Cultural Differences in Child Rearing

The discussion of child-rearing practices presented in this chapter is based primarily on research carried out with middle- and upper-middle-class white American parents and children. In the brief analysis in this chapter, only selected information could be offered. Since there are more middle-class white Americans than any other single type, it seemed most appropriate to concentrate on this group. Numerous studies of social class and ethnic differences in socialization practices within our society have been carried out, however, and if you would like to examine such research, you can consult "Social Class and Ethnic Influences upon Socialization" by Robert D. Hess, Chapter 25 in *Carmichael's Manual of Child Psychology* (3rd ed., 1970), edited by Paul H. Mussen, pp. 457–557. Hess supplies an excellent review of research as well as a bibliography of twenty-three pages.

Investigations of parent-child relationships and of class and ethnic differences in the socialization of children in American society provide a great deal of information on the impact of different child-rearing practices. Additional insight can be gained by examining cross-cultural studies. The socialization approaches used by parents in other cultures differ markedly from American society. The characteristics of children and adults who are products of varying socialization practices have been studied by many psychologists, sociologists, and anthropologists. If you would like information about such cross-cultural studies, perhaps the best single source to consult is "Cross-Cultural Study in Child Psychology" by Robert A. LeVine, Chapter 26 in *Carmichael's Manual of Child Psychology* (3rd ed., 1970), edited by Paul H. Mussen, pp. 559–612.

Peer Interactions in the Nursery School

For a review of research on peer interaction, examine "Peer Interaction and Social Organization" by Willard W. Hartup, Chapter 24 in Volume II of *Carmichael's Manual of Child Psychology* (3rd ed., 1970), edited by Paul H. Mussen. Hartup presents a historical overview of early research, describes patterns of interaction with peers, group formation, popularity, friendships, leadership, peer influences on the individual child, and peer versus adult influence. Another excellent review of social relationships in early childhood is provided by Darrell K. Adams in Chapter 7 of *Infancy and Early Childhood* (1967), edited by Yvonne Brackbill. A briefer review of some of the same topics covered by Hartup and Adams is provided by John D. Campbell on pages 289–322 of *Review of Child Development Research*, (1964), **1**, edited by Martin L. and Lois Wladis Hoffman. Comprehensive discussions of recent research are presented in *Issues in Childhood Social Development* (1978), edited by H. McGurk.

Sex-typing and Socialization

For a concise review of studies on how social factors determine sex-role behavior, see "Sex-typing and Socialization," by Walter Mischel, Chapter 20 in Volume II of *Carmichael's Manual of Child Psychology* (3rd ed., 1970), edited by Paul H. Mussen. Mischel reviews studies of sex-typed behavior, sex-role stereotypes (and how valid they are), consistency and specificity in sex-typed behavior, the acquisition of sex-typed behavior, the extent to which children exhibit sex-typed behavior, and the impact of child-rearing practices on sex roles. A thought-provoking analysis of sex-typing is presented by Jeanne H. Block in "Conceptions of Sex Role: Some Cross-Cultural and Longitudinal Perspectives" in *American Psychologist*, 1973, **28** (6), 512–526.

The Impact of Hormones on Behavior

John Money has devoted his professional life to research on hormonal influences on behavior. In *Man and Woman, Boy and Girl* (1972) (written in collaboration with Anke Ehrhardt) he summarizes not only his own research but that of other scientists as well. Chapter 1 ("Synopsis") provides a concise overview of the main points made in greater detail in later chapters of the book. You might be especially interested in sections of these chapters on types of behavior associated with **XXX, XXY**, and **XYY** chromosome patterns (pp. 29–33); tomboyism due to the impact of hormonal imbalance (pp. 98–103); the impact of cultural traditions on sex roles (Chapter 7); how hermaphroditic males and females struggle with identity (Chapter 8); behavioral differences that appear early and continue to develop in males and females (pp. 179–182); the impact of precocious puberty (pp. 198–202); and the impact of delayed puberty (pp. 202–206).

The Impact of Television on Behavior

Many psychologists, legislators, and parents have speculated about the extent to which children are influenced by television. If you would like information about studies of the impact of television on child behavior, the most convenient source is the series of reports prepared by the Surgeon General's Scientific Advisory Committee. The titles of the five volumes published under the general heading *Television and Social Behavior* are: Vol. I, *Media Content and Control* (1972), edited by G. A. Comstock and E. A. Rubinstein; Vol. II, *Television and Social Learning* (1972), edited by J. P. Murray, E. A. Rubinstein, and G. A. Comstock; Vol. III, *Television and Adolescent Aggressiveness* (1972), edited by G. A. Comstock and E. A. Rubinstein; Vol. IV, *Television in Day-to-Day Life: Patterns of Use* (1972), edited by E. A. Rubinstein, G. A. Comstock, and J. P. Murray; and Vol. V, *Television's Effects: Further Explorations* (1972), edited by G. A. Comstock, E. A. Rubinstein, and J. P. Murray. The final report *Television and Growing Up: The Impact of Televised Violence* (1972) is available from the Superintendent of Documents, U.S. Government Printing Office, Washington, D.C. 20402. For a short article summarizing many of the findings, look for "Television and Violence: Implications of the Surgeon General's Research Program" by John P. Murray which begins on page 472 of the June 1973 issue of *American Psychologist*. An analysis of the Surgeon General's Report (and the research reported in it) by three psychologists who are convinced that television has a definite impact on child behavior is presented in *The Early Window: Effects of Television on Children and Youth* (1973) by Robert M. Liebert, John M. Neale, and Emily S. Davidson. An excellent review of research (not limited to the Surgeon General's Report) is provided by Aletha H. Stein and Lynette K. Friedrich in "Impact of Television on Children and Youth" in *Review of Child Development Research*, 1975, **5**, edited by E. M. Hetherington.

Sex Differences and Aggression

An especially noteworthy difference between males and females is their relative aggressiveness. For a review of research on sex differences in aggressiveness, consult pages 188–195 of Chapter 22 ("Aggression" by Seymour Feshbach) in Volume II of *Carmichael's Manual of Child Psychology* (3rd ed., 1970), edited by Paul H. Mussen; or "Stability of Aggressive Reaction Patterns in Males: A Review" by D. Olweus in *Psychological Bulletin*, 1979, **86**, 852–875. D. E. Barrett describes a naturalistic study of sex differences in aggression in an article that begins on page 143 of *Merrill-Palmer Quarterly*, 1979, **25**.

Prosocial Behavior

Even though written in 1937, *Social Behavior and Child Personality* by Lois Barclay Murphy still provides insights into the early development of sympathy for others. For a review of recent research on prosocial behavior, see "Children's Cooperative and Helping Behaviors" by J. H. Bryan in *Review of Child Development Research*, 1975, **5**, edited by E. M. Hetherington; "The Development of Social Cognition" by Carolyn U. Shantz in the same volume; or "Empathy, Role-Taking, Guilt, and Development of Altruistic Motives" by Martin L. Hoffman in *Moral Development and Behavior* (1976), edited by Thomas Lickona.

Fear, Anxiety, and Emotional Development

If you would like more information about fear and anxiety in children, consult the review of studies on pages 863–883 in "Emotional Development" by Arthur Jersild, Chapter 14 in *Manual of Child Psychology* (2nd ed., 1954). More recent research is reviewed and discussed in *The Development of Affect* (1978), edited by Michael Lewis and Leonard A. Rosenblum.

Use of operant conditioning techniques to help children overcome fears is described in "Behavioral Treatment of Children's Fears: A Review" by A. M. Graziano and others in *Psychological Bulletin*, 1979, **86**, 804–830.

KEY POINTS

The Nature of Preoperational Thought

Preoperational thinking: tendency to focus on one quality, inability to reverse

One-track thinking may "cancel" aspects of understanding

Objects classified in one category at a time

Cognitive development may lead to improved memories

Language Development

Overextensions illustrate assimilation and accommodation

First morphemes acquired in particular sequence

"Inconsistent" grammar may be due to consistent schemes

Confusion of opposites may be due to inability to decenter and reverse

Egocentric thinking: difficulty in taking another's point of view

Socialized thinking may occur early under simplified conditions

Is There a Critical Period in Cognitive Development?

Research and social trends in the 1960s led to cognitive critical-period hypothesis

Research in 1970s led to doubts about cognitive critical-period hypothesis

Piaget: attempts to speed up cognitive development lead to superficial learning

Differences Between Middle- and Low-Income Environments

Impoverished environment has cumulative depressant effect

Extended compensatory programs have positive impact

The Nature and Measurement of Intelligence

General and specific factors in intelligence

Between 6 and 18, 15-point changes in IQ common

What Types of Preschool Experiences Should Parents Try to Provide?

Authoritative child rearing appears likely to promote competence

Full-time mothering does not necessarily promote early cognitive development

Play and Playthings

Play makes it possible for children to experiment without risk

Preschoolers prefer novelty, manageable complexity, incongruity in play

Encouraging Creativity and Fantasy

Children can learn to engage in imaginative play

CHAPTER □ 9

TWO TO FIVE:
COGNITIVE DEVELOPMENT

In the preceding chapter the significance of parent-child interactions during the preschool years was discussed. Such relationships are important at this stage of development primarily because the process of socialization is instituted. Many parent-child interactions during the first two years involve the parents' encouragement and responsiveness. During the first year, for instance, mothers who impress psychologists as being particularly effective at parenting are skillful at sustaining activities initiated by the infant. During the second year, parents of competent children also function primarily as responders, although they occasionally establish limits. Starting a bit before their second birthdays, however, children develop physical and mental capabilities that permit them to function independently. At that point, parents must make the child aware of the needs and desires of others.

Even though it is an oversimplification, it might be said that around the age of two years the role of the parents shifts from that of care*giver* to care*taker*. For the first eighteen months, successful parents *give* the child care. They do everything possible to encourage the baby and toddler to assert independence and try out skills. But after the age of two it appears to be necessary for the parents to take charge (in a democratic manner) if they hope to continue to be effective parents. The young child must learn that certain restrictions are necessary and that the needs of others must sometimes be taken into account. A child who does not learn to control self-centered impulses during this initial period of asserting independence is not only sure to make life miserable for parents but is also very likely to encounter difficulties getting along with teachers and classmates when school begins.

As noted in the preceding chapter, Diana Baumrind found that children of permissive parents (who failed to take charge) seemed to encounter problems in adjustment during the preschool years. They were dependent, immature, and lacking in self-control. The children of authoritarian parents also experienced difficulties, but of a different kind. Such children were likely to be discontented, insecure, and hostile under stress. Children of authoritative parents, by contrast, were found to be sociable, self-reliant, and competent. The authoritative parents *did* take charge. They set limits but also took into account the child's point of view and explained reasons for restrictions. The ability of children to understand explanations for restrictions—and to explain their own reasons for objecting to limits—highlights differences between parent-child relationships before and after children reach the age of two years. Between their second and fifth birthdays, children learn to think in more and more sophisticated ways. They are able to substitute thoughts—and words—for actions. They also master most forms of adult speech and become capable of communicating what they think and feel with considerable clarity. Some of the factors that lead to these developmental changes in thought and language will be discussed in this chapter.

A related topic centers on the question: Are the years from two to five a critical period in intellectual development? In the 1960s a series of scientific articles and books that meshed with contemporary political and social trends in our society aroused great interest in preschool education. The dramatic and impressive nature of cognitive changes between the years of two and five led some psychologists to propose that were children not given the proper kind of "instruction" during the preschool years, they might suffer permanent retardation in intellectual development. Evaluations of this hypothesis, together with an analysis of the nature and measurement of intelligence, will be presented in the final section of this chapter.

The Nature of Preoperational Thought

In Chapter 6 you were acquainted with the six stages in the sensorimotor period of development described by Jean Piaget. During that period children acquire the object concept and learn to coordinate schemes so that they can engage in mental manipulations and think out simple problems. During the next three years children begin to carry out mental manipulations in more complex ways. But their thinking still differs in significant ways from that of older children and adults. Piaget's concept of an *operation* can help explain the distinction between the thinking of three-year-olds and that of ten- or fifteen-year-olds.

Operations, Conservation, Decentration

You are reminded that an operation is a mental action that can be reversed. Two- to five-year-olds are not able to engage in operational thinking, which explains why Piaget refers to this as the *preoperational* period. Preoperational thinking (to reinforce points you learned in Chapter 3) can be clarified by examining the Piagetian concepts of conservation and decentration. Conservation refers to the idea that certain properties of objects (for example, volume, mass, or substance) do not change when the shape or appearance of an object changes. Decentration refers to the ability of a child to keep from centering attention on only one quality at a time. (Or, to put it another way, the ability to concentrate on more than one quality of an object or situation.) Operational thinking, conservation, and decentration are all illustrated by Piaget's experiment in which children are asked to tell what they think happens when water is poured from one container into a different shaped container. When children up to the age of five respond in such situations they reveal that they concentrate on only one quality at a time (for example, height) and are unable to mentally reverse what they have seen. The inability of two- to five-year-olds to handle operations (that is, to mentally reverse actions) is perhaps the most distinctive feature of their thinking. But other aspects of cognitive development are revealed by the ways preschoolers assimilate, accommodate, and form schemes representing their ever-widening experiences.

Preoperational thinking: tendency to focus on one quality, inability to reverse

Schemes, Assimilation, and Accommodation

In his analysis of cognitive development Piaget stresses the formation of schemes. As children perceive people and events and interact with objects and other individuals, they assimilate new experiences to already existing schemes or accommodate their thinking by modifying such schemes. To strengthen your grasp of these various processes, put yourself in the place of a three-year-old who first goes off to nursery school after having been more or less confined to home and neighborhood. The family has a cocker spaniel, and the child has learned that it is called Fluffy and that it is referred to as a dog. On the way to school the first day the child sees a Great Dane and a chihuahua, which represent totally new animals, since Fluffy has been the only dog encountered up to that time. Upon asking what these strange animals are called, the child is told, "They are dogs, like Fluffy." In sorting out the meaning of these first encounters with others dogs and the bit of information that they *are* dogs the child fits some features into an already existing scheme but also alters that scheme. Fluffy has four legs and barks, and so do the other dogs. So those features are assimilated. But Great Danes are much bigger than Fluffy, while chihuahuas are much smaller (among other things), so the child must revise (accommodate) the original scheme for *dog*.

One-track Thinking

When preoperational children are confronted with something that does not fit any already developed scheme (or when they form new schemes), they tend to center their attention on one feature at a time. In Piaget's water experiment, children below the age of five may be misled into saying that a taller glass holds more water than a shorter one (when actually they hold the same) because they concentrate on height. The same tendency to center attention on a single attribute characterizes the spontaneous formation of schemes. The process illustrated by the example of dogs occurs each time a child is exposed to a new experience or a variation of a previous experience. If the number of new experiences, objects, and persons that a child encounters in the first few days in a nursery school (or on excursions away from home) is considered, it is apparent that young children engage in an enormous amount of cognitive activity. Some of the facts that influence the way a preschooler sorts out these various impressions are illustrated by some of the clinical interview procedures devised by Piaget.

If you were to take eight blocks and arrange them about an inch apart in a row, most preschoolers could probably count them. If you then asked a four-year-old child to form a row of the same number of blocks (by selecting from a supply you provided), your subject would probably carry out your request by putting a block just below each of the blocks already in line. But, if you then took the first row of blocks and spaced them about three inches apart, you might be surprised at the confusion this simple change would produce. If you asked the child (who had just demonstrated an ability to form a line containing the same number of blocks) "Do I have more blocks (pointing to the long row), or do you have more blocks (pointing to the short row), or do we have the same?" the likely response would be, "*You* have more blocks." The tendency for the child to concentrate on the single feature of length tends to cancel out the just-demonstrated point that each row contains the same number of blocks.

One-track thinking may "cancel" aspects of understanding

Now, picture yourself carrying out other Piaget experiments. You ask the four-year-old to watch as you put pieces of cardboard down on a table. Some of the pieces are square, some are round, some are triangles. There are large and small pieces of each shape. After you place several of each shape and size in a random order on the table, you say to the child, "Put together things that are alike—that are the same." The child will probably respond to this request by moving the pieces around in a somewhat disorganized way, putting some similar objects together but not following a consistent procedure (for example, putting all large pieces together, or all pieces of the same shape together.)

Next, you ask a five-year-old to observe as you place plastic flowers of different types (say tulips, zinnias, and petunias) on the table. The assortment includes three yellow, two red, and two orange flowers of each type. If you say, "Put together flowers that are alike—that are the same," the child will probably sort flowers either by color or type. Then, you ask, "Suppose a girl (or boy, depending on the sex of your subject) takes all the yellow tulips and makes a bunch of them, or else makes a bunch of all the flowers. Which way does she have a bigger bunch?" Your subject will probably reply, "She would have more tulips." Children at the preoperational level find it difficult to think of an object as belonging to more than one classification category at a time. It is not until children reach the elementary school years that they comprehend that the same object or person can be classified in several ways at the same time.

Objects classified in one category at a time

You try still another Piagetian experiment independently with both the four- and five-year-old children. This time you take several sticks. The smallest is three inches long, the next is three and one-half inches long, and so on by half-inch increments. You put these down in scrambled order in front of each child and say, "Put these sticks in a row from the shortest to the longest." The four-year-old will probably put the sticks in something approximating a row, but it is not likely that they will be arranged in order from shortest to longest. The five-year-old is likely to come closer to carrying out your request, but may experience some difficulty in placing all of the sticks in exact order. After the four- and five-year-olds have arranged the sticks, you put the sticks in the proper order, very neatly arranged. Next, you ask each child first to arrange another set of sticks just like yours and then make a drawing of the arrangement. Now you wait six months and then ask the two children to draw a picture of the sticks that they arranged and drew the last time you saw them. You might be amazed to discover that the four-year-old, who had trouble copying the arrangement of sticks and making a drawing of the arrangement just after it had been done in your initial interview, draws a more accurate picture of the sticks arranged in order a half-year later. Piaget and Inhelder (1973) discovered that preschoolers actually improve their recollections of some arrangements of objects. Apparently, children retain an image of the arrangements they have previously seen. But they later interpret these images more accurately because of the rapid changes in cognitive development that take place during the preschool years.

Cognitive development may lead to improved memories

The block experiment illustrates how the thinking of preoperational children is dominated by their perceptions. When the just-counted blocks are rearranged the child's thinking is dominated by how things look, not by how they must logically be. The experiment in sorting geometric shapes reveals the tendency for preoperational children to group things in loose and confused ways. The flower experiment shows how difficult it is for a preoperational child to deal with relations between a part and the whole to which it belongs. The experiment in arranging sticks reveals the difficulty the preoperational child experiences with ordinal relationships (placing things in order). All of the experiments demon-

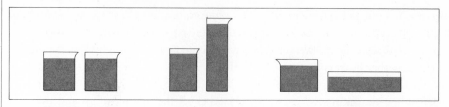

Preschoolers maintain that the amount of liquid in one of two equal-sized containers changes when it is poured into a container of a different shape. (Illustrates the tendency for preoperational thinkers to concentrate on one quality at a time as well as their inability to reverse.)

Preschoolers maintain that a spaced-out row of eight blocks contains a greater number of blocks than a tightly spaced row of eight blocks. (Illustrates how preoperational thinkers tend to be influenced by how things look rather than how they must logically be.)

Preschoolers are likely to group objects in a somewhat unsystematic and inconsistent manner. (Illustrates the tendency for preoperational thinkers to classify objects in loose and disorganized ways.)

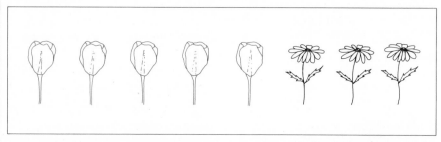

When asked if there are more tulips or more flowers, preschoolers are likely to maintain that there are more tulips than flowers. (Illustrates the difficulty preoperational thinkers have when they are asked to think of an object as belonging to more than one classification at a time and to deal with relations between a part and the whole to which it belongs.)

Preschool children may not be able to arrange a series of sticks in order from smallest to largest. (Illustrates the difficulty preoperational thinkers have dealing with ordinal relationships.)

strate a common characteristic: the inability to think simultaneously about several aspects of a situation. As the memory experiment reveals, however, in just a few months the thinking processes used by children may change quite dramatically.

Relationships Between Thought and Language

The amount of cognitive activity young children engage in and their rapid strides in sorting out their experiences makes Piaget's reference to this stage of cognitive development as *preoperational* a bit misleading. It calls attention to what preschoolers are unable do to. Two- to five-year-olds may not be able to conserve, decenter, or think operationally, but they *are* capable of forming and modifying schemes at an impressive rate. The young child must sort out an immense number of new experiences, and it should not be surprising that preschoolers tend to focus on one attribute at a time. To call attention to the amount of cognitive activity that a child engages in during the first five years, consider vocabulary acquisition. In a sense, each new word a child learns represents a scheme in that it reflects awareness of some particular idea or variation of a basic idea. By the time they reach the age of six years children have acquired a vocabulary of between 8,000 and 14,000 words (Carey, 1977). That is a most impressive performance, even though it does not involve operational thinking.

The point that words might be thought of as representing schemes calls attention to relationships between thought and language. Piaget believes that language development reflects cognitive development. That is, children express in words what they already know. Some linguists (for example, E. Sapir, 1921; B. Whorf, 1956) argue that language precedes thought; others (for example, Lev Vygotsky, 1962) propose that language and thought are separate early in life but begin to merge at around the age of two years. There is, however, quite a bit of support for Piaget's view that thought precedes language. This will become clear as aspects of early language acquisition are examined.

Language Development

To grasp how language development reflects cognitive development, keep in mind points that have just been summarized regarding preoperational thinking. Two- to five-year-olds form schemes through physical or mental manipulation, and these schemes are constantly revised through the processes of assimilation and accommodation. Preschoolers are unable to decenter, which means that they concentrate on one quality at a time. They are also preoperational, which means that they are unable to mentally reverse actions. Aspects of language acquisition that illustrate each of these characteristics of early cognitive development will now be considered.

First Words: Schemes, Assimilation, Accommodation

Most of the words that children learn first (Nelson, 1973) refer to parts of the body, to actions, or to familiar objects or individuals. These types of words reflect initial stages of cognitive development described by Piaget. In the early stages of sensorimotor thinking (described in Chapter 6), children explore their own bodies. Next, they build up schemes through their own actions and by interacting with familiar objects and individuals. While these observations on word acquisition reflect general trends, many children seem to specialize in particular types of first words.

M. F. Bowerman (1976a) found that some children seem to concentrate almost exclusively on objects, others specialize in names of people, and still others favor social phrases (for example, Hi, want). Bowerman hypothesizes that such differences are based on cognitive styles that are present before language is acquired. Cognitive styles, in turn, might be based on innate tendencies influenced by circumstances that lead to the development of particular types of schemes. A girl with many siblings and relatives in the house, for example, might be inclined to develop social phrases; a boy who has contact only with his mother—and dozens of playthings—might concentrate on learning names of objects.

As soon as a child forms a scheme and learns the name of an object, there is a tendency to apply that term to all similar objects. A learning theorist would call this generalization. But some psychologists who study language development prefer the term *overextension* (Clark, 1973). Once a child learns the word *dog*, for example, all four-legged animals may be called dogs. When a parent corrects the child by saying "No, honey, that's not a dog, that's a cat," the child will learn to correct the overextension (or to *discriminate*, in learning-theory parlance). This process is an illustration of the Piagetian principles of assimilation and accommodation. First the child notices similarities between dogs and cats and assimilates these identical elements in forming a revised scheme for *dog*. Then, when the child learns that cats differ from dogs in significant ways, accommodation takes place. The revised *dog* scheme is modified, and a *cat* scheme is formed.

Overextensions illustrate assimilation and accommodation

Early Two-word Utterances: Inability to Decenter

In their initial use of language, children usually concentrate on expressing one idea at a time, a point which is revealed by the earliest two-word utterances formed by children. Before the age of two years most children progress from using holophrastic speech to the point that they begin to use telegraphic speech. Just as one-word expressions serve a variety of purposes, two-word utterances can be used in a variety of ways. Roger Brown, who has written one of the most complete accounts of early language acquisition (1973), describes at least eleven ways that two-word utterances are used. The child may *name* something ("Allgone milk") or indicate the *location* of an object ("Milk table"). Between the ages of two and three, children form more elaborate utterances. Most of these, however, are still telegraphic in that nonessential (to the child, if not to a grammarian) words are omitted.

Brown bases many of his conclusions about early language on records of the spontaneous speech of three children who are quite famous among contemporary students of language acquisition. Their names are Adam, Eve, and Sarah, and their speech was recorded (sometimes in writing, sometimes by microphones sewed in their clothing) when they were between eighteen and twenty-seven months of age. When the children began to use sentences, they almost exclusively used nouns and verbs (with an occasional adjective thrown in). They omitted prepositions (*in, on*), conjunctions (*and, or*), articles (*a, the*), and auxiliary verbs (*have, did*). A rather verbose adult might say "I am eating delicious cake that has been tastefully served on a beautiful plate." A two-year-old might convey the same message by saying "Eat cake." The child maintains the proper word order, eliminating all but the essentials, and is likely to remain faithful to this telegraphic mode of speech even when asked to repeat a sentence. For example, if the verbose adult attempted to encourage a two-year-old to acquire a larger vocabulary by enunciating the elegant sentence about delicious cake served on a beautiful plate and then asked the child to repeat the whole thing, the child might listen attentively and still say, "Eat cake."

Consistent (Mis)Usage: Application of Schemes

Brown traces the sequence of early language acquisition by concentrating on *morphemes*, the smallest units of meaning. Morphemes include words (for example, *milk*) as well as parts of words that have meaning (for example, *ing*). Brown has plotted the appearance of fourteen grammatical morphemes and their order of acquisition. Children learn to add *ing*, for example, before they learn *in* and *on*. They learn to add an *s* to make a word plural before they learn to add an *s* to express possession. Adding an *s* to a verb form (*walks*) comes still later. Even though Adam, Eve, and Sarah acquired types of morphemes in the same sequence, they used different morphemes. Such individuality in the acquisition of language is not surprising. Every child will form a different assortment of schemes because of exposure to different objects, individuals, and experiences.

First morphemes acquired in particular sequence

Other characteristics of early language development are illustrated by the acquisition and use of *wh-questions* (who, what, when, where, why). At first (around two years of age), children use inflections rather than wh-words to ask questions. Next, they use telegraphic-type questions: "What man doing?" At around three years of age, question sentences become longer, but children tend to follow the order of subject and verb that they have learned in declarative sentences. Instead of saying "Why can't the dog come?" for example, the three-year-old will say "Why the dog can't come?" inserting "Why" in front of "The dog can't come."

This is a wug.

Now there is another one.
There are two of them.
There are two _____.

Figure 9–2   Dr. Jean Berko Gleason, "The Child's Learning of English Morphology," *Word*, 1958, **14**, 150–177.

"Inconsistent" grammar may be due to consistent schemes

In their use (and misuse) of language children reveal consistencies that make a great deal of sense. A child who forms a question by simply putting "Why" in front of a previously learned phrase, for example, is applying schemes in a logical way. So is a child who assumes, after learning to form a plural by adding *s*, that all plurals can be formed the same way. Jean Berko demonstrated this tendency when she asked four-year-olds to form the plural of names of imaginary and real animals (see Figure 9–2). If a single imaginary animal in a picture was a *Wug*, four-year-olds reasoned that two of them shown in another picture were *Wugs*. If a single longnecked water bird was a *goose*, two of them were *gooses*.

Other evidence of the extent to which children use language according to their own rules (some of which are more consistent than the rules of English grammar) is provided by ways children respond to premature attempts at instruction in proper usage. A mother and a four-year-old just home from nursery school engaged in this conversation (reported by Cazden, 1968):

Child: My teacher holded the baby rabbits and we patted them.
Mother: Did you say your teacher held the baby rabbits?
Child: Yes.
Mother: What did you say she did?
Child: She holded the baby rabbits and we patted them.
Mother: Did you say she held them tightly?
Child: No, she holded them loosely.

(If the past tense of *scold* is *scolded*, and the past tense of *fold* is *folded*, and the past tense of *mold* is *molded*, why isn't the past tense of *hold*, *holded*?) An example of how a child may find it necessary to adapt to apparent inconsistencies in the speech of parents is illustrated by this interchange. A three-year-old girl was looking at a picture in the book *Three Billy Goats Gruff*. She carefully pointed to each goat and said "Look! Three billy goats eated." Her mother, busily working near her, simply said "Ate." The girl once again counted the figures in the picture and said "Three billy goats eated." Her mother responded again by mechanically saying "Ate." At that point the little girl shrugged her shoulders and said "OK! *Eight* billy goats eated." (Reported by Dennis A. Warner, 1978.)

Confusing Opposites: Inability to Reverse

Still other aspects of early language acquisition can be explained (in part, at least) by focussing on the distinguishing feature of Piaget's concept of an operation. M. Donaldson and R. Wales (1970) became interested in finding out how children acquire understanding of opposites. They showed preschool children two cardboard trees equipped with hooks from which paper apples could be hung. Different numbers of apples were hung from each tree out of the child's view and then displayed. The children were then asked "Does this tree have more (or less) apples than the other?" Donaldson and Wales had expected that the difference between *more* and *less* would be clearly understood by three- and four-year-olds. They were surprised to discover that most preschoolers did not know the difference well enough to use the words correctly with any degree of consistency. The children in their study correctly replied that a tree had more apples sixty-three out of sixty-nine times. The same children were able to correctly explain when a tree had *less* apples only fifteen out of fifty-five times.

Subsequent studies by Eve Clark (1973) have revealed a similar tendency for young children to confuse the opposites *little* and *big, same* and *different, before* and *after*. Clark hypothesizes that the confusion is caused by the tendency of a child to focus on only one end of the continuum implied by opposites, particularly the end that emphasizes the greatest amount or extent. Terms such as *more* and *less* are usually applied to the same objects and situations, and they appear in the same position in a sentence. A three- or four-year-old who is involved in sorting out schemes relating to all sorts of objects and experiences seems to concentrate on the *most* or the *biggest*.

It seems possible that the inability of preschoolers to differentiate between more and less may be related to their inability to explain what happens when water is poured from one container into a container of a different shape. Three- and four-year-olds maintain that a tall container contains more because they center their attention on the single quality (height) that stands out. Perhaps children of the same age who confuse "more" and "less" are misled by the same tendency to focus on a single noteworthy quality. Furthermore, the inability of preschoolers to think operationally may limit understanding of opposites. In a sense, a child has to "reverse" *more* in order to understand *less*. A young child cannot reason out the water problem by mentally pouring water back into the

Confusion of opposites may be due to inability to decenter and reverse

original container. The same inability to mentally reverse may make it difficult for a child to deal with opposites.

Egocentric Speech and Thought: One-track Thinking

A final aspect of early language development that illustrates the way children concentrate on one thing at a time is referred to by Piaget as *egocentric speech* and *thought*. Egocentric, as used by Piaget, does not mean selfish or conceited. It signifies that young children find it difficult to take another person's point of view. In their conversations with others and in experimental situations in which they are asked to describe how something would look if viewed by someone else (Piaget and Inhelder, 1956), preschool children reveal that they have difficulty seeing things from another person's perspective. Quite often, nursery school children will engage in what Piaget calls a *collective monologue*. A pair of children may give the appearance of having a conversation, pausing after having said something to listen to the partner, but their statements and responses will bear little relationship to each other. Each child's utterances will follow a particular line of thought. But there is little reciprocal interchange where something said by one individual elicits an appropriate response from the other. In certain situations, when one child asks another a specific question or when a mutually interesting point comes up, preschool children *do* engage in genuine conversations (Garvey and Hogan, 1973). Piaget suggests, however, that such *socialized speech* does not usually appear with any consistency until after children reach the age of seven years or so.

Piaget's conclusions regarding egocentric and socialized speech were originally based on records of vocal interchanges between children in natural settings. He later devised some simple experiments to determine the extent to which a child is able (or unable) to take another's point of view. One of these experiments features a model of three easily distinguishable mountains. (Each mountain is a different color, one has snow on it, another a house, and the third a red cross.) A child is asked to sit on one side of a table on which the model is placed. Then the examiner produces a doll and puts it at some other position on the table. The child is then asked to indicate what the doll sees by selecting from a set of ten pictures the one that represents the mountains seen by the doll. Piaget and Inhelder (1956) found that children up to the age of seven or eight years tend to pick out a picture that represents their point of view rather than that of the doll. He concluded that despite the fact that children who are approaching eight years of age know that the appearance of something changes when they walk around it, they are prevented from selecting the correct picture by their egocentrism—their inability to visualize something from another's point of view. Egocentric thinking, in turn, can be understood by considering the principle of decentration. Preoperational children typically concentrate on one thing at a time. This

Egocentric thinking: difficulty in taking another's point of view

tendency causes them to focus on their own point of view even when asked to imagine a different point of view.

Questions Regarding Piaget's Description
of Preoperational Thinking

Are Children Less Egocentric than Piaget Says They Are?

A number of psychologists have questioned Piaget's conclusions regarding egocentricity and the explanation that egocentricity manifests a child's inability to decenter. Margaret Donaldson, for instance, suggests that children below the age of seven or eight years "fail" the mountain experiment mainly because they do not understand what they are to do. In *Children's Minds* (1978) she describes experiments that are specifically designed to "make sense" to children. In one experiment, for example, a child is asked to hide a boy doll behind a wall so that a policeman doll cannot see it. In another experiment a simplified version of Piaget's mountain task is presented in a very slow and deliberate manner. Donaldson reports that when children below the age of eight are asked to deal with realistic and familiar problems, they are *not* egocentric. She also suggests that young children have difficulty classifying objects primarily because of problems of communication. She reports that they can solve conservation problems if instructions are presented in language they can understand. Donaldson concludes that parents and teachers might foster cognitive development by talking *about* words (p. 93) to help children acquire language skills. This may in turn lead to deeper and earlier understanding.

Another psychologist who has criticized Piaget's conclusions about preoperational thought is Rochel Gelman. She reports (1979) that when conditions are communicated to young children at their own level, preschoolers are capable of solving simplified versions of many of the Piagetian experiments. Gelman argues, for example, that when children are asked to distinguish between "winners" and "losers" instead of specifying "more" or "less," they are able to correctly answer questions about aspects of conservation. She believes that Piagetian concepts should be tested by specifically devising tasks and experimental settings to suit the preschool child.

The results of the experiments described by Donaldson and Gelman suggest that Piaget may have overemphasized the orderliness of the sequence and timing of aspects of cognitive development. (As noted in the evaluation of Piaget's theory in Chapter 3, John Flavell has observed that Piaget has "a penchant for symmetry and neatness of classification" [1963, p. 38].) On the other hand, simply because researchers have developed ingenious experimental techniques that enable *their* subjects to solve certain types of problems earlier than Piaget's subjects does not mean his observations should be rejected or ignored. If parents and preschool teachers make a concerted effort to see things from the child's point of view, arrange conditions to suit the child, and use terms that are familiar to the child, a child may demonstrate certain types of understanding somewhat earlier than Piaget predicts they will. But if parents, teachers, siblings, or peers do *not* make any special efforts to think and talk as a preschool child does, the trends described by Piaget would probably appear "on schedule."

Socialized thinking may occur early under simplified conditions

While it may make sense for those who interact with preschool children to follow Donaldson's suggestion and talk *about* words, it might not be advisable for adults (outside of experimental situations) to try to frequently adjust their thought and speech to suit the child. If parents and teachers spend too much time deliberately thinking and talking in preoperational terms, it would seem possible that they might slow down the rate at which a child would move to concrete operational thinking. These observations lead to the question: Should parents and preschool teachers make systematic efforts to encourage children to conserve, decenter, and overcome egocentric thinking at a faster-than-normal rate?

Should Efforts Be Made to Speed up Cognitive Development?

Aware that preschool children are typically preoperational and unable to conserve, some psychologists in the 1960s (for example, Hunt, 1961; Engelmann and Engelmann, 1968) speculated about the possibility of speeding up cognitive development. They reasoned that preschool children who learned how to solve conservation problems, for example, might function as concrete operational thinkers at an earlier-than-average age. Precocious concrete operational thinkers might then begin to function as formal thinkers ahead of schedule, making them capable of solving many kinds of problems at a younger age than if they had not received early instruction. There are arguments for and against the policy of trying to accelerate cognitive development. These can be understood more completely by examining background information and assumptions.

Is There a Critical Period in Cognitive Development?

Factors Leading to the Cognitive Critical-Period Hypothesis

In the 1960s a number of discoveries and conditions led to the hypothesis of a critical period in cognitive development. The initial impetus for this hypothesis came from early research on critical periods such as the Lorenz report on imprinting (1952) and the Bowlby report on the impact of institutionalization (1952). These provocative observations led some theorists to speculate that the first years of life might be of crucial significance not only in the formation of attachment behavior but also in the development of cognitive abilities. Benjamin Bloom (1964), for example, analyzed data regarding age changes in cognitive functioning and hypothesized that children achieve 50 percent of their adult intelligence by the age of four, 80 percent by the age of eight. Bloom also argued that if children lived in an impoverished environment for the first four years of their lives, they might lose as many as 2.5 IQ points a year and that this loss would be irreversible. Shortly before Bloom published his book, Martin Deutsch (1964) had reported that disadvantaged children showed gains in cognitive functioning after being exposed to intensive preschool experiences. The reports by Bloom and Deutsch appeared at a time when the Great Society program of the administration of President Lyndon Johnson was being planned. One of the goals of the Great Society program was to attempt to equalize educational opportunities. The hypothesis that deprivation early in life led to permanent decreases in cognitive development motivated the establishment of Head Start schools for disadvantaged children. Psychologists who endorsed the cognitive critical-period hypothesis predicted that enriched preschool experiences, such as those to be provided in Head Start programs, would lead to permanent gains in intellectual functioning.

Research and social trends in the 1960s led to cognitive critical-period hypothesis

The assumption that the preschool years might be a critical period in cognitive development led not only to Head Start and related programs for disadvantaged children but eventually to programs for early instruction for *all* children. A book titled *How to Teach Your Baby to Read* (1964) by Glenn Doman was widely purchased by upper- and middle-class parents, as was *Give Your Child a Superior Mind* (1968) by Siegfried and Theresa Engelmann. Engelmann and Engelmann described techniques parents were to use in efforts to speed up and expand the cognitive abilities (such as concepts described by Piaget) of their preschool children. In addition, the number of middle- and upper-class children who were enrolled in nursery schools increased with the publication of popular reports of Bloom's hypothesis about the critical nature of the first four years. Many parents seem to have believed that children who did not attend nursery school would be unable to compete with those who did during the elementary school years. Parental concern about preschool experiences was influenced by toy manufacturers who stressed (often in distorted fashion) Bloom's hypothesis about the crucial importance of the first four years. One advertisement for "creative" playthings, for example, proclaimed that "New research shows will to learn is established before the first day of school or it's never established at all" (*New Yorker*, October 3, 1964, p. 185).

Factors Leading to Doubts About a Cognitive Critical Period

In the late 1960s and early 1970s many of these initial speculations about a cognitive critical period during the preschool years came to be questioned.

Extensive research on imprinting (for example, Hinde, 1973) led to the conclusion that *sensitive* rather than critical periods seem to occur, and only under certain conditions. Follow-up studies on the impact of institutionalization (for example, Thompson and Grusec, 1970; Dennis, 1973) questioned the hypothesis that lack of stimulation early in life would lead to irreversible retardation. Bloom himself revised his original view regarding irreversibility of early IQ losses when he stated (1968) that while experiences during the preschool years are of great significance, change may take place later in the course of development. Arthur Jensen (1969) analyzed Bloom's data and concluded that if his method of estimating mental growth was applied to physical growth, the resulting prediction would be that the average four-year-old would achieve a height of six feet seven inches by the age of seventeen.

Research in 1970s led to doubts about cognitive critical-period hypothesis

Although Burton White maintained in 1975 that it may be "all over by the age of three" as far as cognitive development is concerned, other specialists in early childhood education who published reports around the same time no longer supported the critical period hypothesis. E. Zigler, who was director of Head Start for a number of years, for instance, noted:

I, for one, am tired of the past decade's scramble to discover some magic period during which interventions will have particularly great pay-offs. . . . My own predilection is that we cease this pointless search for magic periods and adopt instead the view that the developmental process is a continuous one, in which every segment of the life cycle from conception through maturity is of crucial importance and requires certain environmental nutrients. (1975)

Furthermore, twelve psychologists who made up the Consortium on Developmental Continuity, Education Commission of the States, and who directed different types of programs for disadvantaged children, prepared a report titled *The Persistence of Preschool Effects*. Toward the end of the report they express the opinion that "there is as of now no indication of a 'magic age' at which early intervention is most effective" (1977, p. 108). (Other points made in this report will be presented a bit later in this discussion.)

Piaget: attempts to speed up cognitive development lead to superficial learning

When he learned that American psychologists such as Engelmann were referring to his descriptions of cognitive development in their efforts to speed up mastery of concepts, Jean Piaget expressed the opinion that such attempts would lead to superficial rather than genuine learning (1966). To test his accelerated intelligence view (as well as Piaget's contention that it would produce only superficial learning) Engelmann set out to teach six-year-old children the concept of specific gravity. He then invited Constance Kamii and L. Dermon, advocates of the Piagetian view, to test the children to determine whether or not they had gained genuine understanding. Kamii and Dermon (1972) concluded that the children had gained only partial understanding of the concept, that they still functioned at the preoperational level, and that they applied the rule they had learned in rote fashion. Engelmann argued that this seemed to be the case only because the children lacked information that would have been necessary for them to use the rule with understanding. He claimed that they could be taught this information and then would be able to apply the concept. Kamii and Dermon evaluated this argument and discovered that the children had to be told what information they would need. (They were not able to ask for it on their own.)

Florence Goodenough (1939) reported that the IQ gains attributable to the nursery-school experience of middle-class children faded as they moved through the grades. This early review was reaffirmed by Joan W. Swift's later review (1964) of the same type. The same sort of fade reaction was mentioned in a summary of follow-up studies on Head Start programs presented in the *Report of the U.S. Commission on Civil Rights*: "None of the compensatory education programs appears to have raised significantly the achievement of participating pupils within the period evaluated by the Commission" (1967, p. 138).

In commenting on reports that Head Start programs had failed to produce lasting gains in intellectual functioning, Susan W. Gray and Rupert E. Klaus (1970) observed that not even the best possible program could be expected to "inoculate" children and make then "immune" to the impact of continued existence in a poor environment. This observation calls attention to two points: (1) the hypothesis that there is a critical period in cognitive development (which does not seem to be substantiated by available evidence) leads to the assumption that proper experiences during the first few years of life will permanently equip a child with effective cognitive skills; (2) there are significant differences between the home environments of middle-income and low-income children. The first point has just been discussed, the second merits elaboration and analysis.

Differences Between Middle- and Low-Income Home Environments

In recent years it has become increasingly apparent that American children are not "created equal," in the sense that they have equal opportunities to develop their capabilities. Many children from upper- and middle-class homes may be exposed to experiences and reactions that favor cognitive development (an abundance of toys, exposure to many different kinds of situations, parents who have the time to engage in frequent conversations with them). This may not be the case with children who are born into low-income families. It should be emphasized that, as Ainsworth (1974) has shown, there are differences between sensitive and insensitive mothers who came from middle-income backgrounds. Furthermore, because some individuals who come from the worst possible backgrounds achieve eminence and success, it seems reasonable to assume that some parents from low-income homes must provide an extraordinarily effective environment for their children.

It does appear, however, that certain caretaker characteristics may be more likely to appear in low-income homes than in middle-income homes. For example, Robert D. Hess and Virginia Shipman (1965) found that a significant number of children who were born into low-income homes were cared for by mothers who were inattentive and unresponsive, used impoverished language, lacked self-confidence, ran the home in a disorganized way, and often functioned at the preoperational level of cognitive development. Perhaps it struck you that some of these caretaker characteristics are similar to those Baumrind (1971) found typical of permissive middle-class parents (described in the preceding chapter). Such an environment, therefore, might be found at any income level. The research of Hess and Shipman suggests, though, that such ineffective caretakers are more likely to be found in lower-class homes.

Regardless of their sensitivity and effectiveness, mothers from low-income backgrounds may find it extremely difficult, entirely on their own, to overcome the depressant effect of the cumulative impact of conditions associated with poverty in America.

The Cumulative Depressant Effect of an Impoverished Environment

The low-income woman who is expecting a child often receives little or no benefits from health knowledge and services. A low-income woman who seeks medical advice during pregnancy is likely to receive it from a series of different medical practitioners on the staff of a clinic. If she receives medical aid at the time of delivery, the doctor may be a stranger to her. If she is uneducated, she may not know of the availability of programs and information that might contribute to a healthy pregnancy and a safe and uneventful delivery. A low-income mother may not be aware of the importance of a good diet during pregnancy (or even be able to maintain such a diet). She may not protect herself from exposure to infectious diseases. She may take a variety of drugs without realizing that even aspirin or the equivalent may cause abnormalities in fetal development. For all these reasons, a child of a low-income mother may be born with physical defects, some of which may go undetected for several years because regular health care is not available.

The low-income mother may not know about the physical and psychological care of infants and may not even benefit from "tradition" if she has no contact with older female relatives. Because of poverty, the parents may not be able to provide much in the way of clothing or playthings for the child. Also because of poverty, and possibly because both parents must work, the child may only rarely venture beyond the immediate neighborhood. The child from a low-income home may never ride in a car or a bus or be taken to a large department store and may be ignorant of objects and experiences that are completely familiar to more favored children. Many inner-city children, for example, have no conception of a farm or a garden.

When the time comes to enter school, the child may be apprehensive at worst or unenthusiastic at best because of the attitudes of parents and older siblings and playmates. If parents, siblings, or older peers were school dropouts, they may harbor negative feelings about teachers and education. And these may be communicated directly or indirectly to the child. If older children have negative experiences in school, they may describe these in exaggerated fashion and make the uninitiated younger child feel anxious about what lies ahead. Even if the parents do not feel negatively toward education, they may take little interest in what goes on in school, fail to show up for parent conferences, and be indifferent to report cards. Because of lack of familiarity with many objects and situations depicted in instructional materials, together with an absence of encouragement from parents, a child from a low-income home may get off to a poor start in the primary grades. Inability to read or write will then lead to ever-increasing problems and cause the child to fall further and further behind. By the time the student reaches the secondary grades, she or he may have given up on school and may resolve to just put in time until it is legally permissible to drop out. Awareness that many older children in the neighborhood are unable to find employment contributes to attitudes of fatalistic resignation, anger, or resentment. The possibility of higher education seems so remote that it may never be considered at all. Even if an adolescent does respond to the urging of a teacher and resolve to work for high grades, the attempt may be cut short because there is no place at home to study, no desk or reference works to use, no encouragement from parents.

The child from a low-income home may never see a doctor or dentist and may go to school hungry and dressed in hand-me-down clothes. If a language other than English is spoken in the home or neighborhood, the child may find it difficult to understand the teacher, converse with classmates, or read instructional materials. When asked to complete assignments or take tests, the child may have difficulty following instructions, interpreting questions, or supplying answers. If the child becomes aware that parents and neighbors are treated in demeaning ways or are accorded little respect from others, feelings of self-doubt and low esteem may be intensified.

There are exceptions to the portrait just presented, of course, but this description includes most of the elements found in a detailed study of disadvantaged children by Frank Riessman (1962). One of the most significant points about the description just provided relates to ways factors (such as inadequate prenatal care or birth complications) appear to lead to a lasting impact on a child growing up in a poor environment. E. E. Werner, J. M. Bierman, and F. E. French (1971) revealed how potent a poor environment can be when they carried out a longitudinal study of all 670 children born on the island of Kauai in 1955. Each newborn infant was rated on a scale of severity of prenatal and birth complica-

A child who lives in a slum may fail to overcome early handicaps (such as inadequate prenatal care or birth complications) and suffer in many ways from the cumulative depressant effect of a poor environment. George Malave/Stock, Boston.

tions. Later, periodic assessments were made of physical health, intelligence, social maturity, and environmental variables. This comprehensive study found, significantly, that most children from middle and upper-income homes who were judged to have had a poor start because of prenatal or birth complications seemed to have overcome their early handicaps by the time they entered school. On intelligence tests, for instance, they scored only slightly below children from similar backgrounds who were judged to have had uneventful prenatal and birth experiences. Children from lower economic backgrounds who had experienced difficulties at the beginning of their lives, however, seemed to remain at a disadvantage. They scored from nineteen to thirty-seven points lower on IQ tests than children from similar backgrounds who were judged to have had normal prenatal and birth experiences. On the basis of this finding, as well as other analyses of their data, Werner and her associates concluded that the single most important variable leading to retardation or aberrations in development in disadvantaged children is the poor environment in which they mature. This conclusion is supported by other research summarized by Arnold Sameroff and Michael J. Chandler (1975, pp. 205–210).

Impoverished environment has cumulative depressant effect

If the pervasive devitalizing nature of a disadvantaged environment is considered, it is not surprising that brief exposure to an enriched environment (such as that provided in Head Start programs) is insufficient to "inoculate" or "immunize" a child for life. When early reports (such as that of the U.S. Commission on Civil Rights) revealed that the intellectual functioning of children who had participated in special preschool programs had not produced permanent results, psychologists responsible for such programs questioned the critical-period hypothesis and concluded that more extended instruction was necessary. They reasoned that compensatory education for disadvantaged children had not begun early enough, had not lasted long enough, and had not involved the parents enough.

Extended Compensatory Education Programs Have a Positive Impact

In extending the intensity and duration of Head Start programs (some of which had lasted only a few months), two basic strategies were followed. The first consisted of early intervention programs such as the Florida Parent Education Project directed by Ira Gordon (described in Chapter 7); most early intervention programs instruct mothers to be more sensitive, responsive, and confident in interacting with their children before and after they enter nursery school. The second strategy involves Follow-Through programs designed to continue the kind of education provided in Head Start preschools through the primary grades.

Such programs have now been in existence long enough to make it possible to study long-term effects. Information about the later school and intelligence test performance of graduates of such programs is presented in *The Persistence of Preschool Effects*. The psychologists who collaborated in preparing this report provide evidence that compared to control-group children from similar backgrounds, children who participated in such programs were less likely to be assigned to special classes for retarded pupils, less likely to be held back during the elementary school years, and more likely to earn higher scores on the Stanford-Binet intelligence test immediately following graduation from such programs. The authors subsequently note, however, that as the children moved through the grades, the same fade reaction found in earlier studies of the impact of nursery school experience appeared. By the end of the elementary grades initial improvement in IQ score had largely disappeared. This finding suggests that the child who is no longer given special support and enouragement throughout the elementary school years may succumb to the impact of the negative environmental conditions described a bit earlier.

Extended compensatory programs have positive impact

Scores on an intelligence test were used as one of the measures of the success of extended compensatory education programs. Furthermore, the fact that these scores faded has been stressed as an important consideration in evaluating the hypothesis of a critical period in cognitive development. For both of these reasons, it will be fruitful to briefly examine the nature and measurement of intelligence. Such an analysis will not only make it possible for you to evaluate the significance of reports of IQ scores. You should also be able to better comprehend why such scores may change as a child matures.

Recent research leads to the conclusion that extended compensatory programs (such as Head Start and Follow Through) may have a positive and lasting impact on development and academic achievement. Charles Harbutt/Magnum.

The Nature and Measurement of Intelligence

One of the difficulties in drawing conclusions about research on intelligence is that there is no universally agreed upon definition of intelligence. As a result, different people mean different things when they talk about this quality. This should be kept in mind when discussing comparative scores, since much may depend on the test used to determine the scores. The conception of intelligence that test authors have in mind when they start to work determines the questions they write, which in turn determine the final score. Consequently, it is important to know how a writer of an intelligence test defines the quality to be measured.

Definitions of Intelligence

There is general agreement that the two most widely respected tests of intelligence are the Stanford-Binet and Wechsler tests. Lewis Terman, who was assisted by Maud A. Merrill in developing the Stanford-Binet tests (1937, 1960), designed them to measure a general factor (McNemar, 1942) which might be described as the ability to deal with abstractions. David Wechsler, the chief originator of the

Wechsler-Bellevue test (1939), proposed that intelligence is made up of several factors rather than a single factor. The Wechsler-Bellevue served as the model for several subsequent tests—the Wechsler Intelligence Scale for Children, usually abbreviated WISC (1949), the Wechsler Intelligence Scale for Children—Revised, or WISC-R (1974), the Wechsler Preschool and Primary Scale of Intelligence, or WPPSI (1963, 1967), and the Wechsler Adult Intelligence Scale, or WAIS (1955, 1964, 1968). Each of these tests consists of several subtests. And three IQ scores are computed—a verbal score, a performance score, and a full-scale score.

The distinction between general and specific abilities is perhaps the major point of difference in definitions of intelligence. Charles Spearman (1927), one of the earliest authorities on intelligence, spoke of a "g" (for "general") factor, plus several "s" (for "specific") factors. The "ability to deal with abstractions" measured by the Stanford-Binet is an example of the "g" factor. The separate abilities measured by the subtests on the WISC and WAIS are examples of "s" factors. (Verbal subtests of the WISC measure information, comprehension, arithmetic, similarities, and vocabulary. Performance tests measure skills in picture completion, block design, picture arrangement, object assembly, coding, and mazes.) The arrangement of subtests on the Stanford-Binet and the WISC, and the kinds of scores they yield, illustrate that there are different ways of looking at intelligence, and the way it is defined will determine how it is measured.

General and specific factors in intelligence

The appraisal of intelligence is further complicated by the fact that it cannot be measured directly. Therefore, efforts must be confined to measuring the overt manifestations of what ultimately is based on brain function. And that is why intelligence is so elusive. It depends on what manifestations you choose to observe. Some theorists define intelligence as what is measured by an intelligence test. This may sound like double talk, but the intent is not to dodge the issue. Any estimate of intelligence depends first and foremost on the questions asked in the effort to measure it.

The Nature of Intelligence Tests

An intelligence test consists of questions that the test-maker believes will yield an adequate sample of the subject's ability to deal with the types of problems that the test-maker considers indicative of intelligence (as the test-maker defines it). This is the crucial point in appreciating the values and limitations of intelligence tests. Sir Francis Galton, who was instrumental in initiating the mental-test movement, emphasized that a test consists of the *sinking of shafts at critical points* (1890, p. 373). When you set out to measure intelligence, the important question is: What are "critical points"? You have to try to select sample bits of behavior that you hope will be "critical" or indicative of a general ability, yet make your questions fair to all.

The major confounding factor is differences in educational opportunity. An estimate of general learning ability must take into account that some children benefit from an especially rich home and school environment. Obviously, the capacity of a child to learn is a function of both inherited potential and experiences. But the test-maker is interested in a general capacity and wants to avoid, as much as possible, measuring abilities that are largely the result of a particular set of home or school experiences. If questions are too directly related to a specific kind of home or curriculum, they will measure only how well a child has responded to those experiences. What about children who have *not* been exposed to that set of home or curriculum experiences? You can't really say they're dumb, because you haven't given them the chance to demonstrate that they're bright. To avoid this sort of handicap, the test questions should be based on situations common to practically all children. Whether they have learned from the exposure is what you hope to discover, but you must try to make sure they have had the opportunity to learn in the first place.

One more point regarding intelligence tests has to do with the score. No intelligence-test score is an "absolute" measure. Many people fail to grasp this fact. A common misconception is that an IQ score is a once-and-for-all judgment of how bright a person is. In fact, the score of an intelligence test is merely a qualified guess about how successful a child is—as compared to other children—in handling certain kinds of problems at a particular time. If retested, even with the same questions, the child is quite likely to get a different score. This tendency is illustrated by studies where the same individuals have been given intelligence tests at frequent intervals.

The Variability of IQ Scores

Data collected during the course of the Berkeley Growth Study made it possible for Nancy Bayley (1949) to compare intelligence-test scores of the subjects from birth to eighteen years. For the first five years of the study the California Preschool Scale was used; for the years from six to twelve and at fourteen and sixteen the Stanford-Binet was used. At thirteen and fifteen the Terman-McNemar test was administered; and the subjects were asked to take the Wechsler-Bellevue at the ages of sixteen and eighteen. Since each of these four tests is based on different assumptions about intelligence, and since the questions differ, it should not be surprising that there was considerable variability in IQ scores of subjects at different age levels. The scores obtained in the first two years were especially unstable, but consistency became apparent during the elementary school years. In commenting on the results of this survey, Bayley notes that part of the instability from one age level to another, particularly lack of consistency between scores obtained before and after the age of five, might be attributed to differences in the kinds of questions asked. She concluded that sensorimotor

If the same child is given an individual intelligence test every two years, between the ages of six and eighteen the IQ scores are likely to vary by fifteen points or more.

functions were stressed on infant tests at around the one-year level, that adapting to concrete situations was significant up to four years, and that ability to deal with abstractions was the most important single factor thereafter.

Marjorie P. Honzik, Jean W. Macfarlane, and Lucile Allen (1948) analyzed intelligence-test-score data from another University of California longitudinal investigation, the Guidance Study. The California Preschool Scale was used for the first five years; the Stanford-Binet from six to fifteen; the Wechsler-Bellevue at eighteen. The researchers found corroboration of Bayley's conclusions regarding instability of infant test scores, with greater consistency becoming apparent around the age of five. Correlations between scores on tests administered a few years apart were high, but the longer the interval between tests, the lower the relationship tended to be. The researchers also reported that between the ages of six to eighteen, the scores of almost 60 percent of the subjects changed fifteen or more points; the scores of almost a third of the group changed twenty or more points; and the scores of 9 percent of the group changed thirty or more points. In only 15 percent of the cases did IQ scores change less than ten points. Some subjects showed upward or downward changes of as much as fifty points. Honzik

Between 6 and 18, 15-point changes in IQ common

and her associates noted that children whose test scores showed the most extreme fluctuations were known to have been exposed to unusual variations in their lives.

The shifts in scores at various ages can also be explained by the fact that items at the different age levels of the Stanford-Binet measure different kinds of intellectual skills. Just exactly what these different skills are is open to interpretation. Quinn McNemar (1942) analyzed the different types of items included at the various age levels on the Stanford-Binet. He concluded that a large part of the performance at each age was explained by a single factor but that the factor changed in nature for each level. L. V. Jones (1954) did approximately what McNemar did but concluded that there were several factors, not one, and that with age these separate factors became more clearly differentiated. Even though the exact changes at different levels of the Stanford-Binet are not clearly established, it can be assumed that a child's IQ score on that test might change because different abilities are being measured at different ages. After analyzing longitudinal studies in which repeated measurements of intellligence had been made, McCall, Hogarty, and Hurlburt (1972) concluded that there is a qualitative shift in what is defined as intelligence at different ages.

The assumption that intelligence tests measure different abilities at different age levels offers one explanation for the consistent finding that children who are provided with preschool educational experiences show only temporary increases in IQ scores. There are, however, a number of other explanations why early gains in intellectual functioning that appear immediately after preschool experiences are "cancelled" by later experiences and conditions. (All of these will be discussed more completely in later chapters, but they merit brief mention at this point since they are pertinent to an evaluation of the cognitive critical-period hypothesis.)

Factors That May "Cancel" Preschool Experiences

Differences in Cognitive Style

As noted in the discussion of definitions of intelligence, some theorists have proposed that there is a variety of special types of intellectual functioning. Different types of intellectual functioning are sometimes expressed as differences in *cognitive styles*. For example, some children are *impulsive* thinkers, others *reflective;* some are *analytic* thinkers, others *thematic* (Kagan, 1964b, 1964c). Distinctions have also been made between *convergent* and *divergent* thinkers (Guilford, 1967) and between *field dependent* and *independent* types (Witkin et al., 1962). The nature of each of these types of thinking will be explained in Chapter 11. The important point to grasp now is that children may change in their abilities to answer questions on intelligence tests or on school exams because they are inclined to use a particular cognitive style, and cognitive style may not become apparent—or significant—until the elementary school years.

Differences Between Preschool and Elementary School Curricula

Another possible explanation for changes in IQ scores and in school achievement between the preschool and elementary school years may be traced to changes in the school curriculum. (This point is related to differences in types of items that are presented on intelligence tests at various age levels.) The kinds of skills that are stressed in preschool programs are often quite different from those that become crucial in the elementary grades. The most significant differences probably center on the acquisition of the abilities to read and write. Success in the elementary grades is influenced more by skill in reading than by any other single factor. Yet it is difficult to predict, on the basis of preschool performance, how rapidly any particular child will learn to read. Preschool programs typically stress reading *readiness* exercises, but any child's actual ability to read will not be revealed until instruction is provided. And the response of the child to early reading instruction will have a pervasive impact on many aspects of school learning. A child who learns to read easily, for example, will probably develop initial self-confidence as a student because so much of the curriculum is based on reading. A child who experiences difficulties in learning to read, on the other hand, may come to fear and dislike school, even if preschool experiences were favorable.

A related point involves competition with others. Most nursery school programs concentrate on individual improvement. Each child's performance is typically related to his or her previous performance, not to the performance of others. As soon as a child enters the primary grades, though, explicit or implicit comparisons to the performance of other children are made. If traditional report cards are used in an elementary school, a child's performance is rated as superior, average, or inferior compared to the performance of other children. But even in schools which make an effort to stress individual performance and do not use comparative grading, children quickly become aware of how they perform compared to others. A child who is having difficulty learning to read does not need a letter grade or test score to become aware of that fact. Every time successful readers display their skill, nonreaders realize that they are less capable. (The kind of behavior being described here is one facet of what Erikson emphasizes in his distinction between industry and inferiority, which will be discussed more completely in the next chapter.)

Still another difference between nursery school and grade school curricula is a function of the kinds of cognitive skills required. Most nursery school programs try to prepare children for the primary grades. But because of the sequence of stages in cognitive development, it is difficult (if not impossible) to teach certain skills to preschool children that will become important during the elementary school years. The preoperational child is typically unable to handle assignments that *are* within the capability of a concrete operational thinker (for example, the ability to generalize from one experience to a similar experience). Accordingly, a child may not be responsive to instruction that stresses applications to similar

The IQ scores and cognitive functioning of some children may change because of different reactions to the transition from a relaxed, supportive nursery school to a demanding, competitive, elementary school. Guy Gillette/Photo Researchers; Ken Heyman.

situations until after concrete operational thinking is achieved. The evaluation by Kamii and Dermon of Engelmann's attempt to teach specific gravity to six-year-olds leads to the conclusion that preschool children find it difficult to generalize, even when attempts are made to teach them how to become concrete operational thinkers ahead of schedule.

Because of factors such as these, it is possible that both IQ scores and general intellectual functioning may change as a child matures. A child who has enjoyed nursery school and responded favorably to instruction during the preschool years, therefore, will not "automatically" continue to behave that way in the primary grades. Difficulties in learning to read, or the realization that others learn faster, or the increasing need to take responsibility for completing assigned tasks (to mention only a few of the many possibilities) may cause a substantial alteration in a child's self-concept and in attitudes toward school. An erosion of confidence or a failure to acquire basic skills may lead to poor school performance. Poor attitudes and performance may, in turn, eventually have a negative impact on a child's ability to answer questions on intelligence tests. Test-makers try to minimize the impact of such factors, but it is probably impossible to eliminate the impact of schooling on IQ scores.

This outline of a few factors that might lead to differences in intellectual performance over a period of years is not intended to imply that preschool experiences have *no* impact on later behavior. It is merely an attempt to point out some possible reasons why a child who is exposed to excellent preschool experiences may not receive permanent benefits from such experiences. Even if parents and teachers of preschool children may not be able to count on bringing about permanent changes, however, it still makes a great deal of sense to do everything possible to provide two- to five-year-olds with the best possible environment in which to practice and acquire cognitive skills. That point leads to the question: What types of preschool experiences should parents try to provide in their efforts to foster cognitive development?

What Types of Preschool Experiences Should Parents Try to Provide?

Child-rearing Techniques That Favor Cognitive Development

In Chapter 7 techniques used by parents who seem to encourage satisfactory development in one- and two-year-olds were summarized. It seems reasonable to assume that general techniques that were effective with one- and two-year-olds will continue to be effective with three- and four-year-olds. Among the successful techniques used with very young children that might be expected to continue to be effective with somewhat older preschoolers are the following:

- ☐ Letting the child initiate activities and then responding in ways that extend and expand those activities.
- ☐ Taking turns, giving the child ample opportunities for self-expression.
- ☐ Arranging conditions and providing responses so that children develop the feeling that they can produce consequences.
- ☐ Seeing things from the child's point of view.
- ☐ Establishing feelings of mutual delight.
- ☐ Talking, responding, enriching, encouraging, explaining.

Authoritative child rearing appears likely to promote competence

In the preceding chapter Diana Baumrind's research on the impact of different types of child rearing was summarized. Baumrind found that there was a tendency for children to become competent and self-reliant when parents were *authoritative*. Since competence may be as much a cognitive as a personality characteristic, the techniques used by authoritative parents merit mention in a discussion of factors likely to enhance intellectual development. Authoritative parents used these techniques:

☐ Permitted and encouraged the child to do many things independently.

☐ Urged the child to try to achieve mature and skilled types of behavior. (A technique that would seem to be in opposition to making efforts to think and talk at the *child's* level, as in the experimental situations devised by Gelman.)

☐ Established firm control but gave reasons for restrictions.

☐ Respected the child's wishes but also expected the child to take into account the needs of others (while still allowing for the egocentric thinking of young children).

☐ Were warm, supportive, and loving.

☐ Showed their children that achievements were admired and appreciated.

☐ Exuded aura of competence (and thus served as models of competence).

Factors Parents Might Consider Regarding Nursery School

If parents have time to interact extensively with preschool children, if they use techniques such as those just described, and if they *enjoy* interacting with their children, it would seem that they could supply an excellent environment for cognitive development in the home. Unless a child has restricted opportunities to interact with other children in the neighborhood, there may be little reason for parents to feel that attendance at a nursery school is essential. As noted earlier, Joan W. Swift (1964) found that middle-class children who attended nursery school did not seem to perform better in school or on intelligence tests over the long run than children who did not attend. (Swift noted, however, that children from disadvantaged backgrounds *did* benefit, a conclusion later corroborated by the authors of *The Persistence of Preschool Effects*.) Accordingly, the primary factor for middle-class parents to consider (assuming they have the time, inclination, and ability to use techniques such as those listed above) when deciding for or against nursery school might center on the question: Will it be better for parents and child if they each engage in separate activities for part of the day?

In relation to this point it should be noted that full-time mothering may not always be desirable. There is some evidence (Birnbaum, 1975) that educated women who devote themselves to full-time mothering may overinvest in their preschool children. That is, they may provide more attention than a child can handle (a point related to arguments against overstimulating infants that were

Full-time mothering does not necessarily promote early cognitive development

If a middle-class child has opportunities to interact with playmates in the neighborhood, and if the mother enjoys child care, there does not seem to be any reason to assume that nursery school experience is essential as preparation for the primary grades. It appears, however, that some mothers "overinvest" in children who remain at home during the preschool years. Sybil Shelton/ Monkmeyer.

noted in Chapter 7). Furthermore, one study comparing the behavior of children of working and nonworking mothers (Moore, 1975) reported that while boys who received full-time mothering during their preschool years were advanced in cognitive abilities, they were rated as more conforming, fearful, and inhibited as adolescents. It would be a mistake to assume that these findings mean that a woman should *avoid* functioning as a full-time mother, even if she enjoys it and finds it fulfilling. But mothers of preschool children who are indecisive about seeking or accepting a job might take into account that maternal employment during the preschool years does not seem to have negative effects on the development of the young child (L. W. Hoffman, 1979). In fact, there may be advantages since working mothers report that they are more satisfied with their lives than nonworking mothers (Dubnoff, Veroff, and Kulka, 1978). There is evidence that the mother's satisfaction with her role increases her effectiveness as a parent (Gold and Andres, 1978).

If parents do decide (perhaps after consulting with the child) to arrange for nursery school experiences, they may be faced with a choice between schools. Some nursery schools offer a classic Montessori form of instruction, others are based on Piagetian concepts and stress a great deal of self-instruction and interaction between age-mates, still others feature behavior-modification techniques. In small towns, perhaps only one school will be available, but in populated areas there may be several to choose from. Because of the number and complexity of the variables involved, it is all but impossible to carry out a trustworthy comparison of the impact on later child behavior of different kinds of nursery school experience. This probably explains why no comprehensive effort to carry out such a study has been attempted. (It would be essential, for example, to obtain *detailed* information about a child's abilities and attitudes before entering school as well as information about the variety and subtleties of the child-rearing techniques used by the parents in the home. Such information is extremely difficult to obtain.) Furthermore, there are undoubtedly differences between schools that practice the same basic approach that are a function of the personalities of the director and the teachers. Accordingly, parents might select a nursery school by considering questions such as these:

☐ What do parents of children who attended a particular nursery school have to say about it?

☐ What do children who attended a particular nursery school have to say about it?

☐ What impressions do parents form after having visited the school, observed teachers interacting with children, and talked to the teachers?

☐ How does the child feel about the school that is being considered after a few trial sessions?

How Much Home "Instruction" Is Necessary or Desirable?

A final point regarding preschool experience has to do with the question of whether "instruction" should be provided in the home. Statements by toy manufacturers or magazine articles arguing that "the will to learn must be established before the age of five" (or the equivalent) are not nearly as common today as they were in the mid-1960s, but they are occasionally encountered. And books claiming to describe techniques parents can use to "raise" a child's IQ are still to be found in libraries and in book stores. If they read such books, though, parents will discover that the approaches described usually require formal lessons, and that these lessons involve a considerable amount of drill and rote memorization. This schoolroom atmosphere (even including a chalkboard) created in many books of this type conflicts with several of the characteristics of effective parents noted earlier (for example, permitting and encouraging the child to do many things independently). Instead of feeling obliged to act as tutors, therefore, parents might simply urge their preschoolers to watch "Sesame Street" every day. Millions of dollars and thousands of hours of planning by experts in early childhood education have been devoted to preparing programs that teach children concepts (among many other things) in a vivid and entertaining way. And because these concepts are "offered" to children, it is possible for each child to respond in a way that Piaget would approve of. That is to say, each child can assimilate, accommodate, and form schemes at a rate that he or she can determine.

Even though "Sesame Street" may be preferred to formal lessons by parents, there are two kinds of situations where instruction in the home (to parents as well as child) may be desirable. If parents (of any economic level) who are eager to provide an excellent home environment for their preschool children are not satisfied with the efforts, or feel a bit baffled by the behavior of their offspring, they might benefit from assistance, support, and advice. Supportive programs designed to recommend specific interaction techniques and to build parental self-confidence may be of considerable value in such cases. Such programs may be offered by federal, state, and county agencies or by colleges and universities. The second kind of home instruction that may be highly beneficial is the early intervention programs such as the Florida Parent Education Program. For reasons discussed earlier, low-income parents may need systematic and prolonged assistance in providing a home environment that will foster the cognitive development of their children.

The evaluation of home instruction that has just been presented brings us back to points discussed at the beginning of this chapter, that is, Piaget's views on cognitive development. Because he believes that children are born with tendencies to assimilate, accommodate, and form schemes, Piaget recommends that children be allowed to move through the early stages of cognitive development without being "pushed" by parents or teachers. In evaluating Piaget's views on instruction, though, it may be helpful to recall that he based his theories on observations of the behavior of his own children and of Swiss children who came from the equivalent of upper- and middle-class American homes. If a child is routinely exposed to many objects and experiences and has abundant opportunities to interact verbally with parents, it may be reasonable to expect that cognitive development will occur without instruction. But if the child does not have sufficient opportunities to assimilate, accommodate, and form schemes, it may be essential for parents and teachers to try to make up for a sterile environment.

Regardless of how rich a child's environment is, though, parents should not lose sight of the potential value of play. It is possible that the cognitive development of a child might be fostered more by an hour's worth of play with (or even without) age-mates than by an hour-long lesson presented by parents.

Play and Playthings

When children are allowed to engage in self-selected play activities they have opportunities to discover many things at their own pace and in their own way. In

Two-year-olds seem to prefer realistic toys, perhaps because such familiar objects are easier to re-late to existing schemes. Older children often get a great deal of enjoyment out of "abstract" toys, perhaps because they enjoy expanding and embellishing conceptions they have already formed. Constantine Manos © 1967/Magnum; Guy Gillette/Photo Researchers.

Play makes it possible for children to experiment without risk

contrast to formal instruction (at home or in school), self-initiated play makes it possible for a child to explore and experiment without risk. If a child cannot answer a question or carry out a task presented by a parent or teacher, tension may develop. The child may feel inferior or inadequate and become reluctant to try new tasks for fear of failure. But in a play situation there is usually no pressure to produce a particular result and no concern about failure if an intended outcome does not occur. A "wrong" response, in fact, may trigger a new and unexpected way of doing things.

It appears that aspects of the play of two- to five-year-olds are related to habituation in infants. Just as a six-month-old baby becomes bored by a stimulus that is continued for a period of time and perks up when a new stimulus is presented, preschool-age children respond to novelty. They also seem to respond favorably to objects and situations that represent manageable complexity (Berlyne, 1966), as well as to incongruity. Furthermore, just as infants may be more inclined to respond to a few objects in a crib rather than a baffling abundance of objects (as noted in Chapter 6), two- to five-year-olds may be bothered by too much complexity and variety. Two-year-olds, for instance, seem to prefer realistic toys to those that are less familiar (Fein and Robertson, 1975). It is not until they reach the end of the preschool years that children show a preference for "abstract" toys. Such reactions might be interpreted with reference to Piaget's theory. Two-year-olds, who have a comparatively limited repertoire of schemes, may prefer realistic toys because they are easier to relate to existing schemes. Older children, who have had many more opportunities to assimilate and accommodate, may welcome new objects and enjoy expanding, revising, and embellishing conceptions they have formed. If parents and teachers make toys and experiences available to children, the child is able to make the choice of what to play with and how to respond. But if adults turn a game into a test by asking a child to demonstrate proficiency, anxiety may occur, particularly if the play situation is too complex for the child to handle.

Preschoolers prefer novelty, manageable complexity, incongruity in play

Encouraging Creativity and Fantasy

Because they are egocentric thinkers who are not acutely aware of what others are thinking, two- to five-year-olds are usually not self-conscious. As a result, most of them enjoy engaging in role playing and acting out fantasies. While many children are able to engage in creative play by inventing their own plots—or improve on those seen on television—some may need assistance in getting started. J. T. Freyberg (1973) selected a group of disadvantaged children classified as low fantisizers and showed them how they could use objects such as pipe cleaners and blocks to create imaginative adventures. After eight of these demonstration sessions most of the children were rated higher on imaginative play than control group children who had not been exposed to such training.

Children can learn to engage in imaginative play

A different approach to encouraging fantasy in children has been developed by Richard de Mille (1967). He is eager to encourage children to engage in fantasy, but he also feels that it is important for them to learn to distinguish between imagination and reality. De Mille observes that sometimes in childhood there seems to be a war between reality and imagination. On the one side are young children letting their imaginations run free. On the other side are adults insisting that reality must be acknowledged. De Mille suggests that since much can be said for either side, parents and teachers should strive to arrange situations so that imagination and reality can coexist. He observes, "Distinctions between reality and imagination are necessary, and it is important that they be learned. But it is also important to teach the distinctions in a way that does not turn off the imagination" (1967, p. 4). In *Put Your Mother on the Ceiling,* he describes thirty games to be played by an adult and a child. The games are built around statements made and questions asked by the adult. The game referred to in the title, for example, starts out with the adult saying "Mother could climb up a ladder and touch the ceiling, couldn't she? I think so. But could she stand on the ceiling? I never heard of a mother doing that." Then, the adult asks a series of questions intended to encourage the child to imagine that mother is standing on the ceiling—and to do all manner of things. The questions are arranged to help the child gradually move from reality to fantasy.

Here is a sample of the kinds of statements the adult is asked to read. (For the sake of brevity, not all of the questions in a particular sequence are included. The / after each question indicates a pause during which the child either silently imagines something or responds verbally.)

"Let us imagine that Mother is standing right there (pointing). / Let's give Mother a hat. What color hat will you give her? / What color dress will you give her? / All right, change the color of her hat. / . . . Change the color of her dress. / Have her go into another room. / . . . Have her riding on an elephant. / . . . Have her riding on a spaceship to the moon. / . . . Have her walking on the bottom of the ocean. / What would you like to have Mother do now? / " (pp. 63–67)

After the child has been given ample time to have Mother do other things, the adult asks "What was the name of the game we just played?" to signal that fantasy time is over and that it is time to return to the world of reality.

How Critical Are the Years from Two to Five?

In these last two chapters you have read about types of behavior and interrelationships that occur during the years from two to five that may have a profound influence on later behavior. But as the brief comments on differences between preschool and elementary school curricula suggest, exprience that occur between the years from six to twelve may divert the course of development in crucial ways.

At the end of Chapter 7 you were asked to postpone making a decision about the hypothesis that infancy is the most crucial stage in development until you learned about the two- to five-year-old. Perhaps some of the sections you have read in these two chapters have convinced you of the value of examining evidence regarding later age levels. Before you make a decision about how critical the two- to five-year period is, therefore, you will want to take into account aspects of development during the years from six to twelve. These will be discussed in the next two chapters.

Suggestions for Further Study

Piagetian Experiments: Preoperational to Concrete Operational Thought

An excellent way to gain greater understanding of Piaget's description of cognitive development is to carry out some of his clinical interviews. To grasp differences between preoperational and concrete operational thought, ask a child in the four- to seven-year-age range to play the following "games" with you. (It would be even better if you compare the performance of a four-year-old and a seven-year-old.) The simple experiments described below can be carried out with easily obtained "equipment" and should take no more than a few minutes. Begin by asking the age of your subject. (It would be prudent to verify this with a parent or teacher.) Next, explain that you would like her or him to play a few games with you. Then, follow instructions provided below. (Note: if your subject is completely baffled by the first problem, you might avoid confusion and frustration by not presenting the more difficult problems, and you might then select a slightly older subject.)

Conservation of Number

Purpose: To discover if the child grasps that the number of objects in a row remains the same even if the distance between them is changed. Children of four or so will be unable to decenter and are likely to say that a longer row has more blocks—even though they can count the blocks in both rows. Older children will be able to understand that the number is constant, even when the appearance of the blocks is changed.

Equipment: Twenty blocks, poker chips, or the equivalent.

Procedure: Place the blocks (or whatever) in front of the child and space out eight of the blocks about an inch apart in a row. Place the remaining blocks in a pile close to the child. Then say: "Can you count the blocks? How many are there?" (Point to the blocks you have arranged in a row. If the child cannot count them accurately, give assistance.) Then say: "Now take as many of these blocks as you need to make the same number." (Give assistance if necessary.) Describe how the child proceeds.

Next, take the blocks in the row nearest you and space them about three inches apart. Take those in the other row and space them about one inch apart. Point to the longer row and say: "Let's say these are my blocks" (point to the long row) "and these are your blocks" (point to the short row). "Do I have more blocks, or do you have more blocks, or do we have the same?" Record the child's response.

Then ask: "Why do you think so?" Record the child's response.

Finally, take the blocks which were spaced three inches apart and move them so that they are one inch apart, just below the other row. Then say: "Now, do you have more blocks, or do I have more blocks, or do we have the same?" Note the child's response and reaction: (Does the child seem surprised, bothered, unimpressed?)

Conservation of Area

Purpose: To discover how the child handles a different situation involving conservation. A child who is able to handle the problem presented in the preceding experiment may encounter difficulty when confronted with the same basic problem presented in a different form. In solving the conservation of number problem the child must grasp the fact that the number of blocks stays the same even though the space between them is changed. In this experiment the child must understand that four blocks placed on pieces of paper of equal size take up the same amount of space, even though they are arranged differently.

Equipment: Eight small blocks, poker chips, or the equivalent; two pieces of paper or cardboard at least eight-and-a-half by eleven inches.

Procedure: Place the two pieces of paper in front of the child, and arrange the blocks in a pile to one side. Say: "Let's pretend these are fields owned by two farmers. They are exactly the same size, and each farmer has the same amount of space for cows to graze in. One farmer decides to build a barn" (you might say "silo" if you use poker chips), "and we will make believe this is the barn." (Take one of the blocks and place it near one corner of one piece of paper.) "The other farmer builds a barn, too." (Put a block on the other piece of paper in the same position as that on the first.) "Do they still have the same amount of space for their cows to graze in?" Record the child's response.

Then say: "Now let's suppose that both farmers make a lot of money and build three more barns. One farmer's barns are built this way" (place three blocks right next to the block already on one sheet of paper), "the other's barns are built this way" (place three blocks several inches apart at different places on the other piece of paper). "Do they still have the same amount of space for their cows to graze in, or does one farmer have more space than the other?" Record the child's response.

Then ask: "Why do you think so?" Record the child's response.

Finally, take the blocks which were scattered and place them together so that both sets of blocks are arranged in exactly the same way on each piece of paper. Then ask: "Now, does each farmer have the same amount of space for cows to graze in, or does one have more space than the other?" Note the child's response and his or her reaction.

Conservation of Continuous Quantity

Purpose: To discover if a child who can understand conservation of number can also grasp conservation of quantity. Children at the level of concrete operations may be unable to generalize from the block experiment and will solve the following problem only if they have had sufficient experience with liquids in glasses of different size.

Equipment: Two plastic or glass tumblers of the same size, one plastic or glass bowl or vase (or a tall, thin tumbler).

Procedure: Pour water into one of the equal-sized tumblers until it is about two-thirds full, into the other until about one-third full. Put these down in front of the child and say: "Is there more water in this glass (point to one), "or this one" (point to the other), "or are they the same?" Record the child's response.

Then, pour water from the fuller glass into the emptier one until they are equal and ask: "What about now? Is there more water in this glass" (point to one), "or this glass" (point to the other), "or are they the same?" Record the child's response.

(A child who says one has more water can be encouraged to pour liquid back and forth from one glass into the other until satisfied that they are the same.)

Next, empty the water from one glass into the bowl (or vase) and ask: "Is there more water in this one" (point to the full glass), "or this one" (point to the bowl or vase), "or do they contain the same amount of water?" Record the child's response.

Then ask: "Why do you think so?"

Finally, pour the water from the bowl or vase back into the glass and ask: "Now, is there more water in this glass" (point to one), "or this glass" (point to the other), "or are they the same?" Note the child's response and reaction.

Conservation of Substance

Purpose: To discover if a child understands that the amount of a substance remains the same even though its shape is changed. The child who is unable to decenter will concentrate on only one quality and, therefore, will be unable to grasp that the amount stays constant. The older child will be able to allow for both qualities at once and will be able mentally to *reverse* the action which changed the shape of the substance, showing the capability of dealing with *operations*. However, difficulty may be experienced in dealing with an abstract (not actually present) situation of a similar type, indicating that the child is at the level of *concrete operations*.

Equipment: A small amount of plasticene or clay.

Procedure: Take a piece of plasticene or clay and divide it as equally as possible.

Roll the pieces into two balls and ask the child if the two are the same size. If the answer is that one is bigger than the other, ask the child to remove as much as necessary from the larger ball until satisfied that they are identical. Then take one ball, roll it into a sausage shape and ask: "Is there more clay here" (point to ball), "or here" (point to sausage), "or do they both have the same amount of clay?" Record the child's response.

Then ask: "Why do you think so?"

Then, roll the sausage shape back into a ball and ask: "Is there more clay here" (point to one ball), "or here" (point to the other ball), "or are they the same?" Note the child's response and reaction.

Then say: "Suppose I put these two pieces on two scales. Would this piece be heavier, or this piece, or would they be just as heavy?" Record the child's response.

Then, roll one ball into a sausage shape and ask: "What would happen if I weighed these now? Would this one" (point to ball) "or this one" (point to sausage) "be heavier, or would one be as heavy as the other?" Record the child's response.

Then ask: "Why do you think so?"

Early Language Development

If you would like to learn more about language development, one of the best sources of information is *A First Language: The Early Stages* (1973) by Roger Brown. More recent books on language development include *Language and Maturation* (1977) by Paula Menyuk; *Psychology and Language* (1977) by H. H. and E. V. Clark; *Language Development and Language Disorders* (1978) by Lois Bloom and M. Lahey; *Readings in Language Development* (1978), edited by Lois Bloom; *Early Language* (1979) by P. and J. de Villiers.

A Piagetian interpretation of early language development is offered by E. L. Moerk in "Piaget's Research as Applied to the Explanation of Language Development" in *Merrill-Palmer Quarterly*, 1975, **21**, 151–169. Techniques parents might use to encourage language development are described by Moerk in "Processes of Language Training in the Interaction of Mother-Child Dyads" in *Child Development*, 1976, **47**, 1064–1078.

Recording the Speech of Young Children

A different way to gain insight into language development is to keep a record of the utterances of a young child. Subjects two to three years of age are probably the best to choose, since this is a period when children are beginning to use language extensively but without complete awareness of adult sentence structure. Record (on a tape recorder or in writing) everything children of different ages say on several different occasions and analyze their utterances in terms of such factors as consistency in grammar, parts of speech used, pivot words, and other characteristics that attract your attention. You might also compare the speech you have recorded with the utterances of two- and three-year-olds recorded by Brown and Bellugi in an article in *Harvard Educational Review*, 1964, **34**, 133–151, or to descriptions of early language provided by Brown on pages 63–111 of his *A First Language* (1973).

Nature and Measurement of Intelligence

An excellent concise account of theories, tests, and the nature of intelligence is provided by Nancy Bayley in "Development of Mental Abilities," Chapter 16 (pp. 1163–1209) in Volume I of *Carmichael's Manual of Child Psychology* (3rd ed., 1970), edited by Paul H. Mussen. More detailed analyses of intelligence and its measurement can be found in *The Nature of Human Intelligence* (1967) by J. P. Guilford; *Psychological Testing* (4th ed., 1976) by Anne Anastasi; and *Essentials of Psychological Testing* (3rd ed., 1970) by Lee J. Cronbach.

A comprehensive collection of articles on the development of intelligence, issues of measurement, and analyses of conceptual processes is provided in *Intellectual Development* (1971), edited by Pauline S. Sears.

Cognitive Style

A comprehensive analysis of cognitive styles is presented in *Individuality in Learning* (1976) by Samuel Messick and associates.

Play

Discussions of the role of play in development are presented in *Child's Play* (1971), edited by R. E. Herron and B. Sutton-Smith; *The Child's World of Make-Believe: Experimental Studies of Imaginative Play* (1973), edited by J. L. Singer; *Play and Education: The Basic Tool for Early Childhood Learning* (1979) by O. Weininger; *Play: Its Role in Development and Evolution* (1976), edited by J. S. Bruner, A. Jolly, and K. Sylva; and *Play* (1977) by Katherine Garvey.

PART FIVE

SIX TO TWELVE

This part consists of two chapters: Chapter 10, "Six to Twelve: From Family to School"; and Chapter 11, "Six to Twelve: Cognitive and Moral Development."

Theorists whose work is summarized in Chapter 3 consider the following types of behavior and relationships with others to be of significance during the years from six to twelve:

□ Freud: Latency period. Children tend to identify with the parent of the same sex. Libidinal energy is not attached to any part of the body or any particular person.

□ Erikson: Industry versus inferiority. Children should be encouraged to do things and be praised for their accomplishments.

□ Piaget: Concrete operational stage. Children become capable of mentally re-versing actions but can solve problems only by generalizing from concrete experiences.

□ Sears: Phase III. When a child enters school, behavior may be shaped as much by the responses of teachers and classmates as by parents. The child identifies with and imitates selected adults and peers.

KEY POINTS

Six to Twelve as a Crystallization Period
Stable traits: passivity; aggressiveness in males; dependency in females

Sex Differences in Growth and Behavior
Well-established sex differences: girls more verbal; boys better in math, more aggressive
Some evidence that boys more dominant, curious; girls more fearful, compliant
Until puberty, girls and boys equal in strength
Growth spurt in girls two years earlier than in boys
Physically advanced boys more popular, better adjusted

The Influence of Parents and Other Adults
Boys from father-absent homes may fail to acquire masculine traits, be immature
Single parent may have economic problems, be forced to play multiple roles
Working mothers may be more satisfied, serve as appropriate model
Sons of working mothers may have conflict with fathers, be underachievers

The Influence of Siblings and Peers
First-born children more achievement-oriented, may experience more stress
First-born children may benefit from acting as "teachers"
Roles established as early as first grade

The Emergence of a Concept of Self
Successfully doing things beside and with others leads to a sense of industry
Attempts to be successful and popular may lead to conflicts

Problems of Adjusting to Independent Existence
Academic achievement of elementary school children compared to others
Elementary school children acquire roles in unsupervised play situations
Elementary school children expected to obey rules, may experience guilt

Extent and Nature of Behavior Disorders
Clinic referral rates highest in 9-to-15-year span
Some children must cope with more risk factors than others
Early success may mislead; early problems may strengthen

Views of Adjustment
Defense mechanisms protect ego
Repression as explanation of abnormal behavior
Learning-theory view of adjustment: abnormal tendencies shaped by reinforcement
Using behavior modification to control nervous habits
Child must feel comfortable, secure, and loved before experiencing urges to know and appreciate

CHAPTER 10

SIX TO TWELVE:
FROM FAMILY TO SCHOOL

The age spans covered in earlier chapters have been chosen to mark transition points in development. From conception to birth, development takes place in the mother's body; during the first month after birth, the neonate adjusts to independent existence; the period from two months to two years is characterized by initial mastery of locomotor ability, language, and thought; from two to five, children gain considerable control over their bodies, organize their thoughts into quite complex patterns, become capable of using adult forms of language, engage in initial interactions with those outside the home, and experience emotion aroused by other than physical stimuli. The sixth and twelfth years have been selected to mark the age span discussed in this (and the next) chapter for several reasons.

Six to Twelve as a Crystallization Period

During the elementary school years physical maturation and growth lead to significant changes in appearance and behavior. Children grow rapidly and the proportions of the various parts of the body alter to make twelve-year-olds appear much more mature than six-year-olds. Differences in the physiques of males and females become more noticeable, and girls who reach puberty before they leave the sixth grade become directly aware of biological differences between the sexes. Physical changes, in turn, influence social relationships between boys and girls, and also have an impact on emerging concepts of self.

In Freud's view of development, this is the latency period—a time when the libido is not concentrated on any particular part of the body or person, as it was during the oral, anal, and phallic stages. In Erikson's conception of development, these years mark the stage of industry versus inferiority. In Piaget's description of intellectual development, between six and twelve the child achieves mastery of concrete operations and may begin to engage in formal thought. For Sears, this is Phase III; when a child enters school behavior is shaped by teachers and peers, particularly through the processes of identification and imitation.

The importance of this age span has been stressed by Jerome Kagan and Howard A. Moss (1962). Using data accumulated by previous researchers at the Fels Institute, they analyzed the impact of parent-child relationships on the personality development of forty-five females and forty-four males. They traced development not only to the age of five (as was the case with the studies of parent-child relationships mentioned in Chapter 7) but until their subjects were adolescents and adults. Extremely detailed information was available on all of these individuals up to the age of fourteen. Supplementary data were obtained for seventy-one of the eighty-nine in a five-hour interview and battery of tests administered when they were between nineteen and twenty-nine years of age.

Stable traits: passivity; aggressiveness in males; dependency in females

In analyzing this rich accumulation of data, Kagan and Moss paid special attention to stability of behavior. They found that children rated as passive as early as the age of two retained this characteristic to such an extent that they concluded it was apparently due to biological factors. Other traits that appeared to be stable were aggressiveness in males and dependency in females. Kagan and Moss suggested that these traits might be traced to constitutional variables that are later reinforced by "behavioral rules promoted by the child's culture" (p. 119). There were several traits, however, that were characterized as much by change as by stability.

Perhaps the most significant conclusion of Kagan and Moss was based on their discovery that for many traits elementary school behavior was a better predictor of adult behavior than preschool behavior. This led them to conclude that the first four years of school (the years from six to ten) are a critical period in development in that they "crystallize behavioral tendencies that are maintained through young adulthood" (p. 272).

Each of the types of behavior mentioned in this introduction will be examined in this chapter. First, the impact of physical development on behavior will be summarized. This will be followed by analyses of the impact of identification with parents (and older siblings and other adults) and the impact of interactions with peers. Next, the significance of Erikson's stage of industry versus inferiority will be discussed, leading to an analysis of related observations by Karen Horney. Then, differences between the kinds of behavior expected of preschool and elementary school children will be summarized to call attention to the number of adjustments children must make during the years from six to twelve. The following section features an outline of the frequency and nature of behavior disorders that may appear when children experience problems in making such adjustments. The chapter concludes with brief comments on psychoanalytic, learning-theory, and third-force explanations of the process of adjustment.

Sex Differences in Growth and Behavior

Visiting an elementary school and comparing kindergarten pupils with fifth and sixth graders will make you immediately aware of the rapid rate of growth that occurs between the ages of six and twelve. You are likely to be impressed by the physical energy of five- and six-year-olds. But you may also notice that, while differences in height and weight certainly exist, it is difficult to pick out the biggest and smallest pupils. This is not likely to be the case when you observe fifth and sixth graders. Differences in the size and shape of twelve-year-old children may be so extreme that you may wonder if it is possible that they were all born within twelve months of each other. One reason fifth and sixth graders vary so much in size is that they have moved a significant way toward achieving their ultimate adult height. In addition, the proportions of the various parts of the body of a twelve-year-old come quite close to those of a mature individual. This has occurred because the arms and legs have grown at a more rapid rate than other parts of the body during the preceding five years. These changes make differences in size and build more apparent.

Relationships Between Puberty and Sex-typing

The average age of sexual maturity for American girls is between twelve and thirteen years (Tanner, 1970), with a range from nine to sixteen years. For boys, the average age of puberty is fourteen years, with a range from eleven to eighteen years. Many American girls, therefore, reach puberty before they finish the sixth grade. The beginning of menstruation is bound to cause a girl to become aware of the implications of sexual maturity. She will not only begin to develop secondary sex characteristics that will cause her to appear more feminine, she may experience a changed attitude toward boys. If Money and Ehrhardt (1972) are correct in generalizing from the results of their studies of androgenized girls (summarized in Chapter 6), changes in the production of sex hormones at puberty will cause girls to think increasingly about romantic attachments, marriage, and having children. The interest of girls in the housewife-mother role, however, is also influenced by observation, imitation, and indoctrination.

Factors that begin to influence sex-typed behavior starting in the preschool years continue to shape behavior more intensely during the elementary school years. Cognitive awareness of male and female behavior which Kohlberg (1966) suggests is established by the age of five, becomes more pervasive. The observation and imitation of male and female models, which was demonstrated by Bandura and his colleagues (1963a), also continues. Furthermore, many elementary school texts and other books depict boys and girls engaging in different activities. C. Tavris and C. Offir (1977), for example, describe the results of a survey of children's books carried out in 1972: "Boys make things. They rely on their wits to solve problems. They are curious, clever, and adventurous. They achieve; they make money. Girls and women are incompetent and fearful. They ask other people to solve their problems for them. . . . In story after story, girls are the onlookers, the cheerleaders" (p. 177).

The impact of such indoctrination was revealed in interviews carried out by W. R. Looft (1971). Looft asked first and second graders what they would like to be when they grew up. Of the thirty-three boys who responded, nine chose football player and four chose policeman. Less frequent nominations went to doctor, dentist, priest, pilot, and astronaut. Of the thirty-three girls who responded, fourteen chose nurse, eleven chose teacher. Less frequently mentioned were mother, stewardess, and salesgirl. *One* girl said she would like to be a doctor.

Starting in the early 1970s various feminist groups encouraged school districts to select texts that did not reinforce such sex stereotypes. But children still read other books and watch television for several hours a day. (In a survey made in 1974, Sternglanz and Serbin reported that males on television programs were portrayed as aggressive, constructive, and helpful; females as deferential and passive.) Although many television series now feature women who possess traits equal to or exceeding those of the most daring, brilliant, and resourceful men (or supermen), it is possible that commercials may at least partially counteract the impact of such shows. Many of the women depicted in commercials are primarily interested in making themselves attractive to males. Even more are made to appear singlemindedly dedicated to cleaning house, washing clothes, and generally making life as comfortable as possible for husbands and children.

To determine if the women's liberation movement had overcome some of the influence of "sexist" books, television commercials, and the like on career choices, R. F. Biehler repeated the Looft survey (extending it through the sixth grade) in 1979. The career choices of children attending a middle-income elementary school in a medium-sized California city are indicated in Table 10–1. As you can see, by the end of the 1970s girls appear to have overcome many sex-stereotyped ideas about careers for women. Only one girl specified "housekeeping" (which may or may not be the same as "homemaker"), and only one mentioned being a mother, and both of these girls took pains to point out that they intended to

Table 10–1

Career Choices of Elementary School Children

	BOYS	GIRLS
1st Grade	Professional athlete (or coach) 6 Race car driver 5 Police officer 4 Truck driver 3 Construction worker 3 Mechanic, fireman, tree trimmer, welder, computer operator, diamond worker, balloon man at the zoo	Nurse 10 Teacher 7 Ballerina 2 Policewomen 2 Ice skater, person who sells cosmetics
2nd Grade	Motorcycle racer 6 Scientist 5 Professional athlete 4 Police officer 4 Truck driver 2 UPS driver 2 Artist 2 Astronaut 2 Inventor 2 Pilot, cowboy, coffee maker, store clerk, little boy	Teacher 5 Ice skater 4 Artist 3 Jockey 2 Archaeologist, nutritionist, dancer, missionary, ice cream store owner, plant nursery owner, don't know
3rd Grade	Professional athlete 2 Lawyer 2 Doctor, architect, business manager, spy, house builder, physics (fisecx) teacher, army officer, chef, fence builder	Teacher 5 Gymnast 2 Movie actress 2 Nurse 2 Veterinarian 2 Horse trainer 2 Artist, college professor, jockey, ice skater, donut maker, zoo keeper, dental assistant, housekeeper (and artist), paleontologist (and baseball player and mother)
4th Grade	Professional athlete 7 Police officer 5 Truck driver 4 Builder 2	Nurse 9 Teacher 6 Veterinarian 4 Stewardess 3

Table 10–1

Career Choices of Elementary School Children

	BOYS	GIRLS
4th Grade (cont'd)	Race car driver 2 Stuntman 2 Scientist 2 Fireman 2 Cowboy, lumberjack, sky diver, photographer, meter reader, detective, my self	Secretary 2 Singer 2 Movie star 2 Gymnast 2 Dancer, jockey, dental assistant, scientist, nutritionist, plant nursery owner, president (or doctor)
5th Grade	Professional athlete 4 Truck driver 2 Police officer 2 Cartoonist 2 Race car driver, motorcycle racer, driver of street sweeper, bus driver, Air Force pilot, artist, doctor, lawyer, owner of a Mercedez Benz, actor, cabinetmaker, glass blower, space scientist, I think I am too young to know	Teacher 9 Actress, model, singer 5 Veterinarian 4 Jockey 2 Psychologist 2 Lawyer, hairdresser, horse trainer, scientist, nurse, head waitress, athlete, rancher, nuclear scientist, piano teacher
6th Grade	Professional athlete 7 Police officer 3 Architect 3 Veterinarian 2 Contractor 2 Racing car driver, engineer, doctor, demolition expert, forest ranger, artist, author, astronomer, movie star, Playboy photographer	Veterinarian 4 Stewardess 4 Horse trainer 2 Artist 2 Surgeon, nurse, scientist, teacher, model, mechanic, pilot, policewoman, lawyer (and hairdresser on the side), beautician (butishion), owner of an answering service

Source: Unpublished study by R. F. Biehler. Information collected by Lotys Gibb and the teachers of Citrus Elementary School, Chico, California.

pursue a career as well. While teacher and nurse are still popular choices for girls at the end of the 1970s, they also express interest in a wide variety of other occupations, including many that were traditionally considered to be men's jobs (for example, nuclear scientist). Being a professional athlete is the most popular choice for boys, which is probably traceable to the impact of televised sports coverage.

Thus, some of the same general trends reported by Looft in 1971 still seem to prevail in 1979. The interest of girls in teaching and nursing careers might be attributed as much to mature and realistic appraisals of career opportunities, though, as to the impact of sex stereotypes. In terms of actual job opportunities, particularly for females who hope to combine motherhood and a career, teaching and nursing are very sensible choices. The career choices of boys, by contrast, are much less realistic and seem to reflect a romanticized conception of the "Macho" image. Only a tiny proportion of the elementary school boys who aspire to play professional football or make a living racing motorcycles, for instance, will actually pursue those careers. The hypothesis that girls are more realistic is supported by the greater tendency for them to "hedge their bets." Girls in 1979 were more likely than boys (by a ratio of about five to one) to say that they wanted to be, for example, an actress *or* a beautician.

Varying Conclusions Regarding Sex-typed Behavior

Since sex-typed behavior becomes more apparent in the elementary school years than at earlier stages of development, this is an appropriate place to summarize research and conclusions relating to differences in the behavior of males and females. One of the most complete summaries of research on sex differences was carried out by Eleanor Maccoby and Carol Jacklin (1974), who examined 1,600 studies published between 1966 and 1973. They summarized their conclusions (pp. 349–352) under three headings, as follows:

☐ Well-established differences: Girls excel in verbal ability. Boys excel in visual-spatial ability and mathematical ability, and are more aggressive.

☐ Types of behavior where there is insufficient evidence to clearly establish sex differences: Tactile sensitivity; fear, timidity, and anxiety; activity level; competitiveness; dominance; compliance; nurturance and "maternal" behavior.

☐ Types of behavior where the evidence suggests that no sex differences exist: Sociability, suggestibility, self-esteem, complex cognitive abilities, ability to analyze problems, relative impact of heredity and experiences on personality development, motivation toward achievement, auditory or visual orientation.

Well-established sex differences: girls more verbal; boys better in math, more aggressive

Maccoby and Jacklin also concluded that there was little evidence that parents treat girls and boys in different ways (p. 338).

Jeanne H. Block (1976) analyzed many of the same studies as Maccoby and Jacklin, as well as their interpretations, and came to some different conclusions. Block felt that some of the inferences made by Maccoby and Jacklin could be questioned for the following reasons (pp. 289–298): they may have been too demanding in deciding when evidence was conclusive or indicative of tentative differences; Maccoby and Jacklin did not take into account certain significant studies that might have altered some of their conclusions; many of the studies surveyed were done on preschool children whose sex-typed behavior is not clearly established.

After making her own analysis, Block concluded that there is some, although not conclusive, evidence that the following sex differences exist:

Some evidence that boys more dominant, curious; girls more fearful, compliant

- ☐ Boys are better at solving insight problems.
- ☐ Boys are more dominant and have a stronger, more potent, self-concept.
- ☐ Boys are more curious, active, and impulsive.
- ☐ Girls express more fear and are more susceptible to anxiety.
- ☐ Girls seek more help and reassurance.
- ☐ Girls are more compliant with adults (at early ages).

Even when an element of control is established, such as in the Money and Ehrhardt investigation of androgenized girls (summarized in Chapter 7), it is not possible to determine the causes of such types of behavior. Money and Ehrhardt suggest that the brain of each child is programmed to release hormones in certain ways. They believe that this accounts for some of the differences between the behavior of males and females. But all types of behavior are also shaped by observation of models, experiences, reinforcement, and cultural expectations. Maccoby and Jacklin did not find sufficient scientific evidence to support the view that parents treat boys and girls in different ways, but other researchers have come to different conclusions. Inge Broverman and several associates (1972), for example, summarized studies where adults were asked to describe their perceptions of "typical" masculine and feminine traits. Broverman and her colleagues found strong consensus from groups of respondents who differed in sex, age, religion, marital status, and educational level: typical masculine traits centered on competence, rationality, and assertiveness; typical feminine traits reflected warmth and expressiveness. Because these stereotyped conceptions were considered desirable to the majority of men and women from all types of backgrounds, it would seem reasonable to expect that boys and girls would be treated differently by their parents. The hypothesis that stereotyped views of masculinity and femininity lead to differential treatment of daughters and sons is supported, in fact, by a number of research investigations.

In her reanalysis of the research evaluated by Maccoby and Jacklin, Block concluded that the studies on which they based their conclusions regarding parental socialization practices featured very young children. Block also found that the measures used were inappropriate or too broadly defined. Support for Block's contention is provided by Beverly I. Fagot (1978) who observed pre-

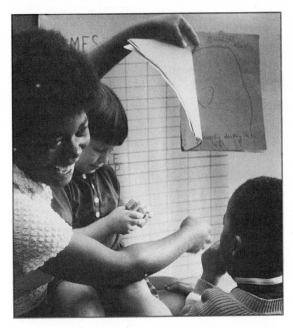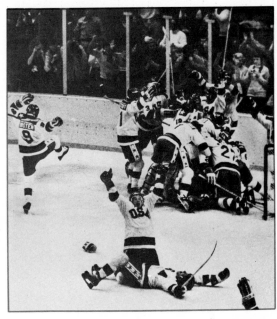

Girls in our society are socialized to learn interpersonal relationships, which may contribute to their interest in such careers as teaching and nursing. The socialization of boys, in contrast, emphasizes achievement and competition, which is reflected in the often unrealistic desire of elementary school boys to become professional athletes. Roger Malloch/Magnum; United Press International.

schoolers and their parents interacting in their homes. She concluded that parents often responded negatively when girls engaged in physical or athletic activities, but responded positively when girls engaged in dependent, adult-oriented behavior. She also found that girls asked for help three times more frequently than boys. Fagot speculates that the tendency for parents to respond positively to requests for help from girls, but not from boys, strengthens dependent behavior in girls and weakens it in boys. Furthermore, the parents themselves were not aware that they responded differently to daughter and son requests for help. Nor were the parents aware that they responded negatively when girls manipulated objects and that they permitted boys to explore more. Fagot concluded that it is only when the subtleties of parent-child interactions are taken into account that differences in socialization practices become clear.

In her reanalysis of studies of socialization, Block concluded that both mothers and fathers emphasize achievement, competition, and independence in boys and stress warmth and physical closeness in dealing with girls. In addition, parents seem to discourage rough-and-tumble play in daughters, are reluctant to punish them, and encourage them to think more about life. These conclusions reaffirmed observations Block had made in an earlier article on sex-typing. After reviewing studies of socialization practices, Block (1973) concluded that boys in our society are encouraged to achieve and be competitive, to control expression of feelings, and to conform to rules. Girls, on the other hand, are encouraged to develop close interpersonal relationships, talk about their troubles, show affection, and give comfort to others. (If you will reexamine Table 10–1 you will note that many of the occupational choices of elementary school boys center on achievement and competition and that many of the choices of girls reflect concern for others.)

In discussing the significance of the differential treatment of boys and girls in our society Block notes that compared to adults in other technological societies, Americans put more emphasis on sex-typing, with particular stress on competitive achievement in males. Americans also seem less concerned about controlling aggression in males. She points out that because of current trends in our society, it would be desirable for children to acquire a conception of sex roles that combine what are presently identified by many people as masculine *or* feminine traits. Boys would seem likely to benefit, for instance, if they became more sensitive to the needs of others. Many girls would benefit if they were encouraged to be less docile and more achievement-oriented. Block also suggests that too much stress on traditional sex-appropriate behavior inhibits introspection and self-evaluation and impedes the development of the ego and of social maturity. She concludes, however, that because of the extent to which sex stereotypes are entrenched in the minds of most Americans (as reported by Broverman and her associates) it may be difficult for children in our society, particularly girls, to develop flexible conceptions of sex-appropriate behavior. Accordingly, parents and teachers might make efforts to encourage elementary school children of both sexes to achieve a balance between self-assertiveness and concern for and relations with others.

Sex-related Changes in Physical Abilities and Development

Despite the impact of sex-role stereotypes, quite a few elementary school girls of the 1980s seem to have rejected the traditional view that they should be the embodiment of "sugar and spice and everything nice." An impressive number have discovered that they can compete successfully in many traditionally male activities. J. M. Tanner (1972, p. 5) reports that until adolescence girls and boys are equal in strength; around the ages of twelve and thirteen girls, on the average, have larger muscles than boys of the same age. Elementary school girls who have discovered that they can compete with boys on Little League teams and the like are personally aware of the strength factors described by Tanner. In fact, girls may have an advantage over boys of the same age because they grow at a more rapid rate. If you were to ask teachers of all the grades in an elementary school to have their pupils line up in order from shortest to tallest, you would become aware not only of increasing differences between extremes in height and variations in body build, but also that many girls would be at the tall end of the fifth- and

Until puberty, girls and boys equal in strength

Because the growth spurt of girls occurs about two years earlier than that of boys, the average eleven- to fourteen-year-old girl is taller than the average boy of the same age. Lawrence Fried/ Magnum.

sixth-grade lines. Many boys, however, would be at the tall end of all the other lines. This tendency for girls to be taller, starting around the fifth grade, is due to a growth spurt just before the advent of puberty. Because girls mature at a more rapid rate than boys, they experience their growth spurt about two years earlier (Tanner, 1970). Some girls begin their spurt as early as seven and one-half years, but the average age is eleven (Maresh, 1964). An eleven-year-old girl athlete who is a fast maturer may be two years ahead of male classmates in physical development and, because of her advanced maturity (coupled with skill), may surpass many boys of the same age in sports prowess.

Growth spurt in girls two years earlier than in boys

After a girl who has enjoyed being the star of a Little League team reaches puberty, however, she may need to accept a revision of her conception of male-female relationships. Physical changes that begin at the time of puberty will not only make her look more feminine, they will also place her at a physical disadvantage compared to most boys. After the growth spurt, the muscles in the average boy's body are larger, as are the heart and lungs. Furthermore, the body of the mature male has a greater capacity than that of the female for carrying oxygen to the blood and for neutralizing the chemical products of muscular exercise. All of these characteristics equip the average post-pubescent male with greater strength and endurance than the average post-pubescent female, which explains why most sports competition after the elementary school years is between members of the same sex.

Because of a combination of biological, physical, and cultural influences, most boys in American society place a great deal of emphasis on sports prowess.

(Elementary school boys mentioned professional athlete more frequently than any other career choice when asked in 1971 and 1979 what they wanted to be when they grew up.) Stress on sports begins in the elementary school years and continues through high school. Accordingly, most boys in our society want to engage in activities that permit them to demonstrate their strength and physical prowess. Paul H. Mussen and Mary Cover Jones (1957) analyzed data from the Berkeley Growth Study and found that boys who matured early and were physically advanced were more popular and better adjusted than slow-maturing, smaller, and weaker boys.

Physically advanced boys more popular, better adjusted

It appears that rate of maturation may not only have an impact on social behavior and personality but on cognitive development and academic performance as well. Early maturing girls, for example, seem to have a slight but significant advantage over late-maturing girls of the same chronological age on academic achievement tests (Tanner, 1962). While slow maturers of either sex may be at a disadvantage in certain areas of behavior, the more rapid maturation rate of females seems to give girls, on the average, quite pervasive advantages over boys. There is some evidence (Witelson and Pallie, 1973), for example, that selected structures of the left cerebral hemisphere of the brain, which is associated with language processing, are more mature in newborn girls than boys. If this advanced brain maturity of girls prevails throughout childhood, which is the case for more easily measured skeletal maturity, at least part of the verbal and language superiority of girls may be due to their more rapid rate of maturation. Language precocity, in turn, may help account for the fact that girls earn higher grades in school, on the average, than boys. The more rapid maturation rate of females may therefore equip them to cope with academic requirements more easily than boys of the same age. Factors such as these led Peter Wolff (1977, p. 17) to conclude that the higher incidence of behavioral disturbances in boys might be attributed, at least in part, to their slower rate of maturation.

These observations regarding the impact of height, physical maturity, and athletic ability on behavior and perceptions of self call attention to ways children acquire roles during the elementary school years. Some forms of behavior are established through interactions with or identification with parents, teachers, and other adults; other characteristic ways of reacting to experiences are shaped by interactions with siblings and peers. Each of these types of influence will be discussed separately.

The Influence of Parents and Other Adults

In Chapter 8, the beginning of the process of socialization was described. All of the factors that lead the preschool child to begin to acquire culturally accepted forms of behavior continue to exert an influence throughout the elementary school years. It seems reasonable to assume, for instance, that parents who function in authoritative, authoritarian, or permissive ways when dealing with two- to five-year-olds will use essentially the same basic approach in their interactions with six- to twelve-year-olds. Although the overall pattern of parent-child relationships will probably remain fairly stable, there are likely to be some modifications in specific techniques (for example, authoritarian parents may be less inclined to spank children as they grow older—and bigger). Furthermore, since the child will spend much of the day at school or playing with peers outside the home, the role of the mother as primary disciplinarian is likely to be altered. As children mature, the father may take an increasing amount of responsibility for handling problem behavior.

Children's Perceptions of Parents

Parent-child relationships have been studied in preschool children through use of techniques described in Chapter 8. The basic method involves rating child personality by observing three- to five-year-olds in free play with peers and comparing these with ratings of parental child-rearing practices based on interviews with parents or observations of them interacting with their children. When they enter first grade, children participate less frequently in free play that can be easily observed and rated. They are, however, mature enough and verbal enough to express their feelings about techniques of child rearing, particularly disciplinary techniques used by their mothers and fathers. J. A. Armentrout and G. K. Burger (1972) asked fourth- to eighth-graders to describe the kinds of control they felt their parents used. The children reported that their parents' use of threats to withhold love decreased steadily but that establishing and enforcing rules increased from the fourth to the sixth grade and then decreased. The researchers hypothesized that as parents recognize their children are becoming more autonomous, they make less use of techniques intended to make the child feel dependent on them. In place of such techniques of control, they substitute rule-making and limit-setting. Once control has been established, however, rules are relaxed to a certain extent.

This outline of children's perceptions of parents is based on the assumption that a typical family consists of mother, father, and children. Until recently this assumption dominated theories about the impact of identification, imitation, and modeling on child behavior. Freud's psychosexual stages, for example, describe shifts in identification with the mother or father depending on the sex of the child and the phase of development. Robert Sears' early investigations of child-parent relationships (1957, 1965) were based on a similar assumption that both parents would be available in the home for children to identify with. Subsequent studies by Sears (1972) and by other social learning theorists have revealed ways children learn sex-appropriate behavior by imitating models, particularly the mother *or* father, during the early years of their lives. In the 1980s, however, the traditional family pattern may not exist for almost half of all school-age children. Many American children now spend at least part of their school years living with one parent, primarily because of divorce. But even in homes where both parents are available as child rearers, the arrangement of mother as homemaker and father as breadwinner may no longer be typical because more and more women are becoming employed outside of the home. These two deviations from the traditional pattern will be discussed separately.

The Impact of Divorce

It is estimated that 40 to 50 percent of the children born in America in the 1970s and 1980s will spend an average of six years living in a single-parent home because of marital disruption. The great majority of these children will live with the mother, but about 10 percent of school-age children will live with the father (Glick and Norton, 1978). Many of these children will eventually reenter into a two-parent family involving a stepparent.

In a review of research, E. Mavis Hetherington (1979) stresses that in assessing the impact of divorce on a child it is important to take into account such factors as the timing of the divorce, the age of the child, the sex of the child, and the attitude of the divorced parents toward each other. The impact of divorce is greatest, for instance, immediately after the disruption of the family occurs. After the first year most children appear to adjust quite satisfactorily to living with only one parent. Young children, though, are less capable of evaluating the impact of divorce and may fail to comprehend their parents' needs, emotions, and behavior (often because of egocentric thinking). They may also be unable to evaluate prospects of reconciliation or harbor fears of total abandonment.

The impact of divorce appears to be more pervasive and enduring for boys than for girls, although girls from father-absent homes may experience difficulties interacting with males in adolescence (Hetherington, 1972). A basic explanation for this sex difference is that the father's leaving home (the most common pattern) deprives the boy of a male model. If the mother continues to be hostile and critical of the father after they separate, boys are particularly likely to experience difficulties. They may either fail to develop masculine traits or make exaggerated attempts to prove their masculinity, have problems relating to peers, and act in immature ways (Biller and Davids, 1973). When divorced mothers have a positive attitude toward ex-husbands (and other males), however, and encourage their sons to be independent and mature, no significant differences between the behavior of boys reared in father-present and father-absent homes are found (Hetherington, Cox, and Cox, 1977). This may be the case because fatherless boys may find adequate substitutes in older brothers, male teachers, youth-group leaders, and the like.

On the basis of his studies of modeling behavior, Albert Bandura concluded that "when children are exposed to multiple models they may select one or more

Boys from father-absent homes may fail to acquire masculine traits, be immature

About half of all American children spend several years living in single-parent homes because their parents are divorced. It appears that boys have a more difficult time adjusting to divorce than girls. One explanation is that they lack close contact with a male model. Arthur Grace/Stock, Boston.

of them as the primary source of behavior, but rarely reproduce all the elements of a single model's repertoire or confine their imitation to that model" (Bandura, Ross, and Ross, 1963a, p. 534). With the hundreds of male models available in the form of characters and sports figures seen on TV, acquaintances, and neighbors, it is not likely that absence of a father will always mean that a boy will fail to develop masculine traits. Even if a father is present, in fact, he may not serve as a significant model for masculine behavior. Paul H. Mussen and E. Rutherford (1963) found that there was little relationship between the masculinity-femininity scores of first-grade boys and the scores of their fathers.

While virtually all children appear to be upset during the first few months after a divorce takes place, they are likely to be better off in the long run if conflict between parents ceases to be an everyday occurrence. In her review Hetherington reports that consistent evidence shows that "children in single parent families function more adequately than children in conflict-ridden nuclear families" (1979, p. 855). Even so, there are a number of problems that the single parent must cope with. One of these is downward economic mobility due to the likelihood that the divorced mother who seeks employment may find that she is able to secure only low-paying part-time jobs. Another difficulty is traceable to the need for the single parent to try to play all of the roles that are split between mother and father in a nuclear family. In addition to the need for one person (in

Single parent may have economic problems, be forced to play multiple roles

many cases) to serve as caretaker, homemaker, *and* breadwinner, the single parent must also take sole responsibility for such matters as socialization and discipline. In a harmonious nuclear family mother and father can alternate in taking care of child-rearing problems, support and encourage each other, and serve as dual models for the child to imitate. (The positive traits of one parent may offset some of the negative traits of the other and vice versa.)

This summary of research findings on the impact of divorce leads to the conclusion that if parents do feel obliged to separate they can minimize the negative impact of divorce on their children by maintaining reasonably cordial (or at least neutral) rather than hostile relations with each other. As Hetherington notes, a child may be better off living in a single-parent home than in a conflict-ridden two-parent home. This may not be the case, however, if the parents are still in active conflict after they terminate their marriage.

The Impact of Maternal Employment

As noted in the discussion of day care in Chapter 7, at the present time over half of all America's mothers who live with their husbands and have school-age children are employed. Employment rates are even higher for mothers in single-parent families. Chapter 9 presented research evidence demonstrating that the development of preschool-age children does not seem to suffer if the mother works and that there may be certain advantages to maternal employment. What applies at the preschool level continues to apply during the elementary school years.

After reviewing studies of the impact of maternal employment on child development Lois Wladis Hoffman (1979) noted that there are a number of positive factors that may operate when a mother has a job outside of the home. First of all (as noted in Chapter 9) working mothers report that they are more satisfied with their lives, on the average, than nonworking mothers. Second, a working mother may serve as a more appropriate model for her children by exemplifying contemporary views of the feminine role and thus contradicting the outdated expectation that women should spend most of their lives as homemakers. Related to this point, school-age children are often expected to take household responsibilities when the mother works. Taking such responsibilities, in turn, often means that the home runs more smoothly when either or both parents are absent and that children learn to become more independent and to develop self-esteem. Finally, it appears that daughters of working mothers admire them more than do daughters of nonworking mothers and are more likely to become higher achievers later in life.

Hoffman notes, though, that the impact of maternal employment on the behavior of boys is not as uniformly favorable as it is for girls. In some studies boys of working mothers have been rated above average in social and personality adjustment. But boys from lower-class families may experience a strain in father-son relationships when the mother works. Apparently, the fact that she has

Working mothers may be more satisfied, serve as appropriate model

a job implies that the father is a failure. There is also some evidence that in middle-class homes the sons of working mothers may be somewhat below average in intellectual functioning and in academic achievement. Hoffman notes that on the basis of available data it is not possible to trace the cause of this slight decrease in the cognitive behavior of sons of working mothers. Perhaps future research might indicate that while middle-class boys may not exhibit strained relationships with their fathers (as is the case with lower-class boys), they may be less likely to view the father as a highly competent person when the mother works. (This might be especially true if the mother has a "better" job than the father.) Failure to think of males as competent might cause boys to be less motivated to achieve.

Sons of working mothers may have conflict with fathers, be underachievers

Even though there are certain exceptions, then, the general conclusion regarding the impact of maternal employment on the school-age child seems to be that in most cases it is not likely to cause excessive negative behavior and that in some instances it may lead to positive forms of behavior.

The Influence of Siblings and Peers

The Impact of Birth Order and Siblings

The behavior of the child after entering school may be influenced not only by how parents establish and enforce discipline in the home, by the presence or absence of the father, and by the fact that the mother has a job, but also by relationships with siblings. Helen Koch (1956) studied nearly four hundred five- and six-year-olds from two-child families and analyzed aspects of family constellations. She found that, compared to girls with older sisters, girls with older brothers were aggressive and tomboyish; compared to boys with older brothers, boys with older sisters were less aggressive and daring. These findings suggest that older siblings serve as models that influence the behavior of their younger brothers and sisters.

A substantial number of studies of the significance of birth order have been carried out. The results are often difficult to evaluate because of the number of possible combinations of siblings and also because of the difficulty of taking into account such factors as genetic differences, family size, spacing of children, socioeconomic status, and special conditions, such as preference of parents for a particular child. Even so, some trends are apparent. First-born children are rated as more achievement-oriented (Altus, 1966) and more cooperative, responsible, and more conforming to social pressures (Becker, Lerner, and Carroll, 1966). They are also more likely to experience guilt feelings (Cobb, 1943) and to encounter psychological problems (Garner and Wenar, 1959). It should be stressed that these are *trends;* many of the great achievers of history were

First-born children more achievement-oriented, may experience more stress

later-born children, and many first-born children do not possess any of the characteristics just noted. Furthermore, after carrying out a review of dozens of studies, C. Schooler (1972) concluded that "The general lack of consistent findings [regarding birth order effects] leaves real doubt whether the chance of positive results is worth the heavy investment needed to carry out definitive studies" (p. 174).

A number of explanations have been proposed to account for differences between first- and later-born children. One hypothesis (White, Kaban, and Attanucci, 1979) is that parents spend more time with first-born children and also engage in more language interchanges with them than they do with later-born children. Parents may also be eager to prove to themselves and others that they are skillful and capable child rearers and may instill in the child a strong need for achievement. When a second child joins the family, the parents are likely to be more relaxed, consistent, and confident about child rearing and less likely to feel compelled to prove themselves.

Another hypothesis (Schachter, 1959) is that first-born or only children will have greater exposure to adult models and will pattern and evaluate their behavior with reference to adult standards, which are not only more demanding but also more consistent than the behavioral standards of siblings. While this may be true during the preschool years, it would seem that as soon as children enter school they would be more likely to evaluate themselves, and be evaluated, with reference to peers. Perhaps tendencies established during the preschool years will be maintained, but a switch to peer standards may be more likely.

Still another hypothesis is that the first-born child will feel driven to regain the parents' undivided attention enjoyed before brothers and sisters entered the family. (In her study of two-child families, Koch found that a two- to four-year difference in the ages of first- and second-born children was most threatening to the older child.)

Competition with siblings might account for some of the higher achievement of oldest children, but it does not explain the equally high achievement of only children. The higher achievement of some only children might be attributed to the fact that middle- and upper-class parents tend to have smaller families than lower-class parents. It might be hypothesized that if individuals in positions of responsibility and wealth are more intelligent and capable than those who work at less demanding and lower-paid jobs, some only children may become high achievers because of superior genetic potential and a richer and more stimulating environment. Another explanation for the higher achievement (and also guilt and adjustment problems) of first-born children is that they may be seen as the primary perpetuators of the "family name" and that parents *expect* more of them.

A final factor that may account for some differences in the behavior of first- and later-born children centers on "tutor-pupil" relationships. R. B. Zajonc and G. B. Markus (1975) report that a study of all of the males in the Netherlands who attained nineteen years of age in the years 1963–1966 revealed that

One explanation for the tendency for first-born children to score high on achievement tests and do well in school is that they act as teachers for younger siblings. These tutorial experiences may solidify their own understanding of many concepts. Peter Vandermark/Stock, Boston.

first-born boys with slightly younger siblings earned the highest scores, on the average, on an intelligence test. A similar tendency for American first-born children was reported by H. M. Breland (1974) who analyzed scores on Merit Scholarship examinations. Zajonc and Markus hypothesize that the superior test performance of first-born children may be due, in part, to a tendency for them to act as "teachers" for siblings who are slightly younger. These experiences contribute to understanding of the kinds of concepts stressed on intelligence and achievement tests.

First-born children may benefit from acting as "teachers"

Hierarchies and Popularity

As soon as organisms interact in groups, they tend to arrange themselves in hierarchies. As chickens in a farmyard establish a pecking order, so children in the elementary grades become interested in discovering who is the best in the class with respect to different qualities. D. C. Freedman (1971) asked elementary grade pupils to rate each other in regard to several types of behavior. He found that as early as the first grade both boys and girls showed substantial agreement about who was the "toughest" in their class. Not until later grades, however, was

Roles established as early as first grade

agreement reached regarding who was "nicest" and "smartest." (Perhaps this was the case because toughness shows up fast and needs to be recognized for reasons of survival, whereas it takes a while to find out who the nice and smart people are.)

In addition to sorting themselves out with reference to specific qualities, children also develop likes and dislikes for each other. When sociometric choices made by elementary grade students are compared with ratings of personality traits (made either by teachers or the children themselves), it appears that the characteristics of popular children change with age. R. D. Tuddenham (1951) found that in the first grade the most frequently chosen girls were quiet little ladies who were neither quarrelsome nor bossy. Lack of quarrelsomeness continued to be a popular trait in older girls, but the quiet little lady lost out in the fifth grade to the attractive, friendly good sport. The qualities of most popular boys stayed constant, however. At all elementary grade levels, such boys were good athletes, good sports, bold, and daring.

The emergence of roles and hierarchies demonstrates that during the elementary school years children become aware of themselves as individuals outside of the protected environment of the home. The significance of the formation of a self-concept based on the reactions of peers and of adults other than parents has been emphasized by Erik Erikson.

The Emergence of a Concept of Self

Erikson's Emphasis on Industry versus Inferiority

Erikson points out that children gain their first experience with life outside the home when they enter school. In the classroom, they get their first taste of what will be a critical part of their lives: applying themselves "to given skills and tasks which go far beyond the mere playful expression of organ modes or the pleasure in the function of limbs" (1963, p. 259). That is, children learn that they need to work and "to win recognition by producing things" (p. 259). A child whose efforts in school are successful will develop a sense of industry. Erikson notes, "This is socially a most decisive stage: since industry involves doing things beside and with others, a first sense of division of labor and of differential opportunity, that is, a sense of the technological ethos of the culture develops at this time" (p. 260). The child who does not do well in school, has no confidence in being able to do things "beside and with others," and fails to achieve any status with peers will develop a sense of inadequacy and inferiority.

Successfully doing things beside and with others leads to a sense of industry

The American child with a sense of the competitive nature of our culture may recognize the opportunities available in a meritocracy but at the same time be intimidated or overwhelmed by what must be done to make the most of these opportunities. This point is emphasized by Erikson, but it was a central argument in the theory developed by another student of Freud, Karen Horney.

Horney's Emphasis on Success versus Acceptance

Horney (pronounced "Horn-eye") was born and educated in Germany. After earning an M.D. degree she became a member of the Berlin Psychoanalytic Institute. She soon found, however, that she was unable to accept some of Freud's teachings, particularly his belief that successful women are motivated primarily by penis envy. In time, professional relationships became uncomfortably strained. This situation, along with the realization that she and her husband had drifted apart, led Horney to decide to make a clean break with all ties in Berlin and come to the United States.

She settled in Chicago during the height of the gangster era of the 1930s, and on her first night in that city a gun duel occurred during a holdup in her hotel. That introduction to America, plus the discovery that mental illness in this country seemed to be substantially different from neurosis in Europeans, led her to have further doubts about orthodox Freudian theory.

Horney became convinced that the culture in which a person lives has a profound influence on behavior, a conclusion also reached by Erikson after he contrasted aspects of European and American culture. But while Erikson came to emphasize how the individual needs to establish a sense of identity, Horney focused on the American preoccupation with success. In her initial contacts with American patients, she was struck by the extent to which they focused on winners and losers. She became aware that this caused a basic conflict: individuals in a meritocratic society who achieve success do so at the expense of many others, who thereby become failures. As she treated American patients, she became convinced that hardly anyone seemed really to win. Some successful individuals developed insecurities because of their awareness that they were both admired and hated by their peers, while unsuccessful people were torn by envy and self-hate.

Horney therefore emphasizes many of the same ideas as Erikson. In Erikson's view, during the years six to twelve American children must become aware that mastery of basic learning skills is essential to existence in a meritocracy. If they are successful, they will develop a sense of industry; if they do not do well, they will acquire a sense of inadequacy and inferiority. Horney emphasizes that American children experience conflicting feelings because they are told to do everything possible to be better than others but at the same time are enjoined to be popular and get along with others. Children who achieve success and feel guilty about it, or those who do not and feel defeated, may experience feelings of inadequacy and inferiority similar to those described by Erikson.

Attempts to be successful and popular may lead to conflicts

When they compare report cards, play games, compete for class offices, and the like, children during the years from six to twelve discover in no uncertain terms that some people are more successful at some things than others. As they interact in school, children acquire definite roles—class "brain," best athlete, class clown, and so forth. One of the reasons that roles become more important as children progress through the elementary grades is that they become increasingly capable of discerning the thoughts of others. Piaget has described preschoolers as egocentric to emphasize the point that young children are usually so busy sorting out their own thoughts they find it difficult to also take into account the thoughts of others. Early in the elementary school years, however, children become capable of socialized thinking. When that occurs, they become much more aware of how their behavior affects others. By the end of the elementary school years many children are very much concerned about what others think of them. (Changes in cognitive development that lead to socialized thinking, as well as to related types of thinking, will be discussed in the next chapter.)

Problems of Adjusting to Independent Existence

Developmental Tasks of the Elementary School Years

When six-year-old children begin to wrestle with the demands of the school curriculum and engage in extensive unsupervised interaction with peers, they are almost sure to be confronted by problems of greater variety and magnitude than those encountered during the comparatively protected preschool years. The nature and impact of these problems are illuminated by what Robert Havighurst refers to as developmental tasks. These he defines as tasks which arise "at or about a certain period in the life of an individual, successful achievement of which leads to his happiness and to success with later tasks, while failure leads to unhappiness in the individual, disapproval by the society, and difficulty with later tasks" (1952, p. 2). Among the developmental tasks expected of the preschooler are learning to walk and talk, forming simple concepts, and learning to relate oneself to others. The developmental tasks expected of six- to twelve-year-olds include:

1   Learning physical skills necessary for ordinary games
2   Building wholesome attitudes toward oneself as a growing organism
3   Learning to get along with age-mates
4   Learning an appropriate masculine or feminine social role
5   Developing fundamental skills in reading, writing, and calculating
6   Developing concepts necessary for everyday living
7   Developing conscience, morality, and a scale of values
8   Achieving personal independence
9   Developing attitudes toward social groups and institutions

(Havighurst, 1952, pp. 15–28)

Even though the nature and significance of some of these tasks (for example, learning sex roles) has changed since Havighurst described them in 1952, they still describe the many kinds of obstacles the elementary school child must surmount on the road to satisfactory later development. (They also reveal multiple reasons

Two of the developmental tasks that children are expected to achieve during the elementary school years are developing fundamental skills in the 3 R's and learning physical skills necessary for ordinary games. If children fail to achieve these developmental tasks, they are likely to encounter problems that may increase in intensity as they move through the grades. Frank Siteman/Stock, Boston; Hella Hammid/Photo Researchers.

why Kagan and Moss seem justified in referring to the elementary school years as a "crystallization period.")

To highlight the many kinds of adjustments children must make when they move from the sheltered environment of the home to the much less protected environments of the school and neighborhood, several of the developmental tasks listed by Havighurst will be discussed. Each task will be analyzed by contrasting aspects of the behavior and environment of preschoolers with the corresponding behavior and environment of elementary school children. (As you read you may realize that the following discussion is an expanded analysis of factors that were noted briefly in Chapter 9 in speculating about causes of changes in IQ scores over a span of time.)

Differences Between Preschool and Elementary School Behavior and Expectations

Building a Wholesome Attitude Toward Oneself   The self-concept of the preschool child centers on the formation of feelings of autonomy and initiative (to focus on the qualities stressed by Erikson). The independence of the preschooler develops, however, in the protective atmosphere of the home, immediate neighborhood, and perhaps a nursery school. A child's self-concept is influenced by the reactions of parents (and perhaps nursery school teachers) who are typically sympathetic and supportive and eager to foster positive traits. Furthermore, because developmental changes during the preschool years are often rapid and dramatic, parents may focus on recent attainments and overlook inadequacies, attributing them to immaturity and assuming that they will disappear with age. The preschool child's self-concept is also somewhat "insulated" because of egocentric thinking. Children below the age of five are not acutely aware of the feelings or responses of others and may therefore fail to comprehend (except in extreme instances) when their behavior is reacted to negatively by others.

By contrast, the self-concept of the elementary school child centers on the establishment of a sense of industry. Failure to experience a sense of industry leads to inferiority, which is likely to be a more pervasive cause of feelings of inadequacy than doubt or guilt experienced by a preschool child. Unlike autonomy and initiative, which are largely shaped by the reactions of parents, a child's conception of his or her ability to work by and with others is also influenced to a significant extent by the reactions of peers and teachers. Teachers, who must divide their attention among twenty to thirty pupils, and who must maintain control of the class and also demonstrate their ability to foster learning, are not as likely as parents to be tolerant and sympathetic when confronted by unsatisfactory behavior. The self-concept of the elementary school child is not only increasingly influenced by the reactions of peers but also by classmates' academic and social abilities. Elementary school children, along with their parents and teachers, become concerned about how well they perform compared to others. As children move through the elementary grades they become progressively capable of socialized thinking. Greater awareness of the feelings of others may lead to previously unrecognized feelings of rejection and embarrassment and perhaps erode the self-confidence that had been established during the preschool years.

Mastery of Basic Academic Subjects   The preschool child is rarely expected to complete formal assignments involving academic skills. Even less rarely is the performance of a preschool child on almost any kind of task publicly compared to the performance of others. If a preschool child "fails" some undertaking, parents and nursery school teachers are likely to respond with sympathy, support, and encouragement.

The elementary school child is expected to master certain prescribed academic tasks. Depending on the school, the teacher, and the grade level, the child might be expected to work more or less independently. Success is likely to be determined as often by comparison to the achievements of others as by evaluation of improvement over each child's previous performance. Failure to do as well as others may be reacted to by teachers or parents with disappointment (or even punishment), and encouragement to improve may involve pressures of various kinds (for example, the promise of money or a gift for higher grades).

Academic achievement of elementary school children compared to others

Getting Along with Age-mates   The preschool child almost always plays with age-mates under the surveillance if not supervision of parents or nursery school teachers. When children experience problems in getting along with others they are likely to arouse a supportive rather than a critical response from adults. Interactions with other children are not very complex, and involve the assignment of temporary rather than stable roles (as Parten discovered in her study of preschool play, summarized in Chapter 8). And as was the case with the formation of a self-concept, the egocentric thinking of preschoolers at least partially "insulates" them from subtle negative responses from others.

The elementary school child engages for the first time in frequent unsupervised play with age-mates. The protected play atmosphere of backyard or nursery school is replaced by more of a "law of the jungle" atmosphere when children are on their own. The games and pastimes that elementary school children participate in with peers are complex and often lead to the assignment of quite stable roles that highlight differences between individuals (for example, the child who is chosen captain of a team versus the child who is the last one picked when choosing sides). The acquisition of socialized thinking causes elementary school children to become aware of how others react to them, and they may become very much concerned about how popular they are with others.

Elementary school children acquire roles in unsupervised play situations

Learning an Appropriate Sex Role   The preschool child is just beginning to become aware of sex roles and is not concerned or self-conscious about behaving in sex-inappropriate ways or of participating in activities with members of the opposite sex. If the family has been disrupted by divorce, or if the mother works, children of this age are not likely to suffer in their relations with peers.

Elementary school children become increasingly aware of sex-appropriate behavior. (They may or may not favor revised conceptions of the liberated female, depending on the attitudes of the parents and the family situation.) Because of greater awareness of the thoughts of others (due to socialized thinking), they may be concerned about how peers respond to sex-inappropriate behavior (for example, a boy may be upset if he is called a sissy). Lack of a male model in father-absent homes may have a significant impact on the behavior, maturity, and academic performance of boys during this age span. If the mother works, the independence and academic achievement of both boys and girls may be influenced.

Learning Skills Necessary for Games   Preschool children typically engage in loosely organized games and quite often children of different ages participate. As a consequence, differences in skill are difficult to evaluate and may not be of any significance. There may be more stress on fantasy, imagination, and getting along with others than on actual physical skills.

Elementary school children frequently engage in competitive games, and by the middle grades they may be involved in Little League or similar adult-directed sports activities. Athletic skill, for boys in particular, may be the single most important factor in determining acceptance by peers. Differences in the athletic prowess of children become clear and are magnified by the reactions of parents to the performance of children in organized competitive sports.

Development of Conscience and Morality   Preschool children (for reasons to be explained in the next chapter) develop only rudimentary understanding of moral codes. If they break rules or behave in immoral ways their behavior may be excused by adults and attributed to immaturity. Since children at this age are egocentric thinkers, they are not likely to grasp how much they may hurt someone else's feelings by thoughtless behavior.

Elementary school children expected to obey rules, may experience guilt

Elementary school children are expected to learn and abide by the laws and regulations of society, community, and school, and to honor rules when they play with age-mates. If they break a law, or ignore a school regulation, or fail to comply with the rules of a game, they may be punished or ostracized. Growing sensitivity to the feelings of others may lead to guilt about behavior that causes distress to others.

Achieving Personal Independence   Many parents do their best to promote competence and independence in preschool children. The competence of the young child is evaluated, however, largely in terms of individual performance in protected and supervised home and nursery school settings. Because preschoolers function in quite circumscribed environments, parents and teachers can often manipulate circumstances to suit the child. (If a four-year-old boy dislikes his nursery school teacher, for instance, or if he is bullied by an older pupil in the school, the parents can easily arrange for him to attend a different school.)

The elementary school child is expected to achieve most of the developmental tasks that have just been discussed outside of the home, either in school classrooms or in interactions with peers. Accordingly, it may be difficult or impossible for parents to manipulate circumstances in efforts to improve a problem. (A fourth-grade boy who doesn't like his teacher, for example, will probably just have to put up with him or her for nine months. And if a bully asserts himself in out-of-school situations, a victim may despair about finding ways to avoid intimidation.) Elementary school children must learn to become independent in the strict sense of that word—they have to learn to make many of their own adjustments and solve many of their own problems.

This analysis of differences between the developmental tasks faced by pre-school and elementary school children helps explain certain aspects of development that have been discussed in earlier chapters. Factors such as those just noted, for instance, help explain why the Berkeley Growth Study researchers found that IQ scores often change as children mature. These factors also reveal many reasons why excellent preschool experiences, whether they are provided in Head Start schools, nursery schools, or in home settings by highly sensitive mothers, may not "immunize" or "inoculate" children and guarantee later success. But this discussion of developmental tasks at the elementary school level has also called attention to related points that have not been previously discussed. Perhaps the most precise way to summarize the overall significance of differences between preschool and elementary school behavior and expectations is to use the phrase, "It's a whole new ballgame." This is not to say that experiences that occur during the first five years of a child's life are of little significance. Theories and evidence presented in earlier chapters make it clear that this is not the case. The use of that phrase is simply a direct way of emphasizing that even children who get off to an excellent start the first five years of their lives have to make many adjustments when they begin school. The great majority of children *do* make the necessary adjustments, which might be considered as a tribute to the resiliency and adaptability of the human organism. Some children, however, are unable to cope with the demands placed upon them and develop behavior disorders of various kinds.

Extent and Nature of Behavior Disorders

Extent of Behavior Disorders

An extensive survey (Rosen, Bahn, and Kramer, 1964) of referrals to psychiatric clinics in all parts of the country revealed that the highest referral rates occur during the nine-to-fifteen age span, with peaks at nine and ten, and fourteen and fifteen. The referral rates and peaks varied for males and females: boys were twice as likely as girls to receive psychiatric treatment; peak referral years for boys were nine and fourteen, peak years for girls were ten and fifteen. The records of

Clinic referral rates highest in 9- to 15-year age span

Children are most likely to be referred to a psychotherapist when they are in the nine- to fifteen-year span. Parents who are anxious and who seem to need consolation appear to be particularly likely to seek professional help if they become convinced that their child has adjustment problems. Robert Spellman.

psychiatric clinics provide detailed data regarding behavior disorders, but such figures should be interpreted with caution because of the impossibility of making allowance for selective factors of various kinds (for example, characteristics of parents that cause them to seek the aid of a therapist). The data on referral peaks are supported, however, by teacher evaluations made for an extensive mental health survey of Los Angeles County (1960). Ten- and eleven-year-olds were rated as emotionally disturbed more frequently than those at other age levels.

Estimates of the prevalence of behavior disorders are difficult to make because of the problem of determining a precise point at which a particular form of behavior becomes "abnormal" or "severe." But a number of surveys have been made. R. Lapouse and M. Monk (1964) carried out intensive interviews with the mothers of a large representative sample of apparently normal six- to twelve-year-olds. They found that mothers reported 80 percent of the children had temper tantrums; approximately half manifested many fears and worries; about one-third had nightmares and bit their nails; and between 10 to 20 percent sucked their thumbs, wet their beds, or showed tics and other physical signs of tension. The researchers concluded that their findings might be interpreted more as an indication of the pressures of meeting the demands of a complex, modern society than as a sign of widespread psychiatric disorders. In another study (Stennett, 1964), data accumulated on a sample of fifteen hundred children between the ages of nine and eleven (a peak period of clinic referrals) led to the estimate that between 5 and 10 percent had "adjustive difficulties" severe enough to warrant professional attention and that 22 percent might be classified as emotionally handicapped.

Researchers who have studied incidence rates often conclude that many supposedly normal children exhibit symptoms that would be judged pathological *if* the children were referred to a clinic for observation. An extensive mental health survey carried out in England (Shepherd, Oppenheim, and Mitchell, 1966), for example, revealed that mothers who sought clinical help were rated as anxious, nervous, and likely to seek consolation. The researchers concluded that many children *not* referred to clinics suffered from behavior disorders as serious as those of children who were receiving professional help.

One phase of the longitudinal research carried out at the University of California provides evidence of adjustment problems in a typical group of children. When the subjects of the Guidance Study were fourteen, Jean Walker Macfarlane, Lucile Allen, and Marjorie Honzik (1954) issued a report of behavior problems shown at different age levels up to that time. Between the years of six to twelve the following types of behavior were noted in one-third or more of the cases: overactivity, oversensitiveness, fears, temper tantrums, jealousy, and excessive reserve. At all age levels boys were found to be more likely than girls to show these problems: overactivity, attention demanding, jealousy, competitiveness, lying, selfishness in sharing, temper tantrums, and stealing. Girls were more likely than boys to suck their thumbs; be excessively modest and reserved; fuss about their food; be timid, shy, fearful, oversensitive, somber; and to have mood swings. (The researchers comment that these differences were undoubtedly due to untraceable interactions between biological and cultural factors.)

Susceptibility to Behavior Disorders

Even an exceptionally fortunate and well-adjusted child (or adult) is almost sure, at some time or another, to have headaches, possess little desire for food, experience a nightmare, stumble over words, engage in nervous habits, suffer pangs of jealousy, feel anxious, become preoccupied about health, or experience similar symptoms that sometimes indicate serious problems of adjustment. In many situations these responses are appropriate, and a person who did not develop such symptoms would be abnormal. A child about to undergo surgery, for example, or go to camp for the first time, or participate in a piano recital, is almost sure to experience a degree of physical and emotional upheaval. Adults usually decide for themselves whether any form of behavior has become extreme or lasting enough to require medical or psychotherapeutic attention. The decision is made *for* the child. As the researchers in the mental health survey in England discovered, some parents have a much greater tendency to seek help than others.

In making a decision about the seriousness of a behavior disorder, parents may not only weigh circumstances and be influenced by their own personalities, they are also likely to take into account their estimate of the child's ability to cope with stress. Some children seem much more capable than others of finding their own solutions to problems. E. James Anthony notes an analogy proposed by Jacques May, a disease ecologist, to account for differences in human vulnerability and resistance to disease. May observed, "It is as though I had on a table three dolls, one of glass, another of celluloid, and a third of steel, and I chose to hit the three dolls with a hammer, using equal strength. The first doll would break, the second would scar, and the third would emit a pleasant musical sound" (1970, p. 692). Anthony notes that this analogy is helpful in clarifying certain points, but that it is an oversimplification.

Some children must cope with more risk factors than others

Anthony suggests that an evaluation of a child's adjustment should involve the appraisal of several types of risks: genetic, constitutional, environmental, situational—which are similar to the constitutional, group membership, and situational determinants of personality described by Murray and Kluckhohn (1948); a fourth consideration proposed by Anthony involves critical points in development, which can be related to the critical-period concept, Freud's stages of psychosexual development, Erikson's stages of psychosocial development, and Havighurst's developmental tasks. May's analogy, Murray and Kluckhohn's set of personality determinants, and Anthony's list of risk factors serve as frames of reference for speculations about why some children are much more likely than others to develop extreme forms of behavior disorders.

A "glass" child, for example, might inherit tendencies to engage in odd and difficult-to-control behavior. From the moment of birth he or she might resist cuddling and be easily irritated. The parents might have had doubts about having the child in the first place, and their attitude toward the child might be cold and resentful. These tendencies might be reinforced by the baby's strange and unresponsive behavior. And the insecurity and indecision of the parents might cause the child to develop a sense of mistrust. The parents might resort to strict toilet training and punitive discipline out of a sense of desperation, which would be likely to produce doubt and shame on the part of the child. At the preschool level the parents might be bothered by the child's tendencies to explore and ask questions. Their discouragement of such forms of behavior might produce in the child feelings of guilt and inferiority. The child might find it difficult to make friends in school, might take little interest in learning, and might mature late and be especially self-conscious at the time of puberty. Such a child might well be characterized as made of fragile crystal, likely to break if handled roughly.

A "steel" child, on the other hand, might inherit a strong physique and a well-functioning body and be exceptionally easy to care for. He or she might be responsive to others and reinforce the confidence of parents who eagerly awaited the birth of the baby and are well adjusted, warm, loving, and supportive. Such a child would begin life with a sense of trust. If the parents use techniques of child rearing such as those described by the Harvard Preschool Project researchers and Diana Baumrind, the child would be likely to develop competence as well as autonomy and initiative. If the child did well in school, industry would be established. If the child experienced few problems at puberty and made an early decision about a career, identity would become clearly established. In terms of theories of adjustment, such an individual would be much better equipped to cope with stress as an adult than the "glass" child.

As Anthony points out, however, human behavior is extremely complex. Some children who had personal histories every bit as unfortunate as those of the hypothetical "glass" child did not break under stress but responded with "highly superior modes of behavior such as creativity, productivity, and constructiveness." Several cases of this type are described by Victor and Mildred Goertzel in *Cradles of Eminence* (1962), an analysis of the biographies and autobiographies of four hundred of the most eminent people of the twentieth century. Here, for example, is a capsule description of a child who seems destined to become preoccupied with behavior problems later in life:

Boy, senior year secondary school, has obtained certificate from physician stating that nervous breakdown makes it necessary for him to leave school for six months. Boy not a good all-around student; has no friends—teachers find him a problem—spoke late—father ashamed of son's lack of athletic ability—poor adjustment to school. Boy has odd mannerisms, makes up own religion, chants hymns to himself—parents regard him as "different." (1962, p. xiii)

Instead of spending his adult life as a patient in a mental hospital, which might have been predicted from the information just provided, this child—Albert Einstein—became, in many people's consideration, the most creative, productive, and constructive thinker of the twentieth century. Anthony's observations on Jacques May's analogy, and case histories such as that of Albert Einstein, raise these questions: Why do some children who are provided with apparently excellent experiences early in life fail to make the most of their abilities? Why do some children who develop under ostensibly undesirable circumstances go on to achieve greatness?

Adaptability, Resiliency, and Unpredictability

After analyzing the data on behavior disorders in the typical group of children noted earlier, as well as all the other information accumulated on the subjects of the Guidance Study, various members of the research staff at the University of California made predictions of how successful and well adjusted each child would be as an adult. After the subjects had reached the age of thirty, comparisons were made between child and adult behavior. Surprisingly, 50 percent of the children in the sample who were later studied as adults became more stable and effective individuals than had been predicted; 20 percent turned out to be less effective than had been predicted. In commenting on these findings Jean Walker Macfarlane observed:

We have found from a review of life histories that certain deficits of constitution and/or environment, and certain unsolvable interpersonal conflicts have long-term effects upon the individual, up to age thirty. We have also found that much of personality theory based on pathological samples is not useful for prediction for the larger number of persons. Many of our most mature and competent adults had severely troubled and confusing childhoods and adolescences. Many of our highly successful children and adolescents have failed to achieve their predicted potential. (1964, p. 125)

As a partial explanation for this conclusion Macfarlane notes:

We had not appreciated the maturing utility of many painful, strain-producing, and confusing experiences which in time, if lived through, brought sharpened awareness, more complex integrations, better skills in problem solving, clarified goals, and increasing stability. Nor had we been aware that early success might delay or possibly forestall continuing growth, richness, and competence. (1964, p. 124)

Macfarlane and her coworkers were impressed by the resiliency of the human organism. Some children, however, seem to lack sufficient adaptability to situations that others take in stride; some children are faced with conflicts and problems of such magnitude that even the most adaptable succumb. The inaccuracies of the predictions of the Guidance Study researchers reveal the difficulties and complexities of tracing the causes of mental health and mental illness. Children who have "ideal" parents and who are exceptionally well adjusted in school, Macfarlane hypothesizes (1964, p. 125), may develop unrealistic expectations about how well they will do when they embark on a career or may spend too much time and energy attempting to maintain an image. Children who come from homes where apparently undesirable techniques of child rearing are used or who experience much misery and unhappiness in school may thereby become equipped to cope with and overcome extreme demands in later life.

Early success may mislead, early problems may strengthen

The impact of a "tempering" process was revealed by Goertzel and Goertzel in *Cradles of Eminence*. The Goertzels estimate that, at most, only fifty-eight of the homes of the four hundred eminent people studied were trouble-free. In the great majority of family backgrounds of famous individuals (as in the case of Albert Einstein) early home and school experiences varied from inadequate to disastrous. The Goertzels comment, "There is no adverse circumstance of the kind commonly thought to induce mental illness, delinquency, or neurosis which some one of the four hundred does not experience in his childhood" (1962, p. 208). Instead of succumbing, however, these individuals were spurred to great achievements.

Less extreme and dramatic evidence of the desirability of a certain amount of "tempering" is provided by Alexander Thomas, Stella Chess, and Herbert G. Birch (1970) in their follow-up study of individuality in children. They found that some easy-to-rear children developed unexpected problems when they left the home environment. They offered this explanation:

On the basis of ratings and observations of subjects in one of the longitudinal studies at the University of California, researchers made predictions of how successful and well-adjusted each child would be as an adult. If Albert Einstein had been one of their subjects, it is quite likely that his behavior as an adolescent would have led to a prediction that he would encounter extreme problems later in life. Yet Einstein, as well as many of the "poor risk" subjects of the California study, turned out to be a successful and well-adjusted adult. It appears that painful early experiences sometimes have a maturing and stabilizing effect. Furthermore, certain traits that lead to adult achievement may not become apparent until an individual becomes fully mature. United Press International.

In general easy children respond favorably to various child-rearing styles. Under certain conditions, however, their ready adaptability to parental handling may itself lead to the development of a behavioral problem. Having adapted readily to the parents' standards and expectations early in life, the child on moving into the world of his peers and school may find that the demands of these environments conflict sharply with the behavior patterns he has learned at home. If the conflict between the two sets of demands is severe, the child may be unable to make an adaptation that reconciles the double standard. (1970, pp. 105–106)

Thomas, Chess, and Birch illustrate their point with a case history of a girl who had been "reared by parents who placed great value on individuality, imagination, and self-expression" (p. 105). When this child entered school, she found it extremely difficult to adjust to classroom routine, did poor work, and found it difficult to make friends. The parents were asked to encourage their daughter to accept the fact that it was necessary to follow the teacher's instructions and that she should occasionally abide by the play preferences of classmates. Within six months the child was enjoying school and making friends. In many respects this case history illustrates one of the same points made by the Guidance Study researchers: a child who seems to have been blessed by favorable determinants of personality may still encounter problems of adjustment.

The University of California researchers were impressed by the adaptive capacity of the children they studied but also by the difficulty of making accurate predictions about later adjustment. Insight into different ways children adapt—and why theories of adjustment do not always permit accurate predictions—is provided by an analysis of psychoanalytic, learning-theory, and third-force views of adjustment.

Views of Adjustment

The Psychoanalytic View of Adjustment

Defense mechanisms protect ego

Defense Mechanisms   In Freudian theory, the ego and superego are engaged in a constant struggle with the id. In some situations the primitive impulses of the id may be so strong that the conscious and rational forces of an individual's personality cannot completely contain them. The most common result is that the individual resorts to defense mechanisms that permit partial expression of the impulses of the id but do not completely compromise the ego. Imagine that a fourth-grade boy is confronted on the same day with an important test and a class election. His id, governed by the pleasure principle, seeks the easy gratification of a high grade on the test and election to the presidency of the class. A struggle between the id and superego may take place if the boy is tempted to cheat on the test or insert some extra slips in the ballot box. If both of these impulses are satisfactorily checked by the superego, the boy may get a low grade on the exam and receive only one vote (his own) in the election. These are both ego-shattering experiences. In efforts to patch up his self-concept, the child might resort (usually in an unconscious way) to some or all of these defense mechanisms:

☐ He might say, "The stupid test wasn't really important, and if I'd won the stupid election, I would have had to do a lot of extra work." (Rationalization)

☐ If the boy came very close to cheating on the test, he might say to himself, "I got a low score on the test because I didn't cheat. I saw others cheat, but I was honest and I'm going to do everything I can to be the most honest person in the class. In fact, I think I'll organize a campaign for everyone to be honest." (Reaction formation)

☐ If the boy desperately wanted to be elected class president because he loved being the center of attention and half recognized this very strong urge, he might say to himself, "It's a good thing Mary was elected president because now maybe she won't be so wild about trying to get everybody's attention all the time." (Projection)

- [ ] During recess just after the exam and election the child might engage in some sensational and reckless stunts on the swings. (Compensation and attention-getting)
- [ ] After recess, the teacher might invite the child to choose a partner to work with on a project. The child might select Mary, who got an A on the test and was elected president of the class. (Identification)
- [ ] On the way home from school, the double disappointment might suddenly overwhelm his thoughts, and the boy might begin to suck his thumb, a habit he had not indulged in since kindergarten days. (Regression)
- [ ] A bit further along, when disappointment had turned to frustration and anger, the boy might encounter a sassy first-grader whose previous taunts had never aroused a response in him. On this occasion, the first-grader's first wisecrack is answered with a sharp cuff administered to the back of the head. (Displacement)

The Significance of Repression   As these illustrations reveal, defense mechanisms are common forms of behavior, and most of us probably resort to one or more of them every day of our lives. Only repeated and extensive use of behavior intended to protect the ego is likely to lead to unfortunate consequences. A child of demanding parents who is unable to meet their standards of schoolwork, for example, may be constantly torn by the urge to cheat and the fear of being caught. One solution to this conflict might be a tendency to say or think or write over and over again "Honesty is the best policy" (obsession). Another solution might be excessive concern about cleanliness (compulsion) where the "dirty" thought of cheating is symbolically purified.

Perhaps the most important contribution Freud made toward the understanding of behavior was his insight that memories repressed at the conscious level but retained in the unconscious may continue to influence thoughts and actions. A child who arouses parental fury by some flagrant act of misbehavior at an early age, for example, and is screamed at, spanked, and then locked in a dark closet as further punishment may suffer from that time on from fear of the dark and enclosed places. The pain, shame, guilt, and anxiety of the incident will be repressed, and the individual will not be able to remember what happened. The experience, however, will be retained at the unconscious level of memory and will influence behavior. If fear of the dark and of enclosed places become so extreme that they dominate the person's life, a psychotherapist's help may be called for. If the individual can be helped to recall the incident, talk about it, and understand why being in a dark, enclosed place was—and is—associated with pain, fear, and guilt that is no longer appropriate, the phobia may be brought under control.

Repression as explanation of abnormal behavior

One of the defense mechanisms described by Freud is regression: the tendency to respond to stress by engaging in a form of behavior that provided comfort at an earlier stage of development. Charles Harbutt/Magnum.

The phobias just described are conditioned fears. Other phobias may be due to displaced anxiety. The child may experience a feeling of intense anxiety because of some threatening or disagreeable feature of relations with parents. If the actual cause of the anxiety is vague, incompletely understood, or threatening to the child, the anxiety may be transferred to some specific object or situation. An example of this type of reaction is *school phobia,* where the child will resist leaving home or find excuses for coming home early. The cause of school phobia may be anxiety about being separated from the mother, but fear is displaced to the school. Another common type of displaced anxiety is *death phobia,* sometimes referred to as "eight-year anxiety" because it typically occurs at that age. E. James Anthony (1967, p. 1395) has suggested that at this age the child first becomes aware of the irreversibility of death, which leads to a sense of helplessness. This vague but intense feeling of uneasiness is expressed as a fear of the child's own death or the death of parents.

School (and sometimes death) phobias may be caused by parent-child relationships that involve dependency and hostility. L. Eisenberg (1958) and S. Davidson (1961) hypothesize that while parents overtly urge a child to go to school, they may also give subtle nonverbal cues, communicating that the child should stay home. Or a child may develop a sense of hostility toward the parents (perhaps as a result of a conflict between feelings of dependency and urges to assert independence) and experience an urgent need to go home, to make sure vaguely sensed wishes for the parents' death or injury have not come true (Lassers, Nordan, and Bladholm, 1973).

Learning-Theory View of Adjustment

Psychoanalysts trace behavior disorders to early experiences, particularly at critical stages of psychosexual development. Compulsive tendencies in a ten-year-old, for example, may be attributed to coercive toilet training and to the fixation of libidinal energy (that ordinarily might be available for coping with adjustment problems) at the anal stage of development. Learning-theory explanations of adjustment and maladjustment also stress the impact of certain types of experiences, but emphasis is on how certain tendencies have been shaped by reinforcement rather than on fixation or the influence of unconscious memories. Compulsiveness in a ten-year-old might be explained, for instance, by the hypothesis that parents frequently rewarded tendencies toward neatness early in life, particularly when the child was dependent on them and eager for their approval. An older child's excessive concern about neatness might be explained as an effort to reexperience the pleasurable sensations associated with early praise.

Learning-theory view of adjustment: abnormal tendencies shaped by reinforcement

Learning-theory explanations of certain types of behavior are usually much less intimidating than psychoanalytic explanations. As a consequence, attempts to eliminate or lessen unfortunate traits do not need to be restricted to the efforts of psychoanalysts or clinical psychologists, but can sometimes be made by parents. The psychoanalytic explanation of a phobia or of a nervous habit, for instance, may lead parents to believe that the only way they can help their child is to arrange for a specialist to uncover repressed memories. Instead of assuming that it is essential to trace causes (which is often extremely difficult to do with children because they are unable to verbalize their feelings, even when a skilled therapist endeavors to help them overcome repression), learning theorists concentrate on reinforcing positive types of behavior. Some theorists specialize in the use of *behavior therapy*, which is based on the principles of learning theory. Quite often parents, though, can use the same techniques in the home.

If a six-year-old boy has such a fear of dogs he is afraid to go out and play, for example, parents might use the technique developed by Albert Bandura and his associates (1967) and arrange for the child to observe playmates having positive experiences with dogs. If an eight-year-old girl bites her nails almost constantly, her parents might help her use techniques recommended by Nathan Azrin and Gregory Nunn (1977). With parental encouragement and assistance the girl might keep a record of the number of times she bites her nails each day (before she starts on her behavior-modification program), list all the annoyances and inconveniences nail biting causes, list all the mannerisms which immediately precede her nail biting, describe exactly how she bites her nails, note situations and activities that seem to lead to nail biting, and identify people who seem to cause her to bite her nails. After she has used these techniques to become thoroughly aware of what was previously an "unconscious" habit, the girl should practice a competing reaction, such as clenching her hands, each time she feels the urge to bite her nails. She should mentally rehearse how she will clench her hands when she feels the impulse to bite her nails and ask her parents and friends to comment on her progress (and gently remind her when she backslides). This

Using behavior modification to control nervous habits

approach to dealing with a nervous habit such as nail biting is obviously much more simple and direct than brooding about unfortunate infantile experiences that might have fixated libidinal energy at the oral stage of psychosexual development. (A psychoanalyst might argue, however, that if the underlying causes of the nail biting are not uncovered, the girl is likely to develop some substitute form of oral activity such as thumb sucking or compulsive gum chewing. A behavior therapist might reply that those habits could also be controlled through use of behavior-modification techniques.)

While the learning-theory view of adjustment (and therapy) often makes it possible to replace unfortunate habits or reactions with neutral or constructive forms of behavior, it does not shed much light on more pervasive reactions such as anxiety or depression. Positive and negative personality traits that influence behavior in a variety of ways can sometimes be understood, though, by interpreting behavior in terms of a description of needs proposed by Abraham Maslow. Maslow's observations call attention to causes of positive and negative forms of behavior, but in a way that may make it possible for parents and teachers (not just psychotherapists) to become aware of inadequacies in a child's life and bring about improvements.

The Third-Force View of Adjustment

As noted in discussing conceptions of development in Chapter 1, Abraham Maslow proposed *third force* psychology as an alternative to psychoanalysis and learning theory. Maslow suggests that "We have, each one of us, an essential inner nature which is instinctoid, intrinsic, given, 'natural,' i.e., with an appreciable hereditary determinant, and which tends strongly to persist" (1968, p. 190). This inner nature is shaped by experiences and interactions with others, but it is also self-created. "Every person is, in part, 'his own project' and makes himself" (p. 199). Because individuals are unique and make themselves, Maslow reasons, they should be allowed to make many of their own choices. Parents and teachers should have faith in children and let them grow and *help* them grow, not try to *make* them grow or attempt to shape their behavior. The best way to help a child grow, Maslow suggests, is to take into account the nature of human motivation.

To explain motivation Maslow has proposed a hierarchy of needs and a basic principle that binds them together. The principle is: "The tendency for a new and higher need to emerge as the lower need fulfills itself by being sufficiently gratified" (p. 55). At the lower level of the hierarchy are *deficiency* (or D) needs: physiological, safety, belongingness and love, esteem. The higher level of the hierarchy is made up of *growth* or *being* (or B) needs: self-actualization, knowing and understanding, aesthetic. (See Figure 10–1.)

There are several significant differences between deficiency and growth needs. Individuals act to get rid of deficiency needs in order to reduce disagreeable tension. Such needs can be satisfied only by other people and therefore make individuals other-directed and dependent on others when in difficulty. By

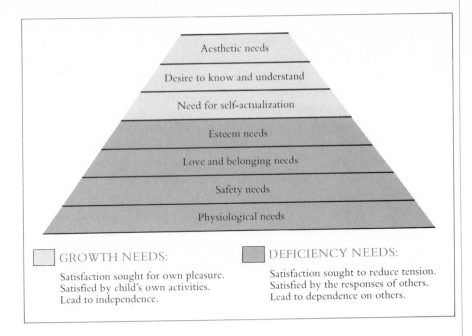

Figure 10–1   Maslow's hierarchy of needs. Redrawn, with permission, from Abraham H. Maslow, "A Theory of Human Motivation," *Psychological Review*, 1943, **50**, 370–396. Copyright 1943 by the American Psychological Association.

contrast, people seek the pleasure of the growth needs, and their satisfaction arouses a pleasurable form of tension. Such needs can be self-satisfied, which means that individuals are self-directed and able to find their own solutions to difficulties.

Maslow's basic principle of motivation, his hierarchy of needs, and the distinctions he makes between deficiency and growth needs can be illustrated by contrasting two hypothetical third-grade boys.

One boy comes from a broken home where he is alternately ignored and physically abused by a bitter, alcoholic mother. The mother stays up late every night, drinks, and watches television. The child gets little sleep and must get ready for school by himself each morning. He eats no breakfast and must search to find sufficient clothes to wear. He is aware that his mother despises him, and his shabby appearance and lack of confidence prevent him from making friends. Instead, he is the butt of many jokes and the chief victim of the class bully. His teacher is repelled by his appearance, bothered by his habit of falling asleep, and well aware that he is the poorest student in the class. When she plays a recording during music-appreciation period, she notes his lack of response and attributes it to low intelligence.

A second boy comes from a home where the parents provide excellent physical care and make it abundantly clear that they love and esteem him. He goes to school feeling physically fit and emotionally secure. These qualities, plus other aspects of his personality and appearance, make him attractive to classmates, and he is elected class president. He is eager to do schoolwork and takes pleasure in delving into things. When the teacher plays a record, he comments excitedly on what the music might mean.

Maslow would explain the behavior of the first boy by pointing out that none of his deficiency needs are being satisfied. He is hungry, tired, afraid of being physically abused, has rarely experienced love or a sense of belonging, and is constantly made to feel inferior. Since a higher need emerges only when lower needs are sufficiently gratified, such an unfortunate child could not desire to learn or develop an appreciation for music. The second boy, by contrast, is in the enviable position of having all the deficiency needs well satisfied. He is therefore primed to devote himself wholeheartedly to learning and to enjoying aesthetic and other self-fulfilling experiences.

Child must feel comfortable, secure, and loved before experiencing urges to know and appreciate

If the first boy is not helped to satisfy his deficiency needs, he is almost sure to become what Maslow refers to as a *bad chooser*. If left entirely to his own devices, he will very likely develop one or more types of problem behavior. Only if some sympathetic and understanding adult helps him to satisfy his deficiency needs is he ever likely to become a good chooser, capable of making his own growth decisions. This is a significant aspect of Maslow's theory that is sometimes overlooked. He recommends freedom of choice only for children who have had deficiency needs well satisfied. This is what he means when he urges parents and teachers to *help* children grow.

Several types of behavior described in this chapter can be more completely understood by interpreting them with reference to cognitive and moral development. Several of the developmental tasks listed by Havighurst, for instance, depend upon cognitive skills as well as understanding of moral principles. Accordingly, cognitive and moral development during the elementary school years merit detailed examination. These two types of behavior will be discussed in the next chapter.

Suggestions for Further Study

Physical Development

Perhaps the leading authority on physical development, particularly at the time of puberty, is J. M. Tanner. He describes aspects of adolescent development in "Physical Growth," Chapter 2 in *Carmichael's Manual of Child Psychology* (Vol. 1, 1970, pp. 77–155), edited by Paul Mussen; and in "Sequence, Tempo, and Individual Variation in Growth and Development of Boys and Girls Aged Twelve to Sixteen" in *Twelve to Sixteen: Early Adolescence* (1977, pp. 1–24), edited by Jerome Kagan and Robert Coles.

Father Absence

For a review of studies of the impact of father absence on child behavior examine "The Effects of Father Absence on Child Development" by E. Mavis Hetherington and J. L. Deur in *The Young Child: Review of Research* (1972, Vol. 2), edited by W. W. Hartup; or "Children in Fatherless Families" by E. Herzog and C. E. Sudia in *Review of Child Development Research* (1973, Vol. 3), edited by B. M. Caldwell and H. M. Ricciuti.

Divorce

For a concise review of studies of the impact of divorce on child development see "Divorce: A Child's Perspective" by E. Mavis Hetherington in *American Psychologist*, 1979, **34** (10), 851–858. For more comprehensive analyses see *Marital Separation* (1975) by R. Weiss; or "Marital Disruption as a Stressor: A Review and Analysis" by B. L. Bloom, S. J. Asher, and S. W. White, *Psychological Bulletin*, 1978, **85**, 867–894.

Maternal Employment

For a concise summary of research on the impact of maternal employment on child development examine "Maternal Employment: 1979" by Lois Wladis Hoffman in *American Psychologist*, 1979, **34** (10), 859–865. For more comprehensive analyses consult "Effects of Maternal Employment on the Child: A Review of Research" also by Hoffman in *Developmental Psychology*, 1974, **10**, 204–228; or "Developmental Comparisons Between 10-Year Old Children with Employed and Non-employed Mothers" by D. Gold and D. Andres in *Child Development*, 1978, **49**, 75–84.

Horney's View of Behavior

If Karen Horney's observations on the conflict between success and acceptance of self arouse your interest you may wish to read a section of one of her books. These not only provide many insights into behavior, they are also a pleasure to read because Horney has a clear, direct style. Her best-known work is *The Neurotic Personality of Our Time* (1937). For a sample of the points made in this book you might read pages 35–40 for a concise description of a neurotic personality; pages 75–78 for an analysis of how Horney's view of anxiety differs from Freud's (a complete description of which is presented in Horney's book *New Ways in Psychoanalysis* [1939]); pages 80–90 for a description of environmental characteristics leading to neurosis. Neurotic competitiveness is discussed in Chapter 11; "Recoiling from Competition" in Chapter 12; "Culture and Neurosis" in Chapter 15. Other books by Horney are *Our Inner Conflicts* (1945) and *Neurosis and Human Growth* (1950).

Types of Maladjustment

For more complete information about causes and symptoms of behavior problems, neuroses, and psychoses, refer to *Child Psychiatry* (4th ed., 1972) by Leo Kanner. The first edition of this classic text was published in 1935, and Kanner might be thought of as the dean of American psychiatrists. He outlines the history of child psychiatry (Part 1), discusses how physical, environmental, and interpersonal factors influence behavior (Part 2), describes clinical methods (Part 3), and provides detailed descriptions of personality problems arising from physical illness, psychosomatic disorders, and disorders of behavior (Part 4). Essentially the same topics are covered in *Behavior Disorders in Children* (4th ed., 1972) by Harry and Ruth Morris Bakwin. Another excellent reference is *Manual of Child Psychopathology* (1972), edited by Benjamin B. Wolman. The part headings of this 1,300-page volume are: "Etiologic Factors" (genetic, organic, sociocultural), "Organic Disorders" (brain damage, epilepsy, mental retardation, etc.), "Sociogenic Disorders" (neuroses, psychoses, delinquency, and so on), "Other Disorders" (speech and hearing problems, learning disturbances, and so forth), "Diagnostic Methods," "Overview of Treatment Methods," "Specific Treatment Methods," "Research in Childhood Psychopathology," and "The Clinical Professions." Briefer discussions of many of the same topics covered in the Kanner, Bakwin, and Wolman books are provided in "Behavior Disorders" by E. James Anthony; and "Childhood Psychosis" by William Goldfarb, Chapters 28 and 29 in *Carmichael's Manual of Child Psychology* (3rd ed., Vol. 2, 1970), edited by Paul H. Mussen.

Psychotherapy with Children

If you would like information about techniques of psychotherapy used with children, a general review of methods is presented in the Kanner and Wolman books mentioned above. For detailed information about specific techniques, consult the following: the psychoanalytic approach is described in *The Psychoanalytic Treatment of Children* (1946) by Anna Freud; and *The Psychoanalysis of Children* (1937) by Melanie Klein.

Carl Rogers describes his nondirective or client-centered approach in *Client-Centered Therapy* (1951) and *On Becoming a Person: A Therapist's View of Psychotherapy* (1970). Two case histories in which nondirective techniques are used with children are *One Little Boy* (1952) by Dorothy W. Baruch; and *Dibs: In Search of Self* (1964) by Virginia Axline. Behavior therapy is discussed in *Handbook of Psychotherapy and Behavior Change* (2nd ed., 1978), edited by S. L. Garfield and A. E. Bergin. Group therapy is discussed in *The Theory and Practice of Group Psychotherapy* (1970) by I. D. Yalom. Family therapy is described in *Progress in Group and Family Therapy* (1972), edited by C. J. Sager and H. S. Kaplan. Milieu therapy is described in *The Empty Fortress* (1966) and *A Home for the Heart* (1974) by Bruno Bettelheim. A fictional account of the reactions of a sixteen-year-old girl to institutionalization and psychotherapy is offered in *I Never Promised You a Rose Garden* (1964) by Hannah Green (a pseudonym used by Joanne Greenberg).

Encouraging Parent-Child Understanding

Carl Rogers developed his technique of client-centered therapy because he wanted to help his patients learn to cope with their own problems. In his sessions with clients, Rogers accepts, reflects, and clarifies the feelings expressed so that people gain insights into their own behavior. A number of psychologists who used nondirective techniques in therapeutic sessions concluded that it might be beneficial to help parents use variations of the basic method in interacting with their children. One of the first therapists to do this was Haim Ginott, author of *Between Parent and Child* (1965), *Between Parent and Teenager* (1969), and *Teacher and Child* (1971). In all of these books Ginott urges those who deal with children to accept, reflect, and clarify feelings expressed by children.

Thomas Gordon has expanded the basic technique outlined by Ginott into a more complete program described in *P.E.T.: Parent Effectiveness Training* (1970). He calls his approach the "No-Lose" method because it involves having parent and child discuss problems and come up with compromise solutions. If a girl refuses to wear a raincoat to school, for example, the parent may force her to wear it (the parent wins) or give in and permit the child to go out in the rain without a coat (the child wins). A no-lose solution involves having the parent and child discuss the problem (the girl doesn't want to wear her raincoat because it is plaid and no one else at school wears a plaid coat) and find a mutually satisfying solution (the girl is allowed to wear her mother's white coat).

If you would like to find out more about how parents and teachers might use techniques derived from nondirective therapy, examine one of the books by Ginott or Gordon's description of P.E.T. (Gordon trains and "licenses" individuals to conduct P.E.T. workshops. You might wish to examine his book for a preview of what would be covered in the eight-week program, so that if a course is offered in your area, you would know whether you would like to take it.) (For critical evaluations of the Ginott and Gordon books, examine "Popular Primers for Parents" by K. Alison Clarke-Stewart in *American Psychologist* (1978, **33**, 359–369) and "The Validity of Popular Primers for Parents" by Robert J. Griffore in *American Psychologist* (1979, **34**, 182–183.)

Maslow's View of Motivation

If the account of Abraham H. Maslow's views of motivation in this chapter aroused your interest more than earlier descriptions of his work, you might wish to read sections of *Toward a Psychology of Being* (2nd ed., 1968) or *Motivation and Personality* (2nd ed., 1970).

KEY POINTS

Cognitive Development

Formal thought: systematic approach, awareness of variables, formation of hypotheses, ability to generalize

Socialized speech and thought: awareness that others may have different views

Impulsive and reflective cognitive styles

Analytic and thematic cognitive styles

Convergent and divergent cognitive styles

Girls may earn higher grades because of desire to please adults

Moral Development

Moral behavior depends on circumstances

Being able to recite principles has no effect on moral behavior

Around 10: from sacred and imposed rules to mutual agreements

Moral realism: sacred rules, no exceptions, no allowance for intentions, consequences determine guilt

Preconventional morality: avoid punishment, receive benefits in return

Conventional morality: impress others, respect authority

Postconventional morality: mutual agreements, consistent principles

Kohlberg: stages of morality universal, sequential

Not all studies support hypotheses of universal, sequential stages

Values clarification: encourage children to choose, prize, and act on beliefs

Many moral decisions must be made on spur of moment

A strong conscience leads to "right" moral decisions but may cause guilt feelings

Children may acquire visible moral attributes through imitation but not acquire judgment

By 12, children understand subtleties of feelings, can take societal perspective

By 12, children can empathize deeply, accurately

Discuss real moral dilemmas, react positively, set consistent example

Show affection, avoid punishment, stress reasons

Use subtle techniques to help children become aware of others' feelings

CHAPTER □ 11

SIX TO TWELVE:
COGNITIVE AND MORAL DEVELOPMENT

In Chapter 9, factors were presented that might account for changes in IQ when intelligence tests are given to the same children over a period of time. Several factors were described under the heading "Differences Between Preschool and Elementary School Curricula." These factors included differences between preoperational and concrete operational thinking, differences in cognitive style, the significance of early success in key subjects such as reading, and competition with others. In order to comprehend the significance of cognitive development during the six- to twelve-year span, each of these factors needs to be considered, and they will be discussed in the first part of this chapter.

While cognitive development is extremely important during the elementary school years, so is moral development. These two types of behavior are related in several ways. First of all, children cannot comprehend or apply general moral principles until concrete operational thinking gives way to formal thought. Second, children find it difficult to understand the feelings of others (which influences awareness of how their behavior affects others) until egocentric thinking is replaced by socialized thinking. Finally, the competitive nature of our schools and our society causes conflicts (as described by Karen Horney) when children may feel obliged to look out for themselves in school situations even though this may involve violating moral codes and regulations. These often interrelated aspects of cognitive and moral development will be discussed in the second part of this chapter.

Cognitive Development

From Concrete Operational to Formal Operational Thought

By the time they leave kindergarten, some children may be capable of certain types of concrete operational thinking. They may be able to handle operations by mentally reversing actions. They are not likely, however, to be able to generalize very effectively because they can deal only with concrete objects and experiences that are actually present or have been experienced directly in the past. In the years from six to twelve, the child gradually acquires cognitive abilities that lead to formal thought. The sixth grader thus will probably be able to solve some problems not restricted to actual experiences and perhaps be able to deal with contrary-to-fact propositions. The way this transition occurs is illustrated by the reactions of children of different ages to experimental situations devised by Piaget.

When six-year-olds are confronted with the problem where equal amounts of water are poured into a vase and a bowl, most are able to explain that the amount of water stays the same. If they are asked to apply the same basic principle (of conservation) to a situation where one of two equal-size pieces of clay is flattened, they may be able to supply the correct answer. But if asked to explain what will happen if heavy and light weights of equal size are placed in tubes containing equal amounts of water, they are likely to fail. Six-year-olds are able to solve problems of conservation only if they have had concrete experience with the objects involved. As they mature, they will gradually comprehend similarities and recognize relationships and be able to solve many different types of conservation problems. Until they reach the point where they can solve such problems in a fairly consistent way (around age twelve), though, they have not demonstrated capability of formal thought.

The same point is illustrated by the way the six- to twelve-year-old masters classification. The six-year-old who can explain when actually confronted with flowers of different types and colors that a yellow tulip is at the same time not only yellow and a tulip but also a flower may be unable to understand similar hypothetical situations. For example, if asked (just after explaining about flowers that are physically present) if a person can be a Catholic and a television star at the same time, a six-year-old may confidently state that it is *not* possible and not see any inconsistency.

When children reach the point of being able to make some consistent generalizations, they have shown that they are beginning to develop their capacity for formal thought. But an incomplete grasp of this kind of thinking is revealed by the way they set about solving problems. If asked to explain how to predict what will happen if objects of varying sizes and weights are placed on a balance, eleven-year-olds are likely to proceed in a disorganized manner. They may make wild guesses before they begin to experiment and then proceed to engage in haphazard trial and error in searching for a solution. Not until they have gained sufficient experience with formal thought will they be able to plan mentally a systematic approach to solving the problem. Only after a considerable amount of experience will they be able to carry out a plan evolved entirely in their minds and then accurately predict the results before they actually balance objects. This kind of intellectual behavior illustrates the essence of formal thought: the ability to solve never-before-encountered problems entirely by mental manipulation of variables. Formal thinking, then, is characterized by a systematic approach to problem solving, consideration of several variables at the same time, skill in forming hypotheses, and the ability to generalize by applying principles to many different situations.

Formal thought: systematic approach, awareness of variables, formation of hypotheses, ability to generalize

From Egocentric to Socialized Speech and Thought

Preschoolers who are in the process of developing a repertoire of schemes tend to organize and adapt to experiences in their own way. As a consequence, their view of a particular object or situation may be quite different from the perception of others. They may also be incapable of decentration and will concentrate on only one aspect of a situation at a time. These conditions lead to egocentric speech and thought, where children tend to assume that everyone else sees things their way and understands their point of view. Conversely, they fail to comprehend that others may have different points of view.

Around the age of eight, most children have gained enough experience and interacted with enough people to grasp the idea that views of the world differ and that it is often wise to find out what others think and to pay close attention to what they say. When this occurs, Piaget says, the child has become capable of socialized speech and thought.

Socialized speech and thought: awareness that others may have different views

While the ability to see things as others see them helps children interact more effectively in many school and social situations, it also tends to make children self-conscious. A first-grade boy who falls off a swing on the playground or splashes paint on his face while at the easel may continue about his business in an unconcerned way. If the same boy does something awkward when he reaches the sixth grade, he is likely to immediately check to see if others have seem him—and if they are laughing at him. One consequence of cognitive development in the elementary school years, therefore, is that children move from being more or less immune to the reactions of others to feeling as if they are "on stage" most of the time. This tendency reaches a peak in early adolescence and will be discussed more completely in Chapter 12.

The Impact of Cognitive Style

Piaget's description of cognitive development provides an outline of general trends that reflect age changes in intellectual functioning found in children in all parts of the world. It has been found, however, that while all children go through the stages of sensorimotor, preoperational, and concrete operational thought in essentially the same sequence, they may differ in cognitive style.

Impulsive and reflective cognitive styles

Jerome Kagan (1964b, 1964c) has performed a series of studies on the styles of conceptualization manifested by different children. He has concluded that some children seem to be characteristically *impulsive*, whereas others are characteristically *reflective*. He notes that impulsive children have a fast conceptual tempo; they tend to come forth with the first answer they can think of and are concerned about giving quick responses in school situations. Reflective children, on the other hand, take time before they speak; they seem to prefer to evaluate alternative answers and to give correct responses rather than quick ones. When taking tests, impulsive pupils may answer more questions but also make more errors than reflective pupils. Kagan also concluded that impulsiveness appears to be a general trait that appears early in a person's life and is consistently revealed in a variety of situations. Other types of thinking Kagan refers to as *analytic* and *thematic*. Analytic students tend to note details when exposed to a complex stimulus, whereas thematic students respond to the pattern as a whole (or in global fashion).

Analytic and thematic cognitive styles

Tamar Zelniker and Wendell Jeffrey (1976) carried out several experiments to check on Kagan's observations regarding cognitive styles. They found that reflective children perform better on tasks requiring analysis of details, while impulsive children seem to do better on tasks requiring global interpretations. They concluded that impulsive children are not necessarily inferior to reflective children in problem-solving ability, as some earlier students of cognitive style had concluded. Impulsive thinkers may do less well on many school and test situations that require analysis of details, primarily because they prefer to look at problems in a thematic or global way. The impulsive thinker may often be a thematic thinker as well, possessing a fast conceptual tempo combined with a tendency to look at the big picture. Reflective thinkers are more deliberate, but their tendencies toward analytic thinking cause them to concentrate on details.

Samuel Messick (1976) has summarized research on other cognitive styles. He notes that some children more than others seem to experience things vividly and also are aware of many more aspects of a situation at a given moment. Some children are more likely than others to be distracted by conflicting ideas. Other children appear to place things in broad categories compared to age-mates who classify experiences into many separate categories. Still other children seem to

Children who are impulsive thinkers have a fast conceptual tempo. They also tend to look at a situation in global (or thematic) terms. As a consequence, they may not do as well on school assignments that require analysis of details (such as multiple-choice tests) as children who are reflective and analytic thinkers. Elizabeth Crews/Stock, Boston.

have a tendency to "level" memories by merging similar recollections, as contrasted with peers who retain distinct recollections of separate experiences. J. P. Guilford (1967) has concluded that some individuals appear to be *convergent* thinkers—they respond to what they read and observe in conventional, typical ways. Others are *divergent* thinkers—they respond in unexpected or idiosyncratic ways. Some children memorize much more easily than others; some are more capable than others of grasping ideas and evaluating their accuracy or appropriateness in a particular situation.

Convergent and divergent cognitive styles

Still another type of cognitive style is referred to as *field dependence* or *field independence*. Herman Witkin and others (1962) developed a technique for measuring how individuals perceive situations and respond to problems. He seated subjects in a specially constructed chair in a darkened room. An illuminated rod and frame that could be moved independently were placed in front of the subject, who was instructed to tell the experimenter how to move the rod so that it would appear vertical. Sometimes the frame would be tilted; in other cases the chair would be tilted; sometimes both would be placed at a angle. Witkin and several associates (Witkin, Dyk, Faterson, Goodenough, and Karp, 1962) carried out a series of studies with subjects of varying ages and found that some individuals were better able than others to perceive the rod independent of the frame (the *field* or background). A *field-dependent* person depends on the visual field (the frame) to make deductions about the position of the rod. If the frame is tilted, the field dependent person will instruct the experimenter to align the rod so that it is parallel to the side of the frame. The *field-independent* person, by contrast, using body position as a guide, does not need to depend on visual cues and is better able to disregard the position of the frame in aligning the rod. Witkin and his colleagues found that as children mature, they tend to become more field independent. Individual differences, however, remain quite stable. That is, some children tend to be field dependent throughout their school years; others tend to be field independent. Witkin also discovered that males at all age levels tend to be more field independent than females.

In subsequent investigations Witkin and Goodenough (1976) found that field independent individuals tend to be active and self-motivated, they assume a participant role and prefer physical science subjects. Field dependent individuals tend to assume a spectator role, they are more sensitive to social situations, and they prefer social science subjects. The fact that males in many cultures tend to be more field independent than females (Witkin and Berry, 1975) may be an indication that there is a genetic factor involved. On the other hand, it is possible that the differential treatment of boys and girls (noted in discussing parental responses to infants and young children in earlier chapters) may favor general independence in males and cause females to function more as spectators who also become concerned about social relationships. (Efforts to determine if specific child-rearing practices are related to field dependence or independence [for example, Witkin, 1969] have not yielded clear-cut results.)

Sex Differences in School Achievement

Sex differences in field dependence and independence suggest that as soon as boys and girls enter the primary grades and are asked to learn basic skills and acquire information, they show different interests and abilities. Some of these center on specific subjects and skills; others involve general attitudes toward school and teachers. Helen L. Bee (1974, p. 7) analyzed sex differences in cognitive functioning and found evidence (similar to that reported by Maccoby and Jacklin [1974] and by Block [1976]) that during the elementary school years girls, on the average, are superior in verbal fluency, spelling, and reading, and that they earn higher grades. Boys, on the average, are superior in mathematical reasoning and in tasks involving understanding of spatial relationships. One possible explanation for boys' superior ability in mathematical reasoning is that their greater tendency toward field independence helps them to concentrate on specific aspects of a situation without being confused by background information. Possible explanations for the verbal superiority of females include the following (some of which have already been noted): girls interact more with their mothers, they are more likely to use words than actions to express their needs, they mature more rapidly.

The average American girl earns higher grades in school than the average boy. The superior academic performance of girls has been attributed to their faster rate of maturity, their superiority in verbal and language skills, and their desire to please adults. Barth J. Falkenberg, staff photographer, *The Christian Science Monitor.*

Females earn higher grades in school, but males are more likely to achieve at a higher level in many activities later in life. Lois Wladis Hoffman (1972) suggests that the better school performance of girls may be due, in part at least, to their desire to please. Boys, by contrast, appear more interested in working on tasks that interest them and less concerned about earning approval. Because of these tendencies, girls may want to earn high grades in order to arouse a positive response from parents and teachers and boys may engage in more self-motivated study. If a boy does not find a particular subject interesting, he may not make much of an effort to learn it, which will lead to poorer overall evaluations on report cards. But the tendency for a boy to study something for its own sake may be beneficial later in life when prolonged self-directed study is called for.

Hoffman speculates that girls may be motivated by a desire to please because they are not encouraged to strive for independence early in life. On the basis of research carried out by Howard Moss (1967), she suggests that mothers tend to think of male infants as sturdy and active and female infants as delicate dolls (despite the fact that female infants are more mature and better able to cope with many forms of stress than male infants). As a result, mothers overprotect female infants and treat them as dependent. This process continues throughout childhood. Hoffman also hypothesizes that a girl may find it more difficult to develop autonomy and independence because she identifies more completely with the

Girls may earn higher grades because of desire to please adults

primary caretaker (almost always the mother) and her first teachers (almost all of whom are women) and also experiences less conflict with them.

The Significance and Ramifications of Academic Achievement

America is a meritocratic society in which persons from the humblest origins can achieve success through their own efforts. In many cases success later in life depends on doing well in school. And a child who does not get a good start during the elementary school years may have an extraordinarily difficult time overcoming this handicap later on. Upper- and middle-class parents tend to be more aware of the importance of early success in school than lower-class parents, partly because they are more likely to have benefited themselves from successful educational experiences. Early intervention, Head Start, and Follow Through programs have been established in an effort to supply children from impoverished backgrounds with the kinds of experiences and motivation that give more favored children advantages in school. A basic premise of such programs is that if disadvantaged children are helped to a good start in responding to educational experiences, they are more likely to later qualify for jobs that will permit them to improve their economic and social standing.

These comments suggest the opportunities provided by school achievement. But the fact that doing well in school is such an important prerequisite to later success causes six- to twelve-year-olds to experience pressure and anxiety. As they move through the elementary grades children become increasingly aware that in order to succeed they must compete against others. They also learn that certain types of abilities contribute more to success than others. A child who learns to read rapidly and easily, for example, will have a substantial advantage in school work over one who experiences problems acquiring that skill. Cognitive style may take on increasing significance as children are asked to deal with more complex aspects of the school curriculum. A field-independent child, for example, may enjoy advantages over a field-dependent pupil when the time comes to learn geometry or to engage in self-directed study.

Because of individual differences in intelligence, background, motivation, specific types of abilities, cognitive style, and related characteristics, some children do better in school than others. As children become aware of differences in academic performance and of the significance of earning high grades, they are likely to experience the kinds of conflicts described by Erikson and Horney. Children who fail to develop a sense of industry and think of themselves as inferior, or children who become aware that success must often be won at the expense of others, are particularly likely to experience conflicting thoughts and emotions.

Even children who develop a sense of industry or who manage to be both successful and popular, however, are faced with conflicts centering on morality. Elementary school children become progressively aware of the nature and significance of moral norms, school rules, and the laws of society. One reason for this developing awareness is that they increasingly interact with others and realize that in order to get along with others certain common understandings and regulations must be established. Another reason is that the gradual transition from concrete operational to formal thinking makes it possible for them to grasp and apply general principles. But even as they become aware of the necessity for codes and rules, and capable of understanding how and when to apply them, elementary school children are faced with temptations to ignore moral codes or break rules or laws that interfere with their needs and desires. A child who finds a wallet must decide whether or not to return it to the owner. A child who needs a particular score on an important test in order to earn an A may feel driven to cheat. A child who covets a toy that is as impressive as that recently given to a friend is tempted to steal it. To complicate matters further, elementary school children become increasingly aware that many adults, sometimes including highly regarded public officials or perhaps their own parents, occasionally behave in thoughtless, immoral, or illegal ways. Furthermore, crimes committed by juvenile offenders have increased sharply in the last few years and only a fraction of adolescents who commit crimes are caught and punished. (Statistical data relating to this point will be presented in Chapter 13.) Accordingly, elementary school children are quite likely to observe or hear about the escapades of peers who committed an illegal act, got away with it, benefited from it, bragged about it, and were admired for it.

Moral development during the six- to twelve-year span is therefore of great significance. During this period of development children acquire the cognitive abilities to begin to comprehend the underlying reasons for honoring moral norms and obeying laws. They also become aware of conflicts between regulations and personal desires that are particularly acute in a competitive, affluent, meritocratic society. And they may also be confused and dismayed by the realization that many adults and older children set a negative example. For all of these reasons, psychologists and educators have been interested in finding ways to encourage moral behavior in children. Such concern is not new, though. The topics of moral development and moral education have been studied for more than fifty years.

Moral Development

The Hartshorne and May Studies of Character

In 1922 the leaders of the Religious Education Association felt so concerned about immorality in America that they passed a resolution to attempt a scientific investigation of the question "How is religion being taught to young people, and with what effect?" They asked Hugh Hartshorne, a professor of religious education, and Mark May, a professor of psychology, to help them find answers to these questions. Hartshorne and May were provided with a substantial budget and supervised a comprehensive series of ingenious studies to discover how children reacted when placed in situations that centered on deceit, generosity, charitableness, and self-control (1929, 1930a, 1930b).

Thousands of children at different age levels were observed reacting in situations that revealed their actual moral behavior. The same children were also asked to respond to questions about hypothetical situations to reveal how much they understood about right and wrong behavior. Elementary school children, for example, were allowed to correct their own papers or record their own scores on measures of athletic skill without being aware that accurate measures were being made independently by adult observers. They were also asked what they *thought* was the right thing to do in similar situations. A comparison of the two sets of data made it possible to determine, among other things, if children practiced what they preached. Hartshorne and May wanted information about these two aspects of moral development to discover if the immoral behavior of young children was due to ignorance. They discovered, however, that many children who were able to describe right kinds of behavior in hypothetical situations indulged in wrong behavior in real-life situations.

One significant discovery of Hartshorne and May was that children behave in situations that call for moral judgment by reacting in specific rather than consistent ways. Even a child who was rated as among the most honest in a group would behave in a dishonest way under certain circumstances. A boy who was an excellent student but an indifferent athlete, for example, would not cheat when asked to correct his own paper, but he *would* inflate scores on sports skills. A girl who was an excellent athlete but a terrible speller would alter dozens of misspelled words on a paper, but be completely accurate in recording her physical performance.

Moral behavior depends on circumstances

After reviewing research carried out in the forty-five years since Hartshorne and May published their findings, Thomas Lickona reported that "A huge and ever-expanding body of research . . . has replicated Hartshorne and May's basic finding: Variations in the situation produce variations in moral behavior" (1976, p. 15). Lickona adds, though, that recent research also supports another conclusion of Hartshorne and May that some children are more "integrated" (or consistent) than others in reacting to moral situations. It would appear to be a mistake, therefore, to assume that there is *no* consistency in moral thinking and behavior. If that hypothesis is endorsed, there would be little reason to assume that a child develops any kind of personal code of ethics or that parents and teachers should try to promote the development of a strong conscience in children.

Another factor to consider regarding consistency of moral behavior is that the various descriptions of stages in moral reasoning that will be summarized later in this chapter all stress that children exhibit characteristic types of thinking at different age levels. Some of the theories, moreover, are based on the assumption that particular children at any given stage will respond to moral situations in the same basic way. Perhaps the best way to summarize the issue of generality versus specificity in moral thinking and behavior, therefore, is to suggest that many children respond in quite consistent ways when confronted with moral decisions. But all children have a breaking point and may behave immorally when the personal stakes are high. This breaking point is probably much higher for some children (who have a well-developed conscience) than it is for others.

Another significant, and dismaying, discovery of Hartshorne and May was that children who went to Sunday School or who belonged to such organizations as the Boy Scouts or Girl Scouts were just as dishonest as children who were not exposed to the kind of moral instruction provided by such organizations. The members of the Religious Education Association learned, therefore, that the effect of religious education at that time seemed to be negligible. Hartshorne and May concluded that one explanation for the ineffectiveness of moral instruction in the 1920s was that too much stress was placed on having children memorize platitudes such as the Ten Commandments or the Boy Scout oath and law. They suggested that many children who could recite "Thou shalt not steal" or who could unhesitatingly reel off "Trustworthy, loyal, helpful, friendly, courteous, kind, obedient, cheerful, thrifty, brave, clean, and reverent," either did not understand what they were saying or saw no connection between such elegant words and actual deeds. Hartshorne and May suggested that a more effective way to arrange moral instruction would be to invite children to discuss real-life moral situations as they occurred. Instead of having children chant "Honesty is the best policy," for example, they urged teachers to call attention to the positive consequences of honest acts. If a pupil in a school reported that he or she had found money belonging to someone else, the teacher might praise the child and ask everyone in the class to think about how relieved the person who had lost the money would be to have it returned.

Being able to recite principles has no effect on moral behavior

Partial explanations for the inability of the children studied by Hartshorne and May to understand moral principles or to apply them in consistent ways were supplied by studies of moral judgment carried out by Jean Piaget.

Piaget's Analysis of the Moral Judgment of the Child

Age Changes in Interpretation of Rules About the time that Hartshorne and May were publishing their reports, Jean Piaget was carrying on a very different kind of investigation of moral development. Instead of obtaining data from thousands of subjects, Piaget started out observing how a handful of Swiss children played marbles. (He first took the trouble to learn the game himself so that he would be able to understand the subtleties of the competition.) Piaget discovered that interpretations of rules followed by participants in marble games changed with age. Four- to seven-year-olds just learning the game seemed to view rules as interesting examples of the social behavior of older children. They did not understand them but tried to go along with them. Seven- to ten-year-olds regarded rules as sacred pronouncements handed down by older children or adults. At about the age of eleven or twelve rules were seen as agreements reached due to mutual consent. Piaget concluded that younger children see rules as absolute and external.

Around 10: from sacred and imposed rules to mutual agreements

Even though children from the age of four to about ten years do not question rules, however, they may frequently break them because of incomplete understanding. After the age of eleven or so, children become increasingly capable of grasping why rules are necessary. At that point, Piaget concluded, they tend to lose interest in adult-imposed regulations and take delight in formulating their own variations of rules to fit a particular situation. Piaget illustrates this point by describing (1962, p. 50) how a group of ten- and eleven-year-old boys prepared for a snowball fight. They divided themselves into teams, elected officers, decided on rules to govern the distances from which the snowballs could be thrown, and agreed on a system of punishments for those who violated the rules. Even though they wasted a substantial amount of play time engaging in such preliminary discussions, they seemed to thoroughly enjoy their newly discovered ability to make up rules to supplant those that had previously been imposed on them by their elders.

Reactions to Stories Involving Moral Decisions   The way children of different ages responded to rules so intrigued Piaget he decided to use the clinical-interview method to obtain more systematic information about moral development. He made up pairs of stories and asked children of different ages to discuss them. Here is a typical pair of stories:

There was a little boy called Julian. His father had gone out and Julian thought it would be fun to play with his father's ink-pot. First he played with the pen, and then he made a little blot on the table cloth.

A little boy who was called Augustus once noticed that his father's ink-pot was empty. One day that his father was away he thought of filling the ink-pot so as to help his father, and so that he should find it full when he came home. But while he was opening the ink-bottle he made a big blot on the table cloth. (1962, p. 122)

After reading these stories Piaget asked "Are these children equally guilty? Which of the two is naughtiest, and why?" As was the case with interpretations of rules, Piaget found that younger children reacted to these stories differently than older children. The way six-year-olds interpreted rules, and the answers they gave when confronted with the pairs or stories, led Piaget to conclude that their moral reasoning is quite different from that of twelve-year-olds.

Piaget refers to the moral thinking of children up to the age of ten or so as *morality of constraint*, but he also calls it *moral realism* or *heteronomous morality*.

(*Heteros* is Greek for *other*; *nomos* is Greek for *law*. Therefore, *heteronomous* means subject to external rules or laws.) The thinking of children of eleven or older Piaget calls the *morality of cooperation*. The terms *autonomous morality, morality of reciprocity, moral relativism,* and *moral flexibility* are sometimes also used. After analyzing the responses of elementary school children in clinical interviews Piaget concluded that the two basic types of moral reasoning differ in several ways which are summarized in Table 11–1. To clarify and illustrate some of the differences between the moralities of constraint and cooperation summarized in Table 11–1, here are some examples and explanations of types of thinking that characterize the thinking of moral realists (that is, those who use the morality of constraint).

The Nature of Moral Realism (or the Morality of Constraint)   The younger child sees rules as *real*—ready made and external. Because rules are imposed by outside authority, it is assumed they should always be obeyed the same way. The letter of the law rather than the spirit of the law must be observed, and no exceptions are allowed. An illustration of these characteristics of moral realism is provided by reactions of younger and older children to a change in rules. Several children of elementary school age were playing baseball in a vacant lot bordered by weeds. One excellent hitter decided to get some additional batting practice by deliberately hitting several foul balls in a row. Each time a ball was hit foul, however, it took quite a bit of time to find it in the weeds. Accordingly, some of the older children proposed that anyone who hit two foul balls in a row was out. Most of the players agreed, but the youngest child in the group was so upset by this change in the official rules of baseball that he refused to play and went home in a huff. The moral realist, in addition, thinks literally and in terms of blind obedience—no allowance is made for motives or intentions. Furthermore, the degree of guilt is equated with the seriousness of the consequences. These characteristics of moral realism are illustrated by the responses of children to the ink-blot stories. Younger children interviewed by Piaget mantained that Augustus was more guilty than Julian because he had made a bigger blot. No account was taken of the fact that Julian was misbehaving and that Augustus was trying to help his father.

Moral realism: sacred rules; no exceptions; no allowance for intentions; consequences determine guilt

Some aspects of these differences in the moral reasoning of younger and older children can be understood by taking into account Piaget's descriptions of cognitive development. The child of six who has not completely mastered decentration will tend to think of only one thing at a time and will therefore not be inclined to weigh alternatives. Before the age of seven, a child who has not made the transition from egocentric to socialized speech will find it difficult to consider different points of view. And a child who has not moved from concrete operational to formal thought will be unable to consider hypothetical situations and anticipate consequences. Because of the tendency to think of one thing at a time, the young child finds it difficult to comprehend situations where a rule might be revised to allow for special circumstances. The same tendency to focus on one thing at a time leads the younger child to reason that a big ink blot,

Table 11–1
Differences Between Morality of Constraint
and Morality of Cooperation

MORALITY OF CONSTRAINT (TYPICAL OF SIX-YEAR-OLDS)	MORALITY OF COOPERATION (TYPICAL OF TWELVE-YEAR-OLDS)
Single, absolute moral perspective (behavior is right *or* wrong)	Awareness of differing viewpoints regarding rules
Conception of rules as unchangeable	View of rules as flexible
Extent of guilt determined by amount of damage	Consideration of a wrongdoer's intentions when evaluating guilt
Definition of moral wrongness in terms of what is forbidden or punished	Definition of moral wrongness in terms of violation of spirit of cooperation

(Note that these first four differences call attention to the tendency for children below the age of ten or so to think of rules as sacred pronouncements handed down by external authority)

Punishment should stress atonement and does not need to "fit the crime"	Punishment should involve either restitution or suffering the same fate as a victim of someone's wrongdoing
Peer aggression should be punished by an external authority	Peer aggression should be punished by retaliatory behavior on the part of the victim[1]
Children should obey because rules are established by those in authority	Children should obey rules because of mutual concern for the rights of others

(Note how these last three differences call attention to the tendency for children above the age of ten or so to see rules as mutual agreements among equals)

[1]Beyond the age of twelve adolescents increasingly affirm that reciprocal reactions, or "getting back," should occur in response only to good behavior, not to bad behavior.

Source: Freely adapted from interpretations of Piaget (1932) by Kohlberg (1969) and Lickona (1976b).

regardless of how it is caused, is worse than a small ink blot. The younger child concentrates on obvious physical properties and does not take into account nonobservable factors such as intentions.

Piaget found that children up to the age of ten or so abide by a morality of constraint: they insist on obedience to fixed rules which they believe are established by external authority. Above the age of ten children become increasingly capable of adopting a morality of cooperation: they view rules as flexible and recognize that they are mutual agreements among equals. Philip Jon Bailey; Nancy Hays/Monkmeyer.

Piaget's description of cognitive development also helps explain some of the conclusions of Hartshorne and May. Concrete operational thinking causes elementary grade children to think in terms of actual experiences, which may account, in part, for the tendency for children to be honest in one situation but not another. Furthermore, children who are not capable of formal thinking are unable to comprehend general principles or apply them in varied situations, which explains the ineffectiveness of moral instruction that stresses the memorization of abstract principles such as the Ten Commandments or the Boy Scout oath and law.

Thomas Lickona (1976b) reviewed research relating to differences between the moralities of constraint and cooperation and concluded that there is quite a bit of experimental evidence to support the general distinction Piaget has made between the moral thinking of younger and older elementary grade children. It appears, however, that these differences are most apparent when the thinking of six- and twelve-year-olds is compared. Children in the middle of this age range are likely to think sometimes as moral realists and function sometimes as moral relativists, depending on the situation and whether or not they have had experience with similar situations.

Kohlberg's Description of Moral Development

Kohlberg's Use of Moral Dilemmas   As a graduate student at the University of Chicago in the 1950s Lawrence Kohlberg became fascinated by Piaget's studies of moral development. He decided to expand on Piaget's original research by making up stories involving moral dilemmas that would be more appropriate for older children. Here is the story that is most often mentioned in discussions of his work:

> In Europe a woman was near death from cancer. One drug might save her, a form of radium that a druggist in the same town had recently discovered. The druggist was charging $2000, ten times what the drug cost him to make. The sick woman's husband, Heinz, went to everyone he knew to borrow the money, but he could only get together about half of what it cost. He told the druggist that his wife was dying and asked him to sell it cheaper or let him pay later, but the druggist said "No." The husband got desperate and broke into the man's store to steal the drug for his wife. Should the husband have done that? Why? (Kohlberg, 1969, p. 376)

Kohlberg's Six Stages of Moral Reasoning   After analyzing the responses of ten- to sixteen-year-olds to this and similar moral dilemmas, Kohlberg eventually (1963) developed a description of six stages of moral reasoning. Be forewarned, however, that Kohlberg has revised some of his original stage designations, and descriptions of the stages have been modified since he first proposed them. In different discussions of his stages, therefore, you may encounter varying descriptions. The outline presented in Table 11–2 is a composite summary of the sequence of moral development as it has been described by Kohlberg, but you should expect to find differences if you read other accounts of his theory.

The scoring system Kohlberg developed to evaluate a given response to a moral dilemma is extremely complex. Furthermore, the responses of subjects are lengthy and may feature arguments about a particular decision. To help you understand a bit more about each Kohlberg stage, simplified examples of responses to a dilemma such as that faced by Heinz are noted below. For maximum clarity, only brief typical responses to the question "Why shouldn't you steal from a store?" are mentioned.

- ☐ Stage 1 Punishment-Obedience Orientation. "You might get caught." (The physical consequences of an action determine goodness or badness.)
- ☐ Stage 2 Instrumental Relativist Orientation. "You shouldn't steal something from a store and the store owner shouldn't steal things that belong to you." (Obeying laws should involve an even exchange.)
- ☐ Stage 3 Good Boy—Nice Girl Orientation. "Your parents will be proud of you if you are honest." (The right action is one that will impress others.)

☐ Stage 4 Law and Order Orientation. "It's against the law and if we don't obey laws our whole society might fall apart." (To maintain the social order, fixed rules must be obeyed.)

☐ Stage 5 Social Contract Orientation. "Under certain circumstances laws may have to be disregarded—if a person's life depends on breaking a law, for instance." (Rules should involve mutual agreements, the rights of the individual should be protected.)

☐ Stage 6 Universal Ethical Principle Orientation. "You need to weigh all the factors and then try to make the most appropriate decision in a given situation. Sometimes it would be morally wrong *not* to steal." (Moral decisions should be based on consistent applications of self-chosen ethical principles.)

Similarities and Differences Between Piaget and Kohlberg   As you examined this list of stages and the examples of responses at each type, you may have detected similarities between Piaget's and Kohlberg's descriptions of age changes in moral development. The first four of Kohlberg's stages are roughly equivalent to moral realism as described by Piaget. Kohlberg's preconventional and conventional moral thinkers and Piaget's moral realists all tend to think of rules as edicts handed down by external authority. The letter of the law is observed and not much allowance is made for intentions or circumstances. The postconventional thinker of Kohlberg shares some similarities with the older children observed by Piaget: rules are established by individuals who come to mutual agreement, each moral decision is made by taking into account special circumstances.

While there are similarities in the conclusions drawn by Piaget and Kohlberg, there are also important differences. Piaget believes that moral thinking changes as children mature. He does not believe that the changes are clearly related to age nor are they considered to be sequential. Piaget feels that the different types of moral thinking he described often overlap and that a child might sometimes function as a moral realist, sometimes as a more mature moral decision-maker. Kohlberg (1969), by contrast, maintains that the order of the stages he has described is universal and fixed and that a person moves through the stages in sequence. Not everyone reaches the top stages, but all individuals begin at stage one and work their way upwards.

Kohlberg: stages of morality universal, sequential

In some respects, there are greater similarities between Piaget's description of *cognitive* development and Kohlberg's description of moral development than between the two outlines of moral development. Piaget describes preoperational, concrete operational, and formal operational stages. Kohlberg describes preconventional, conventional, and postconventional levels. Even though he does not stress an orderly sequence of *moral* development, Piaget does believe that children go through the stages of *cognitive* development in definite order. Piaget's formal operational stage and Kohlberg's postconventional level both stress understanding

Table 11–2
Kohlberg's Stages of Moral Reasoning

☐ Level 1   Preconventional Morality. (Typical of children up to the age of nine. Called preconventional because young children do not really understand the conventions or rules of a society.)

   Stage 1   Punishment-Obedience Orientation. The physical consequences of an action determine goodness or badness. Those in authority have superior power and should be obeyed. Punishment should be avoided by staying out of trouble.

   Stage 2   Instrumental Relativist Orientation. An action is judged to be right if it is instrumental in satisfying one's own needs or involves an even exchange. Obeying rules should bring some sort of benefit in return.

☐ Level 2   Conventional Morality. (Typical of nine- to twenty-year-olds. Called conventional since most nine- to twenty-year-olds conform to the conventions of society because they *are* the rules of a society.)

   Stage 3   Good Boy—Nice Girl Orientation. The right action is one that would be carried out by someone whose behavior is likely to please or impress others.

   Stage 4   Law and Order Orientation. To maintain the social order, fixed rules must be established and obeyed. It is essential to respect authority.

☐ Level 3   Postconventional Morality. (Usually reached only after the age of twenty and by only a small proportion of adults. Called postconventional because the moral principles that underlie the conventions of a society are understood.)

   Stage 5   Social Contract Orientation. Rules needed to maintain the social order should be based not on blind obedience to authority but on mutual agreement. At the same time, the rights of the individual should be protected.

   Stage 6   Universal Ethical Principle Orientation. Moral decisions should be made in terms of self-chosen ethical principles. Once principles are chosen, they should be applied in consistent ways.

Source: Based on descriptions in Kohlberg, 1969, and Kohlberg, 1976.

and application of abstract principles and taking into account unique circumstances in a given situation. A person cannot engage in postconventional moral reasoning, in fact, until after formal thinking is mastered, but only a small proportion of formal thinkers consistently apply universal ethical principles.

Preconventional moral thinkers obey laws because they want to avoid punishment or because they want an even exchange. Conventional moral thinkers obey in order to impress others or because they feel law and order must be maintained. Postconventional moral thinkers obey because they realize that laws are based on mutual agreements and consistent principles. © Sepp Seitz 1979/ Woodfin Camp.

Evaluations of Kohlberg's Theory   In the years since he first proposed his theory, Kohlberg has performed extensive research using the moral dilemmas he wrote and the scoring scheme he devised to evaluate levels of moral thinking. Dozens of other investigators have carried out similar studies. (For a comprehensive review, see T. Lickona, 1976b.) Some psychologists have reported evidence that substantiates Kohlberg's hypotheses that the stages he has described are fixed, sequential, and universal. Other investigators, however, have reported evidence that does not support these hypotheses and have raised questions about Kohlberg's basic approach and some of his conclusions. In summarizing such criticisms, William Kurtines and Esther Greif (1974) point out several weaknesses of the Kohlberg theory:

Not all studies support hypotheses of universal, sequential stages

1   Kohlberg wrote nine moral dilemmas, but an average of six of these have been presented to most subjects. Consequently, not all subjects have responded to the same set of dilemmas.
2   The main characters in almost all of the dilemmas are male, which may help account for the fact that females often earn lower moral development scores than males.

3   The scoring of the responses of subjects is complex, difficult to master, and more or less controlled by Kohlberg who has issued the complete scoring scheme only to selected investigators. (A few years after this criticism was made Kohlberg made available a revised and simplified scoring scheme.)

4   The relationship between moral reasoning and moral behavior has not been established. There is little experimental evidence to indicate that a person who can supply postconventional answers to hypothetical dilemmas will act in a similar way in a real-life situation. (The results of the Hartshorne and May studies would lead to the expectation that there would be substantial differences between what children *say* they would do when responding to the case of Heinz, for example, and what they would actually *do* in a less fanciful situation involving breaking a law under extenuating circumstances.)

Educational Implications of Kohlberg's Theory   Even though serious questions have been raised about the validity of Kohlberg's theory, some individuals (including Kohlberg himself) have speculated about the possibility of using the conception of stages to foster moral development. Several psychologists have undertaken to help or teach children to proceed through the stages of moral development faster and further than they would on their own. Even though most adolescents engage in some aspects of formal operational thinking, very few adolescents or adults reach the postconventional level of moral reasoning. This is unfortunate because postconventional thinkers adapt their responses to unique situations. Elliot Turiel (1966) made the first attempt to induce changes from lower to higher stages. The subjects were twelve- and thirteen-year-old boys with equivalent IQs, drawn at random from a seventh-grade class. The boys were divided into groups and exposed to arguments for and against moral dilemmas that emphasized reasoning one stage below, one stage above, and two stages above their initial stage of moral thinking. The results indicated that arguments one level above a given stage produced more of an effect than the other arguments. The improvement in moral reasoning was quite modest, however.

In a later study, Moshe Blatt (1975) used group discussions instead of arguments to try to improve the moral reasoning of ten- to twelve-year-old boys attending a Reform Jewish Sunday School and four public school classrooms. Asking the children to carry on their own analyses (with supervision by Blatt) led to significant increases in the moral thinking of children attending the Sunday School (most of whom came from academic and professional families). The children in the public school groups registered less impressive improvement. Control group children who had not participated in discussion showed no change. A follow-up investigation (Blatt and Kohlberg, 1978) concluded that the increases were permanent (although the moral reasoning of the children when they were older might have been attributed, in part, to a greater number of intellectual and moral experiences). The results of the Blatt study led Kohlberg himself to experiment with discussion techniques intended to lead individuals to achieve higher levels of moral reasoning. At first he worked with inmates of correctional institutions, then he developed moral education programs with high school students (Kohlberg, 1975). Details and implications of his approach with high school students will be noted in Chapter 13 when moral development during the adolescent years is discussed.

Values Clarification

Even though not explicitly based on Kohlberg's theory, an approach to moral education that became popular in the 1970s merits mention at this point since it is very similar to the group-discussion technique originated by Blatt and now being used by Kohlberg. *Values clarification* was first proposed by Louis Raths for helping children become more aware of their values (some of which are similar to types of moral thinking described by Piaget and Kohlberg). In the first book on the subject, *Values and Teaching* (1966) by Raths, Merrill Harmin, and Sidney B. Simon, the basic approach of values clarification was described. The authors proposed that students are likely to develop a set of values that will help them make confident and consistent choices and decisions if they engage in the following activities:

☐ Choose their beliefs and behavior by first considering and then selecting from alternatives.

☐ Prize their beliefs and behaviors by cherishing and publicly affirming them.

☐ Act on their beliefs repeatedly and consistently.

Values clarification: encourage children to choose, prize, and act on their beliefs

Seventy-nine strategies for helping students engage in such activities are described in *Values Clarification: A Handbook of Practical Strategies for Teachers and Students* (1972) by Sidney B. Simon, Leland W. Howe, and Howard Kirschenbaum. First, students are asked to choose their beliefs freely and from carefully considered alternatives. In Strategy 5, "Either-Or Forced Choice" (pp. 94–97), for example, the teacher asks students, "Which do you identify with more, a Volkswagen or a Cadillac?" Pupils indicate their preference by walking to one side of the room or the opposite; they then team up with a classmate who made the same choice and explain the reasons for the choice. Students are encouraged to cherish and publicly affirm their beliefs by engaging in activities such as that presented in Strategy 12, "Public Interview" (pp. 139–162). In this strategy a student volunteers to be interviewed by the rest of the class and publicly affirms and explains his or her stand on various issues.

Several of the strategies devised by values clarification enthusiasts involve moral dilemmas very similar to those devised by Piaget and Kohlberg. An important difference between the values clarification approach and the discussions supervised by Blatt and Kohlberg is that children not only talk about what they will do in values clarification sessions, they also are encouraged to *act*. Once students have chosen values and publicly affirmed them, they are urged to do something in accordance with those beliefs. If pupils say they are interested in recycling natural resources, for example, they are urged to write letters favoring that view, participate in paper drives, and so on.

The Importance of the Superego (Conscience)

Kohlberg feels character education is necessary because so few adults consistently engage in postconventional thinking. But if the conflicting pressures exerted on a child confronted with *genuine* (not hypothetical) moral dilemmas are considered, the possibility of easy success seems remote. One of the difficulties of moral decisions is that they often have to be made in a split second. The child wrestling with a hypothetical moral dilemma in a discussion has the opportunity to think over responses and also is likely to feel that the decision need not be final. But consider an actual moral dilemma that might be faced by an eleven-year-old boy. Assume he has had his allowance cut for failing to get sufficiently high grades. A few minutes after school has been dismissed on the fateful day, he returns to his classroom to pick up a forgotten book. He hears the school secretary call his teacher to the telephone and as he approaches his room, he sees the teacher hurrying down the empty hall in the opposite direction. When he enters the room, he notices the week's lunch money on the teacher's desk. He is quite sure no one saw him enter the room, and he realizes the teacher will be back in a minute or two, so he must make a snap decision. Should he grab some of the money, or wait by the door until the teacher returns?

Many moral decisions must be made on spur of moment

The response of a person in such a situation is almost "reflexive," since there is no time to weigh the relative merits of different courses of action. The person must act first and think later. In many cases, making an *immoral* decision may permit the person to engage in more analysis and to have more of a choice than making a moral decision. For example, if the boy decides not to take the money, he may never have another opportunity like it; but if he does take it, he can think things over and still exercise the option of returning it to his teacher. He cannot be sure how she will react, however, and since the deed is an accomplished fact, the successful culprit might be inclined to rationalize, "The teacher gave me a lousy grade and that's the reason my allowance was cut, so she really owes me the money," or "They get money for the lunch program from the government, so a couple of dollars won't make any difference."

A strong conscience leads to "right" moral decisions but may cause guilt feelings

Snap decisions and later evaluations of them that represent postconventional thinking both bring into play one's conscience (or in Freudian terminology, one's superego): the internalized values that govern much of a person's behavior. In order to make the right decision in emergency situations, a person needs a strong, clear conscience so that the "reflexive" reaction will be the correct one. But such a conscience can be a source of considerable anxiety when postmortem analyses are made. A person with a weak conscience who acts in a flagrantly dishonest way

Many moral decisions must be made on the spur of the moment. In a situation such as this one, a child's conscience—rather than the ability to evaluate moral dilemmas at a sophisticated level of understanding—may be the key factor. Philip Jon Bailey.

will shrug it off and suffer no pangs of guilt. The individual with a strong conscience, however, may brood for weeks about such a mild thing as an ungracious remark or gesture. This leads to questions regarding the kinds of factors and experiences that lead to the development of the conscience of a child.

Factors Leading to the Development of a Child's Conscience

Martin L. Hoffman, who specializes in the study of moral development, has summarized types of experiences that seem to favor the internalization of moral norms (which might also be referred to as the formation of a child's conscience or superego).

The Impact of Disciplinary Techniques He reports (1979) that moral internalization appears to be initially fostered by disciplinary techniques used by parents when a child is guilty of immoral behavior. Children are most likely to internalize moral norms when the parents point out the harmful consequences of the behavior. Such explanations are most likely to be effective, though, if the parents frequently show affection for the child outside of disciplinary encounters. These two techniques are similar to those Diana Baumrind (1967, 1971) found were used by parents who promoted general competence in children. *Authoritative* parents, to review her findings, explained restrictions and also frequently showed their children that they loved and respected them. And just as Baumrind reported that parents who were *authoritarian* seemed to coerce their children into adopting acceptable forms of behavior, Hoffman found that parents who used excessive power-assertive discipline caused children to behave morally out of fear of punishment, not because of internalized standards. It appears, though, that parents who explain rather than physically punish need to make sure that the child pays attention to the explanation. If children who have just committed a moral offense are not impressed enough by their parents' attitude and behavior, they may ignore what they are told. If they are aroused too much, on the other hand, fear or resentment may interfere with their response to the parents' explanation. If a child has committed a moral transgression, therefore, it would seem wise for parents to treat the matter seriously and sympathetically but not casually or in an extreme or punitive way.

The Impact of Imitation   In addition to showing their children affection and explaining how immoral behavior may cause others to suffer, parents should do everything possible to set a good example. Freud was the first theorist to stress the significance of identification with parents. He proposed that children imitate their parents' moral behavior because of anxiety over either physical attack or loss of love. To reduce anxiety, Freud reasoned, the child tries to be like the parent through defensive (or "If you can't lick 'em, join 'em") identification. In his review, Hoffman notes that there is some evidence that children may acquire certain types of moral reasoning and behavior (for example, helping others) by identifying with their parents. However, identification is not likely to cause them to feel guilty after violating moral standards. One reason guilt is not likely to be learned through identification is that children up to the age of eight or so are egocentric thinkers. Another reason is that parents rarely communicate their own guilt feelings to children.

Children may acquire visible moral attributes through imitation but not acquire judgment

Freud's observations on identification were later interpreted by American psychologists such as Sears and Bandura in terms of social-learning theory as imitation. Hoffman concludes that experiments by social-learning theorists reveal that imitation may be an effective way for children to learn visible moral attributes that require little self-denial (for example, helping others). But these attributes are not likely to lead to the acquisition of moral standards children use in judging their own behavior (for example, resisting the temptation to steal something). Research by social-learning theorists also discloses that if children observe a peer who behaves aggressively or yields to temptation and is *not* punished, they are likely to imitate that behavior. Even if the peer model *is* punished, however, children may not be deterred from acting the same way.

These findings suggest that there may not be much value in parents and teachers making an example of a child who has committed a moral transgression by punishing him or her in front of siblings or classmates. It may be necessary for an elementary school child to have personal experience with moral instruction in order to internalize standards of conduct. It is likely that this is more the case for egocentric thinkers than for socialized thinkers, but direct experience seems to be more effective than observation at all ages. (Perhaps you have observed that drivers who are exceeding the speed limit may slow down when they observe a fellow motorist getting a ticket—but only for a few miles after they have passed the patrol car.)

The Significance of Empathy   An important aspect of conscience development is the ability and tendency for one person to respond in a vicarious way to the distress of others. In the discussion of prosocial development at the preschool level in Chapter 8, young children were reported to appear to be more likely to respond to the plight of others if they have had similar experiences themselves. Also noted were the relationship between aggressiveness and helping behavior, that children who express their own feelings strongly seem more likely to respond to overt expressions of the feelings of others, and that the experience of pleasure when helping someone else seems to strengthen the tendency to respond sympathetically.

In his review of moral development Hoffman traces the development of empathy. He concludes that even infants show certain signs of empathy but that it is not until the late elementary school years that children are capable of realizing that other individuals experience pleasure and pain not just at a particular moment in a given situation but in a variety of ways over a period of time. An eleven-year-old may understand, for example, that a friend whose dog is run over by a car will be unhappy not only just after the incident but for weeks or months after it has occurred. Hoffman also notes that late elementary grade school children show initial signs of recognizing the plight not only of individuals who share their own characteristics but of individuals and groups who possess characteristics they have not directly experienced (for example, starving children in an undeveloped country). These more subtle forms of empathy apparently may occur only after children become capable of formal thought and are able to deal with abstractions.

The Development of Interpersonal Reasoning   Changes in the development of empathy that Hoffman describes in his review have been studied intensively by Robert L. Selman (1976a, 1976b). Selman developed some *interpersonal dilemmas* similar to the moral dilemmas used by Kohlberg which he presents in the form of color-sound films. Here is his description of one of the interpersonal dilemmas he uses in his research:

Tom is trying to decide what present to buy his friend Mike, who will be given a surprise birthday party the next day. Tom meets Mike by chance and learns that Mike is extremely upset that his pet dog, Pepper, has been lost for 2 weeks. In fact, Mike is so upset that he tells Tom, "I miss Pepper so much I never want to look at another dog again." Tom goes off, only to pass a store with a sale on puppies; one or two are left and these will soon be gone. The dilemma is whether or not to buy the puppy for Mike's birthday. (1976b, p. 161)

After showing the film depicting this dilemma, Selman asked six- to twelve-year-old children to respond to a series of standard but open-ended questions designed to elicit the subject's reasoning about interpersonal relationships. Selman concluded that children become progressively more aware of the subtleties of interpersonal relationships as they move through the elementary grades. He describes five stages of interpersonal reasoning which are summarized in Table 11–3.

Some of these changes can be illustrated by responses of children to questions Selman asked after showing the film about Mike and Tom. When asked, "Can Mike be both happy and sad at the same time if he gets a new puppy for a gift?" six-year-olds deny that this is possible (probably because they find it difficult to decenter and therefore concentrate on only one type of feeling at a time). Children of nine years or so recognize that Mike can be sad about the lost puppy and be happy about getting a new one, but they picture these feelings as more or less distinct. That is, Mike will be sad first and then happy. It is not until they approach the end of the elementary school years that children are able to grasp that Mike can feel happy and sad at the same time.

Other aspects of the development of interpersonal reasoning are brought out by the question, "Does Mike really mean it when he says he never wants to see another puppy again?" Six-year-olds tend to take Mike's statement literally, twelve-year-olds begin to realize that Mike is trying to find an outlet for his grief and that he may not really feel the way he says he feels. Still another question, "What sort of boy is Mike?" reveals additional aspects of the development of understanding of the feelings of others. Six-year-olds tend to describe Mike's personality in terms of specific actions, for example, "Mike is a boy who lost his puppy." Twelve-year-olds reveal a more comprehensive understanding of Mike, for example he shows he is sensitive because he is so upset but he also seems to want others to feel sorry for him.

These various responses reveal that during the elementary school years children gradually grasp that a person's overt actions or words do not always reflect inner feelings. They also come to comprehend that there are often multiple facets to a person's reaction to a distressing situation. Toward the end of the elementary school years and increasingly during adolescence, children become capable of taking a somewhat detached and analytic view of their own behavior as well as the behavior of others.

Not surprisingly, the interpersonal sensitivity and maturity of a child seems to have an impact on relationships with others. Comparing the responses of seven- to twelve-year-old boys who were attending schools for children with learning and interpersonal problems with the responses of a matched group of boys attending regular schools, Selman found that the special schools boys were below average for their age in understanding the feelings of others.

Table 11–3

Stages of Interpersonal Reasoning Described by Selman

☐ Stage 0: The Egocentric Level (About ages 4 to 6)

Children do not recognize that other persons may interpret the same social event or course of action differently than they do. They do not reflect on the thoughts of self or others. They can label the overtly expressed feelings of others but do not comprehend cause-and-effect relations of social actions.

☐ Stage 1: Social Information Role Taking (About ages 6 to 8)

Children are able to differentiate between their own interpretations of social interactions and the interpretations of others but in limited ways. They cannot simultaneously think of their own view and the view of others.

☐ Stage 2: Self-Reflective Role Taking (About ages 8 to 10)

Interpersonal relations are interpreted in relation to specific situations where each person understands the expectations of the other in that particular context. Children are not yet able to view the two perspectives at once, however.

☐ Stage 3: Multiple Role Taking (About ages 10 to 12)

Children become capable of taking a third-person view which permits them to understand the expectations of themselves and of others in a variety of situations as if they were spectators.

☐ Stage 4: Social and Conventional System Role Taking (About ages 12 to 15+)

Each individual involved in a relationship with another understands many of the subtleties of the interactions involved. In addition, a societal perspective begins to develop. That is, actions are judged by how they might influence *all* individuals, not just those who are immediately concerned.

By 12, children understand subtleties of feelings, can take societal perspective

---

Source: Adapted from discussions in Selman 1976a and Selman 1976b.

Selman believes that teachers and therapists might be able to aid children who are not as advanced in role-taking skills as their age-mates by helping them become more sensitive to the feelings of others. If an eight-year-old boy is still functioning at the egocentric level, for example, he may fail to properly interpret the behavior of classmates and become a social isolate. Selman describes (1976a, p. 314) how such a boy was encouraged to think continually about the reasons behind his social actions and those of others and acquired sufficient social sensitivity to learn to get along with others.

The ability of children to comprehend how others feel not only contributes to skills in getting along with peers but to related aspects of moral development.

Children who understand the subtleties of the behavior and feelings of playmates, for example, are able to empathize more deeply with them. Children who can take a third-person view are more likely to be able to evaluate their own behavior and that of others when they engage in interactions based on mutually agreed-upon rules. (The baseball-in-the-weeds situation described earlier illustrates how a moral realist may not get along with moral relativists because rules are interpreted differently.) And being able to take a sensitive and comprehensive view of situations is also likely to lead to more mature analysis of moral dilemmas.

Stages in the Development of Empathy and Sympathy Selman's description of stages in interpersonal reasoning may be clarified by a very similar analysis Martin L. Hoffman (1976) has made of the development of empathy and sympathy. Hoffman suggests that there are three stages in the development of understanding of the feelings of others and in the reactions and motives of children who offer assistance to those in distress.

1 Level of person permanence. Children have acquired a sense of other individuals only as physical entities. They are capable of sensing another's distress, and of wanting to help, but they do not understand causes or know exactly *how* to help. Their efforts to help may be motivated primarily by a desire to end their own distress at seeing someone else suffer. (This is essentially the same as Selman's Egocentric Level.)

2 Level of role playing. Children realize that others have feelings and that these feelings may differ from their own, but their understanding is confined to a particular situation. They make an active effort to put themselves in another's place, and their efforts to help may no longer be based on a desire to relieve their own vicarious discomfort but on an altruistic wish to relieve the other person's distress. Efforts to help may proceed in trial-and-error fashion, however, and often feature frequent requests for feedback (for example, "Is there anything I can do?") (This level corresponds to Stages 1 and 2 in Selman's outline.)

3 Level of identity. Children realize that others are continuous persons with their own histories and identities and they grasp distinctions between immediate and chronic distress. When children at this level respond to distress, they can take into account not only situation-specific distress but also the particular characteristics of an individual. There is increasing development of the ability to generalize from one distress experience to another, and to understand the plight of an entire group of people who possess different characteristics. (This level is similar to Stage 4 in Selman's outline.)

By 12, children can empathize deeply, accurately

The observations of Selman and Hoffman reveal that elementary school children not only become increasingly capable of understanding the feelings of

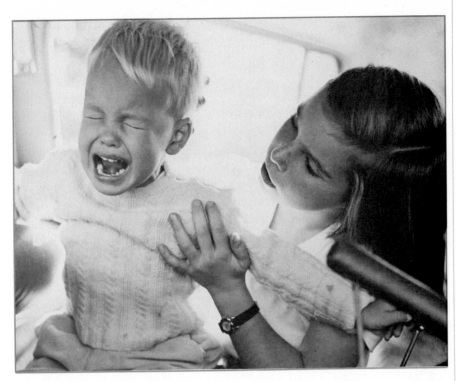

Robert Selman and Martin Hoffman have observed that children may not be able to completely understand someone else's distress, or provide appropriate sympathy or help, until after they reach the age of twelve or so. Suzanne Szasz.

others. They moreover respond sympathetically when they realize other people are in distress. But even as they become more capable of sympathizing with others, six- to twelve-year-old children also may experience such reactions as envy and spite. A child who is an excellent student or one who is elected to a class office, for example, may arouse resentment rather than empathy. When seeking to understand the behavior of elementary school children, therefore, it is not only important to consider relationships between cognitive, moral, and social development, but also to keep in mind some of the conflicts that children face when they sort out their thoughts regarding cooperation and competition, admiration and envy, sympathy and the hope that a more fortunate classmate's luck will change.

Many of the most significant differences between the moral and social thinking of six- and twelve-year-olds are traceable to Piaget's distinction between egocentric and socialized thinking (which in turn can be traced to differences in preoperational and concrete operational thinking). The significance of these differences becomes clear when techniques parents and teachers might use to encourage moral development in elementary school children are considered.

Encouraging Moral Development at the Elementary School Level

Hartshorne and May found that moral instruction that stressed memorization of platitudes was ineffective. Piaget found that younger children are moral realists, that ten- to twelve-year-olds enjoy making up their own rules, and that types of moral behavior can be related to cognitive development. Kohlberg believes there is an invariant sequence of moral development and discussion techniques help children move to more advanced stages of moral reasoning. Enthusiasts for values clarification are convinced that the strategies they have devised will lead children to make more confident and desirable moral decisions. Selman traces the development of social-cognitive understanding, interpersonal reasoning, and role-taking skills. These various observations point to factors that need to be considered by parents and teachers of elementary school children who would like to encourage such traits as honesty, integrity, and consideration for others. Many of the factors just noted can be put into perspective by considering Piaget's descriptions of cognitive development.

During the elementary school years children are primarily concrete operational thinkers. They can solve problems involving factors that they have actually experienced, but they find it difficult to grasp abstractions. They cannot apply a general principle to many different situations and may be unable to deal with hypothetical situations. These characteristics of concrete operational thought help explain why Hartshorne and May found that stress on abstract principles and concepts had little impact on actual moral behavior. They also lead to doubts about the value of asking children below the age of twelve to spend a great deal of time discussing Kohlberg's moral dilemmas or engaging in values clarification exercises. To cite just one example, when they are asked to indicate if they prefer ice cream, Jello, or pie for dessert (a question featured in a values-clarification strategy intended to give children practice in choosing between alternatives), young children will probably react in a quite literal way. They will think about their favorite dessert but not about the principle of choosing between alternatives. There is little reason to believe that when they are faced with a choice involving values they will see any connection between picking a dessert and making a moral or ethical decision.

The characteristics of concrete operational thinkers suggest that discussions of moral dilemmas or values-clarification strategies must be carefully arranged if they are to be successful. Richard Hersh, Diana Paolitto, and Joseph Reimer (1979) have developed techniques of moral education based on the observations of Piaget and Kohlberg that are more elaborate and sophisticated variations of the basic approach recommended by Hartshorne and May in the 1930s. Hartshorne and May recommended (1930, p. 413) that teachers promote discussions of actual situations in detail so that children who found themselves in similar situations would recognize commonalities and be helped to choose a desirable course of action. Hersh, Paolitto, and Reimer recommend to teachers the following procedures for implementing what they refer to as developmental moral education:

1 Recognize that younger children will respond to moral conflicts differently than older children.

2 Try to take the perspective of students and stimulate their perspective-taking abilities.

3 Develop awareness of moral issues by using a variety of real and hypothetical moral dilemmas and by using daily opportunities in the classroom to heighten moral awareness. (Moral education should be an integral part of the curriculum, it should not take place during "Moral Education Period.")

4 Create a classroom atmosphere that will enhance open discussion (for example, arrange face-to-face groupings, be an acceptant model, foster listening and communication skills, encourage student-to-student interaction).

Specific suggestions for supervising classroom discussions offered by Hersh, Paolitto, and Reimer included the following:

1 Highlight the moral issue to be discussed. (Describe a specific real or hypothetical moral dilemma.)

2 Ask "Why" questions. (After asking students what they would do if they were faced with the moral dilemma under discussion, ask them to explain *why* they would act that way.)

3 Complicate the circumstances. (After students have responded to the original dilemma, mention a factor that might complicate matters, for example, if the dilemma involved a best friend.)

4 Use personal and naturalistic examples. (Invite students to put themselves in the position of individuals who are confronted by moral dilemmas described in newspapers or depicted on television.)

Parents might use similar techniques, particularly when encouraging children to think about the consequences of real moral dilemmas. In addition, parents might take into account the points emphasized in the discussion of ways to encourage prosocial behavior in two- to five-year-olds that was presented in Chapter 8. To refresh your memory, studies of the prosocial behavior of preschoolers revealed that young children are more likely to understand the plight of others if they have had similar experiences and have thought about those experiences. The impact of models and of reinforcement of prosocial behavior has also been stressed. The guidelines for encouraging prosocial behavior in preschoolers presented in Chapter 8 can be revised to apply to the fostering of moral behavior in elementary school children as follows:

1 Invite children to talk about real (not hypothetical) situations where they have had to make moral decisions (to make them aware of their feelings and to encourage them to become aware of factors that lead to dishonest behavior).

Discuss real moral dilemmas, react positively, set consistent example

2 Express pleasure when behaving in a moral manner and encourage children to become aware of and to express the pleasure they feel when they behave in an honest or helpful way.

3 Do not berate a child for failing to apply a general moral principle in consistent ways. If a child is honest in one situation but not another, try to take into account circumstances, pressures, and feelings. If possible (and appropriate), help the child think about the factors that led him or her to commit a dishonest act. Awareness of causes of one type of immoral behavior may help the child resist temptation in a similar situation in the future.

4 Try to serve as a positive model to be imitated by exuding warmth and pleasure when acting in honest and helpful ways. Be as consistent as possible in displaying moral behavior and praise children for behaving in similar ways.

In addition to these suggestions based on the earlier discussion of prosocial behavior at the preschool level, additional suggestions for encouraging moral development can be derived from the observations of Hoffman and Selman summarized a bit earlier in this chapter.

Hoffman concluded that parents are most likely to encourage their children to internalize moral standards when they frequently show affection to their children and treat their misdeeds in a serious but sympathetic way, showing how one person's "immoral" behavior may cause others to suffer. If children value the love of their parents it would seem logical for them to want to please their parents by behaving in admirable ways. If children are severely or physically punished for misdeeds, they are more likely to react with fear or resentment than to give thoughtful consideration to how their misbehavior negatively affects others. Furthermore, a parent who uses physical punishment serves as a punitive model the child may imitate when interacting with others. A final point derived from Hoffman's observations, in certain situations it might be desirable for parents to express guilt feelings in the presence of their children, for example, "I really shouldn't have been going 45 in that 25-mile zone. You never know when a child, or someone's dog, will pop out from behind a parked car." Such efforts may be counteracted eventually when the older child learns that a popular reaction to wrongdoing in contemporary America is "*Never* admit you are guilty." Even so, it would seem beneficial for children to realize that in some cases an individual with a well-developed conscience does recognize and admit personal guilt.

Discussion techniques that Selman recommends for use by teachers and therapists might also be used by parents who become aware that their children are not as sensitive to the feelings of peers as they might be. Casual observations about how others feel can be introduced in a natural rather than artificial way and might lead to more mature social reasoning. If a boy is observed to react with physical or verbal abuse when accidentally jostled by a playmate, for example, a parent might say, "You know, people don't always intentionally bump into others. Unless you are absolutely sure that someone has hurt you on purpose, it

Show affection, avoid punishment, stress reasons

Use subtle techniques to help children become aware of others' feelings

Children are more likely to internalize moral standards if their parents frequently show affection, and if explanations, rather than punishment, follow misdeeds. Peter Vandermark/Stock, Boston.

can be a lot pleasanter for all concerned if you don't make a big deal out of it."

A final point about fostering moral development relates to instruction or adult supervision, as contrasted with peer interactions. Piaget concluded that ten- to twelve-year-olds, who are in the process of overcoming the limitations of moral realism, seem to take delight in formulating their own rules. It appeared to Piaget that many children at this stage of moral development were so proud of their newly discovered ability to formulate rules, they preferred to ignore adult-imposed regulations and substitute their own. Accordingly, there may be value, starting when children reach the age of ten or so, to encourage them to participate in rule making. They are not only more likely to understand and accept rules based on mutual agreements with peers, they may also be encouraged to move from conventional to postconventional moral thinking as described by Kohlberg. (The conventional level, you may recall, stresses obedience to external authority, the postconventional level stresses formulation of rules by mutual consent.) Two qualifications to this suggestion to encourage participation should be noted, however.

First of all, most upper-elementary-grade children are still concrete thinkers and they may feel obliged to make up a separate rule for every contingency. A fifth-grade teacher encountered this problem when he asked his pupils to propose class rules. Within twenty minutes over fifty rules had been proposed and when the teacher ran out of blackboard space, he had to call a halt. The major reason for this profusion of regulations was that a separate rule was suggested for variations of a particular type of behavior. For example, there was a rule "Don't run in the hall," followed by a rule "Don't run in the classroom," followed by a rule "Don't run on the way to the boys' room," and so on.

A second reason for exercising caution when encouraging elementary grade school children to participate in making rules is that they may also wish to determine how rule breakers should be punished. When Piaget asked young children to propose punishments he found that many of their choices were often "astonishingly severe" (1962, p. 210). He offered this explanation for the harsh nature of child-determined punishments: "In these children's eyes, punishment consists, as a matter of course, in inflicting on the guilty party a pain that will smart enough to make them realize the gravity of their misdeed. Naturally, the fairest punishment will be the most severe" (p. 213). The same tendency for young children to propose severe punishments was observed by Urie Bronfenbrenner in Russian elementary schools. One of the techniques of character training used in the Soviet Union is to have school councils, made up of elected student representatives, determine if classmates have broken school rules and how guilty children should be punished. The punishments proposed by the children observed by Bronfenbrenner were often so severe that teachers had to intervene and suggest milder penalties (1970, pp. 66–68).

The Significance of All Stages of Development

The beginning of the preceding chapter presented Kagan and Moss's view that the elementary school years represent a crystallization period in development. They supported their conclusion by noting that the behavior of children during the first four years of school serves as a better predictor of adult behavior than their actions and reactions during the preschool years. Now that you have some familiarity with aspects of the development of six- to twelve-year-olds, you are in a position to evaluate the relative importance of this stage. You should not expect to come up with a simple or direct answer, however. Psychologists who have devoted years to the study of the question of critical periods in development have not only reached almost diametrically opposed conclusions, they have also revised their own opinions as new research evidence has been reported. To illustrate, here is a review of opinions regarding the critical nature of different periods of development that have been noted in earlier chapters.

Otto Rank (1929) and Frederick Leboyer (1975) believe that a child's reactions to being born have a permanent impact on personality. Margaret Ribble (1943) maintains that the first experiences of a newborn child give personality its original slant. In a discussion of research on infant behavior Michael Lewis observed, "At no time in its history will the human being again experience more dramatic, intense, and dynamic change" (1967, p. 17). T. G. R. Bower, in the preface to one of his books on infancy, maintained that "Few would dissent from the proposition that infancy is the most critical period of development, the period in which the basic frameworks of later development are established" (1977b, p. vii).

By contrast, William Kessen (1979), Arnold J. Sameroff (1974), and Jerome Kagan, R. B. Kearsly, and P. R. Zelazo (1978) reviewed appropriate research and concluded that there is no clear-cut evidence that behavior during the first two years is predictive of later behavior. All of these theorists questioned the hypothesis that infancy is a critical period of development.

J. M. Hunt (1961) and Benjamin Bloom (1964) were led to believe by evidence that had been reported up to the early 1960s that the preschool years were a critical period in cognitive development, a conclusion later stressed by Burton White (1975). While White still maintains (up to a point) that "it is all over by the age of three" as far as intellectual development is concerned, Bloom and Hunt have revised their earlier opinions. Bloom (1968) noted that changes in cognitive functioning undoubtedly take place after the preschool years, and Hunt observed, "A major share of early losses [in intellectual functioning] can be made up if the development-fostering quality of experience improves, and a great deal of early gain can be lost if the quality of experience depreciates" (1979, p. 136).

In attempting to reconcile these conflicting opinions, theorists have offered a variety of observations. L. Alan Sroufe, for instance, notes that "What children experience, early and later, makes a difference. We cannot assume that early experiences will somehow be cancelled out by later experience" (1979, p. 840). Michael Lewis offered this opinion (in collaboration with Mark D. Starr) twelve years after he had made the just quoted statement about the crucial significance of infancy: "Individual differences in behavior as detected by measurement instruments currently employed are not particularly stable over development" (1979, p. 668). After offering explanations for this conclusion (centering on methodological problems and conceptual differences) Lewis and Starr observe, "Our answer [to the question "Does childhood show the man?"] is both that in principle childhood does show the man and that this principle is not open to denial by fact. Rather, the continuous nature of development should be taken as a premise" (p. 668).

It seems fair to rephrase the observations by Sroufe, Lewis, and Starr in this way: we should assume that there is continuity of development even though we cannot prove it on the basis of current research evidence.

Two psychologists who are convinced that there is continuity in personality development are Jack Block and Jeanne H. Block, who have collaborated in

Table 11-4
Dimensions of Ego Control and Ego Resiliency
(as described by Jack Block and Jeanne H. Block)

DIMENSIONS OF EGO CONTROL (CONTROL OF IMPULSE)

CHARACTERISTICS OF EGO OVERCONTROLLERS	CHARACTERISTICS OF EGO UNDERCONTROLLERS
Constrained and inhibited	Expressive and spontaneous
Show minimal expression of emotion	Express feelings freely
Delay gratification unduly	Desire immediate gratification
Planful and organized	Live life on an impromptu basis
Perseverative and nondistractible	Distractible
Less exploratory than average	Ready to explore
Relatively conforming	Less conforming than average

studying consistency in basic ego traits. Jack Block also carried out an exhaustive analysis (1971) of 171 subjects of some of the longitudinal studies completed at the University of California. Block, who has probably examined more kinds of information about individuals obtained over a period of years than any other researcher, concluded, "The unity or consistency of personality is compellingly apparent in these data and is manifest in so many and so diverse ways as perhaps to establish the unity principle empirically once and for all" (p. 268). The Blocks have individually and jointly published dozens of articles on basic personality traits they refer to as *ego control* and *ego resiliency*. In summarizing their research (1979) they note that some individuals are consistently ego *overcontrolled* or ego *undercontrolled*, others may be characterized as ego *resilient* or *brittle*. (Characteristics of these personality types are summarized in Table 11–4.) On the basis of results to date of a longitudinal study they initiated in 1968 the Blocks conclude that there is subtantial evidence that ego control and ego resiliency are consistent traits of personality. They have also traced background factors that appear to influence each type of behavior. Overcontrolled individuals, for example, come from families that emphasize order and favor conservative values. Undercontrolled individuals come from conflict-ridden homes where the parents do not

Table 11–4
Dimensions of Ego Control and Ego Resiliency
(as described by Jack Block and Jeanne H. Block)

DIMENSIONS OF EGO RESILIENCY (PERSONALITY CONSISTENCY AND ADAPTABILITY)	
CHARACTERISTICS OF EGO BRITTLE TYPES	CHARACTERISTICS OF EGO RESILIENT TYPES
Fixed in patterns of adaptation	Resourceful
Stereotyped in responding to new situations	Able to improvise when confronted by new situations
Rigid under stress	Maintain integrated performance under stress
Anxious when confronted by competing demands	Able to handle conflicting demands
Slow to recover after stress	Quick to recover after stress
Disquieted by changes in life	Take changes of life in stride

Source: J. H. Block and J. Block, 1979.

place much emphasis on socialization and make few demands. In their research, the Blocks are attempting to overcome the limitations of less intensive analyses of personality development. They agree with Lewis and Starr that lack of evidence of personality consistency might be attributed to lack of measuring devices or methods of observation that are sensitive enough to measure subtleties of behavior.

Even if it is assumed that certain personality traits *are* consistent, however, the course of a child's life may be diverted by experiences or circumstances such as those noted in the preceding chapter in summarizing developmental tasks. Jack Block was impressed by the consistency of personality he found when he analyzed the longitudinal data of the University of California studies. Jean Walker Macfarlane (1964), who compared predictions made at the time of adolescence with the later behavior of some of the same subjects studied by Block, was surprised (as noted in Chapter 10) by the extent to which expected and actual adjustment often differed.

At first glance, it might seem that while Block and Macfarlane analyzed the same data, one researcher discovered consistency, the other inconsistency. But the conclusions of these two researchers are not necessarily in conflict. In fact, some of

Block's conclusions about ego resiliency might be used to explain some of the inconsistencies noted by Macfarlane. Perhaps some of the subjects who failed to live up to early promise, for instance, had characteristics similar to those of the ego brittle personality type noted in Table 11–4. When confronted by adjustment problems in early adulthood, when they no longer had the support of parents or teachers, they may have been unable to adapt or recover from the stress they suffered.

The question of precisely how much early experiences influence later behavior is impossible to evaluate on the basis of available evidence. It seems certain (as Sroufe, Lewis and Starr, and the Blocks maintain) that what happens to a child early in life has an impact on personality development and later behavior. On the other hand, it appears (as Kessen, Sameroff, Kagan, and Macfarlane suggest) that it is not always possible to make accurate predictions of what a child will be like as an adolescent or an adult. The course of a child's life may be diverted by changing conditions or unexpected experiences. And personality traits that were appropriate at one age level may not serve a child as well a few years later.

In a comprehensive analysis of the long-term results and implications of their longitudinal study of temperament, Alexander Thomas and Stella Chess (1977) affirm the points just made. They note that in the early phases of their study they were impressed by the consistency of temperament in easy, difficult, and slow-to-warm-up children. As the children matured, however, and were exposed to an ever-widening range of experiences, the behavior of some subjects became less consistent and predictable. Thomas and Chess explain consistency or lack of consistency in personality by noting,

One temperamental characteristic may be enormously influential in the child-environment interactional process at one age period and in certain life situations but not particularly important at a later period. A temperamental trait may assume an importance at the older age period which it did not have earlier. Or the same characteristic may play an important role in development at sequential age stages. (1977, pp. 28–29)

A slow-to-warm-up child with relaxed and understanding parents, for example, may experience few difficulties while at home during the preschool years but become upset if exposed to an impatient and demanding teacher during the elementary school years. This example illustrates what Thomas and Chess refer to as the *goodness of fit* concept, which sheds light on other aspects of personality consistency and inconsistency. Some children, even difficult ones, may be fortunate enough to have parents with characteristics and attitudes that are in harmony with (or at least not in conflict with) their temperaments. A father who prides himself on his drive and dogged competitiveness, for instance, may respond positively to a difficult child because he can boast that his offspring "really has a mind of his own." But goodness of fit may change as the child matures. The father who admired self-willed behavior in his seventeen-month-old son may feel differently by the time the same child matures into a seventeen-year-old adolescent and takes the family car in defiance of a parental directive that it not be used on a particular night.

Perhaps the most satisfactory conclusion regarding the issue of continuity of development has been offered by Richard Q. Bell, G. M. Weller, and M. F. Waldrop (1971) who compared the behavior of children as neonates and preschoolers and then made this observation: "Newborn behavior is more like a preface to a book than a table of its contents yet to be unfolded. Further, the preface is itself a rough draft undergoing rapid revision" (1971, p. 132). Taking into account the significant changes in physical, social, cognitive, and moral development during the six- to twelve-year span that have been discussed in these last two chapters, it seems reasonable to say that the rough draft of each child's personality continues to undergo rapid revision during the elementary school years. It might also be suggested that the plot (to continue to use the book metaphor suggested by Bell and his associates) is beginning to take recognizeable shape. Even so, it is not possible to predict how the story will end. Before the story takes final form, in fact, the plot thickens considerably because of the impact of sexual, social, and cognitive maturity. The nature of changes in behavior that occur during the adolescent years will be discussed in the next two chapters.

Suggestions for Further Study

Piagetian Experiments: Concrete Operational to Formal Thought

To gain greater understanding of differences between concrete operational and formal thought, you might carry out some of the experiments Piaget devised for children in the eight- to fifteen-year age range. If possible, ask a child of eight or so and one of over twelve to solve the following problems. First, ascertain the age of your subject; then follow these instructions.

Approaches to Problem Solving: Physical Science

Purpose: To discover how a child attempts to solve a problem. Children at the level of concrete operations are able to solve problems if they have had actual experience with the kinds of objects and situations involved, but they are likely to experience difficulty handling new and unique situations. In addition, they are likely to approach a problem in a haphazard, unsystematic way. The children at the level of formal operations, on the other hand, can deal with combinations of ideas in a systematic way, propose and test hypotheses, and imagine what might happen in situations never before encountered.

Equipment: A piece of string about six feet long and three fishing weights, one small, one medium, and one large. (Any objects of different weights to which a string can be attached may be substituted for the fishing weights.)

Procedure: Take three pieces of string eighteen inches long, and attach to the end of each a small, medium, and large weight. Pick up the string with the smallest weight and swing it back and forth as a pendulum; hold the string at different positions along its length and let the weight drop (when the string is held taut) from different positions on an arc; push the weight as well as simply letting it fall. Also, call attention to the fact that the strings are equal in length but the weights are different.

Then say "There are four factors involved here: the length of the string, the difference in weight at the end of the string, the height from which the weight is released, and the force with which the weight is pushed. I want you to figure out which of these factors—or what combination of them—determines how fast the weight swings. Experiment with these pieces of string any way you like, and when you think you have it figured out, tell me what your solution is. Or, if you can, give me your solution without actually handling the strings." Describe the subject's procedure and solution.

Ask the subject to prove the solution to you. If you detect an oversight, demonstrate the nature of the error and observe the subject's reaction. (Note: the *length* of the string is the major determinant of the speed of the swing.)

Approaches to Problem Solving: Behavioral Science
Purpose: The problem in the previous exercise involved principles of physical science. Some students may have had courses in science or have done considerable reading in that subject, which will have given them sufficient background to solve the problem. Accordingly, you may also wish to ask your subject to wrestle with this *behavioral* science problem.

Procedure: Ask the subject to explain how to test this hypothesis: "Because many advertisers make exaggerated claims in their television commercials, the government is beginning to ask them to provide conclusive proof that what they say is true. Suppose a fruit company is planning to use the slogan 'An apple a day keeps the doctor away.' In anticipation of being approached by the government, they ask you to set up an experiment to either prove or disprove this statement. You have an unlimited budget and you can proceed any way you like. How would you set about getting conclusive evidence to prove or disprove the statement 'An apple a day keeps the doctor away'? Tell me all the ideas you get as they come into your mind." Describe the subject's proposed procedure.

Hartshorne and May's Studies of Character

The series of studies on character development carried out by Hugh Hartshorne and Mark May have never been equaled in terms of ingenuity, thoroughness, or depth. Even though they were done in the 1920s, the results of these studies are still well worth examining. The authors give detailed descriptions of how they developed and administered their various measures, as well as their results and conclusions, in a three-volume series published under the general title *Studies in the Nature of Character*. Volume I, *Studies in Deceit* (1930) gives the background of the study and then provides a description of the methods and results of the studies of honesty. Volume II, *Studies in Service and Self-Control* (1929) describes methods and conclusions regarding those types of behavior. Volume III, *Studies in the Organization of Character* (1930), reports a follow-up study of interrelationships between the types of behavior reported in Volumes I and II. (The final summary begins on page 382.)

Piaget's Description of Moral Development

Piaget describes his observations on moral development in *The Moral Judgment of the Child* (1932). Thomas Lickona summarizes research investigations stimulated by Piaget's conclusions in "Research on Piaget's Theory of Moral Development" on pages 219–240 of *Moral Development and Behavior* (1976), an excellent compilation of articles on all aspects of morality which he edited.

Moral Realism

Piaget has suggested that children tend to be *moral realists* until about the end of the elementary school years, when they become capable of a morality of cooperation. For insight into this distinction, obtain permission to ask pupils at lower and upper grades in an elementary school to explain how they would react to these situations:

1   Suppose your mother had bought a new dress. She was very proud of it, but you thought it looked terrible. If she asked you what you thought about it, what would you say?
2   Suppose two boys had stolen candy bars in a supermarket. One boy had plenty of money to pay for them, and the other came from a poor family, had no money, and was very hungry. Should both boys be punished in the same way if they are caught?
3   Suppose John was playing ball on the playground and accidentally hit Mary and gave her a bloody nose. During the same recess period David got mad at Jane and hit her. It hurt, but it wasn't nearly so bad as Mary's bloody nose. John caused greater injury to Mary than David did to Jane. Does this mean John should be punished more severely than David?

According to Piaget, younger children are more likely to apply the letter of the law (*never* tell a lie) than the spirit of the law (it is all right to tell a white lie); they are less likely to take into account circumstances (such as hunger and poverty); and they are more likely to judge a person by the practical consequences of the act committed rather than by the motivation behind the act (a child who causes a more serious injury should be more severely punished even if it was an accident). Did the responses from younger and older students fit these predictions? Summarize and comment on your results.

Kohlberg's Stages of Moral Development

If you would like to read Kohlberg's own account of the stages of moral development, examine "Moral Stages and Moralization: The Cognitive-Developmental Approach" in *Moral Development and Behavior* (1976), edited by Thomas Lickona. A review and critique of research on Kohlberg's stage theory is presented in "The Development of Moral Thought: Review and Evaluation of Kohlberg's Approach" by William Kurtines and Esther Blank Greif in *Psychological Bulletin,* 1974, **81**, (8). Techniques for encouraging moral development by taking account of Kohlberg's stages are described in *Promoting Moral Growth* (1979) by Richard Hersh, Joseph Reimer, and Diana Paolitto.

Values Clarification

For more information on values clarification and detailed instructions for putting values clarification strategies into practice, refer to *Values and Teaching* (1966) by Louis E. Raths, Merrill Harmin, and Sidney B. Simon; *Values Clarification: A Handbook of Practical Strategies for Teachers* (1972) by Sidney B. Simon, Leland W. Howe, and Howard Kirschenbaum; or *Personalizing Education: Values Clarification and Beyond* (1975) by Leland W. Howe and Mary Martha Howe.

Social-Cognitive Understanding and Empathy

Robert L. Selman describes his conclusions regarding the development of understanding of the feelings of others in "Social-Cognitive Understanding: A Guide to Educational and Clinical Practice" on pages 299–316 of *Moral Development and Behavior* (1976), edited by Thomas Lickona. Martin L. Hoffman discusses "Empathy, Role-Taking, Guilt, and the Development of Altruistic Motives" on pages 124–143 of the same volume. Carolyn U. Shantz reviews research on all aspects of the development of understanding of the thoughts and feelings of others in "The Development of Social Cognition" in *Review of Child Development Research,* 1975, **5**, 257–324, edited by E. Mavis Hetherington.

PART SIX

ADOLESCENCE AND YOUTH

This part consists of two chapters: Chapter 12, "Physical, Sexual, and Social Development"; and Chapter 13, "Cognitive, Moral, and Emotional Development."

Theorists whose work is summarized in Chapter 3 consider the following types of behavior and relationships to be of significance during adolescence and youth.

□ Freud: Genital stage. Concern about sexual relations. Libidinal energy typically concentrated on a member of the opposite sex.

□ Erikson: Identity versus role confusion. Adolescents and youth need to establish a sense of identity, particularly with regard to sex roles and occupational choice.

□ Piaget: Formal operational stage. Many adolescents become able to deal with ab-stractions, form hypotheses, solve problems systematically, engage in mental manipulations.

□ Sears: Continuation of Phase III. In adolescence and youth behavior may be shaped as much by reactions of peers as by reactions of adults. Identification with and imitation of admired peers is of significance.

KEY POINTS

Significant Tasks and Characteristics of Adolescence and Youth

Youth: transitional stage when college students neither adolescents not adults

Cohort: group influenced in particular ways by historical events

The Impact of Physical Maturity

Girls reach puberty at 12.5; boys at 14 (on the average)

Some complete adolescent development before others start

Early-maturing boys self-confident; late-maturing boys seek attention

Early-maturing girls out of step in high school; self-possessed as adults

Blos: A Psychoanalytic Interpretation of Adolescent Sexuality

Adolescent behavior: attempt to retain or regain psychic equilibrium

Libidinal energy increases at puberty, is sublimated

Common adolescent sublimations: asceticism, intellectualism, uniformism

Erikson: A Psychosocial Interpretation of Adolescent Identity

Identity: acceptance of body, goals, recognition from those who count

Identifications at adolescence involve a sense of urgency

Sex-role confusion may complicate formation of identity

Choice of career has significant impact on identity

Psychosocial moratorium: delay of commitment

Negative identity: adopting forms of behavior considered to be undesirable

The Impact of Sexual Maturity

Substantial increase in premarital intercourse by females

Single sexual standard of permissiveness with affection being accepted

The Nature and Impact of Changing Sex Roles

Traditionally, male identity linked to job; female identity linked to husband

Males eager to be leaders and make money; females want to help others

The Impact of Sex-typed Behavior

Fear-of-success stories influenced by variety of factors

Psychological androgyny can be encouraged in a variety of ways

Stages in Occupational Choice

Search for a satisfying career may extend into the thirties

Realistic occupational choices begin to appear around ninth grade

The Influence of Parents and Peers

Generation gap appears to be exception rather than rule

Democratic approach to encouraging autonomy appears most effective

Parents influence plans; peers influence immediate status

Continuity and Discontinuity in Development

Preadolescent behavior may "reverse" during adolescence

Genotypic continuity: changes in behavior do not necessarily indicate personality lacks stability

CHAPTER □12

ADOLESCENCE AND YOUTH:

PHYSICAL, SEXUAL, AND SOCIAL DEVELOPMENT

The types of behavior listed opposite Freud, Erikson, Piaget, and Sears in the introduction to this final part outline topics that will be discussed in these chapters on adolescence and youth. Freud stressed the impact of sexual maturity on behavior and the significance of sexual relations. Erikson explains how the formulation of sex roles and choice of an occupation influence the formation of a sense of identity. Piaget describes the nature of formal thinking, a distinctive type of cognitive functioning that opens up possibilities for new kinds of moral as well as intellectual reasoning. Sears calls attention to ways that reactions of peers begin to shape certain types of behavior, often to a greater extent than the reactions of parents and other adults do.

Additional descriptions of adolescent behavior in these chapters have been provided by Robert Havighurst and Kenneth Keniston. Havighurst describes developmental tasks for the adolescent years. Keniston has emphasized the need to think about youth as well as adolescence when the development of contemporary young Americans is considered.

Significant Tasks and Characteristics of Adolescence and Youth

Developmental Tasks

In Chapter 10, the developmental tasks children are expected to achieve during the elementary school years were listed and discussed. Robert Havighurst has also proposed developmental tasks for the adolescent years which he describes as follows:

1 Accepting one's physique
2 Achieving new and more mature relations with age-mates of both sexes
3 Achieving a masculine or feminine role
4 Preparing for marriage and family life
5 Achieving emotional independence of parents and other adults
6 Achieving assurance of economic independence and selecting and preparing for an occupation
7 Acquiring a set of values and an ethical system as a guide to behavior
8 Developing intellectual skills necessary for civic competence
9 Desiring and achieving socially responsible behavior (1952, pp. 33–71)

These developmental tasks, together with the points emphasized by Freud, Erikson, Piaget, and Sears noted in the introduction to this final Part will provide the organizational frame of reference for these last two chapters. In this chapter, physical, sexual, and social development during adolescence and youth will be discussed. These topics reflect the first seven developmental tasks listed above and relate to points emphasized by Freud and his followers (sexual maturity), Erikson (sex roles, occupational choice, and identity), and Sears (influence of peers). In Chapter 13, cognitive, moral, and emotional development will be discussed. The first two topics reflect the final three developmental tasks noted by Havighurst and are clarified by the speculations of Piaget (cognitive development) and Kohlberg (moral development). *Emotional maturity* as used in the final chapter title refers to the extent to which adolescents and youth achieve (or fail to achieve) a satisfactory degree of adjustment or self-fulfillment.

Youth as a Stage of Development

These last two chapters are devoted to descriptions of development during adolescence *and* youth for reasons spelled out succinctly by Kenneth Keniston. In the opening paragraphs of *Youth and Dissent* (1970) Keniston observes, "Millions of young people today are neither psychological adolescents nor sociological adults; they fall into a psychological no man's land, a stage of life that lacks any clear definition." (p. 3) He goes on to argue that "the unprecedented prolonga-

Youth: transitional stage when college students neither adolescents nor adults

Kenneth Keniston suggests that *youth* has become a new stage of life in our society because about half of all young Americans prolong their education beyond high school. College students, Keniston notes, are "neither psychological adolescents nor sociological adults . . . they fall into a psychological no man's land." Arthur Grace/Stock, Boston.

tion of education has opened up opportunities for an extension of psychological development, which in turn is creating a 'new' stage of life." Keniston suggests that the word *youth* is preferable to terms such as *protracted adolescence* as a designation for this new stage of development. He notes (p. 5) that in 1900 only 6.4 percent of young Americans completed high school and that there were only 238,000 college students. Today, almost 80 percent of American youth complete high school and approximately 10 million—about half of all Americans in their late teens and early twenties—attend college. Largely because so many young Americans continue their education beyond high school, Keniston feels that discussions of development should not stop at adolescence (typically defined as the years between twelve and eighteen) but should continue through the mid-twenties. Because Keniston's point seems accurate, these last two chapters summarize information and speculations about development through the mid-twenties.

To clarify what he means by youth Keniston notes (pp. 8–12) several major themes that sum up characteristics of young people who are neither adolescents nor adults:

☐ Tension between self and society and pervasive ambivalence: "The adolescent is struggling to define who he is; the youth begins to sense who he is and thus to recognize the possibility of conflict and disparity between his emerging selfhood and his social order."

☐ The concept of the *wary probe*: while adolescents engage in experimentation, youth make "serious forays into the adult world." They are also character-ized by a "testing, exacting, challenging attitude."

☐ Estrangement (feelings of isolation, unreality, absurdity, and disconnected-ness) alternating with omnipotentiality (feelings of absolute freedom and of being in a world of pure possibilities).

☐ Refusal of socialization: attempts to break out of prescribed roles.

☐ Emergence of youth-specific identities and roles; conceptions of self that are somewhere between the ephemeral enthusiasms of the adolescent and the more established commitments of the adult.

☐ Valuation of change, transformation, and movement; abhorrence of same-ness.

☐ Tendency to band together in youthful countercultures.

Having described some of the characteristics of youth, Keniston points out what it is not (as he defines it). It is not the end of development but a transitional stage that may extend from the late teens through the twenties. Neither is youth a universal phase of development since not all post-adolescents (for example, those who begin to work full time after graduation from high school) go through the stage of youth.

Keniston offered his description of youth in 1971. It is based to a considerable extent on observations he made of students, including many who could be classified as activists, attending Harvard and similar institutions during the 1960s. The 1960s were characterized by a substantial amount of student unrest centering on the civil rights movement, American involvement in Vietnam, greater student control of education, and demands for free speech on campus. The following decade has been referred to as the "quiet seventies" by Richard G. Braungart (1980, p. 565), who reviewed research on youth movements. Accordingly, you should keep in mind several important points in evaluating Keniston's descrip-tions of youth. First, the distinction Braungart draws between the activist sixties and the "quiet seventies" calls attention to the impact of rapid political, social, and cultural change on behavior and identity. Second, estimates of the percentage of activist youth vary from 2 to 4 percent of the college population (Braungart, 1980, p. 563). Members of the student bodies at institutions such as those studied by Keniston were more likely to follow the lead of activists than those attending most colleges. Finally, not all definitions and descriptions of youth are similar.

Some psychologists, for instance, agree with Keniston that *youth* should refer to a transitional stage. But they use the term to describe all individuals between the ages of fourteen and twenty-four. This alternative definition is used by the authors of *Youth: Transition to Adulthood* (1974), a report by the Panel on Youth of the President's Science Advisory Committee. The writers of this report also differ from Keniston in their description of distinctive characteristics of young people in this stage of development. They suggest that youth are characterized by inward lookingness, psychic attachment to others of the same age, a drive toward autonomy (as reflected by high regard for youth who successfully challenge adults or who act autonomously with adults), concern for the underdog, and interest in change (1974, pp. 113–125). They also suggest that whereas young people in simple agricultural societies appear to be eager to *hurry* through childhood in order to begin to function as adults, young people in technological societies may be *reluctant* to leave the youth subculture. Many American youth may feel obliged to attend college in order to prepare for an occupation. But as college students they are segregated in many ways from adult society. Because of this segregation they may prefer to remain in the youthful subculture as long as possible.

In these two chapters references to youth will be based more or less on Keniston's interpretation of the term. That is to say, the word *youth* will refer primarily to college students who are in a transitional stage between adolescence and adulthood. The term *adolescent* will be used to refer to high school students between the ages of twelve and eighteen.

The Need to Think in Terms of Cohorts

Keniston's definition of youth calls attention to one recent change in thinking about human development: the fact that the transitional stage from childhood to adulthood extends into the twenties for many young Americans. Another change in recent discussions of adolescence and youth is indicated by the frequent use of the term *cohort*. Though use of the term varies, most often writers will be using it in the sociological sense proposed by N. B. Ryder (1965): a cohort is a group distinctively marked by the life stage it occupies when historical events impinge on it. Such usage focuses on a "generation" of young people who are united not by a desire to achieve some goal through struggle but united by exposure to a given set of cultural conditions. The reason for frequent use of *cohort* in discussions of contemporary adolescence and youth will become apparent if you will compare the conditions in our society when you attended high school with the present conditions or those of a few years earlier. If you have brothers or sisters a few years older and/or younger than you are, you probably belong to different cohorts.

Cohort: group influenced in particular ways by historical events

As you are well aware, conditions in America and in the world today change with sometimes bewildering rapidity. You may not be as aware, however, until you stop to think about it, that social or political conditions that characterize a brief period of time may have a different impact on subgroups of individuals. Some, but not all, adolescents who came to maturity during the Second World War, for example, may have been influenced by the fact that the father was absent from many homes for up to five years because of military service. Another example from a later "wartime" period: the values of youth who were attending

Psychologists who describe research on adolescence and youth often use the term *cohort* to suggest the extent behavior is influenced by a particular set of conditions at a particular time. During the 1960s, for example, when student activism was at a peak, large numbers of youth engaged in demonstrations to express their dissatisfaction with "the establishment." During the 1970s, campuses were quiet because most students concentrated on preparing for careers that would permit them to *become* part of "the establishment." To understand these differences, it is essential to take into account the cohort to which each group belonged. Olive R. Pierce/Photo Researchers; © Arthur Grace/Stock, Boston.

particular universities in the mid-1960s (for example, Kent State) were influenced by events during American involvement in Vietnam in dramatically different ways than the values of draft-free youth the same age who were preparing for jobs in war-related industries. And, to cite just one more example, the impact of inflation, high rates of unemployment, and cuts in government spending on social programs which are features of American life in the early 1980s seem likely to have a different impact on the development of a high school student from a wealthy home than the impact on a school drop-out who lives in an inner-city ghetto. The frequent use of the word *cohort* in discussions of contemporary adolescence and youth, therefore, calls attention to two points: (1) the need to consider conditions during the particular time a given group of adolescents or youth reached maturity; (2) the need to consider how different groups of young people of the same age may have been influenced by these conditions.

Now that you are acquainted with the organizational frame of reference of these last two chapters and with explanations why references to youth and to cohorts will be included, it is time to examine specific types of behavior, beginning with physical development.

The Impact of Physical Maturity

Changes Accompanying the Growth Spurt

Two significant physiological changes usher in adolescence—the growth spurt and puberty. As noted in Chapter 10, most girls experience the growth spurt at eleven or twelve. Boys are likely to have their most rapid period of growth between thirteen and fourteen (Maresh, 1964). The spurt and changes that accompany it are caused by increased output of the growth hormone and gonadotropic hormones controlled by the pituitary gland. The gonadotropic hormones stimulate the sex glands (gonads) so that they not only increase in size but also produce increased amounts of sex hormones: androgens in males and estrogens in females. These in turn act on the pituitary to lead first to an increase and then to a gradual diminution of output of the growth hormone. Thus, there is a reciprocal interaction between the pituitary and the sex hormones, an interaction that produces an increase in overall size and several other physical changes as well. The proportions of the body change, and it assumes close to adult form. The shape of the face alters and comes closer to adult appearance. Internally, the heart and lungs increase in size, and the digestive system assumes almost its final size and shape. The sex organs mature rapidly, and *secondary sex characteristics* appear: breast development, rounded hips, and the appearance of a waistline in girls; broadening of the shoulders, replacement of fat with muscle tissue in boys. Pubic, axillary (armpit), facial, and body hair appear; the texture of the skin changes (often with temporary malfunctioning of the oil-producing glands, which leads to acne); and the voice changes. This latter change is much more apparent in males, since the larynx enlarges and the vocal cords lengthen to such an extent that the voice drops an octave in pitch. All of these changes have a profound impact on the appearance, biological functioning, and psychological adjustment of the young person reaching puberty.

The Nature and Impact of Puberty

The term *puberty* (from the Latin *pubertas,* meaning "age of manhood") refers to the time when a person becomes physiologically capable of reproduction. (The term also means "approach to maturity.") The point at which a girl reaches sexual maturity is often considered to be the first menstrual period. There is evidence (Tanner, 1972), however, that a period of sterility occurs and that conception is not likely to take place until at least ten months after that time. Consequently, if puberty is defined as the point at which the individual becomes capable of sexual reproduction, then it occurs in females a year or so after menstruation begins. There is, therefore, some vagueness about the age of puberty in females, but there is even more confusion about when boys become sexually mature. As a result, a commonly used index of masculine puberty is the emergence of pigmented pubic hair.

Girls reach puberty at 12.5; boys at 14 (average)

Some complete adolescent development before others start

Differences in Rate of Maturation Sexual maturity is usually achieved shortly after the completion of the growth spurt. The average age at which American girls reach menarche (begin menstruation) is between twelve and thirteen; boys reach sexual maturity at an average age of fourteen. J. M. Tanner (1970, 1972), a leading authority on physiological development, suggests that this difference is one of the two most significant facts about human biological development. The other is that some individuals have completed their adolescent development before others have started theirs. The range of individual differences in the age when puberty is reached is graphically depicted in the accompanying illustration and further demonstrated in cases of precocious development. Tanner and G. R. Taylor report (1969, p. 106) that a Peruvian girl five years and eight months old gave birth to a child. Tanner also describes (1970, p. 131) the case of a six-and-a-half-year-old boy whose physiological maturity was that of a fifteen-year-old. His endocrine system caused him to experience a strong sex drive, which he neither understood nor attempted to control. The boy had frequent erotic dreams and when taken to a hospital for examination stared at attractive nurses with such lecherous intensity they felt uncomfortable and were eager to leave the room. While such cases are rare, in almost any secondary school there are likely to be some students who have achieved puberty while classmates have not even started their growth spurt.

Differences in rate of maturation may have a significant impact on several aspects of behavior because the physiological changes that accompany maturity are so obvious. The first menstrual period may be a difficult and traumatic experience for a girl, particularly if she has not been provided with information about sexual maturity. The appearance of secondary sexual characteristics influences the reactions of peers, parents, and teachers. The reactions of others, in turn, influence the young person's self-concept.

The growth spurt and the appearance of the primary and secondary sex characteristics follow such a standard pattern, and individual children tend to be so faithful to a fast, average, or slow rate of maturation, that the timing of maturation must be due primarily to genetic factors. However, it may also be influenced by nutrition. Evidence demonstrating the importance of nutrition is provided by a secular trend in sexual maturity: the average age of menarche in this country has occurred three to four months earlier every ten years since 1850. It appears, however, that the limit of early puberty has been reached in this country and that the average age of menarche is not likely to get much lower than it is at the present time (Tanner, 1970).

Concern About Appearance The timing of puberty and the development of characteristics signaling sexual maturation are extremely important to both boys and girls for many reasons, but an especially compelling one is concern about appearance, particularly attractiveness to members of the opposite sex. During the elementary school years, children tend to prefer the company of peers of the

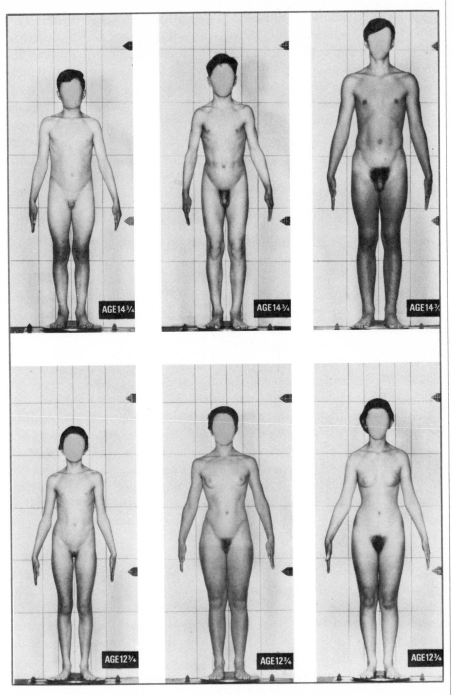

Differing degrees of pubertal development at the same chronological age. The three boys in the upper row are 14.75 years of age. In the lower row, the three girls are 12.75 years of age. From J. M. Tanner, "Growth and Endocrinology in the Adolescent," in L. I. Gardner, ed., *Endocrine and Genetic Diseases of Childhood* (W. B. Saunders Company, 1969).

same sex. If boys and girls do engage in similar activities such as neighborhood games, they are more likely to judge each other on the basis of skill than any other quality. But the growth spurt, sexual maturity, and the discovery that particular members of the opposite sex arouse feelings never before experienced, lead many recently pubescent boys and girls to think seriously for the first time about male-female relationships. A boy who delighted in provoking the girls in his sixth-grade class by a well-phrased gibe may strive to win their approval by what he says and does in high school. A girl who treated boys with ill-concealed contempt in the fifth grade may take great pains to make herself appear attractive to them in junior high school. Suddenly, physical appearance becomes extremely important.

Manufacturers and advertising agencies spend millions of dollars doing their best to convince young people that being attractive to the opposite sex is *the* most important aspect of their lives. If you count the number of TV commercials intended to foster this belief or examine ads in magazines catering to the interests of young males and females, you will appreciate the extent of the bombardment. These ads may have an especially strong impact on adolescents who have just achieved puberty, partly because such young people are not sophisticated enough to recognize the manipulative techniques being used, partly because they may still dream that their appearance will change. The growth spurt pushes the young person quite far in the direction of ultimate adult appearance, but further changes in face and figure are yet to come. Realizing this, the junior-high-age boy or girl who is less than satisfied with the reflection seen in a mirror may hope that—with a bit of assistance from the beauty aids advertised so alluringly on television and in magazines—a final metamorphosis from ugly duckling to beautiful swan may take place. The older high school student, on the other hand, who is near final physical maturity, may accept the fact that no further changes are forthcoming and become more fatalistic about appearance. There is still interest in making oneself attractive, in building muscles or taking off fat, and in using beauty aids to enhance appearance, but the older adolescent is more likely to think when gazing into a mirror, "I'll just have to make the best of it."

Evidence indicating that appearance is of great concern just after puberty is supplied by studies where adolescents are asked what they like and dislike about themselves (for example, Lerner and Karabenick, 1974). Physical characteristics are mentioned more frequently than either intellectual or social ones. But the proportion of disliked appearance characteristics decreases as students move from junior high into senior high school. Such studies also reveal that girls tend to be more concerned about their appearance than boys.

The standards against which teen-agers measure their relative appeal to members of the opposite sex both reflect and enhance their increasing concern about appearance. For girls, the qualities displayed by models in magazine advertisements and TV commercials, contestants in beauty pageants, and stars of films and television series, present a clear standard of the qualities of face and

Concern about appearance reaches a peak during the junior high school years, just after most adolescents achieve puberty. Richard Kalvar/Magnum.

figure considered desirable. For boys, signs of early maturity (for example, face and body hair) and strength may be more of an asset than facial features.

Ellen Berscheid and Elaine Walster (1972) studied reactions to appearance and concluded that for both sexes physical attractiveness exerts a positive impact on many aspects of a child's life and that it may be the single most important factor in determining popularity among college students. Furthermore, they discovered that attractiveness was associated with many positive traits (such as adaptability and academic ability) and unattractiveness with some negative traits. Teachers, for example, were more likely to give attractive children higher ratings and higher grades.

In a review of studies of friendship, however, John C. Coleman (1980) reports that there is evidence that appearance influences popularity (or lack of it) only for adolescents and youth who are the most and least attractive members of a group. He concludes that appearance has little effect on the popularity of most young people who are between the extremes. He also concludes that attractiveness alone is neither a necessary nor a sufficient cause for popularity.

The Impact of Early and Late Maturation

Over a period of years, a number of investigators at the University of California examined longitudinal data to determine the impact of early and later maturation on adolescents. Then, when the subjects were in their thirties, their adult behavior and adjustment was compared to the ratings made when they were in high school. These various investigations are summarized in Table 12–1.

The characteristics noted in Table 12–1 cannot be interpreted too literally for several reasons. First of all, different groups of subjects were studied, and the types of behavior various investigators found typical of early and later maturers were not always consistent. Second, as indicated by the parenthetical notes regarding leadership in early-maturing adolescent males and confidence in later-maturing adolescent girls, the impact of the timing of puberty sometimes varied depending on social class. Third, comparatively small groups of subjects were studied. And thus factors such as attractiveness may have had an influence on some of the characteristics (for example, popularity) studied. Finally, the subjects of these studies attended high school in the 1930s and 1940s. Changes in conceptions of sex roles and sexual behavior in the last few years may have altered the significance of early and later maturation in the 1980s.

It does seem safe to conclude, however, that the behavior and development of individuals who mature substantially earlier or later than most of their peers may be influenced in significant and permanent ways. The exact nature of this influence may be difficult to predict, though, for reasons that become clear in interpretations of the data in Table 12–1. After reviewing research on early and later maturation Norman Livson and Harvey Peskin (1980) speculate that the early-maturing male is likely to draw favorable responses from adults (because of his adult appearance) which promotes confidence and poise (contributing to leadership and popularity with peers). The late-maturing boy, by contrast, may feel inferior and attempt to compensate for his physical and social frustration by engaging in bossy and attention-getting behavior. The very success of the early-maturing boy in high school, however, may cause him to develop an inflexible conception of himself, leading to problems when he must deal with new or negative situations later in life. The need for the early-maturing boy to cope with difficult adjustment situations in high school, on the other hand, may equip him with the ability to adapt to adversity and change later in life.

Livson and Peskin observe that the late-maturing boy is psychologically and socially out of step with peers, and the same applies to the *early*-maturing girl. The *late*-maturing girl, whose growth is less abrupt and whose size and appearance are likely to reflect the petiteness that is a feature of stereotyped views of femininity, shares many of the characteristics (poise, popularity, leadership tendencies) of the early-maturing boy. The advantages enjoyed by the late-maturing girl are not permanent, however. Livson and Peskin report that "The stress-ridden early-maturing girl in adulthood has become clearly a more coping, self-possessed, and self-directed person than the late-maturing female in the

Early-maturing boys self-confident; late-maturing boys seek attention

Early-maturing girls out of step in high school; self-possessed as adults

Table 12–1
The Impact of Early and Late Maturation

	CHARACTERISTICS AS ADOLESCENTS	CHARACTERISTICS AS ADULTS
Early-Maturing Boys	Self-confident, high in self-esteem, likely to be chosen as leaders. (But leadership tendencies more likely in lower-class than middle-class boys.)	Self-confident, responsible, cooperative, sociable. But also rigid, moralistic, humorless, conforming.
Late-Maturing Boys	Energetic, bouncy, given to attention-getting behavior, not popular	Impulsive and assertive. But also insightful, perceptive, creatively playful, able to cope with new situations
Early-Maturing Girls	Not popular or likely to be leaders, indifferent in social situations, lacking in poise. (But middle-class girls more confident than those from lower class.)	Self-possessed, self-directed, able to cope, likely to score high in ratings of overall psychological health
Late-Maturing Girls	Confident, outgoing, assured, popular, likely to be chosen as leaders	Likely to experience difficulty adapting to stress, likely to score low in ratings of overall psychological health

Sources: H. E. Jones, 1946; M. C. Jones, 1957, 1965; P. H. Mussen and M. C. Jones, 1957; Peskin, 1967, 1973; Clausen, 1975; Livson and Peskin, 1980; Petersen and Taylor, 1980.

cognitive and social as well as emotional sectors. . . . It is the late-maturing female, carefree and unchallenged in adolescence, who faces adversity maladroitly in adulthood" (1980, p. 72).

This discussion of the significance of the timing of puberty leads to the broader questions of the impact of sexual maturation on behavior, a topic that has been of particular interest to psychoanalysts.

Blos: A Psychoanalytic Interpretation of Adolescent Sexuality

When adolescents become sexually mature, they experience changes in physical functioning and in reactions toward others that influence many aspects of their behavior. Freud was the first psychologist to speculate about the significance of sexual maturity, proposing that the latency period of the elementary school years was followed by the genital stage of development. While Freud's observations on sexuality are provocative, they are not widely accepted today, partly because he based so much of his theories on the recollections of a small number of disturbed, middle-class, European female patients. Two of Freud's pupils, however, pursued careers in psychoanalysis in America, worked extensively with adolescents, and wrote book-length interpretations derived from Freudian theory.

Chapter 3 described Erik Erikson's introduction to Freud. Erikson, you may recall, was wandering around Europe when he met a friend from high school days, Peter Blos. Blos subsequently journeyed to Vienna and became a tutor to the chldren of a woman being analyzed by and studying with Freud. When Blos was asked to set up a school for children of other patients and students of Freud, he invited Erikson to join him. You are already familiar with the details of how Erikson came to this country and developed his psychosocial view of development. During the time Erikson was treating child and adult patients, living with Indian tribes, and carrying out research, Blos was practicing psychoanalysis, primarily with adolescents. Each man completed a book summarizing his views of adolescent development at about the same point in his career, and their interpretations will now be outlined.

Review of Freudian Theory

Certain aspects of Freudian theory described in Chapter 3 are necessary as background for a psychoanalytic view of adolescence. Freud proposed that psychosexual energy (the libido) centers on the organs of the body that provide the greatest amount of sensual gratification at different ages. The oral, anal, and phallic stages occur during the preschool period, followed by a latency period during the elementary school years. Some critics have interpreted "latency" in a literal way and have argued that Freud was wrong since elementary school children continue to show an interest in sex. Blos points out that such criticisms betray a lack of understanding of what Freud meant—he emphasized "the lack of a new sexual aim . . . rather than the complete lack of sexual activity" (1962, p. 5). When puberty is achieved, however, the libido centers on the sex organs, and that is why it is called the *genital* period. Blos suggests that much adolescent behavior can be understood by thinking of it as a "struggle to regain or to retain a psychic equilibrium which has been jolted by the crisis of puberty" (p. 11).

Adolescent behavior: attempt to regain or retain psychic equilibrium

The Emergence of Heterosexual Desires

Freud theorized that at the beginning of the elementary school years (and during the latency period), the boy admires his mother and female teachers but identifies with his father and other male adults. The girl has repressed her feelings toward her father and identifies with her mother and older females (such as teachers). Blos explains the transition that takes place in the next five or six years by

The psychoanalyst Peter Blos suggests that much adolescent behavior can be understood by thinking of it as a "struggle to regain or retain a psychic equilibrium which has been jolted by the crisis of puberty." The Norwegian painter, Edvard Munch, offered his interpretation of a girl's discovery of her sexual maturity in *Puberty*. Nasjonalgalleriet, Oslo.

suggesting that the child's own achievements and reactions from peers provide satisfactions that previously were supplied by parental approval.

By the end of elementary school, the child becomes quite self-sufficient and confident and is at ease with companions. Then, just as this stability becomes established, it is disrupted by the advent of puberty. With the maturation of the sex organs, adolescents experience a strong attraction to members of the opposite sex. But since genital desires cannot be gratified directly (in many cases), the postpubescent boy or girl may find release through sexual jokes, single-minded interest in things like collections or hobbies, and same-sex group activities. Boys tend to be hostile to girls and belittle them, partly out of fear and envy. Girls, on the other hand, are likely to engage in a strenuous final burst of tomboyish activities (particularly when the growth spurt occurs), and then abruptly switch to interest in boys as boys (when menarche is achieved). All of these tendencies and activities are forms of *sublimation,* a defense mechanism for expressing libidinal energy in socially accepted ways not directly related to sexual activities.

Libidinal energy increases at puberty, is sublimated

In the psychoanalytic view, when the girl reaches puberty and libidinal energy increases, she may be unable to continue to repress heterosexual desires and, as a consequence, may "attach herself to boys often in frantic succession" (p. 66). In an effort to control initial heterosexual interests, the girl may throw herself into friendships, fantasy life, athletic activity, and grooming.

When boys achieve puberty and after girls have had their first heterosexual experience there is a tendency for them to form idealized friendships. The boy is likely to choose one of his peers; the girl may develop a crush on some older woman or man. In boys, the same-sex friendship is usually succeeded by clumsy attempts at heterosexual interaction. These crude overtures may be displaced in short order by what Blos calls a "tender love" experience (p. 101). The object of a boy's affections may be regarded with awe and tender devotion. If relationships with members of the opposite sex seem threatening, both boys and girls may turn to *asceticism* (renouncing comforts and material possessions in favor of an austere or simple life) or *intellectualism* (stressing rational and objective analyses while playing down emotion and feelings) in seeking ways to sublimate sexual energy. In American society, in particular, they also may turn to what Blos terms *uniformism:* seeking security by endorsing a shared code with members of the peer group and depending on mutual recognition of sameness.

Common adolescent sublimations: asceticism, intellectualism, uniformism

Toward Ego Synthesis

In time, the young person develops heterosexual relationships and also consolidates aspects of personality: "It is the task of the late adolescent to arrive at a final settlement which the young person subjectively feels to be 'my way of life'" (p. 127). In some cases, a teen-ager who is unable to achieve this consolidation suffers *prolonged adolescence.* This may occur because "Late adolescence is a decisive turning point, and consequently is a time of crisis" (p. 130). The young person who is afraid of becoming an adult may attempt to remain an adolescent. Or the final adolescent crisis sometimes "overtaxes the integrative capacity of the individual and results in adaptive failures, ego deformations, defensive maneuvers, and severe psychopathology" (p. 130). Thus, the young person on the

One of the most common adolescent sublimations (according to Peter Blos) is *uniformism,* an attempt to gain security through mutual recognition of sameness. © Joel Gordon 1980.

threshold of adulthood may go through a process of "workable and abortive compromises or egosyntheses, of positive and negative adaptations to endopsychic and environmental conditions" (p. 143) and thus satisfactorily find "my way of life." Or the adolescent may try to postpone entry into the adult world or make the effort and fail.

All of these points are described in *On Adolescence,* which was published in 1962. In *The Adolescent Passage,* a collection of articles by Blos published in 1979, additional observations on the transition from childhood to adulthood are presented. Blos observes that "the formation of a conflict between generations and its subsequent resolution is the normative task of adolescence" (p. 11). Without such a conflict, Blos believes, the restructuring of personality that marks the transition from child to adult would not occur. He later suggests, though, that much of the negative and violent behavior of disaffected adolescents is not due to conflicts with their parents. It is rather an expression by young people of their dissatisfaction with societal disorders caused by adults. Furthermore, Blos notes, some types of adolescent behavior that are occasionally interpreted as due to a "generation gap" (for example, use of drugs, promiscuous sexual relations) might be interpreted as attempts on the part of youth to demonstrate that they are no longer dependent on their parents.

Blos suggests that in some respects an adolescent who has had warm, supportive relationships with parents throughout childhood may feel a greater need to indulge in a dramatic demonstration of independence than one who has not felt extremely close to the mother or father. Even if adolescents from congenial homes do not feel obliged to engage in acting out independence, they may be "burdened with family ties" (p. 19) when the time comes to move from dependence to independence. It would seem, then, that parents might ease the final stage of adolescence if they gradually encourage social and emotional independence in their sons and daughters starting at the end of the elementary school years.

Blos believes that the current emphasis on precocious sexual freedom is unfortunate because quite often "childish" needs may be satisfied by sexual activity and that such behavior "impedes rather than promotes progressive development" (p. 12). He expresses the opinion that while the adolescent's "conscious anguish and guilt feelings in relation to sexuality have declined remarkably, if we take his behavior and his words at face value, . . . guilt and anxiety have not disappeared but have simply been removed from consciousness by virtue of the fact that childhood and adolescent sexuality is sanctioned and encouraged by professional expert, parent, and peer" (p. 24).

Blos describes the final phase of adolescence as a time of crisis. The young person feels a need to consolidate and integrate feelings about self. The friend Blos invited to join him in Vienna, and who studied psychoanalysis with him, arrived at essentially the same conclusion. But because Erik Erikson was exposed to different experiences, he proposed a view of the identity crisis that emphasizes social and cultural factors. Erikson's views of adolescent development will now be summarized.

Erikson: A Psychosocial Interpretation of Adolescent Identity

By spending most of his professional life treating the mentally ill, Blos followed the same career pattern as Sigmund Freud. However, Blos's specialization in the treatment of American adolescents led him to revise some of Freud's interpretations derived from analysis of middle-class European females. Even so, Blos remained faithful to the basic principles of psychoanalytic theory. In his descriptions of adolescent behavior, Blos frequently assumes that the libido becomes attached to different objects at different stages of development. In this view, the basic problem confronting the developing person is the transfer of sexual energy from the parents to a member of the opposite sex. In making this transfer, it is necessary for adolescents and youth to resolve the Oedipus complex which involves conflicting feelings regarding the parents. This conception illuminates certain aspects of development and can explain some types of adolescent behavior. But it does not shed much light on the extent of the influence of social and cultural factors on development.

If Erik Erikson had followed the same career pattern as his friend, he might have remained as faithful to orthodox psychoanalytic theory. But, as noted in Chapter 3, the influence of anthropologists led Erikson to carry out field studies of American Indians. Taking part in the Berkeley Growth Study, Erikson also analyzed the development of normal children. These, and other influences, led him to propose a view of development that is based on Freudian principles but also stresses the impact of the culture on personality. Since this will be the last extended reference to Erikson's views in this book, and also because earlier stages serve as the framework for later ones, a brief review of Erikson's concept of development will clarify the description of adolescence that follows.

Review of Erikson's Theory of Development

Erikson based his view of development on the epigenetic principle illustrated by the biological maturation of the fetus. He hypothesized that there is a ground plan for personality development and that out of this, parts arise, "each part having its time of special ascendency, until all parts have arisen to form a functioning whole" (1968, p. 92). He described the "parts" as stages where "ego qualities which emerge from critical periods of development . . . integrate the time table of that organism within the structure of social institutions" (1963, p. 246). The first four of these stages were described in preceding chapters. Infants must develop a sense of trust based on recognition of consistency and continuity in their own behavior and in interactions with their parents. When two- to three-year-olds become capable of mastering their muscles and nerves so that locomotion and toilet control are achieved, they need to experience a sense of autonomy or independence and to avoid feeling shame or doubt about their abilities. At the preschool level, when children energetically engage in many activities, they need to develop a sense of initiative, without feeling guilty about trying new things on their own. During the elementary school years, a sense of industry must emerge as children learn to do things with others and to engage in sustained activities involving specific goals. If children are not accepted by peers or feel that they have failed in efforts to meet standards, they will develop a sense of inferiority.

The Stage of Identity versus Role Confusion

A child who has had favorable experiences during these four stages will develop a stable and positive self-concept. But this is no guarantee that the individual will successfully cope with the problems of the next stage, for reasons described by Erikson in this way:

In puberty and adolescence all samenesses and continuities relied on earlier are more or less questioned again, because of a rapidity of body growth which equals that of early childhood and because of the new addition of genital maturity. The growing and developing youths, faced with this physiological revolution within them, and with tangible adult tasks ahead of them are now primarily concerned with what they appear to be in the eyes of others as compared with what they feel they are, and with the question of how to connect the roles and skills cultivated earlier with the occupational prototypes of the day. In their search for a new sense of continuity and sameness, adolescents have to refight many of the battles of earlier years. (1963, p. 261)

In all of the preceding stages, Erikson stressed the importance of "continuity and sameness." These qualities take on special significance when the child moves toward adulthood because the integration of the ego is perceived to take on aspects of finality, just as physical appearance does. Consequently, the key characteristic of this stage is a search for *identity*, and the primary danger is *role confusion.*

Identity: acceptance of body, goals, recognition from those who count

Definition of Identity   The terms *identity* and *identity crisis* have become so popularized that it is important to review Erikson's original meanings. Here is how Erikson described the basic concept of identity: "An optimal sense of identity . . . is experienced merely as a sense of psychosocial well-being. Its most obvious concomitants are a feeling of being at home in one's body, a sense of 'knowing where one is going,' and an inner assuredness of anticipated recognition from those who count" (1968, p. 165). Erikson suggests adolescence is a critical period in development for the following reasons:

Identifications at adolescence involve a sense of urgency

Adolescence is the last stage of childhood. The adolescent process, however, is conclusively complete only when the individual has subordinated his childhood identifications to a new kind of identification, achieved in absorbing sociability and in competitive apprenticeship with and among his age mates. These new identifications are no longer characterized by the playfulness of childhood and the experimental zest of youth: with dire urgency they force the young individual into choices and decisions which will, with increasing immediacy, lead to commitments "for life." (p. 155)

In Erikson's view, two aspects of behavior are of special significance to the young person on the verge of adulthood: sex roles and occupational choice.

The Significance of Sex Roles   The danger in adolescence is role confusion: failure to experience a sense of consistency or commitment. Sex roles are particularly important because they establish a pattern for many types of behavior. Until recently, there was little confusion about appropriate characteristics and activities for males and females in our society. While such certainty provided a clear code of behavior for those who possessed or were eager to develop these characteristics, it created problems for those who did not. Sex stereotypes also led to the kinds of abuses and forms of discrimination objected to

Identity, as Erik Erikson defines it, involves acceptance of one's body, knowing where one is going, and recognition from those who count. A high school graduate who is pleased with his or her appearance, who has already decided on a college major, and who is admired by parents, relatives, and a particular friend, is therefore likely to experience a sense of psychosocial well-being. Mary Stuart Lang.

by feminists. With recognition of these abuses has come a blurring of sex roles and a trend toward unisex views. This trend may remove pressure from those who reject or are unable to develop "traditional" male and female traits, but it may create problems for the adolescent trying to develop a clear sense of identity.

Sex-role confusion may complicate formation of identity

While sex-role confusion causes problems for many adolescents, occupational choice may be of greater concern and significance.

The Significance of Occupational Choice Erikson proposes that occupational choice is perhaps the major decision leading to a sense of identity. The occupation we choose influences other aspects of our lives perhaps more than any other single factor. Our job determines how we will spend a sizable proportion of our time; it determines how much money we earn; and that, in turn, determines where and how we live. These last two factors determine, to a considerable extent, with whom we interact socially. All of these factors influence the reactions of others, and these reactions lead us to develop perceptions of ourselves. The choice of a career, therefore, is a highly significant decision in a person's life, and

Choice of career has significant impact on identity

the nature of life in a meritocracy makes it an especially difficult choice in America. Competition is necessary for success in most lines of endeavor, which presents the possibility that we will discover that we are less capable than others. Furthermore, as Karen Horney pointed out, the sometimes conflicting desires to be liked by others and to be successful may lead to feelings of guilt. Finally, many careers require an extended period of preparation and training. If we are not absolutely sure about our choice of a particular career we may have frequent doubts as preparation for it proceeds. Erikson notes that occupational choice is particularly difficult in America because of our technological orientation, which features the assembly line and corporate organization, both of which limit individuality. Other complicating factors are the amount of training needed for many jobs in a technological society and the rapidly changing job market.

When confronted with the realization that the time has come to make some sort of career choice, that many careers pose a threat to personal identity, and that the job market fluctuates rapidly, the young person seeking to avoid role confusion by making a firm vocational choice is faced with many unsettling complications. Because of this, Erikson suggests that for many young people a *psychosocial moratorium* may be desirable.

Erikson's Concepts of Psychosocial Moratorium and Negative Identity

Psychosocial moratorium: delay of commitment

A psychosocial moratorium is a period marked by a delay of commitment, which is illustrated very clearly by Erikson's own experiences. You may recall that after leaving high school Erikson spent several years wandering around Europe without making any firm decision about the sort of job he would seek. Under ideal circumstances, such a psychosocial moratorium should be a period of adventure and exploration with a positive (or at least neutral) impact on the individual and society. But in some cases, the young person may engage in defiant or destructive behavior. A young person who is unable to overcome role confusion—or unable to postpone choices leading to identity formation by engaging in a positive psychosocial moratorium—may attempt to resolve inner conflict by choosing what Erikson refers to as a *negative identity*.

The loss of a sense of identity is often expressed in a scornful and snobbish hostility toward the roles offered as proper and desirable in one's family or immediate community. Any aspect of the required role, or all of it—be it masculinity or femininity, nationality or class membership—can become the main focus of the young person's acid disdain (1968, pp. 172–173).

An adolescent boy whose parents have constantly stressed how important it is to do well in school so that he will be admitted to a prestige college, for example, may deliberately act in an unscholarly way or quit school entirely and join a commune.

Adolescents who are dissatisfied with themselves and unable to focus on constructive goals may fashion a negative identity by engaging in forms of behavior that are opposed by their parents. Jeff Albertson/Stock, Boston.

Erikson explains such choices by suggesting that the young person finds it easier to "derive a sense of identity out of total identification with that which he is least supposed to be than to struggle for a feeling of reality in acceptable roles which are unattainable with his inner means" (p. 176). If the young person who chooses a negative identity plays the role only long enough to gain greater self-insight, it may be a positive experience. But in some cases, the negative identity may be "confirmed" by the way the adolescent is treated by those in authority. If forms of behavior adopted to express a negative identity bring the teen-ager into contact with excessively punitive parents, teachers, or law enforcement agencies, for example, the "young person may well put his energy into becoming exactly what the careless and fearful community expects him to be—and make a total job of it" (p. 196).

Erikson notes (pp. 245–247) that one reason for the tendency to develop a negative identity is that the adolescent has achieved Piaget's stage of formal

Negative identity: adopting forms of behavior considered to be undesirable

operations, which makes possible the exploration of possibilities. The number of possible choices of groups, interests, and activities available to the contemporary American youth may seem overwhelming to a young person who lacks a sense of identity. (For a somewhat exaggerated account of some of the choices available, see Chapters 12, 13, and 14 of Alvin Toffler's *Future Shock* (1970). The chapter titles are: "The Origins of Overchoice," "A Surfeit of Subcults," "A Diversity of Life-styles.") Formal thought also makes the adolescent capable of developing what Erikson refers to as a *historical perspective,* the fear that earlier events in one's life are irreversible and may limit the choices available. As a consequence, Erikson suggests, "youth often rejects parents and authorities and wishes to belittle them as inconsequential" (p. 247) because they may stress the irreversible nature of many experiences. Conversely, young people may be attracted to those who propose "mythologies and ideologies predicting the course of the universe" (p. 247) since this implies that choices are yet to be made.

Summary of Points Emphasized by Blos and Erikson

Before proceeding it will be helpful to review points emphasized by Blos and Erikson, which are summarized in Table 12–2. Both theorists emphasize that the adolescent must make new and different kinds of adjustments, an observation that helps explain points noted at the end of the preceding chapter: longitudinal studies of personality development reveal that an individual's behavior does not always remain consistent throughout the span of development. It is therefore not always possible to predict adult adjustment from child behavior. Blos and Erikson also agree that if an individual is to function satisfactorily as an adult, a conception of "my way of life" or a sense of personal identity must be achieved. Failure to achieve such a picture of oneself as a reasonably coherent personality may lead to prolonged adolescence, a psychosocial moratorium, negative identity, or adjustment problems of varying degrees of severity. Blos explains that kinds of behavior can be due to sublimation of sexual urges. Erikson proposes that each adolescent needs to develop an acceptable conception of sex roles and to make an occupational choice.

Both Blos and Erikson based the bulk of their original theories on observations of adolescents made in the 1940s and 1950s. Accordingly, it is of interest to compare their conclusions to points made by Keniston, who based his description of youth on observations made during the 1960s. Keniston emphasizes many of the same points as Erikson but proposes a transitional stage between adolescence and adulthood for those who attend college. He notes, for instance, that "the adolescent is struggling to *define* who he is, the youth begins to *sense* who he is" (1970, p. 8, italics added). He believes that youth formulate conceptions of self that are somewhere between the passing enthusiasms of the adolescent and the

---

Table 12–2

Summary of the Observations of Blos and Erikson on Adolescence

POINTS STRESSED BY BLOS

☐ Much adolescent behavior is a "struggle to regain or retain a psychic equilibrium which has been jolted by the crisis of puberty"

☐ Lack of opportunity to satisfy sexual desires directly leads to sublimations:
Asceticism: renouncing comforts and material possessions in favor of an austere and simple life
Intellectualism: stressing rational and objective analyses while playing down emotions and feelings
Uniformism: seeking security by endorsing a shared code with members of the peer group and depending on mutual recognition of sameness

☐ Basic task of adolescence: arrive at a subjective feeling that "this is my way of life"

☐ Failure to achieve a sense of "my way of life" may lead to prolonged adolescence, adaptive failures, ego deformations, defensive maneuvers, or severe psychopathology

---

POINTS STRESSED BY ERIKSON

☐ Adolescents have to refight many battles of earlier years

☐ Basic task of adolescence: achieve a sense of identity (acceptance of one's body, formulation of goals, recognition by those who count)
Identifications at adolescence may involve lifetime commitments
Formation of identity depends on acceptance of a sex role, occupational choice

☐ Failure to achieve a sense of identity causes role confusion and may lead to a psychosocial moratorium (a period of delay of commitment) or formation of a negative identity

---

more established commitments of the adult. He also makes a distinction between adolescent experimentation and the more "serious forays into the adult world" that are made by youth. Finally, Keniston recognizes points similar to Erikson's concept of negative identity when he writes about youthful estrangement and the possibility of refusing socialization. It might be suggested, therefore, that Keniston's observations on youth extend Erikson's description of adolescent behavior to apply to the behavior of young Americans in their twenties attending college.

In the remainder of this chapter (and the end of the next chapter) amplifications of points raised by Blos and Erikson will be presented. In the following sections of this chapter the nature of sexual relationships during adolescence and youth will be discussed, followed by analyses of sex roles and occupational choice.

Comments on negative identity, adaptive failures, and psychopathological reactions will be offered at the end of the next chapter in the discussion of emotional maturity.

The Impact of Sexual Maturity

Changes in Attitude Toward Sexuality and in Sexual Behavior: 1950–1980

A glance at any book or magazine display or page of movie advertisements calls attention to the extent to which sexuality is stressed and exploited in contemporary American society. It is obvious that sexuality is discussed and depicted much more openly today than it was thirty years ago. Changes in sexual *behavior*, however, are difficult to assess, but some information is available. Alfred Kinsey and his associates found (1948) that 39 percent of the males they interviewed in the late 1940s reported having had premarital sexual intercourse by the age of sixteen, 72 percent by age nineteen. Of the females they interviewed (1953) in the early 1950s 3 percent reported having had sexual relations before sixteen, 20 percent before nineteen. In the early 1970s, R. C. Sorensen (1973) obtained data from a large sample of adolescents and found that 44 percent of the males under sixteen and 72 percent of those under nineteen reported having had premarital intercourse, figures almost identical to those reported by Kinsey. The proportion of *females* fifteen and under who reported having had sexual relations was 30 percent, however, and the figure for females under nineteen was 57 percent. In a different and later survey, M. Zelnik and J. E. Kantner (1977) reported figures of 18 percent for girls under fifteen, 55 percent for those under nineteen. Between 1950 and 1970, therefore, the proportion of women reporting premarital sexual relations appears to have increased from 3 to 20 or 30 percent for those under sixteen, from 20 to 55 or 57 percent for those under nineteen. This might be taken as evidence that the major "revolution" in current aspects of sexual relationships appears to be a tendency for women of the 1970s to be more likely to engage in premarital intercourse.

Substantial increase in premarital intercourse by females

Premarital Intercourse and Birth Control

Changes in assumptions about male-female differences in sex drives and responsiveness may also contribute to the increased premarital intercourse of young women. Up until recently it was widely thought that men enjoyed sex more than women did. William Masters and Virginia Johnson (1970), who specialize in treating couples suffering from sexual inadequacy, have concluded that the physiological capacity for sexual response is greater in females than in males. A recent survey of adolescent girls (Hunt, 1970) revealed that they are aware of and

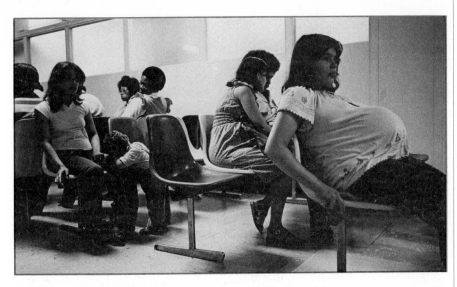

The failure of teenagers to use contraceptives leads to an estimated 700,000 unwanted pregnancies each year. © Mary Ellen Mark/Magnum.

support this view. More than two-thirds of those queried expressed the belief that women enjoy sex as much as men.

Despite a more liberal female attitude toward premarital sex, however, women still tend to be significantly more conservative about sexual relationships than men (Packard, 1970). This is understandable, as it is the woman who gets pregnant. Even with the availability of contraceptives, Zelnik and Kantner (1972) found that three-fourths of all fifteen- to nineteen-year-old unmarried girls who engaged in intercourse used no birth-control device. The consequences are revealed in the National Center for Health Statistics' *Facts of Life and Death* (1974). The report indicates that the proportion of illegitimate births increased from 38 per 1,000 live births in 1940 to 107 per 1,000 in 1970.

Donn Byrne, who has specialized in research on human sexual behavior, estimates that 11 million teen-agers engage in sexual intercourse from time to time. However, not more than 20 percent of them (about the same percentage reported by Zelnik and Kantner) use contraceptives regularly (1977, p. 67). He reports that the result is almost 700,000 unwanted pregnancies each year, followed shortly after by about 300,000 abortions, 100,000 miscarriages, and 200,000 out-of-wedlock births. To try to determine why so few teen-agers make use of contraceptives, Byrne asked eighteen- and nineteen-year-old girls attending a midwestern university to fill out an anonymous questionnaire. Information about birth control methods was provided via films and lectures at the university, and various contraceptives could be obtained at the student health service. Despite the fact that students were knowledgeable about methods of birth control and aware of the availability of contraceptives, only a third of those who were sexually active made systematic efforts to prevent pregnancy. Byrne hypothesizes (on the basis of related research on sexual behavior) that many teen-agers may be reluctant to use contraceptives because they feel anxious or negative about sex. He suggests that they avoid planning ahead and obtaining contraceptives because such thoughts and actions lead to guilt. (As noted a bit earlier, Blos suggests that guilt about premarital sex may no longer be consciously acknowledged by many young people but that unconscious guilt may influence behavior.) In order to reduce the number of unwanted pregnancies in teen-age girls, Byrne recommends (p. 68) that adolescents be exposed to the view that contraception is a significant and legitimate part of sexuality.

While Byrne's recommendation might lead to somewhat fewer illegitimate births to teen-age girls, the results of a survey and analysis by C. Lindemann (1974) lead to the conclusion that not all adolescent females would accept the view that contraception should be a part of sexuality. Lindemann interviewed and counseled over 2,500 young women in public health clinics, high schools, and colleges. When he asked those who failed to use contraceptives why they followed such a policy he found that some young women stressed unpredictability, uncertainty, and spontaneity; others seemed to be ignorant of the need for birth control. Some of his respondents pointed out, for example, that having sexual relations is often unpredictable and cannot always be anticipated. Others agreed with a young woman who said, "Sex is better if it is natural. Birth control is artificial. Getting birth control would shatter romantic ideas. I didn't like the idea of birth control because sex should be spontaneous" (1974, p. 15). Still others endorsed the view of a high school girl who pointed out that she had been having sexual relations for two years without getting pregnant and therefore saw no reason to bother with contraceptives.

Teen-age girls who favor these points of view might not be interested in information about birth control or take advantage of opportunities to obtain contraceptives. Lindemann found, however, that many girls and young women he interviewed were simply ignorant of the need for birth control. Such females would probably be more likely to welcome information about contraception and come to think of it as a part of sexuality.

Additional factors that may determine if a teen-age girl will use birth-control techniques were reported by I. L. Reiss, A. Banwart, and H. Foreman (1975). These investigators found that the life style of a young woman most likely to use contraceptives included these elements: high degree of commitment to a particular heterosexual relationship, a view of sexuality stressing the right of a woman to make decisions about her own sex life, self-assurance concerning her body image, a history of early acquisition of sex information inside and outside her family. In regard to the last point H. D. Thornburg (1970) asked female college students how they had acquired information about sex. Female acquaintances seemed to be the primary source, with articles in magazines and books and school sex education programs next in line, and parents at the bottom of the list.

Unfortunately, peers were often poorly informed about many aspects of sex, and Lindemann found in his survey that many girls hesitated to ask their mothers for information because they assumed that their parents were opposed to premarital sex. He also discovered, though, that contrary to the expectation of adolescent girls, quite a few parents had permissive attitudes about premarital sex. These permissive parents hesitated to offer information to girls about birth control, however, for fear that this would be interpreted as a sign that they were encouraging unrestrained sexual activity. Those who oppose sex education programs in the schools by arguing that adolescents should learn about sex from their parents are usually not aware of the kinds of factors noted by Thornburg and Lindemann.

Attitudes toward and knowledge of methods of birth control reveal aspects of contemporary adolescent and youthful sexuality. In order to comprehend the degree of confusion and ambivalence experienced by some young people regarding sex, however, it is necessary to consider some of the conflicting motives and attitudes to which they are exposed.

Conflicting Feelings About Premarital Sex

In a discussion of the development of sexuality in adolescence, Patricia Y. Miller and William Simon (1980) point out that puberty, a biological event, causes adolescents to function as "self-motivated sexual actors," which is a social event. They go on to comment that in technological societies "young people are defined as sexually mature while simultaneously being defined as socially and psychologically immature" (1980, p. 383). The confusion resulting from conflicts between sexual, social, and psychological conceptions of maturity is intensified by contemporary attitudes toward sex. Miller and Simon observe that, compared to previous cohorts, "contemporary adolescents are expected to be more interested in sex, to become experienced earlier, and once experienced, to approach regular sociosexual activity with greater competence" (p. 390). They go on to observe that "the contemporary adolescent must fashion an interpersonal sexual script from materials provided by a society that is nearly obsessed with the sexual possibilities of adolescence." They add that because of the high rate of divorce and the large number of adults on the "sexual marketplace," the adolescent in contemporary America "increasingly sees the surrounding adult social world as itself more sexually active and sexually interested than it used to be" (p. 390).

In addition to difficulties caused by such factors, the young person may be further confused because "the sex education of the adolescent is emphatically attached to moral education" (p. 392). Miller and Simon believe this is the case because gender-role expectations establish attitudes toward sexual morality. (The traditional view of the "good girl," for example, is that she does not engage in premarital sex.) They note, "Many of the specific images that form the core of the individual's earliest sense of the sexual are thoroughly imbued with vague but powerful moral tones" (p. 392). Evidence to support the point that sex and morality are intertwined was supplied by R. C. Sorensen (1973) who found that 76 percent of the thirteen- to fifteen-year-old girls he interviewed, and 43 percent of the sixteen- to nineteen-year-olds, reported sometimes or often feeling guilty about masturbation. The corresponding figures for males were 43 percent at thirteen to fifteen, 47 percent at sixteen to nineteen. Sorensen also asked his subjects to express their psychological reactions to their first sexual experience. Thirty-six percent of the girls reported that they had felt guilty (compared to 3 percent of the boys); 31 percent of the girls said they felt embarrassed (compared to 7 percent of the boys).

It appears, then, that quite a few adolescents and youth feel consciously guilty about sexual activities. If the conclusion drawn by Blos on the basis of clinical interviews with adolescent patients is valid, at least some young people also experience *unconscious* guilt about sexual relations before marriage. Even though they may consciously or unconsciously endorse the traditional view that premarital sex is wrong, however, adolescents and youth are motivated to engage in such relationships. As Miller and Simon observe, contemporary adolescents and youth may feel that they are *expected* to have early sexual experience and to develop a high level of competence. In addition, engaging in sexual relations may be reinforcing for reasons that have been outlined by S. Jessor and R. Jessor (1975). These researchers point out that adolescents and youth may be motivated to have sexual relations as early as possible because of one or more of these reasons: to prove to themselves and others that they have achieved a mature status, to establish a sense of independence (a point also stressed by Blos), to affirm sexual identity, to gain support for the belief that they are attractive to others, to reject social conventions or behave in a socially unacceptable manner (perhaps out of a desire to establish a negative identity), and to gain respect from peers.

These factors explain why premarital sex may seem appealing to adolescents and youth, even when they at least partially endorse the view that such activity is morally wrong. Jessor and Jessor found, for example, that while 60 percent of their female respondents mentioned fear of pregnancy as a reason for not engaging in premarital sex, 60 percent also mentioned fear of parental disapproval and 55 percent mentioned fear of damaging their reputation.

These figures obviously support the conclusion that females have more potent reasons than males for being concerned about the consequences of premarital sex. Other female-male differences in thinking about premarital sex are revealed by studies of attitudes toward the sexual partner. W. Simon, A. S. Berger, and J. S. Gagnon (1972) found that the first sexual relationship for almost half of all the college males they interviewed was with a female for whom they felt no emotional involvement. By contrast, only 5 percent of the females they interviewed reported no personal involvement with their first sexual partner. Fifty-nine percent of the women said they planned to marry their first partner, an additional 22 percent reported that they were in love with him but did not anticipate marriage.

Simon and Miller (1980) speculate that many males may have their first sexual experience with a "casual" acquaintance because they lack sociosexual competence. This makes it difficult for them to gain access to "good girls." Furthermore, contemporary young men may endorse traditional views of sexual morality and be reluctant to risk damaging the reputation of a female for whom they feel genuine affection, even though they profess to endorse sexual permissiveness.

A further difference between male and female attitudes toward premarital sexual relations was revealed by D. E. Carns (1973). Carns found that 60 percent of the males he interviewed mentioned that they had told friends about the experience within a month and that 80 percent of their audience approved of what they had done. By contrast, only 40 percent of the females shared the experience with others. (Sixty-seven percent of their confidants approved.) Miller and Simon (1980, pp. 395–396) reason that the results of these various surveys lead to two conclusions: (1) many males may tend to engage in premarital sexual relations to impress peers; females may be more motivated to please their partner; (2) the double standard regarding premarital sex has diminished considerably in the last twenty years, but even in the 1980s there still seems to be a tendency for sexual experimentation to be condoned (or even encouraged) in males to a significantly greater extent than in females. Even so, it appears that a single standard which I. L. Reiss (1967) has referred to as *permissiveness with affection* is increasingly being accepted and endorsed as acceptable for both males and females.

Single sexual standard of permissiveness with affection being accepted

Despite the move toward a single standard regarding premarital sex, many more females than males consider such relations to be a prelude to marriage. In order to understand significant aspects of marriage in the 1980s, though, it is necessary to take into account the impact of sex roles.

The Nature and Impact of Changing Sex Roles

Changes in Sex Roles

Contemporary attitudes toward sexuality and marriage reflect and are influenced by changing conceptions of sex roles. Until recently, in our society it was assumed that almost all adult males and females would marry and that husband and wife would then take on well-defined and clearly established responsibilities: the man would function as the breadwinner, the woman would serve as the homemaker and child rearer. During the last twenty years, however, interpretations of appropriate behavior for mature males and females have changed dramatically. As noted previously, about half of all mothers of school age children now are employed. Furthermore, the high rate of divorce has led to a significant number

Douvan and Adelson found that in the 1950s most high school girls had a "diffuse and misty" identity because they assumed that what they would become would depend on the man they would eventually marry. Burt Glinn/Magnum.

of single-parent homes. Distinctions between jobs for men and jobs for women are becoming more blurred all the time, and females are now employed in occupations that were male-dominated up to the last decade or so. These changes have led to advantages as well as to disadvantages for adolescents and youth who are faced with the task of establishing a satisfactory interpretation of a personally acceptable sex role.

Some of these advantages for females are revealed by a comprehensive study by Elizabeth Douvan and Joseph Adelson. These two psychologists supervised extensive interviews of hundreds of adolescents in the late 1950s. They spent several years analyzing the responses and then reported their conclusions in *The Adolescent Experience* (1966). They were particularly interested in identity formation and came to the conclusion that in the 1950s and 1960s there were striking differences in the ways adolescent males and females perceived identity formation. Most of the high school boys they interviewed seemed to have a reasonably clear picture of their future career. As a consequence, Douvan and Adelson speculated, the adolescent boy typically felt that his identity was in his own hands. The girls who were interviewed in the 1950s, however, tended "to keep identity diffuse, and misty" (1966, p. 18) because they assumed that what they were to become as adults would depend to a large extent on the men who would eventually become their husbands.

Until recently, therefore, the typical American adolescent girl felt that she could not achieve a real sense of adult identity until she was married. Once married her identity would depend, to a significant degree, on what her husband did for a living. A high school girl of the 1950s might have picked out some young man she hoped to marry, and she might have used various means to induce him to propose to her, but the young man was expected to take the initiative regarding marriage. The kind of job he secured after marriage, and his success at that job, would influence his wife's conception of herself perhaps more than her own behavior. Douvan and Adelson emphasize the extent to which this set of expectations was accepted at the time they wrote their report by mentioning the results of a survey of sophomores attending a leading women's college in the 1950s. When asked to describe what they thought they would be doing in ten years, forty-seven out of fifty respondents wrote descriptions that included the following elements:

1   Marriage to a successful professional man or junior executive
2   Three or more children
3   A home in the suburbs
4   Daily activities including chauffeuring, shopping, and food preparation
5   A station wagon
6   Membership in community organizations (p. 235)

Douvan and Adelson acknowledge that the sample of this study was highly selected and biased. But even allowing for this, the unanimity of opinion is striking, and the list of traits provides a clear reflection of what had become—until the women's movement developed—a widely accepted view of the feminine role in America.

Changes in the thinking about the roles of women in our society between 1950 and the present are revealed by the replies of female college juniors and seniors attending a state university who were asked to describe what *they* expected to be doing in ten years (Biehler, 1979). About one-third described a specific job (but made no mention of a husband or family), about one-third mentioned both a job and a family, about one-third indicated that they expected to be devoting themselves to rearing a family but that they intended to pursue a career of some

Traditionally, male identity linked to job; female identity linked to husband

sort after the children were grown up. Only two out of seventy females in this group failed to mention pursuing some sort of job or career on either a part-time or full-time basis, none of them gave the sort of description (centering on being a housewife and mother) Douvan and Adelson found so common in the 1950s.

Factors That Perpetuate Sex Roles

It appears, then, that the young female of the 1980s is much more likely to feel that her destiny is in her own hands than her mother did when she was the same age. While the opportunity for self-fulfillment obviously opens up many opportunities, it may also lead to confusion and problems for reasons noted in discussing socialization during the elementary school years. Chapter 10 presented Inge Broverman and several associates' analysis (1972) of perceptions of "typical" masculine and feminine traits. There was considerable unanimity of opinion from respondents of both sexes, all age levels, and all types of backgrounds: men were pictured as competent, rational, and assertive; women were thought of as warm and expressive.

Beverly Fagot (1978) found that many parents appear to treat preschool age boys and girls differently. Parents often respond negatively when young girls engage in physical or athletic activities, but respond positively when girls exhibit dependent, adult-oriented behavior. As a consequence, girls are much more likely than boys to ask for help because this tendency is strengthened by the positive response of parents and teachers. Boys, on the other hand, are often told directly or indirectly to handle things themselves. On the basis of comparisons of interview responses and actual behavior, Fagot concluded that parents often were not aware that they were responding differently to boys and girls. It is possible, therefore, that although contemporary parents may *think* that they have rejected traditional conceptions of sex roles, they still might encourage girls to be dependent and boys to be independent.

Jeanne Block (1973) reviewed research on socialization practices and reached a conclusion similar to that reported by Fagot. Block found evidence that boys in our society are encouraged to achieve and be competitive, to control expression of feelings, and to conform to rules. Girls, on the other hand, are encouraged to develop close interpersonal relationships, talk about their troubles, show affection, and give comfort to others.

Evidence that the differential treatment of boys and girls in our society has an impact on early speculations about careers was revealed by the results of the survey reported in Chapter 10. When they were asked "What do you want to be when you grow up?" many six- to twelve-year-old boys mentioned occupations that centered on competitiveness and achievement (professional athlete, lawyer). While elementary school girls sometimes mentioned such occupations, they showed a much greater tendency to aspire to jobs that would permit them to help others (teacher, nurse). Evidence that these sex differences continue to prevail

Jeanne Block suggests that males in our society are socialized to achieve and be competitive and that females are socialized to develop interpersonal relationships. Such differences in socialization practices help account for the finding that college males are more interested than females in becoming leaders and making money and that females are more interested than males in helping others. Ellis Herwig/Stock, Boston.

through the high school years is offered by W. B. Fetters (1976) who carried out an extensive nation-wide survey of graduates of the high school class of 1972. When asked, "Is each of the following very important to you in selecting a job or career?" 28.6 percent of the males responded "Having a position that is looked up to by others," compared to 22.3 percent of the females. "Making a lot of money" was very important to 28.5 percent of the males, but to only 15.9 percent of the females; the "chance to be a leader" was rated high by 21.9 percent of the males but by only 9.9 percent of the females. By contrast, 61.7 percent of the females were eager for "opportunities to work with people rather than things," compared to 36.0 percent of the males. And 64.0 percent of the females indicated interest in having "opportunities to be helpful to others or useful to society," compared to 42.1 percent of the males.

Males eager to be leaders and make money; females want to help others

The results of the various studies just summarized suggest that even though many young females of the 1980s believe they have unlimited opportunities to seek a variety of jobs, they may still be socialized to prefer to work with people and to help others. Furthermore, independent and competitive types of behavior displayed by girls may be deliberately or unwittingly discouraged by parents and teachers. For these reasons, Block recommended (to repeat points noted in Chapter 10) that it would be desirable for children and adolescents to acquire sex roles that *combine* what are presently identified by many individuals (as reported by Broverman et al.) as masculine *or* feminine traits. Boys might benefit, for instance, if they became more sensitive to the needs of others; many girls would benefit if they were encouraged to be less docile and more achievement oriented. Reasons for encouraging girls to develop higher career aspirations are revealed by studies of *fear of success*. To understand research and conclusions regarding this phenomenon, a bit of background is necessary.

The Impact of Sex-typed Behavior

Speculations About Achievement Motivation

J. W. Atkinson (1964) has developed a view of occupational aspirations that is derived from the conception of *achievement motivation* proposed by David McClelland (1961). McClelland believes that in the course of development people acquire a *need for achievement,* and he has conducted research to demonstrate the degree to which the need varies among individuals. His basic research technique is to show subjects pictures of individuals in different situations (a boy sitting at a desk with a book in front of him, for example) and ask them to write stories about what is happening. Individuals with a high need for achievement tend to write stories emphasizing work, getting things done, and success; those with a low need for achievement do not mention such types of behavior. Atkinson proposes that differences in the strength of the need for achievement can be explained by postulating a contrasting need to avoid failure. Atkinson believes that the tendency to achieve success is influenced by the probability of success and the attractiveness of achieving it. A strong need to avoid failure is likely to develop when people experience repeated failure and set goals beyond what they think they can accomplish.

Research on Fear of Success

Some Females May Perceive Achievement as Inappropriate   As she read reports of research inspired by the work of McClelland and Atkinson, Matina S. Horner became intrigued by the finding that the need for achievement in males seemed to be more fully developed than in females. She decided to make this the subject of her Ph.D. dissertation (1968) and, using a technique derived from studies by Atkinson, asked 178 university students to write a four-minute story from this cue: "At the end of first-term finals Anne finds herself at the top of her medical school class." When she analyzed the stories, Horner found three recurrent themes: (1) fear that Anne would lose friends; (2) guilt about success;

(3) unwillingness to come to grips with the question of Anne's success (in some stories, the cue was more or less ignored). She concluded that all three of these themes reflected a general *fear of success* and discovered that 65.5 percent of the stories written by women could be classified under this heading, contrasted with only 9 percent of those written by men.

As a second part of her study she placed men and women in competitive and noncompetitive situations. She found that women who wrote fear-of-success stories performed much better when working alone than when competing against others. She reasoned that fear of success motivates many women to avoid achievement, particularly in competitive situations.

Reports of Horner's study (1970) attracted attention, and a number of articles in newspapers and magazines led readers to believe that there is a well-established tendency for almost all women to fear success. Because of the publicity and the topicality of the concept, over sixty studies derived from or similar to Horner's original research were carried out in the next three years. David Tresemer (1974, 1977) reviewed these and also analyzed the techniques used by Horner. He concluded that fear-of-success stories may be influenced by a variety of factors, including the type of cues supplied. For example, when a woman in a story is described as the best *psychology* student rather than as the best medical student, Tresemer reports, males write more fear-of-success stories than females.

Fear-of-success stories influenced by variety of factors

Females May Try to Protect the Male Ego　In *The Adolescent Society* (1961) James S. Coleman reported that bright high school girls did not try to qualify for the honor roll because they were afraid it might make them unpopular, particularly with boys. While it appears that more young women of the 1980s have a greater desire to achieve success in school and in a career than their predecessors, there are still many adolescent (and adult) females whose primary goal is marriage and a family. For thousands of years bright and capable women have accepted that marriage may be possible only when a male is attracted to but not threatened by a woman. Recognizing that many males are sensitive about their "masculinity," generations of practical women have avoided display of their abilities and resorted to subtle and indirect ways of achieving success in marriage and life. Awareness of this aspect of male-female relationships may account for at least some of the fear-of-success stories written by females in studies such as Horner's. Perhaps some stories stressing Anne's discomfort about "finding" (a word which leads the reader to believe that Anne is bothered) herself at the top of her class could be attributed to recognition of the need to protect the male ego. (Philip H. Dreyer reports [1975, p. 214], though, that the percentage of women who admit that they pretend to be dumb on dates has dropped considerably in the last thirty years.)

Conflicts Between a Career and Marriage　Additional insight into career problems encountered by females is provided by the observations of Karen Horney. It seems significant that a woman was the first psychoanalyst to reveal the conflict between a desire to achieve success and the desire to be accepted by others. (Maslow's hierarchy of needs calls attention to the fact that the needs for love and belonging usually must be satisfied before the need for esteem emerges.) Perhaps the disintegration of her own marriage led Horney to emphasize the significance of such conflicts. As a young woman she was attracted to her husband and desired to maintain a loving relationship with him, but she also felt impelled to use her exceptional intelligence and abilities. After she had achieved notable success in her career, her relationship with her husband became less meaningful and they separated, a predicament that may confront many successful women in the 1980s. Today, more than at any time in history, choices concerning career and marriage for both males and females may be inextricably intertwined.

In *The Adolescent Experience* (1966) Douvan and Adelson emphasized the extent to which the future of a high school girl of the mid-1950s would depend on the man she married. In the 1980s this is still true of many adolescent females. A significant number of high school and college females, however, are determined to try to alter this pattern by establishing themselves in careers. A young woman's decision to prepare for a career will influence other decisions, particularly those regarding marriage and having children. If she hopes to combine a career and a family, she must decide whether to devote full time to rearing children before or after pursuing a career, whether to interrupt a career only long enough to give birth and then place the child in the care of baby sitters or a day-care center, or whether to ask her husband to share or take over the responsibility for child rearing. This last option, in particular, emphasizes how decisions about a career will have a profound influence on the choice of a husband. A woman who wants to combine a full-time career with marriage will need to try to choose a husband who is willing and able to adapt to deviations from the traditional pattern. While a contemporary young man might profess to be above male chauvinism and be confident in his ability to adjust to marriage with a career-oriented woman, both he and his prospective spouse might not consider some of the practical difficulties that could arise in such a relationship. They may discover that traditional role assignments of female as homemaker and child rearer and male as provider are not easy to disregard.

The Advantages of Psychological Androgyny Broverman and her colleagues (1972) reveal the extent to which traditional conceptions of sex roles are ingrained in the minds of many Americans. Sandra Bem's research (1975, 1976) supports those findings. In discussing early child-parent relationships in Chapter 7, Bem's studies were cited as indicating that adults vary in the extent to which they can be classified as *sex-typed* or as high in *psychological androgyny*. Sex-typed females (who endorse stereotyped conceptions of femininity) may refuse to nail two boards together, for instance, because they feel it is a "masculine" rather than a "feminine" form of behavior. Sex-typed males may refuse to handle a baby or do household chores presumably because engaging in such behavior will make

Couples who attempt to reverse or modify the traditional roles of husband and wife may discover that the adjustment involves more than they anticipated. Such marriages are most likely to succeed if the husband rates high in psychological androgyny. Owen Franken/Stock, Boston.

them appear effeminate or at least unmasculine. Only adults rated high in psychological androgyny appear able to move between masculine and feminine roles without difficulty or self-consciousness.

On the basis of available evidence, it is not possible to trace or precisely evaluate all of the factors that lead to sex-typed behavior or to psychological androgyny. The report of Money and Ehrhardt (1972) comparing androgenized and normal girls leads to the assumption that at least some forms of sex-typed behavior (for example, tendencies for adolescent girls to be interested in marriage and motherhood) may be due to hormonal balances established at the time of conception. The study by Fagot and the analysis of research by Block, on the other hand, call attention to the extent to which sex-typed behavior is shaped by the responses of parents and teachers. Furthermore, the various studies carried out by social learning theorists such as Sears and Bandura suggest that observation of models will have a significant impact on sex-typed behavior. A boy who watches his father unselfconsciously care for an infant or wash the dishes would seem more likely to acquire a flexible view of sex roles than a boy whose father is a sex-typed male. And a girl who observes her mother go off to work should be less inclined to picture women solely as mothers and homemakers.

Even if a girl has tendencies toward sex-typed feminine behavior due to hormonal balances that were programmed at the time of conception, therefore, it would seem likely that she could be encouraged to develop psychological androgyny. Parents and teachers might try to favor the development of flexible conceptions of sex roles by following suggestions offered by Block. Girls might be

Psychological androgyny can be encouraged in many ways

urged to be more competitive and achievement oriented, boys might be encouraged to be more sensitive to the feelings of others and to engage in other than traditional masculine activities without self-consciousness. Without such encouragement, a sex-typed male might experience many problems if he later marries a career-oriented woman or is even asked to share in child-rearing and housekeeping responsibilities.

Stages in Occupational Choice

Super's Description of Vocational Developmental Tasks

This review of research on fear of success and the influence of sex roles on occupational choice calls attention to one way choice of a job may influence a young person's sense of identity. But self-concept is influenced in a variety of ways by vocational choice, a view that has been proposed by Donald Super (1957). Some of Super's observations are similar to Erikson's emphasis on the significance of occupational choice on the formation of identity. Other of Super's points are related to the concept of achievement motivation presented by McClelland and Atkinson.

Super proposes that patterns of behavior emerge during the school years and are expressed in academic performance, peer-group activities, athletics, and part-time work. (In the elementary school years, Erikson would refer to this as the development of a sense of industry or inferiority.) Success and failure in these various activities lead eventually to a concept of self that is publicly proclaimed when the person seeks a more or less permanent occupation.

Evidence to support Super's hypothesis regarding interrelationships between self-concept, success in school, and later occupational attainment is provided in a summary of the results of a longitudinal study of 2,000 boys who entered high school in 1966 (Bachman, O'Malley, and Johnston, 1978). Starting in the tenth grade the boys were studied intensively and their careers were followed for several years after they graduated. Boys rated high in self-esteem in the tenth grade did well academically, and the high grades they earned served to reinforce their confidence in themselves. If they succeeded in finding a satisfying job as soon as they entered the labor market, their self-esteem remained high. But if they remained unemployed for any length of time, their self-concept suffered.

Super proposes that there are vocational developmental tasks similar to the more general developmental tasks described by Havighurst. These tasks are listed and described in Table 12–3. Super's outline of vocational developmental tasks suggests that Erikson's statement about the choice of occupation being "commitment for life" should not be interpreted too literally, particularly in the volatile occupational world of the 1980s. Super's view of an extended period of searching for the "right" job, a search that may often extend into one's thirties, appears to be an accurate reflection of the present occupational situation in America. Because

Search for a satisfying career may extend to thirties

	Table 12–3	
	Vocational Developmental Tasks Described by Super	
AGE	DESIGNATION OF TASK	DESCRIPTION OF TASK
14–18	Crystallization of a vocational preference	Evaluation of self-concept and formulation of initial ideas about work
18–21	Specification of a vocational program	Choice of a college curriculum that leads toward a particular career
21–24	Implementing the vocational preference	Acceptance of an initial job
24–35	Stabilization	Narrowing an area of specialization and searching for personal satisfaction in a career
35–	Consolidation	Developing expertise, strengthening job skills, and acquiring status

Source: D. E. Super, "Vocational Development in Adolescence and Early Childhood: Tasks and Behaviors," in D. E. Super et al., (Eds.), *Career Development: A Self-Concept Theory* (New York: College Entrance Examination Board, 1963).

of rapid advances in technology and abrupt reversals in the economic situation in this country and the world, many adults may change careers several times either out of choice or necessity.

Ginzberg's Description of the Process of Vocational Choice

Another theorist who has stressed the tentative and changeable nature of occupational choice is E. Ginzberg (1972). Ginzberg focuses on a sequence of vocational decision-making that begins a bit earlier than the vocational developmental tasks described by Super. Three periods are described by Ginzberg, the first beginning around the age of eleven or twelve, the last extending into the mid-twenties. These periods are outlined in Table 12–4. Ginzberg proposes that adolescents move from a fantasy stage through a tentative period made up of four substages before thay make a final job choice as adults. There is evidence that this sequence frequently does occur. J. W. Hollender (1967), for example, studied over 4,500 adolescents from the sixth through the twelfth grades and found that realistic occupational choices began to appear around the ninth grade and to increase thereafter. (On the basis of Ginzberg's description of stages and the results of the Hollender study, it might be predicted that the elementary school boys mentioned in Chapter 10 who said they wanted to be professional athletes or

Realistic occupational choices begin to appear at ninth grade

Table 12–4

Stages in the Process of Vocational Choice Described by Ginzberg

AGE	DESIGNATION OF STAGE	DESCRIPTION OF STAGE
11–12	Fantasy	Initial, often unrealistic fantasies about careers. Little realization of opportunities or of training requirements; little awareness of abilities.
11–18	Tentative	
11–12	Interest	Fairly realistic speculations about different careers; formulation of likes and dislikes regarding various occupations.
13–14	Capacity	Awareness of need to evaluate likelihood of being able to succeed in different careers.
15–16	Value	Evaluation of the kind of life-style that will be associated with different careers and appraisal of values associated with different kinds of jobs (e.g. working to make money or to help others).
17–18	Transition	Awareness of the need to make a fairly specific decision regarding finding a job or choosing a college program.
19–25	Realistic	Cycle of exploration and crystallization. Attempts to find a balance between a desired life-style and the realities of the world of work. Such cycles may be influenced by educational and vocational opportunities, changes in aspirations, work experiences, changes in financial resources, and changes in the labor market.

Source: E. Ginzberg, "Toward a Theory of Occupational Choice: A Restatement," *Vocational Guidance Quarterly*, 1972, **20**, 169–176. *Note:* If you have not yet made a firm occupational choice and/or have changed your major one or more times you may find it comforting to discover that both Super and Ginzberg stress that a person may not settle on a vocation until the mid-twenties or even later.

motorcycle racers will have more realistic career aspirations before they leave high school.)

Additional data for evaluating Ginzberg's description of a transition from fantasy to realism are provided by J. C. Flanagan (1972) who analyzed aspects of

Many elementary school boys dream of becoming motorcycle racers or professional athletes when they grow up. J. W. Hollender found that more realistic occupational choices are made toward the beginning of the high school years. Burk Uzzle/Magnum.

Project TALENT, two national surveys of large numbers of adolescents carried out in 1960 and 1970. He found that sometimes political or cultural trends led to somewhat unrealistic occupational choices. Quite a few boys who lacked a high degree of ability in mathematics and the sciences, for example, were inspired by the space race with Russia to become physicists and engineers. Ten years later many girls seemed to set unrealistically high goals for themselves, perhaps because job possibilities for females had just opened up dramatically.

It would seem, though, that females might be better off setting their occupational sights a bit too high rather than the opposite. L. W. Harmon (1971) asked college women about the history of their career choices. Many of them reported that they had made an occupational choice when they were in the elementary grades and that they had seen no reason to change it. Unfortunately, many of the choices they had selected during the grade school years reflected the stereotyped view that females should not seek jobs of leadership or responsibility. Accordingly, the "unrealistically" high career aspirations of girls that were reported in the 1970 Project TALENT survey might be interpreted as a step in the right direction. Evidence to support this contention is supplied by M. S. Richardson (1974) who found that many college women of the mid-1970s were becoming more career oriented. This conclusion fits with the results of the study mentioned a bit earlier where college juniors and seniors were asked to describe what they thought they would be doing in ten years. Both studies lead to the conclusion that many young women of the 1980s seem to be overcoming fear of success.

Career choices reflect personality traits, attitudes, values, abilities and interests, all of which contribute to identity. Since all of these factors are influenced by the reactions of others, the remaining pages of this chapter are devoted to analyses of some of the ways parents and peers influence adolescents and youth.

The Influence of Parents and Peers

Evaluations of the Significance of the Family

In the 1960s and early 1970s a number of theorists argued that the American family had disintegrated and parents had little contact with or influence over their children, particularly during adolescence. The authors of the Report to the President prepared by participants in the 1970 White House Conference on Children noted: "We are experiencing a breakdown in the process of making human beings human" (1971, p. 243). Urie Bronfenbrenner affirmed this point of view by asserting that children are no longer brought up by their parents but by their peers and by television (1972, p. 95). In the late 1970s and early 1980s a number of psychologists have reexamined earlier studies and analyzed recent research and drawn different conclusions. Glen H. Elder, Jr., for example, notes in an essay on "Adolescence in Historical Perspective" that "important studies from the 1950s to the present have consistently documented the central role of the family in the lives of young people" (1980, p. 18). In a review of research on value development Norman T. Feather observes, "One should not discount the family as an important force in the socialization of adolescent values" (1980, p. 280). In a review of research on moral development Martin L. Hoffman stresses the central role played by parents and concludes "it may be a mistake to think of peer groups as exerting an influence apart from the influence of adults" (1980, p. 328). In a review of political thinking at adolescence Judith Gallatin expresses the opinion that while theorists in the 1950s and early 1960s tended to overemphasize the impact of the family on political socialization, some writers of the late 1960s and early 1970s tended to go too far in the opposite direction. She concludes that in the early 1980s the balance seems to be swinging back to a point somewhere between the two extremes. And even at a time when psychologists were discounting the influence of the family, D. Kandel and G. Lesser (1969) estimated that parents had twice as much influence on the career choices of adolescents as peers. It seems reasonable to say, therefore, that it is important to examine how parents influence adolescent sons and daughters as they move from dependence to autonomy.

Factors That Complicate the Move Toward Autonomy

Human beings have a longer period of dependence on parents than any other species. This leads to special difficulties when the time comes for the young person to be independent, partly because the long period of interaction has led to strong

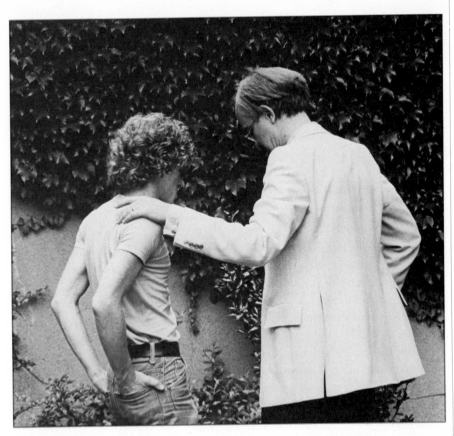

Some theorists have concluded that the family no longer has much of an influence on American adolescents. Other psychologists, however, are convinced that parents still influence the behavior, values, and plans of their teen-age sons and daughters in significant ways. © Joel Gordon 1979.

emotional ties, partly because the adolescent is mature and sensitive enough to comprehend the magnitude and significance of what is happening. In our society, these already substantial problems are magnified by a lack of any clear set of guidelines indicating when a young person has achieved maturity. In many simpler societies, initiation rituals have been established, and once a boy or girl successfully masters or experiences the prescribed forms of behavior, adulthood is proclaimed by dress or ornament or some other tangible sign. But in America, there is considerable confusion about the rights and privileges of adulthood. The most obvious example, up until 1972, was that an eighteen-year-old male was considered to be man enough to engage in warfare but not man enough to vote. At the present time, many legislative bodies are debating the age at which liquor can be legally purchased or consumed. This varies from state to state, as do the ages at which a marriage license or driver's license can be obtained, property owned, or even cigarettes purchased.

These inconsistencies in society at large make the task facing parents and their close-to-adult children even more difficult than it is to begin with. Douvan and Adelson provide an eloquent description of the nature of the problem.

The family must take on tasks of socialization more subtle than they have met before; at the same time it must know how to yield gracefully to such competing socializers as the peer group. It must accommodate itself to the implications and dangers of the child's sexual maturity; it must adjust to his extraordinary, nerve-wracking ambivalence; it must face and respond to his clamor for autonomy, distinguishing those demands which are real and must be granted from those which are token and are used to test the parents or to bargain with them. Above all, the family must allow the child to abandon it, without allowing him to feel that he is himself abandoned or an abandoner. (1966, p. 119)

Because ours is a melting-pot society, there is no single, well-established code of behavior, such as that found in homogeneous and self-contained cultures. Because ours is a technological society, culture change is extremely rapid. Because ours is a meritocratic society, parents are eager to insure that their children will be prepared to compete effectively with others. For all of these reasons, the peer group may exert a degree of influence on parental decisions about adolescent behavior. In the absence of a single set of guidelines, parents who must make decisions about what their teen-age sons and daughters can and cannot do may fall back on their own adolescent experiences. But rapid cultural change has made some of the parents' experiences obsolete or irrelevant. In addition, they may feel apprehensive that too many restrictions—or old-fashioned ones—may handicap their children when the time comes for career and marriage competition with the children of neighbors. Recognizing the parents' uncertainty, the adolescent may try to gain as much freedom and autonomy as possible by describing what peers with the fewest restrictions are allowed to do. Parents, for the most part, will want to continue to exert a degree of control and may disbelieve or discount descriptions of what other families are doing.

Evaluations of the "Generation Gap" Hypothesis

The term *generation gap* is frequently used to explain that the factors just noted may lead to substantial differences between the views of parents and of their adolescent offspring. While such a gap probably exists in some families, it is not inevitable and may be the exception rather than the rule. Daniel Offer (1969) discovered this when he made a comprehensive study of seventy-three normal adolescent boys and their families. Offer felt that too many conclusions about adolescence were based on extreme cases, and he deliberately chose subjects who were *not* identified as maladjusted. He and his associates conducted 6 forty-five-

Daniel Offer concluded that a "generation gap" between parents and their adolescent children may be the exception rather than the rule. Cary Wolinsky/Stock, Boston.

minute interviews with each subject over a period of three years, administered projective and other tests, and also interviewed parents.

They found that disagreements with parents reached a peak in the seventh and eighth grades, but even at that time these were not severe. Eighty-eight percent of the boys felt home discipline was fair, and there were few strong complaints about parents (inconsistent discipline was one of the most common factors mentioned). Most parents were pleased with the behavior of their sons, particularly because they felt that pressure on adolescents had increased since their youth. While the boys were most rebellious at twelve and thirteen, argued with their parents about hair and clothes at thirteen and fourteen, and about the car at sixteen, Offer found that by and large they endorsed the same middle-class values as their parents. He concluded that there was little evidence of parent-child conflict or a generation gap. Apparently, parents recognized cultural changes influencing the behavior of their teen-age sons and adjusted their attitudes accordingly.

Generation gap appears to be exception rather than rule

Although Offer's results and conclusions may have been significantly influenced by his deliberate choice of "normal" subjects (who might have emphasized their normality because of their awareness that he was a psychiatrist), it does seem reasonable to say that conflict between parents and teen-agers is far from inevitable. The conclusions reached by Offer in 1969 regarding lack of evidence of a generation gap have been reaffirmed more recently by A. Tolor (1976), Joseph Adelson (1979), R. Josselson (1980), and J. Gallatin (1980). And in *The Myth of the Generation Gap* S. Coopersmith, M. Regan, and L. Dick observe:

> There are indeed many differences between generations but they are apt to be differences in defining and implementing ideals, in role, in responses to change, and in personal tastes, which generally occur within a context of mutual acceptance, rather than differences that bespeak hostility and disrespect. The gap is largely between the general worlds of adults and young people rather than between parents and children. (1975, pp. 316–317)

Parent-Child Relationships That Favor Autonomy

On the basis of the findings of their study, Douvan and Adelson concluded that four aspects of parent-adolescent relationships were involved in the development of autonomy: parental interest and involvement, the emotional intensity of family interaction, the degree and nature of family conduct, and the nature of parental authority. They offer a detailed analysis of each of these in Chapter 5 of *The Adolescent Experience.* They note that an adolescent is more likely to achieve a satisfactory sense of at least some aspects of autonomy under these conditions: parents manifest a moderate degree of sincere interest; relationships are neither cold nor intense; parents allow a certain amount of conflict (by listening to children explain *their* point of view); adolescents participate in making decisions. They also discovered that girls seemed to progress steadily toward independence but that boys were likely to experience a certain amount of strain. Boys were also more likely to assume an objective-critical view of their parents. In summarizing their analysis, Douvan and Adelson note, "the autonomous have the opportunity for individualism (while the nonautonomous do not)" (p. 173).

G. H. Elder, Jr. (1962) investigated parent-adolescent relationships and autonomy by a method similar to the Douvan and Adelson investigations in many respects. He asked over seven thousand adolescents to rate their parents' behavior. He found that when asked about *fairness,* the most positive ratings were given to parents characterized as *democratic* (the adolescent was invited to participate in discussions, but final decisions were made by the parents), or *equalitarian* (parents and adolescents had equal say). The lowest ratings were given to parents who were *autocratic* (the adolescent was not consulted at all). The democratic approach also seemed to foster confidence and independence. Thus, the results of the Elder study are consistent with the findings of Douvan and Adelson—and with the results of Baumrind's research (1971) on authoritative, authoritarian, and permissive styles of child rearing. Parents who use a democratic approach give their children a chance to gain some experience in making decisions. At the same time they supply a degree of guidance and control. The final move toward autonomy appears to be less threatening under such a regime.

In using a democratic approach with adolescents, however, it appears to be desirable for parents not to exhibit affection too strongly. Douvan and Adelson concluded that sincere (but not smothering) interest and relationships that were neither cold nor intense seemed most likely to promote healthy independence. These conclusions are in harmony with the opinion expressed by Blos that adolescents who come from very close and affectionate homes may be "burdened by family ties" when the time comes to move from dependence to independence.

The Differential Influence of Peers and Parents

It seems clear that parents may influence their teen-age sons and daughters in a variety of ways. But the peer group also has a significant impact, particularly on some types of behavior. Peers may influence adolescent behavior because most teen-agers spend much more time in the company of peers than with their parents. In addition, many types of social behavior can be learned only by interacting with others the same age. Furthermore, the very fact that peers are experiencing similar physical and psychological changes tends to bring them together because they can identify with each others' problems and concerns. (As noted earlier, adolescents report that they are much more likely to learn about sex from peers than from parents.) Because adolescence is a period of rapid change in physical, cognitive, and social development, teen-agers must engage in a considerable amount of trial and error in order to adapt to alterations in their appearance and psychological functioning. Such experimentation takes place largely in the peer group. Finally, rapid social, political, and cultural change tends to lead to cohorts rather than generations of young Americans. For all of these reasons it seems logical to assume that peers will have an impact on the behavior of adolescents. It appears, though, that peers influence different types of behavior than parents.

Factors That Influence Value Development in Adolescence   A number of attempts have been made to compare the beliefs, attitudes, and values of parents and their children, and also compare the extent to which parent-peer and peer-peer opinions agree and conflict. Studies of values (reviewed by Feather, 1980), of political thinking (reviewed by Gallatin, 1980), of moral development (reviewed by Hoffman, 1980), and of occupational choice (reviewed by Rogers, 1972) lead to the conclusion that high school students are probably influenced in these areas of their lives more by parents than by peers. A visit to any high school, on the other hand, will reveal that in terms of dress, hair styles, interests, social

G. V. Brittain proposes that while parents influence the long-range plans of their adolescent sons and daughters, peers have a greater impact on immediate status and identity needs. © George Gardner.

relationships, and the like, the influence of peers is also extremely potent. The hypothesis that parents and peers influence different aspects of adolescent behavior has been developed by G. V. Brittain (1968) who suggests that parents have a greater impact on decisions that have implications for the future (choice of a career) while peers influence decisions that involve current status and identity needs (choice of friends). L. E. Larsen (1972) evaluated Brittain's hypothesis and concluded that the influence of parents was greatest when there was mutual affection and respect. It might be concluded, then, that values, moral and political beliefs, and the long-range plans of high school students are likely to be influenced by their parents. When they seek to establish an immediate sense of identity or status, however, adolescents are more likely to be influenced by peers.

Parents influence plans; peers influence immediate status

This distinction might be clarified by considering principles of social-learning theory that center on observation, imitation, and reinforcement. Sears and other social-learning theorists emphasize the importance of the peer group during adolescence because of the extent to which the behavior of high school students is shaped by the behavior and reactions of classmates. Adolescents may adopt styles of dress or mannerisms of speech and behavior they observe in age-mates they admire. If they receive a positive response from peers when they dress or act in similar ways, such behavior will be strengthened. Only rarely, however, can values or attitudes be acquired by imitating the overt behavior of others. Such beliefs are more likely to be acquired through long-term contact with particular individuals who have expressed opinions or displayed characteristics over a period of time. Most often this description fits the parents more than other adults, although certain high school teachers may have a lasting impact on their students.

Factors That Influence Value Development in Youth   The relative influence of parents and peers on the attitudes and behavior of youth is more difficult to assess than adolescent-parent similarities. But it seems reasonable to expect that many college students will be more inclined than they were in high school to form their own set of values. As they formulate a philosophy of life they may select beliefs that have been encouraged by parents. They will also be likely to take into account attitudes and values favored by peers and by adults other than their parents.

There are a number of reasons to expect youth to be more self-selective than adolescents in formulating a personal code for making decisions. First, and most obvious, youth are more socially, cognitively, and politically sophisticated than adolescents. They have also become legally and perhaps economically responsible for their own behavior, and may no longer feel a strong sense of allegiance to their parents. Furthermore, if they conclude that they are members of a subculture that is between adolescence and adulthood, they may feel an obligation to rethink earlier convictions about values. Finally, to a much greater extent than in high school, college students are likely to be exposed to teachers who espouse values that differ from those of most parents. Some of the courses that college students take (either as requirements or electives), in fact, may force assessment and questioning of traditional beliefs. For all of these reasons it seems logical to expect that parent-youth values will be more divergent than parent-adolescent values. At the same time, it seems reasonable to assume that even older youth will continue to be influenced by the extended contacts they have had with their parents.

Norman T. Feather (1980) supplies evidence in support of these two expectations in a review of research on values. He reports that researchers have found that as college students move from the freshman to the senior class they become increasingly open to new experiences and display greater tolerance. There is also a tendency for them to become more liberal, *provided* they were either a liberal or a moderate to begin with. Students who were conservative when they entered college, though, tend to become more conservative by the time they graduate, even though they have been exposed to liberal ideas. These findings reveal that the extent to which youth will or will not continue to share the values of their parents will depend on a complex group of interacting variables. It may be difficult to predict what will happen in the development of any particular individual because of the interaction of many factors: sex, social class, marital compatibility of the parents, type of discipline used by the parents, geographic area, political background of the home and the home town, the influence of particular peers or teachers, and dozens of other factors.

The nature of some of the push-pull forces that act on youth as they engage in the process of forming their own set of values is illustrated by this statement by a young college woman:

Up to a certain age, I believed everything my parents said. Then, in college, I saw all these new ideas and I said, "Okay, I'm not going to believe all that stuff

Researchers who have asked students to record their values during their college careers have discovered that liberal and moderate youth become more liberal but that conservative youth become more conservative—even though they have been exposed to liberal ideas. J. P. Laffont/Sygma.

you told me," and I rejected everything and said to myself, "Okay, now I'm going to make a new Debbie which has nothing to do with my mother and father. I'm going to start with a clean slate" and what I started to put on it were all new ideas. These ideas were opposite to what my parents believed. But slowly, what's happened is that I'm adding on a lot of the things which they've told me and I'm taking them as my own and I'm coming more together with them. (Josselson, 1973, p. 37)

This discussion of ways adolescents and youth reject, retain, or revise what they have learned from their parents leads to two final questions that will be considered in this chapter: To what extent does behavior in adolescence and youth reflect earlier behavior? To what extent does adolescent and youthful behavior anticipate adult behavior?

Continuity and Discontinuity in Development

In Chapter 10 several differences between preschool and elementary school behavior and expectations were described in making the point that a well-adjusted four-year-old with loving, supporting parents would not automatically become a happy, successful, popular student by the time she or he left elementary school. The six- to twelve-year-old is faced with adjustment situations that are substantially different from those that were met and perhaps easily surmounted during the preschool years. Many of the developmental tasks of adolescence and youth that have been discussed in this chapter are significantly different from those of the elementary school years. (And cognitive, moral, and emotional aspects of adolescent and youthful development have yet to be analyzed.) Accordingly, it might be reasoned that a happy, successful, popular sixth-grader will not automatically become a happy, successful, popular high school senior. And when the time comes for you to attend a high school reunion ten, twenty, or more years after you graduated, you will discover first-hand that happy, successful, popular high school seniors do not automatically become successful adults. This may be true in some cases, but it may also turn out that some adolescents who gave the appearance of being miserable, confused nonentities throughout the high school years surprisingly end up as adults who "have it made."

Several attempts have been made to analyze longitudinal data in an effort to trace continuities of personality from infancy through adulthood. While the results are often inconsistent and difficult to interpret, there is quite a bit of support for the descriptions just given. Some children who get an excellent start in life continue to cope well and become well-adjusted adults. Others, who appear to have had just as much promise as children, seem to make a mess of their lives. Conversely, some children who had many difficulties early in life and during adolescence do not seem to blossom until they reach their thirties or forties. Comments about a few of these longitudinal studies will illustrate some of the complexities and inconsistencies that have been reported.

Jerome Kagan and Howard Moss (1962) analyzed data accumulated by the researchers at the Fels Institute. As noted in Chapter 10 they concluded that the elementary school years are a *crystallization* period in development. They emphasized the significance of the elementary school years because they believed they had discovered a "sleeper effect." Certain types of behavior (for example, academic effort) that were apparent during the six- to twelve-year age span were more predictive of youthful and adult behavior than characteristics the same subjects displayed in high school. Norman Livson and Harvey Peskin (1980), however, question the existence of the sleeper effect, suggesting that the obviousness of certain childhood traits might have masked equally significant but more subtle adolescent traits. They support this argument by citing their own analyses of the longitudinal data of the Berkeley Guidance Study.

On the basis of an early examination of the data they thought they had discovered a variation of the Kagan and Moss sleeper effect. Predictions of adult psychological health based on descriptions of subjects when they were eleven to thirteen were more accurate than predictions based on descriptions when they were younger and older. After reevaluating the data, however, Livson and Peskin concluded that when characteristics at eleven to thirteen were *combined* with

*Preadolescent
behavior may
"reverse" in
adolescence*

characteristics at fourteen to sixteen, predictions became even more precise. Girls most likely to display psychological health as adults, for example, were characterized by independence, self-confidence, controlled temper, and disinclined to whine about disappointments as ten- to twelve-year-olds. *But,* at the ages of fourteen to sixteen they were characterized as dependent, low in self-confidence, possessed of explosive tempers, and given to frequent whining. Putting the two sets of characteristics together improved predictions of adult adjustment. Boys who were stolid and had hearty appetites between ten and twelve *and* who were irritable and had poor appetites between fourteen and sixteen often turned out to have excellent psychological health as adults. While such *stage reversals* quite frequently turned out to improve prediction in girls, this was not as true for boys. The best predictions of psychological health in males occurred when they were rated high in expressiveness, social comfort, and cheerfulness at *both* the ten-to-twelve- and fourteen-to-sixteen-year age spans.

The conclusions of Livson and Peskin, as well as the findings of the impact of early and late maturation summarized earlier in this chapter, point to some of the difficulties of predicting precisely what sort of adult a child or adolescent will become. One explanation for lack of stability or predictability centers on differences between the developmental tasks that must be mastered at different age levels. Different kinds of traits and skills are needed to handle the tasks of adolescence than were appropriate for mastering the tasks of childhood. Another possible explanation is based on a point noted in discussing parent-infant relationships in Chapter 7: a mother or father may possess an ideal set of characteristics for engaging in meaningful play with a baby but not be able to handle heart-to-heart talks with an adolescent.

Still another explanation is offered by Mary Cover Jones (1965), one of the leading researchers at Berkeley. After repeated analyses of the longitudinal data that had been accumulated at the University of California, she became impressed by the extent to which adolescents became *constructive actors* in creating new situations to explore their own capacities to survive and develop. It seems reasonable to expect that this tendency to control one's own destiny becomes even more significant during youth and in adulthood. A related explanation, which questions the expectation that obvious stability and consistency *should*

*Genotypic continuity:
changes in behavior
do not necessarily
indicate personality
lacks stability*

occur, has been offered by Livson and Peskin. They propose the concept of *genotypic continuity* which emphasizes the point that "personality is indeed a substantially predictable multidimensional construct throughout the life span if, *and only if,* we abandon the search for simple persistence or phenotypic continuity of specific characteristics over time" (1980, p. 89, italics in original).

These various observations might be summarized by saying that if one looks beyond the superficial aspects of behavior, which inevitably change with age, any individual is going to be the same person throughout life. And while it seems irrefutable that early experiences will have some influence on later experiences, each individual will also continually change and develop as new experiences are encountered.

Suggestions for Further Study

Impact of the Growth Spurt and Puberty

To appreciate the nature and magnitude of changes that take place at the time of puberty, arrange to visit a seventh-grade and a ninth-grade classroom. Observe the students not only in class but also in the halls and after school. Describe differences in physical appearance and in behavior between the seventh and ninth graders, paying particular attention to differences between boys and girls. You might also try to pick out the most and least mature children in a group and concentrate on their behavior in and out of the classroom. If you make an observation of this type, note your reactions and comment on the implications of differences you detect.

Biological and Physiological Aspects of Adolescence

For more complete information about biological changes at adolescence consult *Growth at Adolescence* (2nd ed., 1962) by J. M. Tanner, whose condensed versions of the material in this book can be found in Chapter 3 of *Carmichael's Manual of Child Psychology* (3rd ed., 1970), edited by Paul H. Mussen; and in Chapter 1 of *Twelve to Sixteen: Early Adolescence* (1972), edited by Jerome Kagan and Robert Coles. Another source you might consult is "The Biological Approach to Adolescence: Biological Change and Psychological Adaptation" by Anne C. Petersen and Brandon Taylor in *Handbook of Adolescent Psychology* (1980, pp. 117–155), edited by Joseph Adelson.

Blos on Adolescence

On Adolescence (1962) by Peter Blos is widely acknowledged as the outstanding psychoanalytic interpretation of this period of development. In Chapter 1, Blos gives a brief outline of the Freudian view of adolescence. In Chapter 2 he gives an outline of the psychosexual development leading up to and culminating in puberty, stressing the need to take into account earlier experiences in order to understand adolescence. (This serves as an excellent brief summary of the overall Freudian view of development.) (Psychoanalytic and other theories of adolescence are analyzed by Rolf E. Muus in *Theories of Adolescence* [3rd ed., 1975].)

Erikson on Adolescence

Although Erik Erikson received the same psychoanalytic training as Blos, his later experiences led him to propose a psychosocial (rather than psychosexual) view of development. The special significance of the stage of identity versus role confusion in Erikson's scheme is explained in *Identity: Youth and Crisis* (1968). In the preface, Erikson notes that identity is so unfathomable and all-pervasive that "I will not offer a definitive explanation of it in this book" (p. 9). (The explanation he offers on page 165 may not be definitive, but it is quite clear.) In Chapter 1, he describes how he first came to use the phrase *identity crisis* and gives a general description of what he means by it. In Chapter 2 he explains how his anthropological studies and treatment of war veterans led him to reinterpret Freud's original explanations of development. Chapter 3 is an overview of all his stages of psychosocial development and emphasizes how they lead up to the stage of identity versus role confusion. Chapter 4 presents brief descriptions of identity crises experienced by George Bernard Shaw, William James, and Freud, and the meaning of *psychosocial moratorium* is explained (pages 156–158). *Negative identity* is described on pages 173–176.

Feelings and Attitudes of Adolescents

In *The Adolescent Experience* (1966), Elizabeth Douvan and Joseph Adelson report on surveys they conducted for the Boy and Girl Scouts of America. They devised extensive questionnaires and used them in interviewing approximately 1,000 fourteen- to sixteen-year-old boys and 2,000 sixth- to twelfth-grade girls. Their results and interpretations reveal many interesting aspects of adolescent development. Almost any chapter of *The Adolescent Experience* makes interesting reading, particularly since the authors write exceptionally well.

Interviewing Adolescents

If you are interested in the revealing insights that the interview technique often yields, you may wish to try this method of obtaining information from adolescents. Douvan and Adelson carried out their interviews in 1955 and 1956. If you would like to use some of their questions to interview adolescents of the 1980s, examine pages 429–449 of *The Adolescent Experience* and pick out provocative questions. Then, ask some high school students to respond to them (you can compare the responses of your subjects with those of adolescents of the 1950s). (If you are unable to find the Douvan and Adelson book, examine the Interview Schedule in the Suggestions for Further Study in Chapter 2 of this book for a sample of questions you might ask.) You may prefer, however, to make up your own questions. In any case, if you carry out some interviews, you might describe how you proceeded, record the responses, summarize trends that emerge, and comment on the implications.

Adolescent Sexuality

The impact of sexual maturity is briefly explained in "The Development of Sexuality in Adolescence" by Patricia Y. Miller and William Simon in *Handbook of Adolescent Psychology* (1980, pp. 383–407), edited by Joseph Adelson. More extensive analyses are presented in *Sexuality in Contemporary America* (1973) by R. C. Sorensen; *Sexual Behavior in the 1970s* (1973) by Morton Hunt; and *The Sexual Experience* (1976), edited by B. J. Saddock, H. I. Kaplan, and A. M. Freedman.

Unwanted Pregnancy

Perhaps the major change in the sexual habits of Americans that has taken place in the last twenty years is the increase in the number of women who engage in premarital intercourse. Despite the availability of birth-control devices, many women, married as well as unmarried, become pregnant by mistake. Katrina Maxtone-Graham interviewed several women who found themselves in this predicament and recorded their reactions in *Pregnant by Mistake: The Stories of Seventeen Women* (1973). In their accounts, the women interviewed express their thoughts and feelings about such options as abortion, adoption, and single parenthood.

The Significance of Sex Roles and Sex Typing

For a concise, thought-provoking discussion of the nature and significance of sex roles examine "Conceptions of Sex Role: Some Cross-Cultural and Longitudinal Perspectives" by Jeanne H. Block, *American Psychologist*, 1973, **28**, 512–526. Sex roles and sex typing are also discussed in *Psychology of Women: A Study of Biocultural Conflicts* (1971) by Judith M. Bardwick; "Sex Roles: Persistence and Change" by D. N. Ruble and I. H. Frieze (Eds.), *Journal of Social Issues*, 1976, **32**(3); and *Masculinity and Femininity: Their Psychological Dimensions, Correlates, and Antecedents* (1978) by J. T. Spence and R. L. Helmreich.

The Influence of Parents and Peers on Adolescents

Ways parents and peers influence adolescents are examined in several chapters of the *Handbook of Adolescent Psychology* (1980), edited by Joseph Adelson. Peruse Chapter 8 (Values), Chapter 9 (Moral Development), Chapter 10 (Political Thinking), and Chapter 12 (Friendships and the Peer Group).

Continuity and Discontinuity in Development

If you are intrigued by the question, How stable are manifestations of personality throughout childhood, adolescence, and adulthood? you will want to read "Perspectives on Adolescence from Longitudinal Research" by Norman Livson and Harvey Peskin in the *Handbook of Adolescent Psychology* (1980, pp. 47–98), edited by Joseph Adelson. The most complete and searching account of continuities in development is provided by Jack Block in *Lives Through Time* (1971).

KEY POINTS

The Nature and Impact of Formal Thinking

Formal thought: possibilities, hypotheses, future, thoughts, speculations

Unrestrained theorizing when formal thought achieved

Adolescent egocentrism: extreme concern about the reactions of others

Transition to formal thinking not abrupt or universal

The Development of Political Thinking

Political thinking of older adolescents more abstract, less authoritarian

Influence of parents on political thinking likely to be indirect

Moral and Interpersonal Development

Morality of cooperation: mutual agreements, allowance for intentions

Understanding of interpersonal subtleties, societal perspective in adolescence

Asceticism in youth may be due to existential guilt

Kohlberg: regressions in moral thinking due to awareness of inconsistencies

Turiel: regressions in moral thinking due to differences in values

Emotions may influence moral decisions more than rational analysis

The Nature and Significance of Identity Statuses

Individuals may not fit in only one identity status category

Identity-status concept not as appropriate for females as for males

Identity Diffusion types avoid thinking about goals, roles, and values

Moratorium types suffering identity crises of various kinds

Foreclosure types unquestioningly endorse goals and values of parents

Identity Achievement types have made satisfying self-chosen commitments

Problems Relating to Failure to Achieve Identity

Academic underachievement may be due to fear of success

Achievement-oriented women of 1980s likely to be self-satisfied

Males may have more problems overcoming sex-typing than females

Boys more likely than girls to gain status by committing delinquent acts

Relationships with parents single most predictive indicator of delinquency

Religious conversions may be due to sublimation, guilt, moratorium

Behavior Disorders in Adolescence and Youth

Preschizophrenic boys negativistic, aggressive; girls shy, inhibited

Depression may be caused by a negative set, learned helplessness, sense of loss

Suicide triggered by inability to solve problems, deterioration of relationships

CHAPTER □ 13

ADOLESCENCE AND YOUTH:

COGNITIVE, MORAL, AND EMOTIONAL DEVELOPMENT

Certain aspects of the types of behavior to be discussed in this chapter were mentioned in the preceding chapter. The cognitive ability of the formal thinker to consider possibilities was noted in discussing Erikson's conceptions of factors that influence identity formation. The opinion of some theorists that sexuality and morality are intertwined was recorded in the section on premarital sexual relations. And emotional adjustment factors were mentioned in discussing early and late maturation, sex roles, and relationships with parents. Even though facets of such topics have already been mentioned, cognitive, moral, and emotional development during adolescence and youth merit the extended coverage supplied in this final chapter.

The Nature and Impact of Formal Thinking

Almost all discussions of cognitive development during adolescence are based on, derived from, or related to Piaget's description of formal thought. As noted in the discussion of cognitive development during the elementary school years (Chapter 11), the transition from concrete operational thinking to formal thought typically begins before children leave elementary school. During the high school years this transition is completed (for many adolescents) and represents a basic reorganization of cognitive abilities.

Characteristics of Formal Thought

Daniel P. Keating (1980, pp. 212–215) summarizes the characteristics of formal thinking by noting that it is based on these abilities:

Formal thought: possibilities, hypotheses, future, thoughts, speculations

- ☐ Thinking about possibilities
- ☐ Thinking about hypotheses
- ☐ Thinking ahead
- ☐ Thinking about thoughts
- ☐ Thinking beyond limits

Piaget (and his chief collaborator Barbel Inhelder) place particular stress on the ability to *think about possibilities.* They state, "There is no doubt that the most distinctive feature of formal thought stems from the role played by statements about possibility relative to statements about empirical reality" (Inhelder and Piaget, 1958, p. 245). The concrete operational thinker concentrates on what can be or has been observed. The formal thinker is able to manipulate abstract ideas and imagine all kinds of possible situations, including those that have never been encountered. These cognitive skills not only influence an adolescent's ability to solve problems and consider contrary-to-fact propositions, they may also influence the process of identity formation. As noted in the preceding chapter, Erikson points out that when older adolescents can anticipate the results of a decision to prepare for a particular job and what it might be like to be employed, they may feel so threatened and confused that they postpone the final choice. Or young people who try to weigh all the possibilities available may find it difficult to choose among them. For youth who attend college, this preoccupation with such possibilities may be extended for four or more years.

Thinking through hypotheses is illustrated most clearly by experiments in which subjects are asked to solve problems such as figuring out relationships between weights and pendulums. (Instructions for carrying out such an experiment were presented in the Suggestions for Further Study section at the end of Chapter 11.) As noted in the discussion of the thinking of elementary school children, concrete operational thinkers typically try to solve problems by trial and error and without following any discernible plan. Adolescents who have mastered formal thought, by contrast, are likely first to plot a course of action and then test hypotheses in a systematic manner by observing and perhaps recording the results of different actions. (Because of the abilities to think about possibilities and think ahead, they may also be able to solve the problem in their heads.)

Thinking about thoughts and *thinking beyond limits* are illustrated by a fascination with abstractions that often characterizes adolescent thinking. Two leading interpreters of Piagetian theory describe this preoccupation with the abstract in the following way:

In the intellectual sphere, the adolescent has a tendency to become involved in abstract and theoretical matters, constructing elaborate political theories or inventing complex philosophical doctrines. The adolescent may develop plans for the complete reorganization of society or indulge in metaphysical speculation. Having just discovered capabilities for abstract thought, he then proceeds to exercise them without restraint. Indeed, in the process of exploring these new abilities the adolescent sometimes loses touch with reality, and feels that he can accomplish everything by thought alone. In the emotional sphere the adolescent now becomes capable of directing his emotions at abstract ideals and not just toward people. Whereas earlier he could love his mother or hate a peer, now he can love freedom or hate exploitation. The adolescent has developed a new mode of life: the possible and the ideal captivate both mind and feeling. (Ginsburg and Opper, 1979, p. 201)

Unrestrained theorizing when formal thought achieved

Adolescent Egocentrism

David Elkind suggests that unrestrained theorizing about ideals without complete understanding of realities tends to make the young adolescent a militant rebel with little patience with parents or other adults who fail to find quick solutions to personal, social, and other problems. Only when the older adolescent begins to grasp the complexities of interpersonal relationships and of economic and social problems will more tempered understanding appear. Elkind also suggests that the egocentrism of early childhood that gave way to socialized speech and thought at the end of the elementary grade years reappears in a different form as *adolescent egocentrism*. This occurs when high school students turn their new powers of thought upon themselves and become introspective. The strong tendency to analyze the self is projected upon others, which helps explain why adolescents are so self-conscious—they assume their thoughts and actions are as interesting to others as to themselves. The major difference between the egocentrism of childhood and of adolescence is summed up in Elkind's observation: "The child is egocentric in the sense that he is unable to take another person's point of view. The adolescent, on the other hand, takes the other person's point of view to an extreme degree" (1968, p. 153).

Elkind believes that adolescent egocentrism also explains why the peer group becomes such a potent force in high school. He observes:

Adolescent egocentrism . . . accounts, in part, for the power of the peer group during this period. The adolescent is so concerned with the reactions of others toward him, particularly his peers, that he is willing to do many things which are opposed to all of his previous training and to his own best interests. At the same

Adolescent egocentrism: extreme concern about reactions of others

When adolescents become capable of formal thinking they tend to turn their new powers of thought on themselves, leading to what David Elkind refers to as *adolescent egocentrism:* extreme concern about the reactions of others. Toward the end of adolescence, the young person comes to realize that other people are much more concerned with themselves. © 1979 Jim Richardson/Black Star.

time, this egocentric impression that he is always on stage may help to account for the many and varied adolescent attention-getting maneuvers. . . .

Toward the end of adolescence, this form of exploitative egocentrism gradually declines. The young person comes to realize that other people are much more concerned with themselves and their problems than they are with him and his problems. (1968, p. 154)

Evaluations of Piaget's Description of Formal Thought

Researchers (for example, Neimark, 1975) who have reviewed investigations of Piaget's hypotheses on the basic characteristics of formal thought have found support for many of his speculations. But there are certain aspects of Piaget's theory that have been questioned. Piaget has proposed a detailed set of *binary operations,* for example, which he uses to explain variations of adolescent thinking. The interaction of these operations is extremely complex. The operations are therefore difficult to evaluate empirically (the major reason that they will not be discussed here). The basic questions raised by critics of Piaget, though, have centered on whether there is a qualitative change in thinking at adolescence, whether this change is gradual or abrupt, and whether the change is universal. In his analysis of Piaget's theory, Keating (1980) concludes that each of these assumptions can be questioned. He interprets the available evidence as indicating that there are *not* distinct stages that distinguish the thinking of older elementary school children from the thinking of adolescents. He also argues that the change is gradual rather than abrupt and that cognitive development is not universal because it is influenced by such factors as schooling and cultural background. It should be noted, however, that Neimark reports greater support for Piaget's hypothesis regarding stages than Keating reports.

Even if strong and consistent support for certain aspects of Piaget's description of formal thinking is lacking, his basic description of cognitive development during preadolescence and adolescence can be used to clarify certain types of behavior. Parents and teachers, for instance, might sympathize with rather than criticize the disorganized efforts of embryonic formal thinkers to solve problems. And they also might try to be more understanding and tolerant of the tendency for adolescents who have just "discovered" formal thinking to engage in unrestrained theorizing. Still another way to benefit from Piaget's observations is to use them to comprehend certain forms of political and moral thinking that become apparent during adolescence.

The Development of Political Thinking

Adelson's Study of Political Thinking

After completing *The Adolescent Experience* with Elizabeth Douvan, Joseph Adelson (1971) used the interview approach to obtain information about the development of political thought during the adolescent years. With the assistance of several colleagues and graduate students, he conducted interviews with 450 eleven- to eighteen-year-olds from all social and intellectual levels in the United States, Great Britain, and West Germany. Fifty members of this original sample were chosen for more intensive, longitudinal analyses. At the start of the interviews, the subjects were requested to imagine that a thousand people ventured to an island in the Pacific for the purpose of establishing a new society. The respondents were then asked to explain how these people might establish a political order, devise a legal system, and deal with other problems of public policy.

The analysis of the interview responses showed no significant sex differences in understanding political concepts and no significant differences attributable to intelligence and social class, although brighter students were better able to deal with abstract ideas and upper-class students were less likely to be authoritarian. The most striking and consistent finding was the degree to which the political thinking of the adolescent changes in the years between twelve and sixteen. Adelson concluded that the most significant changes were: (1) an increase in the ability to deal with abstractions; (2) a decline in authoritarian views; (3) an increase in political knowledge.

The increase in the ability to deal with abstractions is a function of the shift from concrete to formal operational thought. When thirteen-year-olds were asked "What is the purpose of laws?" a typical answer was "So people don't steal or kill" (1972, p. 108). A fifteen-to-sixteen-year-old, by contrast, was more likely to say "To ensure safety and enforce the government" (p. 108). The young adolescent who thinks in concrete terms concentrates on individuals and finds it difficult to take into account society as a whole. When asked about the purpose of laws to require vaccination of children, for example, the twelve-year-old is likely to say it is to prevent sickness in the child who receives the treatment. The fifteen-year-old, who has mastered formal thought, is likely to consider how it will protect the community at large.

Thinking in concrete terms also causes the twelve-year-old to concentrate on the immediate present because of the inability to analyze the significance of past events or to project ideas into the future. And as Piaget noted in his analysis of moral development, the younger child (who is a moral realist) is not likely to take motives into account. When asked to explain why many prisoners are repeat offenders, for example, only older adolescents would mention such motives as having a grudge against society. Adelson and his colleagues found that when twelve-year-olds were asked how prisoners should be treated, many of them recommended that they be punished and taught a stern lesson. Adelson speculates that the tendency for younger adolescents to be punitive and authoritarian might be attributed to several factors: preoccupation with wickedness, the inability of the young adolescent to grasp the concept of rights, and the conviction that laws are immutable. By fourteen or fifteen, the adolescents interviewed by Adelson were more likely to weigh circumstances and the rights of the individual and to recommend rehabilitation rather than punishment.

While Adelson's findings were consistent with Piaget's observations on shifts from morality of constraint to morality of cooperation, Adelson questioned Ginsburg and Opper's conclusion that the young person who has just "discovered" formal thought has a tendency to engage in uncontrolled theorizing. Adelson was led to question this hypothesis by the discovery that respondents rarely discussed utopian schemes. Instead, they demonstrated their grasp of political knowledge. The structured nature of the interviews might have influenced these results and Adelson's conclusions, since a high school student might feel threatened when questioned by a formidably intelligent adult from a prestigious university. Instead of expressing utopian political theories and risking the possibility of appearing naive, the student might simply recite facts.

If Adelson had been able to tape-record spontaneous political discussions between fifteen- and sixteen-year-olds (which would have been closer to Piaget's approach), perhaps he would have found greater support for the hypothesis that adolescents who have just become capable of formal thought have a tendency toward unrestricted theorizing. (Even mature and confident adults who have devoted years of thought to developing utopian schemes hesitate to publish them for fear of being ridiculed by critics. Exchanging ideas in an informal bull session is an entirely different matter.)

Even though they did not discuss utopian schemes in the interviews, older adolescents revealed that they felt a keen sense of involvement in political matters. Subjects who were especially intense about politics were found to come, not surprisingly, from homes where parents were politically active. Other evidence of the influence of parental (and cultural) factors on political thinking was revealed by nationality differences. Adelson concluded that German adolescents disliked confusion and admired a strong leader; British subjects stressed the rights of the individual citizen and the need to equalize wealth; American respondents were concerned about finding ways to balance individual rights and community needs.

The Adelson study has been described in some detail because it focuses on the development of political thinking in ways that can be related to Piaget's description of formal thought. Hundreds of other studies of the political thinking of adolescents and youth have been published. A few brief comments on some of the conclusions noted in these studies will be noted.

Conclusions of Other Studies of Political Thinking

Although it sometimes has been found that many adolescents may not know basic political facts of life such as whether Republicans are more conservative than Democrats, after analyzing many studies Judith Gallatin (1980) concluded that most eighteen-year-olds are quite capable of functioning as well-informed voters.

It appears, though, that they might benefit from instruction in ways to exert political influence. An Education Commission of the States report on political knowledge (1973) revealed that less than half of a representative sample of seventeen-year-olds could identify as many as three ways that citizens can influence their government. Only 25 percent of them could mention four political participation techniques, only 11 percent could list five techniques for exerting political influence, and less than half could interpret and mark a simple ballot correctly. In the absence of comparable data for adults, it is not possible to determine if these weaknesses are due to immaturity or whether they are typical of Americans of all ages.

As mentioned in the preceding chapter in discussing the influence of the family on adolescent development, there is evidence (Gallatin, 1980) that parents often have a significant influence on the political thinking of their sons and daughters. R. W. Connell (1972) speculates that parents do not directly mold the political views of their children but that they place them is a sociopolitical context that leads them to acquire attitudes in subtle and indirect ways. The influence of the parents is most likely to be felt, according to Gallatin, when both parents agree on basic political issues and when there are opportunities for free communication and discussion in the home. Adolescents from such homes tend to earn above-

Influence of parents on political thinking likely to be indirect

average scores on tests of political knowledge and they are more inclined to assume civic responsibilities than are adolescents from permissive or authoritarian homes (to use the terms favored by Baumrind in her studies of child-rearing practices).

There is little evidence that high school teachers have much of an impact on the political views of adolescents (Beck, 1977), but it appears that the mass media do have a significant effect. During the elementary school years television appears to be the most influential medium of communication. Newspapers tend to become a more important source of information about political developments during the high school years (Chaffee et al., 1977).

Political thinking is influenced not only by cognitive development and by child-rearing practices and relationships with parents, but by the values and attitudes that characterize each individual adolescent and youth.

Values in Adolescence and Youth: Cultural Differences

One of the most widely used approaches to studying values is the value survey developed by Milton Rokeach (1973). Respondents are asked to rank the values listed in Table 13–1 in the order of importance to themselves. (Before you read any further you might find it of interest to list the four values in each list you consider to be most and least important. List the numbers 1, 2, 3, 4, and 15, 16, 17, and 18 on a sheet of paper and write value descriptions from Table 13–1 in the appropriate slots.)

The four terminal and instrumental values rated most and least important by male students attending colleges in the United States, Canada, Australia, Israel, and Papua, New Guinea during the late 1960s and early 1970s are shown in Table 13–2.

In commenting on these lists Norman Feather (1980) calls attention to the similarities in terminal values stressed by American, Canadian, and Australian students, all of whom were reared in technological societies. But there are also differences (some of which were revealed more clearly by the middle-range values not listed in Table 13–2 and also by earlier surveys). American youth appear to be more materialistic and achievement-oriented than Australian youth who place more emphasis on peace of mind, an active life, and a cheerful approach to life. The stress and tensions under which Israeli youth live are reflected by their emphasis on peace and national security. Youth in Papua joined with those in Israel in placing world peace at the top of the list, probably because New Guinea was just becoming established as a nation when the survey was made and its citizens were probably apprehensive about their newly won indepen-

Table 13–1
Values Included in the Rokeach Value Survey

TERMINAL VALUES	INSTRUMENTAL VALUES
A comfortable life (a prosperous life)	Ambitious (hard working, aspiring)
An exciting life (a stimulating, active life)	Broad-minded (open-minded)
A sense of accomplishment (lasting contribution)	Capable (competent, effective)
A world at peace (free of war and conflict)	Cheerful (lighthearted, joyful)
A world of beauty (beauty of nature and the arts)	Clean (neat, tidy)
Equality (brotherhood, equal opportunity for all)	Courageous (standing up for your beliefs)
Family security (taking care of loved ones)	Forgiving (willing to pardon others)
Freedom (independence, free choice)	Helpful (working for the welfare of others)
Happiness (contentedness)	Honest (sincere, truthful)
Inner harmony (freedom from inner conflict)	Imaginative (daring, creative)
Mature love (sexual and spiritual intimacy)	Independent (self-reliant, self-sufficient)
National security (protection from attack)	Intellectual (intelligent, reflective)
Pleasure (an enjoyable, leisurely life)	Logical (consistent, rational)
Salvation (saved, eternal life)	Loving (affectionate, tender)
Self-respect (self-esteem)	Obedient (dutiful, respectful)
Social recognition (respect, admiration)	Polite (courteous, well mannered)
True friendship (close companionship)	Responsible (dependable, reliable)
Wisdom (a mature understanding of life)	Self-controlled (restrained, self-disciplined)

Source: M. Rokeach, *The Nature of Human Values* (New York: Free Press, 1973), pp. 358–361. Reproduced with permission of Halgren Tests, 873 Persimmon Ave., Sunnyvale, CA 94087.

dence. Perhaps the most interesting point about the ratings of instrumental values is that *honesty* topped the list of all five groups and *responsibility* was among the top three.

It seems likely that college students of the 1980s in each country (with the possible exception of Israel) might list somewhat different terminal values among the top four because of the impact of changing national and world conditions. If the values you listed, for instance, differ from those stressed by American college students in the early 1970s, it may mean that you belong to a different cohort, even though you are just a few years younger.

Political thinking and values are both influenced by the capability of adolescents and youth to engage in formal thinking. Formal thinking also influences and is related to moral thinking. Morality, in turn, exerts an impact on values as well as interpersonal relationships. Various aspects of moral and interpersonal development during adolescence and youth are explored in the following section.

Table 13–2
**Four Most Important and Four Least Important Values
in Five Groups of Male Students**

RANK OF VALUE	UNITED STATES	CANADA	AUSTRALIA	ISRAEL	PAPUA NEW GUINEA
			TERMINAL VALUES		
1	Freedom	Freedom	Wisdom	A world at peace	A world at peace
2	Happiness	Happiness	True friendship	National security	Equality
3	Wisdom	Mature love	Freedom	Happiness	Freedom
4	Self-respect	Self-respect	A sense of accomplishment	Freedom	True friendship
15	Pleasure	A world of beauty	A world of beauty	A comfortable life	A sense of accomplishment
16	Salvation	Social recognition	Social recognition	Social recognition	Pleasure
17	National security	National security	National security	A world of beauty	Mature love
18	A world of beauty	Salvation	Salvation	Salvation	A world of beauty
			INSTRUMENTAL VALUES		
1	Honest	Honest	Honest	Honest	Honest
2	Responsible	Responsible	Broad-minded	Responsible	Helpful
3	Ambitious	Loving	Responsible	Logical	Responsible
4	Broad-minded	Broad-minded	Loving	Capable	Ambitious
15	Cheerful	Imaginative	Imaginative	Clean	Independent
16	Polite	Polite	Polite	Imaginative	Clean
17	Clean	Clean	Clean	Obedient	Logical
18	Obedient	Obedient	Obedient	Forgiving	Imaginative

Source: N. T. Feather, "Values in adolescence," in J. Adelson (Ed.), *Handbook of adolescent psychology* (New York: Wiley, 1980), p. 266.

Moral and Interpersonal Development

Piaget's View of Moral Development: A Review

In Chapter 11, some of Piaget's observations on moral development were noted. After observing how children devised rules to govern play and listening to them respond to stories involving moral dilemmas, Piaget concluded that younger children are governed by a morality of constraint. At around the age of ten or so, however, when some children begin to function as formal thinkers, a shift to the morality of cooperation begins to occur. Starting around the fifth or sixth grade, children enjoy making up their own rules to supplant those that were formerly imposed on them by adults or older playmates. They think of rules as mutual agreements established to protect the rights of all participants. Children of that age also may evaluate moral situations by taking into account circumstances and intentions. A well-meaning child who makes a big blot of ink on a tablecloth will be considered less guilty than a misbehaving child who makes a small blot.

Morality of cooperation: mutual agreements, allowance for intentions

All of these changes in moral reasoning can be explained by taking into account features of formal thought. The older child is no longer egocentric and can consider another person's point of view, which makes it possible to come to mutual agreement about rules. The older child can think of more than one thing at a time (for example, the physical results of an action and the motives behind that action) and take into account extenuating circumstances.

In an analysis of the transition from the morality of constraint to the morality of cooperation Martin L. Hoffman (1980, p. 296) observes that "Moral growth requires that the child give up egocentrism and realism and develop a concept of self as distinct from others who have their own independent perspectives about events" (1980, p. 296). He suggests that this shift occurs because of two basic developments in cognitive ability and in social interactions that begin in late childhood and continue through adolescence. First, as adolescents mature, they realize that they are gradually attaining equality with adults. As a consequence, they are less inclined to think of regulations as sacred pronouncements handed down by infallible grownups and more inclined to feel that they are just as qualified as anyone else to make up or change rules. A second factor that contributes to the emergence of the morality of cooperation is that interactions with peers make it necessary to assume alternate and reciprocal roles. Assuming a variety of roles in different situations and with different acquaintances leads to the realization that while one person often reacts to situations as others do, sometimes individuals react differently. Awareness of this fact leads the adolescent to become increasingly aware of the inner states that underlie the behavior of others.

Interactions with peers also cause adolescents to think a great deal about relationships with others, particularly when the behavior of friends contradicts expectations. If a friend does not respond in the expected manner, a high school student may brood about it for days.

Changes in Interpersonal Reasoning at Adolescence

Hoffman's observation on the tendency for adolescents to become concerned about the thoughts and feelings of others are similar to Robert Selman's description of the final stages of interpersonal reasoning. To review points noted in Chapter 11, Selman (1976a,b) suggests that ten- to twelve-year-olds are at the *multiple role-taking stage*. They become capable of taking a *third-person* view in that

When adolescents become capable of *social and conventional system role taking* (as defined by Robert Selman) they may take a *societal perspective* because they are able to comprehend the plight of individuals outside of their own limited circle of acquaintances. © Ellen Shub 1980.

Understanding of interpersonal subtleties, societal perspective in adolescence

they are able to evaluate their own behavior and that of others as if they were spectators. Between the ages of twelve to fifteen and beyond, adolescents move into the stage of *social and conventional system role taking.* They increasingly come to understand subtleties of interpersonal relationships and toward the end of the high school years they may begin to take a *societal perspective.* They realize that their actions might influence *all* individuals, not just those who are immediately concerned or affected.

Some of the most interesting examples of this societal perspective take the form of what Hoffman (1980, p. 314) refers to as *existential guilt.* Such guilt occurs when a person who has done nothing wrong still feels culpable because of circumstances that cannot be controlled. Kenneth Keniston (1968) reported that some upper-class activists of the 1960s, for example, occasionally explained that they participated in demonstrations favoring programs for the oppressed or disadvantaged because they felt guilty about their favored backgrounds. In other cases, Hoffman suggests, the existential guilt of 1960s-vintage youth from affluent homes may have caused them to renounce material possessions and join the hippie movement. Hoffman thus proposes an explanation for youthful asceticism

Asceticism in youth may be due to existential guilt

that differs from the interpretation offered by Blos. Blos classifies asceticism as a sublimation, theorizing that it is an attempt to gain release of, or at least limit concern about, sexual energy. Hoffman suggests that such behavior might be explained by thinking of it as a means for reducing feelings of existential guilt.

In making some final comments on existential guilt Hoffman speculates that it may be less common in the 1980s than it was in the 1960s. On the basis of informal interviews with upper- and middle-class contemporary youth he concluded that they place a high value on success and even though they may come from affluent backgrounds, they do not feel they are in a privileged position as they strive to become successful. Two reasons were frequently mentioned by the youth Hoffman interviewed to support their conviction that they are not favored individuals: (1) they expect to have to work hard to find a decent job; (2) because of equal opportunity regulations and Affirmative Action programs they feel that many "disadvantaged" individuals now enjoy a privileged position in the job market.

Information that might be used to evaluate Hoffman's speculations has been provided by J. G. Bachman and L. D. Johnston (1979). They asked 17,000 students who entered college in 1979 to describe "important things in my life." Here are some of the results of the survey, expressed in terms of the percentage of respondents who rated each of the following goals as important:

Strong friendships	69
Finding purpose and meaning in my life	66
Finding steady work	65
Being successful in my work	63
Making a contribution to society	23

The results of this survey seem to support Hoffman's impression that many contemporary youth are more interested in finding a good job and a satisfying life for themselves than in "contributing to society."

Piaget's description of the transition from the morality of constraint to the morality of cooperation has stimulated much research and many speculations about adolescent morality and interpersonal relationships. The theory proposed by Lawrence Kohlberg has been even more provocative.

Kohlberg's Theory of Moral Development

A Brief Review of Kohlberg's Theory   On the basis of responses of ten- to sixteen-year-olds to moral dilemmas such as the story of Heinz (Chapter 11), Kohlberg proposed six stages of moral development:

- ☐ Stage 1 Punishment-obedience orientation. The physical consequences of an action determine goodness or badness.
- ☐ Stage 2 Instrumental-relativist orientation. Obeying rules should bring some sort of benefit in return.
- ☐ Stage 3 Good boy-nice girl orientation. The right action is one likely to impress others.

- ☐ Stage 4 Law and order orientation. To maintain the social order, rules must be established and obeyed.
- ☐ Stage 5 Social contract orientation. Rules should be based on mutual agreement, but the rights of the individual must be taken into account.
- ☐ Stage 6 Universal ethical principal orientation. Moral decisions should be based on consistently applied principles.

Kohlberg believes these stages are universal, fixed, and sequential; that individuals move through the stages in order; and that very few people reach Stage 6. He also believes that moral development can be enhanced by exposing children and adolescents to arguments and discussions of moral concepts that are one stage above their present level.

In a review of research on moral development Martin L. Hoffman comments, "The research, by and large, provides little support for the main tenets of [Kohlberg's] theory" (1980, p. 299). He later adds, though, "whether the theory is confirmed or not, Kohlberg must be given credit for sensitizing researchers to the highly complex nature of moral development and the cognitive dimensions that may be necessary for a mature moral orientation" (p. 301). And he goes on to say, "Although Kohlberg's stages may not form a universal invariant sequence, as he claims, they may nevertheless provide a valid description of the changes in moral thought that occur in our society."

Speculations About "Regression" in Moral Development   An example of how Kohlberg's theory provides insight into both the nature and complexity of moral development is provided by research and interpretations of "regressions" in moral thinking. The subjects of Kohlberg's original research, who supplied the answers to moral dilemmas that were used in establishing the stages, were retested at four-year intervals. Kohlberg and Kramer (1969) reported that most of the respondents followed the predicted pattern and moved through the stages in sequence. About 20 percent of them who had obtained Stage 4 scores at sixteen, however, dropped to Stage 2 at twenty. Most of those subjects moved to higher-than-original levels of Stage 4 by twenty-four, though, and some advanced to Stage 5.

Kohlberg and Kramer concluded that the drop from Stage 4 to Stage 2 reflected a consistent regression in moral thinking. They hypothesized that it was attributable to the impact of the liberal arts curriculum in the colleges the subjects had attended. The youth who slipped from Stage 4 to Stage 2 typically came from middle-class homes. During their college years they came to question and examine their beliefs (as described in the discussion of influences on values offered in the preceding chapter). Kohlberg and Kramer theorize that the college students who regressed were faced with two developmental challenges. First, they learned that the conception of morality they had accepted and formulated as adolescents was just one of many possible conceptions. Second, they discovered

Kohlberg: regressions in moral thinking due to awareness of inconsistencies

Elliot Turiel suggests that some inconsistencies in moral thinking may be due to differences between *universal* values (such as honesty) and *personal* values (such as attitudes toward homosexuality). © Peter Menzel/Stock, Boston.

that there are frequent inconsistencies between moral expectations and the actual behavior of adults. The difficulty of coping with these two challenges caused the young men to regress to a simpler level of moral reasoning. By the time they had completed college, though, they had resolved these conflicts to their satisfaction and emerged with more sophisticated conceptions of morality than they had begun with.

Elliot Turiel (1974) offers a different explanation for apparent regressions in moral thinking. He acknowledges that adolescents and youth may sometimes give answers to moral dilemmas that are below their typical stage of development, but he is not convinced that this means they have moved back to a lower stage. Instead, he suggests, they may simply be rejecting certain types of moral thinking as they become aware of contradictions and of differences between types of moral decisions. Turiel argues that adolescents may develop two distinct value systems. One encompasses principles that are universal and that can be objectively validated (for example, honesty). The other is made up of values (for example, sexual mores) that need to be formulated (up to a point) by each individual living in a particular cultural environment at a particular time. Some of the "regressions" reported by Kohlberg and Kramer, therefore, might not have indicated a consistent shift to simpler moral thinking but merely a tendency for the young men attending college to be in the process of distinguishing between universal-objective and personal-subjective values.

Turiel: inconsistencies in moral thinking due to differences in values

After analyzing data supplied by Turiel, Hoffman concluded (1980, p. 303) that there appears to be more evidence to support the universal-personal conflict hypothesis of Turiel than the regression hypothesis of Kohlberg and Kramer. It might be argued, in addition, that the results of studies that report responses to the Rokeach Value Survey favor the Turiel hypothesis. If you will turn back to Table 13–2 and examine the terminal and instrumental values chosen by college males from different cultures, you will note that honesty (a universal-objective value) is chosen first by all five groups. The terminal values, on the other hand, which are more a function of personal choice and of particular sets of cultural conditions impinging on a particular cohort, vary to a considerable extent. (Even though Kohlberg and Kramer's regression hypothesis may not be completely valid, their analysis of the impact of college on moral thinking seems worthy of consideration.)

Research on varied aspects of Kohlberg's theory continues and eventually more complete understanding of apparent regressions and inconsistencies will undoubtedly be achieved. At the moment, however, Kohlberg's own main interest is moral education.

Kohlberg's Technique of Moral Instruction

Kohlberg's interest in attempting to teach adolescents to acquire higher levels of moral reasoning was stimulated by the work of two graduate students who carried out research projects under his supervision. Elliot Turiel (1966) found that twelve- and thirteen-year-old boys exposed to arguments about moral dilemmas that were pitched one stage above their level of moral thinking seemed to move toward more advanced stages. Moshe Blatt (1975) used discussion techniques with children in religious school and in public schools and reported somewhat greater improvements in moral reasoning than Turiel. Starting in the early 1970s Kohlberg himself began to supervise discussions with young men and women in correctional institutions. After a few years Kohlberg concluded that attempts to improve the moral reasoning of prisoners seemed to depend more on the atmosphere of the prison than on group discussions of moral issues (Muson, 1979, p. 57). Accordingly, Kohlberg and his associates have established what they refer to as *Just Communities* in several high schools, perhaps on the assumption that prevention is better than cure.

The first Just Community, and the one that Kohlberg has worked with most closely, was established within what is called the Cambridge (Mass.) Cluster School. The Cluster School was formed in the 1960s when high school and college students demanded more control over their educational experiences. For half of every day students at Cambridge High who attend the Cluster School meet with their teachers to settle their own problems and make their own rules on a one-person, one-vote basis. In addition, students and teachers discuss how to handle immoral and illegal actions (for example, the theft of stereo equipment from a camp where the members of the Cluster School had gone on an outing).

A Just Community meeting. Participatory democracy in action. © 1979 Lee Lockwood.

Although Kohlberg has not yet completed a comprehensive analysis of the impact of Just Community experiences, he estimates that most of the students are at Stage 2 when they begin to meet with the group and that they progress to Stage 4 by the time they leave (reported in Muson, 1979, p. 68).

While these preliminary reports are promising, two potentially significant factors should be mentioned. First, teachers who have formed and supervise the various Just Communities are not only dedicated to the project (and willing to put up with many frustrations), they also have above-average preparation (including Ph.D. degrees from Harvard). Second, the schools are not typical because administrators were willing to waive requirements and regulations to permit the Just Communities to be established. For both of these reasons, even if Kohlberg eventually supplies impressive evidence that graduates of Just Community groups reach a higher level of moral reasoning than peers who did not participate, it will not be possible to isolate causes. Differences might be attributable to the participatory democracy approach. They might also be traced to the atmosphere of the school and/or the personalities and enthusiasm of the teachers. (Kohlberg himself stressed the significance of the atmosphere of an institution after using his discussion technique in prison.)

Kohlberg's Just Community approach has not been in operation long enough to permit evaluations of its effectiveness. Information on the long-term impact of a very similar approach *is* available, however.

The Summerhill Approach to Moral Education

The participatory democracy that characterizes Kohlberg's Just Communities was practiced in a more complete way for over forty years at A. S. Neill's progressive school, Summerhill. An open meeting was held each Saturday night at Summerhill (which was an all-year, full-time boarding school of about forty pupils and four or five teachers). All pupils and teachers were invited to attend, and each had one vote (the same arrangement as Kolhberg's). If someone at Summerhill infringed on the rights of someone else (by making excessive noise late at night which disturbed the sleep of others, for example), the charge was taken up at one of the weekly meetings (1960, pp. 45–55). If a majority of those present agreed that the complaint was legitimate, the offender had to agree to stop the bothersome behavior and perhaps pay a fine or lose a privilege. Graduates of Summerhill reported (Bernstein, 1968) that they had learned tolerance and sincerity as a consequence of the democratic approach. It is difficult to generalize from these results, however, because the school functioned as an isolated minia-ture world. In addition, much of its success seems to have been due to the unique personality of Neill.

Parents might be able to establish a limited Summerhill atmosphere in a home situation, but they could not duplicate the environment of Neill's school. For one thing, parents cannot isolate their children from the outside world as much as Neill did. Children will thus inevitably come into contact with rules imposed by people in authority who do not give them an opportunity to express their opinions. And given the current emphasis on discipline and the basics in school, it does not seem realistic to expect that many public educational institutions will establish Just Communities that resemble the Summerhill version of self-government.

Alternatives to Kohlberg's Just Community Approach

Because of the difficulty of establishing a Just Community, and the time required for democratic formulation of rules, Kohlberg's approach does not appear to be workable. As soon as more than a few people become involved, participatory democracy procedures become unwieldy. Piaget drew attention to this point when he described how a small group of ten-year-old boys spent as much time agreeing on rules to govern a snowball fight as they did actually playing. While rule-making may be enjoyable when it is a novelty, those who have been involved in a participatory democracy for very long are likely to confess that they sometimes wish an external authority would simply tell them what the rules are so that they can go about their business. Furthermore, comparatively few laws or punishments in adult life are "negotiable" through group discussion. Small groups of citizens do not get together to discuss how tax laws should be established and enforced, for example, nor do they debate what should be done to those who break such laws. Most laws in our society are established by elected representa-tives and they are enforced by the police and the courts.

Because of these potential weaknesses of the Just Community approach, teachers may find that other techniques of moral instruction based on Kohlberg's theory will be more workable. In *Moral Reasoning* (1976) by Ronald E. Galbraith and Thomas M. Jones (subtitled "A Teaching Handbook for Adapting Kohlberg to the Classroom"), several realistic moral dilemmas are presented. In addition, teachers are advised how they might encourage students to write their own moral dilemmas. Both types of dilemmas can be used to stimulate thought and discussion. Techniques of moral instruction that are based on the observations of Kohlberg *and* Piaget have been developed by Richard Hersh, Diana Paolitto, and Joseph Reimer (1979). An outline of their approach was presented in Chapter 11. The same techniques—highlight a moral issue, ask *why* questions, complicate the circumstances, use personal and naturalistic examples—can also be used with adolescents. With older students, however, it is usually not as necessary to keep discussions at a concrete level.

Another alternative to Kohlberg's Just Community approach, or the techniques just described, is the technique of values clarification.

Values Clarification

The values-clarification technique was mentioned briefly in Chapter 11. It consists of asking students to engage in strategies intended to encourage them to prize, choose, and act on their beliefs. In evaluating values clarification in Chapter 11 the point was made that it may not be effective with children below the age of twelve or so because of the tendency for them to be concrete thinkers. This reservation does not apply to adolescents and youth if they are formal thinkers capable of dealing with abstractions and generalizing from one situation to another. In terms of cognitive ability, therefore, many adolescents and almost all youth should be able to respond to values-clarification strategies in ways that its proponents intended.

Typical Values-Clarification Strategies To give you a more complete grasp of what values clarification is like, here are examples of strategies that illustrate the seven steps toward clear understanding of values that have been proposed by the developers of this technique. These strategies are described in *Values Clarification* (1972) by Sidney B. Simon, Leland W. Howe, and Howard Kirschenbaum, and in *Personalizing Education* (1975) by Leland W. and Mary M. Howe.

Prizing and Choosing "Values Lists" (described on pages 119–126 of *Personalizing Education*). Students are asked to list twenty-five things they value, prize, or cherish. The items on the list are then classified under such categories as *possessions, persons, character traits,* and *items similar to those valued by parents.* Then students form small groups to discuss the patterns that they discern in their values.

Publicly Affirming, When Appropriate "Privacy Circles" (described on pages 183–188 of *Values Clarification*). Students are asked to draw a series of five concentric circles. The smallest is labeled *self,* and from there outward the others

One values-clarification strategy involves discussing with others what you might do if you saw a ten-year-old shoplifting and you doubt that he realizes what might happen if he gets caught. © 1978 Sepp Seitz/Woodfin Camp.

are labeled *intimates, friends, acquaintances, strangers*. Then the teacher reads a series of statements and asks pupils to write a key word in the circle that indicates with whom they would discuss that topic. Sample statements: Whether or not you have ever stolen something (Key word: *Stolen*). What you dislike about your best friend (Key word: *Friend*).

Choosing Beliefs from Alternatives   "Rank Order" (described on pages 58–93 of *Values Clarification*). The teacher reads a question and a list of three alternatives and prints them on the board. Six to eight students are then asked to rank these in order and explain why they prefer one over the others. Several hundred questions and alternatives are supplied for use with students of all age levels.

Choosing After Consideration of Consequences   "Alternatives Action Search" (described on pages 198–203 of *Values Clarification*). The teacher reads a vignette and asks students to write out what they would do in that situation. Then students form into groups of three or four to compare and discuss their reactions and to decide which solution would be most desirable. Sample vignette: You see a boy younger than you shoplifting when you are in a store. You doubt that he realizes what might happen if he gets caught. What would you do?

Choosing Freely   The "Free Choice Game" (described on pages 299–302 of *Values Clarification*). The class is divided into groups of five or six. One person in each group volunteers to describe a choice-situation he or she is confronted with. The other members of the group ask questions to help the individual make a decision. The questions follow a five-step progression: (1) to gain understanding of the situation; (2) to help the person clarify her or his perception of the problem; (3) to explore alternatives; (4) to analyze consequences; (5) to explore feelings and movement toward a decision.

Acting on Beliefs   "Values in Action" (described on pages 257–261 of *Values Clarification*). The teacher asks students to make a list of five changes they think would improve some aspect of their school, community, state, or the nation. Then a work sheet is distributed that lists things a person might do to bring about changes (write a letter, go to a meeting). Students check things they have done and indicate things they would be willing to do. A month later they are asked if they carried through on their intentions.

Acting with a Pattern, Consistency, and Repetition   "Taking Action on My Values" (described on pages 316–318 of *Personalizing Education*). Students are given a work sheet that lists a number of things they are to indicate they feel strongly about (helping others, ecology). They are instructed to select three of these and note (1) how they presently act on it; (2) other things they could do to act on it.

Will Discussion of Values Affect Behavior?   It seems likely that students who engage in values-clarification sessions will probably enjoy such discussions and be likely to gain insights from them. The most important question, though, is similar to a question that can be raised about Kohlberg's Just Community technique: Is there likely to be much carryover from classroom discussion to real-life situations? In *Personalizing Education*, Howe and Howe assert that "if our values are clear, consistent, and soundly chosen, we tend to live our lives in meaningful and satisfying ways" (1975, p. 17). The Howes use the phrase "soundly chosen" but they join other values-clarification advocates in stressing that "Values Clarification is not an attempt to teach students 'right' and 'wrong' values. Rather it is an approach designed to help students prize and act upon their own freely chosen values" (p. 19).

There is no reason to assume, however, that students will automatically make sound choices during and after they engage in values-clarification sessions. It is quite possible that when students are encouraged to develop "clear and consistent" values, they will choose those that focus on material possessions, power, self-indulgence, and the like. Considering the nature of high-pressure advertising in America and the kinds of individuals who achieve notoriety in our society, it would be surprising if such values were not favored by many young people. Simply because a person's values are made more consistent as a consequence of values-clarification sessions, therefore, does not guarantee that the individual will live in a "meaningful and satisfying way." It may be just as likely that the opposite could be the case. Furthermore, because of the complexity and unpredictable nature of human relationships, even when individuals do everything possible to make wise choices, they may still select a course of action that will lead to dissatisfaction and unhappiness.

Values clarification may not be a cure-all or a key to happiness, as some of its proponents claim. But the technique may indeed help young people clarify at least some of their values. Suggestions regarding how you might make personal use of values-clarification strategies will be offered at the end of this chapter.

Does Moral Reasoning Necessarily Lead to Moral Actions?

An important point to remember about moral behavior is the specific nature of such behavior. When faced with real-life moral dilemmas, students are likely to react to each situation in specific ways and in terms of personal needs and desires. Hartshorne and May (1930) found that the children they studied behaved honestly or dishonestly depending on the situation and how they perceived it. It appears that Kohlberg is discovering the same thing because he seems to be entertaining doubts about the usefulness (or even the existence) of his Stage 6 (reported in Muson, 1979, p. 57). It may be too much to expect individuals to be completely consistent in applying a personally chosen set of ethical principles.

Perhaps the most important question of all regarding morality, therefore, remains unanswered: Do verbal responses to hypothetical dilemmas make it possible to predict how people will actually respond when faced with everyday moral decisions? It seems reasonable to assume that the same specificity Hartshorne and May found in their studies of honesty in young children might also be found in adolescent and adult reactions to moral situations. That is, the response to any particular real-life moral dilemma will depend on the person's personal strengths and weaknesses and perception of the situation. A male adolescent with understanding parents might readily confess that he is responsible for the dent in the fender of the family car, for example, but if he is having problems in a particular course in school he may take every opportunity to cheat. If asked to respond to a hypothetical moral dilemma regarding cheating, however, the same young man might supply a postconventional answer. Moral decisions are not made solely in terms of intellectual analyses; they involve emotions and needs, many of which may be unconscious.

Emotions may influence moral decisions more than rational analysis

The reasons leading to moral (and other) decisions are not always understood by those who make them, or even by psychologists or psychoanalysts who specialize in analyzing causes. As Freud pointed out, we have a tendency to defend our egos when confronted by evidence that we are less than perfect. We resort to rationalizations and other defense mechanisms to justify our behavior to ourselves and others. If the boy just mentioned was caught cheating and asked to explain why, he might be able to supply a very plausible explanation. If given enough time, he might even supply an answer that would be scored at Stage 6 by Kohlberg. But if the same young man had twice-weekly appointments with a psychoanalyst, he might confess to his therapist that he cheated because he was jealous of a classmate who made out very successfully with girls and who earned higher test scores in that course. Since very few adolescents or adults see psychotherapists frequently for the purpose of discovering why they behave as they do, most individuals are not aware of all of the reasons for many of their actions. That is why it may not be very helpful to ask adolescents to engage in lengthy discussions justifying the behavior of fictional characters in implausible situations. It might be preferable to ask them to think about what the proper action would be in situations they are almost sure to encounter.

The final steps in the process of values clarification emphasize that the individual should make a commitment and act on a particular value decision. Commitment is also stressed in the concept of identity statuses derived from Erikson's description of psychosocial development during adolescence.

The Nature and Significance of Identity Statuses

The Nature of Identity Statuses

Erikson states that the "concomitants of identity are a feeling of being at home in one's body, a sense of knowing where one is going, and an inner assuredness of anticipated recognition from those who count" (1965, p. 165). He also places particular stress on occupational choice and acceptance of a sex role. Erikson hypothesizes that adolescents and youth who possess or acquire these various characteristics of identity will experience a sense of psychosocial well-being. James E. Marcia (1966, 1980) has proposed *identity statuses* which "were developed as a device by means of which Erikson's theoretical notions about identity might be subjected to empirical study. . . . The identity statuses are four modes of dealing with the identity issue characteristic of late adolescents" (1980, p. 161). (Marcia's use of the term *late adolescents* is essentially the same as Keniston's use of the word *youth,* and most research on identity statuses has been carried out with college students.)

Marcia established the four identity statuses after he had conducted semistructured interviews with a selected sample of male youth. All of the interviewees were asked their thoughts about a career, their personal value system, sexual attitudes, and religious beliefs. Marcia proposes that the criteria for the attainment of a mature identity are based on two variables: crisis and commitment. "Crisis refers to times during adolescence when the individual seems to be actively involved in choosing among alternative occupations and beliefs. Commitment refers to the degree of personal investment the individual expresses in an occupation or belief" (1967, p. 119). After analyzing interview records with these two criteria in mind, Marcia established the four identity statuses. Marcia, along with several other investigators, then used a wide variety of measures to determine characteristics of each type. The four identity statuses and some of the results of these various studies which Marcia feels are of significance are summarized in Table 13–3.

Table 13–3
Characteristics of Identity Status Types
Summarized by Marcia

CHARACTERISTIC STUDIED	IDENTITY DIFFUSION (NO APPARENT COMMITMENT TO AN OCCUPATION OR TO A PARTICULAR SET OF VALUES)	MORATORIUM (CURRENTLY STRUGGLING WITH OCCUPATIONAL OR IDEOLOGICAL ISSUES)
Anxiety	High (females)	High
Self-esteem	Low	High
Moral reasoning	Preconventional or conventional	Likely to be postconventional
Autonomy	Low in self-direction. Externally oriented	Internally oriented
Cognitive style	Impulsive. Extreme complexity	Reflective. Cognitive complexity
Sex-role orientation	Femininity (in females)	
College behavior pattern	Choose least difficult college major (females).	Least satisfied with college. Change majors most often.
Intimacy	Engage in stereotyped relationships	Capable of deep relationships
Interpersonal style (subjects were 13 males and 9 females of varying ages)	Withdrawn, feel out of place with the world, feel parents don't understand them, wary of peers and of those in authority	Volatile, eager to be attractive and visible, express feelings quickly and freely, seem to thrive on intense relationships, competitive
Personality profile (subjects were college females)	Fearful, engage in a great deal of fantasy, have tendencies toward flight (as opposed to confrontation and mastery), describe parents as "not there"	Appear to reject mother, identify with father and strive to fulfill his ambitions, daydream a great deal, have an excessive need to be right, ambivalent about interpersonal relationships, give appearance of "wanting everything"

Source: J. E. Marcia, "Identity in Adolescence," in J. Adelson (Ed.), *Handbook of Adolescent Psychology* (New York: Wiley, 1980). *Note:* Not all types of behavior are reported for all four statuses, and information is not always supplied about whether the subjects were male or female. Characteristics that *are* identified as typical of males or females are indicated by parenthetical notations.

Table 13–3
Characteristics of Identity Status Types
Summarized by Marcia

CHARACTERISTIC STUDIED	FORECLOSURE (COMMITTED TO OCCUPATIONAL OR IDEOLOGICAL POSITIONS CHOSEN BY PARENTS)	IDENTITY ACHIEVEMENT (COMMITTED TO OCCUPATIONAL AND IDEOLOGICAL POSITIONS THAT ARE SELF-CHOSEN)
Anxiety	Low	High (females)
Self-esteem	Low (males)/High (females)	High
Moral reasoning	Preconventional or conventional	Likely to be postconventional
Autonomy	Low in self-direction. Authoritarian. Externally oriented.	Internally oriented
Cognitive style	Impulsive. Cognitive simplicity.	Reflective. Cognitive complexity.
Sex-role orientation	Masculinity or androgyny (in females)	Masculinity or androgyny (in females)
College behavior pattern	Most satisfied with college major. Study diligently.	Choose most difficult college majors (females).
Intimacy	Engage in stereotyped relationships	Capable of deep relationships
Interpersonal style (subjects were 13 males and 9 females of varying ages)	Placid, well-behaved, seem happy even in the face of upsetting circumstances, feel parents are loving, keep selves under control	Give appearance of possessing nondefensive strength, seem able to care for others in nonpossessive ways
Personality profile (subjects were college females)	Eager to re-create family closeness, endorse parents' values, inhibited in impulse expression	More interested in pursuing own goals than maintaining approval of parents, trust their own goals, choose men who are cooperative companions (as opposed to "providers and protectors"), more concerned with who they might be than by whom they might be loved

Before you attempt to use the data in Table 13–3 to analyze your own identity status (or to attach labels to your acquaintances) you are asked to consider the following discussion.

Factors to Consider in Evaluating Identity-Status Descriptions

There are a number of factors that ought to be considered when evaluating rapidly accumulating research on identity statuses. Some of these interpretive limitations are unique to the identity-status concept, some are due to limitations of any system of classification.

One of the most vexing problems of classification schemes is that *pure* types are rare or even nonexistent. The psychologist who establishes a typology may tend to smooth out the differences of various types and become convinced that most individuals will fit neatly into one category or another. When classifications are later made of large numbers of subjects, though, this pigeon-holing effect may not be taken into account.

Individuals may not fit in only one identity-status category

Marcia based his original description of identity statuses on semistructured interviews with a small number of male subjects. While this technique makes it possible for an interviewer to probe for subtleties of attitudes, it also increases the possibility that subjective interpretations will be introduced as the interview proceeds. As was the case with Kohlberg's original stage descriptions of moral reasoning (which also were based on interviews with a small number of male subjects), the tentative classification Marcia made of identity statuses was prematurely treated as if it were a well-established typology because it served as a convenient frame of reference for researchers. As data have accumulated, it has become clear that not very many youth can be placed into only one category. The mixed-type problem seems particularly acute with the identity-status approach since identity (as defined by Erikson and Marcia) consists of a combination of somewhat unrelated traits: acceptance of one's appearance, occupational choice, attitudes toward sex roles, feelings of acceptance by others, moral and religious values. A young person may experience commitment in one or more of these facets of identity but not in others. Consider just a few examples of possible combinations:

A young man who has made a firm occupational choice feels insecure about his social acceptance because the woman he loves has rejected his proposal of marriage.

An attractive young woman who is very satisfied with her appearance is confused about how she feels about her boy friend's suggestion that she leave the Catholic church.

A young woman who plans to earn a Ph.D. is elected to Phi Beta Kappa. She is very attracted to a male admirer but gradually becomes aware that he is extremely competitive and that he becomes visibly upset whenever she does anything better than he does.

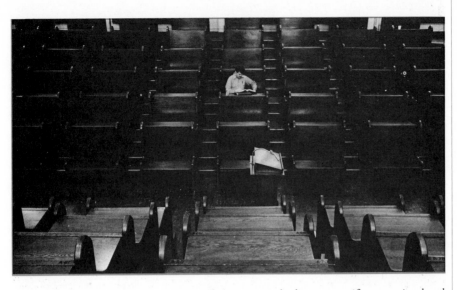

A college student may be committed to a self-chosen major leading to a specific occupational goal and work diligently toward that goal. But he or she might be extremely confused about sex roles and unsure of being accepted by those who count. Such an individual would be difficult to classify into only one of the identity statuses proposed by James Marcia. Jean Claude Lejeune/Stock, Boston.

Each of these individuals is "committed" in one area of identity but "in crisis" in another. Accordingly, they could not be classified in only one of the four identity statuses described by Marcia.

Another problem with the identity-status concept centers on change versus consistency. At one point (1980, pp. 168–170) in his analysis of research on identity statuses Marcia concludes that there is evidence that most male youth begin college as Identity Diffusion or Moratorium types but that between the ages of eighteen and twenty-one they move to Identity Achievement status. This interpretation fits Erikson's description of the process of identity formation. That is, youth may experience a psychosocial moratorium as they seek to clarify values, formulate an acceptable sex role, and make realistic and satisfying occupational choices. But when these problems have been resolved and they make a commitment, they are likely to achieve a sense of identity.

In other sections (pp. 162–164) of his review, however, Marcia summarizes research on personality traits of individuals in each status category without reference to the sequence of identity development. If taken at face value and interpreted literally, some of the data in the first and fourth columns of Table 13–3 suggest that someone who moves from the Identity Diffusion category to the Identity Achievement category would theoretically exhibit the following changes between the ages of eighteen and twenty-one: a switch from impulsive to reflective cognitive style, a shift from femininity to masculinity (if a female), an

Elizabeth Douvan has observed, "The thirty-five-year-old woman who returns to school or work when her last child goes to school undergoes an identity process in many ways comparable to the selection and adaptation process experienced by males in adolescence and early adulthood." Frank Siteman/The Picture Cube.

alteration from an external to an internal orientation, and replacement of stereotyped relationships with deep relationships. Such abrupt reversals of personality seem unlikely, particularly because there is evidence (noted in earlier chapters) that at least some of these traits appear to be quite consistent throughout the span of development.

Identity-status concept not appropriate for females

Still another difficulty with the identity-status scheme is that it does not apply nearly as well to females as to males. Marcia has recently acknowleged this point (1980, p. 179), noting that females are often more concerned about interpersonal relationships than with occupational choice. He also explains that because of marriage-career complications, identity formation typically takes much longer for females than for males. (Elizabeth Douvan has observed that "the thirty-five year old woman who returns to school or work when her last child goes to school undergoes an identity process in many ways comparable to the selection and adaptation process experienced by males in adolescence and early adulthood" [1975, p. 207].)

The identity-status concept is still quite new and the information summarized in Table 13–3 has accumulated in bits and pieces. Most of the studies have featured small numbers of subjects. (The Interpersonal Style description of Identity Achievement types, for example, is based on *two* forty-year-old females.) Not all researchers seem to have taken into account the crisis-and-commitment criteria proposed by Marcia, nor have they always seemed to focus on the process of identity formation. (Failure to consider developmental changes may account for the "prediction" of improbable reversals in cognitive style, masculinity-femininity, and interpersonal relationships noted above.)

Despite all of the cautions and limitations just noted, though, identity-status descriptions *do* make it possible to interpret and understand the behaviors of different types of college students.

Using Identity-Status Descriptions to Understand Youthful Behavior

Identity Diffusion types have yet to experience a crisis because they have not given much serious thought to an occupation, sex roles, or values. As characteristics noted in the first column of Table 13–3 suggest, they give the impression that they may be trying to distract themselves from confronting such issues. They have little self-direction, are disorganized and impulsive, and tend to avoid getting involved in either school work or interpersonal relationships. If these characteristics are displayed only briefly by young people who have just entered college, they might be attributed to immaturity and the initial impact of embarking on an entirely new kind of existence free of parental control. If older students continue to exhibit these forms of behavior, though, they are likely to experience adjustment problems of varying degrees of severity. (Some of these problems will be discussed later.) *Identity Diffusion types avoid thinking about goals, roles, and values*

Moratorium types *have* given a certain amount of thought to identity questions, but they have not come up with any satisfactory answers. They are *aware* that they are "in crisis," as indicated by characteristics noted in the second column of Table 13–3: they are dissatisfied with college, change majors often, daydream a great deal, and engage in intense but short-lived relationships with others. They may also temporarily reject parental values, as illustrated by Debbie's self-analysis quoted near the end of the preceding chapter. After a period of experimentation and restless searching, most Moratorium types are likely to come to grips with themselves and take on characteristics listed in the Identity Achievement column. *Moratorium types suffering identity crises of various kinds*

Foreclosure types are not experiencing a crisis and may never suffer any doubts about key aspects of their identity (particularly occupational choice, sex roles, and values). Erikson suggests that a psychosocial moratorium is a more or less normal phase of identity development, and Peter Blos (1963) and Kenneth Keniston (1971) have proposed that failure to experience some sort of conflict during adolescence may limit personal growth. (In evaluating these opinions you might keep in mind that Erikson experienced a lengthy psychosocial moratorium himself, that Blos is a psychiatrist who treats disturbed adolescents, and that Keniston specialized in studying student activists.)

Some of the traits listed in the third column of Table 13–3 certainly reflect a degree of rigidity, shallowness, and dependency that might be indicative of restricted growth. On the other hand, Foreclosure types *are* satisfied with the goals they have chosen, they have good relationships with their parents, and they seem able to take stress in stride. In a sense, they might be said to possess an *ultra-positive* identity because they endorse and want to acquire traits favored by their parents, which is the opposite of youth who defy their parents by fashioning *Foreclosure types unquestioningly endorse goals and values of parents* a negative identity. Some interpretations of Foreclosure types (particularly when they are compared to Identity Achievement types) imply that personal development will be limited if youth endorse—without a period of questioning or conflict—the values and goals favored by their parents. This seems unfortunate because it suggests that goals selected after a period of conflict are better than goals that have always coincided with those of the parents. Identity Achievement types in Table 13–3 are described as more interested in pursuing their own goals than in mantaining the approval of their parents. But what if the daughter of a female doctor, to note just one example, has *always* wanted to be like her mother and simultaneously pursues that goal *and* earns parental approval? Does this inevitably mean that she will fail to achieve a sense of identity that is as meaningful as that of a medical school classmate whose parents insist that a woman's place is in the home?

Identity Achievement types have made satisfying self-chosen commitments

Identity Achievement types have made self-chosen commitments in at least some aspects of their identity. Because of the variety of factors that make up identity, however, it is not likely that too many individuals experience a triumphant sense of having "put it all together." As the examples provided earlier illustrate, it may be more likely that commitments will have been made in some but not all facets of identity. Furthermore, identity achievement is not a once-and-for-all accomplishment. If an ego-shattering event (loss of a job, being divorced) occurs, Identity Achievement types may be propelled back into a crisis and be faced with the task of rebuilding self-esteem. Because they have already accomplished it once, however, they might be expected to achieve a satisfactory identity again.

Marcia's conclusion that many college students move from the Identity Diffusion and Moratorium categories to the point that they are Identity Achievement types emphasizes the potent effect that a sense of identity can have on overall adjustment. By the same token, youth who fail to achieve a sense of identity are likely to experience a variety of problems. Some of the most common of these will be discussed in the next section.

Problems Related to Failure to Achieve Identity

Some of the identity status data summarized in Table 13–3 point to types of problems adolescents and youth may encounter if they have not achieved a sense of identity. Identity Diffusion and Moratorium types have no clear academic or vocational goals, they may be confused about sex roles and unsure of how they feel about values. Because of uncertainties about such factors they may feel estranged from at least one of their parents, fail to do well in school, and have problems engaging in satisfying relationships with others. (Moratorium types engage in deeper relationships than Identity Diffusion types, but some of the data summarized in Table 13–3 suggest that those classified in the Moratorium category seek intensive relationships primarily to satisfy their own needs without giving much in return.) If adolescents or youth do not feel they are working toward a meaningful academic or vocational goal and/or if they have not established mutually rewarding relationships with others, they may experience a variety of problems traceable at least in part to failure to achieve a satisfying sense of identity. Reactions of this type may include academic underachievement, problems regarding sex, delinquency, use of drugs, and religious conversions. Each of these will be discussed separately.

Academic Underachievement

Between one-third and one-half of young people seen in psychological clinics are referred primarily because of learning problems (Schechter, 1974). Among youth, concern about college grades accounts for over half of all requests for counseling (Blaine and McArthur, 1971). Some school problems are due to learning disabilities of various kinds (perceptual disorders, difficulties in forming concepts, hyperactivity, distractibility), but others appear to be caused by identity or adjustment problems. Both Moratorium and Identity Diffusion types, for instance, who have made no clear choice of an academic or occupational goal, find it difficult to settle down in college. Lack of a clear academic goal undoubtedly is an important cause of poor school work in high school as well, but other factors may contribute to underachievement at both levels. Irving B. Weiner (1980) comments on two causes (other than failure to achieve identity) of poor school work: hostility toward parents and concerns about rivalry.

Weiner reports that many adolescents and youth who seek counseling because of academic performance problems express resentment about parental demands they cannot or prefer not to try to meet. If the resentment is strong enough, the young person may retaliate by making little effort to earn high grades (perhaps as a means for establishing a negative identity). Such attitudes are revealed by characteristics listed in the Identity Diffusion and Moratorium columns in Table 13–3. The most unfortunate aspect of such retaliation is that even if Moratorium and Identity Diffusion types eventually *do* focus on self-chosen academic or occupational goals, they may not be able to overcome the low grade point average they became saddled with during the pre-identity phase of their college careers.

In the preceding chapter research on fear of success was summarized. This type of behavior may not be restricted to females who are concerned about marriage-career conflicts. Regardless of sex or attitudes toward marriage, some students may feel apprehensive about achievement because of fears that they will be unable to compete successfully with their parents, siblings, or acquaintances. Lois Wladis Hoffman (1974) supplied evidence that fear of success is not an exclusively feminine problem. Seven years after Matina Horner had completed her pioneering investigation on fear of success, Hoffman asked students at the same university to record their reactions to stories such as "Ann Goes to Medical School." She found that 60 percent of the females showed fear of success when judged by Horner's criteria. But 70 percent of the males also revealed that they were anxious about attempts to become successful. (The percentage of females is the same as that reported by Horner. The percentage of males jumped from around 10 to 70, which may reflect a change in student values during the 1970s that placed a premium on success.)

David McClelland (1961) and J. W. Atkinson (1964) point out that differences in the need for achievement can often be explained by postulating a contrasting need to avoid failure. Some individuals are success-oriented and set personal goals that they feel confident they can achieve. Others are anxiety-ridden and tend to set goals much too high or too low. Anxious students who set unrealistically high goals are likely to work only half-heartedly, according to Weiner, because they can then rationalize that they *could* have done better but just didn't feel like trying. Those who set goals too low, on the other hand, may rationalize that they did not want to get the reputation of being a "grind."

Academic underachievement may be due to fear of success

Ambivalent feelings about academic achievement are most likely to occur when a student moves from high school to college, often leading to what has been dubbed *big league shock* (Berger, 1961). It seems likely that big league shock might account for at least some of the indecision regarding choice of a college major (as well as other types of behavior) that is experienced by Identity Diffusion and Moratorium types.

Academic underachievement reflects identity confusion regarding occupational choice (and perhaps relationships with parents and peers). But adolescents and youth may also exhibit types of behavior that reveal that they are experiencing problems establishing sex roles.

Problems of Sexual Identity

The Nature of Different Types of Femininity   In their study of adolescents attending high school during the 1950s, Douvan and Adelson (1966) classified their female subjects into six categories: *unambivalent feminine* (consistent choice of feminine traits), *ambivalent feminine* (high score on femininity but some desire to be masculine), *neutral* (no clear-cut or consistent pattern), *boyish* (wanted to be boys), *achievement-oriented* (focused on masculine occupational goals), *antifeminine* (did not want to marry). They found that unambivalent feminine girls (23 percent of their sample) tended to come from upper-middle-class homes, that their future plans centered on marriage, and that they had little motivation for personal achievement. Ambivalent feminine girls (9 percent), by contrast, tended to come from lower-middle-class homes and had a sense of their own competence that led them to want success and individual achievement—in addition to marriage. Girls in all of the nonfeminine groups were judged to have "problematic social development" (p. 250). Achievement-oriented girls (9 percent) were not popular and were perceived as using "the future as an escape from (perhaps a sublimation for) their problems" (p. 250). The boyish girls (22 percent) were judged to be less mature but were active and somewhat resentful of those in authority. The neutral girls (23 percent) were also less mature but were considered to be compliant and inactive. The antifeminine girls (14 percent)— who indicated they had no interest in marriage—were considered to be the most seriously disturbed, and many of them wished they were boys. (For detailed descriptions and explanations of each type, see Chapter 7 of *The Adolescent Experience.*)

Given the dramatic changes that have taken place in conceptions of femininity between the 1950s and 1980s, it seems certain that the proportion of high school girls in each of these categories has changed. It seems even more certain that self-perceptions and perceptions of others of each of the types have changed. In the 1950s, for example, achievement-oriented girls were judged by Douvan and Adelson to be unpopular and to be "using the future as an escape for their problems." The description of the females at the bottom of the Identity Achievement column in Table 13–3, by contrast, demonstrates that contemporary females who focus on career goals have higher self-esteem and are better adjusted than many of their peers. Other evidence to support the hypothesis that attitudes toward feminine achievement have changed is supplied by reports (L. W. Hoffman, 1979) that working mothers tend to be more satisfied with their lives than nonworking mothers. (In speculating about females' changes in thinking about achievement, allowance should be made for the fact that Douvan and Adelson were recording impressions of high school girls; the description in Table 13–3 relates to college women; and Hoffman reported the reactions of women who were in their twenties and thirties. Even so, the career choices of elementary school girls that were listed in Chapter 10 lead to the conclusion that even contemporary preadolescent females have positive attitudes toward careers for women.)

Achievement-oriented women of 1980s likely to be self-satisfied

Nine years after the publication of *The Adolescent Experience,* Douvan recorded some supplementary observations on the nature of sex roles. She observed, "By separating sex and maternity—by dissociating the act of sex from its natural consequences—birth control has led to a separation of maternity from the core of feminine identity and has made possible a new integration in which the woman conceives of herself as fully developed, adult, sexual, and nonmaternal" (1975, p. 33). She notes that perhaps the clearest expression of the separation of the maternal from the sexual is that between the 1950s and the 1970s the proportion of women who said that they would ideally have no children increased from about zero to over 10 percent. Even if the percentage of women who do not wish to have children has increased in the few years since the 1970s data were accumulated, it would seem that an overwhelming majority of women still think favorably about motherhood.

In the 1950s Douvan and Adelson concluded that achievement-oriented high school girls were un-popular and "using the future as an escape for their problems." In the 1980s college girls who are determined to be successful in difficult college programs are rated high in self-esteem and in Identity Achievement. Chris Maynard/Magnum.

As soon as a woman does have a child, she may find, whether she likes it or not, that her identity will center on how well she functions as wife and mother. But when the children reach school age, Douvan points out (as noted a bit earlier), her identity problems will come to resemble those of youthful males. Even so, she suggests the female may have an easier time of it than the male. A contemporary married woman who has children may simply need to bide her time until the children are old enough to go off on their own. At that point, if she decides to embark on a career and establish an identity similar to that of a young man, she will benefit from greater maturity and may experience little difficulty "acquir-ing" previously unneeded "masculine" traits such as competitiveness. If a mother asks her husband to share in early child-care responsibilities, though, he may experience more severe adjustment problems. Douvan points out that American males have been taught to control or reject qualities centering on sensitivity, patience, and tenderness so effectively and for so long that such abilities may have atrophied. Husbands may be so deeply embedded in their sex-typed ruts that they will have a much harder time acquiring traits of psychological androgyny than their wives will. (There is evidence [Elman and Manosevitz, 1972] that parents are more inclined to try to reshape the behavior of a boy who is a "sissy" than the behavior of a girl who is a "tomboy.")

Males may have more problems overcoming sex-typing than females

Philip H. Dreyer (1975) has developed a typology of sex-role preferences among women which serves as an alternative set of descriptions to those formulated by Douvan and Adelson. These types are summarized in Table 13–4. In commenting on his typology Dreyer notes that many contemporary young

Table 13–4
Dreyer's Typology of Sex-Role Preferences Among Women

TYPE DESIGNATION	CHARACTERISTICS
Role synthesizers	Attempt to combine what they feel are the best elements of traditional feminine *and* masculine roles into a life style that emphasizes high levels of personal achievement. Tend to be perfectionists. See men as competitors and seek husbands who will share family roles and chores equally.
Role innovators	Seek new activities, responsibilities, and status for themselves as women. Have practical goals (e.g., getting a good job) and see feminine attributes as means for achieving ends. Do not perceive men as competitors.
Role traditionalists	Conform to stereotyped conceptions of the "ultra-domesticated" woman. Seek husbands who will be good providers and fathers. Have limited occupational and educational goals. Intend to devote their attention to a husband and children with little thought to a career.
Role diffused	Uncertain about almost everything in their lives. Torn between thoughts of a career and speculations about who they will marry. Appear subdued, worried, and embarrassed about their indecision. When doubts become extreme, tend to exhibit traditional feminine forms of behavior.

Source: P. H. Dreyer, "Sex, Sex Roles, and Marriage Among Youth in the 1970s," in R. J. Havighurst and P. H. Dreyer (Eds.), *Youth,* The Seventy-fourth Yearbook of the National Society for the Study of Education (Chicago: University of Chicago Press, 1975).

women think in terms of a sex role that combines marriage, motherhood, *and* a career. (This description fits most of the career projections given by the college females mentioned in the preceding chapter when asked what they thought they would be doing in ten years.)

You might find it of interest to compare Dreyer's sex-role preference descriptions with those of Douvan and Adelson as well as with the identity-status descriptions summarized in Table 13–3. While there are certain similarities, there are also differences, leading to the conclusion that there are many kinds of options regarding contemporary sex roles.

Homosexuality and Identity   If two people of the same sex form a close relationship with each other, they will almost certainly experience some difficulties because of entrenched prejudices against homosexuality. Accordingly, even youth who have formed a satisfying personal conception of themselves as homosexuals may hesitate to proclaim their decision publicly for fear of reprisals or harassment. If homosexuals keep their sexual identity secret, though, they may fail to experience a sense of definite commitment. In a sense, then, the identity problems of homosexuals are caused more by others than by themselves.

Preoccupation with Sexual Relations   Some adolescents and youth, particularly males, may attempt to establish a sense of identity by "specializing" in sexual relations. A number of theorists have concluded that they are not likely to succeed. Peter Blos, for instance, notes that too much stress on sexuality "impedes rather than promotes progressive development" (1979, p. 12). Erik Erikson observes:

> The youth who is not sure of his identity shies away from interpersonal intimacy or throws himself into acts of intimacy which are "promiscuous" without true fusion or real self-abandon.
>
> Where a youth does not accomplish such intimate relationships with others—and, I would add, with his own inner resources—in late adolescence or early adulthood, he may settle for highly stereotyped interpersonal relations and come to retain a deep *sense of isolation*. (1968, pp. 135–136)

R. Josselson, E. Greenberger, and D. McConochie (1977) concluded that high school boys rated low in psychosocial maturity were often preoccupied with heterosexual contacts whereas high maturity boys seemed more able to "take it or leave it." The high maturity boys seemed more concerned about future goals than with immediate sexual gratification. And Ronald Shenker and Mollie Schildkrout observe that "the promiscuous teenager of either sex is more likely to have emotional problems than the youngster who has developed a close relationship and experiences the sex act as a partial expression of . . . commitment to [the] partner" (1975, p. 71). It would seem, therefore, that engaging in sexual intercourse in noncommitted ways is not likely to contribute to a sense of satisfying identity.

Delinquency

Starting in the mid-1940s, the number of adolescents charged with delinquent behavior has steadily increased. Since 1965, the overall increase for girls has been approximately twice that for boys, and in certain crime areas the increase has been substantial. "Between 1960 and 1970 arrests of girls under eighteen years of age increased by 276% for 'violent' crimes, and by 255% for 'property' crimes; for boys the percentage increases were 159% and 75% respectively" (FBI: *Uniform Crime Report*, 1960–1970, pp. 3–4).

Martin Gold and Richard Petronio speculate that delinquency has a masculine character in our society. That is, males are more likely than females to achieve recognition from peers by engaging in illegal acts. Anna Kaufman Moon/Stock, Boston.

Even though the percentage increases for girls are higher than for boys, males still commit many more delinquent acts than females. Martin Gold and Richard J. Petronio (1980, p. 524) speculate that this may be the case because delinquency in our society seems to have a masculine character. They suggest that the range of delinquent behaviors that will be admired by peers is much narrower for females than for males, and so boys are more likely to achieve recognition by engaging in illegal acts.

Boys more likely than girls to gain status by committing delinquent acts

Most records of delinquent behavior are based on actual arrests. Gold (1970), however, obtained data about the number of delinquent *acts* committed by interviewing a representative sample of 522 of the 13,200 thirteen- to sixteen-year-olds in a large midwestern city. Of the 522 adolescents interviewed, 435 confessed that they had committed one or more chargeable offenses (1970, p. 102). Only fifty-four of the boys and twelve of the girls, however, were apprehended by the police. When the total number of acts committed was taken into account, only 3 percent led to arrests. Lower-class adolescents and/or those who committed many delinquent acts were most likely to be caught, booked, and to appear in court. Differences in the number of delinquent acts committed by middle- and lower-class adolescents were not as great as estimates based on arrests indicate.

In recent years, therefore, there has been a trend for more delinquent acts to be committed by youth from all backgrounds. But there has been a disproportionate increase in the number of offenses committed by girls and by upper- and middle-class adolescents living in suburban communities. These figures on delinquency call attention to the variety of causes that impel adolescents to crime.

Causes of Delinquent Behavior   One general explanation for delinquency is supplied by Erikson's concept of negative identity. Other explanations to account for the overall increase in criminal acts include overpopulation, increased mobility leading to the disruption of family and neighborhood ties, frequent separations and divorce making it necessary for the parent with custody of children to hold down a job (and have less time for child care), increasing callousness and indifference to human and property rights, and the general "immoral" tone of our society exemplified by highly publicized acts of dishonesty on the part of public officials and business executives.

Explanations for delinquency also vary depending on the background of particular adolescents. A major cause of delinquent acts by lower-class youth, particularly in inner cities, is unemployment, which may be as high as 70 percent. (Bachman, O'Malley, and Johnston [1978] found that unemployment had a crippling impact on self-esteem.) Other causes of lower-class delinquency center on the conditions of slum living—poverty, rapid population turnover, broken homes, general disorganization. James Coleman (1966) and Michael Harrington (1965) have called attention to the pessimism and despair of inner-city adolescents who feel that they have no control over their future lives and are doomed to remain where they are. Finally, it appears that indulging in delinquent acts is an approved tradition in many inner-city neighborhoods (G. F. Jensen, 1973).

The authors of the FBI Report suggest that the disproportionate increase in delinquent acts by girls may be due to a move away from the traditional passive feminine role to greater aggressiveness and independence. A major cause of the increase in delinquency by middle-class urban youth may be parent-child conflicts. J. G. Bachman (1970) came to the conclusion that the single most predictive indicator of delinquency was relationships between the adolescent offender and parents. The significance of parent-child conflicts as a major cause of delinquency by middle-class youth is highlighted by a distinction between *sociologic* delinquency, which is molded by environmental conditions (as in the case of slum youth) and *individual* delinquency caused primarily by parent-child relationships (A. Johnson, 1959).

Relationships with parents single most predictive indicator of delinquency

W. M. Ahlstrom and R. J. Havighurst (1971) found that adolescents who engage in delinquent acts are likely to have been subjected to erratic and overly strict discipline with physical punishment used instead of reasoning. Furthermore, relationships between delinquent adolescents and their parents are frequently characterized by mutual hostility. The parents of delinquents are more likely to ignore or reject their children, to have personal problems of their own, and to have police records. A final point noted by Ahlstrom and Havighurst is that adolescents from nonbroken homes characterized by hostility or apathy are more likely to commit delinquent acts than adolescents from broken homes where the remaining parent shows affection and provides support.

Characteristics of Delinquents   John J. Conger and W. C. Miller (1966) carried out a longitudinal study of the personality characteristics of delinquent boys. They found that differences between delinquents and nondelinquents were noted as early as the primary grades. Teachers in the first three grades rated future delinquents as less considerate and fair in dealing with others, less friendly, less responsible, more impulsive, and more antagonistic to authority. Because of these tendencies, they were less well liked and accepted by their peers. They were easily distracted when engaged in school work and rarely showed interest (or ability) in the subjects they studied. These general trends continued in the later elementary school years with increasing problems with school work becoming more apparent as the boys progressed through the grades. By the end of the ninth grade there were noticeable differences between delinquents and nondelinquents in virtually all traits measured by Conger and Miller. During the high school years delinquents were rated lower than average in self-confidence and self-respect, less cheerful and happy, less able to get along with either male or female classmates, and more eager for attention. They also were rated as more egocentric, inconsiderate, and thoughtless. They confessed that they often felt discouraged, depressed, and anxious. Finally, they seemed unable to establish close personal relationships with either peers or adults.

D. Magnusson, A. Duner, and G. Zetterblon (1975) reported that sixth-graders who disliked classmates, felt that they were overloaded with school work, were dissatisfied with school, and had low scholastic motivation were likely to have committed delinquent acts by the ninth grade. It would seem that failure to gain satisfaction or recognition in school forced them to seek other means to impress their peers and/or try to bolster their self-esteem.

Drug Use

There are many different kinds of drugs and each has varying effects depending on dosage, circumstances, and individual reactions. Furthermore, drugs are used for many different reasons. Accordingly, perhaps the best way to present information on drug use is to summarize the findings of extensive surveys and permit you to draw your own conclusions. Table 13–5 is based on responses to statements about drug use supplied by over 18,000 high school students who were members of the class of 1978. (Some of the data on trends in Table 13–5 are based on similar surveys carried out in 1975, 1976, and 1977. For details see Johnston, Bachman, and O'Malley [1978].) Table 13–6 summarizes reasons for using various drugs given by a representative sample of 2,510 young men who were twenty-to-thirty years old in 1974. (The data noted at the top of Table 13–6 indicate the number of respondents—out of the total of 2,510—who reported using each drug listed. The figures in the columns at the bottom of the table indicate the percentages of experimental and other users who indicated various reasons for using each drug.) Table 13–7 summarizes the findings of a review of 120 surveys of teenage alcoholism carried out between 1941 and 1975.

Table 13–5
Drug Use Reported by High School Students, Class of 1978:
Selected Findings

ASPECT OF DRUG USE STUDENTS WERE ASKED ABOUT	PERCENT ANSWERED AFFIRMATIVE
Illicit drug use at some time in life	64
Use of marijuana at least once	59
Use of marijuana past year	50
Use of marijuana past month	37
Daily use of marijuana	11
Regular use of marijuana is harmful	35
Disapprove of regular use of marijuana	68
Use of marijuana in public should be prohibited by law	60
It is fairly easy or very easy to obtain marijuana	88
Use of alcohol at some time in life	93
Use of alcohol past month	72
Daily use of alcohol	6
Having four or more drinks a day is harmful	63
Disapprove of having more than two drinks a day	68
Getting drunk in public should be prohibited by law	50
Smoked cigarettes at some time in life	75
Smoked cigarettes past month	37
Daily use of cigarettes	28
Smoking one or more packs a day is harmful	59
Disapprove of smoking a pack or more of cigarettes a day	67
Smoking in public places should be prohibited by law	42

The percentage of high school students who use drugs increased steadily between 1975 and 1978. Most of this increase was due to greater use of marijuana.

More males than females use illicit drugs on a regular basis. Males drink more than females, but there are no sex differences in smoking.

The most widely used drugs other than marijuana are stimulants, tranquilizers, and sedatives.

Seniors who expect to complete college have lower rates of illicit drug use than those who do not plan to continue their education.

The highest rate of drug use is in the Northeast, followed by the North Central, Western, and Southern states. Regional differences are small, however.

The highest rate of drug use occurs in large metropolitan areas, the lowest rate is found in nonmetropolitan areas.

Source: L. D. Johnston, J. G. Bachman, and P. M. O'Malley, *Drugs and the Class of '78: Behaviors, Attitudes, and National Trends* (Rockville, Maryland: National Institute on Drug Abuse, 1979).

		ALCOHOL	MARIJUANA	STIMULANTS	SEDATIVES	HEROIN
NUMBER OF EXPERIMENTAL USERS (USED DRUG LESS THAN 10 TIMES)		93	423	207	177	72
NUMBER OF OTHER USERS (USED DRUG 10 TIMES OR MORE)		2341	959	374	232	76
REASON						
To get high or stoned	Experimental	12	53	48	72	75
	Other	65	93	73	72	99
Because it was expected of you in the situation	Experimental	40	43	19	18	18
	Other	49	40	19	21	29
Because you were bored and it helped to pass the time	Experimental	17	14	18	24	21
	Other	48	56	33	36	46
To help you forget your worries or your troubles	Experimental	8	7	9	24	14
	Other	36	32	18	50	54
To heighten your senses— like taste, touch, or hearing	Experimental	0	11	31	4	8
	Other	6	46	42	8	22
To help you to sleep or relax	Experimental	10	8	5	50	13
	Other	37	47	4	68	50

Table 13–6

Percentages of a Representative Sample of 2,510 Twenty- to Thirty-Year-Old Males Who Indicated Reasons for Using Different Drugs

Source: J. A. O'Donnell et al., *Young Men and Drugs: A Nationwide Survey* (Rockville, Maryland: National Institute on Drug Abuse, 1976).

Table 13–7

Summary of Findings of 120 Surveys of Teen-age Drinking: 1941–1975

☐ The proportion of teenagers who occasionally use alcohol rose steadily from World War II until about 1965. The proportion of occasional drinkers has remained relatively constant since then—approximately 80 percent of boys, 70 percent of girls.

☐ The proportion of high school students who reported having been drunk at least once increased from 19 percent before 1965 to 45 percent after 1966 and up to 1975. The proportion who reported being intoxicated at least once a month increased from 10 percent before 1965 to 19 percent after 1966 and up to 1975.

☐ Percentages of problem drinkers at different grade levels:

	7	8	9	10	11	12
Boys	5.0	15.6	20.9	27.2	33.9	39.9
Girls	4.4	9.1	16.2	18.9	19.9	20.6

(Problem drinking is defined as drunkenness at least six times in the past year or presence of negative consequences from drinking two or more times in the past year. Negative consequences include: getting into trouble with teachers or a principal, getting into difficulties with friends, driving when drunk, being criticized by a date, getting into trouble with the police.)

☐ The average age for the first drink is thirteen years. Drinking typically begins at home and is influenced by parental example. Continued drinking may be influenced by peer pressure.

☐ Some personality characteristics of problem drinkers: alienation, personal dissatisfaction, disturbed relationships with the family, tolerance for deviation.

Source: E. P. Noble, *Alcohol and Health,* Third Special Report to the U.S. Congress (Rockville, Maryland: National Institute on Alcohol Abuse and Alcoholism, 1978).

Religious Conversions

In the late 1960s and early 1970s many dissatisfied adolescents dropped out of society by joining hippie groups or communes. In the late 1970s and early 1980s the most popular subcultures sought by youth who reject prevailing American values appear to be religious cults of various kinds.

In an analysis of the current popularity of religious cults, Harvey Cox (1977), a well-known theologian, speculates that young Americans may turn to such religious groups for the following reasons: to acquire friendship, to gain immediacy of experience, to turn choices and decisions over to a higher authority, to live more natural and simple lives.

Young people may join a religious cult because they are resorting to the sublimation of asceticism, trying to atone for existential guilt, or seeking to postpone key decisions by engaging in a psycho-social moratorium. Donald C. Dietz/Stock, Boston.

Other explanations are supplied by theoretical interpretations of adolescence outlined in the preceding chapter. Many adolescents who join religious cults appear to have chosen to restrict their sexual activities. Accordingly, some of their behavior may take the form of sublimations. In his analysis of adolescence, Peter Blos notes that common sublimations found in adolescents are asceticism, intellectualism, and uniformism. Most religious cults encourage such forms of behavior. Members are required to renounce material possessions (or at least turn them over to the leader), engage in intellectual thought and discussions while playing down emotions and feelings, and submerge their individuality by engaging in uniform types of behavior. An alternative explanation for asceticism in religious conversions is offered by Martin L. Hoffman (1980) who suggests that it may be due to existential guilt.

The desire of some young people to join a religious group can also be understood by taking into account Erik Erikson's concepts of identity, psychosocial moratorium, and negative identity. An adolescent who has been unable to form a sense of positive identity may seek to postpone making decisions. Joining a religious cult eliminates the necessity for the young person to make choices, since many such groups expect members to follow the orders of the leader in unquestioning ways. Venerating and obeying the leader makes it possible for the adolescent to identify with him, and with fellow cult members, and eliminates the need for attempting to develop a unique and independent identity.

Religious conversions may be due to sublimation, guilt, moratorium

The types of behavior just discussed can often be classified, at least in part, as problems due to failure of adolescents and youth to achieve a positive sense of identity. Other, more serious, problems take the form of behavior disorders. Severe disorders that occur during the adolescent years include schizophrenia, depression, and suicidal behavior.

Behavior Disorders in Adolescence and Youth

Schizophrenia

Irving B. Weiner describes schizophrenia, the most common single type of severe psychological disturbance, as "perhaps the major mental health problem in the United States" (1980, p. 450). Schizophrenia (along with autism) was briefly discussed in Chapter 8 in the analysis of interactions between inherited and environmental influences on personality development. Characteristics of schizophrenia noted by Weiner include impaired capacity to think coherently, distorted perceptions of reality, difficulty in establishing and maintaining satisfactory relationships with others, and weakened control over impulses. These characteristics are found in both adolescent and adult schizophrenics, but they may be less clearly defined in younger individuals, which means that the onset of abnormal behavior is more difficult to detect in teen-agers.

Preschizophrenic boys negativistic, aggressive; girls shy, inhibited

Types of behavior that may indicate the likelihood that an adolescent of either sex will later exhibit schizophrenic patterns of abnormality center on withdrawal and lack of interest in social relations. Adolescent boys who later become schizophrenic have been characterized by irritability, aggressiveness, negativism, and defiance of authority. Preschizophrenic adolescent girls tend to be emotionally immature, shy, and inhibited. If an adolescent displays such characteristics in high school and later is diagnosed as a schizophrenic, the prognosis for recovery is less favorable than if abnormal symptoms appear later in life. Weiner notes that follow-up studies reveal that 23 percent of adolescents hospitalized for schizophrenia recover, 25 percent improve but suffer lingering symptoms or occasional relapses, and the remaining 52 percent make little or no progress and remain hospitalized indefinitely. (A fictionalized account of a young woman's experiences with schizophrenia and hospitalization is presented in *I Never Promised You a Rose Garden* [1964] by Hannah Green, a pseudonym for Joan Greenberg. Mark Vonnegut provides an autobiographical account of similar experiences in *The Eden Express* [1975].)

Depression

About 2 percent of the population may be diagnosed as schizophrenics at some time in their lives but about 10 percent of all high school students seen in

Depression may be caused by a cognitive set of negative views toward oneself and the future, learned helplessness, or a sense of loss. Sherry Suris/Rapho Photo Researchers.

psychiatric clinics suffer from depression. Common symptoms of depression include self-depreciation, crying spells, and suicidal thoughts and attempts (Masterson, 1967). Additional symptoms of depression found in adolescents below the age of seventeen involve fatigue, hypochondriasis, and concentration difficulty (Weiner, 1980, p. 455). High school students who experience such symptoms typically try to ward off their depression by restless activity or flight to or from others. They may also engage in problem behavior or delinquent acts carried out in ways that make it clear they are appealing for help. (A depressed fifteen-year-old boy may carry out an act of vandalism, for instance, at a time when a school authority or police officer is sure to observe the incident.) Adolescents over the age of seventeen who suffer from depression are likely to show little self-confidence and feel worthless and discouraged. To combat such feelings they may join antiestablishment groups, manifest a "what's the use of it all?" attitude, or turn to sex and drugs.

A. T. Beck (1970) suggests that depression consists of a *cognitive set* made up of negative views toward oneself, the world, and the future. Martin Seligman (1975) has proposed that depression is caused by *learned helplessness* due to feelings of having no control over one's life. Irving Weiner (1975) emphasizes that depression typically involves a *sense of loss* sometimes caused by the abrupt end of

Depression may be caused by negative set, learned helplessness, sense of loss

a personal relationship through death, separation, or broken friendship. Or an individual may undergo a sharp drop in self-esteem due to failure or guilt. Or the person may experience a loss of bodily integrity following illness, incapacitation, or disfigurement.

Any or all of these factors that lead to depression may eventually lead to thoughts about suicide.

Suicide

Between 1955 and 1974, according to figures reported in *Facts of Life and Death* (1974), death rates from suicide for fifteen- to nineteen-year-olds increased from 2.1 per 100,000 to 8.8 per 100,000. In 1974, suicide was the third leading cause of death among adolescents. (The two leading causes, followed by numbers indicating the rates per 100,000, were: accidents, 68.7; homicide, 11.7.) Males are more likely to commit suicide than females by a ratio of about three to one. Females, on the other hand, are more likely than males to *attempt* suicide by a ratio of about six to one. One explanation for these sex differences in completed and attempted suicide rates is that males are more likely to use firearms when moved to take their lives, females are more likely to use poisons.

It appears that there is a quite typical sequence of experiences that culminates in the attempt of an adolescent to commit suicide (Jacobs, 1971, p. 64):

Suicide triggered by inability to solve problems, deterioration of relationships

1 The individual is likely to have experienced adjustment problems starting in childhood and continuing through adolescence. Many of these problems may have been caused by marital discord between parents, harsh and erratic discipline, and similar negative and ineffective forms of parent–child relationships.

2 A few weeks or days prior to the suicide attempt, problems are perceived to increase.

3 Attempts to deal with the problems are unsuccessful, leading the young person to conclude that he or she has no control over them.

4 Meaningful relationships with others, particularly parents, seem to deteriorate completely. The depressed and desperate adolescent is likely to feel that parents (and others) do not understand his or her problems or that they are unwilling to provide support.

This description of experiences that may cause a young person to attempt suicide underscores the critical need for adolescents and youth to acquire a sense of control over their own behavior. To conclude this book, observations will be offered that you might use to assess and promote your own feelings of self-direction.

Controlling Your Own Future Development

At the very beginning of this book it was noted that thoughtful individuals have always wondered why some individuals are happy and successful, others unhappy and unable to take advantage of their opportunities. Now that you have reached the final pages, you are in a position to evaluate many hypotheses about positive and negative influences on development. The fact that you are reading these words suggest that you are a college student and that you are capable of formal thought. It is also likely that you are in the process of establishing a sense of identity. Because you are a formal thinker you can deal with possibilities and hypotheses and speculate about the future. Because you are probably still sorting out your thoughts on occupational choice, sex roles, and values, you are probably interested in steps you might take to foster identity achievement.

It seems appropriate to conclude this book with a discussion of things *you* might do because so much of what has been discussed earlier has centered on what others have done to you. You had no control over which of your father's sperm fertilized the egg produced by your mother, for instance, so your gender and your genetic structure were given to you. You had no control over the way you were handled immediately after you were born, or whether you were breast- or bottle-fed, or how you were toilet trained. You were unable to request that your parents become well informed about effective techniques of child rearing— although you undoubtedly shaped some of their approaches to child rearing by your reactions to their care. Whether you were exposed to an authoritative, authoritarian, or permissive child-rearing approach, though, was probably determined more by your parents' upbringing and personalities than by your reactions. You probably had very little to say about what your parents deliberately or unintentionally did to persuade you to accept a particular sex role, but you might not have gone along with all of their wishes. In school, you were exposed to a long succession of teachers who nudged you in many different directions. Only recently have you been offered the privilege of choosing at least some of your instructors and of severing relationships with them if you were disappointed or bothered by their behavior.

If you were to undergo intensive and lengthy psychoanalysis with a particularly astute psychiatrist, you might be able to formulate hypotheses about how at least some of these experiences made you what you are. But even if you found out, and felt quite sure that a particular interpretation was correct, you still couldn't change your inheritance or cancel out what happened. Equipped with detailed interpretations of your past you might be able to take into account the impact of certain experiences, particularly negative ones, and try to overcome certain types of behavior that function as handicaps. But there are different, simpler, and much less expensive ways than psychoanalysis to attempt to exert some control over your own destiny.

Some psychotherapists (notably Carl Rogers, 1951) argue that it makes more sense for individuals to concentrate on what they *are* rather than how they have gotten that way when they set out to solve adjustment problems. He maintains that too often psychotherapy makes a patient dependent on the therapist and that the real purpose of therapy should be to promote self-control. He also points out that a potential danger of forms of psychotherapy that concentrate on how past experiences shaped behavior is that a person might be tempted to explain or excuse nonconstructive actions instead of trying to bring about improvements.

An approach that does not require the assistance of any breed of psychotherapist is for you to take steps to form a clearer picture of your own identity. And that is why these concluding remarks center on suggestions you might follow as you seek to influence your future development. Because you are probably engaged in an active search for a sense of identity at this point in your life, the observations that follow are related to descriptions of identity and identity statuses offered earlier in this chapter.

Erikson stresses that a person's sense of identity is most profoundly influenced by occupational choice, sex roles, and self-esteem. Marcia's concept of identity statuses emphasizes the nature and degree of commitment made regarding attitudes toward a career, sexuality, religion, and values. Your first reaction to reading those words might have been, "Hey! That's great! All I have to do is choose a major, decide on a sex role, clarify a few values, and I'll have an identity." It's not that simple, of course, but you might find it helpful to analyze your thoughts and feelings in each of those areas.

Making an Academic or Occupational Choice

If you will examine Table 13–3 once again you will note that characteristics of individuals in the Identity Diffusion and Moratorium categories reflect lack of commitment to a college program. Foreclosure and Identity Achievement types, by contrast, *have* chosen a college major and, because they have a specific goal to shoot for, seem much more inclined to be motivated to study. One way to move toward a sense of identity, then, would be to make a firm (even if temporary) choice about occupational goals (if you have not already done so). In making such a choice you may find it reassuring to keep in mind that both Super and Ginzberg concluded that many individuals do not settle into an occupational groove until they are in their mid-twenties and that changes in occupation frequently occur after an initial choice has been made.

Decisions about sex roles or values are not as simple or straightforward as choice of a college major or selection of an occupation, but there are a number of things you might do to clarify your thinking about such issues.

Formulating an Individually Defined Sex Role

A number of psychologists (Douvan and Adelson, 1966; Broverman and associates, 1972; Bem, 1976; Spence and Helmreich, 1978) have developed various means for measuring masculinity and femininity. No attempt will be made here to reproduce a measure for masculinity or femininity, however, since it is not likely that you could derive a self-constructed score that would be valid or easily interpreted. Furthermore, such a score might cause you to focus on conflicting forms of behavior. Jeanne H. Block (1973) has proposed that the ultimate goal of sex-role development in contemporary America should be the achievement of an individually defined sex role that represents an interaction of masculine *and* feminine aspects of self. You might use that description as a general guide: develop your own conception of a personal sex role and feel free to select your own combination of "masculine" and "feminine" traits. As the sex-role descriptions offered by Douvan and Adelson and Dreyer indicate, the sky is the limit as far as possible combinations are concerned.

Clarifying Values

Attempting to commit yourself to a set of values is a more ambiguous and complex task than deciding on a personal sex role, but there are a number of techniques you might use as starting points. If, for example, you took the trouble to list the four terminal and instrumental values that you consider to be most important (Table 13–1) you might use them as a basis for a bit of self-analysis. Will you be able to satisfy the values you selected, for example, through the kind of job you currently favor? And even though values clarification techniques may have been oversold by enthusiasts, you may find that you will gain insight if you try out some of the strategies. You can do this on your own with many of the strategies. But if a strategy will only work by interaction between members of a group, you might invite friends to participate in values-clarification sessions. Two books you might consult for strategies to use are *Values Clarification* (1972) by Sidney B. Simon, Leland W. Howe, and Howard Kirschenbaum; and *Personalizing Education* (1975) by Leland W. Howe and Mary M. Howe.

If you follow some or all of these suggestions, perhaps you will experience the feeling that you have moved a bit closer to identity achievement. And if you do that, you will have successfully applied some of the things you have learned about human development to your own behavior.

Suggestions for Further Study

The Nature of Formal Thought

Analyses of formal thinking are presented in *Piaget's Theory of Intellectual Development: An Introduction* (2nd ed., 1979) by Herbert Ginsburg and Sylvia Opper; and in "Thinking Processes in Adolescence" by Daniel Keating in the *Handbook of Adolescent Psychology* (1980, pp. 211–246), edited by Joseph Adelson. A review of research on formal thinking is provided by E. D. Neimark in

"Intellectual Development During Adolescence," in *Review of Child Development Research* 1975, **4**, edited by F. D. Horowitz.

Political Thinking

"Political Thinking in Adolescence" is discussed by Judith Gallatin in Chapter 10 (pp. 344–382) of the *Handbook of Adolescent Psychology* (1980), edited by Joseph Adelson. A collection of articles on various aspects of political thinking is provided in the *Handbook of Political Socialization: Theory and Practice* (1977), edited by S. A. Renshon.

Moral Development

Perhaps the best brief discussion of moral development during adolescence is provided by Martin L. Hoffman in Chapter 9 (pp. 295–343) of the *Handbook of Adolescent Psychology* (1980), edited by Joseph Adelson. A collection of articles on moral development is presented in *Moral Development and Behavior: Theory, Research, and Social Issues* (1976), edited by Thomas Lickona.

Identity Statuses

James Marcia reviews research on identity statuses in Chapter 5 (pp. 159–187) of the *Handbook of Adolescent Psychology* (1980), edited by Joseph Adelson. Related research on ego development is summarized by Ruthellen Josselson in Chapter 6 (pp. 188–210) of the same volume.

Delinquency

An excellent brief account of delinquency is supplied by Martin Gold and Richard J. Petronio in Chapter 16 (pp. 495–535) of the *Handbook of Adolescent Psychology* (1980), edited by Joseph Adelson. More comprehensive discussions are presented in *Delinquent Behavior in an American City* (1970) by Martin Gold; and in *Explaining Delinquency* (1971) by L. T. Empey and S. G. Lubeck (with R. L. LaPorte).

Drugs

For more information about drugs, four excellent books to consult are *Drug Awareness* (1970), edited by Richard H. Horman and Allan M. Fox; *Drugs and Youth* (1970), edited by Robert Coles, Joseph H. Brenner, and Dermot Meagher; *Licit and Illicit Drugs* (1972) by Edward M. Brecher and the Editors of Consumer Reports; and *Drugs and American Youth* (1973) by L. D. Johnston.

Behavior Disorders

A brief description of "Psychopathology in Adolescence" is provided by Irving Weiner in Chapter 14 (pp. 447–471) of the *Handbook of Adolescent Psychology* (1980), edited by Joseph Adelson. More comprehensive analyses of severe behavior disorders during adolescence are supplied in *Psychiatric Disorders in Adolescents* (1974) by R. W. Hudgens; and *Current Issues in Adolescent Psychiatry* (1973), edited by J. C. Schooler.

Various interpretations of depression are offered in *Depression: Causes and Treatment* (1970) by A. T. Beck; *Helplessness: On Depression, Development, and Death* (1975) by Martin E. Seligman; and *The Nature and Treatment of Depression* (1975), edited by F. F. Flach and S. C. Draghi.

Suicide is analyzed in *The Gamble with Death* (1971) by Gene Lester and David Lester; *Adolescent Suicide* (1971) by J. Jacobs; and *Suicide* (1972) by Jacques Choron.

BIBLIOGRAPHY

Abramson, E. E. (Ed.). *Behavioral approaches to weight control.* New York: Springer, 1977.

Adelson, J. What generation gap? New York Times Magazine, January 18, 1970, 101–108.

Adelson, J. The political imagination of the young adolescent. In J. Kagan & R. Coles (Eds.), *Twelve to sixteen: Early adolescence.* New York: Norton, 1971.

Adelson, J. (Ed.). *Handbook of adolescent psychology.* New York: Wiley, 1980.

Adelson, J., & Doehrman, M. J. The psychodynamic approach to adolescence. In J. Adelson (Ed.), *Handbook of adolescent psychology.* New York: Wiley, 1980.

Ahlstrom, W. M., & Havighurst, R. G. *Four hundred losers.* San Francisco: Jossey-Bass, 1971.

Ainsworth, M. D. S. The effects of maternal deprivation: A review of findings and controversy in the context of research strategy. In *Public Health Papers,* 14. Geneva: World Health Organization, 1962.

Ainsworth, M. D. S. *Infancy in Uganda: Infant care and the growth of attachment.* Baltimore, Md.: The Johns Hopkins Press, 1967.

Ainsworth, M. D. S. Attachment and dependency: A comparison. In J. L. Gewirtz (Ed.), *Attachment and dependency.* Washington, D.C.: Winston, 1972.

Ainsworth, M. D. S. The development of infant-mother attachment. In B. M. Caldwell & H. N. Ricciuti (Eds.), *Review of child development research* (Vol. 3). Chicago: University of Chicago Press, 1974.

Ainsworth, M. D. S. Attachment as related to mother-infant interaction. In J. S. Rosenblatt, R. A. Hinde, C. Beer, & M. C. Busnel (Eds.), *Advances in the study of behavior* (Vol. 9). New York: Academic Press, 1979. (a)

Ainsworth, M. D. S. Attachment: Retrospect and prospect. Presidential address to the biennial meeting of the Society for Research in Child Development, San Francisco, March, 1979. (b)

Ainsworth, M. D. S., Blehar, M. C., Waters, E., & Wall, S. *Patterns of attachment: A psychological study of the strange situation.* Hillsdale, N.J.: Erlbaum, 1978.

Ainsworth, M. D. S., & Wittig, B. A. Attachment and exploratory behavior of one-year-olds in a strange situation. In B. M. Foss (Ed.), Determinants of infant behavior (Vol. 4). New York: Wiley, 1972.

Alcohol and health: New knowledge. Second special report to the U.S. Congress, National Institute on Alcohol Abuse and Alcoholism, Department of Health, Education, and Welfare. Washington, D.C.: U.S. Government Printing Office, 1974.

Aldrich, C. A., Sung, C., & Knop, C. The crying of newly born babies. II. The individual phase. *Journal of Pediatrics,* 1945, **26**. (a)

Aldrich, C. A., Norval, M. A., Knop, C., & Venegas, F. The crying of newly born babies. IV. A follow-up study after additional nursing care had been provided. *Journal of Pediatrics,* 1946, **27**, 89–96.

Aldrich, C. A., Sung, C., Knop, C., Stevens, G., & Burchell, M. The crying of newly born babies. I. The community phase. *Journal of Pediatrics,* 1945, **26**, 313–326. (b)

Altus, W. D. Birth order and its sequelae. *Science,* 1966, **151**, 44–49.

The American almanac for 1972. The statistical abstract of the United States. New York: Grosset and Dunlap, 1972.

Anastasi, A. *Psychological testing* (4th ed.). New York: Macmillan, 1976.

Andersen, C. M. *Classroom activities for modifying misbehavior in children.* Nyack, N.Y.: Center for Applied Research in Education, 1974.

Anderson, J. E. Methods of child psychology. In L. Carmichael (Ed.), *Manual of child psychology* (2nd ed.). New York: Wiley, 1954.

Annis, L. F. *The child before birth.* Ithaca, N.Y.: Cornell University Press, 1978.

Anthony, E. J. An experimental approach to the psychopathology of childhood: Encopresis. *British Journal of Medical Psychology,* 1957, **30**(3), 146–175.

Anthony, E. J. Psychoneurotic disorders. In A. M. Freedman & H. I. Kaplan (Eds.), *Comprehensive textbook of psychiatry.* Baltimore: Williams & Wilkins, 1967.

Anthony, E. J. Behavior disorders. In P. H. Mussen (Ed.), *Carmichael's manual of child psychology* (3rd ed., Vol. 2). New York: Wiley, 1970.

Apgar, V., Holoday, D. A., James, L. S., Weisbrot, I. M., & Berrien, C. Evaluation of the newborn infant: Second report. *Journal of the American Medical Association,* 1958, **168**, 1985–1988.

Ariès, P. *Centuries of childhood: A social history of family life.* (R. Baldick, Trans.) New York: Knopf, 1962.

Aristotle. *The basic works of Aristotle.* (R. McKeon, Ed.) New York: Random House, 1941.

Armentrout, J. A., & Burger, G. K. Children's reports of parental child-rearing behavior at five grade levels. *Developmental Psychology,* 1972, **7**, 44–48.

Asimov, I. *The genetic code.* New York: Signet, 1962.

Atkinson, J. W. *An introduction to motivation.* Princeton, N.J.: Van Nostrand, 1964.

Axline, V. *Dibs: In search of self.* New York: Ballantine Books, 1964.

Azrin, N. H., & Foxx, R. *Toilet training in less than a day.* New York: Pocket Books, 1976.

Azrin, N. H., & Nunn, R. G. *Habit control in a day.* New York: Simon & Schuster, 1977.

Bachman, J. G. *Youth in transition.* Vol. II. *The impact of family background and intelligence on tenth-grade boys.* Ann Arbor: Institute for Social Research, University of Michigan, 1970.

Bachman, J. G., & Johnston, L. D. The freshmen, 1979. *Psychology Today,* 1979, **13**(4), 78–87.

Bachman, J. G., O'Malley, P. M., & Johnston, J. *Youth in transition.* Vol. VI. *Adolescence to adulthood: Change and stability in the lives of young men.* Ann Arbor: Institute for Social Research, 1978.

Bakwin, H., & Bakwin, R. M. *Behavior disorders in children* (4th ed.). Philadelphia: Saunders, 1972.

Baldwin, A. L. *Theories of child development.* New York: Wiley, 1967.

Bandura, A. *Aggression: A social learning analysis.* Englewood Cliffs, N.J.: Prentice-Hall, 1973.

Bandura, A. Behavior theory and the models of man. *American Psychologist,* 1974, **29**, 859–869.

Bandura, A. *Social learning theory.* Englewood Cliffs, N.J.: Prentice-Hall, 1977.

Bandura, A., Grusec, J. E., & Menlove, F. L. Vicarious extinction and avoidance behavior. *Journal of Personality and Social Psychology,* 1967, **5**, 16–23.

Bandura, A., & Menlove, F. L. Factors determining vicarious extinction of avoidance behavior through symbolic modeling. *Journal of Personality and Social Psychology,* 1968, **8**, 99–108.

Bandura, A., Ross, D., & Ross, S. A. A comparative test of the status envy, social power, and secondary reinforcement theories of identificatory learning. *Journal of Abnormal & Social Psychology,* 1963, **67**, 527–534. (a)

Bandura, A., Ross, D., & Ross, S. A. Imitation of film mediated aggressive models. *Journal of Abnormal & Social Psychology,* 1963, **66**, 3–11. (b)

Bandura, A., Ross, D., & Ross, S. A. Vicarious reinforcement and imitative learning. *Journal of Abnormal & Social Psychology,* 1963, **67**, 601–607. (c)

Bandura, A., & Walters, R. H. *Social learning and personality development.* New York: Holt, Rinehart, & Winston, 1963.

Bardwick, J. M. *Psychology of women: A study of bio-cultural conflicts.* New York: Harper & Row, 1971.

Barnes, K. E. Preschool play norms: A replication. *Developmental Psychology,* 1971, **5**, 99–103.

Barrett, D. E. A naturalistic study of sex differences in children's aggression. *Merrill-Palmer Quarterly,* 1979, **25**, 193–203.

Baruch, D. W. *One little boy.* New York: Dell, 1952.

Baumrind, D. Child care practices anteceding three patterns of preschool behavior. *Genetic Psychology Monographs,* 1967, **75**, 43–88.

Baumrind, D. Current patterns of parental authority. *Developmental Psychology Monographs,* 1971, **1,** 1–103.

Baumrind, D. The development of instrumental competence through socialization. In A. Pick (Ed.), *Minnesota Symposia on Child Psychology* (Vol. 7). Minneapolis: University of Minnesota Press, 1973.

Bayley, N. The development of motor abilities during the first three years. *Monographs of the Society for Research in Child Development,* 1935, No. 1.

Bayley, N. *The California infant scale of motor development.* Berkeley: University of California, 1936.

Bayley, N. Consistency and variability in the growth of intelligence from birth to eighteen years. *Journal of Genetic Psychology,* 1949, **75,** 165–196.

Bayley, N. Some increasing parent-child similarities during the growth of children. *Journal of Educational Psychology,* 1954, **45,** 1–21.

Bayley, N. Comparisons of mental and motor test scores for ages 1–15 months by sex, birth order, race, geographical location, and education of parents. *Child Development,* 1965, **36,** 379–411.

Bayley, N. *Bayley scales of infant development.* New York: Psychological Corporation, 1969.

Bean, C. A. *Methods of childbirth.* Garden City, N.Y.: Doubleday, 1972.

Beck, A. T. *Depression: Causes and treatment.* Philadelphia: University of Pennsylvania Press, 1970.

Beck, P. A. The role of agents in political socialization. In S. A. Renshon (Ed.), *Handbook of political socialization: Theory and research.* New York: Free Press, 1977.

Becker, S. W., Lerner, M. J., & Carroll, J. Conformity as a function of birth order and type of group pressure: A verification. *Journal of Personality and Social Psychology,* 1966, **3,** 242–244.

Becker, W. C. Consequences of different kinds of parental discipline. In M. L. Hoffman & L. W. Hoffman (Eds.), *Review of child development research* (Vol. I). New York: Russell Sage Foundation, 1964.

Beckwith, L. Prediction of emotional and social behavior. In J. D. Osofsky (Ed.), *Handbook of infant development.* New York: Wiley, 1979.

Bee, H. (Ed.). Social issues in developmental psychology (2nd ed.). New York: Harper & Row, 1978.

Bell, R. Q., & Harper, L. V. (Eds.). *Child effects on adults.* Hillsdale, N.J.: Erlbaum, 1977.

Bell, R. Q., Weller, G. M., & Waldrop, M. F. Newborn and preschooler: Organization of behavior and relations between periods. *Monographs of the Society for Research in Child Development,* 1971, **36**(1–2), Serial No. 142.

Bell, S. The significance of activity in child life. *Independent,* 1903, **55,** 911–914.

Beller, E. K. Early intervention programs. In J. D. Osofsky (Ed.), *Handbook of infant development.* New York: Wiley, 1979.

Beloff, H. The structure and origin of the anal character. *Genetic Psychology Monographs,* 1962, **55,** 275–278.

Belsky, J., & Steinberg, L. D. The effects of day care: A critical review. *Child Development,* 1978, **49,** 929–949.

Bem, S. L. Sex-role adaptability: One consequence of psychological androgyny. *Journal of Personality and Social Psychology,* 1975, **31,** 634–643.

Bem, S. L. Sex-typing and androgyny: Further explorations of the expressive domain. *Journal of Personality and Social Psychology,* 1976, **34**(5), 1016–1023.

Bender, L. Schizophrenia in childhood: Its recognition, description, and treatment. *American Journal of Orthopsychiatry,* 1956, **26,** 499–506.

Berg, W. K., & Berg, K. M. Psychophysiological development in infancy: State, sensory function, and attention. In J. D. Osofsky (Ed.), *Handbook of infant development.* New York: Wiley, 1979.

Berger, E. M. Willingness to accept limitations and college achievement. *Journal of Counseling Psychology,* 1961, **8,** 140–144.

Bergner, S., & Susser, M. W. Low birthweight and parental nutrition: An interpretive review. *Pediatrics,* 1970, **46,** 946–966.

Berko, J. The child's learning of English morphology. *Word,* 1958, **14,** 150–177.

Berlyne, D. E. Curiosity and exploration. *Science,* 1966, **153,** 25–33.

Bernstein, E. What does a Summerhill old school tie look like? *Psychology Today*, 1968, **2**(5), 37–70.

Berscheid, E., & Walster, E. Beauty and the best. *Psychology Today*, 1972, **5**(10), 42–74.

Bettelheim, B. *The empty fortress.* New York: The Free Press, 1967.

Bettelheim, B. *A home for the heart.* New York: Knopf, 1974.

Biehler, R. F. Unpublished study. California State University, Chico, 1979.

Bijou, S. W., & Baer, D. M. The laboratory-experimental study of child behavior. In P. H. Mussen (Ed.), *Handbook of research methods in child development.* New York: Wiley, 1960.

Bijou, S. W., & Baer, D. M. *Child development* (Vol. 2). New York: Appleton-Century-Crofts, 1965.

Biller, H. B., & Davids, A. Parent-child relations, personality development, and psychopathology. In A. Davids (Ed.), *Abnormal child psychology.* Belmont, Calif.: Brooks-Cole, 1973.

Binet, A., & Simon, T. Méthodes nouvelles pour le diagnostic du niveau intellectuel des anormaux. *Année Psychologie*, 1905, **11**, 191–244.

Bing, E. Six practical lessons for an easier childbirth. New York: Grosset & Dunlap, 1967.

Birns, B. Individual differences in human neonates' responses to stimulation. *Child Development*, 1965, **36**, 249–256.

Birns, B., Blank, M., & Bridger, W. H. The effectiveness of various soothing techniques on human neonates. *Psychosomatic Medicine*, 1966, **28**, 316–322.

Bishop, B. M. Mother-child interaction and the social behavior of children. *Psychological Monographs*, 1951, **65**, 11 (Whole Number 328).

Blatt, M. Studies on the effects of classroom discussion upon children's moral development. *Journal of Moral Education*, 1975, **42**, 129–161.

Blatt, M., & Kohlberg, L. The effects of classroom moral discussion upon children's level of moral judgment. In L. Kohlberg & E. Turiel (Eds.), *Recent research in moral development.* New York: Holt, Rinehart & Winston, 1978.

Block, J. *Lives through time.* Berkeley, Calif.: Bancroft Books, 1971.

Block, J. H. Conceptions of sex role: Some cross-cultural and longitudinal perspectives. *American Psychologist*, 1973, **28**, 512–529.

Block, J. H. Issues, problems and pitfalls in assessing sex differences. *Merrill-Palmer Quarterly*, 1976, **22**, 283–308.

Block, J. H., & Block, J. The role of ego control and ego resiliency in the organization of behavior. In W. A. Collins (Ed.), *Minnesota Symposia on Child Psychology* (Vol. 11). Hillsdale, N.J.: Erlbaum, 1979.

Bloom, B. L., Asher, S. J., & White, S. W. Marital disruption as a stressor: A review and analysis. *Psychological Bulletin*, 1978, **85**, 867–894.

Bloom, B. S. *Stability and change in human characteristics.* New York: Wiley, 1964.

Bloom, B. S. Learning for mastery. *Evaluation Comment*, 1(2). Los Angeles: Center for the Study of Evaluation of Instructional Programs, University of California, 1968.

Bloom, L. *Language development: Form and function in emerging grammars.* Cambridge, Mass.: MIT Press, 1970.

Bloom, L. Language development review. In F. D. Horowitz (Ed.), *Review of child development research* (Vol. 4). Chicago: University of Chicago Press, 1975.

Bloom, L. (Ed.). *Readings in language development.* New York: Wiley, 1978.

Bloom, L., & Lahey, M. *Language development and language disorders.* New York: Wiley, 1978.

Bloom, L. P., & Hood, L. Structure and variation in child language. *Monographs of the Society for Research in Child Development*, 1975, **40** (2, Serial No. 160).

Blos, P. *On adolescence.* New York: Free Press, 1962.

Blos, P. *The adolescent passage.* New York: International Universities Press, 1979.

Boring, E. G. *A history of experimental psychology* (2nd ed.). New York: Appleton-Century-Crofts, 1950.

Bower, T. G. R. *The perceptual world of the child.* Cambridge, Mass.: Harvard University Press, 1977. (a)

Bower, T. G. R. *A primer of infant development.* San Francisco: Freeman, 1977. (b)

Bower, T. G. R., Broughton, J. M., & Moore, M. K. Infants' responses to approaching objects: An indicator of response to distal variables. *Perception and Psychophysics,* 1970, **9,** 193–196.

Bowerman, M. F. *Early syntactic development: A cross-linguistic study with special reference to Finnish.* London: Cambridge University Press, 1973.

Bowerman, M. F. Commentary. In M. D. S. Braine, Children's first word combinations. *Monographs of the Society for Research in Child Development,* 1976, **41** (1, Serial No. 164). (a)

Bowerman, M. F. Semantic factors in the acquisition of rules for word use and sentence construction. In D. M. Morehead & A. E. Morehead (Eds.), *Normal and deficient language.* Baltimore: University Park Press, 1976. (b)

Bowes, W. A., Jr., Brackbill, Y., Conway, E., & Steinschneider, A. The effects of obstetrical medication on fetus and infant. *Monographs of the Society for Research in Child Development,* 1970, **35**(4), 1–38.

Bowlby, J. *Maternal care and mental health.* Geneva: World Health Organization, Monograph No. 2, 1952.

Bowlby, J. A symposium on the contribution of current theories to an understanding of child development. I. An ethological approach to research in child development. *British Journal of Medical Psychology,* 1957, **30,** 230–240.

Bowlby, J. The nature of the child's tie to his mother. *International Journal of Psycho-Analysis,* 1958, **39,** 350–373.

Bowlby, J. *Attachment and loss.* Vol. I. *Attachment.* New York: Basic Books, 1969.

Bowlby, J. *Attachment and loss.* Vol. II. *Separation: Anxiety and anger.* New York: Basic Books, 1973.

Bowlby, J., Salter, M. D., Boston, M., & Rosenbluth, D. The effects of mother–child separation: A follow-up study. *British Journal of Medical Psychology,* 1956, **29,** 211–247.

Brackbill, Y. (Ed.). *Infancy and early childhood.* New York: Free Press, 1967.

Brackbill, Y. The role of the cortex in orienting: Orienting reflex in an anencephalic infant. *Developmental Psychology,* 1971, **5,** 195–201.

Brackbill, Y. Obstetrical medication and infant behavior. In Joy D. Osofsky (Ed.), *Handbook of infant development.* New York: Wiley, 1979.

Brackbill, Y., Adams, G., Crowell, D. H., & Gray, M. L. Arousal level in neonates and older infants under continuous auditory stimulation. *Journal of Experimental Child Psychology,* 1966, **4**(2), 178–188.

Brackbill, Y., & Thompson, G. G. (Eds.). *Behavior in infancy and early childhood.* New York: Free Press, 1967.

Braine, M. D. S. The ontogeny of English phrase structure: The first phase. *Language,* 1963, **39,** 1–13.

Braine, M. D. S. Children's first word combinations. *Monographs of the Society for Research in Child Development,* 1976, **41** (1, Serial No. 164).

Brandenburg, G. C., & Brandenburg, J. Language development during the fourth year: The conversation. *Pedagogical Seminary,* 1919, **26,** 27–40.

Braungart, R. G. Youth movements. In J. Adelson (Ed.), *Handbook of adolescent psychology.* New York: Wiley, 1980.

Brazelton, T. B. *Infants and mothers: Differences in development.* New York: Delacorte, 1969.

Brazelton, T. B. Effect of prenatal drugs on the behavior of the neonate. *American Journal of Psychiatry,* 1970, **126,** 1261–1266.

Brazelton, T. B. *Neonatal behavioral assessment scale.* (Clinics in Developmental Medicine, No. 50.) London: Heinemann Medical Publications, 1973.

Brecher, E. M. & the editors of *Consumer Reports. Licit and illicit drugs.* Boston: Little, Brown, 1973.

Breland, H. M. Birth order, family size, and intelligence. *Science,* 1974, **184,** 114.

Brill, A. A. (Ed. & Trans.). *The basic writings of Sigmund Freud.* New York: Random House, 1938.

Brittain, C. V. An exploration of the bases of peer-compliance and parent-compliance in adolescence. *Adolescence,* 1968, **2,** 445–458.

Brody, J. E. How doctors can assure more perfect babies. *Woman's Day,* February 1977, **65,** 150, 152, 154.

Brody, S., & Axelrad, S. *Anxiety and ego formation in infancy.* New York: International Universities Press, 1970.

Bronfenbrenner, U. *Two worlds of childhood.* New York: Russell Sage Foundation, 1970.

Brossard, M. The infant's conception of object permanence and his reactions to strangers. In T. G. Décarie (Ed.), *The infant's reaction to strangers.* New York: International Universities Press, 1974.

Broverman, I. K., Vogel, S. R., Broverman, D. M., Clarkson, F. E., & Rosenkrantz, P. S. Sex-role stereotypes: A current appraisal. *Journal of Social Issues,* 1972, **28**(2), 58–78.

Brown, R. *A first language: The early stages.* Cambridge, Mass.: Harvard University Press, 1973.

Brown, R., & Bellugi, U. Three processes in the child's acquisition of syntax. *Harvard Educational Review,* 1964, **34,** 133–151.

Bruner, J. S. *Toward a theory of instruction.* Cambridge, Mass.: Belknap Press of Harvard University Press, 1966.

Bruner, J. S. *Beyond the information given.* (J. M. Anglin, Ed.) New York: Norton, 1973.

Bruner, J. S., Jolly, A., & Sylva, K. (Eds.). *Play: Its role in development and evolution.* New York: Basic Books, 1976.

Bryan, J. H. Children's cooperation and helping behaviors. In. E. M. Hetherington (Ed.), *Review of child development research* (Vol. 5). Chicago: University of Chicago Press, 1975.

Bryant, R. D., & Danforth, D. N. The conduct of normal labor. The first and second stages. In D. N. Danforth (Ed.), *Textbook of obstetrics and gynecology.* New York: Hoeber, 1966.

Bugelski, B. R. *The psychology of learning applied to teaching* (2nd ed.). Indianapolis: Bobbs-Merrill, 1971.

Buss, A. H., & Plomin, R. *A temperament theory of personality.* New York: Wiley, 1975.

Byrne, D. A pregnant pause in the sexual revolution. *Psychology Today,* 1977, **11**(2), 67–68.

Caldwell, B. M., Wright, C. M., Honig, A. S., & Tannenbaum, J. Infant day care and attachment. *American Journal of Orthopsychiatry,* 1970, **40**(3), 397–412.

Campbell, J. D. Peer relations in childhood. In M. L. Hoffman & L. W. Hoffman (Eds.), *Review of child development research* (Vol. 1). New York: Russell Sage Foundation, 1964.

Campos, J. J., Haitt, S., Ramsay, D., Henderson, D., & Svejda, M. The emergence of fear on the visual cliff. In M. Lewis & L. A. Rosenblum (Eds.), *The development of affect.* New York: Plenum, 1978.

Carey, S. The child as word learner. In M. Halle, J. Bresnan, & G. A. Miller (Eds.), *Linguistic theory and psychological reality.* Cambridge, Mass.: MIT Press, 1977.

Carmichael, L. (Ed.). *Manual of child psychology.* New York: Wiley, 1946.

Carmichael, L. (Ed.). *Manual of child psychology* (2nd ed.). New York: Wiley, 1954.

Carns, D. E. Talking about sex: Notes on first coitus and the double standard. *Journal of Marriage and the Family,* 1973, **35,** 677–688.

Carpenter, F. *The Skinner primer.* New York: Free Press, 1974.

Carpenter, G. Mother's face and the newborn. In R. Lewin (Ed.), *Child Alive.* London: Temple Smith, 1975.

Carter, C. O., Homerton, J. L., Polani, P. E., Gunlap, A., & Weller, S. D. V. Chromosome translocation as a cause of familial mongolism. *Lancet,* 1960, **2,** 678–680.

Casler, L. Maternal deprivation: A critical review of the literature. *Monographs of the Society for Research in Child Development,* 1961, **26**(2).

Cazden, C. The acquisition of noun and verb inflections. *Child Development,* 1968, **39,** 433–438.

Chabon, I. *Awake and aware: Participating in childbirth through prophylaxis.* New York: Delacorte, 1966.

Chaffee, S. H., Jackson-Beeck, M., Durall, J., & Wilson, D. Mass communication in political socialization. In S. A. Renshon (Ed.), *Handbook of political socialization: Theory and research.* New York: Free Press, 1977.

Chomsky, N. *Aspects of the theory of syntax.* Cambridge, Mass.: MIT Press, 1965.

Chomsky, N. *Language and the mind.* New York: Harcourt, Brace, Jovanovich, 1968.

Choron, J. *Suicide.* New York: Scribners, 1972.

Clark, E. V. What's in a word? On the child's acquisition of semantics in his first language. In T. E. Moore (Ed.), *Cognitive development and the acquisition of language.* New York: Academic Press, 1973.

Clark, H. H., & Clark, E. V. *Psychology and language.* New York: Harcourt, Brace, Jovanovich, 1977.

Clarke, A. M., & Clarke, A. D. B. (Eds.). *Early experience: Myth and evidence.* London: Open Books, 1976.

Clarke-Stewart, K. A. Popular primers for parents. *American Psychologist,* 1978, **33**(4), 359–369.

Clausen, J. The social meaning of differential physical and sexual maturation. In S. Dragastin & G. H. Elder, Jr. (Eds.), *Adolescence in the life cycle.* New York: Wiley, 1975.

Cohen, J. H., & Filipczak, J. *A new learning environment.* New York: Jossey-Bass, 1971.

Cohen, L. B., De Loache, J. S., & Strauss, M. S. Infant visual perception. In J. D. Osofsky (Ed.), *Handbook of infant development.* New York: Wiley, 1979.

Cohen, L. B., & Salapatek, P. (Eds.). *Infant perception: From sensation to cognition.* Vol. I. *Basic visual processes.* New York: Academic Press, 1975. (a)

Cohen, L. B., & Salapatek, P. (Eds.). *Infant perception: From sensation to cognition.* Vol. II. *Perception of space, speech, and sound.* New York: Academic Press, 1975. (b)

Cohen, S. E. Maternal employment and mother-child interaction. *Merrill-Palmer Quarterly,* 1978, **24,** 189–197.

Coleman, J. C. Friendship and the peer group in adolescence. In J. Adelson (Ed.), *Handbook of adolescent psychology.* New York: Wiley, 1980.

Coleman, J. S. *The adolescent society.* New York: Free Press, 1961.

Coles, R. *Erik H. Erikson: The growth of his work.* Boston: Little, Brown, 1970.

Coles, R., Brenner, J. H., & Meagher, D. *Drugs and youth.* New York: Liveright, 1970.

Committee on Maternal Nutrition, National Research Council. *Maternal nutrition and the course of pregnancy.* Washington, D.C.: National Academy of Sciences, 1970.

Comstock, G. A., & Rubinstein, E. A. (Eds.). *Television and social behavior.* Vol. I. *Media content and control.* Washington, D.C.: U.S. Government Printing Office, 1972. (a)

Comstock, G. A., & Rubinstein, E. A. (Eds.). *Television and social behavior.* Vol. III. *Television and adolescent aggressiveness.* Washington, D.C.: U.S. Government Printing Office, 1972. (b)

Comstock, G. A., Rubinstein, E. A., & Murray, J. P. (Eds.). *Television and social behavior.* Vol. V. *Television's effects: Further explorations.* Washington, D.C.: U.S. Government Printing Office, 1972.

Condon, W. S., & Sander, L. Neonate movement is synchronized with adult speech: Interactional participation and language acquisition. *Science,* 1974, **183,** 99–101.

Conger, J. J., & Miller, W. C. *Personality, social class and delinquency.* New York: Wiley, 1966.

Connell, R. W. Political socialization in the American family: The evidence re-examined. *Public Opinion Quarterly,* Fall 1972, **36,** 323–333.

Consortium on Developmental Continuity, Education Commission of the States. *The persistence of preschool effects.* Washington, D.C.: U.S. Department of Health, Education, and Welfare, 1977.

Coopersmith, S., Regan, M., & Dick, L. *The myth of the generation gap.* San Francisco: Albion, 1975.

Cox, Harvey. *Turning east.* New York: Simon & Schuster, 1977.

Crandall, V. J., Orleans, S., Preston, A., & Rabson, A. The development of social compliance in young children. *Child Development,* 1958, **29,** 429–443.

Cravioto, J., DeLicardie, E. R., & Birch, H. G. Nutrition, growth, and neuro-integrative development: An experimental and ecologic study. *Pediatrics,* 1966, **38** (1, Pt. 2, Supplement), 319–372.

Cronbach, L. J. *Essentials of psychological testing* (3rd ed.). New York: Harper & Row, 1970.

Crowell, D. H. Infant motor development. In Y. Brackbill (Ed.), *Infancy and early childhood.* New York: Free Press, 1967.

Daly, C. J., Heady, A., & Morris, J. N. Social and biological factors in infant mortality. III. The effect of mother's age and parity on social class differences in infant mortality. *Lancet,* 1955, **1,** 499–502.

Danforth, D. N. (Ed.). *Textbook of obstetrics and gynecology.* New York: Hoeber, 1966.

Darwin, C. *The origin of species.* London: Murray, 1859.

Darwin, C. *The expression of emotions in man and animals.* London: Murray, 1872.

Darwin, C. A biographical sketch of an infant. *Mind,* 1877, **2,** 285–294.

Davidson, S. School phobia as a manifestation of family disturbance: Its structure and treatment. *Journal of Child Psychology and Psychiatry,* 1961, **1,** 270–287.

DeCosta, E. J. Cesarean section and other obstetric operations. In D. N. Danforth (Ed.), *Textbook of obstetrics and gynecology.* New York: Hoeber, 1966.

de Mause, L. (Ed.). *The history of childhood.* New York: Psychohistory Press, 1974.

de Mille, Richard. *Put your mother on the ceiling.* New York: Walker, 1967.

Dennis, W. Historical beginnings of child psychology. *Psychological Bulletin,* 1940, **46,** 224–235.

Dennis, W. (Ed.). *Readings in child psychology.* New York: Prentice-Hall, 1951.

Dennis, W. (Ed.). *Historical readings in developmental psychology.* New York: Appleton-Century-Crofts, 1972.

Dennis, W. *Children of the Crèche.* Englewood Cliffs, N.J.: Prentice-Hall, 1973.

Dennis, W., & Dennis, M. G. Cradles and cradling customs of the Pueblo Indians. *American Anthropology,* 1940, **42,** 107–115.

Dennis, W., & Dennis, M. G. Infant development under conditions of restricted practice and minimum social stimulation. *Genetic Psychology Monographs,* 1941, **23**(147), 149–155.

Dennis, W., & Dennis, M. G. Development under controlled conditions. In W. Dennis (Ed.), *Readings in child psychology.* New York: Prentice-Hall, 1951.

Despert, L. Urinary control and enuresis. *Psychosomatic Medicine,* 1944, **6,** 294–307.

de Tocqueville, A. *Democracy in America.* 1835. (Rev. ed., trans. Henry Reeve.) New York: Colonial Press, 1900.

Deutsch, M. Facilitating development in the pre-school child: Social and psychological perspectives. *Merrill-Palmer Quarterly of Behavior and Development,* 1964, **10,** 277–296.

de Villiers, P., & de Villiers, J. *Early language.* Cambridge, Mass.: Harvard University Press, 1979.

Diament, L. Premarital sexual behavior, attitudes, and emotional adjustment. *Journal of Social Psychology,* 1970, **82,** 75–80.

Dick-Read, G. *Childbirth without fear: The principles and practice of natural childbirth* (Rev. ed.). New York: Harper, 1959.

Dollard, J., Doob, L. W., Miller, N. E., Mowrer, O. H., & Sears, R. R. *Frustration and aggression.* New Haven, Conn.: Yale University Press, 1939.

Doman, G. *How to teach your baby to read.* New York: Random House, 1964.

Donaldson, M. *Children's minds.* New York: Norton, 1979.

Donaldson, M., & McGarrigle, J. Some clues to the nature of semantic development. *Journal of Child Language,* 1974, **1,** 185–194.

Donaldson, M., & Wales, R. On the acquisition of some relational terms. In J. R. Hayes (Ed.), *Cognition and the development of language.* New York: Wiley, 1970.

Douvan, E. Sex differences in the opportunities, demands, and development of youth. In R. J. Havighurst & P. H. Dreyer (Eds.), *Youth.* (74th Yearbook of the National Society for the Study of Education.) Chicago: University of Chicago Press, 1975.

Douvan, E., & Adelson, J. *The adolescent experience.* New York: Wiley, 1966.

Dreyer, P. H. Sex, sex roles, and marriage among youth in the 1970s. In R. J. Havighurst & P. H. Dreyer (Eds.), *Youth.* (74th Yearbook of the National Society for the Study of Education.) Chicago: University of Chicago Press, 1975.

Dubnoff, S. J., Yeroff, J., & Kulka, R. A. *Adjustment to work.* Paper presented at the meeting of the

American Psychological Association, Toronto, August 1978.

Du Pont, R. L. *Marihuana and health: Fifth annual report to the U.S. Congress.* Rockville, Md.: National Institute on Drug Abuse, 1975.

Ebbs, J. H., Brown, A., Tisdale, F. F., Moyle, W. J., & Bell, M. The influence of improved prenatal nutrition upon the infant. *Canadian Medical Association Journal,* 1942, **126**, 6–8.

Education Commission of the States. *National assessment of educational progress: Political knowledge and attitudes.* Washington, D.C.: U.S. Government Printing Office, 1973.

Eichorn, D. Physiological development. In P. H. Mussen (Ed.), *Carmichael's manual of child psychology* (3rd ed. Vol. 1). New York: Wiley, 1970.

Eimas, P. D. Speech perception in early infancy. In L. B. Cohen & P. Salapatek (Eds.), *Infant perception: From sensation to cognition.* Vol. II. *Perception of space, speech, and sound.* New York: Academic Press, 1975.

Eimas, P. D., Siqueland, E. R., Jusczyk, P., & Vigorito, J. Speech perception in infants. *Science,* 1971, **171**, 305–306.

Eisenberg, L. School phobia: A study in the communication of anxiety. *American Journal of Psychiatry,* 1958, **114**, 712–718.

Elder, G. H., Jr. Structural variations in the child rearing relationship. *Sociometry,* 1962, **25**, 241–262.

Elder, G. H., Jr. Adolescence in historical perspective. In J. Adelson (Ed.), *Handbook of adolescent psychology.* New York: Wiley, 1980.

Elkind, D. Cognitive development in adolescence. In J. F. Adams (Ed.), *Understanding adolescence.* Boston: Allyn & Bacon, 1968.

Elkind, D. *Children and adolescents: Interpretive essays on Jean Piaget.* New York: Oxford University Press, 1970 (a); 2nd ed., 1974.

Elkind, D. Erik Erikson's eight ages of man. *New York Times Magazine,* April 5, 1970, 25–76. (b)

Elkind, D. Giant in the nursery—Jean Piaget. *New York Times Magazine,* May 26, 1968, 25–80. (Reprinted in D. Elkind, *Children and adolescents: Interpretive essays on Jean Piaget.* New York: Oxford University Press, 1970; 2nd ed., 1974.)

Elman, J., & Manosevitz, M. Sex typing in nursery school children's play interests. *Developmental Psychology,* 1972, **7**, 146–152.

Empey, L. T., & Lubeck, S. G. (with La Porte, R. L.). *Explaining delinquency.* Lexington, Mass.: Heath, 1971.

Endler, H. S., Rushton, J. P., & Roediger, H. L. III. Productivity and scholarly impact (citations) of British, Canadian, and U.S. departments of psychology (1975). *American Psychologist,* 1978, **33**, 1064–1082.

Engelmann, S. *Preventing failure in the elemenatry grades.* Chicago: Science Research Associates, 1969.

Engelmann, S., & Engelmann, T. *Give your child a superior mind.* New York: Simon & Schuster, 1968.

Erikson, E. H. Sex differences in the play configurations of preadolescents. *American Journal of Orthopsychiatry,* 1951, **21**, 667–692.

Erikson, E. H. *Childhood and society* (2nd ed.). New York: Norton, 1963.

Erikson, E. H. *Identity: Youth and crisis.* New York: Norton, 1968.

Etzel, B. C., & Gewirtz, J. L. Experimental modification of caretaker-maintained high rate operant crying in 6- and 20-week old infants. Extinction of crying with reinforcement of eye contact and smiling. *Journal of Experimental Child Psychology,* 1967, **5**, 303–317.

Etzioni, A. Doctors know more than they're telling you about genetic defects. *Psychology Today,* 1973, **7**(6), 26–137.

Evans, R. I. *Dialogue with Erik Erikson.* New York: Harper & Row, 1967.

Facts of life and death. U.S. Department of Health, Education, and Welfare. Rockville, Maryland: National Center for Health Statistics, 1974.

Fagot, B. I. The influence of sex of child on parental reactions to toddler children. *Child Development,* 1978, **49**, 459–465.

Falkner, F., Pernot-Roy, M. P., Habich, H., Sénécal, J., & Massé, G. Some international comparisons of physical growth in the first two years of life. *Courier,* 1958, **8**, 1–11.

Fantz, R. L. Pattern vision in young infants. *The Psychological Record,* 1958, **8**, 43–47.

Fantz, R. L. The origin of form perception. *Scientific American,* 1961, **204**(5), 66–72.

Fantz, R. L. Pattern vision in newborn infants. *Science,* 1963, **140**, 296–297.

Fantz, R. L., Fagan, J. F., & Miranda, S. B. Early visual selectivity as a function of pattern variables, previous exposure, age from birth and conception, and expected cognitive deficit. In L. B. Cohen & P. Salapatek (Eds.), *Infant perception: From sensation to cognition.* Vol. I. *Basic visual processes.* New York: Academic Press, 1975.

Fantz, R. L., & Miranda, S. B. Newborn infant attention to form of contour. *Child Development,* 1975, **46**, 224–228.

Feather, N. T. Factor structure of the Bem sex-role inventory: Implications for the study of masculinity, femininity, and androgyny. *Australian Journal of Psychology,* 1978, **30**, 241–254.

Feather, N. T. Values in adolescence. In J. Adelson (Ed.), *Handbook of adolescent psychology.* New York: Wiley, 1980.

Federal Bureau of Investigation, U.S. Department of Justice. *Uniform crime reports, 1960–1970.* Washington, D.C.: U.S. Government Printing Office, 1972.

Fein, Grace, & Robertson, A. *Cognitive and social dimensions of pretending in two-year-olds.* Children's Bureau Report No. OCD-CB-98. Washington, D.C.: U.S. Government Printing Office, 1976.

Fenichel, O. *Psychoanalytic theory of neurosis.* New York: Norton, 1945.

Feshbach, S. Aggression. In P. H. Mussen (Ed.), *Carmichael's manual of child psychology* (3rd ed., Vol. 2). New York: Wiley, 1970.

Fetters, W. B. *National longitudinal study of the high school class of 1972.* Washington, D.C.: National Center for Health Statistics, Department of Health, Education, and Welfare, Bulletin Numbers 197, 208, 1976.

Fitzgerald, H. E., & Brackbill, Y. Classical conditioning in infancy: Development and constraints. *Psychological Bulletin,* 1976, **83**(3), 353–376.

Flach, F. F., & Draghi, S. C. (Eds.). *The nature and treatment of depression.* New York: Wiley, 1975.

Flanagan, J. C. Some pertinent findings of Project TALENT. *Vocational Guidance Quarterly,* 1973, **22**, 92–96.

Flavell, J. H. *The developmental psychology of Jean Piaget.* Princeton: Van Nostrand, 1963.

Flavell, J. H. *Cognitive development.* Englewood Cliffs, N.J.: Prentice-Hall, 1977.

Fraiberg, S. *The magic years.* New York: Scribners, 1959.

Frazier, T. M., Davis, G. H., Goldstein, H., & Goldberg, I. D. Cigarette smoking and prematurity: A prospective study. *American Journal of Obstetrics & Gynecology,* 1961, **81**, 988–996.

Freda, V. J., Pollack, J. G., & Pollack, W. Rh factor: Prevention of isoimmunization and clinical trial on mothers. *Science,* 1966, **151**, 828–829.

Freedman, D. C. The development of social hierarchies. Paper presented at meeting of World Health Organization, Stockholm, June 28-July 3, 1971.

Freud, A. *Infants without families.* New York: International Universities Press, 1944.

Freud, A. *The psychoanalytic treatment of children.* New York: International Universities Press, 1946.

Freud, A. *Normality and pathology in children: The writings of Anna Freud.* New York: International Universities Press, 1965.

Freud, A., & Burlingham, D. *War and children.* New York: Medical War Books, 1943.

Freud, A., & Dann, S. An experiment in group upbringing. *Psychoanalytic Study of the Child,* 1951, **6**, 127–168.

Freud, S. *An autobiographical study.* New York: Norton, 1935.

Freud, S. *The problem of anxiety.* New York: Norton, 1936.

Freud, S. *An outline of psycho-analysis.* New York: Norton, 1949.

Freyberg, J. T. Increasing the imaginative play of urban disadvantaged kindergarten children through systematic training. In J. L. Singer (Ed.), *The child's world of make believe: Experimental studies of imaginative play.* New York: Academic Press, 1973.

Friedmann, T. Prenatal diagnosis of genetic diseases. *Scientific American,* 1971, **225**(5), 34–51.

Fullard, W., & Rieling, A. M. An investigation of Lorenz's "Babyness." *Child Development,* 1976, **47**, 1191–1193.

Furth, H. *Piaget for teachers.* Englewood Cliffs, N.J.: Prentice-Hall, 1970.

Galbraith, R. E., & Jones, T. M. *Moral reasoning.* Minneapolis: Greenhaven Press, 1976.

Gallatin, J. Political thinking in adolescence. In J. Adelson (Ed.), *Handbook of adolescent psychology.* New York: Wiley, 1980.

Galton, F. *Hereditary genius.* London: Macmillan, 1869.

Galton, F. Statement made in footnote to an article by J. M. Cattell, Mental tests and measurements. *Mind,* 1890, **15**, 373.

Garai, J. E., & Scheinfeld, A. Sex differences in mental and behavioral traits. *Genetic Psychology Monographs,* 1968, **77**, 169–299.

Gardner, L. I. Deprivation dwarfism. *Scientific American,* 1972, **227**, 76–82.

Garfield, S. L., & Bergin, A. E. (Eds.). *Handbook of psychotherapy and behavior change* (2nd ed.). New York: Wiley, 1978.

Garner, A. M., & Wenar, C. *The mother-child interaction in psychosomatic disorders.* Urbana, Ill.: University of Illinois Press, 1959.

Garvey, C., & Hogan, R. Social speech and social interaction: Egocentrism revisited. *Child Development,* 1973, **44**, 562–568.

Garvey, K. *Play.* Cambridge, Mass.: Harvard University Press, 1977.

Geber, M., & Dean, R. F. A. The state of development of newborn African children. *Lancet,* 1957, **272**, 1216–1219.

Geis, G., & Monahan, J. The social ecology of violence. In T. Lickona (Ed.), *Man and morality.* New York: Holt, Rinehart and Winston, 1975.

Gelles, R. J. Child abuse as psychopathology: A sociological critique and reformulation. *American Journal of Orthopsychiatry,* 1973, **43**, 611–621.

Gelman, R. Conservation acquisition: A problem of learning to attend to relevant attributes. *Journal of Experimental Child Psychology,* 1969, **7**, 167–187.

Gelman, R. Preschool thought. *American Psychologist,* 1979, **34**(10), 900–905.

Gerbner, G. The violence profile: Some indicators of the trend in and the symbolic structure of network television drama, 1967–1970. Unpublished manuscript, Annenberg School of Communications, University of Pennsylvania, 1972.

German, J. Studying human chromosomes today. *American Scientist,* 1970, **58**, 182–201.

Gesell, A. L. *Infancy and human growth.* New York: Macmillan, 1928.

Gesell, A. L. Early evidences of individuality in the human infant. *Scientific Monthly,* 1937, **45**, 217–225.

Gesell, A. L. The ontogenesis of infant behavior. In L. Carmichael (Ed.), *Manual of child psychology* (2nd ed.). New York: Wiley, 1954.

Gesell, A. L., & Thompson, H. Learning and growth in identical infant twins: An experimental study by the method of co-twin control. *Genetic Psychology Monographs,* 1929, **6**, 1–124.

Gewirtz, J. L. A learning analysis of the effects of normal stimulation, privation and deprivation on the acquisition of social motivation and attachment. In B. M. Foss (Ed.), *Determinants of Infant Behavior.* New York: Wiley, 1961.

Gewirtz, J. L. (Ed.). *Attachment and dependency.* Washington, D.C.: Winston, 1972.

Gibson, E. J., & Walk, R. R. The "visual cliff." *Scientific American,* 1961, **202**, 2–9.

Ginott, H. *Between parent and child.* New York: Macmillan, 1965.

Ginott, H. *Between parent and teenager.* New York: Macmillan, 1969.

Ginott, H. *Teacher and child.* New York: Macmillan, 1971.

Ginsburg, H., & Opper, S. *Piaget's theory of intellectual development* (2nd ed.). Englewood Cliffs, N.J.: Prentice-Hall, 1979.

Ginzberg, E. Toward a theory of occupational choice: A

restatement. *Vocational Guidance Quarterly,* 1972, **20**, 169–176.

Glass, R. H., & Kase, N. G. *Woman's choice: A guide to contraception, fertility, abortion, and menopause.* New York: Basic Books, 1970.

Glick, P. G., & Norton, A. J. Marrying, divorcing, and living together in the U.S. today. *Population Bulletin,* 1978, **32**, 3–38.

Goble, F. *The third force: The psychology of Abraham Maslow.* New York: Grossman, 1970.

Goertzel, M., Goertzel, V., & Goertzel, T. *Three hundred eminent personalities.* San Francisco: Jossey-Bass, 1978.

Goertzel, V., & Goertzel, M. *Cradles of eminence.* Boston: Little, Brown, 1962.

Gold, D., & Andres, D. Developmental comparisons between 10-year-old children with employed and non-employed mothers. *Child Development,* 1978, **49**, 75–84.

Gold, M. *Delinquent behavior in an American city.* Monterey, Calif.: Brooks/Cole, 1970.

Gold, M., & Petronio, R. J. Delinquent behavior in adolescence. In J. Adelson (Ed.), *Handbook of adolescent psychology.* New York: Wiley, 1980.

Goldfarb, W. Childhood psychosis. In P. H. Mussen (Ed.), *Carmichael's manual of child psychology* (3rd ed., Vol. 2). New York: Wiley, 1970.

Goodenough, F. A critique of experiments on raising the IQ. *Educational Method,* 1939, **19**, 73–79.

Goodrich, F. W., Jr. *Preparing for childbirth: A manual for expectant parents.* Englewood Cliffs, N.J.: Prentice-Hall, 1969.

Gordon, I. J. Early childhood stimulation through parent education. Final report to the Children's Bureau, Social and Rehabilitation Service, Department of Health, Education, and Welfare, Gainsville, Fla., University of Florida, Institute for Development of Human Resources, 1969.

Gordon, I. J., & Guinagh, B. J. A home learning center approach to early stimulation. Final report to the National Institute of Mental Health. Gainesville, Fla.: Institute for Development of Human Resources, University of Florida, 1974.

Gordon, T. P.E.T.: Parent effectiveness training. New York: Wyden, 1970.

Gottesman, I. I., & Shields, J. Contributions of twin studies to perspectives on schizophrenia. In B. A. Maher (Ed.), *Progress in experimental personality research* (Vol. 3). New York: Academic Press, 1966.

Gottesman, I. I., & Shields, J. *Schizophrenia and genetics.* New York: Academic Press, 1972.

Gourlay, N. Heredity vs. environment: An integrative review. *Psychological Bulletin,* 1979, **86**, 596–615.

Gray, S. W., & Klaus, R. E. The early training project: A seven year report. *Child Development,* 1970, **41**, 909–924.

Green, H. [Joanne Greenberg]. *I never promised you a rose garden.* New York: Holt, Rinehart & Winston, 1964.

Greulich, W. W. A comparison of the physical growth and development of American-born and native Japanese children. *American Journal of Physical Anthropology,* 1957, **15**, 489–516.

Griffore, R. J. The validity of popular primers for parents. *American Psychologist,* 1979, **34**(2), 182–183.

Gronlund, N. E. *Sociometry in the classroom.* New York: Harper, 1959.

Gruber, H. E., & Vonèche, J. J. (Eds.). *The essential Piaget: An interpretive reference and guide.* New York: Basic Books, 1977.

Guilford, J. P. *The nature of human intelligence.* New York: McGraw-Hill, 1967.

Guttmacher, A. F. *Birth control and love.* New York: Macmillan, 1969.

Guttmacher, A. F. *Pregnancy, birth, and family planning: A guide for expectant parents in the 1970s.* New York: Viking Press, 1973.

Hafez, E. S. E., & Evans, T. N. (Eds.). *Human reproduction: Conception and contraception.* New York: Harper & Row, 1973.

Hall, G. S. The contents of children's minds. *Pedagogical Seminary,* 1891, **1**, 139–173.

Hall, G. S. Adolescence: Its psychology and its relations to physiology, anthropology, sociology, sex, crime, religion, and education. (2 vols.) New York: Appleton, 1904.

Hall, M. C., et al. *Responsive parent program.* Lawrence, Kansas.: H & H Enterprises, 1977.

Hall, R. V. *Managing behavior: Applications in home and school.* Lawrence, Kansas: H & H Enterprises, 1974.

Halliday, M. A. K. *Learning how to mean: Explorations in the development of language.* London: Arnold, 1975.

Halverson, H. M. An experimental study of prehension in infants by means of systematic cinema records. *Genetic Psychology Monographs,* 1931, **10**.

Hamerton, J. L., et al. Chromosome studies in detection of parents with high risk of second child with Down's syndrome. *Lancet,* 1961, **2**, 788–791.

Hanson, J. W. Unpublished paper, 1977.

Hanson, J. W., Jones, K. L., & Smith, D. W. Fetal alcohol syndrome: Experience with 41 patients. *Journal of the American Medical Association,* 1976, **235**, 1458–1460.

Hardin, G. J. *Birth control.* New York: Pegasus, 1970.

Harlow, H. F. Motivation as a factor in the acquisition of new responses. In *Current theory and research in motivation: A symposium.* Lincoln, Nebr.: University of Nebraska Press, 1953.

Harlow, H. F. The nature of love. *American Psychologist,* 1958, **13**, 673–685.

Harlow, H. F. The heterosexual affectional system in monkeys. *American Psychologist,* 1962, **17**, 1–9.

Harlow, H. F. Early social deprivation and later behavior in the monkey. In A. Abrams, H. H. Garner, & J. E. P. Toman (Eds.), *Unfinished tasks in the behavioral sciences.* Baltimore: Williams & Wilkins, 1964.

Harlow, H. F. Total social isolation: Effects on Macaque monkey behavior. *Science,* 1965, **148**, 666.

Harlow, H. F. *Learning to love.* New York: Ballantine Books, 1971.

Harlow, H. F. Interview with Carol Tavris. *Psychology Today,* 1973, **6**, 64–77.

Harlow, H. F., & Harlow, M. K. Effects of various mother-infant relationships on rhesus monkey behaviors. In B. M. Foss (Ed.), *Determinants of infant behavior* (Vol. 4). New York: Barnes & Noble, 1969.

Harlow, H. F., & Mears, C. *The human model: Primate perspectives.* Washington, D.C.: Winston, 1979.

Harmon, L. W. The childhood and adolescent career plans of college women. *Journal of Vocational Behavior,* 1971, **1**, 45–56.

Harrington, M. *The other America.* Baltimore: Penguin Books, 1965.

Hartshorne, H., & May, M. A. *Studies in service and self-control.* New York: Macmillan, 1929.

Hartshorne, H., & May, M. A. *Studies in deceit.* New York: Macmillan, 1930. (a)

Hartshorne, H., & May, M. A. *Studies in the organization of character.* New York: Macmillan, 1930. (b)

Hartup, W. W. Peer interaction and social organization. In P. H. Mussen (Ed.), *Carmichael's manual of child psychology* (3rd ed., Vol. 2). New York: Wiley, 1970.

Hartup, W. W. Aggression in childhood: Developmental perspectives. *American Psychologist,* 1974, **29**, 336–341.

Hartup, W. W., & Coates, B. Imitation of a peer as a function of reinforcement from the peer group and rewardingness of the model. *Child Development,* 1967, **38**, 1003–1016.

Havighurst, R. *Developmental tasks and education.* New York: Longmans, Green, 1952.

Heinstein, M. C. Behavioral correlates of breast-bottle regimes under varying parent-child relationships. *Monographs of the Society for Research in Child Development,* 1963, **28** (4, Whole No. 88).

Helfer, R. E., & Kempe, C. H. (Eds.). *The battered child* (2nd ed.). Chicago: University of Chicago Press, 1974.

Henry, W. E. Projective techniques. In P. H. Mussen (Ed.), *Handbook of research methods in child development.* New York: Wiley, 1960.

Herron, R. E., & Sutton-Smith, B. *Child's play.* New York: Wiley, 1971.

Hersh, R. H., Paolitto, D. P., & Reimer, J. *Promoting moral growth: From Piaget to Kohlberg.* New York: Longman, 1979.

Herzog, E., & Sudia, C. E. Children in fatherless families. In B. M. Caldwell & H. M. Ricciuti (Eds.),

Review of child development research (Vol. 3). Chicago: University of Chicago Press, 1973.

Hess, E. H. Imprinting in birds. *Science,* 1964, **146**, 1129–1139.

Hess, E. H. Ethology and developmental psychology. In P. H. Mussen (Ed.), *Carmichael's manual of child psychology* (3rd ed., Vol. 1). New York: Wiley, 1970.

Hess, R. D. Social class and ethnic influences upon socialization. In P. H. Mussen (Ed.), *Carmichael's manual of child psychology* (3rd ed., Vol. 2). New York: Wiley, 1970.

Hess, R. D., & Shipman, V. Early experience and the socialization of cognitive modes in children. *Child Development,* 1965, **36**, 869–886.

Hetherington, E. M. Effects of father absence on personality development in adolescent daughters. *Developmental Psychology,* 1972, **7**, 327–336.

Hetherington, E. M. Divorce: A child's perspective. *American Psychologist,* 1979, **34**(10), 851–858.

Hetherington, E. M., Cox, M., & Cox, R. The development of children in mother headed families. Paper presented at the Families in Contemporary America Conference, George Washington University, June 1977.

Hetherington, E. M., & Deur, J. C. The effects of father absence on child development. In W. W. Hartup (Ed.), *The young child: Reviews of research* (Vol. 2). Washington, D.C.: National Association for the Education of Young Children, 1972.

Hilgard, J. R. Learning and maturation in school children. *Journal of Genetic Psychology,* 1932, **41**, 40–53.

Hill, W. F. *Learning: A survey of psychological interpretations* (3rd ed.). New York: Harper and Row, 1977.

Hinde, R. The nature of imprinting. In B. M. Foss (Ed.), *Determinants of infant behavior* (Vol. 2). London: Methuen, 1963.

Hindley, C. B., Filliozat, A. M., Klackenberg, G., Nicolet-Meister, P., & Sand, E. A. Differences in age of walking in five European longitudinal samples. *Human Biology,* 1966, **38**, 364–379.

Hoffman, L. W. Early childhood experiences and women's achievement motives. *Journal of Social Issues,* 1972, **28**(2), 129–156.

Hoffman, L. W. Effects of maternal employment on the child: A review of the research. *Developmental Psychology,* 1974, **10**, 204–228. (a)

Hoffman, L. W. Fear of success in males and females: 1965 and 1971. *Journal of Consulting and Clinical Psychology,* 1974, **42**, 353–358. (b)

Hoffman, L. W. Maternal employment: 1979. *American Psychologist,* 1979, **34**(10), 859–865.

Hoffman, M. L. Developmental synthesis of affect and cognitions and its implications for altruistic motivation. *Developmental Psychology,* 1975, **11**, 607–622.

Hoffman, M. L. Empathy, role-taking, guilt, and development of altruistic motives. In T. Lickona (Ed.), *Moral development and behavior.* New York: Holt, Rinehart & Winston, 1976.

Hoffman, M. L. Toward a theory of empathic arousal and development. In M. Lewis & L. A. Rosenblum (Eds.), *The development of affect.* New York: Plenum, 1978.

Hoffman, M. L. Development of moral thought, feeling, and behavior. *American Psychologist,* 1979, **34**(10), 958–966.

Hoffman, M. L. Moral development in adolescence. In J. Adelson (Ed.), *Handbook of adolescent psychology.* New York: Wiley, 1980.

Hollender, J. W. Development of a realistic vocational choice. *Journal of Counseling Psychology,* 1967, **14**, 314–318.

Holway, A. R. Early self-regulation of infants and later behavior in play interviews. *American Journal of Orthopsychiatry,* 1949, **19**, 612–623.

Honzik, M. The stability of mental test performance between two and eighteen years. In M. C. Jones, N. Bayley, J. W. Macfarlane, & M. Honzik (Eds.), *The course of human development.* Waltham, Mass.: Xerox, 1971.

Honzik, M. P., Macfarlane, J. W., & Allen, L. The stability of mental test performance between two and eighteen years. *Journal of Experimental Education,* 1948, **18**, 309–324.

Horman, R. E., & Fox, A. M. (Eds.). *Drug awareness.* New York: Avon Books, 1970.

Horner, M. S. Sex differences in achievement motivation and performance in competitive and noncompetitive situations. Unpublished doctoral dissertation, University of Michigan, 1968.

Horner, M. S. Femininity and successful achievement: A basic inconsistency. In J. M. Bardwick, E. Douvan, M. S. Horner, & D. Guttman (Eds.), *Feminine personality and conflict.* Belmont, Calif.: Brooks/Cole, 1970.

Horney, K. *The neurotic personality of our time.* New York: Norton, 1937.

Horney, K. *New ways in psychoanalysis.* New York: Norton, 1939.

Horney, K. *Our inner conflicts.* New York: Norton, 1945.

Horney, K. *Neurosis and human growth.* New York: Norton, 1950.

Hotchner, T. *Pregnancy and childbirth.* New York: Avon, 1979.

Howe, L. W., & Howe, M. M. *Personalizing education: Values clarification and beyond.* New York: Hart, 1975.

Hudgens, R. W. *Psychiatric disorders in adolescents.* Baltimore: Williams & Wilkins, 1974.

Hull, C. L. *Principles of behavior.* New York: Appleton-Century-Crofts, 1943.

Hunt, J. M. *Intelligence and experience.* New York: Ronald, 1961.

Hunt, J. M. Psychological development: Early experience. In L. W. Porter & M. R. Rosenzweig (Eds.), *Annual review of psychology* (Vol. 30). Palo Alto, Calif.: Annual Reviews, 1979.

Hunt, M. Special sex education survey. *Seventeen,* July, 1970, 94.

Huntington, D. S. Supportive programs for infants and parents. In J. D. Osofsky (Ed.), *Handbook of infant development.* New York: Wiley, 1979.

Huxley, A. *Brave new world.* New York: Harper, 1932.

Ilg, F. L., & Ames, L. *Child behavior.* New York: Dell, 1955.

Inhelder, B., & Piaget, J. *The growth of logical thinking from childhood to adolescence.* New York: Basic Books, 1958.

Jacobs, J. *Adolescent suicide.* New York: Wiley, 1971.

Jacobs, P., Baikie, A. G., Court-Brown, W. M., & Strong, J. A. The somatic chromosomes in mongolism. *Lancet,* 1959, **2**, 710.

Jacobs, P. A., Brunton, M., Melville, M. M., Brittain, R. P., & McClemont, W. F. Aggressive behavior, mental subnormality and the XYY male. *Nature,* 1965, **208**, 1351–1352.

Jarvik, L. F., Klodin, V., & Matsuyama, S. S. Human aggression and the extra Y chromosome. *American Psychologist,* 1973, **28**(8), 674–682.

Jensen, A. R. How much can we boost IQ and scholastic achievement? *Harvard Educational Review,* 1969, **39**, 1–123.

Jensen, G. F. Parents, peers, and delinquent action: A test of the differential association perspective. *American Journal of Sociology,* 1973, **78**, 562–575.

Jersild, A. T. Emotional development. In L. Carmichael (Ed.), *Manual of child psychology* (2nd ed.). New York: Wiley, 1954.

Jersild, A. T. *Child psychology* (6th ed.). Englewood Cliffs, N.J.: Prentice-Hall, 1968.

Jersild, A. T., & Holmes, F. B. Children's fears. *Child Development Monographs,* No. 20. New York: Teachers College, Columbia University, 1935. (a)

Jersild, A. T., & Holmes, F. B. Methods of overcoming children's fears. *Journal of Psychology,* 1935, **1**, 75–104. (b)

Jessor, S., & Jessor, R. Transition from virginity to nonvirginity among youth: A social-psychological study over time. *Development Psychology,* 1975, **11**, 473–484.

Johnson, A. M. Juvenile delinquency. In S. Arieti (Ed.), *American handbook of psychiatry.* New York: Basic Books, 1959.

Johnston, L. D. *Drugs and American youth.* Ann Arbor, Mich.: Institute for Social Research, 1973.

Johnston, L. D., & Bachman, J. *Monitoring the future: A continuing study of the lifestyles and values of youth.*

Ann Arbor, Mich.: Institute for Social Research, 1975.

Johnston, L. D., Bachman, J. G., & O'Malley, P. M. *Drug use among American high school students, 1975–1977.* Rockville, Md.: National Institute on Drug Abuse, 1977.

Johnston, L. D., Bachman, J. G., & O'Malley, P. M. *Drugs and the class of '78: Behaviors, attitudes, and national trends.* Rockville, Maryland: National Institute on Drug Abuse, 1979.

Jones, E. *The life and work of Sigmund Freud.* Vol. 1. *The formative years and the great discoveries.* New York: Basic Books, 1953.

Jones, E. *The life and work of Sigmund Freud.* Abridged version edited by L. Trilling & S. Marcus. New York: Basic Books, 1961.

Jones, H. E. The adolescent growth study. I. Principles and methods. II. Procedures. *Journal of Consulting Psychology,* 1939, **3**, 157–159, 177–180.

Jones, H. E. Physical ability as a factor in social adjustment in adolescence. *Journal of Educational Research,* 1946, **39**, 287–301.

Jones, L. V. Primary mental abilities in the Stanford-Binet, age 13. *Journal of Genetic Psychology,* 1954, **84**, 125–147.

Jones, M. C. A laboratory study of fear: The case of Peter. *Pedagogical Seminary and Journal of Genetic Psychology,* 1924, **31**, 308–315.

Jones, M. C. The later career of boys who were early or late maturing. *Child Development,* 1957, **28**, 113–128.

Jones, M. C. Psychological correlates of somatic development. *Child Development,* 1965, **36**, 899–911.

Jones, M. C., Bayley, N., Macfarlane, J. W., & Honzik, M. P. (Eds.). *The course of human development.* Waltham, Mass.: Xerox, 1971.

Jones, M. C., & Mussen, P. H. Self conceptions, motivations and interpersonal attitudes of early and late maturing girls. *Child Development,* 1958, **29**, 491–501.

Josselson, R. Psychodynamic aspects of identity formation in college women. *Journal of Youth and Adolescence,* 1973, **2**, 3–52.

Josselson, R. Ego development in adolescence. In J. Adelson (Ed.), *Handbook of adolescent psychology.* New York: Wiley, 1980.

Josselson, R., Greenberger, E., & McConochie, D. Phenomenological aspects of psychosocial maturity in adolescence. Part 1: Boys. *Journal of Youth and Adolescence,* 1977, **6**, 25–56.

Kagan, J. American longitudinal research on psychological development. *Child Development,* 1964, **35**, 1–32. (a)

Kagan, J. *Developmental studies of reflection and analysis.* Cambridge, Mass.: Harvard University Press, 1964. (b)

Kagan, J. Impulsive and reflective children. In J. D. Krumbolz (Ed.), *Learning and the educational process.* Chicago: Rand McNally, 1964. (c)

Kagan, J., Kearsley, R. B., & Zelazo, P. R. (with the assistance of C. Minton). *Infancy: Its place in human development.* Cambridge, Mass.: Harvard University Press, 1978.

Kagan, J., & Moss, H. A. *Birth to maturity: A study in psychological development.* New York: Wiley, 1962.

Kallman, F. J. The genetic theory of schizophrenia: An analysis of 691 schizophrenic twin index families. *American Journal of Psychiatry,* 1946, **103**, 309–322.

Kamii, C., & Dermon, L. The Engelmann approach to teaching logical thinking: Findings from the administration of some Piagetian tasks. In D. R. Green, M. P. Ford, & G. Flamer (Eds.), *Piaget and measurement.* New York: McGraw-Hill, 1972.

Kandel, D. Inter- and intragenerational influences on adolescent marijuana use. *Journal of Social Issues,* 1974, **30**, 107–135.

Kandel, D., & Lesser, G. Parental and peer influences on vocational plans of adolescents. *American Sociological Review,* 1969, **34**, 213–223.

Kanner, L. *In defense of mothers.* Springfield, Ill.: Thomas, 1941.

Kanner, L. Autistic disturbances of affective content. *Nervous Child,* 1942, **2**, 217–250.

Kanner, L. *Child psychiatry* (4th ed.). Springfield, Ill.: Thomas, 1972.

Kaplan, A. R. (Ed.). *Genetic factors in schizophrenia.* Springfield, Ill.: Thomas, 1972.

Karmel, M. *Thank you, Dr. Lamaze: A mother's experiences in painless childbirth.* Philadelphia: Lippincott, 1959.

Keating, D. P. Thinking processes in adolescence. In J. Adelson (Ed.), *Handbook of adolescent psychology.* New York: Wiley, 1980.

Keniston, K. *Young radicals.* New York: Harcourt, Brace & World, 1968.

Keniston, K. *Youth and dissent: The rise of the new opposition.* New York: Harcourt, Brace, Jovanovich, 1971.

Kennell, J. H., Voos, D. K., & Klaus, M. H. Parent-infant bonding. In J. D. Osofsky (Ed.), *Handbook of infant behavior.* New York: Wiley, 1979.

Kessen, W. *The child.* New York: Wiley, 1965.

Kessen, W. The American child and other cultural inventions. *American Psychologist,* 1979, **34**(10), 815–820.

Kessen, W., Haith, M. M,, & Salapatek, P. H. Infancy. In P. H. Mussen (Ed.), *Carmichael's manual of child psychology* (3rd ed., Vol. 1). New York: Wiley, 1970.

Keys, A. J., Brozek, J., Henschel, A., Mickelsen, O., & Taylor, H. L. Growth and development. In *The biology of human starvation* (Vol. 2). Minneapolis: University of Minnesota Press, 1950.

Kidd, K. K., Kidd, J. R., & Records, M. A. The possible causes of the sex ratio in stuttering and its implications. *Journal of Fluency Disorders,* 1978, **3**, 13–23.

Kierkegaard, S. *Either/Or.* (W. Lowrie, Trans.) Princeton, N.J.: Princeton University Press, 1949.

Kierkegaard, S. *Sickness unto death.* (W. Lowrie, Trans.) Princeton, N.J.: Princeton University Press, 1951.

Kinkade, K. A Walden-two experiment. *Psychology Today,* 1973, **6**(8), 35–93. (a)

Kinkade, K. *A Walden two experiment: The first five years of Twin Oaks community.* New York: Morrow, 1973. (b)

Kinsey, A. C., Pomeroy, W. B., & Martin, C. E. *Sexual behavior in the human male.* Philadelphia: Saunders, 1948.

Kinsey, A. C., Pomeroy, W. B., Martin, C. E., & Gebhard, P. H. *Sexual behavior in the human female.* Philadelphia: Saunders, 1953.

Klaus, M. H., & Kennell, J. H. *Maternal-infant bonding.* St. Louis: Mosby, 1976.

Klausner, S. Z. *Two centuries of child rearing manuals.* Technical report submitted to the Joint Commission of Mental Health of Children, Inc. University Park, Pa.: University of Pennsylvania, Project "Hydra," October, 1968.

Klein, M. *The psychoanalysis of children.* London: Hogarth, 1937.

Klein, M. *Contributions to psycho-analysis, 1921–1945.* New York: Anglobooks, 1948.

Knoblock, H., & Pasamanick, B. The developmental behavioral approach to the neurologic examination in infancy. *Child Development,* 1962, **33**, 181–198.

Koch, H. L. Some emotional attitudes of the young child in relation to characteristics of his siblings. *Child Development,* 1956, **27**, 393–426.

Kohlberg, L. The development of modes of moral thinking and choice in the years ten to sixteen. Unpublished doctoral dissertation, University of Chicago, 1958.

Kohlberg, L. The development of children's orientations toward a moral order. I. Sequence in the development of moral thought. *Vita Humana,* 1963, **6**, 11–33.

Kohlberg, L. A cognitive-developmental analysis of children's sex-role concepts and attitudes. In E. E. Maccoby (Ed.), *The development of sex differences.* Stanford, Calif.: Stanford University Press, 1966.

Kohlberg, L. Stage and sequence: The cognitive-developmental approach to socialization. In D. A. Goslin (Ed.), *Handbook of socialization theory and research.* Chicago: Rand McNally, 1969.

Kohlberg, L. Moral stages and moralization: The cognitive-developmental approach. In T. Lickona (Ed.), *Moral development and behavior: Theory, research, and social issues.* New York: Holt, Rinehart, & Winston, 1976.

Kohlberg, L., & Gilligan, C. The adolescent as a philosopher: The discovery of the self in a postconventional world, *Daedalus,* Fall 1971, 1051–1086. (Reprinted in J. Kagan & R. Coles (Eds.), *Twelve to Sixteen: Early adolescence.* New York: Norton, 1971.)

Kohlberg, L., & Kramer, R. Continuities and discontinuities in childhood and adult moral development. *Human Development,* 1969, **12**, 93–120.

Kohlberg, L., & Turiel, E. (Eds.). *Recent research in moral development.* New York: Holt, Rinehart & Winston, 1972.

Kopp, C. B., & Parmelee, A. H. Prenatal and perinatal influences on infant behavior. In J. D. Osofsky (Ed.), *Handbook of infant development.* New York: Wiley, 1979.

Korner, A. F., & Thoman, E. B. Visual alertness in neonates as evoked by maternal care. *Journal of Experimental Child Psychology,* 1970, **10**, 67–78.

Kron, R. E. Instrumental conditioning of nutritive sucking behavior in the newborn. *Recent Advances in Biological Psychiatry,* 1966, **9**, 295–300.

Krumboltz, J. D., & Thoreson, C. E. *Changing children's behavior.* Englewood Cliffs, N.J.: Prentice-Hall, 1972.

Kurtines, W., & Greif, E. B. The development of moral thought: Review and evaluation of Kohlberg's approach. *Psychological Bulletin,* 1974, **81**(8), 453–470.

Lakin, M. Personality factors in mothers of excessively crying (colicky) infants. *Monographs of the Society for Research in Child Development,* 1957, **22** (No. 64).

Lamaze, F. *Painless childbirth: Psychoprophylactic method.* London: Burke, 1958.

Lamb, M. E. (Ed.). *The role of the father in child development.* New York: Wiley, 1976.

Lamb, M. E. Paternal influences and the father's role. *American Psychologist,* 1979, **34**(10), 938–943.

Lambert, W. W. Interpersonal behavior. In P. H. Mussen (Ed.), *Handbook of research methods in child development.* New York: Wiley, 1960.

Lapouse, R., & Monk, M. Behavior deviations in a representative sample of children: Variation by sex, age, race, social class and family size. *American Journal of Orthopsychiatry,* 1964, **34**, 436–446.

Larsen, L. F. The influence of parents and peers during adolescence: The situation hypothesis revisited. *Journal of Marriage and the Family,* 1972, **34**, 67–74.

Lassers, E., Nordan, R., & Bladholm, S. Steps in the return to school of children with school phobia. *American Journal of Psychiatry,* 1973, **130**(3), 265–268.

Leboyer, F. *Birth without violence.* New York: Knopf, 1975.

Leiderman, H., & Leiderman, G. Affective and cognitive consequences of polymatric infant care in the East African highlands. In A. Pick (Ed.), *Minnesota symposium on child development* (Vol. 8). Minneapolis: University of Minnesota Press, 1974.

Leiderman, P. H., & Seashore, M. J. Mother-infant neonatal separation: Some delayed consequences. In R. Porter & M. O'Conner (Eds.), *Parent-infant interaction.* (CIBA Foundation Symposium 33, new series.) Amsterdam: Associated Scientific Publishers, 1975.

Leifer, A., Leiderman, P., Barnett, C., & Williams, J. Effects of mother-infant separation on maternal attachment behavior. *Child Development,* 1972, **43**, 1203–1218.

Lenneberg, E. H. *Biological foundations of language.* New York: Wiley, 1967.

Lerner, R. M., & Karabenick, S. A. Physical attractiveness, body attitudes, and self-concept in late adolescents. *Journal of Youth and Adolescence,* 1974, **3**, 307–316.

Lester, G., & Lester, D. *Suicide: The gamble with death.* Englewood Cliffs, N.J.: Prentice-Hall, 1971.

LeVine, R. A. Cross-cultural study in child psychology. In P. H. Mussen (Ed.), *Carmichael's manual of child psychology* (3rd ed., Vol. 2). New York: Wiley, 1970.

Lewin, K. Behavior and development as a function of the total situation. In L. Carmichael (Ed.), *Manual of child psychology* (2nd ed.). New York: Wiley, 1954.

Lewis, M. The meaning of a response or why researchers in infant behavior should be Oriental metaphysicians. *Merrill-Palmer Quarterly,* 1967, **13**, 7–18.

Lewis, M. Culture and gender roles: There's no unisex in the nursery. *Psychology Today,* 1972, **5**(12), 54–57.

Lewis, M., & Brooks, J. Infants' reactions to people. In M. Lewis & L. Rosenblum (Eds.), *The origins of fear.* New York: Wiley, 1975.

Lewis, M., & Brooks, J. Self-knowledge and emotional development. In M. Lewis & L. A. Rosenblum (Eds.), *The development of affect.* New York: Plenum, 1978.

Lewis, M., & Rosenblum, L. A. (Eds.). *The effect of the infant on its caregiver.* New York: Wiley, 1974.

Lewis, M., & Rosenblum, L. A. (Eds.). *The development of affect.* New York: Plenum, 1978.

Lewis, M., & Starr, M. D. Developmental continuity. In J. D. Osofsky (Ed.), *Handbook of infant development.* New York: Wiley, 1979.

Lickona, T. Reseach on Piaget's theory of moral development. In T. Lickona (Ed.), *Moral development: Current theory and research.* New York: Holt, Rinehart & Winston, 1976. (a)

Lickona, T. (Ed.). *Moral development and behavior: Theory, research, and social issues.* New York: Holt, Rinehart & Winston, 1976. (b)

Liebert, R. M., & Neale, J. M. TV violence and child aggression: Snow on the screen. *Psychology Today,* 1972, **5**(11), 38–40.

Liebert, R. M., Neale, J. M., & Davidson, E. S. *The early window: Effects of television on children and youth.* New York: Pergamon, 1973.

Lindemann, C. *Birth control and unmarried women.* New York: Springer, 1974.

Lipsitt, L. P. Learning in the first year of life. In L. P. Lipsitt & C. C. Spiker (Eds.), *Advances in child development and behavior* (Vol. 1). New York: Academic Press, 1963.

Lipsitt, L. P. Critical conditions in infancy: A psychological perspective. *American Psychologist,* 1979, **34**(10), 973–980.

Lipsitt, L. P., Sturner, W. Q., & Burke, P. Perinatal indicators and subsequent crib death. *Infant Behavior and Development,* 1979, **2**, 325–328.

Livson, N., & Peskin, H. Perspectives on adolescence from longitudinal research. In J. Adelson (Ed.), *Handbook of adolescent psychology.* New York: Wiley, 1980.

Locke, J. *An essay concerning human understanding.* 1690. New ed. New York: Seaman, 1824.

Locke, J. *Some thoughts concerning education.* Abridged in *John Locke on Education* (P. Gay, Ed.). New York: Teachers College, Columbia University, 1964.

Looft, W. R. Sex differences in the expression of vocational aspirations by elementary school children. *Developmental Psychology,* 1971, **5**, 366.

Lorenz, K. Über die Bildung des Instinkbegriffes. *Naturwissenschaften,* 1937, **25**, 289–300, 307–318, 324–331.

Lorenz, K. Die angeborenen formen möglicher Erfahrung. *Zeitschrift für Tierpsychologie,* 1943, **5**, 235–409.

Lorenz, K. *King Solomon's ring.* New York: Crowell, 1952.

Lorenz, K. *On aggression.* New York: Harcourt, Brace & World, 1966.

Lorenz, K. Studies in animal and human behavior (2 vols.). Cambridge, Mass.: Harvard University Press, 1970, 1971.

Lorenz, K. *Civilized man's eight deadly sins.* New York: Harcourt, Brace, Jovanovich, 1974.

Lovaas, O. I. Interview with Paul Chance. *Psychology Today,* 1974, **7**, 76–84.

Lowry, R. J. *A. H. Maslow: An intellectual portrait.* Monterey, Calif.: Brooks-Cole, 1973.

Lynn, D. B. *The father: His role in child development.* Belmont, Calif.: Brooks-Cole, 1974.

Lynn, D. B., & Cross, A. deP. Parent preference of preschool children. *Journal of Marriage and the Family,* 1974, **36**, 555–559.

Lytton, H. Observational studies of parent-child interaction: A methodological review. *Child development,* 1971, **42**, 651–684.

Maccoby, E. E., & Jacklin, C. N. *Psychology of sex differences.* Stanford, Calif.: Stanford University Press, 1974.

Maccoby, E. E., & Masters, J. C. Attachment and dependency. In P. H. Mussen (Ed.), *Carmichael's manual of child psychology* (3rd ed., Vol. 2). New York: Wiley, 1970.

Maccoby, E. E., & Wilson, W. D. Identification and observational learning from films. *Journal of Abnormal and Social Psychology,* 1957, **55**, 76–87.

Macfarlane, J. W. Perspectives on personality consistency and change from the Guidance Study. *Vita Humana,* 1964, **7**, 115–126.

Macfarlane, J. W., Allen, L., & Honzik, M. P. *A developmental study of the behavior problems of normal children between twenty-one months and fourteen years.* Berkeley: University of California Press, 1954.

Magnusson, D., Duner, A., & Zetterblom, G. *Adjustment.* New York: Wiley, 1975.

Maier, H. W. *Three theories of child development* (3rd ed.). New York: Harper & Row, 1978.

Malina, R. M. Secular changes in size and maturity: Causes and effects. In A. F. Roche (Ed.), *Secular trends in human growth, maturation, and development. Monographs of the Society for Research in Child Development,* 1979, **44** (3–4, Serial No. 179).

Manosevitz, M., Lindzey, G., & Thiessen, D. D. (Eds.). *Behavioral genetics: Method and research.* New York: Appleton-Century-Crofts, 1969.

Marcia, J. E. Development and validation of ego identity status. *Journal of Personality and Social Psychology,* 1966, **3**(5), 551–558.

Marcia, J. E. Ego identity status: Relationship to change in self-esteem, "general adjustment," and authoritarianism. *Journal of Personality,* 1967, **35**(1), 119–133.

Marcia, J. E. Identity in adolescence. In J. Adelson (Ed.), *Handbook of adolescent psychology.* New York: Wiley, 1980.

Maresh, M. M. Variations in patterns of linear growth and skeletal maturation. *Journal of American Physical Therapy Association,* 1964, **44**, 881–890.

Marihuana and health. Fifth annual report to Congress from Secretary of Health, Education, and Welfare. Washington, D.C.: U.S. Government Printing Office, 1975.

Martin, B. Parent-child relations. In F. D. Horowitz (Ed.), *Review of child development research* (Vol. 4). Chicago: University of Chicago Press, 1975.

Maslow, A. H. A theory of human motivation. *Psychological Review,* 1943, **50**, 370–396.

Maslow, A. H. *Toward a psychology of being* (2nd ed.). Princeton, N.J.: Van Nostrand, 1968.

Maslow, A. H. *Motivation and personality* (2nd ed.). New York: Harper & Row, 1970.

Maslow, A. H. *The farther reaches of human nature.* New York: Viking, 1972.

Masters, W. H., & Johnson, V. E. *Human sexual inadequacy.* Boston: Little, Brown, 1970.

Masterson, J. F. *The psychiatric dilemma of adolescence.* Boston: Little, Brown, 1967.

Maternity Center Association. *A baby is born.* New York: Maternity Center Association, 1964.

Maternity Center Association. *Guide for expectant parents.* New York: Grosset & Dunlap, 1969.

Maxtone-Graham, K. *Pregnant by mistake: The stories of seventeen women.* New York: Liveright, 1973.

McCall, R. B., Hogarty, P., & Hurlburt, N. Transitions in infant sensorimotor development and the prediction of childhood IQ. *American Psychologist,* 1972, **27**, 728–748.

McCall, R. B., & Kagan, J. Attention in the infant: Effects of complexity, contour, perimeter, and familiarity. *Child Development,* 1967, **38**, 939–952.

McCarthy, D. Language development in children. In L. Carmichael (Ed.), *Manual of child psychology* (2nd ed.). New York: Wiley, 1954.

McClearn, G. E. Genetic influences on behavior and development. In P. H. Mussen (Ed.), *Carmichael's manual of child psychology* (3rd ed., Vol. 1) New York: Wiley, 1970.

McClelland, D. C. *The achieving society.* Princeton, N.J.: Van Nostrand, 1961.

McDonald, R. L. The role of emotional factors in obstetric complications: A review. *Psychosomatic Medicine,* 1968, **30**, 222–237.

McGlothlin, W. H., Sparkes, R. S., & Arnold, D. O.

Effect of LSD on human pregnancy. *Journal of the American Medical Association,* 1970, **212**, 1483–1487.

McGraw, M. *Growth: A study of Johnny and Jimmy.* New York: Appleton-Century-Crofts, 1935.

McGraw, M. Later development of children specially trained during infancy. *Child Development,* 1939, **10**, 1–19.

McGraw, M. *The neuromuscular development of the human infant.* New York: Columbia University Press, 1943.

McGurk, H. (Ed.). *Issues in childhood social development.* London: Methuen, 1978.

McIntire, R. W. *For love of children.* Del Mar, Calif.: CRM, 1970.

McNemar, Q. *The revision of the Stanford-Binet scale.* Boston: Houghton Mifflin, 1942.

Menyuk, P. *The acquisition and development of language.* Englewood Cliffs, N.J.: Prentice-Hall, 1971.

Menyuk, P. *Language and maturation.* Cambridge, Mass.: MIT Press, 1977.

Merminod, A. (Ed.). *The growth of the normal child during the first three years of life.* Basel: Karger, 1962.

Merrill, B. A measurement of mother-child interaction. *Journal of Abnormal and Social Psychology,* 1946, **41**, 37–49.

Messick, S., & associates. *Individuality in learning.* San Francisco: Jossey-Bass, 1976.

Miller, N. E., & Dollard, J. *Social learning and imitation.* New Haven: Yale University Press, 1941.

Miller, P. Y., & Simon, W. The development of sexuality in adolescence. In J. Adelson (Ed.), *Handbook of adolescent psychology.* New York: Wiley, 1980.

Mischel, W. Sex-typing and socialization. In P. H. Mussen (Ed.), *Carmichael's manual of child psychology* (3rd ed., Vol. 2). New York: Wiley, 1970.

Moerk, E. L. Piaget's research as applied to the explanation of language development. *Merrill-Palmer Quarterly,* 1975, **21**, 151–169.

Moerk, E. L. Processes of language teaching and training in the interaction of mother-child dyads. *Child Development,* 1976, **47**, 1064–1078.

Money, J., & Ehrhardt, A. A. *Man and woman, boy and girl.* Baltimore: The Johns Hopkins University Press, 1972.

Moore, K. L. *The developing human: Clinically oriented embryology* (2nd ed.). Philadelphia: Saunders, 1977.

Moore, S. G., & Updegraff, R. Sociometric status of preschool children as related to age, sex, nurturance-giving, and dependence. *Child Development,* 1964, **35**, 519–524.

Moore, T. W. Exclusive early mothering and its alternatives. *Scandinavian Journal of Psychology,* 1975, **16**, 256–272.

Moreno, J. L. *Who shall survive?* Washington, D.C.: Nervous and Mental Disease Publishing Co., 1934.

Morse, P. A. The discrimination of speech and non-speech stimuli in early infancy. *Journal of Experimental Child Psychology,* 1972, **14**, 477–492.

Moskowitz, H. A comparison of the effects of marihuana and alcohol on visual function. In M. F. Lewis (Ed.), *Current research in marihuana.* New York: Academic Press, 1972.

Moss, H. A. Sex, age, and state as determinants of mother-infant interaction. *Merrill-Palmer Quarterly,* 1967, **13**, 19–36.

Murchison, C. (Ed.). *Handbook of child psychology.* New York: Wiley, 1933.

Murphy, L. B. *Social behavior and child personality.* New York: Columbia University Press, 1937.

Murphy, L. B. Development in the first year of life: Ego and drive development in relation to the mother-infant tie. In L. J. Stone, H. Smith, & L. B. Murphy (Eds.), *The competent infant.* New York: Basic Books, 1973.

Murray, H. A. *Thematic apperception test: Manual.* Cambridge, Mass.: Harvard University Press, 1943.

Murray, H. A., & Kluckhohn, C. *Personality in nature, society and culture.* New York: Knopf, 1948.

Murray, J. P. Television and violence: Implications of the Surgeon-General's research program. *American Psychologist,* 1973, **28**, 472–478.

Murray, J. P., Rubinstein, E. A., & Comstock, G. A. (Eds.). *Television and social behavior.* Vol. II. *Television and social learning.* Washington, D.C.: U.S. Government Printing Office, 1972.

Murstein, B. I. (Ed.). *Handbook of projective techniques.* New York: Basic Books, 1965.

Muson, H. Moral thinking: Can it be taught? *Psychology Today*, 1979, **12**(9), 48–92.

Mussen, P. H. (Ed.). *Handbook of research methods in child development.* New York: Wiley, 1960.

Mussen, P. H. (Ed.). *Carmichael's manual of child psychology* (3rd ed.). New York: Wiley, 1970.

Mussen, P. H. (Ed.). *Manual of child psychology* (4th ed.). New York: Wiley, 1980.

Mussen, P. H., & Jones, M. C. Self-conceptions, motivations, and interpersonal attitudes of late and early maturing boys. *Child Development*, 1957, **28**, 245–256.

Mussen, P. H., & Rutherford, E. Parent-child relations and parental personality in relation to young children's sex-role preferences. *Child Development*, 1963, **34**, 589–607.

Muus, R. E. *Theories of adolescence* (3rd ed.). New York: Random House, 1975.

Myers, C. R. Journal citations and scientific eminence in contemporary psychology. *American Psychologist*, 1970, **25**, 1041–1048.

Naeye, R., Messmer, J., III, Specht, T., & Merritt, F. Sudden infant death syndrome temperament before death. *Journal of Pediatrics*, 1976, **88**, 511–515.

National Commission on the International Year of the Child. Unnumbered bulletin. Washington, D.C.: 1979.

Neill, A. S. *Summerhill.* New York: Hart, 1960.

Neill, A. S. *Freedom—not license!* New York: Hart, 1966.

Neill, A. S. *Neill! Neill! Orange peel!* New York: Hart, 1972.

Neilon, P. Shirley's babies after fifteen years: A personality study. *Journal of Genetic Psychology*, 1958, **73**, 175–186.

Neimark, E. D. Intellectual development during adolescence. In F. D. Horowitz (Ed.), *Review of child development research* (Vol. 4). Chicago: University of Chicago Press, 1975.

Nelson, K. Structure and strategy in learning to talk. *Monographs of the Society for Research in Child Development*, 1973, **38**, No. 149.

Nelson, K. Concept, word, and sentence: Interrelations in acquisition and development. *Psychological Review*, 1974, **81**, 267–285.

Newton, N. R. The relationship between infant feeding and later behavior. *Journal of Pediatrics*, 1951, **38**, 28–40.

Nilsson, L., Ingelman-Sundberg, A., & Wirsén, C. *A child is born.* New York: Delacorte, 1966.

Noble, E. P. (Ed.). *Alcohol and health.* Third special report to the U.S. Congress. Rockville, Md.: National Institute on Alcohol Abuse and Alcoholism, 1978.

Northway, M. L. A method for depicting social relationships obtained by sociometric testing. *Sociometry*, 1940, **3**, 144–150.

O'Donnell, J. A., Voss, H. L., Clayton, R. R., Slatin, G. T., & Room, R. G. W. *Young men and drugs: A nationwide survey.* Rockville, Md.: National Institute on Drug Abuse, 1976.

Offer, D. *The psychological world of the teen-ager: A study of normal adolescent boys.* New York: Basic Books, 1969.

Olson, W. C. The measurement of nervous habits in normal children. *Institute of Child Welfare Monograph Series,* No. 3. Minneapolis: University of Minnesota Press, 1929.

Olweus, D. Stability of aggressive reaction patterns in males: A review. *Psychological Bulletin*, 1979, **86**, 852–875.

Orwell, G. *1984.* New York: Harcourt, Brace & World, 1949.

Osofsky, J. D. (Ed.). *Handbook of infant development.* New York: Wiley, 1979.

Packard, V. *The sexual wilderness: The contemporary upheaval in male-female relationships.* New York: Pocket Books, 1970.

Papoušek, H. Conditioned head rotation reflexes in infants in the first months of life. *Acta Pediatrika*, 1961, **50**, 565–576.

Parke, R. D. Perspectives on father-infant interaction. In J. D. Osofsky (Ed.), *Handbook of infant development.* New York: Wiley, 1979.

Parke, R. D., & Collmer, C. W. Child abuse: An

interdisciplinary analysis. In E. M. Hetherington (Ed.), *Review of child development research* (Vol. 5). Chicago: University of Chicago Press, 1975.

Parten, M. B. Social participation among preschool children. *Journal of Abnormal and Social Psychology,* 1932, **27**, 243–269.

Patterson, G. R. The aggressive child: Victim and architect of a coercive system. In L. A. Hamerlynck, L. C. Handy, & E. J. Mash (Eds.), *Behavior modification and families. I. Theory and research.* New York: Brunner/Mazell, 1976. (a)

Patterson, G. R. *Living with children: New methods for parents and teachers.* New York: Research Press, 1976. (b)

Patterson, G. R., Littman, R. A., & Bricker, W. Assertive behavior in children: A step toward a theory of aggression. *Monographs of the Society for Research in Child Development,* 1967, **32**, 5 (Serial No. 113).

Pavlov, I. P. *Conditioned reflexes.* New York: Oxford University Press, 1927.

Peskin, H. Pubertal onset and ego functioning: A psychoanalytic approach. *Journal of Abnormal Psychology,* 1967, **72**, 1–15.

Peskin, H. Influence of the developmental schedule of puberty on learning and ego functioning. *Journal of Youth and Adolescence,* 1973, **2**, 273–290.

Petersen, A. C., & Taylor, B. The biological approach to adolescence. In J. Adelson (Ed.), *Handbook of adolescent psychology.* New York: Wiley, 1980.

Peterson, C. H., & Spano, F. Breast feeding, maternal rejection and child personality. *Character and Personality,* 1961, **10**, 62–66.

Piaget, J. *The moral judgment of the child.* New York: Harcourt, Brace, 1932. Collier Books edition, 1962.

Piaget, J. *The language and thought of the child.* London: Routledge & Kegan Paul, 1952. (a)

Piaget, J. *The origins of intelligence in children.* New York: International Universities Press, 1952. (b)

Piaget, J. How children form mathematical concepts. *Scientific American,* 1953, **189**, 74–79.

Piaget, J. Foreword. In M. Almy, E. Chittenden, & P. Miller, *Young children's thinking: Studies of some aspects of Piaget's theory.* New York: Teachers College Press, 1966.

Piaget, J. *Science of education and the psychology of the child.* New York: Grossman, 1970.

Piaget, J., & Inhelder, B. *The child's conception of space.* London: Routledge & Kegan Paul, 1956.

Piaget, J., & Inhelder, B. *The psychology of the child.* New York: Basic Books, 1969.

Piaget, J., & Inhelder, B. *Memory and intelligence.* London: Routledge & Kegan Paul, 1973.

Pick, H. L., Jr., & Pick, A. Sensory and perceptual development. In P. H. Mussen (Ed.), *Carmichael's manual of child psychology* (3rd ed., Vol. 1). New York: Wiley, 1970.

Pinneau, S. The infantile disorders of hospitalism and anaclitic depression. *Psychological Bulletin,* 1955, **52**, 429–452.

Plato. *The collected dialogues.* A. E. Taylor (Trans.). New York: E. P. Dutton, 1960.

Powell, G. F., Brasel, J. A., & Blizzard, R. M. Emotional deprivation and growth retardation simulating idiopathic hypopituitarism. I. Clinical evaluation of the syndrome. *New England Journal of Medicine,* 1967, **276**, 1271–1278.

Poznanski, E., Maxey, A., & Marsden, G. Clinical implications of maternal employment: A review of research. *Journal of the American Academy of Child Psychiatry,* 1970, **9**, 741–761.

Pratt, K. C. The neonate. In L. Carmichael (Ed.), *Manual of child psychology* (2nd ed.). New York: Wiley, 1954.

Presidential Science Advisory Commission, Panel on Youth. *Youth: Transition to adulthood.* Washington, D.C.: U.S. Government Printing Office, 1974.

Probst, C. A. A general information test for kindergarten children. *Child Development,* 1931, **2**, 81–95.

Proskauer, S., & Rolland, R. S. Youth who use drugs: Psychodynamic diagnosis and treatment planning. *Journal of the American Academy of Child Psychiatry,* 1973, **12**, 32–47.

Provence, S., & Lipton, R. C. *Infants in institutions.* New York: International Universities Press, 1962.

Pulaski, M. A. *Understanding Piaget: An introduction to children's cognitive development.* New York: Harper & Row, 1971.

Rabin, A. I. (Ed.) *Projective techniques in personality assessment.* New York: Springer, 1968.

Rank, O. *The trauma of birth.* New York: Harcourt, Brace, 1929.

Raths, L., Harmin, M., & Simon, S. B. *Values and teaching.* Columbus, Ohio: Merrill, 1966.

Rebelsky, F. G., Starr, R. H. Jr., & Luria, Z. Language development: The first four years. In Y. Brackbill (Ed.), *Infancy and early childhood.* New York: Free Press, 1967.

Reed, E. W. Genetic anomalies in development. In F. D. Horowitz (Ed.), *Review of child development research* (Vol. 4). Chicago: University of Chicago Press, 1975.

Reiss, I. L. *The social context of premarital sexual permissiveness.* New York: Holt, Rinehart & Winston, 1967.

Reiss, I. L., Banwart, A., & Foreman, H. Premarital contraceptive usage: A study and some theoretical explorations. *Journal of Marriage and the Family,* 1975, **37,** 619–630.

Renshon, S. A. *Handbook of political socialization: Theory and research.* New York: Free Press, 1977.

Report to the President: White House Conference on Children. Washington, D.C.: U.S. Government Printing Office, 1971.

Reynolds, S. R. M., & Danforth, D. N. The physiology and course of labor. In. D. N. Danforth (Ed.), *Textbook of obstetrics and gynecology.* New York: Hoeber, 1966.

Rheingold, H. L. The modification of social responsiveness in institutional babies. *Monographs of the Society for Research in Child Development,* 1956, **23.**

Rheingold, H. L. The effect of environmental stimulation upon social and exploratory behavior in the human infant. In B. M. Foss (Ed.), *Determinants of infant behavior* (Vol. 1). New York: Wiley, 1961.

Rheingold, H. L. Independent behavior of the human infant. In A. D. Pick (Ed.), *Minnesota symposia on child psychology* (Vol. 7). Minneapolis: University of Minnesota Press, 1973.

Rheingold, H. L., & Bayley, N. The later effects of an experimental modification of mothering. *Child Development,* 1959, **30**(3), 363–372.

Rheingold, H. L., & Cook, K. V. The contents of boys' and girls' rooms as index of parents' behavior. *Child Development,* 1975, **46,** 459–463.

Rheingold, H. L., & Eckerman, C. U. Fear of the stranger: A critical examination. In H. W. Reese (Ed.), *Advances in child development and behavior* (Vol. 8). New York: Academic Press, 1973.

Ribble, M. *The rights of infants.* New York: Columbia University Press, 1943.

Richardson, M. S. The dimensions of career and work orientation in college women. *Journal of Vocational Behavior,* 1974, **5,** 161–172.

Riessman, F. *The culturally deprived child.* New York: Harper & Row, 1962.

Rimland, B. *Infantile autism: The syndrome and its implications for a neural theory of behavior.* New York: Appleton-Century-Crofts, 1964.

Roazen, P. *Freud and his followers.* New York: Knopf, 1974.

Roche, A. (Ed.). Secular trends in human growth, maturation, and development. *Monographs of the Society for Research in Child Development,* 1979, **44**(3–4, Serial No. 179).

Rogers, C. R. *Client-centered therapy.* Boston: Houghton Mifflin, 1951.

Rogers, C. R. Learning to be free. In S. Farber & R. H. L. Wilson (Eds.), *Conflict and creativity: Control of the mind.* New York: McGraw-Hill, 1963.

Rogers, C. R. *On becoming a person: A therapist's view of psychotherapy.* Boston: Houghton Mifflin, 1970.

Rogers, C. R., & Skinner, B. F. Some issues concerning the control of human behavior. *Science,* 1956, **124,** 1057–1066.

Rogers, D. *The psychology of adolescence* (2nd ed.). New York: Appleton-Century-Crofts, 1972.

Rogerson, B. C. F., & Rogerson, C. H. Feeding in infancy and subsequent psychological difficulties. *Journal of Mental Science,* 1931, **1,** 1163–1182.

Rokeach, M. *The nature of human values.* New York: Free Press, 1973.

Rorvik, D. M., & Shettles, L. B. *Your baby's sex: Now you can choose.* New York: Dodd, Mead, 1970.

Rosen, B. M., Bahn, O. K., & Kramer, M. Demographic and diagnostic characteristics of psychiatric clinic outpatients in the U.S.A., 1961. *American Journal of Orthopsychiatry*, 1964, **24**, 455–467.

Rosenthal, D. *Genetic theory and abnormal behavior.* New York: McGraw-Hill, 1970.

Rosett, H. L., & Sander, L. W. Effects of maternal drinking on neonatal morphology and state regulation. In J. D. Osofsky (Ed.), *Handbook of infant development.* New York: Wiley, 1979.

Ross, D. M., & Ross, S. A. *Hyperactivity: Research, theory, and action.* New York: Wiley-Interscience, 1976.

Rousseau, J. J. *Émile.* (W. Boyd, Trans. & Ed.) New York: Bureau of Publications, Teachers College, Columbia University, 1962.

Rubinstein, E. A., Comstock, G. A., & Murray, J. P. (Eds.). *Television and social behavior.* Vol. IV. *Television in day-to-day life: Patterns of use.* Washington, D.C.: U.S. Government Printing Office, 1972.

Ruble, D. N., & Frieze, I. H. (Eds.). Sex roles: Persistence and change. *Journal of Social Issues*, 1976, **32**(3).

Rugh, R., & Shettles, L. *From conception to birth: The drama of life's beginnings.* New York: Harper & Row, 1971.

Ruppenthal, G. C., Arling, G. L., Harlow, H. G., Sackett, G. P., & Suomi, S. J. A 1-year perspective of motherless-mother monkey-behavior. *Journal of Abnormal Psychology*, 1976, **85**, 341–349.

Rutter, M. *Maternal deprivation reassessed.* Hammondsworth, Eng.: Penguin, 1972.

Rutter, M. Maternal deprivation, 1972–1978: New findings, new concepts, new approaches. *Child Development*, 1979, **50**, 283–318.

Rutter, M., & Schopler, E. (Eds.). *Autism: A reappraisal of concepts and treatment.* New York: Plenum, 1978.

Ryder, N. B. The cohort as a concept in the study of social change. *American Sociological Review*, 1965, **30**, 843–861.

Saddock, B. J., Kaplan, H. I., & Freedman, A. M. (Eds.). *The sexual experience.* Baltimore: Williams & Wilkins, 1976.

Sager, C. J., & Kaplan, H. S. (Eds.). *Progress in group and family therapy.* New York: Brunner/Mazel, 1972.

Salapatek, P. Pattern perception in early infancy. In L. B. Cohen & P. Salapatek (Eds.), *Infant perception: From sensation to cognition.* Vol. I. *Basic visual processes.* New York: Academic Press, 1975.

Salk, L. The effects of the normal heartbeat sound on the behavior of the newborn infant: Implications for mental health. *World Mental Health*, 1960, **12**, 168–175.

Salk, L. Mother's heartbeat as imprinting stimulus. *Proceedings of the New York Academy of Sciences*, 1962, **24**, 753–763.

Sameroff, A. J. Early influences on development: Fact or fancy? *Merrill-Palmer Quarterly*, 1974, **21**(4), 267–294.

Sameroff, A. J., & Cavanagh, P. J. Learning in infancy: A developmental perspective. In J. D. Osofsky (Ed.), *Handbook of infant development.* New York: Wiley, 1979.

Sameroff, A. J., & Chandler, M. J. Reproductive risk and the continuum of caretaking causality. In F. D. Horowitz (Ed.), *Review of child development research* (Vol. 4). Chicago: University of Chicago Press, 1975.

Sapir, E. *Language.* New York: Harcourt, Brace, 1921.

Schachter, S. *The psychology of affiliation.* Stanford, Calif.: Stanford University Press, 1959.

Schaefer, S. A circumplex model for maternal behavior. *Journal of Abnormal and Social Psychology*, 1959, **59**, 226–235.

Schaffer, H. R. *Mothering.* Cambridge, Mass.: Harvard University Press, 1977. (a)

Schaffer, H. R. (Ed.). *Studies in mother-infant interaction.* New York: Academic Press, 1977. (b)

Schaffer, H. R., & Emerson, P. E. The development of social attachments in infancy. *Monographs of the Society for Research in Child Development*, 1964, **29**(3).

Schechter, M. D. Psychiatric aspects of learning disabilities. *Child Psychiatry and Human Development*, 1974, **5**, 67–77.

Scheinfeld, A. *The human heredity handbook.* Philadelphia: Lippincott, 1956.

Scheinfeld, A. The mortality of men and women. *Scientific American*, 1958, **198**(2), 22–27.

Scheinfeld, A. *Your heredity and environment.* Philadelphia: Lippincott, 1965.

Scheinfeld, A. *Heredity in humans.* Philadelphia: Lippincott, 1972.

Schlesinger, I. M. Grammatical development: The first steps. In E. Lenneberg, & E. Lenneberg (Eds.), *Foundations of Language Development: A multidisciplinary approach* (Vol. 1). New York: Academic Press, 1975.

Schooler, C. Birth order effects: Not here, not now! *Psychological Bulletin, 1972, 78,* 161–175.

Schooler, J. C. (Ed.). *Current issues in adolescent psychiatry.* New York: Brunner/Mazel, 1973.

Schramm, D. G. J. Direction of movements of children in emotional responses. *Child Development, 1935, 6,* 26–51.

Scrimshaw, N. S., & Behar, M. Protein malnutrition in young children. *Science, 1961, 133,* 2039–2047.

Sears, P. S. (Ed.). *Intellectual development.* New York: Wiley, 1971.

Sears, R. R. Attachment, dependency, and frustration. In J. L. Gewirtz (Ed.), *Attachment and dependency.* Washington, D.C.: Winston, 1972.

Sears, R. R. Your ancients revisited: A history of child development. In E. M. Hetherington (Ed.), *Review of child development research* (Vol. 5). Chicago: University of Chicago Press, 1975.

Sears, R. R., Maccoby, E. E., & Levin, H. *Patterns of child rearing.* Evanston, Ill.: Row, Peterson, 1957.

Sears, R. R., Rau, L., & Alpert, R. *Identification and child rearing.* Stanford, Calif.: Stanford University Press, 1965.

Seligman, M. E. P. *Helplessness: On depression, development, and death.* San Francisco: Freeman, 1975.

Selman, R. L. Social-cognitive understanding: A guide to educational and clinical practice. In T. Lickona (Ed.), *Moral development and behavior: Theory, research, and social issues.* New York: Holt, Rinehart & Winston, 1976. (a)

Selman, R. L. Toward a structural analysis of developing interpersonal relations concepts. In A. Pick (Ed.), *Minnesota symposia on child psychology* (Vol. 10). Minneapolis: University of Minnesota Press, 1976. (b)

Senn, M. J. E. Insights on the child development movement in the United States. *Monographs of the Society for Research in Child Development, 1975, 40*(3–4, Serial No. 161).

Sewell, W. H., & Mussen, P. H. The effects of feeding, weaning, and scheduling procedures on childhood adjustment and the formation of oral symptoms. *Child Development, 1952, 23,* 185–191.

Shantz, C. U. The development of social cognition. In E. M. Hetherington (Ed.), *Review of child development research* (Vol. 5). Chicago: University of Chicago Press, 1975.

Shenker, R., & Schildkrout, M. Physical and emotional health of youth. In R. J. Havighurst & P. H. Dreyer (Eds.), *Youth.* (74th Yearbook of the National Society for the Study of Education). Chicago: University of Chicago Press, 1975.

Shepherd, M., Oppenheim, A. N., & Mitchell, S. Childhood behavior disorders and the child guidance clinic: An epidemiological study. *Journal of Psychology and Psychiatry, 1966, 7,* 39–52.

Sherman, J. A., & Bushell, D., Jr. Behavior modification as an educational technique. In F. D. Horowitz (Ed.), *Review of child development research* (Vol. 4). Chicago: University of Chicago Press, 1975.

Shirley, M. M. The first two years: A study of twenty-five babies. Vol. I. Posture and locomotor development. *Institute of Child Welfare Monograph Series,* No. 6. Minneapolis: University of Minnesota Press, 1931.

Shirley, M. M. The first two years: A study of twenty-five babies. Vol. II. Intellectual development. *Institute of Child Welfare Monograph Series,* No. 7. Minneapolis: University of Minnesota Press, 1933. (a)

Shirley, M. M. The first two years: A study of twenty-five babies. Vol. III. Personality manifestations. *Institute of Child Welfare Monograph Series,* No. 8. Minneapolis: University of Minnesota Press, 1933. (b)

Shirley, M. M. Development of immature babies during the first two years. *Child Development, 1938, 9,* 347–360.

Shirley, M. M. A behavior syndrome characterizing prematurely-born children. *Child Development,* 1939, **10**, 115–128.

Simon, S. B., Howe, L. W., & Kirschenbaum, H. *Values clarification: A handbook of practical strategies for teachers and students.* New York: Hart, 1972.

Simon, W., Berger, A. S., & Gagnon, J. S. Beyond anxiety and fantasy: The coital experiences of college youth. *Journal of Youth and Adolescence,* 1972, **1**, 203–222.

Singer, J. L. (Ed.). *The child's world of make-believe: Experimental studies of imaginative play.* New York: Academic Press, 1973.

Siqueland, E. R., & DeLucia, C. A. Visual reinforcement of nonnutritive sucking in human infants. *Science,* 1969, **165**, 1144–1146.

Skinner, B. F. *Walden Two.* New York: Macmillan, 1948.

Skinner, B. F. *Science and human behavior.* New York: Macmillan, 1953.

Skinner, B. F. *Verbal behavior.* New York: Appleton-Century-Crofts, 1957.

Skinner, B. F. Baby in a box. In B. F. Skinner (Ed.), *Cumulative record.* New York: Appleton-Century-Crofts, 1961.

Skinner, B. F. Autobiographical sketch. In E. G. Boring & G. Lindzey (Eds.), *A history of psychology in autobiography* (Vol. 5). New York: Appleton-Century-Crofts, 1967.

Skinner, B. F. *Beyond freedom and dignity.* New York: Knopf, 1971.

Skinner, B. F. *About behaviorism.* New York: Knopf, 1974.

Skinner, B. F. *Particulars of my life.* New York: Knopf, 1976.

Skinner, B. F. My experience with the baby-tender. *Psychology Today,* 1979, **12**(10), 28–40. (a)

Skinner, B. F. *The shaping of a behaviorist.* New York: Knopf, 1979. (b)

Skodak, M. Children in foster homes: A study of mental development. *University of Iowa Studies of Child Welfare,* 1939, **16**, No. 1.

Skodak, M., & Skeels, H. M. A follow-up study of children in adoptive homes. *Journal of Genetic Psychology,* 1945, **66**, 21–58.

Skodak, M., & Skeels, H. M. A final follow-up of one hundred adopted children. *Journal of Genetic Psychology,* 1949, **75**, 85–125.

Smoking and Health: A Report of the Surgeon-General. Washington, D.C.: U.S. Department of Health, Education, & Welfare, 1979.

Sontag, L. W. The history of longitudinal research: Implications for the future. *Child Development,* 1971, **42**, 987–1002.

Sorensen, R. C. *Adolescent sexuality in contemporary America: Personal values and sexual behavior.* New York: World, 1973.

Spearman, C. *The abilities of men: Their nature and measurement.* New York: Macmillan, 1927.

Spears, W. C., & Hohle, H. Sensory and perceptual processes in infants. In Y. Brackbill (Ed.), *Infancy and early childhood.* New York: Free Press, 1967.

Speert, H. Historical highlights. In D. N. Danforth (Ed.), *Textbook of obstetrics and gynecology.* New York: Hoeber, 1966. (a)

Speert, H. Premature labor. In D. N. Danforth (Ed.), *Textbook of obstetrics and gynecology.* New York: Hoeber, 1966. (b)

Spence, J. T., & Helmreich, R. L. *Masculinity and femininity: Their psychological dimensions, correlates, and antecedents.* Austin: University of Texas Press, 1978.

Spinetta, J. J., & Rigler, D. The child-abusing parents: A psychological review. *Psychological Bulletin,* 1972, **77**, 296–304.

Spitz, R. A. Hospitalism: An inquiry into the genesis of psychiatric conditions in early childhood. In A. Freud (Ed.), *The psychoanalytic study of the child* (Vol. 1). New York: International Universities Press, 1945.

Spitz, R. A. *The first year of life.* New York: International Universities Press, 1965.

Sroufe, L. A. Wariness of strangers and the study of infant development. *Child Development,* 1977, **48**, 731–746.

Sroufe, L. A. Socioemotional development. In J. D.

Osofsky (Ed.), *Handbook of infant development.* New York: Wiley, 1979.

Sroufe, L. A., & Waters, E. The ontogenesis of smiling and laughter: A perspective on the organization of development in infancy. *Psychological Review,* 1976, **83**, 173–189.

Stark, R., & McEvoy, J. Middle class violence. *Psychology Today,* 1970, **4**, 52–65.

Starr, R. H., Jr. Child abuse. *American Psychologist,* 1979, **34**(10), 872–878.

Stein, A. H., & Friedrich, L. K. Impact of television on children and youth. In E. M. Hetherington (Ed.), *Review of child development research* (Vol. 5). Chicago: University of Chicago Press, 1975.

Stendler, C. B. Sixty years of child-training practices. *Journal of Pediatrics,* 1950, **36**, 122–134.

Stennet, R. G. Emotional handicap in the elementary years: Phase or disease? *American Journal of Orthopsychiatry,* 1966, **36**(3), 444–449.

Stern, D. *The first relationship: Mother and infant.* Cambridge, Mass.: Harvard University Press, 1977.

Sternglanz, S. H., & Serbin, L. A. Sex-role stereotypes in children's television programs. *Developmental Psychology,* 1974, **10**, 710–715.

Stewart, A. H., Weiland, I. H., Leider, A. R., Mangham, C. A., Holmes, T. H., & Ripley, H. S. Excessive infant crying (colic) in relation to parent behavior. *American Journal of Psychiatry,* 1954, **110**, 687–699.

Stone, L. J., Smith, H. T., & Murphy, L. B. (Eds.). *The competent infant.* New York: Basic Books, 1973.

Stott, D. H. The child's hazards in utero. In J. G. Howells (Ed.), *Modern perspectives in international child psychiatry.* New York: Brunner/Mazel, 1971.

Strean, L. P., & Peer, A. Stress as an etiologic factor in the development of cleft palate. *Plastic and Reconstructive Surgery,* 1956, **18**, 1–8.

Sulzer-Azaroff, B., & Mayer, G. R. *Applying behavior analysis procedures with children.* New York: Holt, Rinehart & Winston, 1977.

Suomi, S. J., & Harlow, H. F. Social rehabilitation of isolate reared monkeys. *Developmental Psychology,* 1972, **43**, 337–358.

Super, C. M. Longterm memory in early infancy. Unpublished doctoral dissertation, Harvard University, 1972.

Super, D. E. *The psychology of careers.* New York: Harper & Row, 1957.

Super, D. E. Vocational development in adolescence and early childhood: Tasks and behaviors. In D. E. Super, R. E. Starishevsky, N. Matlin, & J. P. Jordan (Eds.), *Career development: A self-concept theory.* New York: College Entrance Examination Board, 1963.

Swift, J. W. Effects of early group experience: The nursery school and day nursery. In M. L. Hoffman & L. W. Hoffman (Eds.), *Review of child development research* (Vol. 1). New York: Russell Sage Foundation, 1964.

Tanner, J. M. *Growth at adolescence* (2nd ed.). Philadelphia: Davis, 1962.

Tanner, J. M. Physical growth. In P. H. Mussen (Ed.), *Carmichael's manual of child psychology* (3rd ed., Vol. 1). New York: Wiley, 1970.

Tanner, J. M. Sequence, tempo, and individual variation in growth and development of boys and girls aged twelve to sixteen. In J. Kagan & R. Coles (Eds.), *Twelve to sixteen: Early adolescence.* New York: Norton, 1972.

Tanner, J. M., Taylor, G. R., & the Editors of Time-Life Books. *Growth* (Rev. ed.). New York: Time-Life Books, 1969.

Tanzer, D., & Block, J. L. *Why natural childbirth?* Garden City, N.Y.: Doubleday, 1972.

Tavris, C., & Offir, C. *The longest war: Sex differences in perspective.* New York: Harcourt, Brace, Jovanovich, 1977.

Television and growing up: The impact of televised violence. Washington, D.C.: U.S. Government Printing Office, 1972.

Television and social behavior. Washington, D.C.: U.S. Government Printing Office, 1972.

Terman, L. M., & Merrill, M. A. *Measuring intelligence.* Boston: Houghton Mifflin, 1937.

Terman, L. M., & Merrill, M. A. *Stanford-Binet intelligence scale: Manual for the third revision, Form L-M.* Boston: Houghton Mifflin, 1960.

Terman, L. M., & Oden, M. *Genetic studies of genius: The gifted group at mid-life. Thirty-five years' follow-up of the superior child.* Stanford, Calif.: Stanford University Press, 1954.

Thomas, A., Chess, S., Birch, H. G., Hertzig, M. E., & Korn, S. *Behavioral individuality in early childhood.* New York: New York University Press, 1963.

Thomas, A., Chess, S., & Birch, H. G. The origin of personality. *Scientific American,* 1970, **223**(2), 102.

Thomas, A., & Chess, S. *Temperament and development.* New York: Brunner/Mazel, 1977.

Thompson, W. R., & Grusec, J. Studies of early experience. In P. H. Mussen (Ed.), *Carmichael's manual of child psychology* (3rd ed., Vol. 1). New York: Wiley, 1970.

Thornburg, H. D. Age and first sources of sex information as reported by 88 college women. *Journal of School Health,* 1970, **40**, 156–158.

Tinbergen, N. Interview with Elizabeth Hall. *Psychology Today,* 1974, **7**(10), 65–80.

Tinklenberg, J. R. (Ed.). *Marijuana and health hazards: Methodological issues in current research.* New York: Academic Press, 1975.

Tizard, B., & Hodges, J. The effect of early institutional rearing on the development of eight-year-old children. *Journal of Child Psychology and Psychiatry,* 1978, **19**, 99–118.

Toffler, A. *Future shock.* New York: Random House, 1970.

Tolor, A. The generation gap: Fact or fiction? *Genetic Psychology Monographs,* 1976, **94**, 35–130.

Tresemer, D. Fear of success: Popular but unproven. *Psychology Today,* 1974, **7**(10), 82–85.

Tresemer, D. *Fear of success.* New York: Plenum Press, 1977.

Tuddenham, R. D. Studies in reputation. III. Correlates of popularity among elementary school children. *Journal of Educational Psychology,* 1951, **42**, 257–276.

Turiel, E. An experimental test of the sequentiality of developmental stages in the child's moral judgments. *Journal of Personality and Social Psychology,* 1966, **3**, 611–618.

Turiel, E. Conflict and transition in adolescent moral development. *Child Development,* 1974, **45**, 14–79.

U.S. Commission on Civil Rights. *Racial isolation in the public schools.* Washington, D.C.: U.S. Government Printing Office, 1967.

U.S. Public Health Service. *Alcohol and health.* Second special report to the U.S. Congress. Rockville, Md.: National Institute on Alcohol Abuse and Alcoholism, 1974.

Victor, H. R., Grossman, J. C., & Eisenman, R. Openness to experience and marijuana use in high school students. *Journal of Consulting and Clinical Psychology,* 1973, **41**, 78–85.

Vincent, C. E. *Trends in infant care ideas.* Child Development, 1951, **22**, 199–209.

Vygotsky, L. *Thought and language.* Cambridge, Mass.: MIT Press, 1962.

Waddington, C. H. *The strategy of the genes: A discussion of some aspects of theoretical biology.* London: Allen & Unwin, 1957.

Waddington, C. H. *Principles of development and differentiation.* New York: Macmillan, 1966.

Wadsworth, B. J. *Piaget for the classroom teacher.* New York: Longman, 1978.

Walk, R. R. The development of depth perception in animal and human infants. *Monographs of the Society for Research in Child Development,* 1966, **31**(5), 82–108.

Wanderer, Z., & Cabot, T. *Letting go: A twelve week personal action program to overcome a broken heart.* New York: Putnam, 1978.

Warner, D. A. Personal communication, 1978.

Warner, F. *The children: How to study them.* London: Hodgson, 1887–1888.

Watson, J. B. *Animal education: The psychical development of the white rat.* Unpublished doctoral dissertation, University of Chicago, 1903.

Watson, J. B. Psychology as the behaviorist views it. *Psychological Review,* 1913, **20**, 158–177.

Watson, J. B. *Psychology from the standpoint of a behaviorist.* Philadelphia: Lippincott, 1919.

Watson, J. B. *Behaviorism.* Chicago: University of Chicago Press, 1925. (Rev. ed.), 1930.

Watson, J. B. *Psychological care of infant and child.* New

York: Norton, 1928. (a)

Watson, J. B. *The ways of behaviorism.* New York: Harper, 1928. (b)

Watson, J. B. Autobiographical sketch. In C. Murchison (Ed.), *A history of psychology in autobiography* (Vol. 3). Worcester, Mass.: Clark University Press, 1936.

Watson, J. B., & Morgan, J. J. B. Emotional reactions and psychological experimentation. *American Journal of Psychology,* 1917, **28**, 163–174.

Watson, J. B., & Rayner, R. Conditioned emotional reactions. *Journal of Experimental Psychology,* 1920, **3**, 1–14.

Watson, J. D. *The double helix: Being a personal account of the discovery of the structure of DNA.* New York: Atheneum, 1968.

Weathersbee, P. S. Heavy coffee intake, miscarriages linked. *Muncie Evening Press,* Muncie, Ind., Oct. 16, 1975, 19.

Webster, R. L. Postnatal weight and behavior changes as a function of components of prenatal material injection procedures. *Science,* 1967, **7**, 191–192.

Wechsler, D. *The measurement of adult intelligence.* Baltimore: Williams & Wilkins, 1939.

Wechsler, D. *Wechsler intelligence scale for children.* New York: Psychological Corp., 1949.

Wechsler, D. *Wechsler adult intelligence scale.* New York: Psychological Corp., 1955, 1964, 1968.

Wechsler, D. *Wechsler intelligence scale for children—revised.* New York: Psychological Corp., 1974.

Weill, A. T., & Zinberg, N. E. Acute effects of marihuana on speech. *Nature,* 1969, **22**, 434–437.

Weiner, I. B. *Psychological disturbance in adolescence.* New York: Wiley-Interscience, 1970.

Weiner, I. B. Depression in adolescence. In F. F. Flach & S. C. Draghi (Eds.), *The nature and treatment of depression.* New York: Wiley, 1975.

Weiner, I. B. Psychopathology in adolescence. In J. Adelson (Ed.), *Handbook of adolescent psychology.* New York: Wiley, 1980.

Weininger, O. *Play and education: The basic tool for early childhood learning.* Springfield, Ill.: Thomas, 1979.

Weiss, L. A. Differential variations in the amount of activity of newborn infants under continuous light and sound stimulation. *University of Iowa Studies in Child Welfare,* 1934, **9**(4), 9–74.

Weiss, R. *Marital separation.* New York: Basic Books, 1975.

Wellman, B. L. Growth in intelligence under differing school environments. *Journal of Experimental Education,* 1934, **3**, 59–83.

Werner, E. E., Bierman, J. M., & French, F. E. *The children of Kauai: A longitudinal study from the prenatal period to age ten.* Honolulu: University of Hawaii Press, 1971.

Wessel, H. *Natural childbirth and the Christian family.* New York: Harper & Row, 1963.

White, B. L. An experimental approach to the effects of experience on early human behavior. In J. P. Hill (Ed.), *Minnesota symposium on child psychology* (Vol. 1). Minneapolis: University of Minnesota Press, 1967.

White, B. L. *The first three years of life.* Englewood Cliffs, N.J.: Prentice-Hall, 1975.

White, B. L., & Castle, P. W. Visual exploratory behavior following postnatal handling of human infants. *Perceptual and Motor Skills,* 1964. **18**, 497–502.

White, B. L., & Held, R. Plasticity of sensori-motor development in the human infant. In J. F. Rosenblith & W. Allinsmith (Eds.), *The causes of behavior* (2nd ed.). Boston: Allyn & Bacon, 1966.

White, B. L., Kaban, B. T., & Attanucci, J. S. *The origins of human competence. The final report of the Harvard Preschool Project.* Lexington, Mass.: Lexington Books, 1979.

White, B. L., Watts, J. C., & others. *Experience and environment: Major influences on the development of the young child.* Englewood Cliffs, N.J.: Prentice-Hall, 1973.

White, R. W. Motivation reconsidered: The concept of competence, *Psychological Review,* 1959, **66**, 297.

White, S. H. The learning theory tradition and child psychology. In P. H. Mussen (Ed.), *Carmichael's manual of child psychology* (3rd ed., Vol. 1). New York: Wiley, 1970.

Whiten, A. Assessing the effects of perinatal events on the success of the mother-infant relationship. In H. R. Schaffer (Ed.), *Studies in mother-infant interaction.* London: Academic Press, 1977.

Whorf, B. *Language, thought, and reality.* New York: Wiley, 1956.

Widdowson, E. M. Mental contentment and physical growth. *Lancet,* 1951, **1,** 1316–1318.

Wilson, C. *New pathways in psychology: Maslow and the post-Freudian revolution.* London: Gollancz, 1972.

Winick, M. *Malnutrition and brain development.* New York: Oxford University Press, 1976.

Witelson, S. F., & Pallie, W. Left hemisphere specialization for language in the newborn. *Brain,* 1973, **96,** 641–646.

Witkin, H. A. Social influences in the development of cognitive style. In D. A. Goslin (Ed.), *Handbook of socialization theories and research.* Chicago: Rand McNally, 1969.

Witkin, H. A., & Berry, J. W. Psychological differentiation in cross-cultural perspective. *Journal of Cross-Cultural Psychology,* 1975, **6,** 84–87.

Witkin, H. A., Dyk, R. B., Faterson, H. F., Goodenough, D. R., & Karp, S. A. *Psychological differentiation.* New York: Wiley, 1962.

Witkin, H. A., & Goodenough, D. R. *Field dependence revisited.* Research Bulletin 76–39. Princeton, N.J.: Educational Testing Service, 1976.

Witryol, S. L., & Thompson, G. G. A critical review of the stability of social acceptability scores obtained with the partial-rank-order and the paired-comparison scales. *Genetic Psychology Monographs,* 1953, **48,** 221–260.

Wolfenstein, M. Trends in infant care. *American Journal of Orthopsychiatry,* 1953, **33,** 120–130.

Wolff, P. H. Observations on the early development of smiling. In B. M. Foss (Ed.), *Determinants of infant behavior* (Vol. 2). New York: Wiley, 1963.

Wolff, P. H. The natural history of crying and other vocalizations in early infancy. In B. M. Foss (Ed.), *Determinants of infant behavior* (Vol. 4). London: Methuen, 1969.

Wolff, P. H. Critical periods in human cognitive development. *Hospital Practice,* 1970, **11,** 77–87.

Wolff, P. H. Mother-infant relations at birth. In J. C. Howells (Ed.), *Modern perspectives in international psychiatry.* New York: Brunner/Mazel, 1971.

Wolff, P. H. Maturational factors in behavioral development. In M. F. McMillan & S. Henao (Eds.), *Child psychiatry: Treatment and research.* New York: Brunner/Mazel, 1977.

Wolman, B. B. (Ed.). *Manual of child psychopathology.* New York: McGraw-Hill, 1972.

Wright, H. F. Observational child study. In P. H. Mussen (Ed.), *Handbook of research methods in child development.* New York: Wiley, 1960.

Yalom, I. D. Post-partum blues syndrome. *Archives of General Psychiatry,* 1968, **28,** 16–27.

Yalom, I. D. *The theory and practice of group psychotherapy.* New York: Basic Books, 1970.

Yarrow, M. R., Campbell, J. D., & Burton, R. V. *Child rearing.* San Francisco: Jossey-Bass, 1968.

Yarrow, M. R., Scott, P., De Leeuw, L., & Heinig, C. Child rearing in families of working and nonworking mothers. *Sociometry,* 1962, **25,** 122–140.

Yarrow, M. R., Scott, P. M., & Waxler, A. Learning concern for others. *Developmental Psychology,* 1973, **8,** 240–260.

Zahn-Waxler, C., Radke-Yarrow, M., & King, R. M. Child rearing and children's prosocial initiations toward victims of distress. *Child Development,* 1979, **50,** 319–330.

Zajonc, R. B., & Markus, G. B. Birth order and intellectual development. *Psychological Review,* 1975, **82**(1), 74–88.

Zelnik, M., & Kantner, J. F. The probability of premarital intercourse. *Social Science Research,* 1972, **1,** 335–341.

Zelnik, M., & Kantner, J. F. Sexual and contraceptive experience of young unmarried women in the United States, 1976 and 1971. *Family Planning Perspectives,* 1977, **9,** 55–71.

Zelniker, T., & Jeffrey, W. E. Reflective and impulsive children: Strategies of information processing underlying differences in problem solving. *Monographs of the Society for Research in Child Development,* 1976, **41**(5, Serial No. 168).

Zigler, E. Letter to the editor. *New York Times Magazine,* January 18, 1975.

Zimmerman, D. R. Your family's health. *Ladies' Home Journal,* 1976, **93,** 78.

Zinberg, N., & Weil, A. A. A comparison of marijuana users and non-users. *Nature,* 1970, **226,** 119–123.

INDEX

WHAT DO YOU THINK OF THIS BOOK?

We would like to know what you think of this edition of *Child Development: An Introduction*. Your comments will help us not only in improving the next edition of this book but also in developing other texts. We would appreciate it very much if you would take a few minutes to respond to the following questions. When you have finished responding, please return the form to: College Marketing, Houghton Mifflin Company, One Beacon Street, Boston, MA 02107

On a ten-point scale, with 10 as the highest rating and 1 as the lowest, how do you rate the following features of *Child Development: An Introduction*?

Overall rating compared to all other texts you have read. _____

Interest level compared to all other texts you have read. _____

Readability compared to other texts. _____

Clarity of presentation of concepts and information. _____

Value of the *Key Points* as a study and learning aid. _____

Helpfulness of summary *tables* and *diagrams*. _____

Interest level and pedagogical effectiveness of the *illustrations*. _____

Usefulness of the *Suggestions for Further Study*. _____

Do you intend to sell this book _____ or keep it for future reference _____? (Please insert an X in the appropriate space.)

Do you expect to have contact with children or adolescents in any of these capacities during the next ten years? (Check more than one, if appropriate.) Parent _____ Teacher _____ Nurse _____ Social worker _____ Recreational leader _____ Other (Please specify) _____

Please turn to the table of contents and list here the number of all chapters that were assigned by your instructor. _____

If not all chapters were assigned, did you read any others on your own? Please indicate chapter numbers you read on your own. _____

Please indicate the numbers of chapters you found most interesting. _____

Allowing for the fact that some topics are more intrinsically interesting than others, did you find any chapters particularly "deadly" and in need of more effective presentation? Please specify chapter numbers. _____

Were there any topics that were not covered that you thought should have been covered? _____

Please indicate the number of each of the following types of exams that your instructor asked you to take: multiple choice _____ short answer _____ essay _____ oral _____ other (please specify) _____

Did your instructor give you the opportunity to compare your test answers to the answers provided by the person who wrote the questions? Yes _____ No _____

Were you required to write a term paper _____ or complete some sort of term project? (Please specify nature of term project) _____

Did you use the Study Guide? Yes _____ No _____. On a ten-point scale, how do you rate the usefulness of the Study Guide _____? Did your instructor ask you to use the Study Guide _____ or did you obtain it on your own _____?

Are you attending a 2-year college _____, 4-year college _____, university _____?

Is your college or university on the quarter system _____ or the semester system _____?

If you had the chance to talk to the author of this book just before he started to prepare the next edition, what suggestions would you give him for improving *Child Development: An Introduction?*